The African American Baseball
Experience in Nebraska

ALSO FROM ANGELO J. LOUISA

*The Pirates Unraveled: Pittsburgh's 1926 Season* (McFarland, 2015)

*Mysteries from Baseball's Past: Investigations of Nine Unsettled Questions,* edited by Angelo J. Louisa and David Cicotello (McFarland, 2010)

*Forbes Field: Essays and Memories of the Pirates' Historic Ballpark, 1909–1971,* edited by David Cicotello and Angelo J. Louisa (McFarland, 2007)

# The African American Baseball Experience in Nebraska

*Essays and Memories*

EDITED BY ANGELO J. LOUISA

*Foreword by* James E. Overmyer

McFarland & Company, Inc., Publishers
*Jefferson, North Carolina*

LIBRARY OF CONGRESS CATALOGUING-IN-PUBLICATION DATA

Names: Louisa, Angelo Joseph, editor.
Title: The African American baseball experience in Nebraska : essays and memories / edited by Angelo J. Louisa.
Description: Jefferson, North Carolina : McFarland & Company, Inc., Publishers, 2021. | Includes bibliographical references and index.
Identifiers: LCCN 2020047198 | ISBN 9780786479764 (paperback : acid free paper) ∞
ISBN 9781476641560 (ebook)
Subjects: LCSH: African American baseball players—Nebraska—Omaha—History. | African American baseball players—Biography. | Baseball—Nebraska—Omaha—History.
Classification: LCC GV863.N22 O633 2021 | DDC 796.357089/96073—dc23
LC record available at https://lccn.loc.gov/2020047198

BRITISH LIBRARY CATALOGUING DATA ARE AVAILABLE

ISBN (print) 978-0-7864-7976-4
ISBN (ebook) 978-1-4766-4156-0

© 2021 Angelo J. Louisa. All rights reserved

*No part of this book may be reproduced or transmitted in any form or by any means, electronic or mechanical, including photocopying or recording, or by any information storage and retrieval system, without permission in writing from the publisher.*

Front cover: David City baseball team, 1894 (Nebraska State Historical Society)

Printed in the United States of America

*McFarland & Company, Inc., Publishers
Box 611, Jefferson, North Carolina 28640
www.mcfarlandpub.com*

To Joanne Ferguson Cavanaugh,
whose faith in my ability to be a program director
led to the creation of this book

# Acknowledgments

Producing a multicontributor book is like producing a movie, with the editor being the director, the essay writers being the actors, and a host of support people being the grips, gaffers, best boys, and other behind-the-scenes experts. The director and the actors receive much of the recognition, but without the workers who labor outside of the limelight, there would be no movie. And so it is with a multicontributor book, especially this multicontributor book, which had award-worthy support people. Included among those indispensible individuals are:

My lovely wife, the brilliant Pamela Acre Louisa, who has for many years put up with my ambitious projects and high expectations and whose superb computer skills and great proofreading talents made this book 100 times better than it would have been without them.

Joanne Ferguson Cavanaugh, to whom this book is dedicated, for her continued faith in me and for her patience in waiting for this book to be completed.

My dear friend, loyal traveling companion, and former editing partner, David Cicotello, who read most of the manuscript and suggested a number of helpful revisions.

The creative and renowned author-artist Gary Cieradkowski, who produced a beautiful baseball card of Mickey Stubblefield for use in the fifth essay.

Phil Dixon, who discussed the Omaha Tigers with me and who made me aware of certain matters pertaining to that club.

Bill Francis of the National Baseball Hall of Fame, who always takes time from his busy schedule to respond to my requests.

Julie and Bob Gregg, who prepared many of the images in the correct format and size for the book.

Dennis E. Hoffman, my baseball-conversation buddy, whose excellent interviewing skills are equal to his excellent writing skills, for obtaining images of the majority of the interviewees in the second section of the book.

Dennis Mihelich, another dear friend and an outstanding historian and author, who patiently listened to my updates about the progress of the manuscript and who offered encouragement along the way.

John Morse, who confirmed or corrected the accuracy of certain names.

My longtime friend, the always dependable Bob Nash, who not only contributed a essay to the book and co-wrote another essay but who also spent an inordinate amount of time tracking down two images.

And the providers of most of the images found in the book: Rob Anderson and Glen Sisk of Creighton University; Steve Bauermeister; Kelli Bogan and John "Go Big Red!" Horne of the National Baseball Hall of Fame; Al Gilmore; Gary Gilmore; Bill Gonzalez

**viii  Acknowledgments**

of the Durham Museum; Peaches James; Mary-Jo Miller of the Nebraska State Historical Society; Kyle Parkinson of Vanderbilt University; James Redden; Terri Sanders of the Great Plains Black History Museum; Jordan Stepp of the University of California; Rodger Ulmar; Cody Voga of the University of Minnesota; and Phil Wise.
    Many thanks to all of you!

# Table of Contents

*Acknowledgments* — vii

*Foreword*
    James E. Overmyer — 1

*Introduction: Blacks, Baseball and the Cornhusker State*
    Angelo J. Louisa — 3

## Section I—The Long and Winding Road

Prologue
    Angelo J. Louisa — 8

1. The Best in the West: The Lincoln Giants
    Jeremy S. Bloch — 9

2. Integration Before the "Great Experiment": The Nebraska State League of 1892
    William H. Lyons — 25

3. Bud Fowler: Baseball's Black Pioneer Comes to Nebraska
    David C. Ogden — 65

4. The Buffalo Soldiers Play Ball
    Robert P. Nash — 78

5. Shadow Ball in the River City: The Omaha Federals, Tigers and Rockets
    Angelo J. Louisa — 90

6. Satchel Paige Was Here: Rambles Through Nebraska
    Devon M. Niebling — 155

7. When Jackie Came to Town
    John A. Shorey — 172

8. African Americans in the College World Series
    Jerry E. Clark — 184

9. The Pride of Omaha: Bob Gibson
    William R. Lamberty *and* Robert P. Nash — 202

## Section II—Voices from the Omaha Area

Prologue
    Dennis E. Hoffman    216

10. John Morse    219
11. James Redden    225
12. Al Gilmore    229
13. Jerry Bartee    235
14. Steve Bauermeister    242
15. Gary Gilmore    246
16. Rodger Ulmar    253
17. Ron Bartee    258
18. Phil Wise    265
19. Johnny Rodgers    273
20. Kimera Bartee    279
21. Peaches James    286

*About the Contributors*    293
*Index*    295

# Foreword

James E. Overmyer

Baseball history tends to focus primarily on the star players and the most famous teams. For major league baseball followers it's easy to find something to read on Babe Ruth, Ty Cobb, or Mike Trout, or on the New York Yankees, the Brooklyn Dodgers, or the Boston Red Sox. This is also true of the Negro Leagues, which existed before professional ball was firmly integrated beginning in the late 1940s. Folks who follow the history of the black leagues know about Josh Gibson, Satchel Paige, and their fellow Hall of Fame members, and about the top teams they played for, such as the Homestead Grays and Kansas City Monarchs.

To view baseball history (or any history, for that matter) from that angle is like looking up at the tower of an architectural masterpiece while ignoring its foundation, the thing that holds it up. The major leagues grew out of successful local efforts to form baseball teams and leagues, producing the talent that, like cream, rose to the top. But local baseball, at its own level, has experiences worth remembering and documenting. Often, they are remarkably similar to those of the big leagues. I was part of a group that started a local baseball history museum and wrote an accompanying book a few years ago. Other than not being able to boast of a major league franchise, we found an example of just about every important baseball historical milestone in our county, including the birthplaces of two Hall of Famers, one of whom, Frank Grant, was black.

*The African American Baseball Experience in Nebraska: Essays and Memories*, a joint project by 10 researchers and writers, accomplishes this for that Great Plains state, which has its own black Hall of Famer, star pitcher Bob Gibson. This book sets down both the factual history of black ball and the personal reminiscences of a number of relatively recent participants. It lets the readers follow what happened as black players began to excel in baseball beginning in the late 19th century and, at the same time, understand what it meant to them, particularly as they fought their way through discrimination both on the field and off.

Professional black ball in Nebraska goes back to probably 1890, when William Pope, a black hotel waiter, put together the Lincoln Giants. The team, like many in those early days of pro ball, did not draw well enough to survive very long, but it brought good black players into the professional side of the sport. Men from its roster later played with major Eastern and Midwestern black teams, including the Page Fence, Cuban, Chicago Union, Philadelphia, and Leland Giants.

The Lincoln Giants, as an all-black team, didn't make it into the new Nebraska State League (NSL) in 1892, but the capital city had an entry, and six black players, among them the renowned Bud Fowler, were on the rosters of otherwise white clubs. Although an integrated professional league wasn't completely unknown at that time, it was rare. This was progress in baseball for black opportunities, but of course it didn't come easily. The Hastings correspondent to *The Sporting News* called the NSL, "The Nebraska Coon League.... The reason it is called the Coon League is that all the teams with the exception of Hastings and Grand Island have one or more colored players."

The NSL folded after less than a season, putting all its players, both white and black, out of work. Thereafter, opportunities for African Americans were on so-called semipro teams, such as the Omaha Tigers, third-place finishers in the 1935 Nebraska Semipro Baseball Tournament. Also, the state's baseball culture was strong enough to entice barnstorming pro squads, some of them black. A notable game in Omaha in 1936 featured a Negro League all-star team that had Satchel Paige, who pulled his fabled trick of calling in his whole outfield, then striking out the side.

Paige was real, of course, but by now is partly a mythological creature. The second half of the book consists of interviews with former players and coaches from the last 60 years or so who are all real—they played the game in high school, the majority of them played in college, and a few played professionally. They overcame antagonism from white teammates, indifference from some white coaches, and still succeeded, as when Omaha's mostly black Technical High team, coached by a white teacher, John Morse, upset the city's high school baseball world by winning the 1966 state tournament.

One man, unfortunately unavailable for an interview because he had died before the project started, is mentioned over and over as a pivotal figure. He was Josh Gibson, not the Hall of Fame catcher, but Bob Gibson's older brother, who developed black youths' ball skills so they could move up to teams like Tech's champions. As one of his players, Jerry Bartee, put it, "The message Josh communicated was simple: If you're fundamentally sound and play with a big heart, then you're a winner."

This book is a winner, too, for just those reasons.

*James E. Overmyer is a baseball historian specializing in the Negro Leagues, particularly biographies and team histories. A member of the Society for American Baseball Research (SABR) and its Negro Leagues Committee, he is the author of* Queen of the Negro Leagues; Black Ball and the Boardwalk; *and* Cum Posey of the Homestead Grays.

# Introduction

## Blacks, Baseball and the Cornhusker State

### Angelo J. Louisa

Although the state of Nebraska is usually not thought of as being a center for black baseball in the same way that the cities of Chicago, Kansas City, and Pittsburgh were centers for black baseball, it certainly has had its share of contributions to the African American baseball experience. For example, the Lincoln Giants were an outstanding black independent club in the early 1890s and were followed in the capital city by the Kroner Silver Grays in the mid–'90s and the Cuban Giants at the end of the decade.[1] The Nebraska State League was the only integrated league in Organized Baseball in the United States in 1892, with three teams having African American players, one of whom was the famous Bud Fowler. "Buffalo Soldier" regiments stationed at Fort Niobrara and Fort Robinson during the last two decades of the 19th century and the first decade of the 20th century fielded strong nines. The North Loup Sluggers from the African American settlement of DeWitty or, as it was later called, Audacious are said to have had several undefeated seasons during the early 1920s[2] and were known for their colorful on-field buffoonery.[3] And the city of Omaha was the home of various black amateur and semiprofessional clubs, such as the Pickwicks, the Lafayettes, the Beacons, the Western Stars, the Wilcox & Drapers, the Evans Laundrys, the Cudahy Rex, and the Union Pacific Gold Coast Limiteds,[4] and a few that were arguably minor league–caliber professional clubs, including the 1922 Federals, Omaha's entry in the short-lived Western League of Colored Baseball Clubs.[5]

Also, Omaha is the place where Newt Allen, considered by some baseball historians to be the best Negro League second baseman of the 1920s and early 1930s, honed his skills while a member of the Federals; where Piper Davis and Mickey Stubblefield got their professional baseball starts with the Tigers and the Rockets, respectively; and where Jackie Robinson visited in October of 1946. And, of course, Omaha is the birthplace of Bob Gibson, the renowned major league pitcher, who played for Omaha's Technical High School and Creighton University before embarking on a National Baseball Hall of Fame career with the St. Louis Cardinals.

In addition, since 1950, Omaha has been the site of the College World Series, an event in which black college baseball players have showcased their talents, and after Organized Baseball reintegrated itself, a number of African Americans have played for the minor league franchises located throughout the state.

However, even prior to the reintegration period, African American barnstorming teams—including those led by the ageless Satchel Paige—performed at a variety of

**4    Introduction**

Nebraska parks. In fact, the fire that destroyed Omaha's Western League Park in 1936 may have been started by white racists who were reacting against one of Paige's performances.

Other notable black or racially mixed teams that visited the Cornhusker State before the beginning of the reintegration period were the Kansas City Monarchs and the Pittsburgh Crawfords, two of the greatest Negro League franchises of all time, and the All Nations, a touring ball club composed of whites, blacks, Amerindians, and Asians, and featuring such African American stars as John Donaldson and José Méndez.

The first section of this book will cover nine of the most significant contributions that Nebraska has made to the African American baseball experience. Three of the essays are about black teams that represented different parts of the state. Two essays deal with famous black players who came to the state and demonstrated their prowess on local diamonds, whereas one examines how the city of Omaha provided a venue for young African American talent. One essay focuses on the best black player to be born and raised in the state. Another looks at an attempt at integration during the 19th century, and one addresses the appearance of an African American icon.

But why nine contributions and, in particular, why these nine? Well, since nine is one of the mystical numbers of baseball,[6] it is fitting to limit the assortment of topics presented in this type of book to that number. As for the specific topics chosen, they are a good sampling to highlight the state in terms of interest, diversity, and importance. Obviously, not every black player or every team containing black players could be featured, and for many, there was not enough information to write an essay-length study about them.

However, for those topics that were chosen for inclusion in the first section, all the essays were written exclusively for this book, and each contributor has engaged in original research with heavy usage of primary writings, resulting in new interpretations being presented and new questions being raised.[7] Other strengths of this section are that the majority of the topics have not been written about in detail—for that matter, some have not been written about at all—and that many of the contributors are highly qualified authors and/or baseball historians.

The second section contains a collection of memories from individuals who participated in and/or who witnessed Nebraska's African American baseball experience in the Omaha area. Eleven of these reminiscences were gathered through interviews by the "Damon Runyon of Omaha," Dennis E. Hoffman, whereas the remaining one came from an interview that the editor had with James Redden, who served as a batboy for two black teams on their visits to the River City. Taken together, these oral recollections help to bring the book to life by supplying a different dimension of baseball history.

The product of these labors is a mosaic of well-known, somewhat known, and virtually unknown individuals who, despite having to deal with racial injustices on and off the field, did their best to make the African American baseball experience in Nebraska a memorable one.

NOTES

1. James E. Brunson III, *Black Baseball, 1858–1900: A Comprehensive Record of the Teams, Players, Managers, Owners and Umpires* (Jefferson, North Carolina: McFarland & Company, Inc., Publishers, 2019), 142.

2. Carla Garner, "DeWitty/Audacious, Nebraska (1908- )," http://www.blackpast.org/aaw/dewitty-audacious-nebraska-1908 (accessed on June 30, 2015), and Stew Magnuson, "July 4 Ballgame at DeWitty,

1914," http://www.northplattebulletin.com/index.asp?show=news&action=readStory&storyID=32517&pageID=24 (accessed on June 30, 2015).

3. Jean Williams, "Nebraska's Negro Homesteaders Located at DeWitty," *NEBRASKAland* (February 1969) found at http://rootsweb.ancestry.com/~necherry/Negro.htm.

4. Brunson, 142–143; "Here's First League to Finish Season and It Was a Successful One[:] Members of Teams in the Colored Simon Pure Amateur Circuit," *Omaha World-Herald*, July 18, 1926; and "For Colored Title," *Omaha World-Herald*, August 21, 1927.

5. "Colored Western League Is Formed," *Morning Tulsa Daily World*, May 3, 1922. The league has also been formally referred to as the "Western League of Negro Baseball Clubs" but was commonly called the "Colored Western League" or the "Western Colored League." Cf. *ibid.*; "Western Colored League Is Formed," *Oakland (CA) Tribune*, May 3, 1922; "New Monrovia Park Will Be Opened Friday," *Wichita Beacon*, May 31, 1922; and "Coffeyville Nine Beat Monrovians and Tied Up Count," *Wichita Beacon*, June 20, 1922. For the purposes of this book, "Western League of Colored Baseball Clubs" will be used as the league's formal name and "Colored Western League" as its sobriquet.

6. For a fascinating article on the relationship of the number nine with baseball, see Mark Newman, "Baseball Revolves Around Number Nine," http://m.mlb.com/news/article/6837626 (accessed on June 30, 2015).

7. Although the notes have been standardized for consistency purposes, each contributor is responsible for the accuracy of his or her own documentation.

# Section I
# The Long and Winding Road

# Prologue

### Angelo J. Louisa

The African American baseball experience in Nebraska mirrored that of much of the rest of the United States: a long and winding road. During the years before 1899 when Organized Baseball practiced limited integration and all-black clubs began to be formed, Nebraska saw the appearance of the African American Lincoln Giants, the rise and fall of the mostly white, slightly black 1892 Nebraska State League, the coming and going of African American baseball pioneer Bud Fowler, and the arrival of black cavalry and infantry regiments that fielded baseball teams. During the period of complete segregation—1899–1945—the Cornhusker State witnessed the development of African American minor league–caliber clubs and the visits of black barnstorming teams as well as some African American major league–caliber nines. And during the era of reintegration—1946 to the present—Nebraska welcomed Jackie Robinson, became the permanent site of the College World Series, which brought black college players to Omaha, and observed the on-the-field and off-the-field maturation of Bob Gibson.

But what are the details about these matters, and what do these details say about the successes and failures of black baseball players in the 37th state?

The following essays attempt to answer these questions to provide a better understanding of the African American baseball experience in Nebraska.

# 1

# The Best in the West

## *The Lincoln Giants*

### Jeremy S. Bloch

Only 35 years removed from the American Civil War, the progressive city of Lincoln, Nebraska, embraced an all-black baseball team in 1890 and 1891. Lincoln, which had become the capital of Nebraska in 1867 and the home of the University of Nebraska in 1869, proved to be the perfect place for the first African American club west of the Mississippi River. And the club reciprocated by playing a brand of baseball that made its fans proud and that showed that blacks could hold their own against their white counterparts on the diamond.

## *The Omaha Pickwicks and Lafayettes*

No one knows for sure when the first Nebraska African American baseball club was established, but arguably the earliest was the Omaha Pickwicks. Formed in 1887 and apparently gone by 1888, this River City contingent competed against both black and white nines and was considered "the strongest team in the [Big O] barring none."[1] On August 28, 1887, it even played a game against the all-Caucasian C.E. Mayne Base Ball Club for the Nebraska amateur state championship, something that the African American *(St. Paul, MN) Western Appeal* reported that the Pickwicks were "cheated out of ... by the alleged umpire."[2]

Another early black club was the Omaha Lafayettes, who operated during the late 1880s. The Lafayettes, whose "roster drew entirely from employees of the Millard Hotel,"[3] which was located at the corner of Douglas and 13th streets, fielded amateur teams in 1888 and 1889. The first narrowly lost the state championship to the John J. Hardins, two games to one,[4] and the second was touted by the *Omaha Daily Bee* on August 13, 1889, as "the head of the amateur clubs of the state" after concluding a 25-game road trip in which it compiled a 14–11 record.[5] However, just as important as their accomplishments were in and of themselves, the Lafayettes' triumphs made an impression on an enterprising African American waiter who had an ambitious vision.

### February–April 1890

In the spring of 1890, William Pope, that enterprising African American waiter, who just happened to be working at the Millard Hotel,[6] had hopes of forming an all-black baseball club. Seeing the success that the Lafayettes had had, Pope took a chance to better his socioeconomic standing by putting a similar team in Nebraska's proposed state league.[7] Initially, Pope found financial backing from investors in Fremont, Nebraska,[8] but Lincoln provided more potential ticket sales and had shown interest in having a club of its own. The idea of a league was paramount to Pope's vision. His team would need a regular schedule, as well as guaranteed revenue, and Lincoln would be the best place to headquarter his creation. The capital city had been without a professional team since 1888,[9] and Pope thought that Lincoln had a community that enjoyed baseball and facilities to support what would become, for all intents and purposes, a minor league–caliber club. Also, he had the contacts to bring in talented players and supportive fans. Thus, the marriage of Pope, Lincoln, and a new ball club was poised for success.

For his field general, Pope hired William "Blackest" Lewis, a local African American manager, who had served as a waiter with Pope at the Millard Hotel.[10] Lewis, a former member of the Omaha Lafayettes, was in charge of baseball matters. His job included searching the nation for promising athletes, and he found some of his stars in Colorado, Kansas, Michigan, Pennsylvania, and Washington, D.C. In addition, he picked up ace pitcher Joseph "Kid" Miller, another former Lafayette.[11] Pope and Lewis had the team built around three separate pitcher and catcher combinations, though William Jackson, a catcher from Detroit, Michigan, who had played in the Michigan State League, and Bud English, a pitcher from Leavenworth, Kansas, who had been a member of a Topeka nine, were later released when they failed to report.[12]

However, by mid–April it was clear a Nebraska state baseball league would not come to fruition—at least not in 1890. Sadly for proponents of such an idea, only three towns—Kearney, Grand Island, and Lincoln—had secured enough interest and financial backing for representation in the league.[13] But despite the bleak outlook, Pope and Lewis were determined to continue their venture as an independent club.

## May 1890

Starting on May 4, a local paper, the *Daily Nebraska State Journal,* began to ramp up publicity for the Giants. In an article titled "Ready to Play Ball," the Giants were making their last few days of preparations before the start of the season. The paper touted, "Mr. Pope, assisted by Manager Lewis, has spent considerable time in getting together a team of thirteen players which he knows can put up a good game."[14] In particular, there was a buzz in the air for the arrival of George William "Will" Castone, a pitcher who had seen action for Aspen in the Colorado State League[15] as well as at least 11 other teams (See Table 1).

On May 7, the Giants played their first game against an all-white team, the Omaha Reserves. A fair crowd attended to see the new squad, including "not a few ladies."[16] Frank Maupin caught for the Giants and Colorado transplant Castone was the pitcher. Apparently fired up for his first start with his new club, Castone dazzled the team from Omaha, giving up only two hits to the Reserves. The final score was 15–2 in favor of the Lincolnites, with Omaha's runs scored on errors after their hits. The Giants' James Hightower walloped a ball over the center field fence in the eighth inning to add to the opening festivities, and the new squad had great pitching and hitting, much to the delight of the ownership.

On the other hand, the game was not without its shortcomings. Lincoln had three errors, and during the hit parade, one of the Giants was called out for batting out of order.

Also, the team announced that manager Lewis secured John "Jack" Reeves, "a big, heavy" talented pitcher from Kansas City,[17] who had been a member of the Omaha Lafayettes and two Missouri clubs (see Table 1). Obviously, Lewis was not going to rest on his laurels.

The following day pitted the same teams against each other. The Reserves pitched Stevenson, who was considered their best hurler, while Kid Miller was the starting pitcher for the Giants. But Miller pitched poorly, not making it out of the fourth inning before being replaced by Castone. The *Daily Nebraska State Journal* reviewed his performance and noted that "Miller's delivery did not seem to be much of a puzzle, and those who failed to connect with the sphere were presented with a base on balls."[18] Miller left his team in a hole by allowing 11 runs in his four innings, but after Castone entered the game, the Reserves did not score again. And because of Castone's strong relief pitching, the Giants were able to plate four runs in the ninth inning to tie the game and subsequently win in the 10th, 12–11.[19]

On May 10, following a contest that was rained out the day before, Jack Reeves, the new acquisition from Kansas City, pitched his first game,[20] something that the team and fans alike anticipated after the *Daily Nebraska State Journal* reported, "In addition to being a first[-]class twirler[,] Reeves has a good record as an all[-]around player and a heavy batter."[21] And Reeves did not disappoint, tossing a complete game and surrendering three runs, only one of them earned. The Giants' took the field in the ninth, leading 5–1. At this point, Reeves had surrendered just one hit, but the defense almost gave away the game. With two men on, an errant throw by Giant shortstop Hugh Hughbanks caused the Reserves to score two runs, making the score 5–3. Hughbanks then redeemed himself by turning a "neat double play" with George Hughbanks to end what was called "one of the best exhibitions of ball playing ever seen in the city."[22]

After a 3–0 series sweep, the newspapers dubbed the all-black team the Lincoln Giants, and with the team's success, attendance continued to grow. Whereas there were few women in attendance during the first game of the series, by the third game, the papers reported, "There are many admirers of the national game among the fair sex of Lincoln and a large number were on the grounds yesterday."[23]

The Giants played at Association Ballpark at 22nd and Randolph Street, sharing the facilities with the Nebraska Wesleyan University and University of Nebraska baseball squads. The grounds were first class with a "sprinkling apparatus" and a locker room complete with a bath.[24] In anticipation of many fans, club management provided streetcars to transport spectators from 12th and O Streets to the ballpark and back.[25]

After rain cancelled a two-day series with the Nonpareils from Council Bluffs, Iowa,[26] the Giants took on the University of Nebraska's team and defeated it rather handily, 7–3, with the highlight of the game being a triple play. This contest prepared the African Americans to leave on a statewide trip to face the strongest club in Nebraska: the Kearneys.[27]

On May 14, the Giants played in windy conditions against the Kearneys. With the inclement weather wreaking havoc on the field, Castone took the mound throwing a drop. The newspaper raved about his pitching, "When the wind raised[,] it blew with great force against the ball and this aided materially in the drop. When the balls got near the plate[,] they would shoot right down to the ground and the Kearney boys couldn't find them."[28] The Giants also benefited from two new additions to the squad: outfielder George Taylor and middle infielder Jesse Brown scored five of the team's 10 total runs, including a round tripper by the former player, as Lincoln squeaked out a victory with a final score of 10–9.

A major influence on the game's outcome was the officiating provided by the home team. The *Kearney (NE) Daily Hub* described the umpire's performance as:

> [I]f he erred[,] it was lack of knowledge and not the heart....
> If he was at fault and we knew it[,] we wouldn't say so, for the simple reason that no one would believe it. Base ball [*sic*] boys are so accustomed to kicking on the umpire [i.e., complaining about the umpire's decisions] that people never believe their claims even when true.[29]

The second contest in the series was a scoring battle with the Giants winning, 21–15. When Taylor hit another home run, some of the over 800 fans in attendance threw money in appreciation of his extraordinary talent. After the Kearneys lost both games, a local sportswriter referred to the Giants as "coons."[30] But this sort of racist remark was not surprising for the early 1890s, especially after embarrassing a white team.

On the tail end of the road trip, the Giants stopped in Ulysses, Nebraska, where they edged the home nine, 8–7.[31] However, the second game, played on May 16, was won easily by Lincoln in seven rain-shortened innings. The final score, 20–3, garnered Jack Reeves another pitching victory,[32] and the Giants' record improved to 8–0 within the first two weeks of play.

The team returned to the capital city for the much anticipated rematch with the Kearneys, and both the Kearney and Lincoln papers publicized the event. The following poem, "Kearney's Wail of Woe," demonstrates the gravity of the rivalry and the racial tensions prevalent in the late 19th century:

> T'was in the merry month of May—
>     Oh! listen to my wail of woe—
> Nine "cullud gemmen" came this way
> A game of base ball for to play—
>     Are you listening to this wail of woe?
> From "Linkum" City they did come—
>     Oh! horrid is my wail of woe—
> And the way they made the "Kahneys" hum
> And made their physiogs look glum,
>     Would make a million wails of woe.
> They mopped the "Kahneys" up and down—
>     Whoop! was ever such a wail of woe?—
> And when they left the Midway town
> With all our "dollahs" salted down—
>     Resounded then our wail of woe.[33]

The Kearneys were clearly upset with the losses, so they went out and "strengthened [their team] at every point, and with a professional pitcher imported for the occasion."[34] Lincoln prepared for the rematch by purchasing new uniforms and baseball bats. It also hired a band to excite the crowd. The new uniforms were "blue, with maroon stockings, belts and caps."[35] But with all the pomp and circumstance and an attendance of 1,500,[36] the game was a disappointment to both the fans and the ticket office. Poor streetcar service due to a break in the track made getting to the ballpark a challenge, whereas poor defensive playing, especially by the brothers Hugh and George Hughbanks, caused the Giants to lose, 12–10. In front of a small group of rooters, Lincoln suffered its first defeat.

Many of these rooters blamed the loss on the umpiring, probably brought about because one player from each team was chosen to do the officiating,[37] while the Kearney fans declared their team ready for a championship based on this one win.[38]

After the second game of the series, *The Kearney (NE) Daily Hub* reported, "The coons out-play [sic] the Kearneys all around…. The colored gentlemen from Salt Creek mopped the earth with the Kearney boys."[39] The umpiring did not stir up trouble; the Giants simply performed better than the Kearneys in a 10–5 victory, with Reeves striking out an impressive 12 batters.[40]

A large crowd attended the third game against the Kearneys. With both teams boasting a win, the outcome would determine the series victor, but bad officiating played a large part in the Giants' 6–5 loss. The umpire selected for the game was reported as being "a gentleman bred and propagated somewhere on the Mississippi bottoms,"[41] and he was so bad that after his decision to call a clearly foul ball "fair," a riot broke out. Once the game was over, the two managers of the clubs agreed to hire "Joseph McCullough [a supposedly unbiased umpire] to officiate the next series of games with power to impose fines not to exceed over [sic] $50 on each team."[42]

Fresh off their first losing series, the Giants traveled to the River City to again play the Omaha Reserves,[43] but in what was described as "One of the best [']amateur['] games

**To strengthen their team, in late May of 1890, the Giants picked up Will Lincoln, seen here (at the right end of the back row) as a player on the integrated 1894 David City, Nebraska, club (Nebraska State Historical Society, RG3064-26).**

ever played in Omaha," they lost, 2–1. With over 1,000 people in attendance, the Lincolnites' poor fielding resulted in numerous errors and their third defeat of the season.[44]

After this loss, the team elected a new captain. Will Castone replaced James Hightower as the leader of the Giants and management hired a new shortstop, William "Dorcas" Lincoln, in an effort to turn around their recent misfortunes.[45] And apparently, the changes made a difference, as the team went back to Lincoln the next day and defeated the University of Nebraska.[46]

On May 30, following a plea by the newspapers, 1,800 spectators watched the home game versus the Omaha Reserves. This was the largest crowd on record for the Giants, and their fans went away satisfied as Castone pitched a two-hitter in a 6–0 shutout victory,[47] as the team's record went to 11–3.[48]

## June 1890

With a successful May on the books, Pope reported many towns wanted the Giants to play their local ball clubs. Places such as Hastings and Tecumseh touted their squads as up for the challenge of the Lincoln Giants.[49] The all-black team was making a name for itself across the state.

Big changes came in the early days of June. William Lewis, the manager, resigned his post on June 2, but remained with the club as a player. Castone, the captain, then took on the manager position. And Hugh Hughbanks, Kid Miller, and William Newman were released from the team,[50] apparently to lower expenses and for lackluster performances to date.[51]

For the first game of the month, the Giants welcomed the Nonpareils from Council Bluffs and came away with a difficult 9–8 victory, the first loss for the Nonpareils all season.[52] The second contest of the series took place on June 5, and even though the Nonpareils made 12 errors, the Lincolnites "did what they could to make a good game of it,"[53] triumphing, 10–4.

Having swept the short series, the Giants celebrated with another set of new uniforms, which were described by the *Daily Nebraska State Journal* as being, "black with white stockings and trimmings, and are first class in every way."[54]

The next game was against a team of local business representatives. The contest itself did not yield much excitement, as the Giants won, 14–0, after the businessmen gave up in the eighth inning.[55] One of the opposing players was Charlie Hoover,[56] who all season long had been a thorn in the Giants' side. He would volunteer to umpire and purposely make calls against the Giants or he would offer to play for the opposing team if they did not have enough players.[57] It is unknown where his disdain for the Giants originated, but racism and jealousy were likely causes.

On June 10, Manager Castone and his team were granted their dream game against the all-white Omaha Western Association (WA) club. This team was a talented group of professional ballplayers, and the Giants wished to compare themselves to the Omahans in a head-to-head challenge. But unfortunately for the Lincolnites and their fans, the home team lost by a score of 11–5. Fielding was atrocious, and the Giants missed "ten hits which would have been put-outs [sic] had they played their ordinary game."[58] The umpiring also hurt the Giants' chances. According to the *Lincoln (NE) Evening News,* "[The ump] was calling Omaha men safe when they were plainly out, and calling Lincoln men out when they were safe." Then he was replaced in the fifth inning by the infamous Charlie

Hoover.[59] The loss demoralized the team and led to the release of former captain James Hightower.[60]

The next series the Giants played gave them a needed boost in morale and the confidence to continue their season. First, the team went to Ulysses for a quick game, which resulted in a quick victory, and then returned to host the Ulysses club. This contest thrilled the Lincoln fans as Reeves struck out a season high 20 batters, which proved to be not only a career best for the pitcher, but also a single-game record for the city of Lincoln. Also, Reeves helped himself offensively by hitting a home run.[61] Those two victories would be followed by two more, as the Giants swept the four-game series.[62]

On June 20, the African Americans traveled to Genoa, Nebraska, to play the Genoa Indians. The meeting of these two minority teams caused quite the spectacle, and many fans came to see the games. But while the Indians' fielding was acceptable, their batting left a lot to be desired, as they managed only three hits the entire series, and the Giants took both contests with scores of 8–0 and 2–0.[63] "The superiority of the colored man over the Indian in the national game of base ball [sic] was demonstrated yesterday at Genoa, when the Giants crossed bats with the club from the Indian school at that place."[64] Leaving aside the racist tone of that statement, both teams surely recognized the common struggle that they faced as minorities playing America's pastime.

The next week, the Western Association team from Denver stopped to play a game in Lincoln, giving the Giants a chance to redeem themselves for their loss to a previous WA club. Dave Rowe, a famous midwestern ballplayer, managed and played for the Denver team, something that brought out a number of fans.[65] In front of 1,200 spectators, Lincoln got three runs in the first four innings. But unfortunately for the locals, the first four innings were the highlight of the game, with their team surrendering 12 runs over the last five innings to lose, 12–3.[66]

On June 26, Castone arranged a four-game series, of which three contests were played, with a familiar opponent: the Omaha Reserves. The Giants played well and won the first contest, but the management and players were discouraged by poor attendance.[67] Following the game, the *Daily Nebraska State Journal* reported Castone's disappointment:

> I think my team has furnished good ball for the people of Lincoln, but such support as this is very discouraging. The time has come when it is necessary for the public to understand that if they wish the club to exist[,] better support must be given. After this series of games[,] if we receive any encouragement[,] I will agree to secure a league team each week and such other clubs as are available, among them the Chicago Whitings, Kansas City, Topeka, [M]issouri [V]alley[,] and others. Something must be done and it is but fair that the public be apprised of the fact.[68]

The Giants then beat the Reserves, 12–7, in the second game[69] and finished off the series with a 10–4 victory.[70] However, despite the warning from Castone, many fans stayed home and on June 28 the club disbanded. Owner Pope was reported as having "departed for greener fields," but the players planned to stick around Lincoln a while to see if the team would start up again.[71]

In a *Lincoln (NE) Evening News* article, one alleged reason for many of the monetary troubles was reported. According to former Giant captain James Hightower, both owner Pope and manager Castone were cooking the books and taking more money than they deserved. But Pope had already left town and Castone's fellow teammates refused to corroborate the allegations against their manager.[72] So, with the rumors remaining unsubstantiated, no criminal charges were brought against Pope or Castone. Instead, the *Lincoln (NE) Evening News* focused on the positive aspects of the team saying, "They are a gentlemanly set of men, quiet and unobtrusive, and as ball players [sic] they have no equals outside the professional teams. They have given us many good exhibitions of ball, and the *News* hopes they will be able to give many more."[73] The *News* and the Lincoln fans got their wish in early July.

## July 1890

On July 1, amidst rumors of William Pope wanting to swoop up the team and relocate them to Omaha, Will Castone and the players reorganized under their own proprietorship. Pope had hoped that the team would move to establish a better, more consistent fan base, leading to a steady stream of profit. He had plans of taking the team through Iowa and Illinois, but the city of Lincoln and the players had other notions.[74]

The July 2 edition of the *Daily State Nebraska Journal* reported that the Giants would reorganize. Every member on the team signed a contract stating that they were no longer under the employment of Mr. Pope.[75] Instead, each player would receive a portion of the earnings from each game. And without a major investor, the players were able to set their own ticket prices.

Castone, as the club's leader, was busy trying to build a fan base, win games, and support a minority baseball team. In order to do so, he wished to take the Giants on a tour through Iowa, Illinois, Michigan, and possibly New York, saying "This team, one of the strongest aggregations in the [W]est, as it is, will advertise the city of Lincoln far and near and slug its way to fortune and to fame without a doubt."[76]

But before any trip could be made, the Giants hosted the Haverlys, the 1890 amateur champions from Kansas City. The three-game series took place over July 4 and 5, with the Giants winning two of the matchups.[77] Four hundred people attended the doubleheader on July 4, a good turnout considering the Haverlys were not a professional organization.[78] However, a small crowd of 150 people attended the July 5 game, and once again, Castone threatened to disband the team.[79] These threats were a ploy to receive better ticket sales or corporate financial support. And surprisingly, the scheme worked as the *Daily Nebraska State Journal* reported, "It is now pretty certain that the Giants will remain. Several prominent lovers of the game have rendered substantial aid[,] and with a subscription list in circulation which has been liberally signed[,] everything looks favorable for the club."[80] As the team celebrated their new financing, Castone resigned as its manager but continued to pitch, and Ed Carr, a supplemental right fielder, catcher, and pitcher, stepped in as the new manager in mid–July.[81]

Now financially secure, the Giants travelled to Kansas City to face the Haverlys in another series and the Kansas City Maroons in a single game. The first contest in the Haverly series was very well attended, breaking Kansas City records for fans watching a game involving an amateur team.[82] The only loss on the field took place on July 13, 1890, in the second contest against the Haverlys. Once again, the defeat was blamed on poor umpiring and underhanded tricks on the part of the home team.[83] When this sort of dishonest play continued in the final game of the series, the Giants refused to participate any further, forfeiting in the eighth inning.[84]

While in Kansas City, George Taylor, Lincoln's power hitter and a man who could play four positions, and Frank Maupin, Lincoln's primary catcher who also saw action in left field and center field, left the team.[85] Both had been unhappy with the team management since Pope's departure. Now down two players, the Giants travelled to Missouri

Valley, Iowa, to compete against its amateur local nine. There, they lost, 5–2, due to their opponent's incredible pitching display. Missouri Valley's hurler, known only as "Beymer," went all the way, striking out 12 Lincolnites and allowing just six hits.[86]

With the summer coming to a close, the Giants returned home to face Nebraska City on July 25, 1890. This was the last game in their 1890 season, and from what the *Lincoln (NE) Evening News* wrote, one that left something to be desired by both teams:

> Ed Marnell came up from Nebraska City yesterday morning with ten strapping young men, whom he confidentially told the *News* comprised the champion semi-professional [sic] team of Nebraska. It must have been their day off, for when they struck the remnant of the once-famous Lincoln Giants[,] they played like a lot of farmers. As a matter of fact, neither one of the teams acted as though they had seen a ball game [sic]....
> The shortstop and the third baseman of each team early in the game became imbued with the idea that the first basemen were ten feet high and their proper position on the right foul fence.[87]

The game was tied, 5–5, going into the ninth, but timely hitting by the Lincolnites produced two more runs and secured the victory, 7–5.[88]

On July 27, 1890, the *Daily State Nebraska Journal* reported that the Giants were disbanding for the rest of the season. Though the paper did not state the reasons behind the team's folding, money troubles continued to plague the club throughout July. The *Nebraska Journal* also reported that the team played 45 games that season and won 39 of them, whereas the *Omaha Daily Bee* stated that it "lost only four or five games out of about thirty played."[89] But Will Castone claimed that his club finished 40–5, baseball historian Gregory Bond wrote that the correct record is 45–5, and another baseball historian, Kent Morgan, has shown that if the results of each game as found in the various newspaper accounts are added together, the Giants had 30 wins and nine losses.[90]

## 1891 and Beyond

Sol White, in his *History of Colored Base Ball* [sic], states that after the Lincoln Giants folded, there were only three all–African American professional baseball teams in 1890—a slight understatement in that there were at least four such teams operating at that time[91]—and that the Giants were the first completely black team in the West, meaning the area west of the Mississippi River.[92] However, he does not acknowledge the fact that the Giants reorganized for a second season in 1891.[93]

Will Castone tried to resurrect the club throughout the offseason and place it in a league to end the barnstorming-style scheduling, but his efforts came to naught. On the other hand, he did manage to bring the club back to life as an independent team by the middle of the 1891 season, with the Giants playing their first game on July 4 against the Nonpareils of Council Bluffs. He then put out a challenge in *The Sporting News*, declaring that the recently renewed squad would schedule a series against any African American club in the world, hoping that he would get the attention of the famous Cuban Giants. For that matter, Castone and his teammates were so desperate to have a game that they said that they would perform for any amount of money and give the entire gate receipts to their opponent, an offer extended to any black or white semiprofessional team.[94] But this turned out to be a disappointing attempt to kick-start the second season and the club disbanded in August with a 10–7 record.[95]

Some of the players from the Giants' club would be integrated into white Nebraska State League (NSL) teams during the 1892 season, but all-white teams in the league were reluctant to play against clubs that were integrated. Owners and managers alike were not pleased when cities like Plattsmouth, Kearney, and Beatrice signed five former Giant members. These men were talented and intelligent when it came to playing baseball, but the color of their skin was foremost in the eyes of the bigots. It was one thing to lose to an all-black team, but these integrated squads were not well received by some Nebraskans. For example, the Plattsmouth team had three white players who purposely performed badly after the arrival of their black teammates. One was eventually sold to Beatrice and the other two broke their contracts and joined teams located outside of the state.[96]

The NSL eventually folded in the middle of the 1892 season, causing the former Giant players to look for work. Castone continued to attempt to get an all-black team into a league, but his plans ultimately failed, as did any hope of reorganizing the Giants. Thus, following a three-year stint in Nebraska, George William Castone, who Gregory Bond called "the state's most important and versatile black ballplayer,"[97] left the Cornhusker State to join the New York Cuban Giants in 1893. After that, he moved to Chicago and then to St. Paul, Minnesota, serving as a coachman and butler during his stay in the former location and a waiter during his stay in the latter. Also while in the Windy City, he married a German immigrant by whom he had four children, whereas while in the Saintly City, he became an accomplished painter.[98]

Similarly, former owner William Pope and former manager William Lewis, who both said goodbye to the Giants in midseason of 1890, retired from pay-for-play baseball. By 1891, they rejoined Omaha's service industry, with Pope opening a restaurant and catering business in downtown Omaha with his brothers and Lewis going back to waiting tables.[99]

Among the baseball clubs that John Patterson played for after leaving Nebraska was the Adrian, Michigan, Page Fence Giants, who operated from 1895 through 1898. The date of the Giant team in the above image is unclear and depends on the identification of the pictured players. From what is known from different sources, the men shown are (left to right): Walker or Joe Miller, Charlie Grant or Sol White, George Wilson, John Patterson or Bill Binga, Pete Burns, Gus Parsons, unknown or possibly James Chavous, Grant "Home Run" Johnson, unknown or George Taylor, Billy Holland, unknown or John Patterson (National Baseball Hall of Fame Library).

But such was not the fate of all the Giants. William Lincoln, Frank Maupin, Kid Miller, Jack Reeves, John Patterson, and George Taylor played for various teams throughout the 1890s and at least three of the last four, and possibly all four, continued to do so for the first decade of the 20th century (see Table 1). In fact, Patterson performed so well that his name was added to the 2006 Negro Leagues Committee's preliminary ballot for induction into the National Baseball Hall of Fame.[100]

How then should the Lincoln Giants be remembered? Perhaps Kent Morgan said it best when he wrote:

> The tenacity and graceful performance of the team's players and founders contributed positively to the ebb and flow of a still evolving professional sport. [Their] story sketches a microcosm of the trials facing African American baseball players and teams during the late nineteenth century.[101]

## Table 1: The 1890 Lincoln Giants[102]

| Name | Position | Comments |
| --- | --- | --- |
| Jesse Brown | 2B, SS, CF | Played for the Washington, D.C., Douglas, 1882–1883, and the Philadelphia Gorhams in 1889 |
| James Bullock | CF, P | Played for the Lexington, Missouri, Black Stockings, 1888–1890; the Kansas City, Missouri, Maroons in 1890; the Los Angeles Trilbys, 1897–1900; the Salt Lake City Browns in 1899; the Salt Lake City Santiagos in 1899; and the San Diego Coast Giants, 1899–1900 |
| Ed Carr | RF, C, P | Played for the Topeka State House in 1887; the Topeka Capitals in 1888; the Topeka Athletics in ?; the Omaha Lafayettes, 1888–1889; the Omaha Beacons in 1889; the Kansas City, Missouri, Fire Department No. 11, 1892–1893; and the Omaha Colored Giants in 1898 |
| George William "Will" Castone | P, CF, LF, SS, 3B | (1867–1967). Played for the Kansas City, Missouri, Novels, the Topeka Athletics, and the Lawrence, Kansas, Eagles in 1886; the Concordia, Kansas, town team, 1886–1887; the Lawrence, Kansas, town team in 1887; the Kansas City, Missouri, Maroons, 1887–1888; the Colorado Springs Pastimes, the Salt Lake City Salt Lakes, and the Denver Solis in 1888; the Aspen, Colorado, Aspens or Silver Kings of the Colorado State League, the Georgetown, Colorado, team, and a Denver team in 1889; the Fremont town team, the Beatrice town team, the Kansas City, Missouri, Schmeizers, and the Denver Black Champions in 1891; Lincoln/Kearney of the Nebraska State League in 1892; and the New York Cuban Giants in 1893 |
| Dean | RF | Probably James Dean |
| Bud English | P | Released when he failed to report |
| George Hightower | 2B | |
| James Hightower | 1B, SS | Played for the Topeka Athletics in 1886 |
| George Hughbanks | 2B, 1B, LF, CF, SS | Played for the Omaha Pickwicks in 1887; the Omaha Lafayettes in 1888; the Omaha Colored Nine in 1894; and the Wilcox & Drapers in 1895 |
| Hugh Hughbanks | SS, 2B, CF | Played for the Omaha Pickwicks in 1887 and the Omaha Lafayettes in 1888 |
| William Jackson | C | Released when he failed to report |

| Name | Position | Comments |
|---|---|---|
| King | SS | |
| William "Blackest" Lewis | CF, 1B, SS, LF | Played for the Omaha Lafayettes in 1888; the Omaha Beacons in 1889; the Omaha Colored Nine in 1894; and possibly the Kansas City, Missouri, Unions in 1898 |
| James/William "Dorcas" or "Will" Lincoln | SS | Played for the Kansas City, Missouri, Maroons, 1887–1888; the Burlington Railroad team in Plattsmouth, Nebraska, in 1891; the Kansas City, Missouri, Fire Department No. 11, 1892–1893; the Hutchinson, Kansas, Clippers in 1893; the Omaha Hotel Midway in 1894; David City, Nebraska, team, 1894–1895; the Adrian, Michigan, Page Fence Giants in 1895; the Omaha Originals in 1895; the Hutchinson, Kansas, Browns in 1895; the Omaha All Omahas in 1897; the Lincoln Colored Giants, 1897–1898; and the Kansas City, Missouri, Times Hustlers in 1899 |
| Frank Maupin | C, LF, CF | Played for the Kansas City, Missouri, Novels and the Lawrence, Kansas, Eagles in 1886; Kansas City, Missouri, Maroons, 1887–1890, 1896–1897; Burlington Railroad team in Plattsmouth, Nebraska, and the Kansas City, Missouri, Stars in 1891; Plattsmouth of the Nebraska State League and a picked nine in Kansas City in 1892; the Kansas City, Missouri, Fire Department No. 11 in 1893; teams in Hutchinson, Kansas, in 1893 and 1895; the Omaha Colored Nine in 1894; the David City, Nebraska, team, 1894–1895; the Kansas City, Missouri, Times Hustlers, 1898–1899; and the Kansas City, Missouri, Bradburys in 1899 |
| Joseph "Joe" or "Kid" Miller | LF, P | Played for the Omaha Lafayettes in 1889; the Silver City, Iowa, Silver Citys in 1890; Nebraska City in 1891; the Osawatomie, Kansas, Coloreds in 1891; the Omaha Colored Nine, the Omaha Midways, and the Council Bluffs, Iowa, Maroons in 1894; the Adrian Demons of the Michigan State League and the Omaha Wilcox & Drapers in 1895; the Adrian, Michigan, Page Fence Giants in 1895, 1897, 1898, and, depending on the source, 1896; the Kansas City, Missouri, Unions in 1898; the Chicago Columbia Giants, 1898–1900; the Paola, Kansas, Colored Nine in 1899; and the Chicago Union Giants 1901–1903 |
| William Newman | CF, C, 1B | |
| John Patterson | 3B | John W. "Pat" Patterson (1872–1940). Played for the New Orleans Pinchbacks in 1889; the Deadwood, South Dakota, Metropolitans in 1891; Plattsmouth of the Nebraska State League in 1892; the New York Cuban Giants in 1893, 1894, 1896, and, depending on the source, 1895; the Adrian, Michigan, Page Fence Giants in 1895, 1897, and 1898; the New York Colored Giants in 1898; the Chicago Columbia Giants in 1899, 1900, and, depending on the source, 1901; the Chicago Colored Combination in 1900; the Chicago Union Giants in 1902; the Philadelphia Giants in 1903 and, depending on the source, 1908; the Cuban X Giants in 1904, 1905, and, depending on the source, 1906; depending on the source, the Philadelphia Quaker Giants in 1906; and the Brooklyn Royal Giants in 1906 and 1907. Became the manager of the Battle Creek, Michigan, High School baseball team in 1907 and led them to the state title that year. Served as a police officer in Battle Creek from 1909 through 1940.[103] |

| Name | Position | Comments |
|---|---|---|
| John "Jack" Reeves | P, CF, LF | Played for the Springfield, Missouri, Reds in 1888; the Kansas City Maroons, 1888–1890 and 1896–1897; the Omaha Lafayettes in 1889; the New York Cuban Giants in 1890; the St. Louis West Ends in 1891; Plattsmouth of the Nebraska State League and a picked nine in Kansas City in 1892; the Kansas City, Missouri, Fire Department No. 11 and the Springfield, Missouri, Blues in 1893; the David City, Nebraska, team in 1894; the Kansas City, Missouri, Times Hustlers, 1898–1899; and the Kansas City, Missouri, Colored Nine in 1900, for which he managed and may have played |
| Robertson | RF | |
| Smith | LF | |
| George Taylor | LF, 1B, C, 3B | George H. "Colored Prodigy," "Colored Wonder," or "Nellie" Taylor (1869-?). Played for the Aspen, Colorado, Aspens or Silver Kings of the Colorado State League in 1889; the Denver Claytons in 1890; the Denver Black Champions in 1891; Beatrice in the Nebraska State League in 1892; the Denver Denvers, 1892–1893; the Pueblo, Colorado, Pueblos, the Omaha Midways, the Council Bluffs, Iowa, Maroons, and the Findlay, Ohio, Giants in 1894; the Omaha Wilcox & Drapers in 1895; the Adrian, Michigan, Page Fence Giants, 1895–1898; depending on the source, either the Denver Gulfs of the Colorado State League in 1896 or the Denver Grizzlies of the Colorado State League in 1898; the Three Rivers, Michigan, Three Rivers in 1899; depending on the source, the Chicago Columbia Giants in 1900; the Chicago Union Giants in 1903 and 1904; the Leland Giants in 1905 and 1906; and the St. Paul Gophers in 1907 |

## Table 2: The 1891 Lincoln Giants[104]

| Name | Position | Comments |
|---|---|---|
| Harry Banks | P, 2B | Played for the Minton, Nebraska, Mintons in 1894 and the Omaha Wilcox & Drapers in 1895 |
| Broadus | LF | |
| James Bullock | P, OF | See Table 1. |
| Ed Carr | 3B, CF, C | See Table 1. |
| George William "Will" Castone | P, C | See Table 1. |
| Dean | RF | See Table 1. |
| Robert Dobbs (Dodds) | C, CF | Played for the Leavenworth, Kansas, Leapers, 1886–1888; an unspecified ball club in Colorado Springs, 1888–1889; the Aspen, Colorado, Aspens in 1889; the Pueblo, Colorado, West Sides in 1891; the Lincoln Kroner Silver Grays (Lincoln Greys or Silver Greys) in 1895; and the Central City, Colorado, Gilpins in 1899 |
| Harding | P, RF | Played for the Omaha Wilcox & Drapers and the Lincoln Kroner Silver Grays (Lincoln Greys or Silver Greys) in 1895 |
| James Hightower | 1B, SS | See Table 1. |
| George Hughbanks | 2B, CF | See Table 1. |

## 22   Section I—The Long and Winding Road

| Name | Position | Comments |
|---|---|---|
| James/William Lincoln | SS, P, 2B | See Table 1. |
| Frank Maupin | C | See Table 1. |
| Joseph "Kid" Miller | P, 3B | See Table 1. |
| John Patterson | 3B, 2B | See Table 1. |
| John "Jack" Reeves | No position found | See Table 1. |
| Smith | OF | |
| George Taylor | C, 1B, LF | See Table 1. |
| George Timpson | OF | |

## Notes

1. "Omaha, Neb.," *(St. Paul, MN) Western Appeal*, September 3, 1887.
2. Ibid.
3. Kent Morgan, "The 1890 Lincoln Giants: Professional Baseball's Unlikely Return to Nebraska's Capital City," *Nebraska History* 96, no. 2 (Summer 2015): 88.
4. "Hardins vs Lafayettes," *Omaha Daily Bee*, August 23, 1888, and "Lafayette vs Hardin," *Omaha Daily Bee*, August 24, 1888.
5. "Amateur Games" *Omaha Daily Bee*, August 13, 1889.
6. *Omaha City and South Omaha City Directory for 1890* (Omaha: J.M. Wolfe & Co., Publishers, 1890), 657.
7. Morgan, 85–91.
8. "Sporting Notes," *Lincoln (NE) Weekly Herald*, March 22, 1890.
9. For details on Lincoln's 1888 team, see Morgan, 87, and Bruce Esser, "Nebraska Minor League Baseball," http://www.nebaseballhistory.com/before1900.html (accessed on March 28, 2015).
10. Morgan, 85, and *Omaha City and South Omaha City Directory for 1890*, 482, 657.
11. "Ready to Play Ball," *Daily Nebraska State Journal*, May 4, 1890.
12. Ibid., and "They Show Up Well," *Daily Nebraska State Journal*, May 8, 1890.
13. "A Four[-]Town League," *Daily Nebraska State Journal*, April 11, 1890.
14. "Ready to Play Ball."
15. "Ready for the Fray," *Daily Nebraska State Journal,* May 7, 1890.
16. "They Show Up Well."
17. Ibid.
18. "It Took Ten Innings," *Daily Nebraska State Journal*, May 9, 1890.
19. Ibid.
20. "The Sporting World," *Daily Nebraska State Journal*, May 10, 1890.
21. Ibid.
22. "And Giants They Are," *Daily Nebraska State Journal*, May 11, 1890.
23. Ibid.
24. "The Sporting World," *Daily Nebraska State Journal*, May 10, 1890.
25. Ibid.
26. "The Sporting World," *Daily Nebraska State Journal*, May 13, 1890.
27. "Very Seldom Happens," *Daily Nebraska State Journal*, May 14, 1890.
28. "The Base Ball [*sic*] Game," *Kearney (NE) Daily Hub*, May 15, 1890.
29. Ibid.
30. "Base Ball [*sic*] Notes" *Kearney (NE) Daily Hub*, May 16, 1890.
31. "Nearly Met a Match," *Daily Nebraska State Journal*, May 17, 1890.
32. "The Rain Came Down," *Daily Nebraska State Journal*, May 18, 1890.
33. "The Sporting World," *Daily Nebraska State Journal*, May 21, 1890. Originally, this poem was attributed to the *Kearney (NE) Enterprise*, but this mistake was corrected in a later issue and attributed to the *Kearney (NE) Daily Hub*. "Kearney Gets a Gift," *Daily Nebraska State Journal*, May 25, 1890.

34. "Best of the Season," *Daily Nebraska State Journal*, May 22, 1890.

35. "The Sporting World," *Daily Nebraska State Journal*, May 21, 1890. Prior to this, the Giants wore brown uniforms.

36. Ibid.

37. "First Dose of Defeat," *Daily Nebraska State Journal*, May 23, 1890. The game was held up for one hour while a scorebook was delivered to the park, no doubt delayed by the streetcar malfunction.

38. "Glory to Kearney," *Kearney (NE) Daily Hub*, May 23, 1890.

39. "Lincoln's Victory," *Kearney (NE) Daily Hub*, May 24, 1890.

40. "They All Play Ball," *Daily Nebraska State Journal*, May 24, 1890.

41. "Kearney Gets a Gift." The umpire was also seen sitting in the Kearney dugout between innings.

42. "Sporting Notes," *Daily Nebraska State Journal*, May 25, 1890. The game was described as unpleasant due to bad umpiring.

43. This team was also referred to as the City Steams.

44. "The Lively Amateurs," *Omaha World-Herald*, May 26, 1890.

45. "The Field of Sport," *Daily Nebraska State Journal*, May 29, 1890.

46. "The Field of Sport," *Daily Nebraska State Journal*, May 27, 1890.

47. "The First Shut Out [sic]," *Daily Nebraska State Journal*, May 31, 1890.

48. Batting Averages for May: Patterson .355, Castone .308, Hightower .305, Taylor .292, Carr .231, Miller .222, Maupin .208, Reeves .172, Hugh Hughbanks .167, George Hughbanks .160, Brown .148, Newman .111, and after one game, Lincoln's average was .500. "In the Field of Sport," *Daily Nebraska State Journal*, June 2, 1890.

49. "The Sporting World," *Daily Nebraska State Journal*, June 1, 1890; "The Men from Iowa," *Daily Nebraska State Journal*, June 4, 1890; and "The Sporting World," *Daily Nebraska State Journal*, June 3, 1890.

50. "The Sporting World," *Daily Nebraska State Journal*, June 3, 1890.

51. Miller would return to the club in 1891 and Newman may have come back in late July of 1890 because there was a Newman playing first base for the Giants in the July 25 game against Nebraska City.

52. "The Sporting World," *Daily Nebraska State Journal*, June 5, 1890.

53. "A Comedy of Errors," *Daily Nebraska State Journal*, June 6, 1890.

54. "The Sporting World," *Daily Nebraska State Journal*, June 8, 1890.

55. "The Sporting World," *Daily Nebraska State Journal*, June 10, 1890.

56. Ibid. Charlie Hoover was a former Western League player for the Kansas City club, but by 1890, he was no longer playing professional ball.

57. For an example of Hoover's bad umpiring, see "A Rattling Game," *Lincoln (NE) Evening News*, June 5, 1890.

58. "Our Giants Done Up," *Lincoln (NE) Evening News*, June 12, 1890.

59. Ibid.

60. "The Sporting World," *Daily Nebraska State Journal*, June 13, 1890.

61. "It Took Work to Win," *Daily Nebraska State Journal*, June 15, 1890, and "Here's to Mr. Reeves," *Daily Nebraska State Journal*, June 18, 1890.

62. "Keeping Up the Lick," *Daily Nebraska State Journal*, June 20, 1890.

63. "The Same Old Story," *Daily Nebraska State Journal*, June 21, 1890, and "The Sporting World," *Daily Nebraska State Journal*, June 22, 1890.

64. "Little Locals," *Lincoln (NE) Evening News*, June 21, 1890.

65. Dave Rowe did not end up playing in the game against the Giants due to illness, but he did manage the team while in Lincoln.

66. "The Fifth Was Fatal," *Daily Nebraska State Journal*, June 24, 1890.

67. "The Sporting World," *Daily Nebraska State Journal*, June 27, 1890.

68. Ibid.

69. "The Sporting World," *Daily Nebraska State Journal*, June 28, 1890.

70. "Three Times and Out," *Daily Nebraska State Journal*, June 29, 1890.

71. "The Sporting World," *Daily Nebraska State Journal*, June 28, 1890.

72. "A Little Trouble," *Lincoln (NE) Evening News*, June 28, 1890.

73. Ibid.

74. "Will Explode a Bomb," *Daily Nebraska State Journal*, July 1, 1890.

75. Pope no longer had any investment in the Giant ball club after this date.

76. "Better Than Before," *Daily Nebraska State Journal*, July 2, 1890.

77. The Giants won the second and third games and went into the ninth inning of the first game with a lead. However, the Haverlys scored nine runs in that inning to get the victory.

78. "Batted Out Victories," *Daily Nebraska State Journal*, July 5, 1890.

79. "Base Ball [sic] News," *Lincoln (NE) Call*, July 6, 1890.

80. "Resented the Insult," *Daily Nebraska State Journal*, July 10, 1890.

81. "The Sporting World," *Daily Nebraska State Journal*, July 17, 1890.

82. "The Sporting World," *Daily Nebraska State Journal*, July 14, 1890.

83. "Hardly a Fair Shake," *Daily Nebraska State Journal*, July 15, 1890.
84. "Not the Best Treatment," *Daily Nebraska State Journal*, July 21, 1890.
85. Ibid.
86. "Found a Speedy Twirler," *Daily Nebraska State Journal*, July 23, 1890.
87. "A Jay Ball Game," *Lincoln (NE) Evening News*, July 26, 1890.
88. "A Very Pretty Game," *Daily Nebraska State Journal*, July 26, 1890, but cf. "A Jay Ball Game."
89. Cf. "The Sporting World," *Daily Nebraska State Journal*, July 27, 1890, and "Base Ball [sic] Gossip," *Omaha Daily Bee*, September 1, 1890.
90. Cf. Wm. Castone, "Here Is a Good Chance," *The Sporting News*, January 31, 1891, 2; Gregory Bond, "Too Much Dirty Work: Race, Manliness, and Baseball in Gilded Age Nebraska," *Nebraska History*, 85, no. 4 (Winter 2004): 174; and Morgan, 99n52.
91. The three that White mentions—the York Colored Monarchs, the Cuban Giants, and the New York Gorhams—and the Chicago Unions. See Sol White, *History of Colored Base Ball [sic], with Other Documents on the Early Black Game, 1886–1936*, comp. Jerry Malloy (Lincoln: University of Nebraska Press. 1995), 20. But there may have been more.
92. White, 18.
93. Ibid., 20.
94. "They Challenge Everybody," *The Sporting News,* July 11, 1891, 5.
95. "Amateur Teams Standing," *Omaha Daily Bee*, August 9, 1891.
96. For details, see Bond, 181.
97. Ibid., 184.
98. Mark E. Eberle, "George William Castone: An Integrated Baseball Life at the Close of the Nineteenth Century," https://scholars.fhsu.edu/all_monographs/6/ (accessed on August 27, 2019).
99. Morgan, 97; *Omaha City and South Omaha City Directory for 1891* (Omaha: J.M. Wolfe & Co., Publishers, 1891), 519, 710–711; *Omaha City and South Omaha City Directory for 1892* (Omaha: J.M. Wolfe & Co., Publishers, 1892), 389; *Omaha City and South Omaha City Directory for 1893* (Omaha: J.M. Wolfe & Co., Publishers, 1893), 507; and *Omaha City and South Omaha City Directory for 1894* (Omaha: J.M. Wolfe & Co., Publishers, 1894), 493.
100. Morgan, 96.
101. Ibid.
102. The information for this table comes from Bond; White; various issues of the *Daily Nebraska State Journal* and other newspapers; Dick Clark and Larry Lester, eds., *The Negro Leagues Book* (Cleveland, Ohio: The Society for American Baseball Research, 1994); Thom Loverro, *The Encyclopedia of Negro League Baseball* (New York: Checkmark Books, 2003); James A. Riley, *The Biographical Encyclopedia of the Negro Baseball Leagues* (New York: Carroll & Graf Publishers, 1994); James E. Brunson III, *Black Baseball, 1858–1900: A Comprehensive Record of the Teams, Players, Managers, Owners, and Umpires*, 3 vols. (Jefferson, North Carolina: McFarland & Company, Inc., Publishers, 2019); Eberle, "George William Castone: An Integrated Baseball Life at the Close of the Nineteenth Century"; Mark E. Eberle, "Black Baseball in Kansas City, 1870–1899," https://scholars.fhsu.edu/all_monographs/7/ (accessed on September 18, 2019); www.baseball-reference.com (accessed on June 24, 2019); www.seamheads.com (accessed on June 24, 2019); and "St. Paul Colored Gophers," https://en.wikipedia.org/wiki/St._Paul_Colored_Gophers#19 (accessed on July 15, 2019). Although Brunson has provided an extensive number of details on African American baseball prior to 1901, his three-volume work contains inconsistencies and typographical errors. Thus, judgment calls by the author of this chapter and the editor of this book have been made regarding what information from those volumes has been included in this table.
103. Chuck Carlson, "Battle Creek's First African-American Police Officer," *Battle Creek (MI) Enquirer*, September 11, 2015.
104. The information for this table comes from Bond; White; various issues of the *Daily Nebraska State Journal* and other newspapers; Clark and Lester; Loverro; Riley; Brunson; Eberle, "George William Castone: An Integrated Baseball Life at the Close of the Nineteenth Century"; Eberle, "Black Baseball in Kansas City, 1870–1899"; www.baseball-reference.com (accessed on June 24, 2019); and www.seamheads.com (accessed on June 24, 2019). Although Brunson has provided an extensive number of details on African American baseball prior to 1901, his three-volume work contains inconsistencies and typographical errors. Thus, judgment calls by the author of this chapter and the editor of this book have been made regarding what information from those volumes has been included in this table.

2

# Integration Before the "Great Experiment"

## The Nebraska State League of 1892

WILLIAM H. LYONS

## Introduction

Although Nebraska had professional baseball teams in several leagues prior to 1892, efforts to establish a league comprised solely of professional clubs based in Nebraska did not result in teams taking the field until 1892. The first such baseball league, the Nebraska State League (NSL),[1] came into existence on March 1, 1892, and, for a variety of reasons, could not finish its inaugural season, ending play on July 15 of that year. Although not a success, the NSL was the only league in Organized Baseball in the United States in 1892 to allow racially integrated teams[2] and the last league in Organized Baseball in Nebraska to include such teams until after World War II.

## Professional Baseball in Nebraska, 1879–1892[3]

### 1879

The first professional baseball league[4] that included a Nebraska team—Omaha—was the 1879 Northwestern League, which also consisted of Davenport, Iowa; Dubuque, Iowa; and Rockford, Illinois. Apparently, the Omaha Greenstockings did not complete the 36-game season, disbanding with a record of 11 wins and 13 losses, 6–13 in the league.[5]

### 1885

Omaha had a team in the new Western League,[6] but financial problems caused it to move to Keokuk, Iowa, on June 6, 1885, and brought about the demise of the league on June 15. Two teams had black players. Moses "Fleet" Walker[7] played for Cleveland, and John "Bud" Fowler, who later was a member of the Lincoln/Kearney club in the 1892 NSL, played for Keokuk.[8]

## 1886

Lincoln fielded a team in the Western League,[9] the Tree Planters, which finished last with a record of 31 wins and 49 losses, 23 games behind the first-place Denver Mountain Lions.[10] Of the teams in the league, only Topeka had a black player—Bud Fowler—who led the league with 12 triples.[11]

## 1887

Lincoln, Omaha, and Hastings[12] represented Nebraska in the Western League.[13] The Lincoln Tree Planters ended up second, with a 62–34 record, 15½ games behind the Topeka Golden Giants, whereas the Omaha Omahogs and Hastings Hustlers were less successful, going, depending on the source, 36–65 and 33–62 or 41–66 and 36–65, respectively.[14]

## 1888

Lincoln joined the Western League, while Omaha moved from the Western League to the Western Association. The Western League began play with four teams (Lincoln, Denver, Leavenworth, and Hutchinson, Kansas). On June 6, 1888, in last place with two wins and 11 losses and struggling financially, Lincoln disbanded. Newton, Kansas, took Lincoln's place on June 11, posting a record of three wins and five losses. The Western League folded on June 21 and did not operate again until 1892. In the Western Association,[15] Omaha came in fourth, winning 55 games while losing 48 and finishing 13½ games behind the champion, Kansas City.[16]

## 1889

The only Nebraska team in a professional league in 1889 was Omaha, which played in the Western Association[17] and captured the pennant with an 83–38 record.

## 1890

Lincoln joined Omaha in the Western Association,[18] albeit briefly, when Des Moines moved to Lincoln on August 12, 1890. Omaha, 51–69, ended up sixth and Des Moines/Lincoln, 48–73, finished seventh.

The center of baseball attention in Lincoln in 1890 was a professional club known as the Lincoln Giants, comprised entirely of black players. The promoters of that club had hoped that it would be part of a Nebraska state league, but plans for the league never got past the preliminary organization, so the Giants played as an independent team. Although highly successful on the field, the team was not successful financially.

## 1891

Lincoln and Omaha were part of the Western Association, which initially fielded eight teams.[19] Omaha went 51–59 and came in third behind Sioux City and Kansas City, whereas Lincoln, with a 46–49 record, disbanded on August 21, 1891.

## 1892

In addition to the establishment of the Nebraska State League, the Western League returned, opening the season with a team in Omaha[20] before folding on July 17, 1892.[21]

## The 1892 Nebraska State League: Formation

### 1889 Through 1891: Mostly Talk

Perhaps because of the mixed success of Nebraska professional baseball teams, interest in forming a professional league comprised solely of Nebraska clubs took time to develop. The earliest written indication of discussion of a Nebraska state league appeared in a newspaper article in Red Cloud, Nebraska, in 1889.[22] The article mentioned Beatrice, Fremont, Grand Island, Hastings, Kearney, Lincoln, and Plattsmouth as possible team sites. The cities were logical candidates because they each had populations of 10,000 or more and established railroad connections between them, as well as a history of interest in and support for baseball.

*Sporting Life* reported on an organizational meeting of a "Nebraska [s]tate [l]eague" held on March 25, 1890, in Fremont, Nebraska.[23] One of the organizers, listed as "W.M. Pope," likely was William M. Pope, an African American and one of the two founders of the 1890 Lincoln Giants.[24]

Although the 1890 Nebraska State League never operated, hope continued for a Nebraska state league in 1891:

> There will probably be a Nebraska [s]tate [l]eague in the field next season [1891], the circuit to include Kearney, Hastings, Grand Island, Norfolk, Seward, York, Blair, Fremont, and possibly Plattsmouth and Nebraska City. Out of these eleven cities, which have from 10,000 to 20,000 population, it is thought a league could be formed that would be a paying investment, and also furnish the lovers of the national game with good ball playing [*sic*] all season. Sunday ball could be played in all the cities, and there would be rousing old crowds at all Sunday games.[25]

Similarly, an article in the *Omaha Daily Bee* invited renewal of efforts to establish a Nebraska state league:

> And not a word is heard in regard to the proposed state league. It seems to have fallen entirely through for the present, at least. There are a couple of towns that have already organized their teams, and they propose to play ball, league or no league. What has become of the gentleman from Grand Island that advocated so strongly for a league?[26] Wake up, let us hear from you again, and perhaps we may raise a little enthusiasm on the subject.[27]

George William "Will" Castone, who managed the Lincoln Giants in 1890, hoped to revive the Giants in 1891 and offered to locate the team "in some minor league city (Nebraska [s]tate [l]eague preferred)."[28]

> William Castone, manager of the old Lincoln Giants, now with Kearney, is meeting with success in his formation of a state league. A letter was received this morning from Nebraska City to count them in. The league will consist of Kearney, Grand Island, Nebraska City, Blair, Missouri Valley, Fremont, Plattsmouth[,] and Beatrice or Hastings.[29]

Despite this positive news, Castone's efforts to form a state league were ultimately unsuccessful. Instead, he reorganized the Lincoln Giants as a touring team.

## 1892: Things Begin to Come Together

Early in 1892, Castone sent a letter to baseball enthusiasts in Kearney, Grand Island, Hastings, Norfolk, Fremont, Beatrice, Nebraska City, South Omaha, and Plattsmouth, calling for an organizational meeting of a Nebraska state league. On February 7, 1892, he published in the *Omaha Daily Bee* the following call for a meeting:

> The outlook for a state league this season is very promising, and I suggest that a meeting be called [as] soon as possible at the Capitol Hotel this city, February 18 or 19, Lincoln being a more convenient place than either Hastings or Omaha, and a substantial six[-]club league formed which can play the season out, [sic] at a low salary limit could be made a success.
>
> The project has been agitated for the past two years, but for some reason nobody has ventured yet. Now is the time to get your feet wet, wake up you base ball [sic] enthusiasts, and decide upon a place to meet, so we can start the ball rolling for 1892, and have a good and prosperous league.
>
> Last year[,] Hastings, Beatrice, Fremont[,] and Plattsmouth all had good [amateur/semiprofessional] clubs, [sic] and were well supported, [sic] and will be on deck again this season. Norfolk and Grand Island are only waiting for a meeting to be called. Now we want to hear from Kearney. Will the following cities send a delegate to a meeting called here if agreeable to all, February 18 or 19? Kearney, Grand Island, Hastings, Norfolk, Fremont, Beatrice, Nebraska City, South Omaha[,] and Plattsmouth. Answer in [t]he *Bee*.[30]

The *Bee* noted that "Castone will undoubtedly resuscitate the Lincoln [G]iants in case of the much talked of Nebraska league."[31] Castone intended just that, as he indicated in an article published in *The Sporting News*: "Lincoln can be counted on as a member and will be represented by the Lincoln Giants."[32] On Castone's efforts to secure players for his team, the *Omaha Daily Bee* noted:

> G. W. Castone is in correspondence with part of the famous Cuban Giants of New York, and with part of the Lincoln Giants[,] he could put in a team second to none. Kearney, Norfolk, or some other good town would do well to secure Mr. Castone, as he is well up in the business.[33]

At the same time, and apparently in response to Castone's letter and published call, Ulysses S. Rohrer of Hastings made it clear that he and others in Hastings opposed allowing blacks to play on any Nebraska state league team:

> Manager Rohrer, of the Hastings ball team[,] received a letter yesterday [February 6, 1892,] from William Castone, of Lincoln, requesting Rohrer to send a representative to the [s]tate [l]eague meeting to be held at Lincoln Feb. 20. Rohrer, upon receipt of the letter, consulted a number of the fans as to the advisability of sending a representative. There seems to be strong opposition here to entering the State League if colored players are to be permitted to play in [sic] any of the teams. Hastings stands ready to put a team in the Nebraska State League, providing it is composed entirely of white players. The people here say they witnessed too much dirty work by colored players last season.[34]

The *Hastings Daily Nebraskan* opined that "Castone, the colored gentleman from Lincoln, is being ignored in the formation of a base ball [sic] league for the state. This is right and proper."[35]

Shortly after Castone announced his intentions to form a Nebraska state league, Will Houseworth[36] of Lincoln announced similar plans, calling for an organizational meeting on February 20, 1892, "for the purpose of creating a Nebraska amateur base ball [sic] league."[37] Houseworth emphasized "that the meeting called by him will be separate and independent of the one called by William Castone."[38] The *Omaha Daily Bee* reported that "Mr. Houseworth of Lincoln is corresponding with the different delegates [from Beatrice, Fremont, Grand Island, Norfolk, Plattsmouth, Lincoln, and possibly Hastings and Kearney] and all are very enthusiastic over the prospect of a league."[39]

The supporters of a Nebraska state league envisioned a geographically compact confederation with teams located in midsized cities and with good railroad service connecting the cities.[40] Some supporters, recognizing that the collapse of Lincoln's Western League team in 1891 meant that Lincoln would not have a team in a professional league in 1892, desired a Nebraska state league team in the state capitol.[41] Others questioned whether Lincoln would support a team in the proposed state league.[42] All supporters understood the importance of keeping player salaries and other costs under control.[43]

## March 1, 1892: The Organizational Meeting in Lincoln

An enthusiastic coterie of baseball devotees met in the parlor of the Capital [H]otel[44] [on March 1, 1892,] with the view of organizing a state league. There were present W.A. ["Pa"] Rourke of Grand Island, Tom Patterson and Phil Greusel of Plattsmouth, S.C. Coman of Fremont, H.L. Ewing and Harry Gatewood of Beatrice, N.A. Lockwood of Norfolk[,] and T.J. Mickey [sic—actually Hickey], Will Housewurth[,] and Castone of Lincoln.[45]

The group chose Hickey as chair and Coman as temporary secretary.[46] All agreed that "the proposed league did not contemplate and could not stand any ostentatious expenditure of means, and the discussion developed the fact that there are a good many hitherto expensive ball players [sic] now looking around pretty industriously for an opportunity to put in the summer at salaries such as men commanded in other walks of life."[47] Those attending chose Hickey, Coman, Patterson, Rourke, Housewurth, J.W. Cutright of Lincoln, and E.G. Drake of Beatrice as the initial board of directors of the NSL. Hickey was elected president, Cutright as vice president, and Coman as secretary-treasurer. Ewing, Coman, and Patterson formed a committee to draft a constitution and bylaws for the league.[48]

The delegates agreed that the league should include six teams, but raised concern over whether Norfolk was geographically too distant from Beatrice, Fremont, Grand Island, Lincoln, and Plattsmouth to be a viable location. There was discussion of whether to allow Norfolk to have a team if it would make a $35-per-game guarantee, as opposed to the $25 guarantee agreed upon for all other teams, but the Norfolk delegate, Lockwood, "did not feel that he ought to do so; although his town was anxious to get in." In the end, the delegates authorized a committee consisting of Rourke and Housewurth to visit Hastings and Kearney "with a view of inducing one of them to go into the organization."[49]

Issues discussed at the meeting included[50]:

1. A $25 Guaranteed Payment. A home team would pay the visiting team $25 "before the time for calling the game, rain or shine, except on holidays, when the receipts are to be equally divided between the two clubs." This guaranteed payment would haunt several teams as a result of multiple rainouts in May.

2. A $600 Per Month Salary Cap. The cap would be enforced by requiring each team to post a $500 bond that would be forfeited for any cap violation. As the season progressed, there were rumors that Beatrice had gone over the salary limit, but there is no evidence of any action by the league against Beatrice (or any other team) on these bonds.[51]

3. Monthly Team Budgets. "Calculating upon the theory that the full salary limit of $600 per month is reached, and that it will take about $50 per month from each club as dues to the [l]eague to pay umpire and secretary salaries, and the purchase of balls and other supplies, it was estimated that $650 a month would cover the authorized expense per club."[52] "The representatives from Grand Island and Beatrice said that their towns had organized with such backing that they would be able to play through the six-months [sic] season on a $600 a month salary limit if not a dollar was taken in at the gate." In contrast, Lincoln and Plattsmouth had significant difficulties raising initial funds.[53] Apart from capital contributions made to the teams by supporters, the only source for payment of these monthly bills

would be the gate receipts. A number of early rainouts and later single-admission doubleheaders greatly reduced the vital gate receipts for many teams.

4. A League Season. The announced season was May 1 through November 1. However, before the start of play, the NSL replaced the six-month schedule with a shorter one starting on Sunday, May 1, and ending in September.[54] But even that shortened schedule drew criticism as too long for an inaugural season in Nebraska.

5. Umpires. The league would hire three umpires (one umpire per game) and would pay them not more than $75 per month each.[55]

6. The Type of League Ball. "After considerable discussion of the merits of the respective kind of balls, it was decided to use the Reach ball."

7. Team Uniforms. Lincoln would have white with brown trimmings; Fremont, grey; Grand Island, dark blue; Beatrice, black with white trimmings; and Plattsmouth, maroon shirts and blue pantaloons.[56]

Prior to adjournment, the delegates instructed Secretary-Treasurer Coman to take steps to secure protection for the league according to the National Agreement's rule against outside tampering with the league's players under contract.[57] The delegates also levied an assessment on each team to meet advance expenses of the league. As the meeting concluded, the delegates stated that they were "fully confident that they could make the [l]eague a complete success"[58] and they agreed on a $500 cash prize to be awarded to the pennant winner to "insure good, hard ball [sic] playing."[59]

## Hastings Joins the NSL

Despite Norfolk's interest in the league, organizers decided to try to attract either Hastings or Kearney to join as the sixth team. Grand Island manager Rourke and Lincoln manager Houseworth, the NSL delegates, focused their attention on Hastings, apparently considering Kearney as an alternative should Hastings decline to join. What they found in Hastings was very encouraging. Supporters had raised "sufficient funds ... to see the team through the season," and the Hastings correspondent for *Sporting Life*, identified as Doc, exuded:

> We can't afford to stay out. Hastings is the best every-day [sic] base ball [sic] town in Nebraska, not excepting Omaha. The ample railroad facilities of this city afford an excellent opportunity for base ball [sic] fans living in contiguous towns to witness the [l]eague games here without much inconvenience, and this fact was thoroughly demonstrated when Hastings held a membership in the old Western League and held her own with such towns as Denver, Omaha, Topeka[,] and Kansas City.[60]

Reports from Hastings indicated that Ulysses S. Rohrer, who had managed the Hastings team in the Western League in 1887, would likely be named the manager of the new Hastings team, and that he was "receiving a dozen letters per day from players all over the country inquiring as to the prospects of Hastings."[61] Echoing the sentiments about black players expressed by Rohrer, Doc noted:

> Good, steady, sober players[62] will do well to correspond with the Hastings manager. It is reported that Plattsmouth has signed several colored players. I think that is a mistake. The colored men who played with visiting teams in this city last year gave exhibitions of dirty ball, and the base ball [sic] fans here will not attend games where colored players participate.[63]

The Hastings supporters expressed concern about the length of the proposed NSL season, noting the chances of bad weather in April, May, and September, and suggesting a Memorial Day to September 1 season.[64] The league ultimately did reduce the length of the season, but the concern about the weather in May proved prescient.

## Early Financial Problems: A Preview of Things to Come

### Plattsmouth

On March 11, 1892, the *Lincoln (NE) Evening News* reported that the Plattsmouth committee assigned to raise funds for the Plattsmouth team "have been out hustling for two days, but have met with such poor success that they have concluded to let the matter drop, and it now looks as if this city will do without any club in the coming season."[65] Fortunately for the 1892 NSL and Plattsmouth, these reports stimulated financial support for the team.[66]

### Lincoln

The *Daily Nebraska State Journal* reported that the attempt to organize a league team in Lincoln appeared to have failed because backers could not raise the required money.

> Manager Houseworth had gone ahead securing contracts with players and making such arrangements as could be made without any outlay relying upon T.J. Hickey, president of the league, at whose solicitation he claims to have gone into the movement, to come to the front with the needed capital when it became necessary to make any outlay.

Matters came to a head after Houseworth asked Hickey for money to purchase "uniforms and paraphernalia and meet other necessary preliminary expenses." When Hickey explained that "he did not intend to put up the cash," Houseworth released the players he had signed to contracts and advised them not to travel to Lincoln.[67]

Secretary-Treasurer Coman made an emergency trip to the capital city with the hope of keeping Lincoln in the league.[68] The *Daily Nebraska State Journal* reported that Coman persuaded the other teams to provide cash to assist the Lincolnites if necessary.[69] As it turned out, however, support for the Lincoln club came from local sources. At some point during the afternoon of April 13, 1892:

> [President] Hickey presented to Manager Houseworth a simple little slip of paper upon which were inscribed the names of the Lincoln Street Railway [C]ompany and the Lincoln Park [C]ompany for $100 each and Mr. Hickey for $25, all payable on demand to meet immediate expenses necessary. Mr. Hickey has also consented to assist in carrying the paper about the city this afternoon to secure such other contributions as may reasonably be expected.[70]

Ultimately, the Lincoln club received $500 in subscriptions. Although far short of the fund-raising results in Beatrice, Grand Island, and Hastings, "[t]his so encouraged Manager Houseworth that he determined to run the club, and accordingly he notified his players to report for duty. All is therefore once more lovely in the Nebraska League."[71]

## Approval of the Initial Schedule

Several problems faced the drafters of the initial NSL schedule.[72] First, Beatrice and Hastings apparently did not permit professional baseball games to be held in those cities on Sundays.[73] Second, the question of which teams should play at home on the Fourth of July holiday provoked contention. And third, although the teams in the league were located relatively close to each other, the challenge of determining an equitable travel schedule proved difficult.

On Saturday, March 19, 1892,[74] the managers of the six teams—Harry Gatewood, Beatrice; Ulysses S. Rohrer, Hastings; William "Pa" Rourke, Grand Island; Norman Baker,[75] Fremont; Tom Patterson, Plattsmouth; and Will Housewoorth, Lincoln—met in Lincoln. The managers appointed Baker "as a committee of one" to draft the schedule.[76] Baker presented a proposed schedule on Monday, March 21, 1892, "but it was not adopted by the [l]eague."

> Manager Rohrer, of the Hastings team, is arranging a new schedule of games for the State League that will be fairer than the one already arranged. The schedule is arranged on the circuit plan and the mileage is greatly reduced. Sunday games will be given to Fremont, Lincoln, Grand Island and Plattsmouth, while Hastings and Beatrice will get Fourth of July games. In the schedule no team will have the advantage, and as two or three of the other managers favor it[,] there will be no trouble about its adoption.[77]

Despite this optimistic view, complaints about the schedule continued. The *Beatrice (NE) Daily Democrat* noted that "the schedule is the subject of some contention. One has finally been prepared, which four clubs have accepted, but which seems to hang fire so far as Beatrice and another city are concerned." The principal complaint by the Beatrice team was that the schedule called for "an extra trip at the end of the season that will cost about $200." The team ownership seemed pleased that it would play Hastings in Beatrice on the Fourth of July because Hastings, its "keenest rival[,] ... will draw better than any other club that could come."[78]

On April 5, 1892, the board of directors of the league approved the revised schedule.[79] Opening Day was set for Sunday, May 1, 1892. Each team would play 100 games, 20 with each of the other teams, 10 on the road and 10 at home.[80] With the beginning of the season coming quickly, the teams arranged a short series of exhibition games and set to work on remaining matters, such as preparing the playing fields and completing team rosters.

## *Preseason Preparations in the League Cities*

### Beatrice

The supporters of the team organized as the Beatrice Baseball Association.[81] By the beginning of April, Manager Gatewood provided the following information on the Beatrice players[82]:

> **PITCHER:** J. Edinger (with Ottumwa, Illinois-Iowa League, in 1891).
> **CATCHER:** Jones (with Dubuque, Illinois-Iowa League, in 1891)
> **FIRST BASE:** George H. Taylor (with Denver, Western Association, in 1891) "is a way-up man."
> [**SECOND BASE:** Harry Gatewood]
> **SHORTSTOP:** William[83] Van Arnam (with Los Angeles[84] in 1891) "is considered one of the hardest hitters in the State League."[85]
> **THIRD BASE:** Not yet selected
> **LEFT FIELD:** Bradford is "a local man of Omaha."
> **CENTER FIELD:** Thompson (with Cedar Rapids, Illinois-Iowa League, in 1891).
> **RIGHT FIELD:** Fred[86] Holmes, "local man ... and is one of the best all round men in the team."[87]

Before opening day, Beatrice obtained a second pitcher, John A. Slagle[88]; a third baseman, Holohan; and a new shortstop, Randall.[89]

## Fremont

Fremont baseball supporters met on March 2, 1892, at the Eno Hotel and formed the Fremont Base Ball [sic] Club.[90] S.C. Coman of Fremont, just elected as secretary-treasurer of the NSL, discussed the financial aspects of the operation of the 1891 Fremont team, which was "under pay" from May 28, 1891, to August 9, 1891. That team's operating expenses were about $1,000 per month, and revenue "under the most unfavorable circumstances" was over $2,200. In contrast, he explained that the $550 salary limit, plus league expenses of about $100, would result in total monthly expenses of $650, which would be about $350 less per month than in 1891. "It was thought that a fund of $800 should be raised to equip the club and insure at least one month's running expenses." E.N. Morse, Bruce Smith, and Mayor Fried, as well as Coman, were appointed to raise the $800.[91]

The *Fremont (NE) Daily Tribune* gave the Fremont team the nickname "Colts" because the players were relatively young[92]:

L. J. Finch (Center Field)–Age 31–Bloomington, Illinois (1888), independent Illinois and Nebraska teams (1889), Illinois-Iowa Interstate League (1890), and Fremont, Nebraska (1891)

J. L. Graver (Catcher)–Age 23–Ottumwa, Iowa (1886), "Missouri Valley and other principal teams in Iowa and Nebraska" (1890–1891)

Harry Stoney (Second Base)–Age 19–Canadian by birth, Hamburg, Iowa (1890), Hot Springs, South Dakota (1891)

Dick Purcell (Shortstop)–Age 20–Lead City, South Dakota (1891) "He is one of the best shortstops ever on a diamond in Nebraska."

Charles Bowman (First Base)–Age 22–West Omaha, Nebraska (1889), Omaha City Steams (1890), and Cranes of Omaha (1891).

Horace Butler (Left Field, Utility Infielder)–Age 19–Fort Omaha (1889), Omaha City Steams (1890), Cranes of Omaha and Chadron, Nebraska (1891).

Norman Baker, a former major league pitcher, managed the team and also pitched for Fremont.[93]

Without the opportunity for the modern extended preseason "spring training," and with less than perfect weather, the Fremont team held indoor practices in the "old opera house."[94]

## Grand Island

The Grand Island Base Ball Club [sic] was formed at the end of March or beginning of April 1892.[95] William "Pa" Rourke was named player-manager. Grand Island had a baseball team in 1891, but rather than use the baseball grounds the 1891 team had used, the club decided to construct a new venue for the 1892 season. A streetcar operator in Grand Island, the Grand Island Motor Company, offered $800 toward construction of the new grounds. *Sporting Life* reported that Grand Island had picked a location for the new grounds and that work would commence shortly.[96]

The first reported players for Grand Island were Hoffmaster, Rourke, and Wood.[97] Hoffmaster/Hoffmeister started in center field on opening day. Rourke managed, started at third base, and provided relief pitching in that game. But Wood did not play for the team after the regular season began.

## Hastings

Hastings selected Ulysses S. Rohrer, a local business person and baseball player, as manager. Although Rohrer did not participate in every game, he often played shortstop.

His decision to play that position after he succeeded S.C. Coman as secretary of the NSL created controversy because the league secretary was responsible for hiring and firing umpires. In addition to being vocal in his opposition to black players, Rohrer had a reputation as a complainer with the other teams in the league.[98]

Like Grand Island, Hastings had a team in 1891, but elected to build new baseball grounds for the 1892 season. The park was being "ploughed and graded, and then the fences and grand stand [sic] will be built, and Manager Rohrer expects to have it ready for practice about [April 20], and when the same are finished will be hard to beat in the [l]eague."[99]

The NSL resolved a dispute over rights to second baseman Byron McKibben, awarding him to Hastings. McKibben, who had played for Hastings in 1891 and was attending college in Des Moines, "accepted a clerical position in M. Levy's New York and Boston clothing store, where he will work when not playing ball." Hastings also signed pitcher Kid Fuller of Philadelphia.[100]

## Lincoln

> All things indicate that the coming season will prove successful for the Nebraska State League. Lincoln undoubtedly has the winning team of the [l]eague, as the efficient manager, Will I. Houseworth, has been most particular in the selection of his men. They are all men whose names are familiar with the base ball [sic] world.[101]

Lincoln would, however, be the first team in the league to fold, after accumulating a dismal 1–3 record, enduring many rainouts, and suffering financial collapse.

Will Castone had hoped to revive the Lincoln Giants as Lincoln's team in the NSL. This hope would not come to fruition, but Will Houseworth was able to sign Castone to play for Lincoln that season.[102] Lincoln also signed John "Bud" Fowler, regarded as the first black professional baseball player in the United States. Although nearing the end of a long and distinguished playing career, Fowler performed well for Lincoln and its successor, Kearney.

## Plattsmouth

After weathering the early problems with financing, the Plattsmouth club signed eight players: Frank Maupin, catcher; John Reeves and George Yapp, pitchers; Gibson, first base; McKibben, second base; C.W. Porter, third base; Clark, short stop [sic], and Bradford, outfielder.[103] "This is the first team to be completed and we regard it as good as any in this league considering the fact that the salary limit is so low the players signed so far for the league are very good men."[104] A more complete list of the players included: pitchers John Reeves, George Yapp, and Al Perrine; catcher Frank Maupin; first baseman Gibson; second baseman McKibben; third baseman Kennedy; shortstop Clark; and outfielders Porter and Sam Patterson.[105]

The first two black players signed, Maupin and Reeves, received positive recognition in the press. Maupin "our crack catcher is a colored man but is as fine a catcher as any in the state.... Reeves, [one of the three pitchers], is also a colored man and is said to be a strong man for the club. He is but little known here and hails from Kansas City."[106] Later, Plattsmouth signed a third black player, John "Pat" Patterson.[107]

*Sporting Life* reported that the Plattsmouth ballpark was being placed in shape and active arrangements were "being made to have the team put into trim for the season."[108]

## The Black Players

### George William "Will" Castone—Lincoln/Kearney

Prior to coming to Lincoln in 1890, George William "Will" Castone had performed for various baseball teams. He was first a player for and then player-manager of the Lincoln Giants in 1890 and 1891, was involved in several attempts to form a Nebraska state league, and had hoped to make the Lincoln Giants the capital city's entry in the 1892 NSL. Also, he served as a correspondent for *The Sporting News* in the early 1890s. One of two starting pitchers for Lincoln/Kearney in the 1892 NSL, he joined the New York Cuban Giants in 1893 before leaving professional baseball and eventually becoming "an artist, best known for his oil-on-canvas paintings."[109]

### John W. "Bud" Fowler—Lincoln/Kearney

John W. "Bud" Fowler (real name John W. Jackson, Jr.) was born in Fort Plain, New York, on March 16, 1858, and died in Frankfort, New York, on February 26, 1913. Credited

Bud Fowler (at the right end of the middle row) as a member of the integrated 1894 Findlay, Ohio, Sluggers (National Baseball Hall of Fame Library).

with being the first black in Organized Baseball, Fowler played professionally in many places, starting with Lynn, Massachusetts, in the International League. His career was replete with instances of racial prejudice, so much so that in 1891, after failing to get a position with Plattsmouth for that season, he joined independent teams in St. Louis; Beloit, Wisconsin; Watertown, Wisconsin; Findlay, Ohio; and finally Milwaukee.[110]

Fowler joined Lincoln/Kearney, became its second sacker, and received his share of praise. "Bud Fowler, our colored second baseman and captain, is a whole team in himself. He is everywhere at all times and keeps the boys moving."[111] An article in *The Sporting News* said: "Fowler, [sic] on second needs no introduction as he has played ball all over America.... He covers more ground in his position, makes as many hits and runs and has more stolen bases and is probably worth more to a team than any other man in the league."[112] He "appeared in 35 games, batting an unusually low .273, but led the league in stolen bases with 45."[113] After the 1892 NSL collapsed, Fowler returned to an independent team in Findlay, Ohio, and formed the all-black Adrian, Michigan, Page Fence Giants in September of 1894. The following year, he and several of the Page Fence Giants joined the Adrian Demons of the integrated Michigan State League. But Fowler did not stay long, moving after a few games to the Lansing Senators, also of that league, the last team that he played for in Organized Baseball.[114] For the remainder of his life, he was involved in organizing, promoting, managing, and/or playing for black baseball clubs, playing for integrated clubs prior to 1899, and organizing and promoting black leagues.[115]

### Frank Maupin—Plattsmouth

The Lincoln Giants recruited Frank Maupin from the Kansas City Maroons in 1890, and he remained with the team in 1891. Maupin joined Plattsmouth in 1892, playing catcher for the entire time the club stayed in the NSL. After that, he was a member of seven or eight teams that were located in Missouri, Kansas, or Nebraska, including the Omaha Colored Nine in 1894 and the David City squad in 1894 and 1895.[116]

### John W. "Pat" Patterson—Plattsmouth

John W. "Pat" Patterson was born on March 2, 1872, in Omaha and died on August 23, 1940, in Battle Creek, Michigan. He played baseball for the New Orleans Pinchbacks in 1889, the Lincoln Giants in 1890 and 1891, and the Deadwood, South Dakota, Metropolitans in 1891 before becoming a member of the Plattsmouth team in the 1892 NSL.[117] And when the NSL shut down, he headed east and was a player or a player-manager on various black teams, such as the New York Cuban Giants, the Page Fence Giants, and the Cuban X Giants.[118]

### John "Jack" Reeves—Plattsmouth

Like Frank Maupin, John "Jack" Reeves was signed by the Lincoln Giants in 1890 after being a member of the Kansas City Maroons, and he stayed with the club in 1891.[119] However, unlike Maupin, Reeves saw action with the Springfield, Missouri, Reds in 1888 and the Omaha Lafayettes in 1889.[120] Following his days with Lincoln, the New York Cuban Giants, with whom he spent some time in 1890, and the 1891 St. Louis West Ends, he joined Plattsmouth as a pitcher. His post–Plattsmouth career consisted of playing for at least five other nines, possibly six, one of which was the 1894 David City squad that Maupin played for.[121]

## George H. Taylor—Beatrice

George H. Taylor was a member of the Aspen Aspens or Silver Kings of the Colorado State League in 1889, the Denver Claytons in 1890, the Lincoln Giants in 1890 and 1891, and the Denver Black Champions in 1891 before becoming the first baseman for Beatrice in the 1892 NSL.[122] The existing NSL box scores show that he was a durable player who usually batted second or third in the lineup, but on occasion would bat fourth or fifth. He performed well in the field, collecting very few errors in a league that, overall, was at best below average defensively.

After the NSL folded, Taylor had a long career with a number of black clubs—some of which were famous, such as the Page Fence Giants, whereas others were of the Nebraska-Iowa local variety, such as the Omaha Midways, the Council Bluffs Maroons, and the Omaha Wilcox & Drapers—as well as the integrated Denver, depending on the source, Gulfs or Grizzlies of the Colorado State League.[123]

## *The Regular Season Begins—In the Rain*

"The Nebraska Coon League will open the season Sunday, May 1st [*sic*].... The reason it is called the Coon League is that all the teams with the exception of Hastings and Grand Island have one or more colored players."[124] *The Sporting News* report, which came from Hastings, was inaccurate—Fremont also had no black players—but captured the atmosphere of racial intolerance in Hastings. How prevalent racism was in other league cities and on the other league teams is unclear. As the season progressed, some Plattsmouth players attributed the team's problems on the field to conflicts between the black and white members of the team. In addition, some of the players who breached their contracts and signed with other teams offered racial issues as justification for their actions. Despite allegations of racially based problems among the players, there was only one documented incident of apparent racially motivated violence. Newspaper stories relating to the league games and teams included what today would be racial slurs but at the time may simply have been accepted descriptive language.[125] Other comments, however, were racist in any context,[126] with racism being evident at the formation of the league and playing a role in the problems the league faced. But there were nonracist problems as well. And one such problem—heavy and sustained rain—started on opening day.

The 1892 NSL season began on Sunday, May 1, with extreme weather interfering with the quality of play, discomforting spectators, and preventing one of the opening games from being played. Plattsmouth hosted Lincoln, Grand Island hosted Hastings, but rain prevented Fremont from hosting Beatrice either on Sunday, May 1, or Monday, May 2.

### Lincoln versus Plattsmouth

Lincoln defeated Plattsmouth, 8–2, in a game played at Plattsmouth's Chicago Avenue ballgrounds under extremely difficult conditions. The field was "three inches deep in mud"[127] and threatening weather limited attendance to about 300.[128] Castone pitched a complete game for Lincoln, giving up one earned run (two runs overall) and seven hits. But despite the terrible state of the grounds, Lincoln's "fielding ... was simply marvelous."[129] Plattsmouth's fielding, however, was simply awful.[130] Fowler, leading off and playing second base, had one hit in five at bats, and scored one run. In addition to his strong performance on the mound, Castone went 3-for-5 at the plate. Plattsmouth's three black players, Maupin (catcher), Reeves (pitcher), and John Patterson (second base), all started the game. Maupin's "batting was a feature in [the] game," though, unfortunately for him, the catcher once hit into hard luck: "One of his drives went over the center fielder's head, but the ball stuck in the mud and he got but one base."[131] John Patterson was 1-for-4, Maupin was 3-for-5, and Reeves, who pitched in relief of the starter Yapp, also played first base and was 2-for-4.

## Hastings versus Grand Island

Hastings defeated Grand Island, 11–4, on Sunday, May 1, at Grand Island.[132] "Several hundred" spectators attended the game and the number of Hastings supporters equaled the number of Grand Island supporters.[133] Grand Island catcher Keefe had the first hit of the game, a double. Hofer started the game for Grand Island but was replaced by manager–third baseman Pa Rourke. Hastings manager Ulysses Rohrer, who later in the season played shortstop, was not in the lineup that day. The newspapers in both cities agreed that Grand Island did not play well while Hastings played very well and earned the victory. The *Grand Island (NE) Independent* was particularly blunt: "It's true that a poor article was dished out by our club, an article that almost gagged some of the spectators who were anxious to see their boys win."[134]

## Beatrice versus Fremont

The NSL schedule called for Beatrice and Fremont to play two games in Fremont to start the season, but rain forced cancellation of both contests. The *Beatrice (NE) Daily Democrat* observed that the bad weather actually benefited the Beatrice team. "As under the rules the visiting club is guaranteed $25 a game, play or not, the towns where the season began are out of pocket.... As it is our boys are making expenses sitting around the Fremont hotel stove."[135] Fremont manager Baker complained that he was tired of paying the $25 guarantees.[136]

## Rain

Rain on Monday, May 2, also prevented the second game between Lincoln and Plattsmouth, whereas the game between Hastings and Grand Island was stopped by the rain at the end of the fourth inning with the game tied 2–2.

## Beatrice Finally Opens

Playing at the Plattsmouth grounds on Chicago Avenue, the Beatrice team won its first League game, 9–6. The game "was full of vim and vigor throughout the entire contest, and was 'anybody's game' until the last man was retired in the ninth inning."[137] Another account stated that the game "abounded in brilliant playing."[138] But despite the enthusiasm reflected in these newspaper accounts, the game was sloppy: 15 errors (seven for Beatrice and eight for Plattsmouth) and only seven of the 15 runs were earned. Taylor played first base for Beatrice, going 1-for-5. For Plattsmouth, Patterson went 1-for-4, Maupin went 1-for-5, and Reeves, now at first base and in the outfield, went 2-for-5. Slagle, pitching for Beatrice, "hit a ball into a chicken-coop next to the right field fence in the sixth and made the second home run of the game before it was recovered."[139] Player-manager Harry Gatewood was fined by Umpire Greusel "for too much kicking [i.e., complaining] during the third inning" of the game.[140]

### More Rain

The scheduled May 4 game between Beatrice and Plattsmouth was called on account of rain. "This makes two postponed games out of the four scheduled to occur in [Plattsmouth]. The weather which prevailed during the two games that have been played has been so cold and rainy that the gate receipts were only sufficient to pay the [$25.00] guarantee. We must have better weather."[141]

### Fremont Finally Opens

Fremont played its first home game on May 3 against Hastings, winning 4–2. Weather, again, was poor: "[T]he grounds were heavy, the air full of ice and general gloom was rampant." As to the game, the *Fremont (NE) Daily Tribune* applauded the quality of play by the Fremont team, writing, "It was a pretty game from start to finish and Fremont was 'strictly in it.'" The newspaper report did not list the paid attendance, but it stated that "a goodly number of ... cranks [i.e., fans] were assembled in the grand stand [*sic*]."[142]

Jack Reeves when he was with the 1894 David City, Nebraska, amateur champions. As with many African Americans who had been on all-black teams, Reeves could play more than one position and would be destined to play on more than one club (Nebraska State Historical Society, RG3064-26).

## *The Plattsmouth Minstrel Show*

On May 6, with the Plattsmouth team struggling on the field (no wins, three losses) and on the balance sheet as a result of the terrible weather, several of the Plattsmouth members participated in a minstrel show to raise funds for the players.[143] Admission was

50 cents for the first performance at the Waterman Opera House. A "fair[-]sized crowd greeted the base ball [sic] minstrels [in the opera house] and every one [sic] in it will tell you that he or she was agreeably surprised at the merit of the entertainment." Praised as "first class from beginning to end," the show featured Frank Maupin, who "brought down the house."[144] The players repeated the show on May 7 at reduced prices of 35 and 25 cents per ticket. Attendance was lower, but "the program was even better rendered than the night before." The show netted the players about $73, a significant supplement to their regular pay.[145]

## *The Lincoln Team Transfers to Kearney*

Despite beginning the season with an 8–2 win in Plattsmouth, everything went downhill from that point for the Lincoln team. The next three scheduled games—one at Plattsmouth and two at Grand Island—were rained out. Although Lincoln was entitled to a $25 guarantee for each of the road games, the first game produced only the $25 guarantee because of the bad weather and the three rainouts produced only the guaranteed amount of $75, for a total of $100.

Lincoln played its home opener on Thursday, May 5, against Beatrice, losing 8–2. Fowler led off and played second, gaining one base hit in four at bats and committing one error, and he combined with third baseman Smith and first baseman Hillis for a 5–4–3 double play. Because he was not pitching, Castone played right field and batted fourth, but got no hits in four at bats. Overall, Lincoln committed four errors and Beatrice two. George Taylor, stationed at first base, batted second and had one hit in four at bats. He also committed one of the two Beatrice errors when he misplayed a ground ball hit by Lincoln pitcher Albert Hopp. The *Daily Nebraska State Journal* described Beatrice as "the strongest team in the league," and noted that Lincoln's good defensive play prevented Beatrice from increasing the margin of victory.[146]

The second game against Beatrice, played on May 6, epitomized the season for Lincoln. Leading 2–1 in the sixth inning, the Lincolnites saw the game abruptly end with a forfeit to Beatrice because the team could not produce a suitable baseball. Manager Houseworth brought three new balls to the game. One ball had been used in practice and was dirty. The second had been ripped and was discarded. And the third, in the course of play, was hit on top of the grandstand and rolled off behind it. In the fifth inning, someone gave the dirty practice ball to Umpire Hart, who put it in his pocket. After the third ball disappeared, Hart offered the practice ball for use in the game, but Beatrice, relying on NSL rules, rejected the dirty ball and demanded a new ball. Houseworth argued that Hart had accepted the practice ball and thus that it should be used, but to no avail. "At the end of about five minutes[,] Umpire Hart announced that he had awarded the game to Beatrice because Lincoln had failed to produce a new ball."[147]

Lincoln played its third home game, against Hastings, on Saturday, May 7, 1892, on "a cold, raw, windy day and not at all adapted to athletics. It was especially cold and raw for Lincoln, as she got the worst of it in every way possible." The capital city nine committed five errors, losing 9–4. Castone, playing left field, had one hit in four at bats and Fowler had two hits also in four at bats. In addition, Fowler was involved in a 3–4–3 double play started by first baseman Hillis.[148]

Rain cancelled the home game against Hastings scheduled for Sunday, May 8, and the home games against Grand Island scheduled for Monday, May 9, and Tuesday, May 10. On May 10, the *Daily Nebraska State Journal* announced that the Lincoln team likely would be moved to Kearney. S.C. Coman, the NSL secretary-treasurer, met with a majority of the league board of directors in Lincoln to discuss the financial problems of the Lincoln team. Coman shared a telegram from Kearney stating that $1,500 had been raised to establish a team in that town. Although the directors present in Lincoln hoped to keep the Lincoln team in Lincoln, when they sought help from "hitherto well-known supporters of base ball [sic] in Lincoln ... [t]hey met with no encouragement." The directors decided that the Lincoln team would remain in Lincoln for the rest of the week (Wednesday, May 11, through Sunday, May 15), during which period the league would try to arrange the move to Kearney. The alternative to moving the team was to continue as a five-team league. The paper noted that "[a]n effort will be made to have Will Houseworth taken in as manager at Kearney."[149]

While Kearney awaited a decision on this matter, the Lincoln club faced the remaining scheduled home contests as a lame duck. Perhaps fittingly, rain caused cancellation of games scheduled for Tuesday, May 10, Thursday, May 12, Friday, May 13, and Saturday, May 14.

Lincoln played Fremont on Wednesday, May 11, losing 6–4 in 14 innings before a small number of attendees. "Castone pitched a splendid game, striking out twelve men, but whenever they found him they hit him hard."[150] Fowler, batting second and playing second base, went 2-for-7 and stole two bases, but poor baserunning and 10 errors cost Lincoln the game.

The *Daily Nebraska State Journal* reported last minute efforts to raise money to keep the team in Lincoln, including talk of "two or three gentlemen of means and influence [who] announced their intention of raising $500 to put the team on its financial feet." There was also talk of Lincoln getting a franchise in the Western League, perhaps the financially troubled St. Paul club.[151]

Hope of somehow retaining the team ended on May 14, when the NSL admitted Kearney as Lincoln's replacement club.[152] The league directors elected J.A. Healy of Kearney to join them. T.J. Hickey of Lincoln, president of the NSL, was replaced by Harry Brewer of Hastings. Manager Clark of Kearney[153] announced his intent to "sign the Lincoln team at once [so that] the league will go on uninterrupted."[154]

Lincoln played its final game, treated as an exhibition game by the league, on Sunday, May 15, against Plattsmouth, winning by a score of 4–1 before about 350 spectators. For a team plagued by rainouts, the description of the M Street grounds for the final game seems fitting:

> The grounds were simply horrible. Inside of the diamond it was not so bad, but there were picturesque lakes all around it, forming a continuous circle from thirty to fifty feet back of the bases and extending to the fences. This picturesque slough contained water from one to three inches deep.

Fowler, as usual playing second base, but batting fourth, was hitless in five at bats. Castone pitched a complete game, giving up six hits and only one run (in the first inning). His defense drew particular praise: "Castone played the fielding game yesterday almost single-handed, as he has several games recently." Because Lincoln was short two players—Smith was disabled and Hillis was "not in town in time to play"—two local men, Kimerer and Gauger, substituted. Kimerer, who played left field, made a "phenomenal leaping catch of a long fly to center." For the Plattsmouth team, the three black members,

John Patterson, Maupin, and Reeves, did not have especially strong games. Patterson, the second baseman, and Maupin, the catcher, had no hits, and Reeves, who was on the mound and played first base, "pitched a wild game until the sixth," when he left the mound.[155]

## *The May 29, 1892, Incident in Grand Island*

Kearney and Grand Island had met earlier in May in a two-game series held in Grand Island on May 23 and May 24. Grand Island won both games (7–2 and 8–3), with no incidents reported by either the Kearney or Grand Island newspapers.[156] However, when the two clubs met again on May 29, there was a clash on the base paths involving Kearney's second baseman, Fowler, and Grand Island's manager–third baseman, Pa Rourke. According to the *Grand Island (NE) Daily Independent*:

> The principal feature of the game was the scrap between Rourke and the [N]egro, Fowler. Rourke was on first, Kipp [the shortstop, batting seventh] knocked a grounder to second. Fowler fielded it. All the latter had to do to put Rourke out was to touch his base and throw the ball to first. Instead of that he pounded both his fists and the ball into Rourke—where he lives—and knocked the wind out of him. Rourke's temper took a flight and it then looked as if a coroner's inquest would follow. Rourke grabbed Fowler, but the other players immediately separated them. It was a disgusting exhibition all around. Both men are perhaps equally to blame, and if the patronage of the majority of the people is to be retained[,] these things must stop at once. We don't believe that any captain could have kept himself in a lovely mood under the circumstances, but if fighting is to be indulged in[,] let it be done when there's no one about.[157]

The newspaper story concluded: "The second base incident was virtually a debate on the question: 'Should colored players be allowed in the state league[?]' The judges decide in favor of the negative."[158] Exactly who "the judges" were is unclear.

Jeffrey Michael Laing describes this confrontation as "the only on-field fight of [Fowler's] more-than-three-decade involvement with the national pastime."[159] Laing makes two additional points. First, in prior years, to avoid the spikes of white players, Fowler had devised wooden shin guards. Second, despite his age, Fowler still had significant speed and stole 45 bases while playing in the NSL. Thus, although the tone of the article in the *Grand Island (NE) Daily Independent* strongly suggests racism ("the [N]egro Fowler" and the "debate" language), Fowler's performance as a player suggests that "in all likelihood, race was not the only reason that Fowler was targeted by his white opponents in 1892."[160]

## *June 20, 1892: The Fremont Team Leaves the NSL*

On June 21, the *Daily Nebraska State Journal* announced that Fremont "Serves Notice of Withdrawal" from the league.[161] Bruce E. Smith, president of the Fremont team, and George O. Hickok, secretary of the team, wrote to League President Brewer:

> We are reliably informed that the secretary of the Nebraska [S]tate [L]eague [Ulysses S. Rohrer] is also acting as manager of one of the clubs [Hastings] belonging to the league and is playing the position of shortstop in [*sic*] his club in the league games. As the secretary of the league has general charge and control of all league umpires, this condition of things is manifestly unfair. As we find no remedy for this

in the constitution of the league, nor in any of the laws or regulations of which we have been informed, we desire to surrender our charter as a member of the league. You will therefore take notice that after this date [June 20, 1892,] we do not consider ourselves bound by the constitution, nor any of the bylaws or regulations of the league.[162]

The first secretary-treasurer of the NSL was S.C. Coman of Fremont, but Coman resigned as secretary—nothing was said about the treasurer's position—on May 26, "on account of an intended European trip, which will take him from home for the greater part of the summer."[163] To elect his replacement, the league directors met in Hastings. Beatrice hoped to secure the position,[164] but the directors elected Rohrer instead. "Rohrer did not desire to accept, but he was prevailed upon to do so and will make the [l]eague a splendid secretary."[165] Although not well documented, apparently Rohrer stated that he would not play for Hastings if elected secretary.[166] This he did for a while, but box scores and newspaper reports show that he returned to the field well before June 20.[167]

There apparently was no rule in the league constitution or bylaws preventing Rohrer from serving both as an officer of the NSL and player-manager of the Hastings team, but Fremont's directors properly called attention to the conflict of interest relating to selection and control of the umpires. Rohrer's power, as league secretary, to terminate the employment of an umpire, created at least the impression of a conflict of interest when coupled with his position as a player-manager for Hastings. In the heat of a game, with Rohrer either on the field as a player or on the sidelines as manager, an umpire might consciously or unconsciously make close calls in favor of Hastings.[168]

Some commentators noted that, while Fremont's allegations about this matter were legitimate, Fremont might have had other or at least additional reasons to withdraw. The *Beatrice (NE) Daily Democrat* observed that "there is a lingering suspicion that financial and other causes are the real reason for [Fremont's] quitting." Was one of "the causes" Fremont's lack of interest in a team with a losing record? According to the *Daily Democrat*, "Fremont, it appears from reading the papers up there, cannot support and takes little interest in a club that is not a head ender."[169] True, the Fremont team had not had great success on the field, being in fifth place, having won 11 games and lost 18 as of June 20. Nevertheless, this assertion seems unfair. The Fremont press was critical of the team's play on the field, but no more so than the newspapers in the other league cities were of their teams from time to time.

Following the withdrawal of the Fremont team, the players, who had not been paid in full under their contracts, made their grievance public. Writing to the *Omaha Daily Bee*, they stated that Fremont dropped out of the league because the owners "thought it cheaper to drop out than to pay us what was coming to us, which was almost one thousand dollars ($1,000), not having been paid us as a cost since the season opened."[170]

There was a strange postscript to the withdrawal. The *Fremont (NE) Daily Tribune* reported that the *Lincoln (NE) Journal* printed a telegram claiming that the NSL, having received the June 20 letter from Fremont, nonetheless met in Fremont and voted to expel the club from the league for nonpayment of dues. The *Daily Tribune* went further to say, "As no meeting of the state league was held in Fremont last night, nor at any other time lately, it is very evident that there is a big mistake somewhere. It has been suggested that some enemy of the Fremont management might have invented the story and sent it to the *Journal*."[171]

## June 26, 1892: The Plattsmouth Team Disbands

The Plattsmouth club's play throughout its time in the league was not of the quality expected by the citizens of that city. Despite a few glimpses of hope, Plattsmouth generally remained in fifth place in the six-team league.[172] On May 18, with the Plattsmouthers on the road with a record of two wins and four losses, the *Plattsmouth (NE) Daily Journal* reported that rumors of "a general shakeup in the entire team" as soon as it returned home.[173] On May 30, Plattsmouth manager Al Perrine resigned and was immediately replaced by Ves Green, the right fielder.[174] Poor attendance was taking its toll,[175] and the *Daily Journal* suggested that the team should hire an advertising manager to address that matter.[176] But unfortunately for the franchise, the poor attendance was merely a symptom of a larger problem.

On June 11, 1892, *The Sporting News* published a report dated May 31, 1892, in which its correspondent in Plattsmouth provided an assessment of the team. The writer was blunt: "If there is a worse loser than our team[,] we want to see it."[177] Acknowledging that bad weather had been an issue, the report listed other serious problems: Frank Maupin's asthma left him unable to catch[178]; the pitchers had only recently gained regular season form; and Jack Reeves had been forced to play first base. Although John Patterson "has played fine ball at second and has done everything in his power to make the team a winning one," first baseman [William] Kennedy "has played ragged ball. The man is dissatisfied with the team and is opposed to playing with [N]egroes and wants to leave." "[W. M.] Myers ... has played a spiritless fielding game and pitched indifferent ball. He is in the same boat with [F. M.] Long and Kennedy and does not like the colored boys." The correspondent catalogued many other deficiencies, concluding that "[t]he boys seem to have a fit of the blues. Their ball playing is certainly lifeless and spiritless."[179]

On June 2, the *Plattsmouth (NE) Daily Journal* reported that "[t]he town's pretty well vacated this afternoon. Most of the population is at the ball park [sic]."[180] Immediately following was a report that Kearney had defeated Plattsmouth, 12–4, in the first game of a doubleheader. Perhaps the reference to attendance at the doubleheader was tongue-in-cheek, because on June 3, the *Plattsmouth (NE) Daily Journal* reported "[a]n assembly of less than two hundred souls paid admission at the Chicago [A]venue ball park [sic] yesterday afternoon and were unwilling witnesses to the horrible slaughter of the Plattsmouth base ball [sic] team." Kearney swept the doubleheader, 12–4 and 7–5. "Two losses in one day is not much out of the ordinary, but the humiliation caused by yesterday's misfortune is that Kearney jumped out of last place and assigned that 'peg' to the home team. This is why we weep." Will Castone pitched both ends of the doubleheader for Kearney, yielding only 10 hits. Jack Reeves pitched the second game for Plattsmouth, "and although quite wild, held his opponents down to stingy singles, none of which should have been responsible for runs." John Patterson managed only two hits in eight at bats for Plattsmouth; Maupin fared slightly better, with three hits in eight at bats.[181]

A significant reason for the problems besetting the Plattsmouth team seemed to be racial tension. The *Omaha Daily Bee* reported that

> [Plattsmouth's problems] can only be laid to the fact that the club is torn with dissensions. The white players are said to be combined against the colored men, and it is said that three of the men will jump their contracts and go to Lemars [sic], Ia. These men have played sulky ball ... and seem to take no interest in the team.[182]

On June 3, the *Plattsmouth (NE) Evening News*, recognizing these issues, suggested a radical solution: release all the white players on the current team and replace them with the players from the 1890 Lincoln Giants.

> This meets with favor in some quarters and disfavor in others. To our mind it seems best to give our new Manager [A. V.] Green, full and unlimited control of the team. Let him sign whom he pleases so long as he gets a team. If he wants white players and can ... sign them, let him do it. If colored players are what he wants[,] let [him] have them. Give us a ball team by all means.[183]

The losing streak reached seven games when Plattsmouth was defeated by Grand Island, 4–3, before the smallest audience "which has ever been assembled in" Plattsmouth,[184] though John Patterson, Maupin, and Reeves all played well.

In an effort to improve the team, manager Ves Green signed Lee Pond, "a former Iowa-Illinois league player," and Norman Baker, who obtained his release from Fremont. Green "figure[d] on recruiting the club to such an extent that by July 1st [*sic*] Plattsmouth will have a team of which she may well feel proud."[185] His efforts seemed to have an immediate effect when Plattsmouth swept a doubleheader from Fremont on June 5. John Patterson had seven hits in 10 at bats, Reeves won the first game, 11–2, and "Maupin caught two brilliant games yesterday. One stolen base and no passed balls is a great record."[186] The *Plattsmouth (NE) Daily Journal* observed that "[f]or the first time since the opening of the season the locals exhibited some team work [*sic*], and their improvement in all departments pleased the large audience immensely."[187]

But unfortunately for the team and its fans, there was no long-term improvement. Plattsmouth dropped its second game with Fremont, 12–9, when Jack Reeves, in relief of starter Yapp, blew a three-run lead, giving up six runs and losing the game in the eighth inning.[188] Notwithstanding a three-day rest before opening a series in Beatrice, Plattsmouth was defeated in the first game, 16–9, while committing 14 errors.[189] The team bounced back (after a fashion) to beat Beatrice, 15–11,

Referred to by the *Omaha Daily Bee* as "a fine backstop, [a] good hitter[,] ... a speedy base runner[,] ... and ... the most popular man on the ... team" when he played for the Lincoln Giants, Frank Maupin was one of the stars of the Plattsmouth club. Along with his fellow former Giants Will Lincoln and Jack Reeves, he would later be a member of the 1894 David City, Nebraska, amateur champions (Nebraska State Historical Society, RG3064-26).

**46   Section I—The Long and Winding Road**

while committing only seven errors to Beatrice's 12,[190] but then lost five games in a row,[191] including a forfeit to Kearney.[192]

After a scheduled three-game series against nonleague opponent Springfield,[193] the team returned to Plattsmouth for three games against league-leading Beatrice and was greeted with a newspaper report that "the rumor is quite prevalent among ballists that the local team had best disband."[194]

> From the beginning[,] the club has been a financial failure and it is stated on authority that unless a decided improvement is accorded in attendance, the coming series of games on the home grounds will be the last in which the state league club of Plattsmouth will take a part.[195]

Plattsmouth and Beatrice played a single game on June 25 and a doubleheader on Sunday, June 26. Admission to both games of the doubleheader was announced as 35 cents.[196] On June 25, the *Plattsmouth (NE) Daily Journal*, which went to press before the 4:00 p.m. scheduled start time for the Saturday game, reported that the Sunday doubleheader probably would be the final league games played by Plattsmouth.[197] Despite recent additions to the team, "poor playing and poor attendance tell the tale, so the inevitable must be accepted with as much grace as is possible."[198] Plattsmouth forfeited the Saturday game under rather strange circumstances when "no Reach balls were at hand when the time came for calling the game.... A little investigation disclosed that Green, one of the local players, after promising to take the balls out to the grounds had locked all the club's Reach balls in his room."[199] Plattsmouth and Beatrice played an "exhibition" game after the forfeit, with Plattsmouth winning, 9–8.[200]

The end came on Sunday, June 26. Plattsmouth played the scheduled doubleheader, losing both games, the first, 13–4, and the second, 7–2. The team committed six errors in the first game and five in the second. In the first game, Patterson did not play, Reeves played center field, and Maupin played third base. "Old man Reeves' fielding" was a feature, and he collected two hits in three at bats, scoring one run, while Maupin collected two hits in three at bats and scored two runs. Plattsmouth's pitcher, Parvin, had already signed a contract with Beatrice in anticipation of Plattsmouth disbanding, and "did not pitch in his usual style."[201] After the final game, the *Plattsmouth (NE) Daily Journal* offered the following editorial opinion:

> The disbandment of the local team is a misfortune which the town can ill withstand, but to allow the players to go without their salaries would make Plattsmouth the laughing-stock [sic] of the entire state. It is the duty of the city to see that every cent due the players is paid.[202]

The next day, the paper called attention to the "endless amount of undesirable advertising [Fremont had received] for not paying the players of her defunct ball club" and urged that "Plattsmouth should shun such methods."[203]

## *July 5, 1892: The Beatrice Team Disbands*

Beatrice, one of the strongest teams in the NSL, played very well, despite having three players—Howe, Edinger, and Thompson—jump their contracts and Harry Gatewood and George Taylor out with injuries.[204] After sweeping a doubleheader with Plattsmouth on May 30, Beatrice was leading the league with a record of nine wins and four losses. Grand Island, in second place with a record of 11 wins and six losses, also swept a doubleheader from Kearney.[205] On June 15, Beatrice was 18–6 and in first place and Grand

Island was 18–11 and in second place. On June 30, Beatrice and Grand Island were still battling, with Beatrice 25–8 and Grand Island 25–13. Kearney then dealt Beatrice a setback on July 2, sweeping a doubleheader by identical 6–2 scores. "Both games were gifts, every error, except perhaps the one charged to [right fielder] Slagle in the second game, being of the rankest and most inexcusable sort."[206] But despite those two bad games, Beatrice continued to lead the NSL with at 25–10 record, followed in second place by Grand Island at 25–13.

After a day off on July 3, Beatrice and Grand Island played two games on the Fourth of July. Beatrice won both of them, shutting out the visiting Grand Island team 6–0 in the first game and 8–0 in the second game. About 1,000 people paid 50 cents apiece to watch those games, described as "two of the … prettiest shut-outs [sic] ever seen" and as "the best games ever put up on the home grounds."[207] Taylor played left field and batted second in both contests. Although going 0-for-4 in the first one, he scored two runs and had two putouts. In the second one, he was 1-for-5, scoring one run and recording four putouts. Combined, the games took about four hours to play, and at the end of the day, Beatrice, at 27–10, was in first place and Grand Island, at 25–15, was in second.

On July 5, however, the directors and shareholders of the Beatrice club met in Beatrice and voted to disband the team. "This move is the result of the action of the league directors in demanding a $40 guarantee from the Beatrice team for games played at home and the announcement that the Beatrice team was to get but $25 from the other cities. The whole transaction was considered manifestly unfair."[208] Grand Island, Hastings, and Kearney agreed to continue the NSL as a three-team league.[209] Hastings signed Holmes, the Beatrice catcher, and expressed pleasure that Beatrice had disbanded because "the jump to that town was too far and expensive and [Beatrice had] overreached itself on the salary question."[210] *Sporting Life* carried a biting comment from Hastings: "Well, there are but three of us left. Plattsmouth and Beatrice have dropped out since my last letter; that's the way it goes with these one-horse towns that have an idea that they can support a first-class ball club, when they can hardly support a town lot nine."[211]

On July 9, the *Daily Nebraska State Journal* noted that "[a] benefit game of ball was played this afternoon for the players of the defunct Beatrice team, six of whom are still here."[212]

## July 9, 1892: The Grand Island Team Disbands

Grand Island, which for most of the season had battled Beatrice for first place, lost its final league game to Hastings by a score of 3–2 and then disbanded on July 9.[213] The previous day, it had defeated Hastings, in Hastings, by a score of 8–6 in a game "that would please anyone. The fielding was lively and the hitting of both teams was excellent."[214] The contest took 11 innings and was described as "[t]he most exciting and closest ball game [sic] played [in Hastings] this season."[215] Grand Island had two wins and two losses in the reconfigured three-team league when it folded.

The reason for the demise of the team was financial:

> [T]he departed cities in the Nebraska league are now reaping the harvest of so much salary lost. That is the secret of the sudden demise of Fremont, Plattsmouth[,] and the city of the braves of the blue. Hastings was the only team in the organization that confined herself to the salary limit and now comes out with flying colors.[216]

## 48   Section I—The Long and Winding Road

On July 11, the *Daily Nebraska State Journal* reported that:

> There was a rumor afloat to-night [sic] that several of the players had made contracts with other clubs. The same was investigated, some claiming that they understood the team was all right and others say it was disbanded. Manager O'Rourke [sic] stated that to-day's [sic] [July 10, 1892,] game would certainly be the last and that the club was as good as disbanded to-night [sic].[217]

Manager Rourke added: "What is the use to continue? We'll only run into the hole deeper, and I have seen too much of base ball [sic] to let my players play for nothing. I want them to quit while there's money enough to pay all indebtedness."[218] The *Grand Island (NE) Independent* concluded that "even a winning club cannot be supported in Grand Island just now."[219] According to the article, some subscribers "have not paid up their subscriptions and stolidly and unblushingly say they will not."[220]

Apparently, the Grand Island team played a nonleague exhibition game against local ballplayers on July 10: "The game today was with a picked nine and was uninteresting."[221]

## *July 13–15, 1892: The Kearney Team, the Hastings Team and the NSL Disband*

The final league game, between Hastings and Kearney, was played on July 11 in Hastings and went to Hastings by a score of 5–3. Perhaps the two teams saved their best for last because they played 15 innings and impending darkness may have allowed Hastings to break the 3–3 tie in the last inning: "had darkness not interfered with fielding there is no telling how many innings would have been played." Fowler, leading off and playing second base for Kearney, had one hit in five at bats, but scored two runs, and had three putouts and five assists—a fitting end to his NSL career. Castone did not play for Kearney because Kearney pitcher Albert Hopp was in for the entire game. As the *Daily Nebraska State Journal* observed, "[t]he Nebraska [S]tate ... [L]eague, like Banquo's ghost, is hard to down."[222]

Despite the exciting final game, the league ended on Friday, July 15, with a notice issued by the Hastings team:

> The Nebraska State League of Base Ball [sic] Clubs is a thing of the past. It collapsed altogether by the withdrawal of Grand Island and Kearney on Saturday [July 9, 1892,] and Wednesday last [July 13, 1892,] respectively, which necessitated the Hastings [c]lub to disband also, which was done last night. The players were all paid off in full and are departing for their respective homes. We have the satisfaction of being the last club to give up the sponge after being the last club to join the [l]eague last spring.[223]

## *What Went Wrong?*

After the collapse of the NSL, *Sporting Life* asserted that "[t]he principal cause of this [l]eague giving up so early in the season was, firstly, the bad wet weather at the opening of the season, and the contract-jumping [sic] of some of its best talent so as to weaken several of the clubs."[224] Both the weather and the contract jumping were contributing factors, but neither separately nor together do these factors explain the collapse. Rather, a combination of weather-related problems, players refusing to honor their contracts, racial tensions, insufficient initial capital, and failure to abide by league salary limits proved fatal.

## Bad Weather

Terrible May weather created problems for the teams and the league, but the weather problems were regional, not confined to Nebraska. The newspapers in the NSL cities carried stories about both local and national disasters caused by the incessant rain.[225] Comments on the length of the league season noted that beginning before the end of May risked weather problems and that risk very quickly became reality. The weather not only created financial difficulties due to rainouts and severely reduced attendance but also prevented any meaningful preseason training period during which players could get into playing shape. When games were played despite poor weather conditions, attendance was low and ticket receipts could not cover actual operating expenses and league fees. Postponement of games as a result of bad weather caused two serious financial effects. First, the home team had to pay the $25 guarantee to the visiting team despite having no game revenue. Second, so many games had to be postponed that the games actually made up before the league collapsed were usually the second contests of single-admission doubleheaders, and the teams lost the ticket revenue that separate makeup games would have produced.

## Problems with Player Contracts: Jumping and Other Issues

The NSL requested protection under the National Agreement in part to avoid interference with player contracts from other participating leagues. Unfortunately for league franchises, though, clubs from other leagues did attempt to entice league players from their teams, with a rather alarming rate of success. But even within the NSL, there were disputes over which teams had rights to particular players.

### Player Contract Problems within the League

Three examples illustrate this type of contract problem. The first involved Plattsmouth, Beatrice, and a third baseman named Kennedy, who had accepted offers from both Plattsmouth and Beatrice. At a meeting of the NSL board of directors held on April 5 in Lincoln, the directors awarded Kennedy to Plattsmouth. Although Beatrice indicated it would appeal the decision, Kennedy was playing third base for Plattsmouth on Opening Day.[226]

The second example, reported by *Sporting Life*, involved a conflict between Plattsmouth and Hastings over a player named Byron McKibben. This problem was a bit more complicated than the dispute over Kennedy. There was evidence that McKibben had signed contracts with Plattsmouth and Grand Island and later with Hastings. Further, McKibben was a minor, and his father would allow him to play only for Hastings. The league directors concluded: "While the equity of the situation was undoubtedly with Plattsmouth, the law was not entirely one-sided, and a compromise was finally effected, by reason of which McKibben went to Hastings."[227] McKibben was in the Hastings lineup, playing second base, for the team's first game against Grand Island.[228]

The third example involved shortstop William Van Arnam. Van Arnam signed with Beatrice but before the season began made it clear that he would not play for the club. Without apparent intervention from the league, Beatrice agreed to release Van Arnam to Lincoln in return for "money considerations." Beatrice suffered a similar defection after the season had started when the team's left fielder and catcher, Howe, requested his release so he could join the Plattsmouth team. He even threatened to jump to Plattsmouth if Beatrice did not honor his request.[229]

### Interference from Clubs in Other Leagues and Independent Clubs

Despite the ostensible protection of the National Agreement, the league clubs lost many players to clubs in other leagues and a few to independent clubs. The usual reason was the promise of additional money.[230] As discussed below, however, a few players, such as Hastings catcher Pierce Chiles, asserted a racial basis for jumping to a new team. Such assertions seem weak attempts to justify a decision made in fact for financial reasons.[231]

Reports of contract jumping abounded,[232] despite the fact that the primary punishment for doing so was blacklisting by the league. Some jumpers, however, were warned of more than temporal punishment for breaching their contract obligations: "The ball player [sic] who has any regard for the hereafter should think twice before jumping a contract entered into with a club that is operated under the [N]ational [A]greement."[233] Some jumps produced colorful stories,[234] with certain teams bidding departing players good riddance.[235] In other instances, the jump was accepted with what seemed to be fatalism.[236]

## Racism

To suggest that racism played no role in the demise of the 1892 NSL would be to ignore the reality that in Nebraska, as in the rest of the United States, pre–Civil War attitudes and prejudices lingered.[237] Racial epithets appeared in many newspapers,[238] and newspapers reporting baseball news often felt obligated to remind readers of the race of a player or players on teams.[239] Among the municipalities represented in the 1892 NSL, Hastings was, as previously described, the most vocal opponent of racially integrated baseball. At the same time, the newspapers in the league cities—including Hastings—and in Omaha also gave the black players apparently genuine praise for the quality of their play on the field.[240]

In a few instances, players jumping teams tried to justify their breach of contract on racial grounds, but that justification is suspect.

> Catcher [Pierce] Chiles, who jumped his Hastings, Neb., contract, and is now playing with the independent St. Joseph [c]lub, writes that his reason for treating the Hastings [c]lub so meanly is that colored players are employed in the Nebraska State League and that he was compelled to associate with them. That was more than his proud Caucasian spirit could brook.[241]

Whether the final sentence reflects a sarcastic response to Chiles's justification might be debated, but the financial enticement offered by the St. Joseph team was important and, as Gregory Bond has pointed out, Chiles had never previously expressed objections to playing against blacks.[242] More to the point, Chiles also left Hastings owing $40 and did not raise the racial justification until criticized about the unpaid debt.[243] In a postscript, the *Hastings Daily Nebraskan* noted, caustically, that "Chiles seems to be more service to Hastings in St. Joe than he was [on] the team." In the same article, the writer acknowledged the strong play of Plattsmouth's black players: "The colored troops fought nobby [*sic*—presumably the writer meant 'nobly']. 'Twas not their shame, that Plattsmouth lost the game."[244]

Newspaper accounts strongly suggest racial discord on the Plattsmouth team, at least as the season progressed. And it would be tempting to generalize from these accounts and the statements of players like Chiles that racial issues played a prominent role in the demise of the league. The evidence, however, does not support such a conclusion. The Plattsmouth team never performed to the expectations of the citizens of that city and, as financial problems increased for it, it is hardly surprising that many of the players became discontented and performed with less than full enthusiasm. It is also significant that there was no reported racial discord on either of the other two teams with black players.

Nor should it be surprising that, after the collapse of the league, a person from Hastings wrote to *Sporting Life* posing the following question: "In order to settle a dispute here, I would like you to inform me through your paper if there are any colored players playing with any league which is under the protection of the National Agreement at present, and if so[,] with what clubs." The editor responded: "None that we know of."[245] The apparent point of the question was to emphasize that the league was out of step with the rest of Organized Baseball in permitting teams to have black players—a final "I told you so" from the home of the most vocal opponents of integrated baseball in Nebraska.

## Inadequate Financing and Disregard of League Player Salary Limits

Of the six teams that comprised the NSL on opening day, only Hastings, the last club to disband, seemed to have adequate resources to handle its financial obligations. Two of the original clubs, Beatrice and Grand Island, which had boasted that each had raised sufficient capital to permit it to meet its monetary commitments to its players and to the league even if the teams played no games,[246] began to have financial troubles as the season progressed. Fremont, although well supported initially, encountered fiscal problems that probably contributed to its decision to withdraw from the league. Lincoln and Plattsmouth both suffered financial difficulties from the outset, with Lincoln's being serious enough to force the city's team to move to Kearney and Plattsmouth's ultimately contributing to its collapse.

Even before the regular season began, complaints surfaced about clubs disregarding the $600 per month player salary limit agreed to at the time of the formation of the league. "There is a suspicion [in Hastings], apparently well founded, that Beatrice has over-stepped [*sic*] the salary limit."[247] Although each team agreed to provide a $500 bond "to be forfeited upon a violation of the salary limit rule,"[248] there is no evidence that the league ever attempted to collect against such a bond. As noted earlier, much of the reported blame for the collapse of the league was assigned to the refusal of many teams to abide by the salary limit. The assertion by the Hastings executives that it was the only club to abide by the salary limit may or may not be true.[249]

## Poor Quality of Play

Although some of the league games were well played, quite a few were marred by excessive fielding errors and seemingly indifferent play. Taking into account the fact that

**52  Section I—The Long and Winding Road**

the gloves used by the fielders were much smaller than those in use today, the number of errors in many games suggested player skill levels well below those of upper-level minor leagues, such as the Western League.[250] And despite the fact that the locals understood that the players in the NSL were not all of a caliber to perform on teams in the higher minor leagues, the newspaper commentary made it clear that the fans found it difficult to support sloppy play.

## Conclusion

A perfect storm—literally and figuratively—of rainouts caused by horrible weather in May of 1892, inadequate initial financing for Lincoln and Plattsmouth and perhaps other teams, refusal of many teams to abide by league player salary limits, players jumping their contract obligations, lack of fan support for the less successful teams, highly variable quality of play, and, to a certain extent, racial tensions involving

Following his time with Beatrice, George Taylor saw action with a number of teams from 1892 through 1907, including the 1896 Adrian, Michigan, Page Fence Giants. Here he is pictured with some of his Giant teammates (left to right): (front row) Fred Van Dyke, Bill Binga, Charlie Grant, Vasco Graham; (middle row) Billy Holland, Gus Parsons, Pete Burns; (back row) George Taylor, George Wilson, Grant "Home Run" Johnson, Walker or Joe Miller (National Baseball Hall of Fame Library).

some players, forced the NSL to end operation in mid–July. Attempts to assign any single factor the ultimate responsibility for the failure are futile. For example, although the financial losses caused by the May rainouts were serious, even with ideal weather, the many other problems besetting the league could have been sufficient to doom its existence.

Although it might be tempting to cast the NSL as a last, if quixotic, attempt to stem the tide of the "gentleman's agreement" in Nebraska, the facts do not support that view. Ulysses S. Rohrer and others from Hastings spoke loudly against integration and likely prevented the all-black Giants from representing Lincoln in the league. But despite Rohrer's efforts, three of the six teams in the league had black players, though those six players seem to have been selected based on talent, not because they were black.

However, none of these problems prevented the NSL from being the first professional baseball league comprised only of teams from Nebraska, and it deserves to be remembered for that fact, if for no other. Just as importantly, the NSL must also be remembered as the last instance of an integrated professional baseball league in the Cornhusker State for over 50 years. The six black players performed very well, were team leaders, and remained with their clubs for as long as the clubs were part of the league. Although Castone ceased making his living from baseball when he was in his mid–20s, Maupin and Reeves continued their careers at least through 1899 and 1900, respectively, and Fowler, Patterson, and Taylor played major roles in black professional baseball long after the NSL vanished. The contributions of these six men are a significant part of the rich baseball history of Nebraska.

Notes

1. Starting in 1910, several professional baseball leagues used the name "Nebraska State League." The second Nebraska State League, formed in 1910, lasted through 1915. The third Nebraska State League lasted two years (1922 and 1923), the fourth lasted 11 years (1928–1938), and the fifth, and final, one lasted four years (1956–1959). When the classification system for minor league teams first appeared in 1902 through the final season of the Nebraska State League in 1959, the league was labeled Class D. From 1902 through 1962, Class D was the lowest level of minor league baseball (with the exception of Class E, which actually operated only in 1943). The current lowest classification is the Rookie League, created as part of the 1963 reorganization of minor league baseball. That reorganization moved former Class D leagues to the new Class A, one step above the new Rookie League classification. See Paul Dickson, *The Dickson Baseball Dictionary*, 3rd ed. (New York: W.W. Norton & Company, 2009), 191.

2. Jeffrey Michael Laing, *Bud Fowler: Baseball's First Black Professional* (Jefferson, North Carolina: McFarland & Company, Inc., Publishers, 2013), 126. Many writers have described and analyzed the history of the antipathy of white baseball players to black baseball players and the gradual exclusion of such players from white professional baseball teams under what is often referred to as the "gentleman's agreement." See, e.g., Tom Gilbert, *Baseball and the Color Line* (New York: Franklin Watts, 1995); Leslie A. Heaphy, *The Negro Leagues, 1869–1960* (Jefferson, North Carolina: McFarland & Company, Inc., Publishers, 2003); Robert Peterson, *Only the Ball Was White: A History of Legendary Black Players and All-Black Professional Teams* (Englewood Cliffs, New Jersey: Prentice-Hall, 1970); Mark Ribowsky, *A Complete History of the Negro Leagues, 1884 to 1955* (New York: Citadel Press, 1995); Scott Simkus, *Outsider Baseball: The Weird World of Hardball on the Fringe, 1876–1950* (Chicago: Chicago Review Press, 2014); Ryan A. Swanson, *When Baseball Went White: Reconstruction, Reconciliation, & Dreams of a National Pastime* (Lincoln: University of Nebraska Press, 2014); and Sol White, *Sol White's History of Colored Base Ball [sic] with Other Documents of the Early Black Game, 1886–1936*, compiled and with an introduction by Jerry Malloy (Lincoln: University of Nebraska Press, 1995). See also James E. Brunson, III, *The Early Image of Black Baseball: Race and Representation in the Popular Press, 1871–1890* (Jefferson, North Carolina: McFarland & Company, Inc., Publishers, 2009).

3. As professional baseball became established, the distinction between "major league" and "minor league" professional teams developed quickly, as did basic agreements between and among professional leagues

## 54  Section I—The Long and Winding Road

relating to protection of player contract rights. See Neil J. Sullivan, *The Minors: The Struggles and the Triumph of Baseball's Poor Relation from 1876 to the Present* (New York: St. Martin's Press, 1990). Minor leagues that joined in the so-called National Agreement received such protection, and starting in the early 1890s such leagues were given designations under a rudimentary classification system. Lloyd Johnson and Miles Wolff, eds., *The Encyclopedia of Minor League Baseball*, 3rd ed. (Durham, North Carolina: Baseball America, Inc., 2007), 15. "It was a loose system, and these classifications, A to F, while in some cases reflecting the level of play, often were assigned in response to the amount of dues paid." *Ibid.* The 1892 NSL was designated a Class B league under this system. "Official News," *Sporting Life*, April 9, 1892, 1.

    4. The dividing line between amateur and professional baseball has sometimes been fuzzy. In many states, local "amateur" baseball teams recruited players by finding them jobs with local businesses. Nebraska newspapers reported the games played by the 1891 Lincoln Giants as "amateur" contests despite the fact that the players were paid by the team. See, e.g., "Amateur Teams Standing," *Omaha Daily Bee*, August 9, 1891. This chapter includes only Nebraska teams that played in clearly professional leagues. With the exception of those parts otherwise noted, information about the professional baseball leagues discussed in this section comes from Johnson and Wolff.

    5. Various issues of the *Omaha World-Herald* between May 8, 1879, and July 9, 1879. "Each team had a color assigned to them with Davenport being the Brown Stockings. The Omaha team had green stockings, Rockford was white and Dubuque was red." http://nebaseballhistory.com/before1900.html (accessed on July 2, 2015). "Dubuque won the league pennant that year. It went on to defeat Providence and the Chicago Cubs, the top two teams in the National League. The 1–0 win over the Cubs led Dubuque, with such talent as [Charles] Comiskey and Charles ["Hoss"] Radbourne, to claim the world championship." http://www.encyclopediadubuque.org/index.php?title=BASEBALL (accessed on July 2, 2015).

    6. The other cities with teams were Cleveland; Indianapolis; Kansas City, Missouri; Milwaukee; and Toledo. For a history of the Western League, including the development of the American League from the Western League, see W.C. Madden and Patrick J. Stewart, *The Western League: A Baseball History, 1885 through 1999* (Jefferson, North Carolina: McFarland & Company, Inc., Publishers, 2002).

    7. See David W. Zang, *Fleet Walker's Divided Heart: The Life of Baseball's First Black Major Leaguer* (Lincoln: University of Nebraska Press 1995).

    8. Laing, 83–86.

    9. The other cities with teams in the 1886 Western League were Denver; Leadville, Colorado; Leavenworth, Kansas; St. Joseph, Missouri; and Topeka.

    10. Although the Lincoln team was not a success, one of the team's players, Percival Wheritt "Perry" Werden, led the league in home runs with 11. Werden, who began his professional baseball career in 1884, later played for Minneapolis in the Western League, where in 1894 he hit .417 with 43 home runs. In 1895, he hit .428 with 45 home runs. He also played at the major league level with the St. Louis Maroons (1884), Washington Nationals (1888), Toledo Maumees (1890), Baltimore Orioles (1891), St. Louis Browns (1892–1893), and Louisville Colonels (1897). "Perry Werden," www.baseball-reference.com (accessed on October 31, 2015).

    11. Laing, 87–88.

    12. Ulysses S. Rohrer, who later helped form and served as player-manager for the Hastings entry in the 1892 NSL, managed the Hastings Western League team for a portion of the season. Johnson and Wolff, 149, and Madden and Stewart, 307. Baseball ran in the Rohrer family. The All-American Girls Professional Baseball League (AAGPBL) website page on Kay Rohrer, a catcher for the Rockford Peaches of the All-American Girls Professional Baseball League, states that her father, William Rohrer, was a minor league catcher, and her grandfather, Ulysses Rohrer, was a 19th-century minor leaguer. http://www.aagpbl.org/index.cfm/articles/rohrer-kay-6-9-1922-3-17-1962/222 (accessed on July 2, 2015). William Rohrer, born in Hastings, Nebraska, worked as a scout for the AAGPBL and managed the Fort Wayne Daisies of the AAGPBL in 1947. http://www.aagpbl.org/index.cfm/profiles/rohrer-william/795 (accessed on July 2, 2015). The AAGPBL site says that William Rohrer's father was a "catcher and manager," but Ulysses S. Rohrer was the player-manager for the Hastings club in the 1892 NSL and, when he played, he was usually the team's shortstop.

    13. The other cities with teams in the 1887 Western League were Denver; Emporia, Kansas; Kansas City, Missouri; Leadville, Colorado; Leavenworth, Kansas; St. Joseph, Missouri; Topeka; and Wichita. Teams folded like bad poker hands in 1887. The Leadville franchise disbanded at the start of the 1887 season, but Omaha and Hastings in Nebraska, and Kansas City, Missouri, were added. Leavenworth was forced to quit after a game on July 8 due to lack of fan support. It was replaced by Wichita, which came over from the Kansas State League, on July 26. Two days later, St. Joseph ceased. It was replaced by Emporia, Kansas, on Aug. 13. Then Wichita folded on Sept. 5, followed quickly by Emporia on Sept. 9. Madden and Stewart, 20.

    14. Cf. *Ibid.*, 25, and Johnson and Wolff, 149.

    15. The Association began with teams in Chicago; Des Moines; Kansas City, Missouri; Milwaukee; Minneapolis; Omaha; St. Louis; and St. Paul, Minnesota. On July 4, 1888, Sioux City, Iowa, replaced St. Louis, which had disbanded on June 20, 1888. In August, Minneapolis sold its franchise to Davenport, Iowa.

    16. Frank Selee, who later managed the Boston and Chicago National League franchises, was the Omaha manager. See Angelo J. Louisa and Robert P. Nash, "Growing Pains in the River City: The Development of Professional Baseball in Nineteenth-Century Omaha," *Nebraska History* 85, no. 4 (Winter 2004), 148–155.

17. The cities with teams in the 1889 Western Association were Denver; Des Moines; Milwaukee; Minneapolis; Omaha; St. Joseph, Missouri; St. Paul, Minnesota; and Sioux City, Iowa.

18. The cities with teams in the 1890 Western Association were Denver; Des Moines/Lincoln; Kansas City, Missouri; Milwaukee; Minneapolis; Omaha; St. Paul, Minnesota; and Sioux City, Iowa.

19. The other six teams were in Denver; Kansas City, Missouri; Milwaukee; Minneapolis; St. Paul, Minnesota; and Sioux City, Iowa. St. Paul moved to Duluth, Minnesota, on June 16, 1891. Milwaukee withdrew from the Western Association and joined the then major league American Association on August 16, 1891.

20. The cities with teams in the 1892 Western League were Columbus, Ohio; Indianapolis; Kansas City, Missouri; Milwaukee; Minneapolis; Omaha; St. Paul, Minnesota; and Toledo. St. Paul moved to Fort Wayne, Indiana, on May 25, 1892. Fort Wayne and Milwaukee disbanded on July 7, 1892. Columbus and Minneapolis disbanded on July 15, 1892.

21. Johnson and Wolff, 162. Madden and Stewart list July 11, 1892, as the date of the League's demise. "Contributing factors to the league's demise included rainy weather and poor fan interest." Madden and Stewart, 32.

22. "Nebraska State News," *Red Cloud (NE) Chief*, October 25, 1889. Columbus, Seward, and York would also later be considered as potential sites for the league.

23. "A conference of base ball [sic] men was held at Fremont, Neb., March 25, at which there were present Dr. H.C. Miller, Grand Island; A.J. Shepherd, Kearney; John F. Patterson, Plattsmouth; W.M. Pope, Lincoln, and Editor Corcoran, of the York *Democrat*. A Nebraska State League was formed with W.H. Harrison, of Fremont, president; Shepherd, of Kearney, secretary; and Dr. Miller, of Grand Island, treasurer. The next meeting of the association will be held in the latter city April 10." "A Nebraska League Started," *Sporting Life*, April 5, 1890, 15. See also "The Local World of Sport," *Omaha Daily Bee*, February 2, 1890.

24. Although Gregory Bond identifies William M. Pope as a "white businessman from Lincoln" and William Lewis as a "local black manager," Kent Morgan shows Pope and Lewis were African Americans from Omaha, both employed as waiters in the dining room at the Millard Hotel. Morgan relied on information in Omaha city directories to identify the race of Pope and Lewis. Cf. Gregory Bond, "'Too Much Dirty Work': Race, Manliness, and Baseball in Gilded Age Nebraska," *Nebraska History* 85, no. 4 (2004), 174, and Kent Morgan, "The 1890 Lincoln Giants: Professional Baseball's Unlikely Return to Nebraska's Capital City," *Nebraska History* 96, no. 2 (Summer 2015), 85.

25. "Another State League," *Sporting Life*, December 6, 1890, 11. By the time the 1892 NSL was formed, Beatrice and Hastings had banned Sunday baseball. Charles Grimes, "The Plattsmouth Club," *The Sporting News*, March 26, 1892, 6. As discussed later in this chapter, even Sunday baseball did not save the 1892 NSL.

26. Perhaps the "Grand Island gentleman" was Dr. H.C. Miller mentioned in the April 5, 1890, article in *Sporting Life*.

27. "Activity in Sporting Circles" *Omaha Daily Bee*, February 1, 1891. See also "The Local Sporting World," *Omaha Daily Bee*, February 22, 1891.

28. Wm. Castone, "Here Is a Good Chance," *The Sporting News*, January 31, 1891, 2:

I would like to locate in some minor league city (Nebraska State League preferred) a first-class club which represented Lincoln last season [1890]. It was one of the strongest amateur [sic] clubs in Nebraska, playing forty-five games and losing but five. The clubs which won the five games are as follows: Kearney, two; Denver and Omaha Western Association teams one each; and Haverly's [sic] of Kansas City, champion amateur club of Missouri, one.

The players, with their batting averages, are: J. Patterson, third base, .355; George Taylor, first base, .305; William Castone, pitcher, .349; Ed Carr, right field, .292; F. Maupin, catcher, .238; J. Reeves, pitcher, .208; William Lincoln, short stop [sic], .245; George Hubanks [sic], left field, .215.

I will complete the team with some of the strongest players in the East. All the players are of good habits. The team in full can be secured at a salary not exceeding $600 per month.

Wm. Castone

Tremont House, Lincoln, Neb.

29. "The State League," *Omaha Daily Bee,* June 18, 1891.

30. "Sports of Early Spring," *Omaha Daily Bee*, February 7, 1892.

31. *Ibid.*

32. George W. Castone, "A Nebraska State League," *The Sporting News*, February 13, 1892, 5.

33. "Breezy Sports of Spring," *Omaha Daily Bee*, February 28, 1892.

34. "The Color Line," *Sporting Life*, February 13, 1892, 1. See also "Opposed to Colored Players," *Daily Nebraska State Journal*, February 6, 1892.

35. "Not Favorable," *Hastings Daily Nebraskan*, February 12, 1892.

36. "Houseworth" sometimes appears as "Housworth" in newspaper articles. *Hoye's City Directory of Lincoln for 1892* lists a William I. Houseworth, "clerk, land department" with the Burlington & Missouri River Railroad, rooming at 905 G Street.

37. "Not Favorable." The reference to the league being "amateur" seems odd because both Castone and Houseworth envisioned a league of professional teams. Perhaps Houseworth used the term "amateur" to refer to what would be called a minor league today.

38. *Ibid.*

39. "Breezy Sports of Spring."

40. "If properly managed with [a] small salary list and with the short jumps, Beatrice, Nebraska City, Fremont, Kearney, Hastings[,] and Grand Island would prove a paying circuit. All are good towns of ten thousand or over." "The Local Sporting World."

41. "The State League Project," *Daily Nebraska State Journal*, January 31, 1892.

42. *Ibid*. As the Lincoln team was collapsing, the same sentiment reappeared. See, e.g., "Were Not in It," *Beatrice (NE) Daily Democrat*, May 11, 1892.

43. "Nebraska's Start," *Sporting Life*, March 12, 1892, 1.

44. The Capital Hotel, located on the southwest corner of 11th and P Streets in downtown Lincoln, was initially a commercial building (1869), converted into a hotel (the Douglas House) in 1870, enlarged in 1873–1874 (the Commercial Hotel), and renamed the Capital Hotel in 1886. It was, at one time, something of a political hub. http://www.waymarking.com/waymarks/WM6NF_Capital_Hotel_Lincoln_NE (accessed on July 2, 2015).

45. "Baseball News," *Fremont (NE) Daily Tribune*, March 2, 1892.

46. "Nebraska's Start," 1. *Sporting Life* reported, "Mr. Hickey will be found a good man for the presidency of the [l]eague, as he has had much experience in the [l]eague, being in 1890 the president of the Lincoln team." "Nebraska's League," *Sporting Life*, March 19, 1892, 14. The references to Hickey's "experience in the *[l]eague*" and being "president of the Lincoln team" are confusing. The Western *League* did not operate in 1890. Lincoln had a team in the Western *Association* in 1890 ( Des Moines moved to Lincoln during the season), but the identity of the president of that team is unclear. The reference to Hickey as president of the Lincoln team cannot be to the presidency of the Lincoln Giants, so perhaps it is to the presidency of Lincoln's 1890 Western *Association* team. T.J. Hickey also served as president of the new Western League, formed in 1900 in Omaha when the old Western League declared itself a major league and challenged the National League. Madden and Stewart, 57, 63. As for Coman, see "Nebraska's League," *Sporting Life*, March 19, 1892, 14.

47. "Nebraska's Start," 1.

48. For the election of the board directors and the officers and the choosing of the members of the writers committee, see *ibid*. There is no evidence that the league was organized as a Nebraska corporation. Similarly, there is no evidence that the "constitution" and "bylaws" still exist. In keeping with the legal practice at the time, the "constitution" likely was a relatively short document with little actual detail about the operation of the league. The "bylaws," the more detailed operating rules for a business corporation, likely would have contained basic administrative rules for the league, such as procedures for electing directors and officers, methods for calling meetings, quorum requirements for meetings, and essential financial obligations of and operating rules for the league teams.

49. *Ibid*.

50. All the information regarding the issues came from *ibid*., with the exception of those matters that are otherwise documented.

51. At least one team, perhaps Plattsmouth, apparently complained to the league:

> The Beatrice team is very likely to encounter a large-sized snag. It is a notorious fact that they have exceeded the salary limit to the extent of several hundred dollars, and it is noised in base ball [*sic*] circles that the league directors will give the matter thorough investigation in a called meeting to occur within the next two weeks. If guilty[,] they should be bounced out of the league.

"The Wheel Turned," *Plattsmouth (NE) Daily Journal*, May 2, 1892.

52. *Ibid*.

53. "The League Falls Down," *Daily Nebraska State Journal*, April 13, 1892, and "Getting Shaky," *Lincoln (NE) Evening News*, March 11, 1892.

54. "Nebraska's League," *Sporting Life*, April 9, 1892, 1.

55. "Nebraska's Start," 1 ("[I]t was stated that [$75] was ample to secure good ones who would pay their own expenses out of that salary."). The initial umpires hired by the NSL were Phil Greusel of Cedar Rapids, Iowa; Frank E. Hart of Sheboygan, Wisconsin; and John M. Fulmer of Schuyler, Nebraska. "Condensed Dispatches," *Sporting Life*, April 30, 1892, 1. The practice of using a single umpire to call a game was common at the time.

56. When Hastings joined the league, it apparently selected red as its color. "Won in the Fourth," *Grand Island (NE) Independent*, May 16, 1892 ("Rohrer's Red Leglets"), and "Won One," *Grand Island (NE) Independent*, July 8, 1892 ("Rohrer's rustling red legs").

57. The National Association granted the 1892 NSL the requested contract protection and assigned the league a Class B designation.

58. "Baseball News," *Fremont (NE) Daily Tribune*, March 2, 1892.

59. "Nebraska's League," *Sporting Life*, March 19, 1892, 14.

60. Doc, "Hastings Redivivus," *Sporting Life*, March 26, 1892, 13.

61. Earlier reports suggested that Rohrer would not be the manager because of his growing business. "Breezy Sports of Spring."

62. Remember Castone's statement that all the players he would recruit "are of good habits." Castone, "Here

Is a Good Chance," 2. He was certainly aware of the aspersions cast on the character of black ballplayers by people like Rohrer. See generally Bond, 172–185.

63. Doc, 13.

64. "Six months is entirely too long for an infant organization. The attendance would be much better if the playing season only covered three or four months. To play ball in Nebraska in the months of April, May[,] and the latter part of September every one [sic] knows here would be at a loss, as the weather is too uncertain during this period. If the season were opened Memorial Day and closed Sept. 1[,] base ball [sic] would be a success in Nebraska. It is to be hoped that this matter will receive attention at the next [l]eague meeting." *Ibid.*

65. "Getting Shaky."

66. "Money has been liberally subscribed in the last few days and a club here is now an assured fact." "Plattsmouths' [sic] Club," *Sporting Life*, April 2, 1892, 2.

67. The information for this paragraph came from "The League Falls Down." The two black players, Fowler and Castone, were in Lincoln, as were third baseman Smith and first baseman Hillis. "The only player here now who came from abroad is Fowler. Smith, Hillis[,] and Castone are local men." *Ibid.*

68. "To Remain in the League," *Daily Nebraska State Journal*, April 14, 1892 ("Secretary S.C. Coman of Fremont came flying into Lincoln on the first train, closely followed by Banker Drake of Beatrice"). "Base Ballists [sic]," *Fremont (NE) Daily Tribune*, April 13, 1892.

69. "To Remain in the League." A later article in *Sporting Life* suggests greater ambivalence from the other teams about providing financial support for Lincoln. According to the article, the rest of the teams in the league initially expressed concern that the NSL could not continue without Lincoln but later concluded that it could continue without Lincoln. "A Flurry," *Sporting Life*, April 23, 1892, 1.

70. "To Remain in the League."

71. "A Flurry," 1. Expressing the same level of enthusiasm, the *Daily Nebraska State Journal* noted: "It is estimated by those familiar with the details of the prospective expense account that the club will be more than self-sustaining from the moment the command is given to 'play ball.'" "To Remain in the League."

72. The drafts of the initial schedule were not published and there is no evidence that the drafts have been preserved. Thus, the problems facing Fremont manager Baker must be inferred from the public discussions of the process in the newspapers.

73. The Nebraska Legislature had, well before 1892, enacted a statute providing:

> If any person, of the age of fourteen years or upwards, shall be found on the first day of the week, commonly called "Sunday," sporting, rioting, quarreling, hunting, fishing, or shooting, he or she shall be fined in a sum not exceeding twenty dollars, or be confined in the county jail for a term not exceeding twenty days, or both, at the discretion of the court.

The question of whether the word "sporting" in the statute included professional baseball games was, until late 1892, subject to interpretation. Some cities and towns enforced the statute against Sunday baseball, while others did not. On Sunday, April 26, 1891, Lincoln attempted to enforce the state statute, apparently against the Lincoln team in the Western Association. The trial court and an intermediate appeals court ruled against the city. Following the announcement of the appeals court decision in 1892, *Sporting Life* reported that "[t]he case will be appealed to the Supreme Court immediately, as the opponents of Sunday base ball [sic] desire a decision before the base bal [sic] season opens." "Sunday Ball," *Sporting Life*, April 9, 1892, 3. On November 10, 1892, the Nebraska Supreme Court resolved the debate, holding that the statute did apply to professional baseball. *State v. O'Rourke*, 35 Nebr. 614, 53 N.W. 591 (1892). Although decided after the demise of the 1892 NSL, the court's opinion helps to explain the importance of the issue in Nebraska in the late 1800s. Despite noting that baseball is well within the dictionary meaning of "sport," the court provided an extended justification, grounded in Christian theology, for the prohibition in the statute.

74. The report in *Sporting Life* has a byline of March 25 but states that the meeting was held "last Saturday," which was March 19.

75. Usually referred to in the newspapers, including those in Fremont, as "Manager Baker," an article in the *Fremont (NE) Daily Tribune* refers to him as "Norman Baker." "Baseball," *Fremont (NE) Daily Tribune*, April 28, 1892 (quoting from the *Omaha World-Herald*).

76. "Nebraska's League," *Sporting Life*, April 2, 1892, 1.

77. *Ibid.*

78. The information for this paragraph came from "Base Ball [sic] Matters," *Beatrice (NE) Daily Democrat*, March 28, 1892. Without the original schedule for guidance, it is impossible to know whether Beatrice had to make more road trips than other teams. Beatrice apparently would have had the very last road trip (September 14–15, 1892) on the NSL's original schedule.

79. "Nebraska's League," *Sporting Life*, April 16, 1892, 1. For the schedule, see "Nebraska's League," *Sporting Life*, April 9, 1892, 1.

80. "Base Ball [sic] Matters." This article does not reproduce the entire Beatrice schedule. It shows 10 home games each with Hastings, Grand Island, Lincoln, and Plattsmouth, but omits home games against Fremont.

81. Local citizens H.L. Ewing, A.T. Cole, I.L. Fiske, John Dwyer, and E.G. Drake were elected directors. Ewing was elected president and Cole was elected secretary and treasurer. "Beatrice Club Organized," *Sporting Life*, April 9, 1892, 12.

58   Section I—The Long and Winding Road

82. "Nebraska's League," *Sporting Life*, April 2, 1892, 1. Although not mentioned in this *Sporting Life* article, Manager Gatewood seems to have been the regular second baseman for Beatrice. See, e.g., *Beatrice (NE) Daily Democrat*, May 6, 1892 (box score, Gatewood playing second base and batting seventh), and "Nebraska's League," *Sporting Life*, March 19, 1892, 14 (noting that Beatrice had signed Taylor, Gatewood, Van Arnam, Kennedy, Jones, Thompson, Edinger, and Howe).

83. "Base Ball [sic] Briefs," *Omaha Daily Bee*, May 1, 1892 ("Billy Van Arnam").

84. The *Daily Nebraska State Journal* reported that Van Arnam played in the Oregon State League in 1891 with a fielding percentage of "away above" .900 and a batting average of .333. "Local Sports," *Daily Nebraska State Journal*, May 1, 1892.

85. Van Arnam subsequently refused to play for Beatrice, causing Beatrice to release him to Lincoln "for a money consideration." "Base Ball [sic] Briefs." He played shortstop for Lincoln in its opening game. "The Wheel Turned."

86. "Late News by Wire," *Sporting Life*, April 23, 1892, 1.

87. "Nebraska's League," *Sporting Life*, April 2, 1892, 2.

88. "Late News by Wire," 1.

89. "All Played Ball," *Beatrice (NE) Daily Democrat*, May 6, 1892.

90. They elected E.N. Morse, Gus Reitz, George A. Hickok, H.D. Dunning, C.B. Nicodemus, John Dern, and Alex Arries as directors. Morse was elected president, Reitz was elected vice president, and George A. Hickok was elected secretary and treasurer. "A Baseball Club," *Fremont (NE) Daily Tribune*, March 3, 1892. "Among those present were Mayor Fried, L.D. Richards, Frank Fowler, H.D. Dunning, J.A. Elliott, S.C. Coman, Gus Reitz, C.B. Nicodemus, George Hickok, G.B. Garvis, I.B. Hickox, John Dern, Bruce Smith, Frank Roberts." The remaining information for this paragraph was also taken from "A Baseball Club."

91. The fundraising appears to have been done on a very informal basis, in part because the law at that time did not impose restrictions of the sort imposed by current federal and state securities laws.

92. "Manager Baker says his team are [sic] the youngest, on the average, of any in the league, but that it is young blood that will keep up its end on the diamond." "Base Ballists [sic]." The team also had a less complimentary nickname: the "Freaks." See, e.g., "The Fatal Eighth," *Plattsmouth (NE) Daily Journal*, June 7, 1892.

93. "Pitcher Baker has often fanned out the St. Louis Browns, the New Yorks, and all the heavy teams of the American [A]ssociation and National League. He ought to be able to keep the boys in the State League guessing." "Base Ballists [sic]." Norman Leslie Baker, who was born on October 14, 1862, in Philadelphia, Pennsylvania, and who died on February 20, 1949, in Hurffville, New Jersey, was a pitcher and outfielder for the Pittsburgh Alleghenys (American Association 1883), Louisville Colonels (American Association 1885), and Baltimore Orioles (American Association 1890), as well as for various minor league teams, including the Omaha Lambs in the Western Association in 1891. Despite the reference in the newspaper article to the National League, there is no evidence that Baker played for a National League team. "Norm Baker," www.baseball-reference.com (accessed on July 11, 2015).

94. "Base Ballists [sic]."

95. The shareholders elected James Rourke, James Foley, William Winters, E.C. Hockenberger, and A.W. Buchpest as directors. *Sporting Life* reported that the directors would elect officers "at an early date." "Grand Island in Line," *Sporting Life*, April 9, 1892, 2. This article was dated Saturday, April 2.

96. *Ibid.* Streetcar lines often served baseball grounds, benefitting both the baseball teams and the streetcar companies. "Fremont has fine grounds, [is] centrally located, good street car [sic] accommodations, and is one of the best drawing towns in the [s]tate." "Nebraska's League," *Sporting Life*, March 19, 1892, 14.

97. "Nebraska's League," *Sporting Life*, March 19, 1892, 14. Game reports used the name "Hoffmeister" for Hoffmaster.

98. See, e.g., "A Great Game," *Fremont (NE) Daily Tribune*, May 25, 1892.

99. W.S.S., "Hastings News," *Sporting Life*, April 23, 1892, 15.

100. The information for this paragraph came from *ibid.*

101. Fred Dunham, "Lincoln Lines," *Sporting Life*, April 23, 1892, 15.

102. "Nebraska's League," *Sporting Life*, March 19, 1892, 14.

103. "Plattsmouths' [sic] Club," 2.

104. Grimes, "The Plattsmouth Club," 6.

105. "Yapp was our pitcher last year and he was a good man. In addition to being a good pitcher[,] he is also a fair all-around man and is quite a sticker. Perrine was also one of our pat pitchers last year. He is a big man and has terrific speed. He will make himself heard of this year. Gibson first base and change catcher, is from Fairfield, Iowa, and is highly recommended. McKibben, second base, played with Hastings last year and Rohrer was after him this year[,] but we got him. He is a fine player and an element of strength not to be despised. Kennedy, third base, was with Beatrice last year and made himself a name as a fielder and batter. Clark, shortstop, was a member of the famous Carroll, Iowa, team last year and is a good man. Porter is from Pueblo, Colorado, and looks like he was onto his job. [And] Sam Patterson was last year the heaviest hitter in the state and many of our victories can be laid to his strong hitting. He is a good outfielder and can pitch a good game." *Ibid.* The claim that Plattsmouth had "got" McKibben was premature because the NSL

subsequently awarded McKibben to Hastings. "Nebraska's League," *Sporting Life*, April 16, 1892, 1. Also, the *Plattsmouth (NE) Daily Journal* reported some intrigue involving Kennedy:

> It is apparent that Kennedy is not desirous of playing with the locals if it can be avoided, but there is some excuse for his actions when the fact is known that he has been under the influence of Manager Gatewood of Beatrice during the greater part of last month. Gatewood was detected in an attempt to defraud the local team out of Kennedy's services, and now he is unprincipled enough to endeavor to induce the latter to jump to the South Dakota league.

"Base Ball [*sic*] Babble," *Plattsmouth (NE) Daily Journal*, April 8, 1892.

106. Grimes, "The Plattsmouth Club," 6.

107. After losing McKibben, Plattsmouth signed John Patterson, its third black player, to play second base. "Base Ball [*sic*] Babble," *Plattsmouth (NE) Daily Journal*, April 8, 1892.

108. "Plattsmouths' [*sic*] Club," 2.

109. Mark E. Eberle, "George William Castone: An Integrated Baseball Life at the Close of the Nineteenth Century," https://scholars.fhsu.edu/all_monographs/6/ (accessed on August 27, 2019). For more information on Castone, see *ibid.*; Bond, 174–181, 184; Dick Clark and Larry Lester, eds., *The Negro Leagues Book* (Cleveland: Society for American Baseball Research, 1994), 178; and James E. Brunson III, *Black Baseball, 1858–1900: A Comprehensive Record of the Teams, Players, Managers, Owners, and Umpires*, 3 vols. (Jefferson, North Carolina: McFarland & Company, Inc., Publishers, 2019), vol. 2, 586–587.

110. Brian McKenna, "Bud Fowler," SABR Baseball Biography Project, http://sabr.org/bioproject (accessed on July 2, 2015).

111. Abe, "The Lincoln Team at Work," *The Sporting News*, April 30, 1892, 1.

112. Admirer, "Kearney Playing Great Ball," *The Sporting News*, June 25, 1892, 6.

113. McKenna.

114. *Ibid.*

115. For an excellent discussion of this period of Fowler's life, see Laing, chapters 7 and 8.

116. For more information on Maupin, see Mark E. Eberle, "Black Baseball in Kansas City, 1870–1899," https://scholars.fhsu.edu/all_monographs/7/ (accessed on September 18, 2019); Bond, 172–173; Clark and Lester, 206; and Brunson, *Black Baseball, 1858–1900: A Comprehensive Record of the Teams, Players, Managers, Owners, and Umpires*, vol. 1, 331, 335, 340, 346, 361, 365, 379, 385, 391, 396.

117. Brunson, *Black Baseball, 1858–1900: A Comprehensive Record of the Teams, Players, Managers, Owners, and Umpires*, vol. 3, 1033, and Clark and Lester, 213.

118. For more information about Patterson, see Brunson, *Black Baseball, 1858–1900: A Comprehensive Record of the Teams, Players, Managers, Owners, and Umpires*, vol. 3, 1033; Clark and Lester, 213; and "John Patterson," http://www.seamheads.com/NegroLgs/player.php?playerID=patte01joh (accessed on July 12, 2019).

119. "And Giants They Are," *Daily Nebraska State Journal*, May 11, 1890 (reporting on Reeve's first start as a member of the Lincoln Giants), and Brunson, *Black Baseball, 1858–1900: A Comprehensive Record of the Teams, Players, Managers, Owners, and Umpires*, vol. 1, 347, and vol. 3, 1078.

120. Brunson, *Black Baseball, 1858–1900: A Comprehensive Record of the Teams, Players, Managers, Owners, and Umpires*, vol. 3, 1078.

121. For more information on Reeves, see Brunson, *Black Baseball, 1858–1900: A Comprehensive Record of the Teams, Players, Managers, Owners, and Umpires*, vol. 1, 335, 340, 346, 353, 379, 385, 391, 397, vol. 3, 1078; Eberle, "Black Baseball in Kansas City, 1870–1899"; Clark and Lester, 217; and Bond, 172–173, 174.

122. Brunson, *Black Baseball, 1858–1900: A Comprehensive Record of the Teams, Players, Managers, Owners, and Umpires*, vol. 1, 353, vol. 3, 1191–1192, and Bond, 174.

123. For more information on Taylor, see Brunson, *Black Baseball, 1858–1900: A Comprehensive Record of the Teams, Players, Managers, Owners, and Umpires*, vol. 1, 353, vol. 3, 1191–1192; Clark and Lester, 55, 57–58; "George Taylor," http://www.seamheads.com/NegroLgs/player.php?playerID=taylo01geo (accessed on July 15, 2019); White, 164, 168 (accessed on July 15, 2019); "George Taylor," www.baseball-reference.com (accessed on July 15, 2019); James A. Riley, *The Biographical Encyclopedia of the Negro Baseball Leagues* (New York: Carroll & Graf Publishers, 1994), 764; and "St. Paul Colored Gophers," https://en.wikipedia.org/wiki/St._Paul_Colored_Gophers#19 (accessed on July 15, 2019).

124. B.W.E., "Hasting's [*sic*] League Club," *The Sporting News*, May 7, 1892, 5.

125. See, e.g., "Base Ball [*sic*]," *Hastings Daily Nebraskan*, May 18, 1892 ("'Dusty' Maupin will act as back stop for the Plattsmouths. He won't be bothered with dust today."), and "No Longer in the League," *Daily Nebraska State Journal*, June 21, 1892 ("Kearney has a handsome pitcher named Castone, and the way this gentleman of Spanish descent mowed down Hastings' imported ball tossers with his invincible drop was a marvel to all.").

126. See, e.g., "Baseball News," *Fremont (NE) Daily Tribune*, May 28, 1892. In a report on a game between Fremont and Kearney, which had two black players (Castone and Fowler), the reporter observed that "[s]ome dark colored individual seems to have hidden in the fuel heap who ought to be dislodged." This thinly veiled reference to the derogatory phrase "nigger in the woodpile" is no less offensive for the rewording. The same report refers to the Kearney team as the "Cotton Pickers," but that reference almost certainly is to the prominent cotton milling industry in Kearney and not an oblique racial comment. Other stories in other

newspapers use this nickname, as well as the nickname "Lambs," which also seems to derive from the cotton milling industry. See also "Joy for the Fans," *Hastings Daily Nebraskan*, May 25, 1892 ("Yesterday was a day for great rejoicing by the Hastings fans, and the somber hue of the Beatrice club's uniform, though intensified by the presence of an ebony colored first baseman, must now appear a shade darker.").

127. "Lincoln Leads." *Lincoln (NE) Evening News*, May 2, 1892. A league team needed strong attendance to meet operating expenses, including player salaries and league fees. If it is assumed that admission was 50 cents a ticket, 300 tickets produced $150, which Plattsmouth had to share equally with Lincoln, leaving Plattsmouth with $75 to be applied to its monthly operating expenses. As rainouts began to multiply and home teams had to pay out $25 guarantees to visiting teams, team finances became strained.

128. "The Wheel Turned." As the reporter colorfully put it:

> Jupiter Pluvius contributed on Saturday night [April 30, 1892,] to the extent of a large-sized rain storm which transformed the local ball grounds into a huge puddle of mud, and not satisfied with the havoc already created[,] he whipped up a bank of black-looking clouds during all of yesterday [May 1, 1892,] afternoon for no apparent reason other than that of cooling the ardor of the ball cranks who had manifested their attention of witnessing the opening league game between the home team and Lincoln.

*Ibid.*

129. *Ibid.*

130. "Lincoln Leads." ("The locals ... put up an abominable fielding game."). See also "The Wheel Turned."

131. "The Wheel Turned."

132. "Won the First," *Hastings Daily Nebraskan*, May 2, 1892, and "Eleven to Four," *Grand Island (NE) Independent*, May 2, 1892.

133. "Eleven to Four."

134. *Ibid.* ("Grand Island lost the game yesterday through errors—and good playing on the part of Hastings."). See also "Won the First." The time of the game was two hours and 15 minutes. Umpire Frank E. Hart officiated.

135. "Base Ball [sic] Notes," *Beatrice (NE) Daily Democrat*, May 3, 1892.

136. "Baseball," *Fremont (NE) Daily Tribune*, May 3, 1892.

137. "Beatrice Is in Luck," *Plattsmouth (NE) Daily Journal*, May 4, 1892.

138. "At Plattsmouth," *Fremont (NE) Daily Tribune*, May 4, 1892.

139. "Beatrice Is in Luck."

140. *Ibid.* The game was played in two hours and 10 minutes.

141. *Ibid.*

142. The information for this paragraph came from "First Victory," *Fremont (NE) Daily Tribune*, May 4, 1892. The game took a brief one hour and 15 minutes to play under the direction of Umpire John Fulmer.

143. Minstrel shows, a popular form of entertainment at the time, capitalized on racial stereotypes. Two of Plattsmouth's black players—catcher Frank Maupin and second baseman John Patterson—participated in the two shows, and Maupin was apparently the star. However, two white players—shortstop Harry Green and right fielder Sam Patterson—also participated. "Beatrice Is in Luck."

144. Information for the first show came from "We Are Still Alive," *Plattsmouth (NE) Daily Journal*, May 7, 1892.

> "O, watch Maupin," "Ain't he cute," "He's as handsome and graceful on the stage as behind the bat." "Do you see him?" "He's the one in the check dress," and similar expressions from the feminine admirers of the stalwart catcher were heard from all over the opera house last night. Maupin seems to have captured the hearts of base ball [sic] enthusiasts—male and female. He was the lion of the show.

145. Information for the second show came from "We Keep A Winnin.'" *Plattsmouth (NE) Daily Journal*, May 9, 1892.

146. "Beatrice Plays Ball," *Daily Nebraska State Journal*, May 6, 1892.

147. "Forced to Forfeit It," *Daily Nebraska State Journal*, May 7, 1892. The problem of a shortage of game balls was not unique to Lincoln. On May 25, 1892, in the sixth inning of a game between Fremont and, ironically, Kearney, Fremont had to send a boy into town on a pony to obtain new baseballs. "It was a four[-]mile ride and had to be accomplished in fifteen minutes. He got there just ten seconds ahead of time, the Fremont cranks meanwhile holding their breath." Fremont won, 5–0. "Still in It."

148. The information for this paragraph came from "Won It at Pleasure." Although the textual report in the *Daily Nebraska State Journal* states there were six errors, the box score shows only five: one by Fowler, the second baseman, three by Smith, the third baseman, and one by Van Arnam, the shortstop. But the textual report states that Castone, in left field, "misjudged" a fly ball and gave the batter two bases, which might account for the sixth error.

149. The information for this paragraph was taken from "Lincoln Is Left Out," *Daily Nebraska State Journal*, May 10, 1892. Among the directors attending were Drake (Beatrice), Baker (Fremont), Rourke (Grand Island), and Rohrer (Hastings). Plattsmouth was not represented. In addition to what was stated in the text, the board decided that Lincoln would not be liable for the $25 guarantee for any games that were not played during that period—a fortunate decision for the Lincoln team because four of the six scheduled games were rained out.

150. "Was Long Drawn Out," *Daily Nebraska State Journal*, May 12, 1892.
151. The information for this paragraph came from *ibid*.
152. "Again in Good Trim," *Daily Nebraska State Journal*, May 15, 1892.
153. Clark was identified as the Kearney manager in *ibid*. The next day, the *Daily Nebraska State Journal* reported that, as a result of the meeting of the board of directors of the Kearney team, Will Housewworth, the Lincoln manager, was "left out and a financial sufferer from the transfer to Kearney." "Take Well to Water," *Daily Nebraska State Journal*, May 16, 1892.
154. "Again in Good Trim." Fowler and Castone joined the Kearney team. "Six or seven of the local team will not go to Kearney, as they have better offers. Fear [a catcher] has three offers, two from teams in the state league and one from Warsaw. If Kearney does not pay up the back salaries[,] those who desire will probably claim their releases." "Take Well to Water."
155. The information for this paragraph was taken from "Take Well to Water."
156. According to the box scores, Castone started both contests for Kearney and pitched two complete games. "Won Again," *Grand Island (NE) Daily Independent*, May 24, 1892, and "'Once More' Rourke's Pretty Young Men Have No Mercy on Mr. Offitt," *Grand Island (NE) Daily Independent*, May 25, 1892.
157. "Kearney Downed," *Grand Island (NE) Daily Independent*, May 30, 1892.
158. *Ibid.*
159. Laing, 7.
160. *Ibid.*, 8. For Laing's additional points, see *ibid*., 7–8.
161. The *Daily Nebraska State Journal* article also noted, a bit prematurely, that "[i]t is also understood that the Plattsmouth team … will be disbanded at once." "No Longer in the League." Plattsmouth disbanded on June 26, 1892.
162. *Ibid.* The letter ended with the following statement: "By order of the board of directors of the Fremont [B]ase ball [*sic*] [A]ssociation."
163. "Nebraska League," *Sporting Life*, June 4, 1892, 2. The *Plattsmouth (NE) Daily Journal* reported that "ill-health" prompted the resignation. "Base Ball [*sic*] Babble," *Plattsmouth (NE) Daily Journal*, May 21, 1892.
164. "Still in It" ("An effort will be made at Hastings today to secure the secretaryship to Beatrice.").
165. *Ibid.*
166. "Fremont Has Flunked," *Beatrice (NE) Daily Democrat*, June 21, 1892.
167. See, e.g., "Won by Hastings," *Hastings Daily Nebraskan*, June 8, 1892 (textual description of Rohrer's at bats and fielding). On May 31, 1892, the author of an article in the *Beatrice (NE) Daily Democrat* raised the conflict of interest issue: "Wonder if 'Baby' Rohrer had anything to do with changing the umpires at Fremont yesterday." "Still on Top," *Beatrice (NE) Daily Democrat*, May 31, 1892.
168. "Fremont Has Flunked."

> Everybody knows what sort of an influence the appearance of the secretary on the diamond would have on the least susceptible of umpires, whose tenure of office is dependent on the will of the secretary. Rohrer's playing has invited criticism of the severest nature and his continued appearance on the field, a menace to clean ball playing. Will he take the hints.

One might question the impartiality of the *Beatrice (NE) Daily Democrat* because Beatrice had sought to have its man elected secretary of the NSL, but the appearance of conflict, whatever the reality, lends credence to the assertions in the article.
169. The quotations for this paragraph came from "Fremont Has Flunked."
170. "What the Players Say," *Omaha Daily Bee*, June 28, 1892. The players who signed the letter were Lou Graver, Mel Marsh, Al Watson, C. Bowman, O. Gitchell, B. Palmer, C.F. Austin, Dick Percell, C. Timms, B. Butler, and B. Kimmel.
171. "That State League Affair," *Fremont (NE) Daily Tribune*, June 22, 1892.
172. Perhaps consistent with the team's poor performance on the field, an offer intended to benefit Plattsmouth players resulted in a visiting player winning a suit. Mayer & Morgan, a Plattsmouth men's clothier, offered a new suit to every Plattsmouth player who hit the firm's advertising sign at the ballpark. The firm, nevertheless, felt obliged to provide a new suit to a Beatrice player (shortstop Thompson, who at one time had played for Plattsmouth), whose double hit the Mayer & Morgan sign. "Mr. Morgan offered a suit to every Plattsmouth man who hits this sign, but as this fact was not generally known, the suit was given to an outsider. Hereafter foreign ball players [*sic*] are barred from these prizes." "In and Around the Town," *Plattsmouth (NE) Daily Journal,*" May 30, 1892. Beatrice also won the game, 3–0, although managing only two hits, largely because Plattsmouth committed eight errors. *Ibid*.
173. "It is currently rumored in local base ball [*sic*] circles that a general shakeup in the entire [Plattsmouth] team will be administered upon its return home from the present trip. The team is evidently mismanaged. There is no doubting the fact that it contains talent which is abundantly able to win a big majority of its games but unless a change of some sort is made in the near future it is extremely likely that the Plattsmouth team will not cut much of a figure in the race. A meeting of the subscribers to the base ball [*sic*] fund is called for Friday evening [May 20, 1892,] at the council chamber and it is then the intention to discuss the situation as it really exists. All in the city who are interested in base ball [*sic*] are requested to attend." "Base Ball [*sic*] Babble," *Plattsmouth (NE) Daily Journal*, May 18, 1892. "The base ball [*sic*] meeting at the council chamber

tonight will be of considerable importance. Every subscriber to the fund in the city should attend." "Base Ball [sic] Babble," *Plattsmouth (NE) Daily Journal*, May 20, 1892.

174. "Another Waterloo," *Plattsmouth (NE) Daily Journal*, May 31, 1892.

175. "Matters have reached a crisis as far as the local club is concerned and it must be better supported. The attendance has been positively shameful since the club has returned home. There is considerable expense connected with running a salaried ball club [sic] and the management had hoped to meet most of the expense by realizing on gate receipts. It would be a burning disgrace for the city to lose its place in the league and all lovers of the great national game must turn out to the games or go down in their pockets and subscribe a liberal amount toward the maintenance of the club." *Ibid*.

176. "The Plattsmouth ball association is badly in need of an advertising manager. The employment of a good one would make a vast difference in the gate receipts." *Ibid*. The comment is interesting because the league teams did virtually no newspaper advertising of their games. Newspaper reports of games sometimes mentioned future games, but not on a systematic basis.

177. Charley Grimes, "Plattsmouth Doing Poorly," *The Sporting News*, June 11, 1892, 3.

178. This reference to Frank Maupin's asthma and inability to play is singular and without corroboration. The box scores and reports of Plattsmouth games show Maupin catching regularly and apparently playing entire games. On May 24, 1892, the *Plattsmouth (NE) Daily Journal* praised Maupin as a catcher and noted that he was hitting about .300. "Base Ball [sic] Babble," *Plattsmouth (NE) Daily Journal*, May 24, 1892. Although box scores are not available for every Plattsmouth game, Maupin appears as the catcher in each game for which there is a box score.

179. All the descriptions about the players' performances came from Grimes, "Plattsmouth Doing Poorly," 3.

180. "Base Ball [sic] Babble," *Plattsmouth (NE) Daily Journal*, June 2, 1892.

181. The information about the doubleheader came from "Over the Fence," *Plattsmouth (NE) Daily Journal*, June 3, 1892.

182. "State League," *Omaha Daily Bee*, May 31, 1892.

183. "Old, Old Story," *Plattsmouth (NE) Evening News*, June 3, 1892.

184. "Better Playing," *Plattsmouth (NE) Daily Journal*, June 4, 1892. Even the arrival of new uniforms from Brooklyn did not seem to help. *Ibid*.

185. *Ibid*.

186. "Jumped Up a Notch," *Plattsmouth (NE) Daily Journal*, June 6, 1892.

187. *Ibid*.

188. "The Fatal Eighth."

189. "Base Ball [sic] Babble," *Plattsmouth (NE) Daily Journal*, June 11, 1892. Beatrice committed seven errors.

190. "Base Ball [sic] Babble," *Plattsmouth (NE) Daily Journal*, June 13, 1892.

191. Losses to Hastings (12–2 and 13–3), Kearney (8–1 and a 9–0 forfeit), and Grand Island (8–5). A bright note from the *Hastings Daily Nebraskan*: "Maupin is one of the best ball players [sic] in the state league. He is quick as a cat and always plays ball." "Made an Even Half Dozen," *Hastings Daily Nebraskan*, June 14, 1892.

192. "Base Ball [sic] Babble," *Plattsmouth (NE) Daily Journal*, June 17, 1892 ("Green had just scored for Plattsmouth when [Umpire] Fulmer made one of his notoriously rotten decisions and called him out for not touching third base. [Manager] Baker kicked and Fulmer gave the game to Kearney by a score of 9 to 0."). The newspaper reports that the two teams played an "exhibition game" after the forfeiture, with Kearney winning, 12–2.

193. The inducement for the nonleague series was a $150 winner-take-all purse. "Base Ball [sic] Babble," *Plattsmouth (NE) Daily Journal*, June 23, 1892. Plattsmouth won the first game, lost the second, and won the third, capturing the money—no doubt a welcome bit of financial news even if too little too late for the survival of the team.

194. "Base Ball [sic] Babble," *Plattsmouth (NE) Daily Journal*, June 24, 1892.

195. *Ibid*.

196. *Ibid*. There is no record of a ticket price fixed by the NSL. One game report mentioned a 50 cent ticket for a doubleheader. Perhaps Plattsmouth reduced the ticket price to attract a larger Sunday crowd.

197. "Base Ball [sic] Babble," *Plattsmouth (NE) Daily Journal*, June 25, 1892.

198. "The addition of Parvin, Miller, and Mulhearn has so strengthened the team that it is fully as strong as any in the league and thus it is extremely unfortunate that disbandment is to occur." *Ibid*.

199. "Gave Up the Ghost," *Plattsmouth (NE) Daily Journal*, June 27, 1892.

200. *Ibid*.

201. For the details on the two games, see "But Four Teams to Finish," *Daily Nebraska State Journal*, June 27, 1892.

202. "Gave Up the Ghost," *Plattsmouth (NE) Daily Journal*, June 27, 1892.

203. "Base Ball [sic] Babble," *Plattsmouth (NE) Daily Journal*, June 28, 1892.

204. The *Plattsmouth (NE) Daily Journal* reported that the Beatrice team offered Plattsmouth money for Plattsmouth's third baseman Kennedy. "It is unlikely that this deal will go. A trade for [George] Taylor would

be more acceptable." "Better Playing." Beatrice did, however, purchase Kennedy from Plattsmouth for $50. "Jumped Up a Notch." Kennedy has "been dissatisfied since the first of the season and was even so anxious to leave that he threatened to jump to St. Joseph, Mo., unless released at once. Under the existing circumstances[,] Manager Baker thought it best to let him go." *Ibid.*

205. For the standings of the NSL teams after the games played on May 30, see "Still on Top."
206. "Beatrice Cranks Are Sad," *Daily Nebraska State Journal*, July 3, 1892.
207. "Suffered Two Shut-Outs [sic]," *Daily Nebraska State Journal*, July 5, 1892.
208. "And Now There Are Three," *Daily Nebraska State Journal*, July 6, 1892.
209. "Will Rise from the Ruins," *Daily Nebraska State Journal*, July 7, 1892.
210. *Ibid.*
211. W.S.S., "Still Undismayed," *Sporting Life*, July 16, 1892, 11.
212. "Base Ball [sic] Notes," *Daily Nebraska State Journal*, July 9, 1892.
213. "But Two Clubs to Finish," *Daily Nebraska State Journal*, July 10, 1892.
214. "Full of Snap and Ginger," *Daily Nebraska State Journal*, July 9, 1892.
215. "But Two Clubs to Finish."
216. *Ibid. Sporting Life* made the same point about teams other than Hastings ignoring the salary cap. "Nebraska League Reduced," *Sporting Life*, July 16, 1892, 1.
217. "Gave Up the Ghost," *Daily Nebraska State Journal*, July 11, 1892.
218. "One More Unfortunate," *Grand Island (NE) Independent*, July 11, 1892.
219. *Ibid.* "When the city has grown again as much as its present size and population it may be opportune to talk of putting another club into the league." *Ibid.*
220. *Ibid.* "We are informed that several law suits [sic] are liable to bob up serenely unless some of the subscribers who promised to pay and won't come up and toe the mark. The directors have acted fairly and openly in this matter and those whom they represent should do the same." *Ibid.*
221. *Ibid.*
222. The information for the final league game came from "Played Six Extra Innings," *Daily Nebraska State Journal*, July 12, 1892.
223. H.S.S., "Done For," *Sporting Life*, July 23, 1892, 4.
224. *Ibid.*
225. See, e.g., "Like Noah's Time," *Hastings Daily Nebraskan*, May 13, 1892, and "An Isolated City," *Gage County (NE) Democrat*, May 19, 1892.
226. For information about the Kennedy example, see "Base Ball [sic] Babble," *Plattsmouth (NE) Daily Journal*, April 8, 1892; "Nebraska's League," *Sporting Life*, April 16, 1892, 1; and "The Wheel Turned."
227. For information about the McKibben example, see "Nebraska's League," *Sporting Life*, April 16, 1892, 1.
228. "Eleven to Four."
229. "Base Ball [sic] Babble," *Plattsmouth (NE) Daily Journal*, May 19, 1892. Holmes had "become dissatisfied by reason of internal dissensions in the [Beatrice] club." *Ibid.*
230. Money was not always the only incentive: "Shorty Howe, the crack pitcher of the Beatrice team, leaves to-day [sic] for his home in La [sic] Mars, Ia. He has an offer of better money there, and what is more potent, has, if rumor be true, a chance to sign a life contract with a feminine manager." "Base Ball [sic] Notes," *Daily Nebraska State Journal*, May 18, 1892. Discord on the Beatrice team may also have played a role in Howe's decision. The *Plattsmouth (NE) Daily Journal* reported that Howe, like Holmes, had "become dissatisfied by reason of internal dissensions in the [Beatrice] club." "Base Ball [sic] Babble," *Plattsmouth (NE) Daily Journal*, May 19, 1892.
231. See Bond, 183 ("Regardless of their true motives, [Plattsmouth first baseman A.S.] Kennedy and [Hastings catcher Pierce] Chiles understood that the rhetoric of race provided political cover for their questionable actions. Normally ungentlemanly activities like jumping a contract and skipping out on a debt or playing intentionally 'ragged ball' to orchestrate a trade would have incurred the wrath of the sporting community. With the integrated diamonds of Nebraska already in turmoil, however, Kennedy and Chiles could plausibly justify their actions and successfully confuse the issue by mimicking the deeds of other segregationists.").
232. "[F.M.] 'Froggy' Long jumped the [Plattsmouth] team this morning and left for his home in Chicago. He expects to join an independent team at Watertown, Wis. Needless to state[,] he will be blacklisted along with Keefe of Grand Island and Howe, Thompson[,] and Edinger of Beatrice." "Over the Fence." "Catcher Keefe has jumped the Grand Island team of the Nebraska League and will be blacklisted." "Condensed Dispatches, "*Sporting Life*, June 4, 1892, 1.
233. "Over the Fence." Apparently, the threat of punishment in the afterlife did no more to deter jumpers than did the secular punishment of blacklisting.
234. "Graver, the catcher of the late Fremont ball team, is in the toils of the law. He accepted terms with the Hastings team, also advance money Friday morning. Barnes, of the Lead City, S.D., ball team, arrived here and induced Graver to jump his contract and sign with Lead City. Barnes and Graver took the early B. & M. train for Lead City via Fremont this morning. As soon as Manager Rohrer heard of the move[,] he wired the officers of Fremont to arrest Graver and Barnes for obtaining money under false pretenses. Word was received

**64  Section I—The Long and Winding Road**

here late this evening that the prisoners were captured. Chief Warzer leaves on the flyer to-night [sic] for Fremont to bring the prisoners back. Barnes and Graver will receive a reception here that they will not soon forget and will have an opportunity to repent at leisure." "Came to Grief," *Sporting Life*, July 2, 1892, 1. "Graver … was arrested and brought back here for obtaining money under false pretenses, and at his trial before Justice Morledge was found guilty and fined $10 and costs, in total about $100. His attorneys will appeal to the District Court." W.S.S., "Still Undismayed," 11.

235. "Lou Johnson, the south-paw [sic] of our [the Hastings] club, jumped his contract the 25th ult., and is now playing at Lawrence, Kas. Although a fine pitcher[,] the management was not sorry to see him go as he was a lusher and a rank disorganizer, and has done more harm than good for the club." Ibid.

236. "The [Hastings] management received notice from catcher Holmes that he could not come to Hastings as he had accepted a position with the Illinois-Iowa League. Hard luck with catchers." Ibid.

237. Newspapers in Nebraska State League cities in 1892 regularly carried lurid articles about racially charged incidents in Nebraska and other states. See, e.g., "White and Black," *Grand Island (NE) Independent*, March 7, 1892 ("Negroes Threaten the Torch," "Negro desperado," and "Every white man in town is a walking arsenal"), and "The Fate That Befell a Farmer," *Daily Nebraska State Journal*, June 3, 1892 ("Charles Meyers Robbed in a Colored Dive" in Lincoln).

238. A report of the May 23, 1890, game between the Lincoln Giants and Kearney in the *Kearney (NE) Daily Hub* used the headline "The Coons Out-Play [sic] the Kearneys All Around," *Kearney (NE) Daily Hub*, May 24, 1890. The text of the story, however, continued somewhat more moderately: "The colored gentlemen from Salt Creek mopped the earth with the Kearney boys in the game of ball yesterday. The defeat was the fault of no one in particular. The Kearneys were simply out-played [sic].… The Kearneys made seven errors and this with poor batting cost them the game.… The features of the game were [Lincoln left fielder George] Taylor's home run and [Kearney center fielder] Beardsley's running catch.… Lincoln has far better batters than Kearney. Taylor, [James] Hightower, and [John] Patterson cannot be beaten wielding the willow, even among the league players, while [Frank] Maupin and [Will] Castone are not slow by any means." The strong racial tone returned two days later. The Kearney reporter described the situation in the top of the ninth inning, with Lincoln leading, 5–1: "This will never do, never! Never!! NEVER. Cram stepped to the plate and said 'By the ebon-hued hide of the Lincoln coons[,] the Kearneyites can't roast me when I go home.'" "Glory for Kearney," *Kearney (NE) Daily Hub*, May 26, 1890. Cram hit a double and Kearney rallied to win the game, 6–5.

239. See, e.g., "They Forfeited the Game," *Omaha Daily Bee*, May 25, 1890 ("The Lincoln Giants are a colored team, and the strongest professional team outside of Omaha in the state."); "Omaha Wins from St. Paul," *Omaha Daily Bee*, May 26, 1890 ("The Lincoln Giants, as is probably generally known, is composed of colored men and it is safe to say that there isn't a stronger amateur [sic] team in the whole western country."); and "Activity in Sporting Circles" ("'Bud' Fowler, the crack colored second baseman, wishes to sign with the Plattsmouth team. Fowler is one of the best men at his position that can be found and would be a good acquisition to the team.").

240. See, e.g., Grimes, "Plattsmouth Doing Poorly," 3 ("John Patterson has played fine ball at second and has done everything in his power to make the team a winning one."); "Jumped Up a Notch" ("Maupin caught two brilliant games yesterday. One stolen base and no passed balls is a great record."); and "Made an Even Half Dozen" ("Maupin is one of the best ball [sic] players in the state league. He is quick as a cat and always plays ball."); and the sources cited in the previous endnote.

241. "Editorial Views, News, Comment," *Sporting Life*, July 2, 1892, 2.

242. Bond, 183.

243. *Ibid.*

244. "They Couldn't Help It," *Hastings Daily Nebraskan*, June 15, 1892.

245. H.S.S., 4. The editor's comment is accurate for 1892. Between 1893 and 1898, a few leagues had integrated teams, but the gentleman's agreement was on the verge of winning the day. See Jules Tygiel, *Extra Bases: Reflections on Jackie Robinson, Race, and Baseball History* (Lincoln: University of Nebraska Press, 2002), 56.

246. "Nebraska's Start," 1.

247. "A Game of Ball," *Beatrice (NE) Daily Democrat*, April 29, 1892 (citing a "Hastings special.").

248. "Nebraska's Start," 1.

249. "But Two Clubs to Finish." *Sporting Life* made the same point about teams other than Hastings ignoring the salary cap. "Nebraska League Reduced," 1.

250. For example, in a game that Plattsmouth lost to Beatrice on June 10, 1892, by a score of 16–9, Plattsmouth committed 14 errors and Beatrice committed seven.

3

# Bud Fowler

*Baseball's Black Pioneer Comes to Nebraska*

David C. Ogden

## Introduction

It is one of the ironies of baseball history: A black man would grow up in Cooperstown in the 1870s, would learn baseball on the grounds of the Cooperstown Seminary, and then would launch a career that would change the game. Nebraska baseball claimed its rightful place in that career in 1892 when Bud Fowler played in what at that time was the only integrated league in Organized Baseball in the United States.

Like many of his African American baseball contemporaries, Fowler lived like a gypsy to maintain playing and managing professionally. His stopover in the Nebraska State League (NSL) was brief—about three months. But that was also the longevity of many of the teams on which he played and was typical of many of the leagues in which Fowler appeared.

Jim Crow was a constant companion during Fowler's travels and the itinerant black man had to navigate the racial politics wherever he played. But in risking physical injury on the diamond and in confronting simmering racial tensions off the diamond, Fowler used ingenuity and organizational skills that would change baseball for whites and blacks. As one of the first, if not *the* first, African Americans in Organized Baseball, Fowler became part of a handful of black players recruited to play in the fledgling Nebraska State League in 1892. But how he got there demonstrates the perilous existence of an African American trying to play professional baseball in the last quarter of the 19th century.

## Early Years

Born in Fort Plain, New York., on March 16, 1858, Fowler was named after his father, John W. Jackson, a hop-picker turned barber.[1] The latter profession became Fowler's off-season occupation during the 1890s. Historians give various accounts as to why Fowler changed his name when he began his baseball career. Brian McKenna speculates that Fowler did it to avoid family interference.[2] Fowler biographer Jeffrey Michael Laing agrees with McKenna but adds that Fowler also may have feared endangering his amateur status if he played professionally.[3] As for "Bud," Ben Hill, a writer for MiLB, noted that Fowler was known for calling other people by that name and the nickname stuck to him.[4]

## 66  Section I—The Long and Winding Road

Only 12 years old when his family moved to Cooperstown, the young Bud learned baseball near the military school that provided Abner Doubleday, the mythical father of baseball and a decorated Civil War general, with his soldierly training.[5]

Fowler debuted as a pitcher in 1878 with the Lynn, Massachusetts, Live Oaks. According to McKenna, the Live Oaks were part of the International Association, and one of two minor leagues that "operated in cooperation with the National League."[6] As McKenna has written, "Fowler became the first African-American [sic] to integrate a team in minor league history and thus the game's first African-American [sic] pro and the first in what would become known as Organized Baseball."[7] The following year, Fowler played in the semiprofessional eastern Massachusetts League. In 1881, he headed north to play for Ontario's Guelph Maple Leafs, supposedly one of the most successful teams in semipro ball.[8] In 1882, he crossed the country to play for a New Orleans team, the Pickwicks. Although all black, the Pickwicks were sponsored by a private white social club of that name. As Laing explained, "It was quite typical in the 1860s and 1870s for black employees who organized baseball teams to take the name of their employers' elite club."[9] Later that summer, Fowler left New Orleans and began his managerial career, acting as the player-manager of the Richmond, Virginia, Black Swans. He then moved to St. Louis in 1883 and worked with a local politician to form a national league for African American players. He also signed with the St. Louis Black Sox, but the league fell through and Fowler left to play in Ohio.[10]

**Bud Fowler with his teammates on the integrated 1885 Keokuk, Iowa, Hawkeyes (left to right): (front row) Ted Kennedy, Bill Van Dyke, Dan Dugdale, Nat Hudson, George Harter; (middle row) William Harrington; (back row) Otto Schomberg, Darby O'Brien, Bud Fowler, David Corcoran, Decker (National Baseball Hall of Fame Library).**

In 1884, the itinerant pitcher began his years-long jaunt through the Midwest, first in Minnesota, playing for a Stillwater team in the Northwestern League, and then on to Iowa in 1885 to play for the Keokuk team, which later joined the Western League, replacing the Omaha Omahogs, which dissolved because of financial problems. For the next six years, Fowler played for teams in Colorado, Kansas, New York, New Hampshire, Indiana, New Mexico, Maine, Michigan, Illinois, and Wisconsin. And in 1892, he added Nebraska to that list. By then, Fowler had been playing for 14 years, a period when fielding gloves and overhand pitching were relatively new to the game. In 1884, Fowler's sore arm forced him to switch positions, so he was entrenched at second base by the time he became a member of the Nebraska State League.

## The Nebraska State League

At its outset, the league consisted of six teams: Beatrice, Fremont, Grand Island, Hastings, Lincoln, and Plattsmouth. Lincoln pitcher George William Castone recruited Fowler, who had been playing ball in Findlay, Ohio, though Lincoln was not the first Nebraska team to attempt to get Fowler. The *Omaha Daily Bee* reported in 1891 that Plattsmouth was also on the verge of signing him. The *Bee* added that Fowler was "one of the best men in his position that can be found and would be a good acquisition to the team."[11] Plattsmouth was attempting to form a club in anticipation of the development of the state league. But for whatever reason, Fowler never joined the team, and accounts vary as to where he played before coming to Nebraska. According to the Negro Leagues Baseball Museum, he spent the 1891 season in Findlay.[12] Laing places him in Ohio, but he also claims that Fowler played in St. Louis and Wisconsin.[13] However, the newspapers covering the earliest days of the Nebraska State League never mention Ohio or St. Louis as his previous stops. For example, the *Daily Nebraska State Journal* reported that he came from a team in Wakesha [sic], Wisconsin.[14]

When he finally travelled west to join the Lincoln team, Fowler created little fanfare. Perhaps that was due to the ambivalence toward black players, although several were playing for Lincoln and other teams in the NSL. But Plattsmouth had the most blacks, prompting white players on that team to threaten to jump to other teams.[15] Another reason for the subdued press coverage of Fowler's entrance into the league may have been his teammate of color, George William Castone. The *Omaha World-Herald* described Castone as a Mexican-Indian, "who claims to be the best [pitcher] in the league."[16] Castone, who came from playing in the Colorado State League,[17] also served as business manager for the Lincoln Giants, the state capital's first all-black team that competed against and usually defeated area all-white teams in 1890 and 1891. Gregory Bond wrote that "Castone's arrival had a profound effect on the course of black baseball in Nebraska. During his three-year stay in Lincoln, he became the most well-known black ball player [sic] in the state, variously filling the roles of pitcher, batter, captain, manager, promoter, sportswriter, and league booster."[18] Nebraska newspapers put Castone at the center of a controversy surrounding the formation of the new Nebraska State League. Castone hoped that his highly successful Lincoln Giants would be part of the league. But Lincoln businessman Will Houseworth had other plans. Houseworth leveraged the racist leanings of his fellow white baseball owners, who were opposed to an all-black team in the league, and mustered enough opposition to Castone. Because of this, Castone reluctantly abandoned his idea to keep the Giants together and signed with Houseworth's Lincoln team.[19]

The press coverage on Fowler never equaled that of Castone, who was already hailed as a star by the time Fowler arrived in the Cornhusker State. But the *Daily Nebraska State Journal* gave some recognition to Fowler, stating that he was an important addition to the Lincoln team. The *Journal* noted Fowler's national reputation as a player and manager and described his approach at the plate as: "It is said that he always hits the ball and hits as if he was mad about something."[20] At the same time, discriminatory language tinged the *Journal*'s compliment, a precursor of the racial discord that would plague the league throughout its brief existence:

> Bud Fowler will be put on second base so that he can play everywhere. Every one [sic] knows who he is. His fame is not as obscure as his face. The latter is very obscure in the dark. But he can play ball.[21]

Fowler and his teammates had a rocky start to the season. In the team's home opener, Lincoln lost to Beatrice, 2–0, before a crowd of about 300 at the M Street grounds.[22] Lincoln committed three errors and Beatrice one, although the rest of the game must have been played crisply, judging from the one hour and 40 minutes it took to complete it. Castone received what little praise was offered by the *Daily Nebraska State Journal*, which noted that there were no "regrets" by fans regarding Castone being on the mound. "His arm has lost none of its cunning and his judgment is always good."[23] A few days later, Lincoln travelled to Beatrice, where the latter team won again by a score of 7–4. The *Daily Nebraska State Journal* tried to soften Lincoln's poor start in its coverage of the game: "Yes, well, Beatrice won, but by a small margin; that is, it wasn't as big as a hundred."[24] The *Journal* noted the chilly conditions of the April 28 game between Lincoln and the home team, Beatrice, "but Dad Fowler soon warmed 'em up when once the grounds were reached."[25] The newspaper did not elaborate further on any defensive or offensive contributions Fowler made in Lincoln's loss to Beatrice. Lincoln again played Beatrice on May 6, beating the team, 2–1, but in a strange twist, the umpire awarded Beatrice the victory when Lincoln failed to produce a new ball after the game ball had been hit and landed on the roof of the grandstand, then rolled behind it.[26] The Beatrice team objected to playing with a soiled ball offered by Lincoln and complained to the umpire who upheld the protest and ruled that Lincoln forfeited the game by not having a new ball. According to the account by the *Daily Nebraska State Journal*, the umpire's decision "created a great deal of excitement and indignation, but old Bud Fowler wrote out a protest, secured the umpire's signature[,] and will appeal to the board of directors."[27] The Lincoln team played on its home turf against Hastings the day after the Beatrice game and lost again, 9–4. The *Omaha Daily Bee* lauded Fowler for his defensive play, though the team had five errors in the game.[28]

Lincoln also had problems off the field. Poor attendance at games and shaky finances doomed the franchise. S.C. Coman, secretary of the league, wired other team owners that he had contacted baseball organizers in Kearney and offered the team to them. At the beginning of the 1892 season, *Sporting Life* reported rumors that the Lincoln team was on shaky financial footing and that it might fold and bring down the league with it.[29] The rumors turned out to be true, and on May 9, the *Kearney (NE) Daily Hub* announced that the team would be transferred to Kearney.[30] The Kearney group, eager to have a team in the Nebraska State League, had raised $1,500 to secure the Lincoln franchise. Praising the efforts of the organizers, the *Hub* encouraged its readers to support the new enterprise:

"There is no reason to back down and out now that we have obtained what we were after. Kearney must put her best foot forward and win the pennant if hearty cooperation and support will do it."[31]

Fowler, Castone, and four others from the Lincoln team signed with Kearney, now called the Cotton Pickers, so organizers had to shop for other players to fill the roster. The *Hub* expressed concern that with only six players joining the town's club, "the team will be weak in the box for [upcoming] games, but this difficulty will soon be surmounted."[32] Organizers also had to raise more money to build a ballpark for the team. The *Hub* reported on May 19, 1892, that the team had secured a location and work had begun to build the "amphitheater" and fence and to prepare the playing field.[33] Team management targeted May 30 for the inaugural game at the park. In the meantime, Kearney played all its games on the road. On Memorial Day weekend, the team proudly unveiled its new structure, "probably the only base ball [sic] grounds in the world run by electricity."[34] The *Hub* attempted to stir public anticipation in the days before Kearney's first home games by writing: "The grounds, which are on the electric street railway line, and lie directly south of Juan Boyle's residence, are the largest in the state, and no better can be found anywhere."[35]

The migration of the Lincoln team to Kearney personified Fowler and his career. Like him, the team could not establish roots and had to find a new home. The financial and racial instability of the minor league organizations, including the Nebraska State League, made life uncertain for the teams and their players. Such uncertainty plagued Fowler throughout his career. It meant constant travelling; and long before Robert Peterson labeled Satchel Paige as "The Travelin' Man" in Peterson's book, *Only the Ball Was White*,[36] Fowler rightfully claimed that moniker, boasting that there were few states where he had not played. "He regaled writers with stories of playing match games for trappers' furs and playing in farming communities, pioneer settlements, mining camps[,] and Old West towns."[37] As previously noted, Fowler did not seem to stay with any team more than a couple of months, and sometimes just days. For example, in the course of three months in 1885, Fowler played with three teams: Keokuk; St. Joseph, Missouri; and Pueblo.[38]

Fowler shared another characteristic with Paige: He kept his age a mystery and used the ruse to promote his tenacity, longevity, and seniority in the game. By the time he played in the Nebraska State League, he billed himself as the "oldest active ballplayer," black or white, in baseball. "Playing up his veteran status to the hilt, Fowler claimed he was 48 years old (when he was actually much younger) so he could be perceived as older than…. Adrian 'Cap' Anson, with whom the African American pioneer was, consciously or unconsciously, competing for national recognition and paying fans for his on-field appearances."[39] Fowler was 34 during his Nebraska playing days, and he based his self-comparison to Anson on more than just gaining public recognition. Anson was one of the most outspoken critics of integration in baseball during the late 19th century, so Fowler's reference was more of a poke in the eye to the famous player-manager than a nudge of acknowledgment.

Regardless of Fowler's motive for the age-shifting, Nebraska newspapers picked up the theme and enhanced the myth. The *Daily Nebraska State Journal* referred to him as "Grandpa Fowler"[40] and reported that he had "been in the arena now for twenty-four years."[41] Five days later, the *Journal* called him "Dad Fowler."[42] *The Sporting News*, as noted by Gregory Bond, took the myth a step further, citing a rumor that Fowler "used to play with an Indian team long before America was discovered."[43]

The Lincoln team (later Kearney) also recognized his veteran status by naming him captain, but his performance in the Nebraska State League did not match his previous exploits on the field. According to Laing, "Grandpa" hit .273 for the short season and had eight extra-base hits in 172 at bats.[44] In essence, Fowler had one of his worst seasons while playing in the league. For example, he hit almost .320 playing for Galesburg, Illinois, and other Midwestern teams in 1890. He also registered 17 doubles, five triples, and two home runs.[45] And two years after playing in the NSL, he batted .331 in the Michigan State League.[46]

But despite his lackluster numbers in the Nebraska State League, newspapers touted Fowler's speed and savvy. In reporting on Lincoln's home opener, the *Daily Nebraska State Journal* exclaimed that Fowler "was a team in himself and carried away the honors of the day," despite Lincoln's loss to Beatrice.[47] The *Kearney (NE) Daily Hub* provided sketchier information on Fowler's performance. In one of its rare line scores, the *Hub* showed that Fowler had a double in an 18–2 loss to Hastings. The hit came in the team's second game after moving from Lincoln to Kearney.[48] Regarding a June 3 contest between Plattsmouth and Kearney, the *Omaha Daily Bee* reported that Fowler "did some fine base running" to help Kearney win a doubleheader.[49] According to the *Hub*, Fowler stole five bases during the second game.[50] Later that month, the *Daily Nebraska State Journal* cited Fowler's contributions to Kearney's first victory of the year over Grand Island. "Fowler, as usual, stole several bases and fielded his position admirably."[51] In an Independence Day doubleheader, Fowler had six hits, including a double, in 11 at bats and stole four bases, as Kearney split the two games with Hastings.[52] In a July 6 game, Kearney clobbered Grand Island, 11–1, with "Cole's batting, Pender's playing at third, Fowler's base running [sic][,] and Hopp's pitching" sealing the victory.[53] Box scores from the *Daily Nebraska State Journal* show Fowler's ability to score runs once he was on base. In 18 games between June 7 and July 7, Fowler scored 27 runs. He hit safely in all but one of those games and had six extra-base hits. However, his defense left something to be desired. Although Fowler was known for his slick fielding, the box scores for that month show otherwise. The second sacker committed 14 errors in the 18-game stretch, but he helped to turn nine double plays.

Despite the team's moments of admirable play, the speed of Fowler, and the pitching of Castone, Kearney remained mired in fourth place most of the season. Whether Fowler's dip in career numbers contributed to Kearney's poor standing in the league is a matter of speculation. Certainly, the begrudging acceptance of black players by white players and managers in the NSL did not make African Americans feel appreciated or welcome to the games. Such a racially hostile environment probably did little to enhance the on-field performances of the league's black participants.

Unfortunately for teams and players, racial tensions crept into the coverage of the NSL. One matter brought those tensions to a boiling point and renewed the debate about whether African Americans should be playing in the league. The incident occurred during Kearney's inaugural games on its new home field. The team was playing a doubleheader against Grand Island, and W.A. Rourke, manager of the visiting team, was a runner on first base when a ground ball was hit to Fowler at second base. Fowler allegedly tagged Rourke so hard that it "knocked the wind" out of the Grand Island player.[54] Rourke then tried to assault Fowler, but players from both teams broke up the fray. One newspaper account said that Fowler had purposely hit Rourke when applying the tag, whereas another reporter criticized the play and the subsequent melee, laying blame on both Fowler and Rourke. The *Kearney (NE) Daily Hub* used more diplomatic terms in defending its home team: "The *Hub* does not care to go into details of these alleged games, so excruciating to every lover of the national game. It is best, so far as the Kearney victims are concerned, and in keeping with the sentiment of the day, to 'let the dead and the beautiful rest.'"[55] On the other hand, the *Hub* was not so diplomatic in describing the playing of Fowler and his teammates. It called the two games a "double disaster" and reported that the Grand Island Sugar Beats "walloped the Kearney aggregation unmercifully both forenoon and afternoon."[56] As for the brawl between Fowler and Rourke, the league levied no fines or disciplinary action against either player. League officials promised to investigate the confrontation while questioning whether African Americans should be playing in the first place. "[Though] President Brewer and Secretary Rohrer are opposed to colored players, they are inclined to see them have fair play as long as they remain in the league."[57]

Although the *Kearney (NE) Daily Hub* gave sketchy coverage of the NSL, the *Daily Nebraska State Journal* provided more depth to its reporting, calling itself "the official newspaper" of the league.[58] Neither newspaper, however, reported on what would come to be Fowler's long-lasting contributions to the game. During his time in Nebraska, Fowler was using innovations that would have a historic impact on baseball. One of those innovations was in response to the racially charged behavior of white players, who allegedly attempted to injure the black second baseman at his playing position. Shin guards, standard equipment for catchers today, were first used by Fowler to protect himself from spikes of white base runners sliding into second. In Jerry Malloy's resurrection of *Sol White's History of Colored Baseball*, an article from an 1889 edition of *The Sporting News* noted that Fowler wore wooden slats stuffed into his pants and over his shins.

> He knew that about every other player that came down to second base on a steal had it in for him, and would, if possible, throw the spikes into him. He was a good player, but left the base every time there was a close play in order to get away from the spikes.
> 
> I have seen him muff balls intentionally, so that he would not have to try to touch runners, fearing that they might injure him.[59]

And Fowler had the scars to show for his defensive play. In May 1884, a runner slid into second base and spiked Fowler, breaking his toe. Also, he was sidelined the next month when a pitch knocked him unconscious and may have broken one or two of his ribs, causing him to miss three games.[60]

Robert Peterson notes that some historians credit another second baseman—Frank Grant—with developing the shin guards. Grant was a contemporary of Fowler's, playing for Buffalo in the International League in the 1890s, while Fowler played for Binghamton. According to *The Sporting News* article, white base runners made a habit of attempting to spike Grant when they slid into second. However, even wearing leg guards, Grant found that avoiding injury proved too great a challenge, and he eventually moved to right field.[61] Fowler never switched positions, so the wooden slats became standard equipment for him, though there is no reference by Nebraska newspapers that he wore them in the NSL. But considering the white players' animosity toward blacks in general, it is not far-fetched to assume that Fowler used them in the spring and summer of 1892. Jeffery Laing contends that white players had motives, in addition to race, for trying to spike Fowler. "The taunts and high spikes of his adversaries were probably attempts to slow the African American speedster's base-running [*sic*] abilities."[62]

W.A. "Pa" Rourke, seen here as the owner and manager of the Omaha franchise in the Western League in 1902, was the manager of the Grand Island team in the Nebraska State League in 1892 (The KM3TV/Bostwick-Frohardt Photograph Collection at The Durham Museum).

Fowler may have contributed to another baseball convention, albeit indirectly. Players' attempts to spike Fowler and other black infielders made the feet-first slide standard in base running. While historian Robert Peterson calls the claim "fanciful," he lends some credence to the notion when he wrote: "[I]f the slide was not developed with the purpose of maiming Fowler and Grant, it seems likely that some players perfected the art with that aim in view."[63]

Fowler did not remain silent before coming to Nebraska about such harsh treatment of African American players. He was not only the first black star in Organized Baseball, but he was also among the first to be outspoken about the racial hostility and discrimination in Organized Baseball, an issue that still looms over the sport more than 135 years after Fowler drew attention to it. For example, while playing for Stillwater, Minnesota, in 1884, Fowler was benched for several days for refusing to catch a white pitcher apparently for racially based reasons. As Brian McKenna surmised, "Fowler, rarely docile, was perhaps reacting to the pitcher's reluctance to work in cohesion with the catcher."[64] In 1888, while playing in Indiana and New Mexico, he complained "loudly and publicly in the newspapers about racial bias"[65]; and in 1890, he filed a racial discrimination suit in Iowa. The Ballingall Hotel in Ottumwa refused to let Fowler eat in its dining room when he was playing for a Galesburg, Illinois, team.[66] By the time he got to Nebraska, Fowler was either more subdued, or the newspapers did not give Fowler a voice in exposing racial tensions in the Nebraska State League. Even newspaper coverage of Fowler's scrap with Rourke was muted.

Fowler's "silence" on racial issues in the NSL may have had more to do with the

Nebraska newspapers' unwillingness to provide black players with a public podium than it had to do with Fowler's reluctance to speak. After all, Fowler faced overt racism from teammates and opponents alike, so he had plenty about which to complain; and as captain for the Lincoln/Kearney team, he might have expected some respect from the press, regardless of his skin color. But the press gave him little. Although the NSL was the only integrated league in Organized Baseball in the nation during its existence, that did not mean that league officials, white players, and the press would tolerate any dissension from black players, despite the fact that white players dissented over having to play with black players. The tightening noose of segregation in all Organized Baseball, plus the nation's deepening economic problems, strangled any outcry, much less discussion, about the stark racial imbalance in its ranks.

Besides being one of the earliest civil rights advocates in sport, another Fowler trait was ignored by Nebraska press: baseball entrepreneur and developer. If newspaper accounts molded perceptions, Nebraskans heard about Fowler only as a player, though in other parts of the country, he was known as a driving force in the development of teams, as well as being a player. In addition, he had a hand in attempts to create all-black professional leagues. How much he contributed to the management of the Kearney team, besides being captain, is difficult to determine based on stories in Nebraska newspapers and other historical accounts. Certainly the NSL could have used Fowler's organizational skills for obvious reasons. One by one, teams began folding in late June. The *Kearney (NE) Daily Hub* reported the dissolution of the Fremont team on June 21[67] and reported on June 28 that the league had also lost Plattsmouth.[68] The Beatrice club was the next to fold and the Hastings and Grand Island teams followed suit within a few days. In the July 17 edition of the *Daily Nebraska State Journal*, a NSL official said the league "had passed into a state of innocuous desuetude."[69] It may be coincidental that the Kearney team was the lone team left standing, and Kearney management made it clear that it "has only quit because there is nobody to play with. See you all later."[70]

On July 18, the *Hub* reported that Fowler and other players from Kearney, plus a few from other baseball clubs, formed a barnstorming team to play in Missouri and Kansas.[71] The team, the Kearney Stewarts, held an exhibition game earlier that month against an amateur team from Callaway, Nebraska, to raise funds for the tour, a game that the Stewarts won, 8–7, in 10 innings.[72] Apparently Fowler did not stay with the Stewarts and returned to Findlay, Ohio, later that summer and also played in Galesburg, Illinois. He would remain in Galesburg to play in 1893.[73]

## Fowler's Post-Nebraska Career

In 1894, after again playing for the Findlay Sluggers, Fowler turned entrepreneurial and attempted to build another ball club in Findlay, which he would call the Colored Western Giants. He partnered with a young African American from the Findlay team: power hitter Grant "Home Run" Johnson. While in Findlay, Fowler bought ad space in the September 22, 1894, issue of *Sporting Life* and wrote:

> Next season the Western States will be represented with the best-equipped colored club ever organized, which will equal any National League Club, and will travel in their own palace dining and sleeping car. Their daily parade through the principal cities will be made on bicycles. All clubs wishing early spring dates can address Bud Fowler, 822 North Main [S]treet, Findlay, Ohio, Manager.[74]

74  Section I—The Long and Winding Road

But he could not arrange financing for the team, so he moved to Adrian, Michigan, where he worked as a barber and again attempted to form a touring black club. Some historians feel that his success in establishing the club became one of his greatest contributions to African American baseball: the Page Fence Giants. Fowler organized the Giants after gaining the sponsorship of the Page Fence Company of Adrian and a local bicycle

Fans celebrate the dedication of Bud Fowler Way in Cooperstown, New York, in 2013 (National Baseball Hall of Fame Library).

business. The result was the creation of one of the best known touring clubs in black baseball history. *Sporting Life* called the Giants "one of the strongest teams in the country"[75] and a series of games was arranged between them and the Cuban Giants, the first African American salaried team, to determine the "colored championship of the world."[76] In addition, Fowler had planned to take the Lansing Colored Capital All-American team on a two-month tour of England in 1895, where the club would barnstorm with the Minneapolis team from the Western League.[77] Later, he scrapped that idea and proposed a four-month tour for the Paige Fence Giants and a nine-man all-star team from the Michigan State League to barnstorm in Hawaii, Australia, and New Zealand. But nothing came of that plan as well.

Part of the reason for the Giants' success—besides playing well enough to have a record of 118 wins and 36 losses in 1895—stemmed from Fowler's recognition that entertainment and promotions were as important in selling black baseball to white communities as the competition was.[78] Fowler would have his Giant players ride bicycles and parade through the town in which they were playing. Not only did the activity showcase the product of one of the team's sponsors, but it was also a good way to stir interest in that evening's game and to engage potential spectators.

Fowler played on and managed several other touring black teams after the Page Fence Giants, but by the end of the first decade of the 20th century, he had faded from the public's consciousness, though he was still active as a baseball entrepreneur and promoter. In 1908, *Sporting Life* reported that Fowler was in "destitute circumstances" and dying from consumption.[79] The story was premature. Indeed, Fowler had suffered a health setback from an old injury, possibly when he was struck by the ball that had put him out of action in 1884, but he bounced back with renewed vigor to organize other black teams. In fact, Fowler was busy assembling a team in 1909 in Frankfort, New York, where he also set up a barbershop. The next year, he tried to put together a touring club to play throughout the United States. However, that and another attempt to form a team fell through, and after those failures, Fowler's health deteriorated, with him dying of pernicious anemia in 1913 at the home of his sister in Frankfurt.[80]

While there is no record of Fowler returning to the Cornhusker State during the last two decades of his life, the pioneering player graced the annals of Nebraska baseball history through those short months that marked the life of the Nebraska State League. It would be more than 60 years before another African American player of such historic magnitude would be a member of a Nebraska professional team, and that man would be National Baseball Hall of Fame pitcher Bob Gibson. Does Fowler deserve a place in the Hall, in the ultimate baseball shrine located in his hometown? According to *New York Times* reporter Hillel Kuttler, there are baseball historians who think that he does. As Kuttler wrote, "Some baseball historians believe that Fowler deserves acclaim … for his record and for prevailing in the face of consistent discrimination."[81] And the village of Cooperstown has taken the first step to honor its hometown hero by naming the street leading to Doubleday Field "Bud Fowler Way." In the ceremony to rename the street, baseball historian John Thorn referred to Jackie Robinson in commemorating Fowler: "Jackie walked across a bridge that others built. If Jackie Robinson walked across a bridge, he also would have walked across Fowler Way."[82]

## Notes

1. Brian McKenna, "Bud Fowler," SABR Baseball Biography Project, http://sabr.org/bioproject (accessed on July 11, 2013).
2. *Ibid.*
3. Jeffrey Michael Laing, *Bud Fowler: Baseball's First Black Professional* (Jefferson, North Carolina: McFarland & Company, Inc., Publishers, 2013), 65.
4. Benjamin Hill, "Fowler: A 19th-century Baseball Pioneer," February 9, 2006, http://www.milb.com/gen/articles/printer_friendly/milb/y2006/mo2/d09 (accessed on July 11, 2013).
5. Laing, 64.
6. McKenna.
7. *Ibid.*
8. *Ibid.*
9. Laing, 71.
10. *Ibid.*
11. "The Gossip of the Amateurs," *Omaha Daily Bee*, February 1, 1891.
12. "John 'Bud' Fowler," Negro Leagues Baseball eMuseum, 2006, http://www.coe.ksu.edu/annex/nlbemuseum/history/players/fowler.html (accessed on July 11, 2013).
13. Laing, 126.
14. "Base Ball [sic] for Nebraska," *Daily Nebraska State Journal*, April 24, 1892.
15. "State League," *Omaha Daily Bee*, May 31, 1892.
16. "The Nebraska State League," *Omaha World-Herald*, May 24, 1892.
17. "Ready to Play Ball," *Daily Nebraska State Journal*, May 4, 1890.
18. Gregory Bond, "Too Much Dirty Work: Race, Manliness and Baseball in Gilded Age Nebraska," *Nebraska History* 85 (2004): 174.
19. *Ibid.*, 179–180.
20. "Base Ball [sic] for Nebraska."
21. *Ibid.* The *Journal*'s race-baiting in making its point about Fowler's color serves as a contrast to statements made six years earlier by officials of the Binghamton, New York, team for whom Fowler played in 1886. At that time, the officials questioned Fowler's color, but that may have had something to do with them defending their stance on retaining a black man. After another team tried to recruit him, the officials feigned ambiguity regarding Fowler's skin: "Some say Fowler is a colored man, but we account for his dark complexion by the fact that ... in chasing after balls [he] has become tanned from constant and careless exposure to the sun." McKenna.
22. "First to Feel Defeat," *Daily Nebraska State Journal*, April 24, 1892.
23. *Ibid.*
24. "Lincoln Loses Again," *Daily Nebraska State Journal*, April 29, 1892.
25. *Ibid.*
26. In the Nebraska State League, the teams furnished the baseballs for the game. "By the rules of the game, when a ball goes out of sight[,] a new one, or one which has been in use at the game, shall be produced." For the May 6 game, it was Lincoln's responsibility to supply a new game ball for the last few innings. Lincoln manager Will Houseworth brought three new balls to the game. "One of them had been used in practicing, at catching and was soiled thus. Another had been ripped a little and discarded. The third was behind the grand stand [sic]." "Forced to Forfeit It," *Daily Nebraska State Journal*, May 7, 1892. The *Journal* reported that Houseworth had given the umpire the practice ball to use, but Beatrice refused to play with a dirty ball, and the umpire upheld Beatrice's objection. More than one week later, the Nebraska State League board of directors threw out the umpire's decision and declared that the May 6 game would not count in the standings and had to be played over again. "Again in Good Trim," *Daily Nebraska State Journal*, May 15, 1892.
27. "Forced to Forfeit It."
28. "Won It by Slugging," *Omaha Daily Bee*, May 8, 1892.
29. "A Flurry," *Sporting Life*, April 23, 1892, 1.
30. "Kearney Gets There Again," *Kearney (NE) Daily Hub*, May 9, 1892.
31. *Ibid.*
32. "Base Ball [sic] Notes," *Kearney (NE) Daily Hub*, May 18, 1892.
33. "Base Ball [sic] Grounds," *Kearney (NE) Daily Hub*, May 19, 1892.
34. "A Boom at Base Ball [sic] Park," *Kearney (NE) Daily Hub*, May 26, 1892.
35. *Ibid.*
36. Robert Peterson, *Only the Ball Was White* (New York, Gramercy Books, 1970), 129.
37. McKenna.
38. Peterson, 19–20.
39. Laing, 128, taken from Merl Kleinknecht, "Blacks in 19th Century Black Baseball," *SABR Research Archives*: 1–2.
40. "First to Feel Defeat."

41. "Base Ball [sic] for Nebraska."
42. "Lincoln Loses Again."
43. Bond, 177.
44. Laing, 127.
45. *Ibid.*, 123.
46. "John 'Bud' Fowler."
47. "First to Feel Defeat."
48. "Hastings 18, Kearney 2," *Kearney (NE) Daily Hub*, May 21, 1892.
49. "State League," *Omaha Daily Bee*, June 3, 1892.
50. "Won Both Games," *Kearney (NE) Daily Hub*, June 3, 1892.
51. "Kearney Kills Her Hoodoo," *Daily Nebraska State Journal*, July 1, 1892.
52. "Nebraska State League," *Daily Nebraska State Journal*, July 5, 1892.
53. "But Didn't They Play?" *Kearney (NE) Daily Hub*, July 7, 1892.
54. Bond, 181.
55. "Two in One Day," *Kearney (NE) Daily Hub*, May 31, 1892.
56. *Ibid.*
57. "State League Gossip," *Daily Nebraska State Journal*, June 1, 1892.
58. "Again in Good Trim," *Daily Nebraska State Journal*, May 15, 1892.
59. Jerry Malloy, comp., *Sol White's History of Colored Base Ball [sic], with Other Documents on the Early Black Game, 1886–1936* (Lincoln: University of Nebraska Press, 1995), 137.
60. McKenna.
61. Malloy, 138.
62. Laing, 8.
63. Peterson, 43.
64. McKenna.
65. Laing, 123.
66. *Ibid.*
67. "Surrenders Her Charter," *Kearney (NE) Daily Hub*, June 21, 1892.
68. "New Schedule of Games," *Kearney (NE) Daily Hub*, June 28, 1892.
69. "The State League is Dead," *Daily Nebraska State Journal*, July 17, 1892.
70. "Oh Yes," *Kearney (NE) Daily Hub*, July 16, 1892. *Sporting Life* casts some doubt over which team was the last one standing. According to that publication, the Hastings team had "the satisfaction of being the last club to give up the sponge after being the last club to join the [l]eague last spring." "Done For," *Sporting Life*, July 23, 1892, 4. But one week earlier in its July 16 issue, the *Kearney (NE) Daily Hub* reported that the Cotton Pickers were slated for three games that week against Hastings, and the latter team never showed, thus ending the league.
71. "The Kearney Nine," *Kearney (NE) Daily Hub*, July 18, 1892.
72. "A Neat Game at Callaway," *Daily Nebraska State Journal*, July 4, 1892.
73. Laing, 128.
74. "This Will Be Gorgeous," *Sporting Life*, September 22, 1894, 4.
75. "Some More Giants," *Sporting Life*, December 8, 1894, 2.
76. Laing, 132.
77. "Fowler Admits It," *Sporting Life*, July 20, 1895, 11.
78. Laing, 132.
79. "A Veteran's Distress," *Sporting Life*, September 19, 1908, 2.
80. Laing, 193.
81. Hillel Kuttler, "Acclaim Comes Late for Baseball Pioneer," *New York Times*, April 14, 2013.
82. Greg Klein, "Cooperstown Celebrates Bud Fowler Day," *Cooperstown (NY) Crier*, April 25, 2013.

# 4

# The Buffalo Soldiers Play Ball

ROBERT P. NASH

During the American Civil War, nearly 180,000 African American soldiers served in the ranks of the Union Army. Organized into racially segregated units, they were grouped together under a separate branch of the Army called the United States Colored Troops. With the end of the war in April 1865, the Union forces quickly demobilized, and there was no provision for black soldiers in the postwar U.S. Army. In July 1866, however, the U.S. Congress passed "An Act to Increase and Fix the Military Peace Establishment of the United States."[1] That legislation included specific orders for the creation of six new units to be composed entirely of black enlisted men. These would become the Ninth and Tenth Cavalry and the Thirty-eighth, Thirty-ninth, Fortieth and Forty-first Infantry. Less than three years later, in March 1869, legislation was enacted further decreasing the size of the Army.[2] The Ninth and Tenth Cavalry survived the resulting reductions, but the four black infantry regiments were consolidated. The Thirty-eighth and Forty-first became the Twenty-fourth Infantry, and the Thirty-ninth and Fortieth became the Twenty-fifth Infantry.

While African Americans were not officially prevented from serving as officers in the black units, in practice those regiments were led by white officers because initially there were no black officers. None of the black officer veterans of the Civil War's United States Colored Troops received commissions in the post-war Regular Army. Nor would any black enlisted men be promoted from the ranks during the remainder of the 19th century. Not until 1870 would the first black cadet be accepted into the United States Military Academy at West Point, and of the 12 black cadets who entered the academy during the 19th century, only three would survive the harsh racist conditions long enough to graduate: Henry O. Flipper (1877), John H. Alexander (1887), and Charles Young (1889). Upon earning their commissions, all three black West Pointers were posted for service with either the Ninth or Tenth Cavalry. After Young's graduation in 1889, it was nearly 50 years before the fourth black cadet, Benjamin O. Davis, Jr., would graduate from the Academy in 1936. Five black chaplains were also commissioned as officers during the 19th century and assigned to the black regiments, but their positions did not give them military command of troops. In 1901, two black soldiers, Benjamin O. Davis, Sr., of the Ninth Cavalry (and later Tenth Cavalry) and John E. Green of the Twenty-fourth Infantry were commissioned from the ranks.[3]

Soon after their formation, all four black regiments were sent to the American West where they would remain on duty until the end of the century. They played an active and important role in the Indian Wars, with 18 of their soldiers earning Medals of Honor in the process.[4] In time, the black Regular troops would become collectively known by their famous nickname: "Buffalo Soldiers." While the exact origins of the appellation are not known with certainty, it is generally agreed that the term was first applied to them by their Native American adversaries. The soldiers' dark skin and hair, it was said, called to mind the buffalo. There is no clear evidence that black soldiers of the era ever used the term themselves, but the Tenth Cavalry ultimately did incorporate a buffalo into their regimental crest.

In August 1885, after years of service in the Southwest and the southern plains, the first troops of the Ninth Cavalry arrived in Nebraska. Over the next two decades, the Cornhusker State would be home to three of the four Buffalo Soldier regiments: the Ninth Cavalry, the Tenth Cavalry, and the Twenty-fifth Infantry. In fact, from 1885 through 1907, the only period during which one or more of those regiments were not resident in Nebraska was during the Spanish-American War (1898) and the Philippine-American War (1899–1902), when much of the U.S. Army, including the Buffalo Soldiers, were on active duty overseas.

Although the fourth black regiment, the Twenty-fourth Infantry, was never stationed in Nebraska, it does provide an interesting footnote in the context of baseball's storied history. From 1871 to 1872, in his last posting before retirement from the U.S. Army, Abner Doubleday (1819–1893) served as the Twenty-fourth Infantry's commander at Fort McKavett, Texas. He is best known, of course, as the purported inventor of the game of baseball, though it is important to note that Doubleday himself never made such a claim. His supposed role in baseball's creation mythology did not emerge until more than a decade after his death and was debunked long ago. The renowned baseball historian, John Thorn, has asserted that Doubleday's only known association with baseball was a letter he wrote in June 1871 while in command of the Twenty-fourth Infantry. In that letter to the Adjutant General of the U.S. Army, Doubleday indicated that he "would … like to purchase baseball implements for the amusement of the men."[5]

By the time that the Ninth Cavalry arrived in Nebraska, the Indian Wars had largely drawn to a close, and the soldiers found that they had more leisure time on their hands.[6] Baseball had become the country's most popular team sport, and numerous sources reported that one of the soldiers' favorite off-duty pursuits was to play it. In addition, Army officers sanctioned and encouraged baseball as a way to boost morale and keep their troops physically fit. Even at the height of the Indian Wars, soldiers had still found occasions to play the sport. Frederick W. Benteen, for example, is best known for his role as an officer with the Seventh Cavalry at the Battle of the Little Bighorn (June 25, 1876). Less well known is that several years earlier, in 1873, his Company H troopers formed a formidable baseball team dubbed the "Benteen Base Ball [sic] Club" in honor of their commander. The Benteens regularly bested their military rivals as well as civilian opponents.[7]

Upon their arrival in Nebraska, troops of the Ninth Cavalry were assigned to garrison both Fort Robinson and Fort Niobrara. The rest of the regiment, including the regimental headquarters, was stationed at posts in Wyoming.[8] Fort Robinson had been established in 1874 in the northwestern corner of the Nebraska panhandle, just west of the present-day town of Crawford. Fort Niobrara, 160 miles to the east in north central Nebraska, was founded in 1880 near the future town of Valentine. The original purpose of both forts was to keep watch over the nearby Native American tribes. In the case of Fort Robinson, it was the Pine Ridge Reservation, while for Fort Niobrara, it was the

Rosebud Reservation. In May 1887, less than two years after the first troops' arrival, Fort Robinson became the regimental headquarters for the Ninth Cavalry and would remain so until 1898.

The years when the Buffalo Soldiers were stationed in Nebraska coincided with an era which saw the expansion of institutional racism and racial segregation throughout American society. In 1896, the U.S. Supreme Court handed down its infamous *Plessy v. Ferguson* decision upholding the separate-but-equal doctrine of racial segregation and sanctioning the growth of Jim Crow laws. It would be more than half a century before the Supreme Court's landmark *Brown v. Board of Education* decision in 1954 effectively overturned *Plessy v. Ferguson*. Unfortunately for African Americans, baseball was no different than other areas of American society. In 1887, the International League barred black players from being members of their teams, and by the late 1890s, the notorious "gentleman's agreement" kept African Americans from participating at any level of Organized Baseball. While the segregated U.S. Army certainly reflected the rest of America, it nevertheless offered blacks greater opportunities than most American institutions of that day. Baseball, for one, provided the chance for black ballplayers to compete against white teams at a time when such opportunities were rare or nonexistent.

Baseball competition took place in three ways: between teams at the same fort, against military teams from other posts, and against civilian teams. For the first nine years that the Ninth Cavalry was stationed at Fort Robinson, it shared the post with white infantry units. As a result, the black soldiers played both against and with their white counterparts. In his classic work on the frontier army, *Forty Miles a Day on Beans and Hay*, Don Rickey indicated that during the 1880s the black soldiers of the Ninth Cavalry and the white soldiers of the Eighth Infantry played together on Fort Robinson's all-post team.[9] When his father, Andrew S. Burt, was stationed at Fort Robinson in the 1880s,

**Unidentified black soldiers playing baseball in Nebraska during the late 19th or early 20th century (Great Plains Black History Museum).**

Reynolds Burt later remembered a hard-fought contest between the Ninth Cavalry and a visiting Seventh Infantry team. In the bottom of the ninth inning with men on base and two outs, a Ninth Cavalry trooper clouted a massive home run to apparently win the game. The umpire, however, who happened to be an infantry officer, called the batter out for "'stepp[ing] clear across the plate' to strike the ball."[10] A "near riot" was averted only when it was judiciously decided to call the game a tie.[11]

Both Fort Robinson and Fort Niobrara were in remote areas of Nebraska, and because the nearby towns were small and predominantly white, games were frequently scheduled between the black cavalrymen and white civilian teams. A local correspondent for the *Cleveland Gazette*, a prominent African American weekly newspaper, reported on the "very pleasant game of base ball [sic]" that was played at Fort Robinson in June 1886 between the Ninth Cavalry and the Magic City nine from nearby Chadron. A good crowd of soldiers and civilians watched as the Ninth Cavalry, managed by Sergeant J.J. Jackson of Troop C, came from behind to tie the Chadron team at 17–all in the fifth inning, with runners at second and third base. At that point, the game ended in a tie due to the muddy field conditions and the arrival of the return train from Chadron.[12] In the following month, the Ninth Cavalry team traveled the 35 miles by rail to Chadron for a rematch. One hundred dollars was riding on the outcome of the game with a reported additional five hundred dollars in bets on the side. When the soldiers arrived to play, however, no sign of the Chadron team could be found. The assembled crowd of spectators left disappointed as the cavalrymen claimed a victory by forfeit.[13]

The Fourth of July was often an occasion for a baseball game between the Ninth Cavalry and a nearby civilian team, though even when the baseball team was not scheduled to play, the men of the Ninth were an integral part of the holiday festivities with the white townspeople. In July 1897, for example, while a baseball game was to be played between civilian teams from Crawford and Chadron, the *Crawford Tribune* announced that the "celebrated Ninth [C]avalry band and glee club will furnish excellent music during the entire day."[14]

In 1896, the *Omaha Daily Bee* called the Ninth Cavalry's baseball team "one of the strongest in the army." To face such a powerful nine for a June 1896 game at Fort Robinson, the towns of Chadron and Crawford not only formed a combined squad, but they also recruited a pitcher from a team in Omaha.[15] Even more dramatically, the outcomes of a series of games between the civilian nine from Alliance show how difficult it was to take on the Ninth Cavalry. After losing games to the horse soldiers in May and in July 1896, 17–10[16] and 12–4,[17] respectively, Alliance joined forces with the town of Hemingford for a game later in July.[18] Though they earned a split in two contests against the team from Chadron, they again fell short to the "colored boys at Fort Robinson" by a score of 12–7. But despite the losing effort, the manager of the Hemingford-Alliance team spoke "highly of the treatment accorded them" at the fort.[19]

In August, the Ninth Cavalry faced a more formidable opponent, as a large contingent of the Twelfth Infantry traveled from Fort Niobrara for a three-game series at Fort Robinson. It was reported that "[t]he entire population of Crawford and the surrounding country witnessed the games." Fort Niobrara dropped the first game, 15–9, due, it was said, to "being out of form owing to their long night ride and the strange grounds." The foot soldiers rebounded the following day, however, to win an "old time [sic] slugging match" by a score of 23–17. They then went on to take the rubber game of the series by coming from behind in a wild ninth inning which saw them score five runs to edge Fort

Robinson, 10–9. As usual, wagering on the games was heavy, and the men of the Twelfth Infantry reportedly returned to Fort Niobrara "loaded down with wealth." Among the spoils was a bulldog which had previously belonged to a Ninth Cavalry officer. For their part, the victors graciously acknowledged the "courteous treatment" and "good will" extended to them by the men of the Ninth Cavalry.[20]

In the following year, the Ninth Cavalry again faced the redoubtable Twelfth Infantry in another three-game series played at Fort Robinson in June 1897. The horse soldiers dropped the first game when the foot soldiers rallied to triumph, 16–14, in the ninth inning. After also losing the second game, 17–7, the cavalry recovered nicely to win the "prettiest" game of the series. In a thrilling back-and-forth contest, the Robinson men outscored their Niobrara rivals three runs to two in the ninth inning to gain a 10–9 victory.[21]

In early April 1898, after 13 years of uninterrupted service in Nebraska, the Ninth Cavalry left Fort Robinson shortly before the outbreak of the Spanish-American War. All four black regiments in the Regular Army subsequently took part in the fighting in Cuba, with five troopers of the Tenth Cavalry receiving the Medal of Honor for their heroism. As a result of the war, the United States seized control of the Philippines from Spain, and over the next four years, each of the black regiments spent significant time in the Philippines as the Americans fought to suppress Filipino resistance to U.S. rule. Soon after the Philippine Insurrection officially ended in July 1902, all four regiments were back in the States. The Ninth Cavalry never returned to Nebraska, but in May 1902, the horsemen of the Tenth Cavalry arrived from their most recent posting in Cuba to take up residence at Fort Robinson. Three months later, the Twenty-fifth Infantry arrived back in the United States from duty in the Philippines, and Fort Niobrara became its new regimental headquarters.

Baseball was just as popular an off-duty activity with the men of the Tenth Cavalry and Twenty-fifth Infantry as it had been with their Ninth Cavalry counterparts. If anything, the new arrivals to Nebraska were even more avid baseball players. In his 1921 book on the Tenth Cavalry, Major Edward Glass commented:

> For the first time in its history, our men had the leisure and opportunity to take up athletics. From the start[,] the regiment made good records. In the words of one old non-com [sic]: "What it took to win, we had nothing else but."[22]

Thomas Clement of the Tenth Cavalry's Troop K echoed those sentiments in noting the "keen and unprecedented interest taken in athletics" and in particular, baseball, since the regiment's return from overseas.[23] A regimental baseball league was soon organized at Fort Robinson.

> During the summer season we have a regular base ball [sic] league, and each troop, the band[,] and hospital corps, have scheduled games, which are played on the dates set apart by the Athletic Committee of the regiment, composed of officers; and at the end of the season[,] the team having the highest percentage of winning games is presented with a pennant.[24]

Major Glass dutifully documented the regiment's annual baseball champions, showing that during their stay at Fort Robinson three different units claimed the post championship: the Band (1903), Troop I (1904), and Troop K (1905 and 1906).[25]

Like the Ninth Cavalry before them, the Tenth Cavalry also scheduled games with white civilian teams. The "post team" composed of the Tenth's best baseball players was described as being of "excellent calibre" and played numerous games against teams from nearby towns.²⁶ Evidently, the Fort Robinson nine had to initially work off some of the rust from their overseas service. For example, on July 4, 1902, they played a game in Crawford against a team representing the towns of Alliance and Burlington. Although the final score was not reported, the *Alliance (NE) Herald* crowed that the Alliance-Burlington team "demonstrated their superiority over the Tenth [C]avalry fellows, fairly wiping up the earth with them."²⁷

But the Fort Robinson team's struggles were clearly of short duration. By the following year, it went undefeated according to a report made by the Tenth Cavalry's Albert S. Lowe in *The Colored American Magazine*. Lowe further disclosed the "curious fact" that a number of men on the baseball team also played in the regiment's band and orchestra.²⁸

Regimental "field days" provided another opportunity for the soldiers to compete on the baseball diamond. These competitions featured standard track and field events, along with more military-related activities such as tent-pitching, horse races, mounted team wrestling, and even tug-of-war from atop horseback. The day's events were typically capped off with a baseball game between rival units.²⁹ Field day competitions were of sufficient interest that they drew the attention of the civilian press, which often carried the results. In July 1903, for example, the *Omaha Daily Bee* reported that the Tenth Cavalry's First Squadron team had overwhelmed the team drawn from the Tenth's Band and the Hospital Corps, 22–5.³⁰

The very strong 1903 Tenth Cavalry team (left to right): (front row) Harris, Richard Hay with his dog, Lewis, Howard C. Roan; (middle row) Vaughan, John Buck, Hambright, Forby; (back row) Shorter, unknown, William K. Porter, Beverly F. Thornton, Jones, unknown.

At Fort Niobrara, the Twenty-fifth Infantry was also involved with baseball. Richard Johnson indicated that his regiment "was long known for its leading role in baseball, an activity in which it took great pride."[31] The regiment's exploits on the baseball diamond are better documented than those of most military teams due to the efforts of Master Sergeant Dalbert P. Green, who penned a brief history of the Twenty-fifth Infantry's teams from 1894 to 1914. Green was certainly well-qualified to produce such an account. Not only was he a star player from 1894 to 1908, but he also served at various times as the team's captain, manager, and coach. He identified the 1903–1905 Fort Niobrara teams as among the greatest nines in the regiment's storied baseball history, along with those stationed in the Philippines between 1899 and 1902 and those based in the Hawaiian Islands from 1914 to 1918.[32]

Sergeant Green traced the origins of the Twenty-fifth's baseball program to 1894 when the regiment was stationed at Fort Missoula, Montana. At that time, the regiment was commanded by Colonel Andrew S. Burt, a well-known baseball enthusiast who established baseball teams at all the military posts where he served.[33] He charged Green with forming a team at Fort Missoula, and during that era, white officers even played alongside the black enlisted men.[34] By the time the Twenty-fifth Infantry arrived at Fort Niobrara 12 years later in August 1906, the regiment's baseball teams had already compiled a distinguished record in competition wherever they had been posted. Unfortunately for the regiment, though, some of its best players were then with its second battalion, which had been sent to garrison Fort Reno in Oklahoma Territory. During the baseball team's first year in Nebraska, its fortunes also suffered a major blow when Private Ashby, "a most promising catcher and a sure heavy batter, … lost one of his hands in a railroad accident."[35]

Upon the Twenty-fifth's arrival at Fort Niobrara, Theophilus Steward, the regiment's chaplain and its only black officer, reported that the new quarters were teeming with snakes. Over the next several weeks, much of the soldiers' time was spent reducing the reptilian population of the fort.[36] Nevertheless, the baseball nine from Fort Niobrara was soon in action against local civilian competition. In September, in what the *Valentine (NE) Democrat* called "one of the best games of baseball ever played in Valentine," Fort Niobrara lost, 7–6, in extra innings to a tough team from Gordon, Nebraska. But even though they did not win on the field, the men of the Twenty-fifth earned "praise for the quiet and gentlemanly manner in which they conducted themselves and the skill which they exhibited."[37] The soldiers came back the next day to defeat Gordon, 6–3, and interest in the game was so high that "every available rig in town was brought into service" to transport spectators to the game.[38] Later that month, in a game with a reported attendance in the thousands, the Fort Niobrara squad easily defeated an "ordinarily good" team from Newport.[39]

The African American soldiers appear to have been well-received by the predominately white civilian population of nearby Valentine. Chaplain Steward indicated that Colonel Bowman, the Twenty-fifth's commander, proudly congratulated his men on a report in the *Valentine (NE) Republican* that "[a] more gentlemanly, or better behaved lot of men never garrisoned Fort Niobrara, than they have thus far proven themselves to be, and may it be said to their credit, they show a disposition to create less disturbance and noise than did many white soldiers who have been stationed here."[40] Steward went on to indicate that "[o]ur relations with the town people of Valentine were friendly and we often shared the Christian hospitality of the good Methodist families."[41]

In the autumn of 1903, the Army's Department of the Missouri scheduled large-scale training exercises to be held at Fort Riley, Kansas. At that time, the Department of the

Missouri included military posts in Nebraska, Iowa, Kansas, Missouri, Arkansas, and Oklahoma Territory. The maneuvers were to involve thousands of Regular Army and National Guard troops and resulted in one of the more interesting stories regarding the baseball exploits of the Buffalo Soldiers during their time in the Cornhusker State. Instead of immediately traveling by train to Fort Riley, the men of the Twenty-fifth Infantry embarked on a two-week march of more than 200 miles across central Nebraska before entraining at Norfolk. All along the route of the march, baseball games were scheduled with civilian teams from the towns through which they passed. As Richard Johnson noted, "the fame of our baseball team seemed to have gone ahead of us and we were challenged in most of these towns by the local teams."[42] In spite of all their marching, the soldier's baseball-playing capabilities were evidently little affected, for none of the civilian teams they faced were able to win a single game. A story in the O'Neill newspaper is illustrative of the excitement generated by the arrival of the black soldiers, as well as the typical outcome of a baseball game between the soldiers and the town team:

> The Twenty-fifth [I]nfantry from Ft. Niobrara, mostly colored, pulled into town Monday from the west, remaining here till Tuesday morning, pitching their tents and stacking their arms near the base ball [sic] ground. Things at once took on somewhat of the holiday aspect, as the soldiers were very sociable and proceeded to make the most of a stop in a good town. Flags were run up by many lovers of the stars and stripes and some business places closed in the afternoon when a ball game [sic] was pulled off between the soldiers and local players.... The ball game [sic] also drew a big crowd and, while very much one-sided, created a good deal of interest. The soldiers won on a score of 9 to 1.[43]

The subsequent training maneuvers at Fort Riley lasted for several weeks and were capped off by a series of athletic competitions which included an elimination baseball tournament. Regular Army teams from six forts were scheduled to play for the championship of the Department of the Missouri. According to Sergeant Green, the Twenty-fifth Infantry was not expected to do well because of the long march it had undertaken before the maneuvers, as well as the fact that the Fort Niobrara team was relatively new. Nevertheless, Fort Niobrara triumphed against the team from Fort Sill, Oklahoma Territory. It then defeated its regimental brethren, the favored Twenty-fifth Infantry's second battalion team from Fort Reno, Oklahoma Territory. Having reached the championship game of the tournament, the Fort Niobrara nine discovered that they would face a formidable opponent: their fellow Buffalo Soldiers from Nebraska, the team of the Tenth Cavalry out of Fort Robinson.[44] En route to the championship game, the Tenth Cavalry had vanquished the teams from Fort Riley, Kansas, and Fort Leavenworth, Kansas, with the latter ending up on the wrong end of a 5–0 shutout.[45]

The ensuing championship game was a hotly contested affair which went into extra innings before the Twenty-fifth Infantry finally scored the winning run in the bottom of the 11th inning to defeat the Tenth Cavalry, 4–3.[46] Dalbert Green reported that "play after play of the sensational order were made." He also paid tribute to the defeated Tenth Cavalry ballplayers by commenting that "their excellent playing and gameness will be long remembered by the fortunate ones who witnessed that hard-fought contest."[47] According to Richard Johnson, "the climax would have done credit to a World Series competition, and I am sure it made a lasting impression on the minds of all real fans who saw it."[48]

The *Plaindealer*, the African American newspaper of nearby Topeka, Kansas, proudly proclaimed that the "Tenth Cavalry and Twenty-fifth Infantry are the [f]lowers of the United States Army. At the [m]aneuvers[,] they were the center of attraction."[49] The results of the athletic competitions even attracted attention at the national level with

**The Twenty-fifth Infantry baseball players from Fort Niobrara displaying the pennant that they won by defeating the Tenth Cavalry from Fort Robinson in the Department of the Missouri championship game in 1903.**

the *Evening Star* and the *Colored American* of Washington, D.C., both carrying the following story:

> According to reports received at the War Department, the popular notion of [N]egro inferiority in athletic sports was completely upset by the result of the field games held at Fort Riley during the recent maneuvers. The base ball [*sic*] championship of the [R]egular [A]rmy was won by the nine from the 25th Infantry, with the nine from the 10th Cavalry as next in order. Both of the regiments named are composed of colored men, and they won games from all their white competitors. Representatives of the 25th Infantry won eleven medals in general athletic contests, carrying off all that were offered to the infantry, and in addition won the cup for wall-scaling and the department cup for having the best athletic battalion on the ground. A squad of the 10th Cavalry won the cup in the dangerous game of wrestling on horseback. These athletic sports were participated in by soldiers in all branches of the [R]egular [A]rmy.[50]

After the Twenty-fifth's triumphant return to Fort Niobrara, the *Valentine Democrat* succinctly reported that the foot soldiers had "won a lot of prizes in competition with other regiments while at Ft. Riley and showed some of the boys how to play base ball [*sic*]."[51]

The Twenty-fifth's baseball team did not rest on the laurels it had earned at the Fort Riley tournament. In what was presumably a regular occurrence, a July 1904 game saw the soldiers defeating the local civilian team from Valentine, 11–5, without having to bat in their own half of the final inning.[52] Over the next three years, they continued their successful run against "strong semi-professional [*sic*] teams" which according to Sergeant Green included players who would later go on to play in the major leagues. If Green is to be believed, during the entire time that the Twenty-fifth Infantry was in the Cornhusker State, it lost only three games—once to a team from Deadwood, South Dakota, and twice to the team from Gordon, Nebraska.[53] In July 1906, after nearly four years in Nebraska, the Twenty-fifth left Fort Niobrara to take up its new assignment in Texas. The following spring found it back in the Philippines. In March 1907, the Tenth Cavalry departed Fort Robinson, and it too was sent overseas to the Philippines.

The African American soldiers certainly did not stop playing baseball after their years in Nebraska but rather continued to play the game at a high level wherever they went. The teams representing the Twenty-fifth Infantry were particularly successful on the baseball diamond. In addition to routinely besting their white counterparts in the Army, they also were competitive in games played against civilian teams, including exhibition games against teams from the Pacific Coast League, the highest level below the major leagues. During the years that the Twenty-fifth Infantry was stationed in Hawaii, from 1913 to 1918, the regiment's dominant baseball team became known as the Wreckers. In fact, many of the Twenty-fifth Infantry's players eventually went on to play professionally in the Negro Leagues. They included, among others, such future stars as Wilbur "Bullet" Rogan, Walter "Dobie" Moore, Oscar "Heavy" Johnson, and William "Big C" Johnson. And, in 1998, Rogan was duly honored for his stellar career in the Negro Leagues by being inducted into the National Baseball Hall of Fame.[54]

Despite the U.S. Army's early record of providing more opportunities for African Americans than most other institutions, in a relative sense at least, it ironically would be overtaken by professional baseball. Shortly after Japan's attack on Pearl Harbor in December 1941, a young Jackie Robinson was drafted into the Army and sent to Fort Riley, Kansas, for basic training with a black cavalry unit. He was subsequently commissioned as a second lieutenant and transferred to the 761st Tank Battalion at Fort Hood, Texas. While there, he was court-martialed for events surrounding his refusal to move to the back of a bus serving Fort Hood. Although ultimately acquitted of all charges, he was honorably discharged from the Army shortly thereafter in November 1944.[55] Less than two-and-a-half years later, on April 15, 1947, Robinson dramatically broke major league baseball's longstanding color line when he took up his position on Brooklyn's Ebbets Field for the first time. On July 26, 1948, more than a year after Robinson's historic achievement, President Harry S. Truman issued Executive Order 9981 formally desegregating the United States armed forces. During their time in Nebraska, the soldiers of the Ninth Cavalry, Tenth Cavalry, and Twenty-fifth Infantry, made their own contributions to the long struggle for civil rights and racial equality by performing their soldierly duties with honor and distinction, and yes, by playing baseball and playing it well.

Notes

1. *An Act to [I]ncrease and [F]ix the Military Peace Establishment of the United States, U.S. Statutes at Large* 14 (1863–1867): 332–338.

2. *An Act [M]aking Appropriations for the Support of the Army for the Year [E]nding June [T]hirtieth, [E]ighteen [H]undred and [S]eventy, and for [O]ther Purposes. U.S. Statutes at Large* 15 (1859–1869): 315–319.

3. In the same year, President William McKinley also made John R. Lynch, a black former U.S. Congressman from Mississippi, a Regular Army paymaster with a captain's rank. Bruce A. Ragsdale and Joel D. Treese, *Black Americans in Congress, 1870–1989* (Washington, D.C.: Government Printing Office, 1990), 85.

4. See Frank N. Schubert, *Black Valor: Buffalo Soldiers and the Medal of Honor, 1870–1898* (Wilmington, Delaware: Scholarly Resources, 1997).

5. John Thorn, "Abner Cartwright," *Nine: A Journal of Baseball History and Culture* 18, no. 1 (Fall 2009): 127.
6. The Ninth Cavalry took part in the Army's last major action of the Indian Wars during the Ghost Dance movement, which tragically ended with the massacre at Wounded Knee, South Dakota, on December 29, 1890.
7. See Harry H. Anderson, "The Benteen Base Ball Club: Sports Enthusiasts of the Seventh Cavalry," *Montana: the Magazine of Western History* 20 (Summer 1970): 82–87.
8. *Annual Report of the Secretary of War for the Year 1885* (Washington, D.C.: Government Printing Office, 1885), I: 151.
9. Don Rickey, *Forty Miles a Day on Beans and Hay: The Enlisted Soldier Fighting the Indian Wars* (Norman: University of Oklahoma Press, 1963), 187.
10. Charles L. Kenner, *Buffalo Soldiers and Officers of the Ninth Cavalry, 1867–1898: Black & White Together* (Norman: University of Oklahoma Press, 1999), 18, citing Reynolds J. Burt, "Memories," manuscript, Rickey Collection, U.S. Army Military History Institute, Carlisle, Pennsylvania.
11. *Ibid.*
12. "The Robinsonians and Magic City's Play a 'Tie Game,'" *Cleveland Gazette*, June 26, 1886.
13. "A Ball Game a Failure," *Cleveland Gazette*, July 31, 1886.
14. "Crawford's Celebration," *Crawford (NE) Tribune*, July 2, 1897.
15. "Will Meet at Fort Robinson," *Omaha Daily Bee*, June 6, 1896.
16. "On the Diamond," *Hemingford (NE) Herald*, May 29, 1896.
17. *Hemingford (NE) Herald*, July 17, 1896.
18. *Hemingford (NE) Herald*, July 24, 1896.
19. *Hemingford (NE) Herald*, July 31, 1896.
20. "Fort Niobrara," *Valentine (NE) Democrat*, August 20, 1896.
21. "Twelfth Infantry vs. Ninth Cavalry," *Valentine (NE) Democrat*, June 17, 1897.
22. Edward L.N. Glass, *The History of the Tenth Cavalry, 1866–1921* (Tucson, Arizona: Acme Printing, 1921), 43.
23. Thomas J. Clement, "Athletics in the American Army," *The Colored American Magazine* 8 (January 1905): 21, 25.
24. *Ibid.*, 25.
25. Glass, 44–45.
26. Clement, 25.
27. *Alliance (NE) Herald*, July 11, 1902.
28. Albert S. Lowe, "Camp Life of the Tenth U.S. Cavalry," *The Colored American Magazine* 7 (March 1904): 205.
29. Clement, 25.
30. "Soldiers' Field Day Contests," *Omaha Daily Bee*, July 29, 1903.
31. Richard Johnson, "My Life in the U.S. Army, 1899–1922," unpublished manuscript in the Richard Johnson Papers, U.S. Army Military History Institute, Carlisle, Pennsylvania, 73.
32. Dalbert P. Green, "History of the 25th Infantry Baseball Teams, 1894 to 1914," in *History of the Twenty-fifth United States Infantry, 1869–1926* by John H. Nankivell ([Denver: The Smith-Brooks Printing Company, 1927]; repr. *Buffalo Soldier Regiment: History of the Twenty-fifth United States Infantry, 1869–1926*, Lincoln: University of Nebraska Press, 2001), 163.
33. Merrill J. Mattes, *Indians, Infants and Infantry: Andrew and Elizabeth Burt on the Frontier* (Denver: The Old West Publishing Company, 1960), 3.
34. Green, 164.
35. *Ibid.*, 167.
36. T.G. Steward, *Fifty Years in the Gospel Ministry from 1864 to 1914* (Philadelphia: A.M.E. Book Concern, [1921]), 354.
37. "Additional Local," *Valentine (NE) Democrat*, September 11, 1902.
38. *Ibid.*
39. "Talk of the Town," *Valentine (NE) Democrat*, October 2, 1902.
40. Steward, 354.
41. *Ibid.*, 356.
42. Johnson, 75.
43. "2[5]th Infantry on March," *(O'Neill, NE) Frontier*, October, 8, 1903.
44. Green, 167–168.
45. Clement, 25.
46. Johnson, 76, and "The Soldiers at Ft. Riley," *(Topeka) Plaindealer*, October 30, 1903. Alternately, Dalbert Green remembered the game as being decided in the 12th inning by a score of 3-2. Green, 168.
47. Green, 168.
48. Johnson, 76.
49. "The Soldiers at Ft. Riley."

50. "Colored Boys on Top," (*Washington, D.C.*) *Evening Star*, November 16, 1903, and "Colored Troops Fought Nobly," (*Washington, D.C.*) *Colored American*, November 28, 1903. The version cited in this chapter comes from the *Evening Star*, whose composition of the report varies slightly in style from the version found in the *Colored American*.

51. "Talk of the Town," *Valentine (NE) Democrat*, November 5, 1903.

52. "Talk of the Town," *Valentine (NE) Democrat*, July 14, 1904.

53. Green, 168.

54. See William F. McNeil, "25th Infantry Regiment Baseball Team," in *Black Baseball Out of Season: Pay for Play Outside of the Negro Leagues* by William F. McNeil (Jefferson, North Carolina: McFarland & Company, Inc., Publishers, 2007), 52–61, and Jerry Malloy, "The 25th Infantry Regiment Takes the Field," *The National Pastime* 15 (1995): 59–64.

55. For the details of Robinson's time in the military, see Jackie Robinson, *I Never Had It Made: An Autobiography* (Hopewell, New Jersey: Ecco Press, 1995), 12–23.

# 5

# Shadow Ball in the River City
## *The Omaha Federals, Tigers and Rockets*

### Angelo J. Louisa

Although the city of Omaha did not have any major league–caliber African American baseball clubs, it did have various lesser ones that deserve recognition, three of which particularly stand out: the Federals, the Tigers, and the Rockets. Unfortunately for baseball historians, though, the remaining information about these teams is so sketchy that a complete picture may never be painted. James Riley, the author of *The Biographical Encyclopedia of the Negro Baseball Leagues*, has written that the topic of Negro League statistics is a miasmic quagmire.[1] However, anyone who has done any kind of research on black baseball teams knows that Riley's label fits the study of black baseball history as a whole.

Part of the problem is that white or mainstream newspapers did not cover black baseball teams on a day-to-day basis, as they usually did with white major and minor league teams. But another part of the problem stems from the lack of coverage by African American newspapers. To quote baseball historian Jules Tygiel:

> Black newspapers could not afford to send writers to accompany clubs on the road and depended heavily on reports submitted by the teams. This source proved highly unreliable, and the traveling squads often failed to call in or refused to reveal losses. In addition, since many of the black weeklies appeared on Saturday, they tended to focus on previews of the following day's contests, rather than results of the previous week, making it difficult for fans to follow a team with any consistency.[2]

And the final part of the problem is that when box scores can be found, oftentimes only the last names of the players are used, creating quite a challenge to identify who was who.

But having said all that, there are some people who are daring enough or foolish enough to explore miasmic quagmires. Thus, the first of the selected Omaha clubs is the 1922 Federals, the initial reference to which is found in an article published in the April 7, 1922, issue of the *Omaha World-Herald*:

> Guy Jackson and John Love [the men in charge of the Federals] of Kansas City are in the city [Omaha] and this morning closed with Rhinie Mohr, the local park's [Western League Park's] concession man, who is acting for [m]agnates [Michael J. "Mike"] Finn and [J. Feagin "Barney"] Burch [the owners of Omaha's white minor league club], to bring their great colored ball team—the former famous Monarchs—to Omaha for the summer. They will have their headquarters here and will play at Rourke [P]ark [another name for Western League Park[3]] on all Saturdays, Sundays[,] and holidays during the absence on the road of the Burch Rods [the name or nickname of Omaha's white minor league club]. They will be called the Omaha Federals and will also fill open dates in the State [L]eague cities [the then all-white Nebraska State League] throughout the summer.... [A]nd they will open the season at the Omaha park with [former major leaguer] Pat Ragan's Waterloo, [Iowa], team one week from Sunday, April 16.[4]

Now, a lot can be gleaned from that article: who was running the Federals, where the team would have its headquarters, where it would play its games, on what date it would start its season, and who its first opponent would be. But there is one piece of incorrect or misleading information found among the details: that Jackson and Love were bringing "their great colored ball team—the former famous Monarchs—to Omaha." Well, wrong. This was not the 1922 Kansas City Monarch team moving to Omaha. What the Federals consisted of was a combination of several former Monarchs; a few future Monarchs, including the young and eventually great second baseman Newt Allen, who would play for both the Federals and the Monarchs that season; player-manager Guy Jackson, a third baseman, second baseman, and shortstop who had been a member of various black teams between 1909 and 1915[5]; and an unknown group of African American players, some of whom would never see action in a Monarch uniform or, for that matter, in a uniform of any other major league–caliber black club (see Table 1).

As for their origins, the Federals may have been one of the ideas of J.L. Wilkinson, the white owner of the Kansas City Monarchs and the All Nations club.[6] Beginning in the early 1920s, due to roster limits, Wilkinson would put young Monarchs who needed more playing time and veterans who were slowing down on the All Nations team or on certain independent black teams. These teams were commonly referred to as semiprofessional clubs because they were not members of one of the major league–caliber black leagues, even though they were really minor league–caliber professional clubs. Robert Gilkerson's Union Giants were one such club. Winfield Welch's Acme Giants of Shreveport, Louisiana, were another.[7] And it appears that the Omaha Federals served the same purpose. The primary source of income during the baseball season for the men who comprised these teams was playing baseball, but not at a major league–caliber level, as opposed to individuals who were working for a company as their primary source of income and making extra money by playing baseball for that company after their work hours.

This is not to say that there was a minor league system in place for the Negro Leagues because such a formal organization never existed. What Wilkinson was doing was an unofficial way of hanging on to surplus players, who he then might "call up" to the Monarchs in the future,[8] and Newt Allen, who would star for the Monarchs for many years, is a prime example of this practice.

The son of a laborer and a laundress, Newton Henry Allen was born in Austin,

J.L. Wilkinson, the owner of the Kansas City Monarchs and the All Nations club, may have been the visionary behind the creation of the Omaha Federals (National Baseball Hall of Fame Library).

Texas—though he told John Holway in 1971 that it was Kansas City[9]—sometime between 1900 and 1903. When talking with Holway, Allen said that his year of birth was 1902, a year that the information on his World War II draft card and the United States Social Security Death Index agrees with. But on ship passenger lists in 1934, his birth date is May 19, 1903, while on one such list in 1925, his year of birth is given as 1902, but his age printed next to it implies 1903, and the 1910 United States Federal Census records state that he was nine on April 21 of that year, indicating that he was born in 1900. Layton Revel and Luis Muñoz of the Center for Negro League Baseball Research believe 1902 is correct, but certain other sources, including some standard reference works, cite the year as 1901. And baseball historian Merl Kleinknecht and whoever compiled Allen's information for Baseball-Reference.com cast their votes for 1903.[10] A miasmic quagmire indeed.

However, no matter when Allen was born, it appears that he moved with his family to Kansas City, Missouri, after his father's death in 1910 and grew up in the same neighborhood as future Negro Leaguers Reuben "Rube" Currie or Curry and Frank Duncan, Jr.[11] It was there that Allen became interested in baseball, playing the sport with his friends, helping to organize and being a member of a sandlot team named the Kansas City Tigers,[12] and assisting and working out with the Kansas City Monarchs. As Allen recalled in 1971:

> Baseball was my whole life.... Frank Duncan and I were boys together on the Paseo at 17th Street.... Another fellow with us was Rube Currie.... He and Frank Duncan lived almost next door to one another. We all used to play sandlot ball in school. We'd put in twenty cents apiece and the winner take the pot.
> Later I used to go out and practice with the Monarchs, and when the ball game [sic] was over, I'd pull the canvas across the ball field. That's the way I would get two or three balls from the groundskeeper—that's how we got our balls to play with.[13]

While Allen played for the Tigers, the Monarch brain trust kept an eye on him and eventually invited him to try out for a place on their club. It would be Allen's ticket to performing on the biggest baseball stage that blacks could perform on in the '20s and '30s, but Allen remembered that the process did not produce immediate results:

> They'd been watching me, and they asked me to come try out with them. I went out twice, but at that time the manager didn't think I could make it. So I went to a semipro club in Omaha [the Federals], and we had a pretty good ball club. They put us in the Nebraska State League [he probably means the Western League of Colored Baseball Clubs], and when we started winning, the Monarchs began to watch me again. When they came through and played us an exhibition, I showed up good, and I left and went with them.[14]

As can be seen from Allen's story, the elderly second sacker was both a product of his times and not completely accurate in his recollections. He referred to the Federals as "a semipro club," which was what many people in the 1920s would have labeled it, and he said that the Omaha team was "put ... in the Nebraska State League," an obvious mistake because the 1922 Nebraska State League was a group of six all-white franchises, none of which were located in Omaha.[15]

Once Allen had won a spot on the Monarch roster in late 1922, he made sure that he kept it, serving the famous Kansas City club for all or part of 23 seasons. He also spent a season or less with the St. Louis Stars, Homestead Grays, Detroit Wolves, Columbus Blue Birds, Chicago American Giants, and Indianapolis Clowns. And during that long and distinguished career, he played on 10 pennant winners, two World Series champions, and the West squad in four East-West All-Star Games while developing a reputation as a talented and fierce competitor. Offensively, he was a line drive hitter and an excellent bunter with good bat control who displayed great speed, an aggressive nature, and baseball smarts when running the bases. Defensively, he had quick hands, exceptional range, and a strong, accurate throwing arm and was outstanding at turning the double play. In fact, Allen made much more of a name for himself with his glove and his arm than he did with his bat. As Phil Dixon wrote about him in 1988:

> [Allen] rates with Elwood "Bingo" DeMoss and Frank Warfield as the greatest [k]eystone players in baseball history.
>
> [He] picked up several tricks from DeMoss, one of which was throwing to first without looking at the base. Allen was an exclusive fielder of the first order. He had soft hands and could handle any kind of throw and was an excellent tager [sic]. On the pivot, his was the best and his low beeline throws kept runners from taking him out on double plays.
>
> Allen had a unique throwing arm in that he could throw a ball over 400 feet.
>
> As fellow Monarch..., Chet Brewer stated, "Many men could throw harder than Newt but few could throw further."[16]

Added to Dixon's glowing assessment and Brewer's compliment, Negro Leaguers Jesse Williams, John "Buck" O'Neil, and Ray Dandridge, as well as J.L. Wilkinson himself and Wilkinson's son, Richard, sung Allen's praises. Williams said that "Allen looked better missing a ball than most people looked catching it. And I never saw him make a bad throw to first."[17] O'Neil commented that "Newt had Hall of Fame credentials. He was the best I have ever seen, making the double play,"[18] whereas Dandridge described seeing "Allen field the ball with his left hand, transfer it to his right hand as he went across second base, and backhand it to the shortstop to start a double play."[19] The Wilkinsons went further with J.L. noting, "In his prime, [Allen] never had an equal,"[20] and Richard stating, "Newt Allen could play much better infield than Jackie [Robinson]...."[21] Moreover, Allen's arm strength served him well in making the transition to shortstop, third base, and the outfield when he was asked to do so.

For his stellar play, Allen was named to the 1952 *Pittsburgh Courier's* All-Time African American All-Star second team as a utility man[22] and was chosen by a panel put together by James Riley in the early 1980s as the third best second baseman of all time in a close race with the versatile Martin Dihigo, Bingo DeMoss, Sammy T. Hughes, and Jim Gilliam. Allen received 11 first-place votes to Dihigo's 15, DeMoss' 14, and 10 each for Hughes and Gilliam.[23]

But Allen had a dark side, too. As he admitted to John

Newt Allen, pictured here during his career with the Kansas City Monarchs (1922-1944), was the most famous player to wear an Omaha Federal uniform (National Baseball Hall of Fame Library).

Holway, "A lot of times I had a nasty feeling within myself, not against a ballplayer. I was pretty bad playing ball, yes, I was pretty bad—run over a man, throw at him."[24] And that nasty feeling would show itself in different ways. For example, in retaliating against Dave Malarcher for slicing his shin with a high slide, Allen not only waited three years to drill him in the forehead with a throw—acceptable baseball etiquette for an infielder teaching a runner to keep his spikes down when sliding—but he also later purposely hit Malarcher in the back of the head with a throw when Malarcher was attempting to move from first to third on a single—a totally uncalled for act.[25] Or his harassment of slow-talking catcher Frazier Robinson had a deliberately cruel twist to it. In Robinson's words:

> While most of my teammates on the 1940 Monarchs welcomed me to the ballclub [sic], it could be pretty rough on a new guy. Newt Allen … was the one that did all the dirty work. He was kind of snobbish to begin with, and then he'd pull a whole lot of jokes or tricks on you that would make you feel not welcome, make you want to go home. A young ballplayer come up there—he would make life hell for them….
> 
> He did little things like sneak into your room while you'd be sleeping and put soap in your eyes and slip out. Then he'd be laughing about it the next day and say, "[I] put the soap in your eyes so you'd be sharp and see good." … He'd do anything to try to upset you…. And if you did something wrong, you could count on Allen to rub it in and put you in the doghouse.[26]

It is not known if Allen's dark side surfaced during the time that he was with the Federals or if it was a consequence of the way he himself had been treated when he began playing ball for the Monarchs, but with or without his dark side, Allen was the most famous player to wear a Federal uniform (see Table 1).

Turning to who the Federals' opponents were, a search of the Omaha newspapers and those of select other towns shows as of November 1, 2019, 27 scheduled games and the results for 20 of them, of which Omaha won nine, lost seven, tied one, and experienced three cancelations. Also, in reporting on a game that the Federals had played on July 22, 1922, against Tekamah, Nebraska, an unknown sportswriter for the *Omaha World-Herald* mentioned that this was the third meeting of the two teams, with Tekamah winning twice. And since it is known that Tekamah lost to the Federals on July 8 and defeated them on July 22, this means that the Omahans suffered at least one more loss, bringing their totals to 28 scheduled games, 21 results found, and an overall record of 9–8–1, with three cancelations (see Table 2).

As with other African American teams, the Federals would play anyone anytime. In fact, in the June 1, 1922, issue of the *Omaha Daily Bee*, Guy Jackson advertised for "games with fast teams in Nebraska and Iowa."[27] But because of the racial climate of 1922, most of the Federals' games were against local black semipro or white semipro or amateur clubs, with at least two being against the All Nations (see Table 2).

However, in addition to having an independent schedule, the Federals joined the Western League of Colored Baseball Clubs in June of 1922 and played their first league game on the 10th of that month.[28] Consisting of franchises in Coffeyville, Independence (Kansas), Kansas City (Kansas), Oklahoma City, St. Joseph (Missouri), Topeka, Tulsa, and Wichita, as well as Omaha,[29] the Colored Western League (CWL), as it was commonly called, appears to have been established as the black equivalent of the white Western League, which had franchises in five of the previously mentioned cities.[30] The games were to be played on Saturdays, Sundays, and possibly Fridays, with white Western League parks to be used in the cities that had them, and scheduled so that they would not conflict with those of the white Western League.[31]

Because of a lack of CWL records, the exact number of league games that the Federals played is not known, but what is known is that they won at least four of them (see Table 2) and that they did not capture the league championship, something that the Wichita club did.[32] For that matter, Omaha may have dropped out of the CWL after its first four games.[33]

Whatever Omaha's league record was, the CWL vanished after the '22 season, and with the exception of a notice found in the April 19, 1923, issue of the *Omaha World-Herald* stating that "The Omaha Federal colored nine has reorganized and wants out of town games," so did the Federals.[34] Thus, apparently the reorganization led to nothing, and today, most of the Federal players are forgotten men—even by historians who write about black baseball.

The other two black Omaha franchises that can arguably be labeled minor league–caliber professional clubs were both touring units—independent squads that traveled from place to place. Like the Federals, these clubs were called semiprofessional at the time that they played, but they were in fact minor league–caliber professional clubs and were comprised of one or more players who had performed on major league–caliber black teams and a number of younger players hoping to get a chance to play on a major league–caliber black team. But unlike the Federals, neither of these clubs was part of a league.

The first of these two was the 1935–1936 Tigers. And the Tigers were the brainchild of Christopher Columbus Curry, better known as C.C. Curry, a black butcher and laborer who had been employed by the Cudahy Packing Company since at least 1925 and who lived with his wife, Callie, in North Omaha during those years.[35] Curry was born in the Lone Star State on July 4, 1882, and had worked as a day laborer in Sherman, Texas, a butcher, a meat handler, and a laborer doing odd jobs in Gainesville, Texas, a butcher in Sapulpa, Oklahoma, and a retail grocer and a meat handler in Tulsa, Oklahoma.[36] In the last residence, he also was the Tulsa baseball team's representative for the Colored Western League, prior to moving to the River City sometime before 1925.[37] Then, once in Omaha, he served as the manager of the Cudahy Rex, an African American amateur club, in 1926 and either as its manager or co-manager, depending on the source, in 1928 and led it to capturing the Omaha Colored Baseball League pennant both seasons.[38] In 1927, he founded his first version of the Tigers, a black semipro team that played an independent schedule and then defeated the Union Pacific Gold Coast Limited, the 1927 Omaha Colored Baseball League champions, 13–4, to claim the title of the city's best African American baseball team.[39] These successes were followed in 1929 by his proposing a new team for the Colored Baseball League—a team that did not materialize—and his forming a black all-star team that played regional games.[40]

Still working for the Cudahy plant but wanting to field an African American professional team in Omaha, Curry established his second version of the Tigers by February 12, 1935, sharing the ownership with his wife and Homer "Goose" Curry, probably one of C.C.'s relatives.[41]

C.C. held the position of president, Callie was the treasurer, while Goose, primarily an outfielder-pitcher on various major league–caliber black clubs and a few minor league–caliber ones from 1928 through 1955, was "the heavy stockholder" and served as the player-manager for the '35 season.[42] However, the next year, Goose left to resume his major league–caliber career and was replaced by Charles "Suitcase" or "Corporal" Mason. Mason was a large man—6'2" and very wide, with size 14 feet—who had been a power-hitting outfielder and occasional pitcher for six major league–caliber black clubs, including the Atlantic City Bacharach Giants and the Homestead Grays. But by the time he started playing for the Tigers, he had moved himself to first base for the most part, though sometimes he still played the outfield or pitched.[43]

Under Goose Curry's leadership, the Tigers trained in Clarksdale, Mississippi, and then played exhibition games against teams in Mississippi, Louisiana, Texas, Missouri, and Illinois before arriving in Omaha to begin their regular-season games, which were all scheduled at Iowa, Nebraska, or Minnesota parks.[44] Under Mason, the Tigers trained in Memphis and then traveled to Omaha after playing some exhibition games in the South.[45] From the River City, Mason's men journeyed to compete against teams in the Midwest and Northwest, going as far east as Albion, Michigan, as far west as the Pacific Coast, as far north as Bonners Ferry, Idaho, and, based on scheduled games, as far south as Denver, Colorado (see Table 4). This transformation from a regional team to a touring unit began on May 24 with a game against Albion and continued with another change that took place later that month when someone from Omaha called the officials in charge of a game that the Tigers had scheduled with the Tekamah town team to tell them that the black squad had folded.[46] However, one day earlier, an article in the *Great Falls (MT) Tribune* reported that the Tigers, like the phoenix rising from its ashes, would be playing the Great Falls nine on June 6 as the Omaha Monarchs.[47] No reason for either change was given, but the obvious explanation would be to make more money.

Homer Curry (third from the left), the player-manager of the 1935 Omaha Tigers, was a former and future member of various major league–caliber clubs, including the Philadelphia Stars, with whom he performed from 1942 through 1947 (National Baseball Hall of Fame Library).

As for the Tiger records, the newspapers examined for this essay show that the 1935 team scheduled at least 26 exhibitions, winning six of them, losing four, and cancelling one, with another one tentatively planned (see Table 3). In comparison, during the regular season, a minimum of 35 games were scheduled, including two cancellations, with the Tigers going 13–12–1 and no scores being found for the remaining seven (see Table 3). Two more games may have been scheduled, but no scores were found for them either (see Table 3).

The 1936 season was different yet similar. Here, at least five exhibition games were scheduled, with the Tigers winning one, losing two, and two scores not being found (see Table 4). The regular season consisted of 52 known scheduled games, of which 14 were won, 13 were lost, five were either cancelled or apparently rained out, and the outcome of 20 have not been unearthed for this essay (see Table 4). One other game was postponed and may not have been played (see Table 4).

In addition, an indefinite number of games were played between June 1 and June 13, with the Monarchs allegedly winning all of them, when in reality they lost at least two (see Table 4). And finally, an article in the June 24, 1936, issue of the *Salt Lake (City, UT) Tribune* reported that the team had played 65 games through June 23 and emerged victorious 62 times, though the author of that article may have been singing the praises of the wrong Monarch club (see Table 4).

But if nearly 40 percent of the results were not available, an impressive array of statistics were. An article in the June 12, 1936, issue of the *Spokane Daily Chronicle* reported that, to date, the Monarchs had hit 107 doubles, 59 triples, and 74 home runs in 41 games, while at the same time, their pitching staff had struck out 378 and walked only 26 and their defense had turned 63 double plays, 16 on throws from the outfield.[48] As for individuals, the trio of Johnson in left, Wall in center, and Dufos in right were hitting .358 and had committed just one error as a unit.[49]

Now, the Tigers are best remembered—when they are remembered at all—for two things:

First, for their performance in the 1935 Nebraska Semipro Baseball Tournament (NSBT), a double-elimination tournament for the best teams in Nebraska that were considered semiprofessional at that time, with the winner getting to advance to the National Semipro Baseball Tournament in Wichita, Kansas. Well, the Tigers came very close to winning the NSBT. They defeated teams from Kearney (the state runner-up), Bellwood, and Dannebrog and twice beat the Iowa-Nebraska Powers of Lincoln, but they could not get past the Ford V-8s of Omaha and had to settle for third place and a payout of the grand sum of $57.07.[50] Still, they showed that an all–African American team could hold its own with many of the best white teams in the state. And it is interesting to note that the Ford V-8s, who had beaten the Tigers twice—the second time by only one run—finished fourth out of 32 teams in the national tournament, so there was no shame in losing to them.

And second, the Tigers are known as the team that gave Lorenzo "Piper" Davis his professional baseball start in 1936. Born in Piper, Alabama, in 1917, the son of John West Davis (1882–1970), a coal miner, and his wife, Georgia Cox (1902–1994), Davis was a football, basketball, and baseball star in high school and had received a partial basketball scholarship to Alabama State College but dropped out after one semester because his family would have had a difficult time providing him with future tuition money.[51] From there, he tried his hand at coal mining, but this experience lasted about as long as his college career. In Davis' words:

> I worked for about three or four months, and then we had a series of accidents that was responsible for me getting out of the mines and into baseball. I guess you might say I struck out as a miner.
> We had some loose coal where the mules go down in the mines, and as one miner went down, he passed the mule and pushed him over and hit that bank of loose rock and coal and it covered him up. As soon as that mule touched it, he was gone. That was strike one.
> The next incident happened when a rock had fallen on the cable and they had a guy following the line trying to find the end of it. Somebody accidently turned the juice on and when he put his hand on that raw spot, it burned him up. I remember it distinctly. That was strike two.
> Then we had a rock with a crack in it and it grumbled and this fellow looked to see what happened and it caved in and broke his leg. And that was the third one. That was strike three. And I was out—out of the mines![52]

Fortunately for Davis, though, it was around this time that Suitcase Mason and his '36 Omaha Tigers showed up in Piper to play an exhibition game against the First Nine, Piper's adult town team of which Davis was a member.[53] Mason liked what he saw in the teenage Lorenzo and offered Davis an invitation to try out for a position on the Tigers during spring training in Memphis, something Davis eagerly accepted.

Once in Memphis, the new recruit became acquainted with the realities of playing minor league–caliber ball[54]:

1. He would receive $91 a month if he made the team, but each player had to make the team each day or else he was cut.
2. The bottom line was the bottom line. The top priority of the team was to earn as much money as it could, so Davis would receive coaching only if he was perceived as being able to help the team financially through his play on the field.

But Davis had two things working in his favor. First, while on his high school baseball team, he taught himself how to play a variety of positions, something that increased his value. And second, "the [Tigers' starting] shortstop got so drunk that he came down with alcohol poisoning" in Memphis and, four days after arriving in Omaha and being sent to a hospital, he died, which forced Mason to thrust the 18-year-old Davis—he would turn 19 that July 3—into the breach.[55]

Playing for the Tigers also had its positives and negatives, and Davis' recollections of those days paints a vivid picture of life on a black touring baseball club. On the plus side, Davis visited a number of midwestern and western states, which proved to be an education in and of itself, competed against both black and white teams, which boosted his confidence, and was paid for his services. But as Davis recalled, "[There was] [t]oo much traveling and not enough money.... Besides, they [presumably C.C. Curry and Mason] didn't finish paying us what little we were supposed to get. We just traveled, traveled."[56] And while traveling, Davis got a taste of the underbelly of life on the road: racial slurs, usually having to sleep on the Tigers'/Monarchs' bus because many hotels would not admit blacks, and not knowing where or when he would be eating his next meal.[57]

After his adventures and misadventures with the Omaha club, Davis returned to Alabama, went to Fairfield, got a job with Tennessee Coal and Iron or Stockham Pipe and Fittings Company (the original name of Stockham Valves and Fittings), depending on the source, and played for the company's team in the Birmingham Industrial League in 1937.[58] This was followed by spending the 1938 season with the Washington Browns, an African American club located in Yakima and then returning again to the Birmingham area to work for the American Cast Iron Pipe Company (ACIPCO) and to play for its semipro baseball club in the Industrial League from 1939 through early 1943.[59] It was either while performing at second base for the company's best team—the 1942 edition—or while moonlighting for the Birmingham Black Barons on weekends that Davis was noticed by Winfield Welch, then the Black Barons' manager, and was offered $500 a month to join the team during the latter part of the '42 season.[60] Although he agreed to those terms, he did not completely sever his ties with ACIPCO until into the next season. And the rest is history.

Using his versatility on the diamond to his advantage, with his best positions being second base, first base, which was his favorite, and shortstop, Davis went on to star for the Barons and helped to lead them to Negro American League (NAL) pennants in 1943, 1944, and 1948, the last one as the club's player-manager.[61] While in a Baron uniform, he also played in seven East-West All-Star Games, pounding out eight hits in 26 at bats, scoring five runs, and driving in four,[62] but just as important, he served as the mentor for the young Willie Mays. It was in this latter capacity that Davis taught the future superstar how to hit a curveball by changing his batting stance—Davis himself was an excellent curveball hitter—how to charge a groundball that was hit into the outfield and throw it on one hop to the plate, and how to discourage pitchers from throwing at him by stealing bases if he was struck.[63] In fact, Mays would later say, "In so many ways[,] Piper was the most important person in my early baseball years."[64]

After his Negro League days, Davis became the first African American signed by the Boston Red Sox organization, and even though he was never called up to the majors, he played nine seasons of minor league ball for various teams in Organized Baseball.[65]

Another version of the Omaha Monarchs would come on the scene in 1938, but it evolved into the Omaha Black Panthers the following year, with Suitcase Mason as its manager, before vanishing after one season.[66] Then, the moniker Tigers or Monarchs was used by various Omaha baseball, softball, basketball,

Lorenzo "Piper" Davis, who was only 18 years old when he became the starting shortstop for the 1936 Omaha Tigers/Monarchs, rose to become the player-manager of the pennant-winning 1948 Birmingham Black Barons (National Baseball Hall of Fame Library).

soccer, and roller hockey teams after 1938, but none of them should be confused with C.C. Curry's club of the mid–1930s.

The final member of the minor league–caliber trio was the Omaha Rockets. And the Rockets operated from 1947 through early August of 1950 and were owned and managed by an African American named Will Calhoun. A native of Texas, Calhoun arrived in Omaha shortly before World War II and became the proprietor of a hotel in North Omaha that provided a place to stay for touring black athletes.[67] In 2010, Ernest "Schoolboy" Johnson, a pitcher and outfielder for the Kansas City Monarchs from 1949 through 1953 and for six seasons in the minor leagues of Organized Baseball, told the author of this essay that he remembered playing against the Rockets and, in particular, encountering Will Calhoun. However, what he recalled best about Calhoun was not his business acumen or his managerial skills but rather the amount of food the man could eat, which consisted of large and multiple portions of a variety of items.[68] And interestingly, in 1948 Calhoun was hospitalized for some undisclosed ailment, which may or may not have been caused by his prodigious appetite.[69]

Leaving Calhoun's eating habits aside, the Rockets were similar to the Federals in that they served as a "farm team" for the Kansas City Monarchs and similar to both the Federals and the Tigers in several ways:

First, they, too, would play anyone anytime. Newspaper articles show that they scheduled games to be held in Colorado, Iowa, Kansas, Minnesota, Missouri, North Dakota, South Dakota, Wisconsin, Wyoming, and even as far north as Canada, as well as a number of towns in Nebraska (see tables 7–10). Also, Leo Adam Biga reports that the Rockets saw action in the Pacific Northwest.[70]

Second, they were capable of playing competitive ball. For example, according to an article in the August 21, 1947, issue of the *Council Bluffs (IA) Nonpareil*, they had gone 51–29 in their previous 80 games, whereas an article in the September 26, 1947, issue of the *Nonpareil* claims they played approximately 70 games and had a winning percentage of over .650.[71] Or based strictly on games found for this essay, they were 30–24–1 in 1947, 22–17 in 1948, and 20–16 in 1949 for a total record of 72–57–1. Unfortunately for baseball historians, only 10 results were discovered for 1950 and none for 85 games that were scheduled from 1947 through 1949 (see tables 7–10), again lending support to Tygiel's words.

And finally, like the Federals and the Tigers, the Rockets had a standout player who got his professional start in Omaha and for whom they are best remembered. As seen earlier in this essay, for the Federals, it was Newt Allen, and for the Tigers, it was Piper Davis. Well, for the Rockets, it was Wilker Harrison Thelbert "Mickey" Stubblefield, who was a member of their 1947 team. The records of Stubblefield's life have more than their share of discrepancies, but a careful comparison of the best of these writings yields a fascinating picture of a man known to some people as "Little Satch."

Born in Mayfield, Kentucky, on February 26, 1926, Stubblefield is said by most sources to have been named Wilker Harrison Thelbert. Wilker was his mother Mary's family name, while Harrison was his father's first name. However, his birth certificate shows his name to be Thelbert W. Stubblefield, and in the 1930 federal census records, he is listed as Thelbert. The sixth of seven children, the future baseball star was orphaned before the age of 12, his mother having died when he was six and his father, a veteran of World War I who had been a highway laborer and a farmer, passing away when he was 11. After his mother's death, Wilker or Thelbert and his younger sister Ollie Bee lived with their father on land that Harrison farmed near Paducah, Kentucky. Then, when Harrison died, they probably moved in with their older siblings, though Stubblefield himself would later say that he had "a lot of homes." But wherever he resided, it was in 1937 that he became a batboy for Mayfield's Kentucky-Illinois-Tennessee League—the so-called KITTY League—team, the Clothiers, and it was during his early teen years that he got his first nickname, "Mickey." This sobriquet came about because the hand-me-down shoes that Stubblefield wore were too big for his feet and made him look like the popular cartoon character, Mickey Mouse.[72]

According to Mickey's daughter Mary Arvin, Stubblefield graduated from Dunbar High School in Mayfield and subsequently attended a trade school in Paducah to become a chef.[73] Apparently nothing more came of this cooking venture as the future Rocket served for two and a half years in the Navy during World War II but was not sent overseas.[74] Then, after being honorably discharged in 1946, he embarked on his baseball career, or as Stubblefield tells the story:

> I got out of the Navy in 1946 and I fooled around here [Mayfield] with the local ballclub [sic] [probably the Blackhawks, Mayfield's African American semipro club]. In 1947, a friend of mine was playing in Nebraska and he called me and asked me did I want to play ball and I told him yes. He said that they would send me money for a ticket, so I got the money and I went to Omaha.... I played with a team called the Omaha Rockets, owned by a black guy [Will Calhoun].[75]

Stubblefield continued that, while with the Rockets, he saw action at three or four positions, with his primary one being shortstop and his secondary one that of pitcher.[76] However, he made a name for himself with the Kansas City Monarchs in 1948 and 1949 at the latter position, though again controversy enters the picture. Some sources say that Stubblefield was a member of the Monarchs in only 1948, and at least one source does not mention him ever having performed for the famous Kansas City club.[77] But a thorough search of newspaper articles proves that Stubblefield was correct when he told Brent Kelley:

> In 1948, I went to Kansas City with the Monarchs. I spent two years there. In the book [an unspecified reference work, possibly James Riley's *The Biographical Encyclopedia of Negro Baseball Leagues*], they only have a year, but it's two years.[78]

Stubblefield also told Kelley, "I was maybe 15–10 for the first year and maybe 12–6 for the next year, or something like that," of which the first win total was later reported to have been 20—records that no standard reference work contains.[79] The problem here, though, stems from how Stubblefield was used by the Monarchs. From the newspaper accounts that were found for this essay, Stubblefield mostly pitched in games against semipro and amateur teams, not Negro American League teams, and therefore his statistics are even more hidden than they would have been if he had opposed NAL competition. Statistics are difficult enough to discover for contests between major league–caliber black teams, but they are extremely difficult, if not impossible, to discover for contests between a major league–caliber black team and teams such as the Amarillo Colts, the Roseburg Chiefs, and Harolds Club. Of course, this is not to say that Stubblefield never saw action in NAL contests. According to author-artist Gary Cieradkowski, "it is documented that [in 1948] he won the two league games he appeared in, both complete games, giving up a total of 10 hits and 3 runs."[80] And he very well may have appeared in some more league games.

In addition to his time spent with the Monarchs in 1948, Stubblefield was a member of the Kansas City Stars, another Monarch "farm club."[81] This period may have been when he was taught by Satchel Paige, who co-managed the team and performed with them, to throw a curveball with a variety of deliveries: overhand, sidearm, and underhand. Stubblefield's daughter Mary goes further to say that Paige also taught her father "how to pitch" (probably meaning how to be a more effective pitcher since Stubblefield already knew how to pitch) and "his [Paige's] stance."[82] This led to Stubblefield becoming "known as 'Little Satch' because he had almost as many pitches and deliveries as his legendary mentor" and Paige himself saying that "[i]f [Stubblefield] was a foot taller[,] he could use him for a double on the mound."[83]

Besides Paige, Stubblefield's stint with the Monarchs and the Stars introduced him to other Negro League legends, such as James "Cool Papa" Bell and Willard Brown. In the case of Bell, the standard reference books do not list him on the Monarch roster for either 1948 or 1949, but newspaper articles show that he was indeed a member of those teams, at least at certain times during those seasons, and he definitely was a member of the Stars, serving as co-manager with Paige.[84]

In the latter part of the 1949 season, Stubblefield was purchased by the McCook Cats of the semiprofessional Nebraska Independent League (NIL) and helped the club to capture its second straight league championship, three games to two over Holdrege in the final round of the playoffs. Little Satch showed that he was appropriately nicknamed by pitching a 4–1 four-hitter, 4–0 five-hitter, and the 5–2 clincher and being credited with all three victories.[85] One of his teammates, Hobart "Hobe" Hays, who was the Cats' starting second baseman and who would later publish a loving memoir of his semipro days, described Stubblefield at that time as "a muscular five-foot-nine athlete who pitched and could play all the other positions as well—especially second base," and then added:

> When I learned this last fact, I rechecked my batting average from the year before. I remembered hitting .324 for the regular season, so I thought they must have Mickey here for other reasons, like pitching.[86]

Stubblefield continued to perform for McCook in 1950 and 1951, reportedly having a 13–6 won-lost record during the former season, before returning to Mayfield in 1952 to pitch for the African American semipro Blackhawks and to work at the Dr. Pepper bottling plant.[87]

It was while pitching in Mayfield that Stubblefield was noticed by two Pittsburgh Pirate scouts, one of whom was either Branch Rickey's son, Branch Jr., or brother, Frank, and signed to a contract to pitch for the Clothiers, the Pirates' Class D affiliate in Mayfield.[88] Thus, Little Satch became the first African American to play in the KITTY League, debuting on June 26, 1952. And, based on what Mary Arvin has published online, what a debut it was. Receiving a standing ovation from a sellout crowd of 1,500 white and black fans at the start of the game, the Clothier's "Jackie Robinson" went the distance, tossing a 5–4 victory while striking out six, walking five, and giving up six hits.[89] The rest of Stubblefield's season was not too shabby either. Appearing in 15 games—13 as a starter and two as a reliever—he won seven, lost six, and finished with a 3.71 ERA.[90] But, as J.G. Preston has shown, what makes Stubblefield's stats more impressive is that:

> He had a 7–6 record for a team that was 40–64 in other games. His 3.71 ERA was not among the league leaders, but it was a good ERA in a league where the weakest-hitting team averaged more than five runs a game and the best-hitting club averaged nearly eight.[91]

However, unfortunately for both the Clothiers and their new acquisition, Stubblefield was prevented from seeing more action because only two other clubs in the league—Paducah and Jackson—would permit him to play in their parks. It is possible that he pitched a game at the home field of another league member—Union City—sometime during the '52 season, but no more than one source cites the contest and no date for it is given.[92]

Controversy also surrounds why Stubblefield left the Clothiers after 1952 and what team or teams he was a member of the following year. Mary Arvin says that her father got "a tip from a Mayfield friend nicknamed 'Dubb Duffy' … [and] joined Duffy in 1953 to play baseball for the Duluth Dukes,"[93] a Northern League club that was not affiliated with any major league franchise. But an article in the April 2, 1953, issue of the *(Greenville, MS) Delta Democrat-Times* reports a sinister reason for his departure:

> [B]oycotts in the Kitty [*sic*] League last year forced the Mayfield, [Kentucky], club to let out pitcher Mickey Stubblefield. The club said it couldn't afford players who could not play without restriction.[94]

Stubblefield himself acknowledged pitching for Duluth, though without disclosing why he was no longer in a Clothier uniform, but there is newspaper evidence that he was on the mound again for the Mayfield Blackhawks in August of '53, despite the fact that the Northern League season did not end until September 7.[95]

As for stats and why he did not stay in Duluth longer, Stubblefield claimed to have "'bout [a] 10–8 [record], something like that," and that he had "left because [his] arm got bad," but J.G. Preston discovered that Stubblefield actually "pitched in six games (less than 15 innings, the exact number is not known) and had a 2–0 record," and as seen above, his arm recovered enough for him to be on the mound for the Blackhawks as late as August of that same season.[96]

Sometime after August 15, 1953, Stubblefield returned

Mickey Stubblefield integrated the KITTY League when he debuted as the Mayfield Clothiers' starting pitcher on June 26, 1952 (Gary Cieradkowski).

to McCook and began playing again for the Cats in 1955.[97] The previous year, he was honored by receiving votes as a utility player on the NIL's All-Time All-Star Team that was chosen by the sports correspondents of the *Lincoln (NE) Sunday Journal and Star*.[98]

But if Stubblefield was the most famous baseball player to wear a Rocket uniform, the most famous sports figure to be one of Will Calhoun's men was Richard "Night Train" Lane.

Better known for his gridiron exploits, Lane was a switch-hitting center fielder-right fielder for the 1947 Rockets. He stayed for only that season, saying "It was so dull. I had to get where the action was. There wasn't enough action in baseball, especially when you're trying to make a name for yourself."[99]

Lane would go on to carve out a 14-year professional football career with the Los Angeles Rams, Chicago Cardinals, and Detroit Lions that led to him being inducted into the Pro Football Hall of Fame in 1974 and being selected for the National Football League's All-Time All-Pro Team in 1969 and its 75th Anniversary All-Time Team in 1994. However, he did have a few fond and not-so-fond memories of his days with the Rockets. As he told an Austin, Texas, sportswriter:

> The guys were all different. It was an experience just to hear them talk.
> We played all over Idaho, Wyoming, Nebraska. We played towns where they'd never seen blacks. Sometimes we'd play with a rodeo or a fair, and we played about 23 games in 16 days one time….
> [And when he received his first Louisville Slugger bat, he remembered that] I ate with it and I slept with it.[100]

Beyond places visited, winning records, and standout players, there was one other thing that the Omaha Federals, Tigers, and Rockets had in common—leaving aside Night Train Lane, whose nature lent itself more to football than baseball—a deep affection for the sport with which they were involved. These were men who mainly played baseball in obscurity—in the shadows—and who put up with racial abuse, long road trips, and a lack of job security, but none of this stopped them from playing because they loved the game. So, perhaps this is the most important thing that can be learned from these men: it is the love of the game that matters above all else. Not the recognition. Not the money. But the love of the game.

### Table 1: The 1922 Omaha Federals[101]

| Name | Position | Comments |
| --- | --- | --- |
| Allen | 2B | Newton Henry "Colt" or "Newt" Allen (c.1900–1988). Primarily a second baseman who also saw action as a shortstop, third baseman, outfielder, and first baseman, Allen played for the Kansas City Tigers in 1920 and 1921, the All Nations in 1922 and 1923, the Kansas City Monarchs from 1922 through 1944, the St. Louis Stars in 1931, the Homestead Grays and Detroit Wolves in 1932, the Columbus Blue Birds in 1933, the Chicago American Giants and the Kansas City Colored All-Stars in 1945, and the Indianapolis Clowns in 1947. |
| Brown | P | |
| Carald | CF | |
| Daniels | LF, CF | |
| Davis | 3B, C | |

| Name | Position | Comments |
|---|---|---|
| Foster | 3B | |
| Gray | C | |
| Hamilton | P, CF, RF | Probably the Hamilton who was a pitcher for the Kansas City Monarchs in 1921, the Atlantic City Bacharach Giants in 1923, the Cleveland Browns in 1924, and the St. Louis Stars in 1924 |
| Harper | RF, P | Probably Chick or Chalky Harper, a pitcher and right fielder for the Kansas City Giants in 1911; a pitcher for the Kansas City Royal Giants in 1912; a pitcher for the Chicago Union Giants in 1916; a right fielder, center fielder, and left fielder for the Kansas City Monarchs in 1920; a right fielder, left fielder, and pitcher for the Detroit Stars in 1920; and a left fielder for the Detroit Stars in 1925 |
| Jackson, Guy | 3B | (1882–?). A third baseman, second baseman, and shortstop who played for the Illinois Giants in 1909, the Chicago Giants from 1911 through 1913, the Kansas City Giants in 1912, the New York Lincoln Stars and the Schenectady Mohawk Giants in 1914, and the Chicago Giants in 1915 |
| Larue | P | |
| Lee | C | |
| Leroy | CF | |
| Napure (Nepure) | C | |
| Nature | P | |
| Pappio | P | |
| Ragion | P | Possibly Hurland Earl (Herlin) Ragland (Raglan) (1896–1960), a pitcher for Jewell's ABCs in 1919, the Indianapolis ABCs in 1920, the Dayton Marcos in 1920, the Columbus Buckeyes in 1921, and the Kansas City Monarchs in 1921 |
| Ray | C, 1B | Probably Otto C. "Jay Bird" or "Jaybird" Ray (1893–1976), a catcher and right fielder for the Kansas City Monarchs in 1920 and 1921; a catcher, right fielder, and center fielder for the Chicago Giants in 1921; a catcher for the Kansas City Monarchs in 1922; a catcher, left fielder, right fielder, and first baseman for the St. Louis Stars in 1922; a catcher, left fielder, center fielder, and right fielder for the St. Louis Stars in 1923; a catcher and center fielder for the Cleveland Tate Stars in 1923; a catcher, first baseman, left fielder, right fielder, and pitcher for the Cleveland Browns in 1924; and, depending on the source, a catcher for the Kansas City Monarchs in 1924 |
| Redd | 3B | Probably Eugene "Gene" Redd (1899–1955), a third baseman, shortstop, and left fielder who played for the Kansas City Monarchs and Cleveland Tate Stars in 1922, the Milwaukee Bears in 1923, and, depending on the source, the Pittsburgh Keystones in 1922 and the Kansas City Monarchs and New Orleans Crescent Stars in 1923 |
| Richie | P | |
| Right (Wright) | 1B, C | |

| Name | Position | Comments |
|---|---|---|
| Rollins (Rolon) | SS | |
| Shiled | P | |
| Smith | 1B | |
| Staple (Staples) | SS, LF | |
| Stewart (Staurt) | C, LF, RF | |
| Sunny | LF | |
| Vaughn | Not found | Possibly Harold Vaughn, an outfielder for the Kansas City Monarchs in 1926 and 1927 |
| Washington | P | |
| Williams, L. | 1B | Possibly the L. Williams who played for the Kansas City Monarchs in 1928 |
| Williams (no first name found) | P, RF | |
| Young | P | Possibly William Young, a pitcher for the Kansas City Monarchs in 1927 |

## Table 2: Found Games Scheduled by the 1922 Omaha Federals[102]

| Date | Team | Location | Results | Comments |
|---|---|---|---|---|
| April 23, 1922 | All Nations | Western League Park, Omaha, Nebraska | Lost; 7–2 | The first game of a doubleheader. Omaha's battery: Ragion and Gray |
| April 23, 1922 | All Nations | Western League Park, Omaha, Nebraska | Tied; 5–5 | The second game of a doubleheader; stopped by darkness in the seventh inning. In the third inning, Redd hit a triple with the bases loaded which drove in three runs. Omaha's battery: Williams and Ray |
| May 13, 1922 | Kennedy All-Stars | Western League Park, Omaha, Nebraska | Not found | The game started at 3:30 p.m. |
| May 14, 1922 | Kennedy All-Stars | Western League Park, Omaha, Nebraska | Not found | The game started at 2:00 p.m. |
| May 28, 1922 | Herman, Nebraska | Herman, Nebraska | Won; 4–2 | Vaughn hit a home run with one on in the ninth. Hamilton gave up only two hits. |
| May 30, 1922 | Herman, Nebraska | Herman, Nebraska | Won; 6–5 | Hamilton pitched a one-hitter. Line score totals: Omaha 6–11–0; Herman 5–1–0. Omaha's battery: Hamilton and Davis |
| June 4, 1922 | Dunlap, Iowa | Dunlap, Iowa | Not found | |

| Date | Team | Location | Results | Comments |
|---|---|---|---|---|
| June 4, 1922 | Hamburg, Iowa | Hamburg, Iowa | Won; 6–5 | Hamilton scattered seven hits and the Federals scored three runs in the 14th inning to win. Line score totals: Omaha 6-10-2; Hamburg 5-7-3. Omaha's battery: Hamilton and Davis |
| June 7, 1922 | Syracuse, Nebraska | Syracuse, Nebraska | Lost; 4–2 | Line score totals: Omaha 2-6-0; Syracuse 4-8-4. Omaha's battery: Washington and Wright |
| June 8, 1922 | Missouri Valley, Iowa | Western League Park, Omaha, Nebraska | Lost; 7–3, according to the June 9, 1922, issue of the *Omaha Daily Bee*, or 8–3, according to the June 9, 1922, issue of the *Omaha World-Herald* | The game started at 3:30 p.m. and lasted for an hour and 50 minutes. Line score totals: Missouri Valley 7/8-13/14-1; Omaha 3-5-4. The *Omaha Daily Bee*'s hit total for Missouri Valley does not equal the individual hits the newspaper attributes to each player. Omaha's battery: Harper and Napure |
| June 10, 1922 | Des Moines Independents, Des Moines, Iowa | Omaha, Nebraska | Cancelled | |
| June 10, 1922 | St. Joseph, Missouri | Western League Park, Omaha, Nebraska | Won; 15–3 | The debut game in the Colored Western League, it was played for an hour and 40 minutes. Every Federal except Jackson had at least one hit, with Harper going 4-for-5, and seven of the Federal players scored at least one run, with Allen scoring four and Smith three. Line score totals: St. Joseph 3-10-9; Omaha 15-17-2. Omaha's battery: Williams and Nepure |
| June 11, 1922 | Des Moines Independents, Des Moines, Iowa | Omaha, Nebraska | Cancelled | |
| June 11, 1922 | St. Joseph, Missouri | Western League Park, Omaha, Nebraska | Won; 7–6 | The first game of a doubleheader, it took an hour and 50 minutes to complete. Allen went 3-for-5, stole a base, and scored three runs. Harper also scored three runs. Line score totals: St. Joseph 6-11-4; Omaha 7-7-4. Omaha's battery: Harper and Nepure |
| June 11, 1922 | St. Joseph, Missouri | Western League Park, Omaha, Nebraska | Won; 6–5 | The second game of a doubleheader, it lasted an hour and 25 minutes, with the Federals triumphing in the bottom of the sixth inning, when Pappio drove in Hamilton with the winning run. Allen tripled and scored a run. Line score totals: St. Joseph 5-6-8; Omaha 6-6-3. Omaha's battery: Williams and Stewart |

## 108    Section I—The Long and Winding Road

| Date | Team | Location | Results | Comments |
|---|---|---|---|---|
| June 12, 1922 | St. Joseph, Missouri | Western League Park, Omaha, Nebraska | Won; 12–2 | The time of the game was one hour and 40 minutes, with Harper, Daniels, and Smith each having two hits, including a triple by Smith. Line score totals: St. Joseph 2-5-13; Omaha 12-9-6. Omaha's battery: Williams and Nepure |
| Probably June 15, 1922 | Herman, Nebraska | Not found | Lost; 2–1 | The game went 10 innings, with Fitch of Herman striking out 13 and winning his 10th straight game and Hamilton of the Federals striking out eight. |
| June 18, 1922 | Armour & Company, Omaha, Nebraska | Western League Park, Omaha, Nebraska | Not found | The first game of a doubleheader, which was scheduled to start at 2:00 p.m. |
| June 18, 1922 | Cudahy Packing Company, Omaha, Nebraska | Western League Park, Omaha, Nebraska | Not found | The second game of a doubleheader |
| July 8, 1922 | Tekamah, Nebraska | Tekamah, Nebraska | Won; 5–1 | The Federals scored four runs in the top of the 11th. Omaha's battery: Shiled and Lee |
| July 8, 1922 | Randolph, Nebraska | Randolph, Nebraska | Lost; 3–2 | The game went 12 innings. Omaha's battery: Young and Staurt |
| July 9, 1922 | Shenandoah, Iowa | Not played | Cancelled | |
| July 16, 1922 | Bellevue town team, Bellevue, Nebraska | Bellevue, Nebraska | Won; 8–6 | Omaha's battery: Brown, Williams and Lee |
| July 22, 1922 | Tekamah, Nebraska | Tekamah, Nebraska | Lost; 7–5 | According to an article in the July 23, 1922, issue of the *Omaha World-Herald*, this was the third meeting of the two teams, with Tekamah winning two out of three. The date, place, and score of one of the previous games were not found. Line score totals: Omaha 5-6-4; Tekamah 7-9-4. Omaha's battery: Nature and Lee, with Nature striking out 11 |
| July 31, 1922 | Bennington, Nebraska | Bennington, Nebraska | Not found | |
| August 17, 1922, at the latest, but probably earlier | Tabor, Iowa | Tabor, Iowa | Lost; 7–1 | Part of the Tabor baseball tournament |
| September 17, 1922 | Pottawattomie, Iowa, All-Stars | Council Bluffs, Iowa | Not found | The game was scheduled to start at 3:00 p.m. |

## Table 3: Found Games Scheduled by the 1935 Omaha Tigers[103]

| Date | Team | Location | Results | Comments |
|---|---|---|---|---|
| Not found | Austin Black Senators, Austin, Texas | Not found | Not found | A tentatively scheduled exhibition game |
| March 31, 1935 | Clarksdale, Mississippi | Clarksdale, Mississippi | Not found | An exhibition game that was scheduled to be played |
| April 4, 1935 | Piney Woods, Mississippi | Piney Woods, Mississippi | Not found | An exhibition game that was scheduled to be played |
| April 5, 1935 | Piney Woods, Mississippi | Piney Woods, Mississippi | Not found | An exhibition game that was scheduled to be played |
| April 7, 1935 | Clarksdale Ginners of the East Dixie League, Clarksdale, Mississippi | Clarksdale, Mississippi | Cancelled | |
| April 7, 1935 | Greenwood All-Stars, Greenwood, Mississippi | Greenwood, Mississippi | Won; 8–1 | An exhibition game in which Mason hit two home runs |
| April 14, 1935 | Alcorn College Braves, Alcorn, Mississippi | Alcorn, Mississippi | Won; 3–2 | An exhibition game which Alcorn gave away by making five errors. Line score totals: Omaha 3-6-2; Alcorn 2-4-5. Omaha's battery: Jefferson and Taylor |
| April 14, 1935 | Alcorn College Braves, Alcorn, Mississippi | Alcorn, Mississippi | Lost; 7–6, according to the April 20, 1935, issue of the *Chicago Defender*. But see Robert Phipps, "Odds, Ends from Sports," *Omaha World-Herald*, April 16, 1935, for a different score. | An exhibition game that was 6–6 going into the bottom of the last inning when an Alcorn player named Barnes hit a solo homer to win it. Line score totals: Omaha 6-8-1; Alcorn 7-10-5. Omaha's battery: Clement, Harvey and Taylor |
| April 14, 1935 | Zulu Cannibal Giants, Louisville, Kentucky | New Orleans, Louisiana | Lost; 2–0 | An exhibition game |
| No date found, but probably played between April 15 and April 19, 1935 | New Orleans Black Pilgrims, New Orleans, Louisiana | Probably New Orleans, Louisiana | Won; 12–2 | An exhibition game |
| No date found, but probably played between April 15 and April 19, 1935 | New Orleans Black Pilgrims, New Orleans, Louisiana | Probably New Orleans, Louisiana | Won; 2–0 | An exhibition game |

| Date | Team | Location | Results | Comments |
|---|---|---|---|---|
| No date found, but probably played between April 15 and April 19, 1935 | New Orleans Black Pilgrims, New Orleans, Louisiana | Probably New Orleans, Louisiana | Won; 12–2 | An exhibition game |
| No date found, but probably played between April 15 and April 19, 1935 | New Orleans Black Pilgrims, New Orleans, Louisiana | Probably New Orleans, Louisiana | Lost; 7–5 | An exhibition game |
| No date found, but probably played between April 15 and April 19, 1935 | New Orleans Black Pilgrims, New Orleans, Louisiana | Probably New Orleans, Louisiana | Lost; 3–0 | An exhibition game |
| According to the March 19, 1935, issue of the *Omaha World-Herald*, exhibition games were scheduled to be played on 14 days from April 16 through May 6, 1935. | Not found | Baton Rouge, Louisiana; Hattiesburg, Mississippi; Bogalusa, Louisiana; Kilgore, Texas; Wiley College, Marshall, Texas; Texas College, Tyler, Texas; Dallas, Texas; and Wichita Falls, Texas | Not found | Exhibition games that may not have been played |
| May 4, 1935 | El Dorado, El Dorado Springs, Missouri | El Dorado Springs, Missouri | Not found | An exhibition game |
| May 19, 1935 | St. Louis Blues, St. Louis, Missouri | Metropolitan Park, St. Louis, Missouri | Not found | Probably an exhibition game |
| No date found, but reported on May 24, 1935 | Black Barons; possibly the Birmingham Black Barons, Birmingham, Alabama | Harrisburg, Illinois | Won; 9–2 | An exhibition game |
| May 26, 1935 | Monroe Monarchs, Monroe, Louisiana | Clarksdale, Mississippi | Not found | Probably an exhibition game |
| May 26, 1935 | Harford Colored Giants | Sparta Stadium, Chicago, Illinois | Cancelled | The cancellation was caused by the Tigers being involved in a train wreck at Bloomington, Illinois. |

## 5. Shadow Ball in the River City (Louisa)

| Date | Team | Location | Results | Comments |
|---|---|---|---|---|
| May 31, 1935 | Forest City Collegians, Forest City, Iowa | Forest City, Iowa | Lost; 9–0 | The first game of a doubleheader |
| May 31, 1935 | Forest City Collegians, Forest City, Iowa | Forest City, Iowa | Lost; 10–3 | The second game of a doubleheader |
| June 1, 1935 | Omaha Packers, Omaha, Nebraska | Omaha, Nebraska | Not found | May not have been played |
| June 2, 1935 | Oakland Cowboys, Oakland, Nebraska | Oakland, Nebraska | Not found | |
| June 6, 1935 | Sheridan, Iowa | Sheridan, Iowa | Won; 11–2 | |
| According to the May 11, 1935, issue of the *Omaha World-Herald*, the Schuyler, Nebraska, team "probably will book the Omaha Tigers for June 7[, 1935]." | Schuyler, Nebraska | Schuyler, Nebraska | Not found | May not have been played |
| June 8, 1935 | Monroe Monarchs, Monroe, Louisiana | Western League Park, Omaha, Nebraska | Lost; 13–4 | Performing before only 204 spectators, the Tigers wore "gaudy, tight-fitting uniforms" for a game that lasted two hours and 18 minutes. Curry homered in a losing cause. Line score totals: Monroe 13-18-2; Omaha 4-5-4. Omaha's battery: Bubbles, Mason and Taylor |
| June 9, 1935 | Monroe Monarchs, Monroe, Louisiana | Western League Park, Omaha, Nebraska | Lost; 20–7 | The first game of a doubleheader, which took two hours to play. Line score totals: Monroe 20-15-1; Omaha 7-11-7. Omaha's battery: Walker, Morgan, Bubbles and Taylor |
| June 9, 1935 | Monroe Monarchs, Monroe, Louisiana | Western League Park, Omaha, Nebraska | Won; 14–11 | The second game of a doubleheader, which took an hour and 25 minutes to play and which saw Mason blast a three-run homer over the center field fence and Reynolds slug a grand slam. Line score totals: Monroe 11-13-4; Omaha 14-8-1. Omaha's battery: Bubbles and Taylor |
| June 12, 1935 | St. Cloud Saints, St. Cloud, Minnesota | St. Cloud, Minnesota | Cancelled | The Tigers had called the Saint Cloud management at 10:00 a.m. that day to tell them that they were having automobile trouble near Austin, Minnesota, but that they would still be able to make it to St. Cloud by 6:00 p.m., the scheduled start of the game. However, they did not show up. |

| Date | Team | Location | Results | Comments |
|---|---|---|---|---|
| June 21, 1935 | Humboldt Red Caps, Humboldt, Iowa | Humboldt, Iowa | Won; 29–6 | Not many details were found, but it is known that during one inning the Tigers scored 10 runs after making two outs. |
| June 23, 1935 | Lakeview town team, Lakeview, Iowa | Probably Lakeview, Iowa | Won; 2–0 | |
| Not found, but reported on July 3, 1935 | Carroll Merchants, Carroll, Iowa | Probably Carroll, Iowa | Won; 5–2 | |
| July 21, 1935 | Oakland Cowboys, Oakland, Nebraska | Oakland, Nebraska | Not found | Scheduled for Ladies Day |
| July 21, 1935 | Kearney Independents, Kearney, Nebraska | Lincoln, Nebraska | Won; 6–5 | Played during the Nebraska Semipro Baseball Tournament, the game went 10 innings and lasted two hours and three minutes before the Tigers squeaked out the victory. Bubber was credited with the win and helped his own cause by hitting a triple and then scoring the winning run on a bad throw to the plate by Kearney's Andy Jensen. Curry also hit a triple, added a single, and scored a run. Every Tiger except for Lee had at least one hit and three had two hits. Line score totals: Kearney 5-9-0; Omaha 6-11-0. Omaha's battery: Bubber and R. Smith |
| July 24, 1935 | Ford V-8s of Omaha, Omaha, Nebraska | Lincoln, Nebraska | Lost; 7–3 | Played during the Nebraska Semipro Baseball Tournament, the game was completed in an hour and 42 minutes. Mason went 3-for-4 and Longley pounded out two hits and scored two runs, but Curry gave up four V-8 runs on two hits and a walk, and Tiger errors led to three more. Line score totals: Ford V-8s 7-7-2; Tigers 3-6-3. Tigers' battery: Curry, Mason and R. Smith |
| July 25–26, 1935 | Bellwood, Nebraska | Lincoln, Nebraska | Won; 7–5 | Played during the Nebraska Semipro Baseball Tournament, the game started on the 25th but ended an hour and 51 minutes later on the 26th. Every Tiger except Meadows had at least one hit and Jesse had two. Line score totals: Bellwood 5-9-2; Omaha 7-10-0. Omaha's battery: Bubber and R. Smith |

| Date | Team | Location | Results | Comments |
|---|---|---|---|---|
| July 26, 1935 | Dannebrog, Nebraska | Lincoln, Nebraska | Won; 19–10 | Played during the Nebraska Semipro Baseball Tournament, the slugfest lasted two hours and one minute, with Curry going 3-for-6, Curry, Mason, and Jesse each scoring three runs, and Mason getting the win. Line score totals: Dannebrog 10–14–4; Omaha 19–18–4. Omaha's battery: Benson, Walker, Mason and R. Smith |
| July 27, 1935 | Iowa-Nebraska Powers of Lincoln, Lincoln, Nebraska | Lincoln, Nebraska | Won; 9–6 | Played during the Nebraska Semipro Baseball Tournament, the game took two hours and 17 minutes to complete and saw the Tigers score four runs in the bottom of the eighth to rally from a 6–5 deficit to a 9–6 lead. R. Smith, Curry, and Grimm each socked triples and James drove in the tying run and then scored what proved to be the winning tally. Line score totals: Lincoln 6–11–3; Omaha 9–12–1. Omaha's battery: Lee, Walker, Mason and R. Smith, Longley |
| July 27, 1935 | Ford V-8s of Omaha, Omaha, Nebraska | Lincoln, Nebraska | Lost; 10–9 | Played during the Nebraska Semipro Baseball Tournament, the length of the game was an hour and 58 minutes. The V-8s scored two runs in the bottom of the ninth to win. Curry, R. Smith, and Jesse each hit triples, with Curry scoring three runs, Longley and R. Smith each scoring two, and Mason and Jessie scoring one apiece. Line score totals: Tigers 9–10–4; Ford V-8s 10–10–2. Tigers' battery: Bubber and R. Smith |
| July 28, 1935 | Iowa-Nebraska Powers of Lincoln, Lincoln, Nebraska | Lincoln, Nebraska | Won; 10–9 | The third-place game of the Nebraska Semipro Baseball Tournament, it was called after seven innings and an hour and 14 minutes by agreement between Mason and the Power manager, Johnny Bretzer (no reason was given as to why Homer Curry was not consulted). R. Smith, Grimm, Jesse, and Benson each had two hits: a pair of singles for Smith; a double and a triple each for Grimm and Jesse; and a single and a double for Benson. Line score totals: Lincoln 9–18–2; Omaha 10–11–2. Omaha's battery: Mason and R. Smith |
| No date found, but reported on August 8, 1935 | Waterloo, Iowa | No place found | Tied; 4–4 | |

## 114   Section I—The Long and Winding Road

| Date | Team | Location | Results | Comments |
|---|---|---|---|---|
| No date found, but reported on August 8, 1935 | York Central Nebraska League team, York, Nebraska | York, Nebraska | Won; 3–0 | Mason gave up only two singles. Line score totals: Omaha 3-10-1; York 0-2-2. Omaha's battery: Mason and Smith |
| August 11, 1935 | Oakland town team, Oakland, Nebraska | Oakland, Nebraska | Won; 10–7 | |
| August 14, 1935 | Council Bluffs Rails, Council Bluffs, Iowa | Broadway Park, Council Bluffs, Iowa | Lost; 4–3 | The game went to 12 innings and was not well attended. Burber pitched for Omaha. |
| August 15, 1935 | Defiance town team, Defiance, Iowa | Defiance, Iowa | Won; 10–5 | |
| To be scheduled sometime between August 26 and August 29, 1935 | Kearney Independents, Kearney, Nebraska | Kearney, Nebraska | Not found | Planned as one of the games for the Buffalo County Fair |
| August 27, 1935 | Oakland, Nebraska | West Point, Nebraska | Not found | One of the games for the Cuming County Fair |
| August 28, 1935 | Japanese All-Stars | Arlington, Nebraska | Lost; 3–2 | Played during the second day of the Eastern Nebraska Tournament, the game was part of a doubleheader that was attended by 2,000 people. Line score totals: Japanese 3-7-2; Omaha 2-7-4. Omaha's battery: Johnican and Benson, Smith |
| August 30, 1935 | Dannebrog, Nebraska | Dannebrog, Nebraska | Not found | |
| September 2, 1935 | Hubbard Aces, Hubbard, Iowa | Hubbard, Iowa | Not found | |
| September 7, 1935 | Sioux City Cowboys, Sioux City, Iowa | Sioux City, Iowa | Lost; 17–4 | Nearly 500 people attended the game, which was played on a muddy field. Lefty Henderson, Sioux City's starting pitcher, struck out 13 Tigers. McNeil and Lomax had the best offensive performances for Omaha, with the former going 3-for-5 and scoring a run and the latter going 2-for-4, including a double, and driving in a run. Line score totals: Omaha 4-8-6; Sioux City 17-15-0. Omaha's battery: Johnsicano, Lomax, McNeil, Mason and Benson |
| September 15, 1935 | Stromsburg, Nebraska | Stromsburg, Nebraska | Lost; 4–0 | Line score totals: Omaha 0-4-1; Stromsburg 4-9-4. Omaha's battery: Mason and Klum |

| Date | Team | Location | Results | Comments |
|---|---|---|---|---|
| September 20, 1935 | Sioux City Stock Yards team, Sioux City, Iowa | Primghar, Iowa | Not found | According to the September 21, 1935, issue of the *Sioux City (IA) Journal*, "[t]here was to be a baseball game between the Omaha Tigers and the Sioux City Stock Yards teams." |
| September 30, 1935 | Kearney, Nebraska | Kearney, Nebraska | Lost; 5–4 | |
| October 8, 1935 | Kearney, Nebraska | Kearney, Nebraska | Lost; 9–6 | |

## Table 4: Found Games Scheduled by the 1936 Omaha Tigers/Monarchs[104]

| Date | Team | Location | Results | Comments |
|---|---|---|---|---|
| Not found, but after April 12, 1936 | Not found | Birmingham, Alabama | Not found | An exhibition game |
| April 25, 1936 | Memphis Red Sox, Memphis, Tennessee | Martin's Park, Memphis, Tennessee | Lost; 10–7 | An exhibition game |
| April 26, 1936 | Memphis Red Sox, Memphis, Tennessee | Martin's Park, Memphis, Tennessee | Lost; 10–9 | An exhibition game that was attended by 2,500 fans. Omaha's battery: Dixon and Langford |
| April 27, 1936 | Memphis Red Sox, Memphis, Tennessee | Memphis, Tennessee | Not found | An exhibition game |
| Presumably May 9, 1936 | A North Omaha team (no specific name was given) | Fontenelle Park, Omaha, Nebraska | Won; 10–0 | Referred to as a practice game, so it may have been an exhibition game. |
| May 10, 1936 | Metz Brothers Brewing Company, Omaha, Nebraska | Western League Park, Omaha, Nebraska | Cancelled | The game was cancelled because of wet grounds. |
| May 15, 1936 | Miller-Knuths, Omaha, Nebraska | Western League Park, Omaha, Nebraska | Cancelled | The game was cancelled because only 117 paying fans showed up for it. |
| May 17, 1936 | Roberts Dairy Company, Omaha, Nebraska | Western League Park, Omaha, Nebraska | Not found | Scheduled to start at 3:30 p.m. |
| May 24, 1936 | Albion town team, Albion, Michigan | Albion, Michigan | Won; 2–1 | The Tigers scored two runs in the top of the first and then hung on as Woodson scattered eight hits. Davis and Langford each scored a run and Mason and Johnson each drove one in. Omaha's battery: Woodson and Langford |
| May 28, 1936 | Four-Ls Rapid City Baseball League team | North Side Park, Rapid City, South Dakota | Won; 12–7 | Langford had three hits, including a triple. Line score totals: Omaha 12-8-2; Four-Ls 7-7-4. Omaha's battery: Eastman, Mayweather, Woodson and Langford |

## 116   Section I—The Long and Winding Road

| Date | Team | Location | Results | Comments |
|---|---|---|---|---|
| May 31, 1936 | Tekamah town team, Tekamah, Nebraska | Tekamah, Nebraska | Cancelled | The Tigers did not show up for the game, leading to the paying spectators having their money refunded. |
| June 1, 1936 | Billings town team, Billings, Montana | Billings, Montana | Cancelled | |
| Before June 4, 1936 | Miles City, Montana | Miles City, Montana | Won; 12–6 | |
| June 4, 1936 | Glasgow, Montana | Glasgow, Montana | Not found | |
| June 6, 1936 | Great Falls, Montana | Great Falls, Montana | Not found | |
| June 7, 1936 | Helena Vigilantes, Helena, Montana | Legion Park, Helena, Montana | Not found | Apparently rained out |
| June 8, 1936 | Colored Giants, Butte, Montana | Clark Park, Butte, Montana | Won; 3–0 | Woodson struck out nine Giants. Line score totals: Omaha 3-3-2; Colored Giants 0-4-2. Omaha's battery: Woodson and Langford. |
| June 9, 1936 | University Store Grizzlies, Missoula, Montana | South Higgins Park, Missoula, Montana | Lost; 14–5 | The game was scheduled to start at 6:20 p.m. Despite the fact that the Monarchs were crushed by the Grizzlies, Harris went 3-for-4, including a double, scored a run, and had two assists; Davis went 2-for-4, including a double, stole two bases, scored a run, and had four assists and a putout; and Mason hit a solo homer in three at bats, stole a base, had five assists and two putouts, and struck out four opposing players. Line score totals: Omaha 5-7-3; University Store 14-18-3. Omaha's battery: Mayweather, Woodson, Mason and Langford. According to the June 11, 1936, issue of the *(Missoula, MT) Daily Missoulian*, before the Monarchs had lost this game, they "had won their tenth straight at Butte 3 to 0." |
| June 10, 1936 | Pearce Drugs, Kalispell, Montana | Kalispell, Montana | Lost; 6–4 | The Monarchs played well offensively but badly defensively. |
| June 11 or 12, 1936 | Kellogg Miners, Kellogg, Idaho | Kellogg, Idaho | Won; 14–8 | |
| June 13, 1936 | Naples, Idaho | Bonners Ferry, Idaho | Won; 3–1 | Outhit seven to three, the Monarchs made the most of what they got. |

| Date | Team | Location | Results | Comments |
|---|---|---|---|---|
| No specific date, but sometime between June 1 and June 13, 1936 | No team names were given, but the *Pittsburgh Courier* reported on June 13, 1936, that the Monarchs have been traveling about the northwestern states and winning all their games, which, as can be seen from the June 9 and June 10 contests, is an obvious exaggeration. | Northwestern states | Not found | Multiple victories and at least two losses. Also, it is in early June that the Tigers changed their name to the Monarchs and became a touring club that played in various states west of the Mississippi. |
| June 14, 1936 | Silver Loaf Bakery, Spokane, Washington | Natatorium Park, Spokane, Washington | Won; 6–0 | The first game of a doubleheader, it was scheduled to start at 2:00 p.m. Davis hit a pair of triples and a single and scored two runs; Woodson hit a pair of doubles and a single and scored two runs; Mason added another double and single, stole two bases, and scored a run; Dubose singled twice, stole a base, and scored a run; and Langford singled and stole three bases. Collectively, the Monarchs stole seven bases. Line score totals: Omaha 6–13–1; Silver Loaf 0–8–1. Omaha's battery: Woodson and Langford |
| June 14, 1936 | Sons of Italy, Spokane, Washington | Natatorium Park, Spokane, Washington | Lost; 3–2 | The second game of a doubleheader. The Sons of Italy scored a run in the bottom of the ninth to edge the Monarchs. Davis and Reed each had two hits, and Dubose and Reed each scored a run. Line score totals: Omaha 2–9–3; Sons of Italy 3–6–2. Omaha's battery: Reed and Langford. Total attendance for the entire doubleheader was approximately 1,000. |
| June 16, 1936 | Walla Walla, Washington, of the Oregon-Washington League | Walla Walla, Washington | Lost; 7–2 | |
| June 23, 1936 | Pocatello Bannocks, Pocatello, Idaho | Pocatello, Idaho | Won; 6–5 | |

| Date | Team | Location | Results | Comments |
|---|---|---|---|---|
| No specific date, but up to June 24, 1936 | No team names were given, but according to the June 24, 1936, issue of the *Salt Lake (City, UT) Tribune*, the Monarchs had played 65 games through June 23, 1936, and won 62 of them. | Various states | Not found | Since the article also says that the Monarchs had come in second in the Denver Post Tournament in 1935—something that they did not do, but the Kansas City Monarchs did—it appears that the author of the article confused the two Monarch clubs. |
| June 24, 1936 | Salt Lake Federation All-Stars, Salt Lake City, Utah | Community Park, Salt Lake City, Utah | Won; 11–4 | Spearheading an offensive attack that produced a total of 20 hits, Davis and Powell each had four of them and Powell scored three runs, whereas Davis and Harris scored two apiece. Mason struck out eight and walked only two, though he gave up 13 hits in a game that was scheduled to start at 4:00 p.m. Omaha's battery: Mason and Langford. The price of admission was 40 cents for adults and 25 cents for children. According to an article in the July 1, 1936, issue of the *(Missoula, MT) Daily Missoulian*, the Monarchs had "won 30 games and lost only four on their recent northwestern tour." |
| No date, but reported on July 5, 1936 | White Elephants, Denver, Colorado | Denver, Colorado | Lost; 8–5 | The first game of a doubleheader |
| No date, but reported on July 5, 1936 | White Elephants, Denver, Colorado | Denver, Colorado | Lost; 18–8 | The second game of a doubleheader |
| July 8, 1936 | Reed's Oilers, Greeley, Colorado | Island Grove Park, Greeley, Colorado | Won; score not found | The game was scheduled to start at 5:00 p.m. |
| July 24, 1936 | Charles City Lions, Charles City, Iowa | Charles City, Iowa | Lost; 7–5 | The Monarchs had led, 4–2, until the seventh. |
| July 27, 1936 | Forest City Collegians, Forest City, Iowa | Forest City, Iowa | Lost; 10–2 | The time of the game was an hour and 50 minutes. Langford went 2-for-3 with a single and a double. Line score totals: Omaha 2-5-3; Forest City 10-11-4. Omaha's battery: Moody, Eatman and Langford |

## 5. Shadow Ball in the River City (Louisa)

| Date | Team | Location | Results | Comments |
|---|---|---|---|---|
| An article in the July 28, 1936, issue of the *St. Cloud (MN) Daily Times and the Daily Journal Press*, reported that "The [Monarchs have] just returned from a tour to the Pacific [C]oast and recently played with International Falls on the border." | No team names were given. | The Pacific Coast and International Falls, Minnesota | Not found | Based on the gap between July 8 and July 24, the Pacific Coast tour and the game with the International Falls team may have occurred during that time. However, the article said nothing of the losses to the Charles City Lions and the Forest City Collegians. |
| July 29, 1936 | St. Cloud Saints, St. Cloud, Minnesota | St. Cloud, Minnesota | Won; 5–2 | Depending on the source, the game began at 6:15 p.m., with the admission price being 40 cents, including grandstand seats, or began at 4:00 p.m., with the admission price being 35 cents. But in either case, it lasted for an hour and 30 minutes. Davis went 3-for-5 with a double and two singles, and Langford had two singles in four at bats and stole a base. Line score totals: Omaha 5-7-4; St. Cloud 2-8-3. Omaha's battery: Mason and Langford |
| July 30, 1936 | Pilot Mound town team, Pilot Mound, Iowa | Presumably Pilot Mound, Iowa | Won; 8–6 | |
| August 3, 1936 | Mando Baseball Club, International Falls, Minnesota | International Falls, Minnesota | Lost; 13–1 | The Monarchs had five hits, but Eatman and Moody gave up 17 hits. |
| August 4, 1936 | Mando Baseball Club, International Falls, Minnesota | International Falls, Minnesota | Won; 5–3 | The Mandos got their runs on seven hits; the Monarchs got their runs on three hits and four errors. |
| August 5, 1936 | Probably the Kearney Independents, Kearney, Nebraska | Kearney, Nebraska | Postponed | The game was postponed. |
| August 9, 1936 | Not found | Oxford, Nebraska | Not found | |
| August 11, 1936 | Not found | McCook, Nebraska | Not found | |

| Date | Team | Location | Results | Comments |
|---|---|---|---|---|
| August 12, 1936 | Iowa-Nebraska Powers of Lincoln, Lincoln, Nebraska | Landis Field, Lincoln, Nebraska | Lost; 8–5 | The game was scheduled to start at 8:30 p.m., with the admission price being 25 cents. The Powers, who were referred to as the Juice Peddlers, scored seven runs in the third inning and held on to clinch the victory. For the Monarchs, Langford went 2-for-4, Dubose scored two runs, and Davis, Mason, and Johnson scored one run apiece. Line score totals: Omaha 5–7–3; Powers 8–10–4. Omaha's battery: Mayweather, Eatman, Mason and Langford. 500 people attended the game, which lasted for an hour and 57 minutes. |
| August 13, 1936 | Not found | Bruning, Nebraska | Not found | |
| August 14, 1936 | Texas Black Spiders | Hubbard, Iowa | Not found | |
| August 15, 1936 | Algona Grays, Algona, Iowa | Titonka, Iowa | Not found | The game was scheduled to start at 2:00 p.m. |
| August 17, 1936 | Probably the Kearney Independents, Kearney, Nebraska | Kearney, Nebraska | Lost; 5–4 | Kearney scored the winning run with two out in the bottom of the ninth. |
| August 19, 1936 | Charles City Lions, Charles City, Iowa | Rudd, Iowa | Lost; 9–4 | |
| August 27, 1936 | An all-star team from the Mid-State Baseball League | Wood River, Nebraska | Won; 6–4 | Played before a large crowd |
| September 5, 1936 | Not found | Rulo, Nebraska | Not found | |
| September 6, 1936 | Hildreth town team, Hildreth, Nebraska | Hildreth, Nebraska | Not found | |
| September 7, 1936 | Not found | Kearney, Nebraska | Not found | |
| September 8, 1936 | Not found | Summerfield, Kansas | Not found | The game was scheduled to start at 3:00 p.m. and the price of admission was 20 cents (probably for adults) and 10 cents (probably for children). |
| September 9, 1936 | Not found | Oberlin, Kansas | Not found | |
| September 10, 1936 | Not found | Bertrand, Nebraska | Not found | |
| September 11, 1936 | Not found | Bertrand, Nebraska | Not found | |

| Date | Team | Location | Results | Comments |
|---|---|---|---|---|
| September 13, 1936 | Bruning town team, Bruning, Nebraska | Bruning, Nebraska | Not found | |
| September 18, 1936 | The winner of the Kearney-Schuyler game that was scheduled to be played on September 17, 1936 | Albion, Nebraska | Not found | |
| September 21, 1936 | Stromsburg, Iowa | Stromsburg, Iowa | Lost; 12–4 | Line score totals: Omaha 4-11-6; Stromsburg 12-9-0. Omaha's battery: Moody and Davis |

## Table 5: The 1935 Omaha Tigers[105]

| Name | Position | Comments |
|---|---|---|
| Benson | 3B, P, 2B, C | Possibly Augusta Benson, a pitcher for the Washington Elite Giants in 1937 and the Memphis Red Sox in 1940 |
| Bubbles (Bubber, Bubbe, Bubler, Burber) | P, 1B, 3B | Possibly Bubber "Bubbles" Berry, a pitcher for the Ethiopian Clowns and the Atlanta Black Crackers in 1938 |
| Curry (Currie), Homer | CF, RF, P | Homer "Blue Demon" or "Goose" Curry (1905–1974). A fast contact hitter, Curry played all three outfield positions, pitched, and occasionally saw action as a first baseman, second baseman, and third baseman during a long career with the Cleveland Tigers in 1928, the Memphis Red Sox from 1929 through 1933, 1937, 1949, 1950, 1953, and 1955, the Monroe Monarchs in 1932, the Nashville Elite Giants in 1933 and 1934, the Columbus Elite Giants in 1935, the Washington Elite Giants in 1936, the Indianapolis Athletics in 1937, the New York Black Yankees from 1938 through 1940, the Baltimore Elite Giants in 1938, 1940, and 1941, the Philadelphia Stars from 1942 through 1947, the Louisville Black Caps in 1954, and the Birmingham Black Barons in 1955. |
| Graham (possibly Grimm) | 3B, LF | |
| Grimm | LF, 1B, 3B, 2B | |
| Gunn (possibly Grimm) | 3B | |
| Henson | P | |
| Hubert | 1B, LF | |
| James | SS | Possibly Tice Livingston (Livingstone) "Selassie," "Tarzan," or "Winky" James (1914–1989), a shortstop for the Chicago American Giants in 1936 and 1941; a shortstop for the Memphis Red Sox in 1936; a shortstop and third baseman for the Memphis Red Sox in 1941; a shortstop and second baseman for the Cincinnati-Cleveland Buckeyes in 1942; a second baseman for the Cincinnati Clowns in 1942; and, depending on the source, a player (no position given) for the Birmingham Black Barons in 1938, a shortstop for the Ethiopian Clowns from 1939 through 1940 and again in 1942, and a shortstop for the Cincinnati-Indianapolis Clowns in 1946 |

| Name | Position | Comments |
|---|---|---|
| Jesse (Jessie) | RF, LF, 2B, SS | |
| Johnican (Johnsicano, Johnson?) | P, RF | Possibly the Johnson who played for the Memphis Red Sox in 1938 or J. "Lefty" Johnson, a pitcher, first baseman, and outfielder for the Memphis Red Sox from 1929 through 1933 |
| Jordan | RF, LF | |
| Klum | C | |
| Lee | CF, RF, P | |
| Lomax | LF, RF, P, 2B | |
| Lonezo | 3B | |
| Longley (Longlgey) | 2B, C | |
| Mason, Charles "Charlie," "Corporal," or "Suitcase" | 1B, P, RF, CF | A good-hitting, run-producing left fielder-right fielder with a strong arm, who sometimes played first base and center field and occasionally pitched, Mason (1894-?) saw action with the Richmond Giants in 1922, the New York Bacharach Giants in 1922, the Atlantic City Bacharach Giants from 1923 through 1925, the New York Lincoln Giants from 1925 through 1928, the Newark Stars in 1926, and the Homestead Grays in 1929 before joining the Omaha Tigers in 1935. |
| McNeil | SS, 2B, P, 1B | |
| Meadows | CF, RF | |
| Morgan | 2B, P, 3B | |
| Reynolds | LF, 1B, RF | Was listed as playing third base against the Monroe Monarchs on June 8, 1935, but based on internal and external evidence, he was the team's left fielder. |
| Smith, L. | 3B, 2B | |
| Smith, R. | C | Was listed as playing center field against the Kearney Independents on July 21, 1935, but based on internal and external evidence, he was the team's catcher. |
| Taylor | C | Possibly Raymond "Broadway" Taylor (1910-?), a catcher who played for the Memphis Red Sox from 1931 through 1933 and again in 1937 and 1938, the Kansas City Monarchs in 1938 and 1944, the New York Black Yankees in 1942, the Cincinnati-Cleveland Buckeyes in 1942, the Cleveland Buckeyes in 1943, the Cleveland Clippers in 1946, and, depending on the source, the Memphis Red Sox in 1934, the Córdoba Cafeteros in 1939 and the Veracruz Azules in 1940 and 1941 |
| Walker | P | |

## Table 6: The 1936 Omaha Tigers/Monarchs[106]

| Name | Position | Comments |
|---|---|---|
| Brooks, Smiling | P | Possibly E. Brooks, a pitcher for the Kansas City Monarchs in 1936 |

| Name | Position | Comments |
|---|---|---|
| Davis, Piper | SS, C | Lorenzo "Piper" Davis (1917–1997). A multitalented player who performed at every position at one time or another during his baseball career but whose best spots were second base, first base, and shortstop, Davis saw service with the Piper Second Nine prior to, depending on the source, July 3, 1931, or July 2, 1932, the Piper First Nine from sometime between July 3, 1931, and July 2, 1932, to the early part of 1936, the Tennessee Coal and Iron or Stockham Pipe and Fittings Company (the original name of Stockham Valves and Fittings), depending on the source, in 1937, the Washington Browns in 1938, the American Cast Iron Pipe Company from 1939 through 1943, the Birmingham Black Barons from 1942 through 1950, the Jalisco Charros in 1950, the Scranton Miners in 1950, the Ottawa Giants in 1951, the Oakland Oaks from 1951 through 1955, the Los Angeles Angels from 1955 through 1957, the Fort Worth Cats from 1957 through 1958, and the Stockham Valves and Fittings from 1962 through 1964 |
| Dubose (Dubos, Dubsow, Dufos, Dufose, Dufore) | RF, 2B | |
| Eatmon (Eatman, Eastman, Eaton), Lefty | P, LF | Possibly Elbert Eatmon or Eaton (1914–1998), a pitcher for the Birmingham Black Barons in 1937 and 1938 |
| Harris, M. "Steel Arm" | 3B, 2B, RF | |
| Herman, Booker | UT | |
| Hughes | P, RF | |
| Johnson | LF, 1B | See Johnican in Table 5 |
| Langford | C, 3B | |
| Lee | RF, 2B | |
| Mason (Macon, Magon), Charles "Charlie," "Corporal," or "Suitcase" | 1B, RF, CF, P | See Table 5. |
| Mayweather (Mayweathers, Maeweathers, Maweathers, Maryweathers), Submarine | P | Possibly Elliot Mayweather, a pitcher for the Memphis Red Sox in 1929 and, depending on the source, 1928 |
| Moody | P, LF | Possibly Frank Moody, a pitcher for the Birmingham Black Barons in 1940 |
| Powell, Joe "Step Infetchit" | CF, LF, RF | |
| Reed | P | |
| Reese | C | He was 20 years old in early June of 1936. |
| Smith, Rufus | 2B, 3B | |
| Watts (Wall, Walts) | CF, RF | |
| Woodson, Speedball or Lefty | P, RF | |

## Table 7: Found Games Scheduled by the 1947 Omaha Rockets[107]

| Date | Team | Location | Results | Comments |
|---|---|---|---|---|
| May 17, 1947 | Huron Elks, Huron, South Dakota | Fair Grounds Park, Huron, South Dakota | Not found | The game was scheduled to start at 5:00 p.m. at Fair Grounds Park. |
| May 20, 1947 | Rock Valley, Iowa | Rock Valley, Iowa | Lost; 14–3 | The game was scheduled to start at 8:00 p.m. Collins homered. Line score totals: Omaha 3-4-6; Rock Valley 14-10-4 |
| May 21, 1947 | Creighton, Nebraska | Creighton, Nebraska | Not found | |
| May 22, 1947 | Oakland, Nebraska | Oakland, Nebraska | Lost; 11–3 | Oakland was a member of the Iowa-Nebraska Semipro League. Line score totals: Omaha 3-6-2; Oakland 11-7-3. Omaha's battery: Oliver, Daniels, Collins and Wright, Sanders, Williams |
| May 23, 1947 | Akron town team, Akron, Iowa | Akron, Iowa | Lost; 9–8 | The game was scheduled to start at 8:15 p.m. under "100 1,500-watt light units mounted in banks on 70-foot poles." |
| May 24, 1947 | House of David | American Legion Park, Council Bluffs, Iowa | Lost; 10–8 | The game started at 8:15 p.m. and the price of admission was 75 cents for adults and 35 cents for children under 16. Attendance was a paid crowd of 650. Jewel Day hit a three-run homer in the first and the Rockets scored two more runs in the bottom of the fifth and three more in the bottom of the ninth, but it was not enough to secure the win. Line score totals: House of David 10-15-4; Omaha 8-12-4. Omaha's battery: Napoleon and Jackson |
| May 27, 1947 | Rock Valley, Iowa | Rock Valley, Iowa | Lost; 14–3 | |
| May 27, 1947 | Flandreau, South Dakota | Flandreau, South Dakota | Not found | |
| May 28, 1947 | Woodbine, Iowa | Woodbine, Iowa | Not found | |
| May 29, 1947 | Wayne, Nebraska | Wayne, Nebraska | Not found | |
| May 30, 1947 | House of David | Soos Park, Sioux City, Iowa | Lost; 3–2 | The scheduled staring time of the game was 8:15 p.m. and the attendance was 2,100. The score was tied at two going into the top of the eighth when Gardner, the right fielder for the House of David, hit a home run to win the contest. Depending on the source, the line score totals were: House of David 3-8-2; Omaha 2-8-1, or House of David 3-9-1; Omaha 2-7-9. Omaha's battery: Dunbar and Oliver, Duffy. The time of the game was one hour and 45 minutes. |

5. *Shadow Ball in the River City* (Louisa)   125

| Date | Team | Location | Results | Comments |
|---|---|---|---|---|
| May 31, 1947 | Madison, Nebraska | Madison, Nebraska | Not found | |
| June 1, 1947 | Norfolk, Nebraska | Norfolk, Nebraska | The results of this game and the ones against the Alliance VFW on June 5 and Hemingford on June 7 are one win and probably two cancelations. | According to the June 11, 1947, issue of the *Omaha World-Herald*, the Rockets went 5–1 during the week of June 1–June 7, 1947. However, seven games were scheduled to be played that week, not including a game against the Lennox Browns that was played. The results of the Benkelman, Wray, Lennox, and two Scottsbluff games are known, so the Rockets defeated one of the following three teams and apparently did not play the other two: Norfolk, Alliance VFW, and Hemingford. |
| June 2, 1947 | Benkelman, Nebraska | Benkelman, Nebraska | Won; 10–3 | Mickey Stubblefield was the winning pitcher. |
| June 3, 1947 | Wray, Colorado | Wray, Colorado | Won; 12–0 | Teddie Epinosa was the winning pitcher. |
| June 4, 1947 | Scottsbluff, Nebraska | Scottsbluff, Nebraska | The Rockets record against Scottsbluff for this week was 1–1. | The Rockets either won this game and lost their game against Scottsbluff on June 6 or vice versa. |
| June 5, 1947 | Lennox Browns, Lennox, South Dakota | Lennox, South Dakota | Won; 9–1 | Espinosa pitched a four-hitter, walked six, and struck out 14, and Stubblefield had two hits. Line score totals: Omaha 9-8-5; Lennox 1-4-6. Omaha's battery: Espinosa and Thompson |
| June 5, 1947 | Alliance Veterans of Foreign Wars (VFW), Alliance, Nebraska | Alliance, Nebraska | The results of this game and the ones against Norfolk on June 1 and Hemingford on June 7 are one win and probably two cancelations. | According to the June 11, 1947, issue of the *Omaha World-Herald*, the Rockets went 5–1 during the week of June 1–June 7, 1947. However, seven games were scheduled to be played that week, not including a game against the Lennox Browns that was played. The results of the Benkelman, Wray, Lennox, and two Scottsbluff games are known, so the Rockets defeated one of the following three teams and apparently did not play the other two: Norfolk, Alliance VFW, and Hemingford. |
| June 6, 1947 | Scottsbluff, Nebraska | Scottsbluff, Nebraska | The Rockets record against Scottsbluff for this week was 1–1. | The Rockets either won this game and lost their game against Scottsbluff on June 4 or vice versa. |

126  Section I—The Long and Winding Road

| Date | Team | Location | Results | Comments |
|---|---|---|---|---|
| June 7, 1947 | Hemingford, Nebraska | Hemingford, Nebraska | The results of this game and the ones against Norfolk on June 1 and the Alliance VFW on June 5 are one and probably two cancelations. | According to the June 11, 1947, issue of the *Omaha World-Herald*, the Rockets went 5–1 during the week of June 1–June 7, 1947. However, seven games were scheduled to be played that week, not including a game against the Lennox Browns that was played. The results of the Benkelman, Wray, Lennox, and two Scottsbluff games are known, so the Rockets defeated one of the following three teams and apparently did not play the other two: Norfolk, Alliance VFW, and Hemingford. |
| June 11, 1947 | McCook, Nebraska | McCook, Nebraska | Not found | |
| June 12, 1947 | Superior, Nebraska | Superior, Nebraska | Not found | |
| June 13, 1947 | Superior, Nebraska | Superior, Nebraska | Not found | |
| June 14, 1947 | Geneva, Nebraska | Geneva, Nebraska | Not found | |
| June 15, 1947 | Goetz Country Club (Sandy's), Lincoln, Nebraska | Lincoln, Nebraska | Cancelled because of wet grounds | According to the June 16, 1947, issue of the *Omaha World-Herald*, the Rockets played .800 ball for the first half of June. |
| June 15, 1947 | Odell town team, Odell, Nebraska | Odell, Nebraska | Lost; 2–1 | Depending on the source, the game was scheduled to start at either 2:00 p.m. or 2:30 p.m. Admission was 60 cents for adults and 35 cents for children. Line score totals: Omaha 1-4-1; Odell 2-6-0. Omaha's battery: Napoline and Duffy |
| June 16, 1947 | Norton, Kansas | Norton, Kansas | Not found | |
| June 17, 1947 | Holdrege, Nebraska | Holdrege, Nebraska | Not found | |
| June 18, 1947 | Hastings Sultans, Hastings, Nebraska | Hastings, Nebraska | Won; 3–2 | Jewel Day drove in Dusty Rhodes with the winning run on a single in the top of eighth. Hastings loaded the bases in the bottom of the ninth but Omaha prevented them from scoring. Line score totals: Omaha 3-5-6; Hastings 2-7-2. Omaha's battery: Espinosa and Saunders. According to the June 18, 1947, issue of the *Muscatine (IA) Journal*, the Rockets had won nine of their last 10 games. |
| June 19, 1947 | York, Nebraska | York, Nebraska | Not found | |
| Depending on the source, June 20 or 22, 1947 | Glenwood, Iowa | Glenwood, Iowa | Not found | |
| June 21, 1947 | Edina, Missouri | Edina, Missouri | Not found | |

## 5. Shadow Ball in the River City (Louisa)

| Date | Team | Location | Results | Comments |
|---|---|---|---|---|
| June 22, 1947 | Muscatine Red Sox, Muscatine, Iowa | Muscatine, Iowa | Won; 9–2 | The game was scheduled to start about 3:30 p.m. Michie went 4-for-5 with two runs scored, Rhoades went 3-for-4 with a run scored, and Saunders went 3-for-6 with a run scored. Line score totals: Omaha 9–16–2; Muscatine 2–5–2. Omaha's battery: Napoleon and Saunders |
| June 22, 1947 | Veterans of Foreign Wars Post 788, Cedar Rapdis, Iowa | Daniels Park, Cedar Rapids, Iowa | Not found | |
| Week of June 22–28, 1947 | Dyersville, Iowa | Dyersville, Iowa | Won; score not found | |
| Week of June 22–28, 1947 | Woodbine, Iowa | Woodbine, Iowa | Won; score not found | |
| June 24, 1947 | Senior Legion, Osage, Iowa | Osage, Iowa | Tied; 2–2 | Called because of darkness after 10 innings. The Rockets were leading going into the bottom of the ninth when Osage tied the game. |
| June 27, 1947 | Sioux City Sportland Independents (Rudy's Sportland), Sioux City, Iowa | Soos Park, Sioux City, Iowa | Lost; 6–4 | The game was scheduled to start at 8:15 p.m. and the paid attendance was 577. Murphy went 3-for-4 with a double and two runs driven in, and Napoleon went 2-for-3 with a double. Line score totals: Omaha 4–12–6; Sioux City 6–10–1. Omaha's battery: Massie and Glenn, Day. The time of the game was one hour and 40 minutes. |
| June 29,1947 | Sioux City Sportland Independents (Rudy's Sportland), Sioux City, Iowa | Soos Park, Sioux City, Iowa | Lost; 11–6 | The game was scheduled to start at 3:00 p.m. and the entrance fee was 75 cents for general admission for adults, 50 cents for bleacher seats for adults, and 10 cents for children. Layne went 3-for-5, and Rhodes went 3-for-4 with a double and a run driven in. Line score totals: Omaha 6–11–2; Sioux City 11–16–2. Omaha's battery: Oliver and Saunders. The time of the game was one hour and 33 minutes. |
| June 29, 1947 | Oakland Larks, Oakland, California | American Legion Park, Council Bluffs, Iowa | Rained out | The game was scheduled to start at 8:15 p.m., with the admission price being 75 cents. |
| Sometime before July 6, 1947 | Mitchell Kernels, Mitchell, South Dakota | Not found | Lost; score not found | |
| July 6, 1947 | Manning town team, Manning, Iowa | Manning, Iowa | Lost; 3–1 | In a night game scheduled to start at 8:30 p.m., the Rockets outhit Manning, six to four, but could get only one run across the plate. |

128    Section I—The Long and Winding Road

| Date | Team | Location | Results | Comments |
|---|---|---|---|---|
| July 7, 1947 | Seneca, Kansas | Seneca, Kansas | Not found | |
| July 8, 1947 | Seneca, Kansas | Seneca, Kansas | Not found | |
| July 8, 1947 | Kansas-Nebraska League All-Stars | Seneca, Kansas | Lost; 15–10 | Referred to as "an exhibition baseball game," it was attended by 1,500 people. |
| July 9, 1947 | Topeka Owls, Topeka, Kansas | Topeka, Kansas | Not found | |
| July 10, 1947 | Wayne town team, Wayne, Nebraska | Wayne, Nebraska | Lost; 5–4 | The Rockets were leading 4–0 going into the bottom of the seventh inning, but Wayne scored one run in the seventh and three in the ninth to tie the game. Then, with two out in the 10th, a Wayne player named Weber hit a long home run to win the contest. Line score totals: Omaha 4-8-3; Wayne 5-10-4. Omaha's battery: Gibson and Glenn |
| July 11, 1947 | Scotland, South Dakota | Scotland, South Dakota | Not found | |
| July 13, 1947 | Canby, Minnesota | Canby, Minnesota | Not found | |
| July 13, 1947 | Hansonville, Minnesota | Hansonville, Minnesota | Not found | |
| July 15, 1947 | Marshall, Minnesota | Marshall, Minnesota | Not found | |
| July 15, 1947 | Goetz Country Club (Sandy's), Lincoln, Nebraska | Unknown | Won; 10–2 | |
| July 16, 1947 | Lake Benton, Minnesota | Lake Benton, Minnesota | Not found | |
| July 17, 1947 | Worthington, Minnesota | Worthington, Minnesota | Not found | |
| July 18, 1947 | Harlan, Iowa, of the Iowa-Nebraska League | Harlan, Iowa | Won; score not found | |
| July 20, 1947 | Goetz Country Club (Sandy's), Lincoln, Nebraska | Sherman Field, Lincoln, Nebraska | Postponed | The game was supposed to start at 3:00 p.m., but wet grounds forced it to be postponed. General admission was 75 cents; Knothole Kids were 10 cents. |
| July 20, 1947 | Stromsburg, Nebraska | Stromsburg, Nebraska | Lost; 6–2 | Line score totals: Omaha 2-3-2; Stromsburg 6-10-0. Omaha's battery: Stubblefield and Saunders |
| July 22, 1947 | Fonda, Iowa | Fonda, Iowa | Not found | |
| July 23, 1947 | Gowrie, Iowa | Gowrie, Iowa | Won; score not found | |
| July 24, 1947 | Glenwood town team, Glenwood, Iowa | Glenwood, Iowa | Won; 16–0 | Line score totals: Omaha 16-20-1; Glenwood 0-7-7. Omaha's battery: Espinosa and Saunders |

| Date | Team | Location | Results | Comments |
|---|---|---|---|---|
| July 25, 1947 | Stanton, Iowa | Stanton, Iowa | Won; 10–6 | The Rockets rallied in the ninth, scoring five runs on two hits, three errors, a walk, and a fielder's choice, to pull out the victory. Line score totals: Omaha 10-10-5; Stanton 6-5-5. Omaha's battery: Burgin, Napoleon and Saunders |
| July 26, 1947 | Norfolk, Nebraska | Norfolk, Nebraska | Not found | |
| July 27, 1947 | Franklin, Nebraska | Franklin, Nebraska | Won; score not found | |
| July 27, 1947 | Oxford, Nebraska | Oxford, Nebraska | Won; score not found | |
| July 29, 1947 | Fonda Indies, Fonda, Iowa | Fonda, Iowa | Not found | |
| Sometime during the week of July 27–August 2, 1947 | Superior, Nebraska | Superior, Nebraska | Won; score not found | |
| Sometime during the week of July 27–August 2, 1947 | McCook, Nebraska | McCook, Nebraska | Won; score not found | |
| July 30, 1947 | Lexington, Nebraska | Lexington, Nebraska | Lost; score not found | |
| August 1, 1947 | Winner, South Dakota | Winner, South Dakota | Lost; 5–4 | |
| August 3, 1947 | Bismarck Veterans, Bismarck, North Dakota | Bismarck, North Dakota | Won; 3–2 | |
| August 4, 1947 | Pierre, South Dakota | Pierre, South Dakota | Not found | |
| August 5, 1947 | Tyndall, South Dakota | Tyndall, South Dakota | Not found | |
| August 5, 1947 | Canistota, South Dakota | Canistota, South Dakota | Not found | |
| August 6, 1947 | Huron Elks, Huron, South Dakota | Huron, South Dakota | Cancelled | |
| August 6, 1947 | Bloomfield, Nebraska | Bloomfield, Nebraska | Not found | |
| August 7, 1947 | Ainsworth, Nebraska | Ainsworth, Nebraska | Lost; 3–2 | |
| August 8, 1947 | Mitchell, South Dakota | Mitchell, South Dakota | Not found | |

| Date | Team | Location | Results | Comments |
|---|---|---|---|---|
| Sometime between August 3 and August 9, 1947 | Various teams in the Dakotas | South Dakota and North Dakota | Presumably the victory over the Bismarck Veterans and the games against Pierre, Tyndall, Canistota, and Mitchell, as well as two other games | According to the August 10, 1947, issue of the *Omaha World-Herald*, the Rockets won four games and lost three during their trip to the Dakotas the week of August 3. |
| August 10, 1947 | Creston, Iowa | Creston, Iowa | Won; score not found | |
| August 10, 1947 | Red Oak, Iowa | Red Oak, Iowa | Won; 9–5 | Murphy had three hits in five at bats and McParea "shared fielding honors" with Laire of Red Oak. Line score totals: Omaha 9-13-1; Red Oak 5-8-6. Omaha's battery: Gibson and Saunders |
| August 12, 1947 | Wayne, Nebraska | Wayne, Nebraska | Won; 13–2 | |
| August 13, 1947 | Fort Dodge, Iowa | Fort Dodge, Iowa | Not found | |
| August 14, 1947 | Fullerton, Nebraska | Fullerton, Nebraska | Not found | |
| August 15, 1947 | Alliance VFW, Alliance, Nebraska | Alliance, Nebraska | Not found | |
| August 16, 1947 | Torrington, Wyoming | Torrington, Wyoming | Not found | |
| August 17, 1947 | Scottsbluff, Nebraska | Scottsbluff, Nebraska | Not found | The first game of a twi-night doubleheader |
| August 17, 1947 | Scottsbluff, Nebraska | Scottsbluff, Nebraska | Not found | The second game of a twi-night doubleheader |
| August 19, 1947 | North Platte, Nebraska | North Platte, Nebraska | Not found | |
| August 20, 1947 | Norton, Kansas | Norton, Kansas | Not found | |
| August 21, 1947 | Osceola, Nebraska | Osceola, Nebraska | Not found | According to the August 21, 1947, issue of the *Council Bluffs (IA) Nonpareil*, the Rockets were 51–29 to date. |
| August 22, 1947 | Plainview, Nebraska | Plainview, Nebraska | Not found | |

## 5. Shadow Ball in the River City (Louisa)

| Date | Team | Location | Results | Comments |
|---|---|---|---|---|
| August 23, 1947 | Bassett, Nebraska | Bassett, Nebraska | Not found | |
| August 23, 1947 | Albion, Nebraska | Albion, Nebraska | Not found | |
| August 24, 1947 | Bassett, Nebraska | Bassett, Nebraska | Not found | |
| August 24, 1947 | Creighton, Nebraska | Creighton, Nebraska | Not found | |
| August 25, 1947 | Mankato, Kansas | Mankato, Kansas | Won; 8–3 | |
| August 26, 1947 | Topeka, Kansas | Topeka, Kansas | Not found | |
| August 26, 1947 | Wausa, Nebraska | Wausa, Nebraska | Not found | |
| August 27, 1947 | Audubon, Iowa | Audubon, Iowa | Lost; 5–2 | In a game that was scheduled to begin at 8:15 p.m., Audubon scored four runs in the bottom of the eighth to win. Line score totals: Omaha 2-4-5; Audubon 5-7-2. Omaha's battery: Pedie and Walter |
| August 27, 1947 | Council Bluffs Browns, Council Bluffs, Iowa | American Legion Park, Council Bluffs, Iowa | Cancelled | Part of the Class A section of the Southwest Iowa Baseball Tournament. The game was scheduled to begin at 8:15 p.m., but it was announced on August 22 that the Rockets had withdrawn from the tournament "because their schedule is too heavy and dates are confusing." |
| August 28, 1947 | Council Bluffs Browns, Council Bluffs, Iowa | Arlington, Nebraska | Won; 7–6 | Part of the Class A section of the Arlington Baseball Tournament (Dodge County Fair Tournament). The game was scheduled to begin at 3:30 p.m. |
| August 29, 1947 | Omaha Storzes, Omaha, Nebraska | Arlington, Nebraska | Lost; 8–4 | The championship game of the Class A section of the Arlington Baseball Tournament (Dodge County Fair Tournament). Line score totals: Rockets 4-8-1; Storzes 8-16-2. Rockets' battery: Napolian, Gibson and Saunders |
| August 31, 1947 | Manning Firemen, Manning, Iowa | Manning, Iowa | Won; 12–4 | The Rockets led 8–0 after two innings and had a total of 19 hits for the game, with Walters, Murphy, Sanders, and Napolian each getting three. Omaha's battery: Gipon and Sanders |
| September 1, 1947 | Schuyler, Nebraska | Schuyler Ball Park, Schuyler, Nebraska | Won; 13–5 | The game was scheduled to start at 8:15 p.m. |

132   Section I—The Long and Winding Road

| Date | Team | Location | Results | Comments |
|---|---|---|---|---|
| September 2, 1947 | Wausa, Nebraska | Wausa, Nebraska | Not found | |
| September 5, 1947 | House of David | West Point, Nebraska | Not found | |
| September 6, 1947 | House of David | Hastings, Nebraska | Lost; 8–3 | The Rockets led 3–0 going into the seventh inning. |
| September 11, 1947 | Montgomery County All-Stars | Stanton, Iowa | Not found | |
| September 15, 1947 | Goetz Country Club (Sandy's), Lincoln, Nebraska | Sherman Field, Lincoln, Nebraska | Won; 12–4 | The game started at 8:15 p.m., with admission costing 75 cents for adults and 40 cents for children under 12. But the weather was cold, and according to the September 16, 1947, issue of the *Lincoln (NE) Star*, "[l]ess than 300 frigid fans were in the stands." However, an article that can be found in the September 16, 1947, issues of the *Lincoln (NE) Evening Journal* and the *Nebraska State Journal* specifically states "200 chilled fans." The Rocket offensive attack was led by McCrey, Stubblefield, and Clark, who each hit a single and a double, and Allen who had a pair of singles, and the entire Rocket team stole 10 bases. Line score totals: Omaha 12-16-3; Goetz 4-7-7. Omaha's battery: Gibson and Saunders |
| September 21, 1947 | Rock County All-Stars | Bassett, Nebraska | Not found | |

## Table 8: Found Games Scheduled by the 1948 Omaha Rockets[108]

| Date | Team | Location | Results | Comments |
|---|---|---|---|---|
| Sometime after April 28, 1948 | Chillicothe Merchants, Chillicothe, Missouri | Chillicothe, Missouri | Not found | |
| May 16, 1948 | Red Oak Red Sox, Red Oak, Iowa | Red Oak, Iowa | Lost; 8–0 | In relief, Cliff Burgin struck out 11 and gave up only two hits in six and a half innings. Line score totals: Omaha 0-2-2; Red Oak 8-8-4. Omaha's battery: Bishop, Burgin and J. Webb. Attendance was 1,500. |
| May 23, 1948 | Lamar, Colorado | Lamar, Colorado | Won this one and lost the one on the 24th or vice versa | |

| Date | Team | Location | Results | Comments |
|---|---|---|---|---|
| May 24, 1948 | Lamar, Colorado | Lamar, Colorado | Won this one and lost the one on the 23rd or vice versa | |
| May 27, 1948 | Pueblo, Colorado | Pueblo, Colorado | Won; score not found | |
| May 29, 1948 | St. Francis, Kansas | St. Francis, Kansas | Won; score not found | |
| May 30, 1948 | Stanton, Nebraska | Stanton, Nebraska | Won; 6–3 | |
| Sometime before May 31, 1948 | A team from Colorado or Kansas | A place in either Colorado or Kansas | Lost; score not found | |
| June 2, 1948 | Van Dyke Colored House of David | American Legion Park, Council Bluffs, Iowa | Lost; 13–2 | In a game that was scheduled to start at 8:15 p.m. and had an admission price of 75 cents, the Van Dyke Colored House of David scored three runs in the top of the first and never gave up the lead. Kenny Morris had two hits in four at bats for the Rockets. Line score totals: Colored House of David 13-19-4; Omaha 2-8-6. Omaha's battery: Senters, Bergin and Barnett |
| June 3, 1948 | Harlan Cardinals, Harlan, Iowa | Harlan, Iowa | Lost; 20–3 | Harlan outhit the Rockets 15-3. Omaha's battery: Barnett, Bishop and Austin. Mercifully, the game was called after seven innings. |
| June 6, 1948 | Fonda Indies, Fonda, Iowa | Fonda, Iowa | Lost; 7–4 | The game was scheduled to start at 8:15 p.m. and was tied at two in the top of the fifth inning, but during the next two innings, Fonda scored five runs to pull out the victory. |
| Sometime between June 6 and June 12, 1948 | Norton, Kansas | Norton, Kansas | Won; 14–4 | |
| Sometime between June 6 and June 12, 1948 | Delphos, Kansas | Delphos, Kansas | Won; 10–3 | |
| Sometime between June 6 and June 12, 1948 | Oxford, Nebraska | Oxford, Nebraska | Won; 16–10 | |

## 134    Section I—The Long and Winding Road

| Date | Team | Location | Results | Comments |
|---|---|---|---|---|
| June 16, 1948 | Stanton Vikings, Stanton, Iowa | Stanton, Iowa | Lost; 9–8 | The Rockets had an 8–1 lead after six and a half innings but could not secure the victory as the Vikings won in the bottom of the 11th. Line score totals: Omaha 8-11-2; Stanton 9-13-3. Omaha's battery: Massey, Johnson and Bonders |
| June 17, 1948 | Aurora, Nebraska | Aurora, Nebraska | Lost; 5–4 | Outhit 14–7, the Rockets lost the game in the bottom of the 12th. Omaha's battery: Bennett and Saunders. Bennett struck out eight, but Korte of Aurora whiffed 14. |
| June 18, 1948 | Tilden, Nebraska | Omaha, Nebraska, or Council Bluffs, Iowa | Not found | |
| June 19, 1948 | Osmond, Nebraska | Osmond, Nebraska | Not found | |
| June 20, 1948 | Winside, Nebraska | Winside, Nebraska | Not found | |
| June 22, 1948 | Mankato, Kansas | Mankato, Kansas | Not found | |
| June 24, 1948 | Odell, Nebraska | Odell, Nebraska | Postponed | |
| Probably sometime between June 25 and June 29, 1948 | McCook, Nebraska | McCook, Nebraska | Lost; 6–4 | |
| Probably sometime between June 25 and June 29, 1948 | Scottsbluff, Nebraska | Scottsbluff, Nebraska | Won; 9–4 | |
| Probably sometime between June 25 and June 29, 1948 | Lynam, Nebraska | Lynam, Nebraska | Won; 6–3 | |
| Probably sometime between June 25 and June 29, 1948 | Gering, Nebraska | Gering, Nebraska | Won; 8–3 | |
| Probably sometime between June 25 and June 29, 1948 | Torrington, Wyoming | Torrington, Wyoming | Won; 3–1 | |

| Date | Team | Location | Results | Comments |
|---|---|---|---|---|
| June 30, 1948 | Manning, Iowa | Manning, Iowa | Won; 14–11 | The Rockets had a slight lead in hits, 14–13, Saunders hit a home run, and Jahn pitched a complete game. |
| July 5, 1948 | Van Dyke Colored House of David | Nicollet Park, Minneapolis, Minnesota | Won; 10–4 | |
| July 6, 1948 | Annandale, Minnesota | Annandale, Minnesota | Not found | |
| July 7, 1948 | Glencoe, Minnesota | Glencoe, Minnesota | Not found | |
| July 8, 1948 | Waukon, Iowa | Waukon, Iowa | Not found | |
| July 9, 1948 | Harpers Ferry, Iowa | Harpers Ferry, Iowa | Won; 18–2 | Line score totals: Omaha 18-21-0; Harpers Ferry 2-4-1. Omaha's battery: Cannon, Saunders and Rinitz |
| July 10, 1948 | Stanley Legion Lions, Stanley, Wisconsin | Memorial Park, Stanley, Wisconsin | Lost; 14–12 | The game was scheduled to start at 8:15 p.m. |
| July 10, 1948 | Neillsville, Wisconsin | Neillsville, Wisconsin | Not found | |
| July 11, 1948 | Black River Falls, Wisconsin | Black River Falls, Wisconsin | Won; 10–8 | |
| July 18, 1948 | Elkader Vets, Elkader, Iowa | Elkader, Iowa | Lost; 4–2 | Line score totals: Omaha 2-5-3; Elkader 4-10-2. Omaha's battery: McCarley and Saunders |
| July 23, 1948 | Exira, Iowa | Woodbine, Iowa | Not found | The game was scheduled to start at either 8:00 p.m., according to an article in the July 18, 1948, issue of the *Omaha World-Herald*, or 8:15 p.m., according to an article in the July 23, 1948, issue of the *Omaha World-Herald*. |
| Probably July 24, 1948 | Humboldt Cardinals, Humboldt, Nebraska | Humboldt, Nebraska | Won; 7–5 | Ross hit a home run. |
| July 25, 1948 | Odell, Nebraska | Odell, Nebraska | Lost; 6–4 | Down 4–0 after five innings, the Rockets scored two runs in the top of the sixth and two more in the top of the seventh to tie the game before Odell scored twice in the bottom of the seventh to clinch the victory. John struck out six, but the Odell pitchers struck out 13. Line score totals: Omaha 4-5-1; Odell 6-9-4, though the run totals for both teams and the error total for the Rockets do not agree with what is found in the box score. Omaha's battery: John, Walters and Saunders |

## 136  Section I—The Long and Winding Road

| Date | Team | Location | Results | Comments |
|---|---|---|---|---|
| July 30, 1948 | Hamburg, Iowa | Hamburg, Iowa | Lost; 13–6 | The game was tied 4–4 going into the bottom of the third when Hamburg scored nine runs in four innings. Line score totals: Omaha 6-9-3; Hamburg 13-17-4. Omaha's battery: Senters, Massey, Bishoff and Saunders |
| Probably July 31, 1948 | Humboldt Cardinals, Humboldt, Nebraska | Humboldt, Nebraska | Lost; 4–1 | |
| August 1, 1948 | Breda Eagles, Breda, Iowa | Memorial Park, Breda, Iowa | Won; 4–2 | The Rockets pulled out the victory in the 11th inning. Admission was 50 cents (probably for adults) and 25 cents (probably for children). |
| August 13, 1948 | Fairfax, South Dakota | Fairfax, South Dakota | Won; 8–3 | |
| August 15, 1948 | Lusterville, South Dakota | Lusterville, South Dakota | Won; 10–5 | |
| August 16, 1948 | Avon, South Dakota | Avon, South Dakota | Won; 9–5 | |
| August 17, 1948 | Lake Andes, South Dakota | Lake Andes, South Dakota | Won; 13–8 | |
| August 18, 1948 | Fullerton, Nebraska | Fullerton, Nebraska | Not found | |
| August 23, 1948 | Wagner, South Dakota | Probably Wagner, South Dakota | Won; 11–0 | According to the August 25, 1948, issue of the *Omaha World-Herald*, this was the 10th victory in a row for the Rockets, indicating that the team had four wins that are not recorded in this table. |
| August 25, 1948 | Chicago Brown Bombers | Scotland, South Dakota | Not found | |
| August 27, 1948 | Monona County All-Stars | Woodbine, Iowa | Not found | |
| August 29, 1948 | Stromsburg, Nebraska | Stromsburg, Nebraska | Lost; 6–4 | Line score totals: Omaha 4-7-0; Stromsburg 6-13-1. Omaha's battery: Bishop, Massy and Walters |
| September 5, 1948 | Odell, Nebraska | Odell, Nebraska | Not found | The game was scheduled to start at 8:15 p.m. |
| September 8, 1948 | Hawarden Eagles, Hawarden, Iowa | Hawarden, Iowa | Lost; 10–3 | The Rockets arrived late because their bus broke down near Sioux City, so the game was shortened to seven innings. |
| Probably September 11, 1948 | Central Nebraska All-Stars | St. Paul, Nebraska | Lost; 1–0 | Sante Fe gave up only three hits, but one of them came in the ninth inning after a walk and an error, and it drove in the winning run. |

## Table 9: Found Games Scheduled by the 1949 Omaha Rockets[109]

| Date | Team | Location | Results | Comments |
|---|---|---|---|---|
| May 13, 1949 | Alexandria, Nebraska | Alexandria, Nebraska | Not found | A night game |
| May 15, 1949 | Stromsburg, Nebraska | Stromsburg, Nebraska | Not found | An afternoon game |
| May 18, 1949 | Crescent, Iowa | Crescent, Iowa | Not found | |
| May 19, 1949 | Carroll Merchants, Carroll, Iowa | Woodbine, Iowa | Rained out | Had been scheduled to start at 8:15 p.m., according to an article in the May 17, 1949, issue of the *Council Bluffs (IA) Nonpareil*, or 8:30 p.m., according to an article in the May 15, 1949, issue of the *Omaha World-Herald*. |
| May 20, 1949 | Osmond, Nebraska | Osmond, Nebraska | Not found | |
| The last third of May 1949 | Tilden, Nebraska | Tilden, Nebraska | Won; 7–0 | Hurler Cotton pitched a no-hitter. |
| May 22, 1949 | Bassett, Nebraska | Bassett, Nebraska | Either this game was won and the June 30 game with Bassett was lost or vice versa | Scheduled for the afternoon |
| May 22, 1949 | Bonesteel, South Dakota | Bonesteel, South Dakota | Won; 14–1 | Scheduled for the evening |
| The last third of May 1949 | Chamberlain, Nebraska | Chamberlain, Nebraska | Lost; 5–4, according to an article in the July 18, 1949, issue of the *(Sioux Falls, SD) Daily Argus-Leader*, or 6–4, according to an article in the May 26, 1949, issue of the *Omaha World-Herald* | |
| The last third of May 1949 | Lexington, Nebraska | Lexington, Nebraska | Won; 7–1 | |
| The last third of May 1949 | Ogallala, Nebraska | Ogallala, Nebraska | Won; 6–2 | |
| The last third of May 1949 | Wray, Colorado | Wray, Colorado | Won; 16–2 | |
| Probably May 30, 1949 | Minatare, Nebraska | Minatare, Nebraska | Won; 15–9 | Afternoon game |
| Probably May 30, 1949 | Minatare, Nebraska | Minatare, Nebraska | Lost; 3–2 | Night game. According to the May 31, 1949, issue of the *Omaha World-Herald*, after the loss to Minatare, the Rockets had won seven of 11 games, but this may have meant seven of the last 11 games played. |

138  Section I—The Long and Winding Road

| Date | Team | Location | Results | Comments |
|---|---|---|---|---|
| May 31, 1949 | Scottsbluff, Nebraska | Scottsbluff, Nebraska | Won; 10–3 | The first game of a double-header |
| May 31, 1949 | Scottsbluff, Nebraska | Scottsbluff, Nebraska | Lost; 8–4 | The second game of a double-header |
| May 31, 1949 | Peetz Merchants, Peetz, Colorado | Peetz, Colorado | Lost; 10–0 | The Rockets were held to four hits. |
| June 1, 1949 | North Platte, Nebraska | North Platte, Nebraska | Not found | |
| June 2, 1949 | Hemingford, Nebraska | Hemingford, Nebraska | Not found | |
| June 3, 1949 | Chadron, Nebraska | Chadron, Nebraska | Not found | |
| June 6, 1949 | Ravenna, Nebraska | Ravenna, Nebraska | Not found | |
| June 8, 1949 | Stanton Vikings, Stanton, Iowa | Stanton, Iowa | Lost; 8–4 | Stanton scored four runs in the bottom of the eighth to break a 4–4 tie and win the game. Line score totals: Omaha 4-7-4; Stanton 8-9-3. Omaha's battery: Russell, Vinson, and Webb |
| June 9, 1949 | Odell, Nebraska | Odell, Nebraska | Not found | The game was scheduled to start at 8:30 p.m. and admission was 50 cents for adults and 25 cents for children. |
| June 10, 1949 | Humboldt Cardinals, Humboldt, Nebraska | Humboldt, Nebraska | Won; 6–5 | Rockets scored two runs in the sixth inning to break a 4–4 tie. |
| June 11, 1949 | Vermillion, South Dakota | Vermillion, South Dakota | Not found | The game was scheduled to start at 9:00 p.m. |
| June 12, 1949 | Gregory, South Dakota | Gregory, South Dakota | Won; 9–1 | In a game that was scheduled to start at 2:00 p.m., Buford Conley scattered five hits. Line score totals: Omaha 9-10-3; Gregory 1-5-4. Omaha's battery: Conley and Massingale |
| June 12, 1949 | Wessington Springs, South Dakota | Wessington Springs, South Dakota | Not found | The game was scheduled to start at 8:30 p.m. |
| No date, but probably played on either June 15, 1949, or June 16, 1949 | Bloomfield, Nebraska | Bloomfield, Nebraska | Lost; 2–1 | Vinson was pitching a shutout going into the bottom of ninth when Bloomfield tied the score and then won in the 10th. Line score totals: Omaha 1-5-3; Bloomfield 2-7-2. Omaha's battery: Vinson and Massingale |

## 5. Shadow Ball in the River City (Louisa)

| Date | Team | Location | Results | Comments |
|---|---|---|---|---|
| June 17, 1949 | Hamburg, Iowa | Hamburg, Iowa | Won; 14–1 | Cooley hit a three-run homer in the seventh inning. Line score totals: Omaha 14-10-0; Hamburg 1-5-10. Omaha's battery: Cooley and Webb |
| June 18, 1949 | Belleville, Kansas | Belleville, Kansas | Lost; 5–4 | |
| June 23, 1949 | Rock Valley, Iowa | Rock Valley, Iowa | Lost; 23–7 | Verno slugged a home run and Webb and Hack socked triples, but Rock Valley pounded out 26 hits to Omaha's nine. Conley struck out four and walked three. Omaha's battery: Conley and Webb |
| No date, but probably played on either June 23, 1949, or June 24, 1949 | Lesterville, South Dakota | Lesterville, South Dakota | Won; 16–7 | According to an article in the June 24, 1949, issue of the *Omaha World-Herald*, Bishop and Connon "were the Rocket standouts" in both this game and the game against Wagner, South Dakota (see below). |
| No date, but probably played on either June 23, 1949, or June 24, 1949 | Wagner, South Dakota | Wagner, South Dakota | Won; 13–3 | |
| June 24, 1949 | Humboldt, Iowa | Humboldt, Iowa | Not found | Scheduled for the afternoon |
| June 24, 1949 | Humboldt, Iowa | Humboldt, Iowa | Not found | Scheduled for the evening |
| June 26, 1949 | Algona K.C.s, Algona, Iowa | The K.C.s' ballpark, Algona, Iowa | Lost; 14–5 | In a game that was scheduled to start at 2:30 p.m., the K.C.s got 13 hits and held the Rockets to only five, two of which, including a home run, were made by James Stephens. Omaha's battery: Jamerson, Vinson and Webb. Admission was 60 cents for adults and 25 cents for children. |
| June 26, 1949 | Wall Lake Lakes, Wall Lake, Iowa | Wall Lake, Iowa | Lost; 7–6 | The Rockets lost in the bottom of the ninth. |
| June 30, 1949 | Bassett, Nebraska | Bassett, Nebraska | Either this game was won and the May 22 game with Bassett was lost or vice versa | |

| Date | Team | Location | Results | Comments |
|---|---|---|---|---|
| July 3, 1949 | Belleville, Kansas | North Central Kansas Free Fairgrounds, Belleville, Kansas | Lost; 5–4 | The game was scheduled to start at 2:30 p.m., with admission being 60 cents for adults and 30 cents for children. Down 4–0 after five innings, the Rockets tied the game in the bottom of the seventh, but Belleville pulled out the victory in the 10th. Andy Varga, the Belleville pitcher, struck out 20 Rockets. Line score totals: Omaha 4-7-3; Belleville 5-11-3. Omaha's battery: McCray and Massingale |
| No date found, but the score was reported in the July 10, 1949, issue of the *Omaha World Herald*. | Ansley, Nebraska | Ansley, Nebraska | Won; 15–4 | |
| No date found, but the score was reported in the July 10, 1949, issue of the *Omaha World Herald*. | Norton, Kansas | Norton, Kansas | Won; 5–2 | |
| No dates found, but the results were reported in the July 17, 1949, issue of the *Omaha World Herald* | Three teams from South Dakota | Three places in South Dakota | Won three games | |
| No date found, but the score was reported in the July 17, 1949, issue of the *Omaha World Herald*. | Lennox, South Dakota | Lennox, South Dakota | Won; 14–4 | Line score totals: Omaha 14-16-1; Lennox 4-6-3. Omaha's battery: Vinson and Webb |
| July 24, 1949 | St. Paul, Nebraska | St. Paul, Nebraska | Not found | |
| July 26, 1949 | Kingsley, Iowa | Kingsley, Iowa | Not found | |
| July 27, 1949 | Lyons town team, Lyons, Nebraska | Lyons, Nebraska | Lost; 4–3 | Lyons pitcher Roy Pounds struck out 20 Rockets. |

## 5. Shadow Ball in the River City (Louisa)

| Date | Team | Location | Results | Comments |
|---|---|---|---|---|
| No date found, but the score was reported in the July 27, 1949, issue of the *Omaha World-Herald*. | Humphrey, Nebraska | Humphrey, Nebraska | Won; 8–5 | Line score totals: Omaha 8-10-1; Humphrey 5-7-2. Omaha's battery: McCray and Webb. According to the July 27, 1949, issue of the *Omaha World-Herald*, this was the Rockets' sixth win in seven games. |
| July 31, 1949 | Bancroft, Iowa | Memorial Park, Bancroft, Iowa | Lost; 4–0 | A plethora of errors hurt the Rockets. Line score totals: Omaha 0-4-8; Bancroft 4-6-1 |
| August 3, 1949 | Wall Lake Lakes, Wall Lake, Iowa | Wall Lake, Iowa | Not found | The game was scheduled to start at 8:30 p.m. |
| The tournament began on August 10 and continued through August 14, 1949. | | Blair, Nebraska | Not found | The Blair Invitational Baseball Tournament |
| August 23, 1949 | Clarkson town team, Clarkson, Nebraska | Clarkson, Nebraska | Rescheduled for August 30, 1949 | |
| August 26, 1949 | Red Oak Red Sox, Red Oak, Iowa | Red Oak, Iowa | Lost; 9–8 | The Rockets had a one-run lead going into the bottom of the ninth, but they could not hold it. Line score totals: Omaha 8-12-3; Red Oak 9-12-3. Omaha's battery Macrae and Massingale |
| August 30, 1949 | Clarkson town team, Clarkson, Nebraska | Clarkson, Nebraska | Lost | |
| September 4, 1949 | Kingsley town team, Kingsley, Iowa | Kingsley, Iowa | Not found | The game was scheduled to start at 8:00 p.m. |

### Table 10: Found Games Scheduled by the 1950 Omaha Rockets[110]

| Date | Team | Location | Results | Comments |
|---|---|---|---|---|
| April 30, 1950 | Minneapolis Clowns | Herman, Nebraska | Not found | |
| May 1, 1950 | Minneapolis Clowns | Burr Oak, Kansas | Not found | |
| May 2, 1950 | Minneapolis Clowns | Damar, Kansas | Not found | |
| May 3, 1950 | Minneapolis Clowns | Franklin, Nebraska | Not found | |
| May 4, 1950 | Minneapolis Clowns | Atwood, Kansas | Not found | |
| May 5, 1950 | Minneapolis Clowns | St. Francis, Kansas | Not found | |

142  Section I—The Long and Winding Road

| Date | Team | Location | Results | Comments |
|---|---|---|---|---|
| May 6, 1950 | Minneapolis Clowns | Glasco, Kansas | Not found | |
| May 7, 1950 | Unknown; possibly the Sabetha town team, Sabetha, Kansas | Sabetha, Kansas | Not found | |
| May 7, 1950 | Minneapolis Clowns | Odell, Nebraska | Not found | The game was scheduled to start at 8:00 p.m. and the admission was 75 cents for adults and 25 cents for children. |
| May 10, 1950 | Minneapolis Clowns | Franklin, Nebraska | Not found | |
| May 11, 1950 | Minneapolis Clowns | Hamburg, Iowa | Not found | The game was scheduled to start at 8:00 p.m. |
| May 12, 1950 | Cary's Travelers, Waterloo, Iowa | Waterloo, Iowa | Not found | The game was scheduled to start at 8:00 p.m. |
| May 17, 1950 | Superior Knights, Superior, Nebraska | Superior, Nebraska | Lost; 18–1 | The Rockets were held to four hits. |
| May 21, 1950 | AFL Athletic Association Ballteam [sic], La Crosse, Wisconsin | Copeland Park, La Crosse, Wisconsin | Won; 4–1 | The game was scheduled to start at 2:30 p.m. and the admission was 75 cents for adults and 35 cents for children. Cannon struck out five and did not give up any walks. Biship and Cannon each went 2-for-3 and scored a run. Line score totals: Omaha 4-6-1; AFL 1-8-1. Omaha's battery: Cannon and Walters. |
| May 24, 1950 | Superior, Nebraska | Superior, Nebraska | Lost; score not found | |
| May 26, 1950 | Sibley Majors, Sibley, Iowa | Sibley, Iowa | Lost; 6–5 | Cotton pitched for the Rockets, who lost when Sibley scored a run in the ninth inning. |
| May 27, 1950 | Akron Indees, Akron, Iowa | Akron, Iowa | Not found | The game was originally scheduled for May 25, 1950, and had a starting time of 9:00 p.m. |
| May 28, 1950 | Newman Grove, Nebraska | Newman Grove, Nebraska | Not found | |
| May 29, 1950 | Winner Pheasants, Winner, South Dakota | Winner, South Dakota | Lost; 8–6 | |
| May 30, 1950 | Scottsbluff, Nebraska | Scottsbluff, Nebraska | Not found | The afternoon game of an afternoon-evening doubleheader |

| Date | Team | Location | Results | Comments |
|---|---|---|---|---|
| May 30, 1950 | Scottsbluff, Nebraska | Scottsbluff, Nebraska | Not found | The evening game of an afternoon-evening doubleheader |
| May 31, 1950 | Alliance, Nebraska | Alliance, Nebraska | Not found | |
| June 1, 1950 | Chadron, Nebraska | Chadron, Nebraska | Not found | |
| June 4, 1950 | Rapid City Red Sox, Rapid City, South Dakota | Camp Rapid, Rapid City, South Dakota | Lost; 4–3 | The game was scheduled to start at 8:00 p.m. Omaha scored two runs in the top of the ninth, but it was too little too late. Cannon went 2-for-4; Bishop, Wells, and Hack each scored a run; and Wells, Collins, and Cotton each had an RBI. Line score totals: Omaha 3-6-3; Rapid City 4-8-2. Omaha's battery: Cotton and Wells |
| June 5, 1950 | Rapid City Red Sox, Rapid City, South Dakota | Camp Rapid, Rapid City, South Dakota | Won; 13–6 | Stevens went 4-for-5, with a double, a triple, a pair of singles, and two runs scored; both Cannon and Hack went 3-for-5, with the former hitting a home run, scoring three runs, and driving in four and the latter stealing a base, scoring a run, and driving in two; and everyone else in the lineup got at least one hit. Line score totals: Omaha 13-19-3; Rapid City 6-11-4. Omaha's battery: Schaggs and Wells |
| June 15, 1950 | Edgemont, South Dakota | Edgemont, South Dakota | Won; 5–2 | Line score totals: Omaha 5-5-2; Edgemont 2-6-3. Omaha's battery: Walters and Wells |
| July 7, 1950 | Estevan Maple Leafs, Estevan, Canada | Estevan, Canada | Lost; 10–7 | |
| July 8, 1950 | Estevan Maple Leafs, Estevan, Canada | Estevan, Canada | Lost; 13–11 | Bishop was the losing pitcher. |
| July 30, 1950 | Rapid City Red Sox, Rapid City, South Dakota | Camp Rapid, Rapid City, South Dakota | Not found | The game was scheduled to start at 8:15 p.m. |
| July 31, 1950 | Rapid City Red Sox, Rapid City, South Dakota | Camp Rapid, Rapid City, South Dakota | Not found | |

144    Section I—The Long and Winding Road

## Table 11: The 1947 Omaha Rockets[111]

| Name | Position | Comments |
|---|---|---|
| Allen | RF, LF | Probably James Allen. See Table 12. |
| Bryant, Clarence | P | |
| Burgin | P | Probably Clifford Burgin. See Table 12. |
| Clark, James or Eddie | 3B | |
| Collins, Eugene "Gene" | P, 3B | Eugene Marvin Collins (1925–1998), a left-handed pitcher and outfielder who played for the Kansas City Monarchs from 1947 through 1951, the Waterloo White Hawks in 1951, the Wisconsin Rapids White Sox in 1952, the Colorado Springs Sky Sox and the Superior Blues in 1952 and 1953, the Veracruz Águila from 1955 through 1957, the Poza Rica Petroleros from 1958 through 1961, and the Mexico City Diablos Rojos in 1961 |
| Daniels, Robert Lee "Lefty" | P | |
| Davis | 1B | |
| Day, Jewel (Jewell) "Mighty" | 1B, C | Was a right-hand throwing and hitting first baseman for the Los Angeles White Sox and an outfielder for the San Francisco Sea Lions in 1946, and according to an article in the May 28, 1947, issue of the *Sioux City (IA) Journal*, he was from Bluefield, West Virginia, and had played for Bluefield State College |
| Douglas, Del | LF | |
| Duffy, W.C. | C | Billy Duffy, a catcher for the Kansas City Monarchs in 1947 |
| Dunbar | P | |
| Espinosa (Ecpinosa, Epinosa, Espinola), Teddie (Teddy, Ted) | P, 3B, RF | A Puerto Rican who was probably the pitcher with the last name of Espenosia who played for the Indianapolis Clowns in 1947. Also, according to an article in the June 29, 1947, issue of the *Council Bluffs (IA) Nonpareil*, he had played in the Cuban League during the previous winter. |
| Gibson (Gipon), Welda | P | Welda H. Gibson (1929– ), a right-handed hurler and bad switch-hitter who saw action for the Houston Eagles in 1949 and 1950, the Oklahoma City Indians and the Yuma Sun Sox in 1955, the Nuevo Laredo Tecolotes and the Victoria Eagles in 1956, and the Tucson Cowboys and the Hobbs Sports in 1957 |
| Glen (Glenn), Edgar | P, RF, C | |
| Jackson | C | Possibly Isiah (Isaiah) "Ike" or "Stonewall" Jackson (1923–1964), a catcher, outfielder, first baseman, and pitcher who played for the Kansas City Monarchs from 1951 through 1953, the Carlsbad Potashers from 1953 through 1955, and the Midland Indians in 1956. For his career in Organized Baseball, he batted .355, with a .586 slugging average and 87 home runs. |
| Lane (Lainne, Layne) | CF, RF | Richard "Night Train" Lane (1928–2002), a Pro Football Hall of Fame defensive back who played for the Los Angeles Rams in 1952 and 1953, the Chicago Cardinals from 1954 through 1959, and the Detroit Lions from 1960 through 1965. For five seasons, he also saw action as an offensive end. |

| Name | Position | Comments |
|---|---|---|
| Massey (Massie) | 3B, P | Probably James Massie. See Tables 12 and 13. |
| McKay (McCarey, McCrey) | CF, RF | |
| McParea | SS | |
| Michie | SS | |
| Morris, Kenny | CF, LF | A football star at Boys Town |
| Murphy, Sylvester "Syl" | 2B, RF | |
| Napoleon (Napolian, Napoline), Charles "Lefty" | P, RF, LF | Lawrence "Larry" or "Lefty" Napoleon, a small left-handed pitcher for the Cincinnati Crescents in 1946 and the Kansas City Monarchs in 1946 and 1947 |
| Oliver, Herschel | P, C, SS | |
| Pedie | P | |
| Rhodes, Dusty | 1B, LF | |
| Robertson | 2B, RF | |
| Roe | 1B | Probably Dusty Rhodes |
| Sanders | P, C | Probably Horatius Saunders |
| Sanderson | SS, 1B | |
| Saunders (Sanders), Horatius "Dedee" ("Dee Dee") | C, 3B | The team captain |
| Stafford, Clifford "Lefty" | P, OF | A good hitter and a fast base runner |
| Stubblefield, Mickey | P, SS | Wilker Harrison Thelbert (or Thelbert W.) "Little Satch," "Mickey," or "The Mayfield Mounder" Stubblefield (1926–2013). Best known as a pitcher, Stubblefield could play any position and saw action with the Kansas City Stars in 1948, the Kansas City Monarchs in 1948 and 1949, the McCook Cats from late 1949 through 1951, 1955, and perhaps some additional seasons, the Mayfield Blackhawks in 1952, 1953, and possibly 1946, the Mayfield Clothiers in 1952, and the Duluth Dukes in 1953. |
| Thomas or Thompson | C | |
| Vertam | P | |
| Walter | C | Probably Chophouse Walters. See Table 12. |
| Walters | LF | Chophouse Walters? |
| West, Tom | P | |
| Williams, Ralph | C, OF | |
| Wright, Bill | RF | Bill Wright, an outfielder for the Kansas City Monarchs in 1948 |
| Wright, Charles | P | |
| Wright, ? | C | |

## Table 12: The 1948 Omaha Rockets[112]

| Name | Position | Comments |
|---|---|---|
| Allen, James "Jim" | OF | |
| Austin | C | |
| Barrett (Barnett), A.G. | C, P | |
| Bennett | P | Probably Jerry Bennett, a pitcher for the Kansas City Monarchs in 1951 |
| Bishop (Bishoff), Donald "Don" | P | |
| Borders | C | |
| Burgin (Burdin, Bergin, Berrigan, Barrigan), Clifford "Cliff" | P | |
| Cannon | LF, P | Probably Ernest Cannon. See Tables 13 and 14. |
| Clark, Ed, Eddie | 1B | |
| Jahn (John) | P | |
| Johnson | P | Possibly Curtis Johnson, a pitcher for the Kansas City Monarchs in 1950; or James D. "J.D." Johnson, a pitcher for the Philadelphia Stars in 1950, the Birmingham Black Barons in 1952, and the Kansas City Monarchs in 1952 and 1953; or L. Johnson (who may have been Leonard Johnson), a pitcher for the Kansas City Monarchs in 1948; or Leonard Johnson, a pitcher for the Chicago American Giants in 1947—he was also a left fielder in at least one game for the club that season—and 1948, the Kansas City Monarchs in 1948, the Nuevo Laredo Tecolotes from 1949 through 1951, and the Minot Mallards in 1951 |
| Massie (Massey, Massy), James "Jim" | P, 3B | |
| McCarley | P | Probably William McCreary, a pitcher for the Fargo-Moorhead Twins in 1949 and, according to an article in the April 24, 1949, issue of the *Omaha World-Herald*, the first African American to play in the Northern League |
| McCrary | SS | William L. "Bill" or "Youngblood" McCrary (1929–2018), a reserve shortstop for the Kansas City Monarchs in 1946 and 1947, who also played for the Fargo-Moorhead Twins in 1949 and the Janesville Cubs in 1951 |
| Morris, Kenny | 3B, CF | See Table 11. |
| Murphy | 2B | Probably Sylvester Murphy. See Table 11. |
| Rinitz | C | |
| Ross | RF | |
| Sante Fe | P | |
| Saunders (Sunders) | C, P | Probably Horatius Saunders. See Table 11. |
| Senter (Senters), John | P | |
| Stevens, James "Jim" | P, CF | |

| Name | Position | Comments |
|---|---|---|
| Walters, Chophouse | OF, P, C | |
| Watts, Al | INF | |
| Webb, Jim | C, INF | |
| Webb, Zip | OF | |
| Williams, Cotton | P | Probably Robert A. "Bob" or "Cotton" Williams (1917–2000), who saw action with the Newark Eagles as a shortstop, second baseman, and third baseman in 1943, as a third baseman, left fielder, shortstop, second baseman, and pitcher in 1945, as a pitcher in 1946, as a pitcher and third baseman in 1947, and as a pitcher, left fielder, and right fielder in 1948; with the Houston Eagles as a pitcher in 1949 and a left fielder and pitcher in 1950; with the New Orleans Eagles as a pitcher in 1951; and with the Philadelphia Stars as a left fielder and pitcher in 1951. He was sometimes referred to with the last name of "Cotton." |

## Table 13: The 1949 Omaha Rockets[113]

| Name | Position | Comments |
|---|---|---|
| Bishop, Donald | P, LF | |
| Cannon (Connon), Ernest "Cannonball" | P, RF, LF | |
| Conley (Connely), Buford "Tex" | P, 2B, 3B | A right-hander who pitched for the Kansas City Monarchs in 1948, he was 17–11 with the Rockets this season. |
| Cooley | P | Possibly the Dooley—no first name has been found—who was a pitcher for the Kansas City Monarchs in 1951 or possibly Buford Conley |
| Cotton, Hurler | P | See Cotton Williams in Table 12. |
| Green, Robert | UT, P | Possibly the Green—no first name has been found—who was a center fielder for the Chicago American Giants in 1946 or the Green who was a left fielder for the Kansas City Monarchs in 1952 |
| Hack (Hock) | SS | |
| Jamerson (Jameson), Londell | P | Londell "Tincy" Jamerson (1931–1975), a pitcher for the Kansas City Monarchs in 1950 and 1951 |
| Massie (Massey), James | 3B, 2B | |
| Massingale (Massingole), Mack | C | The manager of the team |
| McCreary (McCrary, McCray, Macrae), William | P | William McCreary, who pitched for the Omaha Rockets in 1948 and for the Fargo-Moorhead Twins earlier in 1949 |
| Nash, Jim | P | |
| Russell | P | |
| Stephens, James | CF, UT | Probably James Stevens. See Table 12. |
| Stephenson | 2B | Probably James Stevens. See Table 12. |

| Name | Position | Comments |
|---|---|---|
| Utley, Charles | SS | |
| Varona (Verono, Verone, Verno, Vanora), Gilberto (Jilberto) | 1B, P | Gilberto Varona (1930–?), a first baseman for the Memphis Red Sox from 1950 through 1955 and the Bryan/Del Rio Indians in 1954 |
| Vinson, Billie | P, RF | |
| Webb, Joe | C, UT | |

### Table 14: The 1950 Omaha Rockets[114]

| Name | Position | Comments |
|---|---|---|
| Bagtime | RF | |
| Bishop (Biship) | LF, P | Probably Donald Bishop. See Tables 12 and 13. |
| Cannon (Connon), Ernest "Cannonball" | P, RF | |
| Collins | 1B | |
| Cotton | P, 1B | See Cotton Williams in Table 12. |
| Freeman, Jim | 2B, 1B | Played for the Cuban Las Palomas. Was dropped during the season. |
| Hack | 3B, 2B | |
| Saunders (Sanders), Horatius "Dedee" ("Dee Dee") | C | The 37-year-old player-manager, who had played for the Van Dyke Colored House of David in 1948 and the Broadway Clowns in 1949. Also, see Table 11. |
| Saunders | SS | |
| Skagges (Schaggs), Edward | P | A 22-year-old left-handed hurler from Paducah, Kentucky, who was 17–2 for the Rockets when he joined the Estevan Maple Leafs on July 11, 1950. |
| Stevens | CF | Probably James Stevens. See Table 12. |
| Walters (Walter) | C, 3B, P | Probably Chophouse Walters. See Table 12. |
| Wells | C | |

### Notes

1. James A. Riley, *The Biographical Encyclopedia of the Negro Baseball Leagues* (New York: Carroll & Graf Publishers, 1994), xxii.

2. Jules Tygiel, *Extra Bases: Reflections on Jackie Robinson, Race, and Baseball History* (Lincoln: University of Nebraska Press, 2002), 73.

3. Western League Park, which was located between 13th and 15th streets and Castelar and Vinton streets, went by several names: Western League Park (for the league that Omaha's white minor league team belonged to), League Park (a shortened form of Western League Park), Rourke Park (for William "Pa" Rourke, the former owner and manager of Omaha's white minor league team), and Vinton Street Park (for its location).

4. "Colored Ball Team to Play at League Park," *Omaha World-Herald*, April 7, 1922.

5. For more information about Jackson, cf. Riley, *The Biographical Encyclopedia of the Negro Baseball Leagues*, 413; Thom Loverro, *The Encyclopedia of Negro League Baseball* (New York: Checkmark Books, 2003),

150; and "Guy Jackson," http://www.seamheads.com/NegroLgs/player.php?ID=1167 (accessed on November 3, 2019).

6. "Omaha May Be Represented in National Colored Base Ball [*sic*] League Next Year—Organize Team," *Omaha Daily Bee*, September 19, 1921, but many of the other details in the article are not correct. For more information about Wilkinson, see Janet Bruce, *The Kansas City Monarchs: Champions of Black Baseball* (Lawrence, Kansas: University Press of Kansas, 1985), 14–26; Charles F. Faber, "J.L. Wilkinson," SABR Baseball Biography Project, http://sabr.org/bioproject (accessed on July 2, 2015); John B. Holway, *Blackball Stars: Negro League Pioneers* (Westport, Connecticut: Meckler Books, 1988), 327–343; Loverro, 310–311; and Riley, *The Biographical Encyclopedia of the Negro Baseball Leagues*, 842–843.

7. For more information about Wilkinson's "farm system," see Bruce, 25–26, though Bruce incorrectly states that in the early 1920s, Wilkinson had based the All Nations club in Omaha. Perhaps she confused the headquarters of the All Nations with that of the Federals.

8. Ibid.

9. John Holway, *Voices from the Great Black Baseball Leagues*, rev. ed. (New York: Da Capo Press, 1992), 91. Cf. California Passenger and Crew List, 1882–1959; United States World War II Draft Registration Card for Newton Henry Allen; United States Social Security Applications and Claims Index, 1936–2007; and Find a Grave Index for Burials at Sea and Other Select Burial Locations, 1300s-Current.

10. Cf. Holway, *Voices from the Great Black Baseball Leagues*, 91; United States Social Security Death Index, 1935–2014; United States World War II Draft Registration Card for Newton Henry Allen; Honolulu, Hawaii, Passenger and Crew Lists, 1900–1959; California Passenger and Crew Lists, 1882–1959; Florida Passenger Lists, 1898–1964: the date given is May 19, 1902, but Allen's age is listed as 21 on February 17, 1925, implying that he was born in 1903; 1910 United States Federal Census; Layton Revel and Luis Muñoz, "Forgotten Heroes: Newton 'Newt' Allen," Center for Negro League Baseball Research, 2011, 1; Ohio, Death Records, 1908–1932, 1938–2007; Global, Find a Grave Index for Burials at Sea and Other Select Burial Locations, 1300s-Current; Loverro, 4; Riley, *The Biographical Encyclopedia of the Negro Baseball Leagues*, 31; Mark Chiarello and Jack Morelli, *Heroes of the Negro Leagues* (New York: Abrams, 2007), 82; "Newt Allen," www.seamheads.com (accessed on November 15, 2019); Merl F. Kleinknecht, "Newton Henry 'Newt' Allen," in *Biographical Dictionary of American Sports: Baseball*, edited by David L. Porter (Westport, Connecticut: Greenwood Press, 1987), 6; and "Newt Allen," www.baseball-reference.com (accessed on November 15, 2019).

11. Revel and Muñoz, 1.

12. Ibid.

13. Holway, *Voices from the Great Black Baseball Leagues*, 91–92.

14. Ibid., 92.

15. "Nebraska State League," www.baseball-reference.com (accessed on January 21, 2016).

16. Phil S. Dixon, "Newt Allen, Great Star of the Monarchs, Dies in Cincinnati," *The (Kansas City, MO) Call*, June 17 to June 23, 1988.

17. Phil S. Dixon, *John "Buck" O'Neil: The Rookie, the Man, the Legacy, 1938* (Bloomington, Indiana: AuthorHouse, 2009), 71.

18. Ibid.

19. John B. Holway, *Blackball Stars: Negro League Pioneers*, 359.

20. Dixon, *John "Buck" O'Neil: The Rookie, the Man, the Legacy, 1938*, 71.

21. Holway, *Blackball Stars: Negro League Pioneers*, 342.

22. Ibid., 384.

23. James A. Riley, *The All-Time All-Stars of Black Baseball* (n.p.: TK Publishers, 1983), iv–viii, 65, 72.

24. Holway, *Voices from the Great Black Baseball Leagues*, 95.

25. Ibid., 94–95.

26. Frazier "Slow" Robinson with Paul Bauer, *Catching Dreams: My Life in the Negro Baseball Leagues* (Syracuse, New York: Syracuse University Press, 1999), 57.

27. "Federals Want Games," *Omaha Daily Bee*, June 1, 1922.

28. "Federals Win Initial Game Colored Loop," *Omaha World-Herald*, June 11, 1922.

29. Jason Pendleton, "Jim Crow Strikes Out: Interracial Baseball in Wichita, Kansas, 1920–1935," in *Baseball History from Outside the Lines: A Reader*, ed. John E. Dreifort (Lincoln: University of Nebraska Press, 2001), 147. Different sources offer somewhat different groups of cities that had franchises, but Pendleton's list appears to be the correct one.

30. Oklahoma City, Omaha, St. Joseph, Tulsa, and Wichita. "1922 Western League," www.baseball-reference.com (accessed on January 21, 2016).

31. "Colored Ball Loop Formed, Middle West," *Omaha World-Herald*, May 4, 1922.

32. Pendleton, 147.

33. The games against St. Joseph were played on June 10, 11 (a doubleheader), and 12, but an article containing the standings of the CWL published in the June 20, 1922, issue of the *Wichita Beacon* does not mention the Federals. "Federals Win Initial Game Colored Loop," *Omaha World-Herald*, June 11, 1922; "Federals Win Twin Program," *Omaha World-Herald*, June 12, 1922; "Federals Win the St. Joseph Series," *Omaha*

## 150   Section I—The Long and Winding Road

*World-Herald*, June 13, 1922; and "New Players May Help Monrovians in Colored League," *Wichita Beacon*, June 20, 1922.

    34. "Federals Want Games," *Omaha World-Herald*, April 19, 1923. Interested parties were asked to write to Virgil Davis at 5402 South 28th Street or to call Lacy Steward at Webster 2940.

    35. *R.L. Polk & Co.'s Greater Omaha City Directory, 1925* (Omaha, Nebraska: R.L. Polk & Co., 1925), 221; *Polk's Greater Omaha City Directory, 1926* (Omaha, Nebraska: R.L. Polk & Co., 1926), 214; *Polk's Omaha (Nebraska) City Directory, 1928* (Omaha, Nebraska: R.L. Polk & Co., 1928), 243; 1930 United States Federal Census; *Polk's Omaha (Nebraska) City Directory, 1931* (Omaha, Nebraska: R.L. Polk & Co., 1931), 268; *Polk's Omaha (Douglas County, Neb.) City Directory, 1935* (Detroit, Michigan: R.L. Polk & Co., 1935), 250; and *Polk's Omaha (Douglas County, Neb.) City Directory, 1936* (Detroit, Michigan: R.L. Polk & Co., 1936), 175.

    36. Although the 1900 United States Federal Census records and Curry's World War I Draft Registration Card state that Curry's year of birth was 1881, Curry's World War II Draft Registration Card and the United States Social Security Applications and Claims Index, 1936–2007, indicate 1882, and the 1920, 1930, and 1940 United States Federal Census records imply the latter year. Cf. 1900 United States Federal Census; United States World War I Draft Registration Card for Columbus Curry; United States World War II Draft Registration Card for Christopher Columbus Curry; United States Social Security Applications and Claims Index, 1936–2007; 1920 United States Federal Census; 1930 United States Federal Census; and 1940 United States Federal Census. For Curry's jobs before 1925, see 1900 United States Federal Census; *R.L. Polk & Co.'s Gainsville City Directory, 1907* (Sioux City, Iowa: R.L. Polk & Co., 1907), 53; *R.L. Polk & Co.'s Gainsville City Directory, 1910* (Sioux City, Iowa: R.L. Polk & Co., 1910), 50; 1910 United States Federal Census; United States World War I Draft Registration Card for Columbus Curry; 1920 United States Federal Census; *Polk-Hoffhine Directory Co.'s Tulsa City Directory, 1920* (Tulsa, Oklahoma: Polk-Hoffhine Directory Co., 1920), 158; *Polk-Hoffhine Directory Co.'s Tulsa City Directory, 1921* (Tulsa, Oklahoma: Polk-Hoffhine Directory Co., 1921), 146; and *Polk-Hoffhine Directory Co.'s Tulsa City Directory, 1922* (Tulsa, Oklahoma: Polk-Hoffhine Directory Co., 1922), 164.

    37. "New League Proposed," *Wichita Beacon*, April 23, 1922, shows that Curry was the Tulsa club's representative for the Colored Western League, and *R.L. Polk & Co.'s Greater Omaha City Directory, 1925* (Omaha, Nebraska: R.L. Polk & Co., 1925), 221, shows that he was living in Omaha by 1925.

    38. "Here's First League to Finish Season and It Was a Successful One[:] Members of Teams in the Colored Simon Pure Amateur Circuit," *Omaha World-Herald*, July 18, 1926, and cf. "Simmons Re-elected for Fourth Term as Colored Loop Prexy," *Omaha World-Herald*, February 19, 1929, and "One Veteran Starts," *Omaha World-Herald*, April 14, 1929.

    39. "'Tigers' Organized," *Omaha World-Herald*, March 11, 1927; "For Colored Title," *Omaha World-Herald*, August 21, 1927; and "Omaha Tigers Beat Gold Coast Men for Colored Ball Title," *Omaha World-Herald*, August 22, 1927. For results of some of the other '27 Tiger games, see Archie Baley, "Simon Pure and Semi Pro [sic]," *Omaha World-Herald*, July 18, 1927; "Tigers Claw Ravens," *Omaha World-Herald*, August 8, 1927; and "Tigers Win at Malvern," *Omaha World-Herald*, August 15, 1927.

    40. "Simmons Re-elected for Fourth Term as Colored Loop Prexy," and "Curry's All Stars [sic] to Play," *Omaha World-Herald*, September 24, 1929.

    41. *Polk's Omaha (Douglas County, Neb.) City Directory, 1935*, 250; "Negro Nine Ready for Season Here," *Omaha World-Herald*, February 12, 1935; and Robert Phipps, "Odds, Ends from Sports," *Omaha World-Herald*, March 20, 1935.

    42. "Negro Nine Ready for Season Here." For further information on Homer Curry, see "Homer Curry," www.baseball-reference.com (accessed on August 26, 2017); Dick Clark and Larry Lester, eds., *The Negro Leagues Book* (Cleveland, Ohio: The Society for American Baseball Research, 1994), 97, 100, 103, 106, 109, 112, 114, 119, 120, 122, 123, 125, 127, 128, 129, 132, 134, 136, 139, 142, 144, 147, 149, 152, 153, 181; Riley, *The Biographical Encyclopedia of the Negro Baseball Leagues*, 206–207; and "Goose Curry," www.seamheads.com (accessed on August 26, 2017).

    43. For information on Charles Mason, see John Klima, *Willie's Boys: The 1948 Birmingham Black Barons, the Last Negro League World Series, and the Making of a Baseball Legend* (Hoboken, New Jersey: John Wiley & Sons, Inc., 2009), 13–16; "Charlie Mason," www.baseball-reference.com (accessed on April 9, 2017); "Charlie Mason," www.seamheads.com (accessed on April 9, 2017); "Price Slashed to Tourney Customers," *Lincoln (NE) Star*, July 22, 1935; Riley, *The Biographical Encyclopedia of the Negro Baseball Leagues*, 519; Loverro, 193; and Clark and Lester, 83, 86, 89, 91, 94, 96, 100. Most sources differentiate between Charles Mason and Jim Mason, a center fielder for the 1931 Cuban Stars (West), a right fielder for the 1931 Cuban House of David, a first baseman for the 1932 Pollock's Cuban Stars, a first baseman for the 1932 Washington Pilots, and a right fielder for the 1933 and 1934 Memphis Red Sox. However, see R.S. Simmons, "Nebraska State News," *Chicago Defender*, April 4, 1936, and "Charlie Mason," www.seamheads.com (accessed on April 9, 2017).

    44. For spring training details, see "Suitcase Mason Will Bat 'Em Far for the Tigers," *Omaha World-Herald*, March 2, 1935. For details about the exhibition and regular-season games, see Table 3 and the sources cited there.

    45. For spring training details, see Klima, 15. For details about the exhibition and regular-season games, see Table 4 and the sources cited there.

46. "Omaha Tigers Disband," *Omaha World-Herald*, June 1, 1936.
47. "Local Team Travels," *The Great Falls (MT) Tribune*, May 29, 1936.
48. "Monarchs Loom Tough to Whip," *Spokane Daily Chronicle*, June 12, 1936.
49. *Ibid.*
50. "Fords Grab [a] Slice [of] Tourney Receipts," *Lincoln (NE) Star*, July 29, 1935.
51. United States World War I Draft Registration Card for John West Davis; 1930 United States Federal Census; 1940 United States Federal Census; Alabama, Deaths and Burial Index, 1881–1974; 1910 United States Federal Census; United States Social Security Death Index, 1935–2014; Klima, 12; and James A. Riley, *Of Monarchs and Black Barons: Essays on Baseball's Negro Leagues* (Jefferson, North Carolina: McFarland & Company, Inc., Publishers, 2012), 192, 194.
52. Riley, *Of Monarchs and Black Barons: Essays on Baseball's Negro Leagues*, 194.
53. Klima, 14.
54. *Ibid.*, 15.
55. *Ibid.*, 15–16.
56. *Ibid.*, 16.
57. *Ibid.*, 14–16.
58. *Ibid.*, 16–17, supplies the most details for this period of Davis' life and states that Davis played for the Tennessee Coal and Iron team. However, Davis himself in an interview with Christopher D. Fullerton said that he played for Stockham, though he may have been thinking about a later time when it is known that he did play for Stockham. Cf. *ibid.*, 16, Christopher D. Fullerton interview with Lorenzo "Piper" Davis, Part I, Birmingham, Alabama, no date given, Birmingham Black Barons Oral History Collection, Birmingham Public Library, Birmingham, Alabama, http://bplonline.cdmhost.com/digital/collection/p15099coll2/id/1/rec/5, and "Birmingham Industrial League," http://negrosouthernleaguemuseumresearchcenter.org (accessed on August 25, 2017). For information on Stockham Valves and Fittings, see John D. Fair, "Stockham Valves and Fittings," http://www.encyclopediaofalabama.org/article/h-1392 (accessed on August 25, 2017). For information on the Birmingham Industrial League, see "Birmingham Industrial League," http://negrosouthernleague museumresearchcenter.org (accessed on August 25, 2017). For the year during the 1930s that Davis played in the Birmingham Industrial League, see Riley, *The Biographical Encyclopedia of the Negro Baseball Leagues*, 217, though Riley refers to the league as "Alabama's Coal and Iron League."
59. Both Klima, 17–19, and Riley, *The Biographical Encyclopedia of the Negro Baseball Leagues*, 217–218, provide information for this segment of Davis' life, but both contain errors. The correct name of the team that Davis played for in 1938 is the Washington Browns, an all-black club that did not fold until after the 1938 season. See "Bears History," http://www.milb.com/content/page.jsp?sid=t419&ymd=20060130&content_id=39718&vkey=team4 (accessed on November 28, 2019). For select articles on the 1938 Browns, see "Yakima First into Semi-Pro [*sic*] Contract Fold," *Dixon (IL) Evening Telegraph*, March 11, 1938; "Yokima [*sic*], Wash.," *Pittsburgh Courier*, May 28, 1938; "Cherry Team Wins and Loses," *Chilliwack (BC) Progress*, June 8, 1938; "Elks Will Face Traveling Nine," *Bend (OR) Bulletin*, June 8, 1938; "Albany Upsets Browns with Barrage in 9th," *Albany (OR) Democrat-Herald*, June 10, 1938; "Browns Wallop Drakes, 9 to 4," *Eugene (OR) Register-Guard*, June 11, 1938; "Elks to Meet Washington Browns on Bend Field Sunday Afternoon," *Bend (OR) Bulletin*, June 11, 1938; "Elks Come from Behind to Defeat Washington Browns Sunday," *Bend (OR) Bulletin*, June 13, 1938; "Garage Defeated by Washington Browns 9–2," *Reno (NV) Evening Gazette*, June 20, 1938; "Browns Avenge Lassen Defeat," *Reno (NV) Evening Gazette*, June 21, 1938; "Washington Browns Will Play East Helena This Sunday," *Helena (MT) Independent*, June 25, 1938; "Bruising Bats of Davids Beat Out 13–4 Win from the Washington Browns," *Helena (MT) Independent*, July 1, 1938; "Kellogg Loses," *Ogden (UT) Standard-Examiner*, July 18, 1938; "Woodmen-Link Game Postponed Saturday," *Lincoln (NE) Evening Journal*, August 27, 1938; "Caps Beaten by Browns," *Omaha World-Herald*, August 30, 1938; "Washington Club Edges Dows Squad," *Mason City (IA) Globe-Gazette*, August 31, 1938; "Worthington Nine Loses; Plays S.F. Again on Tuesday," *(Sioux Falls, SD) Daily Argus-Leader*, September 2, 1938; and Jeb Stewart, "Piper Davis," SABR Baseball Biography Project, http://sabr.org/bioproject (accessed on June 13, 2019). For information on the 1939–1942 ACIPCO teams and Davis' batting averages while a member of those teams as well as his home run total for the 1942 season, see "Birmingham Industrial League," http://negrosouthernleaguemuseumresearchcenter. org (accessed on August 25, 2017).
60. Cf. Klima, 21, and Riley, *Of Monarchs and Black Barons: Essays on Baseball's Negro Leagues*, 194. However, Stewart wrote, "By 1941[,] the Birmingham Black Barons had taken notice and tried to sign Davis," which indicates that the club had been observing Davis playing baseball prior to 1942. Stewart (accessed on June 15, 2019).
61. Riley, *The Biographical Encyclopedia of the Negro Baseball Leagues*, 217–218, and Fullerton. Also, it is interesting to note that Davis played for the Harlem Globetrotters "for three straight winters, from 1943-[19]44 to 1945-[19]46, and later played with them briefly in the early 1950s." Stewart (accessed on June 15, 2019).
62. Larry Lester, *Black Baseball's National Showcase: The East-West All-Star Game, 1933–1953* (Lincoln: University of Nebraska Press, 2001), 417–418.
63. Willie Mays with Lou Sahadi, *Say Hey: The Autobiography of Willie Mays* (New York: Simon & Schuster,

## 152   Section I—The Long and Winding Road

1988), 15, 18–20, 34–35, and Riley, *The Biographical Encyclopedia of the Negro Baseball Leagues*, 218.

64. Mays with Sahadi, 33.

65. "Lorenzo Davis," www.baseball-reference.com. For more information on Davis' life, see Stewart.

66. For information on the 1938 Omaha Monarchs, see "Monarchs Seek Openers," *Omaha World-Herald*, March 17, 1938; "York Independents Tip Omaha Monarchs," *Omaha World-Herald*, June 6, 1938; "Games Wanted," *Omaha World-Herald*, July 27, 1938; "Bennington A.C. Nips Omaha Monarchs, 5–1," *Omaha World-Herald*, August 1, 1938; "Omahans to Compete in Bennington Meet," *Omaha World-Herald*, August 23, 1938; "Bennington Defeats Yutan Leaguers, 3–2," *Omaha World-Herald*, August 29, 1938; "Baseball Games Top Boone Fair Program," *Omaha World-Herald*, September 14, 1938; and "Feller Fans Ten Omaha Monarchs," *Omaha World-Herald*, October 6, 1938. For information on the 1939 Omaha Black Panthers, see "Suitcase Mason Calls for Baseball Players," *Omaha World-Herald*, March 30, 1939; "Suitcase Mason Back for Diamond Warfare," *Omaha World-Herald*, May 10, 1939; "Bluffs Boosters Play Mason Today," *Omaha World-Herald*, May 28, 1939; "Boosters Wallop Black Panthers," *Omaha World-Herald*, May 29, 1939; "Black Panthers Win Sixth Straight Tilt," *Omaha World-Herald*, July 31, 1939; and "Play Omaha Nine," *Omaha World-Herald*, August 6, 1939.

67. Maurice Shadle, "Omaha Plans a Negro Nine," *Omaha World-Herald*, January 19, 1947.

68. Angelo J. Louisa conversation with Ernest Johnson, Omaha, Nebraska, June 26, 2010.

69. "Rockets Annex Five; Calhoun to Hospitalized," *Omaha World-Herald*, July 2, 1948.

70. Leo Adam Biga, "Baseball and Soul Food," http://omahamagazine.com/articles/tag/omaha-rockets/ (accessed on August 18, 2017).

71. "Rockets First Foe for Browns," *Council Bluffs (IA) Nonpareil*, August 21, 1947, and "Famed Paige Will Chuck Here Friday," *Council Bluffs (IA) Nonpareil*, September 26, 1947.

72. "Mickey Stubblefield," http://mickeystubblfield.com./bio.html (accessed on June 16, 2019).

73. *Ibid.*

74. Brent Kelley, *The Negro Leagues Revisited: Conversations with 66 More Baseball Heroes* (Jefferson, North Carolina: McFarland & Company, Inc., Publishers, 2000), 255, and J.G. Preston, "On Mickey Stubblefield, Who Broke the Color Barrier in the Kitty League," https://prestonjg.wordpress.com (accessed on March 29, 2017).

75. Kelley, 253.

76. *Ibid.*

77. Cf. Clark and Lester, 145, 147, 225; Loverro, 282; Riley, *The Biographical Encyclopedia of the Negro Baseball Leagues*, 751; and Bruce, 141.

78. Kelley, 253.

79. Cf. *ibid.* and "Mickey Stubblefield," http://mickeystubblfield.com./bio.html (accessed on June 16, 2019).

80. Gary Cieradkowski, "Mickey Stubblefield: Integrating the KITTY League," http://infinitecardset.blogspot.com/2013/06/153-mickey-stubblefield-integrating.html (accessed on March 29, 2017).

81. Hobe Hays, *Take Two and Hit to Right: Golden Days on the Semi-Pro Diamond* (Lincoln: University of Nebraska Press, 1999), 117.

82. "Mickey Stubblefield," http://mickeystubblfield.com./bio.html (accessed on June 16, 2019).

83. *Ibid.*

84. For example, see "Kansas City Monarchs, Shortys Play Tonight," *Rhinelander (WI) Daily News*, June 15, 1948, and "Satchel Paige," *Lincoln (NE) Star*, June 2, 1948. However, the first article mistakenly states that Bell was the manager of the 1948 Monarchs, which he was not—John "Buck" O'Neil was.

85. "McCook Takes 1st Playoff Tilt, 4–1," *Lincoln (NE) Star*, September 2, 1949; "McCook Gains Series Edge Over Holdrege," *Lincoln (NE) Star*, September 7, 1949; and "McCook Wins 2nd Straight NIL Title," *Nebraska State Journal*, September 12, 1949.

86. Hays, 117.

87. "Mickey Stubblefield," http://www.kittyleague.com/history/players/s/stubblefield.htm (accessed on June 16, 2019).

88. Cf. William P. Lanier, "Pirates' Farm Club Breaks 50-Year League Color Bar," thought to be *Louisville Defender*, June 1952, found in the gallery section of "Mickey Stubblefield," http://mickeystubblefield.com/gallery6.html (accessed on June 16, 2019) and the bio section of "Mickey Stubblefield," http://mickeystubblfield.com./bio.html (accessed on June 16, 2019).

89. "Mickey Stubblefield," http://mickeystubblfield.com./bio.html (accessed on June 16, 2019).

90. Preston.

91. *Ibid.*

92. *Ibid.*

93. "Mickey Stubblefield," http://mickeystubblfield.com./bio.html (accessed on June 16, 2019).

94. "Four of CSL Towns Boycott Negro Players," *(Greenville, MS) Delta Democrat-Times*, April 2, 1953.

95. Cf. Kelley, 254; "Legion Edged by Mayfield, 10–9," *(Harrisburg, IL) Daily Register*, August 1, 1953; "Legion Loses to Mayfield, 6–3," *(Harrisburg, IL) Daily Register*, August 17, 1953; and Johnson and Wolff, 470.

96. Cf. Kelley, 254; Preston; "Legion Edged by Mayfield, 10–9"; and "Legion Loses to Mayfield, 6–3."

97. "Mickey Stubblefield," http://mickeystubblfield.com./bio.html (accessed on June 16, 2019).
98. Bill Fitzgerald, "'Lefty' Haines Tops NIL All-Time All-Star Choices," *Lincoln (NE) Sunday Journal and Star*, August 15, 1954.
99. "Richard Night Train Lane," *Austin (TX) American-Statesman*, October 23, 1994.
100. Ibid.
101. The information for this table was taken from various issues of the *Omaha World-Herald* and other newspapers; Bruce; Loverro; Revel and Muñoz; Riley, *The Biographical Encyclopedia of the Negro Baseball Leagues*; Clark and Lester, eds.; Terry Bohn, "Saul Davis," SABR Baseball Biography Project, http://sabr.org/bioproject (accessed on February 1, 2016); www.baseball-reference.com (accessed on February 1, 2016); and www.seamheads.com (accessed on February 1, 2016).
102. The information for this table was taken from various issues of the *Omaha Daily Bee* and *Omaha World-Herald*. The spelling of a player's name for a particular game was kept the same as it was spelled in the newspaper that contained the article of that game.
103. The information for this table was taken from "El Dorado Defeats Rockville," *El Dorado Springs (MO) Sun*, May 2, 1935; "Blues to Play Tigers," *St. Louis Globe-Democrat*, May 18, 1935; "Monroe Monarchs Off On Long Road Jaunt," *Monroe (LA) Morning World*, May 26, 1935; "Wreck Postpones Omaha Ball Game [sic] with Giants," *Berwyn (IL) Life*, May 31, 1935; "Oakland Team to Play Negro Club," *Fremont (NE) Tribune*, June 1, 1935; "Monarchs Beat Omaha Nine, 13–4," *Omaha Bee-News*, June 9, 1935; "Red Caps to Play Omaha Tigers at Humboldt Friday," *Humboldt (IA) Republican*, June 21, 1935; "Humboldt Lost to Bancroft Players in a Tight Game," *Humboldt (IA) Independent*, June 25, 1935; "Athletic Program for Fair," *Lincoln (NE) Evening Journal*, August 8, 1935; "Want Public Wedding," *Lincoln (NE) Star*, August 22, 1935; "Eastern Nebraska Tourney Advances to Final Rounds," *Fremont (NE) Tribune*, August 29, 1935; "Hubbard Busy," *Des Moines Register*, September 1, 1935; "Stromsburg Defeats Tigers," *Lincoln (NE) Star*, September 16, 1935; and various issues of the *Chicago Defender, Mason City (IA) Globe-Gazette, Nebraska State Journal, Omaha World-Herald, St. Cloud (MN) Daily Times and the Daily Journal Press*, and *Sioux City (IA) Journal*. The spelling of a player's name for a particular game was kept the same as it was spelled in the newspaper that contained the article of that game.
104. The information for this table was taken from "Albion Loses to Omaha in 2–1 Classic," *(Madison, WI) Capital Times, May 25, 1936*; "Melter Lost as Mates Lose Tilt by 12 to 7 Score," *Rapid City (SD) Daily Journal*, May 29, 1936; "Billings Team Cancels Game," *Billings (MT) Gazette*, May 30, 1936; "Omaha Club Tours," *Pittsburgh Courier*, June 13, 1936; "Pilot Mound Locals," *Ogden (IA) Reporter*, July 30, 1936; "Power vs. Hardys Tonight at Muny," *Lincoln (NE) Star*, July 30, 1936; "Russ Sieck Named to Start Monarch Tilt," *(Lincoln, NE) Evening State Journal*, August 12, 1936; "Third Inning Sortie Gives Powers Game," *(Lincoln, NE) Evening State Journal*, August 13, 1936; "Baseball," *Summerfield (KS) Sun*, September 3, 1936; "Stromsburg Piles It on Colored Monarchs," *Lincoln (NE) Star*, September 21, 1936; and various issues of the *Chicago Defender, Great Falls (MT) Tribune, Greeley (CO) Daily Tribune, Mason City (IA) Globe-Gazette, Minneapolis Star (Missoula, MT) Daily Missoulian (Butte) Montana Standard, Omaha World-Herald, Salt Lake (City, UT) Telegram, Salt Lake (City, UT) Tribune, Spokane Chronicle, Spokane Spokesman-Review, St. Cloud (MN) Daily Times and the Daily Journal Press*, and *Waterloo (IA) Courier*. The spelling of a player's name for a particular game was kept the same as it was spelled in the newspaper that contained the article of that game.
105. The information for this table was taken from various issues of the *Omaha World-Herald* and other newspapers; Bruce; Loverro; Riley, *The Biographical Encyclopedia of the Negro Baseball Leagues*; Clark and Lester; www.baseball-reference.com (accessed on May 19, 2019); and www.seamheads.com (accessed on May 19, 2019).
106. The information for this table was taken from Bruce; Loverro; Riley, *The Biographical Encyclopedia of the Negro Baseball Leagues*; Clark and Lester; Stewart (accessed on June 13, 2019); various issues of the *Omaha World-Herald* and other newspapers; www.baseball-reference.com (accessed on May 19, 2019); and www.seamheads.com (accessed on May 19, 2019).
107. The information for this table was taken from "V.F.W. Nine Has Seven Games Set," *Cedar Rapids (IA) Gazette*, April 29, 1947; "Rock Valley Wins," *(Sioux Falls, SD) Daily Argus-Leader*, May 23, 1947; Hazel Dearborn, "Rock Valley News," *Sioux Center (IA) News*, May 29, 1947; "Baseball," *Marshall County (KS)*, June 12, 1947; "Odell vs. Rockets," *Beatrice (NE) Times*, June 14, 1947; "Muscatine Red Sox to Play Coal Valley," *(Davenport, IA) Daily Times*, June 17, 1947; "Odell Defeats Omaha, 2 to 1; Malicky Homers," *Beatrice (NE) Times*, June 18, 1947; "Osage Plays 2–2 Tie With Omaha Rockets," *Mason City (IA) Globe-Gazette*, June 25, 1947; "Kernels Face State Stars at Mitchell," *(Sioux Falls, SD) Daily Argus-Leader*, July 6, 1947; "Rocket Nine Beats Lennox Browns, 9–1," *(Sioux Falls, SD) Daily Argus-Leader*, July 6, 1947; "All-Stars Triumph," *St. Joseph (MO) Gazette*, July 11, 1947; "Rockets to Appear Here Sunday Against Sandy's," *Lincoln (NE) Evening Journal*, July 17, 1947; "Baseball," *Nebraska State Journal*, July 19, 1947; "Knoke News," *Pomeroy (IA) Herald*, July 31, 1947; "Bismarck Veterans to Play Eagles at Jamestown Sunday," *Bismarck (ND) Tribune*, August 14, 1947; "Baseball," *Fremont (NE) Tribune*, August 30, 1947; "Schuyler to Loop Finals," *Columbus (NE) Telegram*, September 2, 1947; "Rockets Club Sandy's, 12–4," *Lincoln (NE) Evening Journal*, September 16, 1947; and various issues of the *Sioux City (IA) Journal, Carroll (IA) Daily Times Herald, Council Bluffs (IA) Nonpareil (Huron, SD) Huronite and the Daily Plainsman, Lincoln (NE) Star, Muscatine (IA) Journal*, and *Omaha World-Herald*. The

**154  Section I—The Long and Winding Road**

spelling of a player's name for a particular game was kept the same as it was spelled in the newspaper that contained the article of that game.

108. The information for this table was taken from "Merchants to Open Ball Season Sunday," *Chillicothe (MO) Constitution-Tribune*, April 28, 1948; "Brown Bombers at Odell," *Marshall County (KS) News*, June 21, 1948; "Midwestern Elks Parade in Loop, See Ball Game," *Minneapolis Star*, July 5, 1948; "Omaha Rockets Slated to Play Stanley Club," *Marshfield (WI) News-Herald*, July 9, 1948; "Omaha Rockets Whip Harpers Ferry, 18–2," *La Crosse (WI) Tribune*, July 11, 1948; "Legion-Lions to Play Spring Valley July 14," *Marshfield (WI) News-Herald*, July 13, 1948; "Indian News," *(Madison, WI) Capital City News*, July 18, 1948; "Faber Hurls 4–2 Win Over Rockets," *Oelwein (IA) Daily Register*, July 19, 1948; "Helmsing Hurls Humboldt Past Omaha Rockets, 4–1," *Lincoln (NE) Sunday Journal and Star*, August 1, 1948; "Eagles to Play Ireton Tonight in Last Game of the Season Here," *Hawarden (IA) Independent*, September 9, 1948; and various issues of the *Beatrice (NE) Daily Sun*, *Carroll (IA) Daily Times Herald*, *Council Bluffs (IA) Nonpareil*, and *Omaha World-Herald*. The spelling of a player's name for a particular game was kept the same as it was spelled in the newspaper that contained the article of that game.

109. The information for this table was taken from "Baseball Schedule for May and June; List of Players," *Humboldt (IA) Independent*, May 3, 1949; "Host to Rockets," *Lincoln (NE) Evening Journal*, June 8, 1949; "Night Baseball," *Beatrice (NE) Daily Sun*, June 9, 1949; "Special Exhibition Game," *Algona (IA) Upper Des Moines*, June 23, 1949; "K.C. Nine Clouts Omaha Team for 14 to 5 Win," *Algona (IA) Upper Des Moines*, June 30, 1949; "Bancroft Wins 1; Drops 2," *(Algona, IA) Kossuth County Advance*, August 2, 1949; "Clarkson," *Colfax County (NE) Call*, August 11, 1949; "Clarkson," *Colfax County (NE) Call*, September 1, 1949; and various issues of the *Belleville (KS) Telescope*, *Carroll (IA) Daily Times Herald*, *Council Bluffs (IA) Nonpareil*, *Sioux City (IA) Journal (Sioux Falls, SD) Daily Argus-Leader*, and *Omaha World-Herald*. The spelling of a player's name for a particular game was kept the same as it was spelled in the newspaper that contained the article of that game.

110. The information for this table was taken from "Rockets, Clowns Vie at Herman April 30," *Omaha World-Herald*, April 22, 1950; "Travelers Open Against Omaha Rockets Friday," *Waterloo (IA) Daily Courier*, May 9, 1950; "Night Game Thursday," *Hamburg (IA) Reporter*, May 11, 1950; "Superior Raps Rockets," *Lincoln (NE) Evening Journal*, May 18, 1950; "Semipro-Amateur," *Des Moines Tribune*, May 19, 1950; "Republic Has 250 at Farewell Social," *Belleville (KS) Telescope*, May 25, 1950; "Akron Indees Redate Rocket Fray Saturday," *Sioux City (IA) Journal*, May 26, 1950; [No title] *(Sioux Falls, SD) Daily Argus-Leader*, May 28, 1950; "Rockets, Clowns Vie," *Omaha World-Herald*, May 28, 1950; Wally Provost, "NIL Fans Await Tuesday Night Verdict at Fremont," *(Lincoln, NE) Sunday Journal and Star*, July 9, 1950; "Estevan Edges Omaha Tourists," *(Regina, SK) Leader-Post*, July 10, 1950; Spence Sandvig, "On the Ball," *(Sioux Falls, SD) Daily Argus-Leader*, July 17, 1950; and various issues of the *Beatrice (NE) Daily Sun*, *La Crosse (WI) Tribune*, and *Rapid City (SD) Daily Journal*. The spelling of a player's name for a particular game was kept the same as it was spelled in the newspaper that contained the article of that game.

111. The information for this table was taken from various issues of the *Omaha World-Herald* and other newspapers; Bruce; Loverro; Riley, *The Biographical Encyclopedia of the Negro Baseball Leagues*; Clark and Lester; www.baseball-reference.com (accessed on April 7, 2017); www.seamheads.com (accessed June 15, 2019); "Mickey Stubblefield," http://mickeystubblfield.com./bio.html (accessed on June 16, 2019); Kelley; Preston; Cieradkowski; Hays; and "Mickey Stubblefield," http://www.kittyleague.com/history/players/s/stubblefield.htm (accessed on June 16, 2019).

112. The information for this table was taken from various issues of the *Omaha World-Herald* and other newspapers; Bruce; Loverro; Riley, *The Biographical Encyclopedia of the Negro Baseball Leagues*; Clark and Lester; www.baseball-reference.com (accessed on May 19, 2019); www.seamheads.com (accessed June 15, 2019); and Linda Pennington Black, *A Legend Among Us: The Story of William "Youngblood" McCrary* (n.p.: Linda Black, 2014).

113. The information for this table was taken from various issues of the *Omaha World-Herald* and other newspapers; Bruce; Loverro; Riley, *The Biographical Encyclopedia of the Negro Baseball Leagues*; Clark and Lester; www.baseball-reference.com (accessed on May 19, 2019); and www.seamheads.com (accessed June 15, 2019).

114. The information for this table was taken from various issues of the *Omaha World-Herald* and other newspapers.

6

# Satchel Paige Was Here
*Rambles Through Nebraska*

Devon M. Niebling

LeRoy[1] "Satchel" Paige died on Tuesday, June 8, 1982, three days after Kansas City named a youth baseball park for him.[2] He was 75, if the accuracy of a July 7, 1906, birthdate is accepted.[3] Internet searches, microfilm viewing, and plain old thumbing through the photos in books and articles reveal Paige in hats and jerseys representing multiple United States' cities and towns, Canadian provinces, and teams in Cuba, the Dominican Republic, Mexico, and Puerto Rico. By sheer miles traveled, he should have been 101 when he died. His career took him (seemingly) everywhere on the map. And he continues to be found everywhere, a bit of an elusive character, a self-made myth by virtue of his age, the stories he told about himself, the tales told by others, headline snippets, and the maxims that have survived the quick clip of the social media era. Pieces of a life, a long life that ran parallel to two World Wars, Jim Crow laws, both the written and the unwritten, and the story that the United States continues to tell itself. Pieces of Paige.

In the preface to his biography on Paige, Larry Tye notes that "[i]t was a fastball wrapped in a riddle that first drew [him] to Satchel Paige."[4] Tye interviewed many, including Pullman porters, for his book, *Rising from the Rails*, who heard Paige himself talk of his feats while taking the train from stop to stop in the 1930s. Buck O'Neil told Tye about his teammate and friend, "a pitcher who threw so hard that catchers tried to soften the sting by cushioning their gloves with beefsteaks, with control so precise that he used a hardball to knock lit cigarettes out of the mouths of obliging teammates."[5] Paige himself, in a 1935 interview with the *Omaha World-Herald*'s Robert Phipps, admitted that he was 27 years old and compared his pitching prowess to that of Joe Louis, offering, "[D]o you think any one [sic] taught him to fight? Did you ever hear of any one [sic] being taught to knock out men with a six-inch blow? It's just born with you."[6] In the same interview, the young Paige tells Phipps that he does not expect to see Negroes admitted to Organized Baseball for the simple reason that he does not believe the Jim Crow laws will ever be changed. Furthermore, he does not believe the best team of whites could beat the best team of blacks. We see a Paige at this time breaking onto the national scene between the World Wars and making a name for himself, while tossing hot, poignant potatoes into the public discourse.

It does not take a great stretch of the imagination to suggest that Satchel Paige enjoyed his own press—a press that he used to prod the status quo, to make his points while trying to live in a world of barriers and still do the work that he was obviously born to do.

Paige fed the rumor mills by leaving people guessing on topics as mundane as his very age. According to Larry Tye:

> The mystery over Satchel's age mattered because age matters in baseball. It is a way to compare players, and to measure a player's current season against his past performance. No ballplayer gave fans as much to debate about, for as long, as Satchel Paige. At first he was Peter Pan—forever young, confoundingly fast, treacherously wild. Over time his durability proved even more alluring…. He started pitching professionally when Babe Ruth was on the eve of his sixty-home-run season in 1926; he was still playing when Yankee Stadium, "The House That Ruth Built," was entering its fifth decade in 1965. Over that span[,] Satchel Paige pitched more baseballs, for more fans, in more ballparks, for more teams, than any player in history.[7]

During his career, Paige kept moving. And when he was standing still, his verbal jousting and humor made it seemingly impossible for anyone to set the record straight in a sport where statistics are sacred. Yet baseball is also primed for the tale, particularly in the decades when Paige played. And because Paige played in the '30s, '40s, '50s, and '60s, he spanned a time when baseball was segregated, blatantly divided between the major leagues and the Negro Leagues. Tye notes that "[f]ew records were kept or stories written of [Paige's] games in the strictly segregated Negro Leagues."[8] Local newspapers were less than reliable sources for details about Negro League games and/or barnstorming contests on small town sandlots. And even if the box score of a contest landed in the local sports pages, was the article also going to tell the story of the game itself, of the city or town, of those in attendance? Of how black teams were received?

Satchel Paige, ca. 1935–1947. The lyrics of the North American version of Geogg Mack's "I've Been Everywhere" fit Paige well (National Baseball Hall of Fame Library).

Conditions were ripe for anyone and everyone to claim a Paige sighting or tell of a few cuts taken at Paige's fastballs, whether served up overhand, sidearmed, or three-quarters. Or to fuel wonder over whether Paige did in fact win three games in one day, or on an August night in 1936, in Omaha, Nebraska, call in his outfield with the bases loaded against an all-white House of David team. Paige was everywhere. In fact, in circa 1949, "Thomas F. Michaels of Grand Island learned that the used car he [had] bought in Kansas City ... was once owned by Satchel Paige."[9]

In the appendix to his biography of Paige, Tye breaks Paige's career down by the numbers and category, with the categories including the Negro Leagues, East-West All-Star Games, North Dakota, the California Winter League, the Latin leagues, the major leagues, and the minor leagues. And those categories do not mention the parts of Paige's career that perhaps crystallized his myth, his status as legend: the barnstorming tours. Mark Ribowsky suggests that:

> [I]f Satchel Paige hadn't existed, someone in art or literature almost surely would have invented him. Such characters are always needed to guide and provoke us. And Satchel Paige did that. He even counseled us: "Don't look back, something might be gaining on you," went his most famous peroration. If he had said or done nothing else in his long lifetime, that declaration alone would put him right up there with the great Zen masters.[10]

In a sense, however, Paige invented himself despite the odds presented by the times in which he lived. Larry Tye believes that Paige had to stump for himself to be remembered.

> It worked. That very ambiguity—our not knowing where reality left off and embellishment began—helped catapult Satchel from the realm of hero to the rarefied universe of icon. In that respect he was like Babe Ruth. Both rose above reform school roots. Both were boyish men with oversize appetites in everything from food to women to sports. Both understood Satchel's seventh rule for living: do things so big they invite exaggeration, ballyhoo what you have done, then let the press and the public weave it into lore.[11]

Paige gave the sportswriters their due within the constraints of language and the times, while creating a persona for himself that defied convention, even logic—and was brilliant in its delivery.

Paige the Mortal passed away in early June of 1982 in Kansas City, Missouri, and his name was invoked not a week later on a softball diamond in Omaha, Nebraska.

I was 12 in the summer of 1982, nearing the end of my brief tenure as a power hitter in my recreation softball league. My batting eye would not last beyond the summer of 1983, and as the other girls in the league started growing more serious about the game itself (though not yet so serious that each carried an individual bat bag and other assorted gear), I found more joy in the stories on and off the field, in the history and characters of softball and baseball, and in the complex poetry of the game as it seemed to unfold on the landscape of American culture.

Oh, those magical seasons of 1982 and 1983 when physics and a growth spurt aligned with the bat and the ball. All it took each trip to the plate was a pitch slightly low and outside and a tap in the sweet spot, and the ball carried to gaps in the infield and outfield. All I had to do was run.

But I was in a slump at the beginning of June 1982. It had been three or four games since I had gotten a hit, probably nothing for a high school or college player, but for a 12-year-old, it was a vast depressing drought with implications.

On a particular Saturday afternoon, I struck out the first time up to the plate with the bases loaded. The second time up, I tried out a different bat, took a few swings before entering the batter's box, and stepping in heard a voice near the backstop ... not a loud voice, but a distinct voice saying, "Hey, kid. Do it for Sa...." My father's voice. My dad. But what did he say? "Do it for the Sox? Do it for Sax? Steve Sax ... why would I get a hit for Steve Sax." I was not much of a Dodger fan at the time, and Steve Sax was not even one of the players I followed back then. In 1982, I was a Robin Yount, Cecil Cooper, Harvey's Wallbangers fan, and I suffered from Red Sox angst. Even then I suffered from Red Sox angst, even before I knew of the wonderful, epic beauty of Red Sox angst. I followed the Cardinals, of course, because of family ties.

Lost in my own thoughts, I completely missed the next pitch. Two strikes. Turning to the backstop, I asked, "Who?" Clapping his hands together, grinning, my dad said, "Paige. Do it for Satch."

I struck out on the next pitch trying to understand why my dad thought invoking the name of Satchel Paige, recently deceased, might ease my slump. After all, Satchel Paige was a pitcher. I needed the kindness of the batting gods. But such a correlation was typical of my dad. You had to be patient and wait for the logic to unfold. The backstory. The map connecting the dots. And sometimes there simply was no logic or tidy explanation.

In the case of Paige, my dad and I had talked about his passing that week, and in the years I had been playing ball and finally expressing interest in the Game of the Week, my dad gave me bits and pieces of baseball history, rolling together Stan Musial, Buck O'Neil, Brooks Robinson, Jackie Robinson, Lou Gehrig, Roger Maris, Josh Gibson, Cool Papa Bell, and Paige. We did not like the Yankees on principle, though I long suspected that my dad was a closet Yankee fan. But the tidbits. The poignant minutiae that my dad pulled out of his head. He liked Paige because he was a character in a story of his own crafting. He played and he performed, and he was always several steps ahead of the curve. He had to be.

The Satch of all Trades, the Satch of all Teams. The one and only Satchel Paige. The barnstorming era was either made for Paige, or he made the era. A road-not-taken way to learn geography might be to get a map of the United States, dot it with pins for each city or town visited by Satchel Paige during his barnstorming tours, and hold on for the ride. Barnstorming brought Satchel Paige to Nebraska many times over the course not only of his playing career but also in the later years of his life when he made appearances with Meadowlark Lemon and the Harlem Globetrotter basketball team.

*Merriam-Webster* defines barnstorming, an intransitive verb, as "1. to tour through rural districts staging usually theatrical performances and 2. to travel from place to place making brief stops (as in a political campaign or a promotional tour)." In Paige's case, it was almost a case of both, as well as the third component of the *Merriam-Webster* definition: "3. to pilot one's airplane in sight-seeing flights with passengers or in exhibition stunts in an unscheduled course especially in rural districts." In 1946, Bob Feller rented two Flying Tiger aircraft for a dollar a mile and toured the country. Paige and his fellow black all-stars worked their way to California by plane, barnstorming.[12] By way of barnstorming, Negro League players were able to supplement income not available to them in the major leagues due to the color barrier. According to Paige in his autobiography:

> Home isn't a place you stay around too long when you're a barnstormer. I was back on the road, out-traveling any salesman, in no time.
> 
> Barnstorming against major leaguers brought me and a few of the other boys some big money. But the fellows who played only regular-season ball in the Negro [L]eagues didn't have it so good.

> The Negro [L]eague teams played to crowds that was [sic] nearly always colored and there wasn't [sic] enough of those fans so you could make real big money, like the major leagues.
> That meant the Negro [L]eague teams couldn't pay most of the players real high.[13]

Likewise, barnstorming made it possible for towns and cities without major league baseball teams to catch a glimpse of the great baseball talent of the day. Cities such as Omaha, Lincoln, and Council Bluffs hosted all-star "tilts" that were essentially postseason contests between black and white ballplayers. Throughout the late '30s as well as the '40s and '50s, Dizzy Dean All-Stars, Bob Feller All-Stars, and Satchel Paige All-Stars appeared in the area.

Behind the Negro Leagues and tours were characters such as Gus Greenlee, Abe Saperstein, Candy Jim Taylor, and J.L. Wilkinson. The agents of their day. The movers and shakers who kept the work flowing and (sort of) kept the free-spirited Paige on a schedule and a payroll over the course of decades. In a 1973 column, *Lincoln (NE) Evening Journal* sports editor Virgil Parker wrote about his own brief brush with sports promotion and Satchel Paige. In the early '50s, Paige was finishing up his time in the majors with the St. Louis Browns and had started touring with Abe Saperstein's Harlem Globetrotter baseball team (playing against the House of David). Parker writes of receiving a call from Saperstein, "You provide the place to play, the baseballs[,] and the umpires. I'll provide the two teams—with Satchel Paige guaranteed to pitch. You pay for your part out of 20 percent of the gate and keep the rest. We get 80 percent."[14] Parker went further to note that there was no contract; Saperstein's word was his bond. Parker leased the 1,500 seat city-owned field (Sherman), hired the umpires, and purchased a dozen baseballs.[15]

On game day, Parker had 50 dollars in singles for change, which disappeared quickly when a handful of retired railroaders showed up. Still, 30 minutes before the game, neither team had appeared and there were not enough people in the stands to pay for the umpires, the field, or the baseballs. But then, Parker recalls:

> In a matter of minutes, there were 3,000 people in the park trying to sit in the 1,500 seats. One section started to crack from the overweight....
> Just at game time one problem was averted, however The two ball clubs pulled up inn [sic] a pair of broken down buses. But, no Satchel Paige.
> [This problem was also averted when,] during the fourth inning, up drives this big limousine with [a] chauffeur and all. [And] out steps Satchel.[16]

Paige pitched the fifth inning, struck out the side, and left. And Parker offered a lesson learned: "The other guy's job may look like an easy racket. They say the grass always looks greener on the other side of the fence. But beware. There may be some crabgrass hidden underneath."[17] On a local scale, Omaha, Council Bluffs, and even greater Nebraska had Mat Pascale. Over the course of several decades, Pascale and Paige would cross paths and headlines, and grow into roles as elder statesmen of the game.

In the early 1920s, Pascale was living in Florence, working as an insurance agent. The *Omaha World-Herald* listed a classified ad in 1923: "AGENTS[—]In every town and county in Iowa and Nebraska. Apply or write M. Pascale Co., 2914 Cuming St. Omaha."[18] By the mid–1920s, Pascale had moved over to the sports pages as the manager of the Sam Ellas team of the Metropolitan League, trying to strengthen his lineup by signing George Holtscher.[19] The following year, he became a member of the Omaha Concrete Stars company team in a mid-season effort to fortify the lineup. By the end of the 1920s, Pascale was the newly elected secretary of the North Omaha Athletic Club, organized to sponsor baseball, football, and basketball teams,[20] and on his way to establishing his own foothold in sports promotion, an agent in the making.

Satchel Paige first visited Nebraska in the 1930s. And he returned often in various uniforms and hats. The press coverage of a 1935 appearance by Paige in a Kansas City Monarchs' uniform against the House of David notes:

> Paige is not overly particular whom he pitches for. He worked with this very David club to win the Denver tournament in 1934.
>
> A friend of Dizzy Dean's, he is looking forward to exhibition games with the Cardinal eccentric. He has pitched against Dean before on late fall tours.[21]

In perhaps his first mound appearance in Nebraska, 1932, Paige wore the colors of the Pittsburgh Crawfords against the Omaha Packers at Western League Park. Later that year, Paige pitched for the Gilkerson Union Giants against Norfolk. The following year, fans at Western League Park watched Paige pitch for the Memphis Red Sox against Dutch Wetzel's Packers. Press accounts of Paige at this time describe him as the "lanky fire-ball chucker,"[22] "fire-ball twirler,"[23] and even "the greatest colored pitching machine in America."[24] How about perhaps being the greatest pitching machine of his day, sans modifier?

Around this time, Paige was also tossing for Bismarck—as in Bismarck, North Dakota. Paige found his way to League Park in 1935 with the Bismarcks in a game against the Omaha Ford V-8s from the Metropolitan League. Pregame buzz for the contest acknowledged Paige as "[t]hat black Paul Bunyan of the baseball diamond … is expected to attract more than two thousand fans to League [P]ark."[25] The article goes on to describe Paige's pitching delivery as a balk or half-balk motion and concludes that "[i]t is a moot question whether he would be permitted this idiosyncrasy by umpires in a good professional league."[26] Not a handful of weeks later, Paige was back at League Park to pitch two innings for the Kansas City Monarchs, striking out five of the six batters faced. Paige rounded out 1935 appearing in both Omaha and Lincoln with the Kansas City Monarchs against the Clink Clair's All-Stars and Lincoln All-Stars, respectively. Both teams were augmented by Tommy Bridges, Charlie Gehringer, and Schoolboy Rowe of the World Champion Detroit Tigers. Five thousand fans turned out for the Western League game. Paige struck out five and allowed no hits in the first three innings on the way to an 8–2 Monarch victory. In the Lincoln contest at Landis Field,

Similar to Satchel Paige in certain ways, Jay Hanna "Dizzy" Dean competed against his black counterpart in barnstorming games (National Baseball Hall of Fame Library).

Paige pitched two innings and struck out four, including Charlie Gehringer, in a 4–1 Monarch win.

Perhaps the most auspicious game at which Satchel Paige was present took place at Western League Park on August 13, 1936. Paige brought his All-Stars to town with the lineup including Cool Papa Bell, Josh Gibson, and Chet Williams (all from the Pittsburgh Crawfords); Jerry Benjamin, Ray Brown, and Buck Leonard (all from the Homestead Grays); Sammy Hughes, Felton Snow, and Bill Wright (all from the Washington Elite Giants); and Ted "Double Duty" Radcliffe (from the Claybrook Tigers). The All-Stars faced the House of David, with Charley Clements, Dick Wykoff, and Bill Mizeur. The game itself attracted approximately 2,900 fans and was remarkable for the caliber of play, as well as the fact that Western League Park burned to the ground later that night.

The 1936 game at League Park was also a contest in which Paige called in his outfield and then proceeded to strike out the side. Decades later, Scoop Mason, in an interview with Dennis E. Hoffman, remarked that most of the fans that night were white and some of them were angered by Paige's actions. Rather than being amazed and appreciative of Paige's feat, the fans thought Paige was not deferring to the times. He was in effect "showing up the all-white House of David team [and violating] Jim Crow etiquette."[27] Mason was talking about what never appeared in accounts of that game, the reality of the story around the story taking place on the field. According to him, 1930s Omaha was not an easy place, not a safe place for a fellow like Satchel Paige:

> [D]iscrimination reared its ugly head in all aspects of life in Omaha during the 1930s. About the only time whites and blacks came into contact was at the packing houses where they worked together. Whites came into North Omaha to operate shoe stores, grocery stores, and other commercial establishments. But, in general, blacks could not go into South Omaha.[28]

Mason's interview gives us pause. The story on the field is only one story at a baseball game, and often we are deprived of the bigger, deeper story. Paige, on that night in 1936 Omaha, was claiming his lane. Telling his own story.

Paige rounded out the decade with appearances at Lincoln's Landis Field, first in 1937 as a member of his own Ciudad Trujillo All-Stars, champions of the Dominican Republic and the Denver Post Tournament for that year. The team faced Johnny Bretzer's Nebraska semipro champion Powers, with the All-Stars winning, 10–5, as Paige pitched in the ninth inning of the overflow-crowd game.[29] Paige brought his All-Stars back to Landis in 1939 to face Pug Griffin's Lincoln Links. A pregame article noted:

> Satchel Paige has appeared in Lincoln two or three times, the last two summers ago. He is said to be the greatest pitcher in [N]egro baseball and definitely will appear in the Saturday night game. Whether he starts or goes in later will not be decided until game time, but the contract calls for Paige to mount the mound.[30]

The question of whether or not Paige would show up, as well as the issue of contracts and holding Paige to them, becomes more prevalent with the unfolding decades and Paige's evolving story. Paige did take the mound against the Links, pitching one inning, the ninth, striking out four, and walking one.[31]

At the same time Paige was developing a following in the Midwest, Mat Pascale was organizing the sandlot schedule for the Fontenelle Athletic Club and organizing his own All-Stars for games at Miller Park against nines such as the Labor Temple team. In addition, Pascale began stepping up his promotional efforts with regard to barnstorming tours, an effort that required patience and standards. Unlike Abe Saperstein, Pascale got things in writing, particularly when he started scheduling games for Council Bluffs' Legion Park.

Pascale and Paige crossed paths perhaps for the first time via Legion Park and the scheduled October 1946 contest between the Bob Feller All-Stars and the Satchel Paige All-Stars, though earlier that year, a Robert Phipps column mentions that the Kansas City Monarchs wanted more money to bring Satchel Paige along, $2,500 per night. To this request Pascale replied, "I don't remember asking for Paige. The Monarchs are well known around here without Paige."[32] Pavilion seats for that game were available for $2.40, with the best seats going for $3.60. Omaha's Mel Harder, with Bill Veeck's Cleveland Indians at the time, was slated to pitch for the Feller All-Stars, and speculation was whether Paige would go against Harder or Feller. As it turned out, 4,000 chilled fans saw Paige relieve Lefty LaMarque in the sixth inning. "Satch, the string-bean [sic] with a hundred deliveries, brought the crowd to its feet by catching a 'sleeping' Frank Hayes off first and tagging him out in the seventh inning."[33] Writing after the fact, Robert Phipps shared some of the pregame drama, reporting that:

> A little adroit fencing took place before the game last Saturday in Legion Park. Satchel Paige showed up in street clothes. When questioned[,] he said he did not think he would pitch after all.
> "Well[,] in that case," remarked Mat Pascale, "we'll revise the figures on the contract. Your agreement was to pitch three innings, you know."
> A few minutes later[,] Paige appeared again, in uniform and ready to play.[34]

Without benefit of tone, one speculates on the conversation that took place between Pascale and Paige. In the 1940s, by the time of the Feller-Paige All-Star contest, Jackie Robinson was in the Brooklyn Dodger farm system, poised to break the major league color barrier. In fact, a few days after the Feller-Paige contest, Robinson was in Council Bluffs with his own team of All-Stars to face a group of players organized by the Omaha Fire Department. Paige himself would get the nod from Bill Veeck and the Cleveland Indians, but not until 1948 and most definitely beyond his prime as an athlete. In the 1940s, Paige was already an old man, worked by the system. But he also flirted with the system as evidenced by his exchange with Pascale.

Pascale himself branched out in the '40s, perhaps in anticipation of changes he glimpsed on the horizon of barnstorming ball. In the latter half of the decade, he assumed booking responsibilities for Will Calhoun's new basketball Omaha Rockets. Calhoun already owned the baseball Omaha Rockets and anticipated using his bus, baseball contacts, and current baseball players who also played basketball, including Mickey Stubblefield, William McCreary, James Clark, and former Boys Town star Kenny Morris to pull together a viable team.

With the arrival of the Omaha Cardinals, Pascale assumed the role of concession manager. Likewise, he was the secretary-treasurer of the Omaha Umpires' Association, as well as a candidate for the executive secretary position of the Western League. At this time, Pascale also began noticing a shift in Negro baseball in the Midwest and perhaps the country at large. In 1949, the Kansas City Monarchs and Philadelphia Stars were scheduled to appear in Omaha. According to the author of an article in the May 25, 1949, issue of the *Omaha World-Herald*, Pascale noted that he had been told the Stars were one of the better teams in the East, but that the "revamping of Negro baseball has caused wholesale changes in the league." In the same article, Pascale stated:

> I could give you lineups and a complete rundown on both teams, but it would be a waste of space. People in this part of the country don't know or care about individuals.

> Satchel Paige and Goose Tatum are about the only Negroes who mean anything in a baseball way to people around here. Satch has quit the Monarchs for major league ball. The Goose will be coming through with Indianapolis one of these days.[35]

As for Satchel, when on the cusp of his first major league appearance, the *Omaha World-Herald* ran the following editorial:

> Satchel Paige is a man who lived about 20 years too early.
>
> At 39, or possibly a little older, he is still considered a first-rate pitcher, good enough to win a job with the Cleveland Indians as a relief man.
>
> But for 20 years or so Satchel has been a whale of a pitcher, and only the race barrier that prevailed in [O]rganized [B]aseball for so many years kept him from competing with the Lefty Groves and the Fellers.
>
> Satchel has made a lot of money, possibly as much or more than he could have made in the major leagues. He has won a reputation and he has gotten around. Probably no ball player [*sic*] has played in more cities more often than the perambulating Satchel.
>
> The *World-Herald's* Sports Department has lost count of the times he has appeared in Omaha, but 12 or 15 would be a good guess. He pitched on one spectacular occasion here, the night the old Western League ball park [*sic*] burned down.
>
> Money and Fame, it seems, weren't quite enough. The major leagues are still Valhalla for any ballplayer and, rounding 40, Satchel wants to try.
>
> Anybody who ever saw him pitch a baseball, and there must be many millions, will hope he makes good.[36]

Paige had a connection, a relationship with the Midwest. Nebraska enjoyed a slice of the legend, a claim that, yes, Satch played here. Of course, Paige made the circuit, even Alaska, before he was done. He outlasted many of his former teams or witnessed their slow fade due to changes in the times, the wearing down of the color barrier, and a lack of general interest. In the early part of the 1940s, Robert Phipps wrote of the surviving Kansas City Monarchs. He mourned the passing of the Gilkerson Union Giants, the Ethiopian Clowns, and the Canadian Clowns. The Clowns. From a 21st-century perspective, the nomenclature is problematic. The color barrier is problematic, and the part-athlete, part-carnival playbill of the Negro Leagues is a challenge. Phipps described the current Monarch teams:

> All trips are made in a shiny new bus with good tires and lots of lettering on the sides. The team carries 18 players including, at times, the celebrated Paige. No one has explained what kind of contract Satchel has, but apparently he draws his own schedule.
>
> A super-attraction [*sic*], he can write his own terms.[37]

A little more than 10 weeks later, Paige went on record as saying that he was not interested in leaving the Negro Leagues for the major leagues, that, "[a]ll the nice statements in the world from both sides aren't going to knock out Jim Crow."[38] In response, Sam Lacy, "one of the better-known colored sports-writers [*sic*] of Chicago," wrote a letter in which he supported Paige's assertion on the grounds that Paige knew he is in a good spot, offering that:

> Paige realizes he has dominated Negro baseball simply because he has been fortunate enough to occupy the limelight in the small amount of publicity that has been given to colored baseball in the white press. He has personality. Superior colored players who lack his personality just don't get publicity.[39]

Lacy, however, takes issue with Paige's proposal for a colored team in the big leagues, asserting that there cannot be compromise with prejudice.

The time is no riper now than it was four or five years ago. To my way of thinking[,] there should be no psychological time to erase bigotry in sports. Democracy is a fair process. No one should have to lay a knife on your throat to make you play fair. There is no "best" time to seek something that is your constitutional due.[40]

Baseball and Paige in the '40s were participating in a dance of larger import and scope than a game played on a field with a ball and a bat and bases. For all of the beauty of the game, there existed a violent, seemingly immovable underbelly. Paige himself started to speak out more, too.

Throughout the rest of the '40s, Paige continued to bounce around, to seemingly dictate his own schedule, but he also started using his clout to ripple the water, including a threat in 1944 to lead an All-Star walkout strike for "G.I. Joe and his fellow fighters."[41] Paige announced that unless the management of the Negro National and American leagues gave the proceeds from the annual East-West All-Star Classic at Comiskey Park to war relief, at least 16 players would walk. Paige pointed out that the Negro Leagues had grown up, and:

> I built this game up. Like I told the owners, 20 years ago we used to get $125 a month and play in little parks. Now we play at Comiskey [P]ark, get around six hundred dollars a month[,] and in the big cities[,] it's awful close if there ain't more white than black folks in the stands.[42]

**Paige visited Nebraska a number of times in different uniforms (National Baseball Hall of Fame Library).**

Management was not particularly moved, but Paige had made a point.

Towards the end of the decade, Paige did make it to Lincoln and Legion Park in Council Bluffs, pitching for the Kansas City Stars against Tom Kelley and the Omaha Storzes, playing a month before his call from Cleveland. Paige was already 41, though a news report of the day quoted his mother, Lula Paige, as insisting that he was 44.

And Pascale set his sights on booking tours for Richie Ashburn, Rex Barney, Johnny Hopp, and other barnstormers through Odell, Tilden, Spencer, Hastings, North Platte, Alma, Wausa, and Albion. Pascale also ended the decade as the booking agent for two black teams exclusively in 10 states, the Omaha Rockets and the Ligons of Hondo, Texas.

Rolling into the 1950s, Pascale further expanded his booking portfolio to include the

All-American Girls Professional Baseball League, a coda of sorts on the league formed by Phil Wrigley, owner of the Chicago Cubs, in 1943. Pascale also handled the cards for boxing and wrestling in Council Bluffs, and though by the early '50s Satchel Paige was pitching (and performing) for the St. Louis Browns, Pascale was likewise still trying to keep track of the pitcher for games in Nebraska.

For approximately a week in both 1951 and 1952, the *Omaha World-Herald* carried brief updates on ticket availability for games with Paige. Pascale is often quoted saying, "No Paige, no play," and at one point City Commissioner John Rosenblatt stepped in to elaborate on behind-the-scenes concerns over the possibility of a game at Omaha Stadium, which was commonly called Municipal Stadium, between a team of major leaguers and a team put together by Paige. As Rosenblatt said, "It's in the contract that Paige must pitch at least three innings or he won't collect a cent. There are no strings on the major league pitchers."[43] In a subsequent article, Rosenblatt suggested that Paige was close to signing but that tickets were still not being sold in order to protect fans. In fact, the game never occurred.

In general, traveling clubs in the '50s were struggling. Leagues had scooped up many teams, consolidating schedules and making it challenging to find opposition for barnstormers. The Omaha Rockets and Minneapolis Clowns disbanded due to weather and perhaps a lack of interest.

A legend in his own right, Grantland Rice wrote about Paige and National League pitching in the early '50s:

> The National League has drawn good pitching this season. One trouble is that, in the main, it has been spotty. Such headliners as [Sal] Maglie, [Preacher] Roe[,] and others have had trouble finishing what they started.
> 
> The main actor might be the boy wonder, Satchel Paige. Here is the remnant of possibly the greatest pitcher of all time. He has certainly thrown more baseballs at the plate than even Cy Young, who pitched more than nine hundred games.
> 
> No one can say how long Paige has been pitching. But those who knew him long ago report his age now around 50 years and his period of pitching servitude at 30 seasons.
> 
> And there were many times when he worked four and five games a week. Ol' Satchmo must have an arm composed largely of rubber and steel.[44]

Old Paige, timeless and elusive Paige, with his arm of rubber and steel, was honored by the National Baseball Congress in 1953 for his participation in its national semipro tournaments. Paige was named the all-time pitcher for his performances with the 1935 Bismarck, North Dakota, team that won the national title, and as of 1953, he "still [held] the all-time tournament strikeout record with 60 in five games."[45] While being honored for his past, Paige was also working on the future. The '50s brought a revival of Abe Saperstein's baseball barnstorming Harlem Globetrotters, and Saperstein brought Paige aboard as the general manager. Paige and the Globetrotters came to Nebraska and played against the Herman Independents, from Herman, Nebraska, as well as the House of David.

Also in the '50s, Robert Phipps carried Paige's axioms for healthy living and long life:

> First ... you avoid the fried foods. They angry up the blood.
> 
> If there comes the time when the stomach disputes you, ... you lie down and pacify it with cool thoughts.
> 
> Keep the juices flowing. You do this by jangling around gently as you move.
> 
> Go very lightly on the vices, such as carrying on in society. The social ramble ain't restful.

Avoid running at all times.
Don't look back. Something might be gaining on you.[46]

One wonders what Mat Pascale might have said about receiving a copy of Paige's rules for living, particularly while in contract negotiations with the pitcher.

In 1965, Satchel Paige threw three scoreless innings for the Kansas City Athletics against the Boston Red Sox to end his major league career. The game itself was part publicity stunt orchestrated by A's owner, Charles O. Finley and was dubbed Satchel Paige Appreciation Night, with Paige himself sitting in a rocking chair near the bullpen. His appearance set a record for longevity. At the age of 59 years, two months, and eight days, Paige "was two years older than the runner-up and thirty-three more than his catcher that evening. He seemed as old as baseball itself."[47]

And yet, even as he brought his short career in the majors to a close, Paige continued his touring and barnstorming. Throughout the '60s, he made several appearances in Nebraska, including several stops at Lincoln's Sherman Field. In an interview after Paige and his Press All-Stars defeated the Lincoln Air Force Base All-Stars, Paige talked about Bill Veeck's ways to bring people to the ballpark, offering:

> I hate to see baseball slip at any level. And Bill Veeck's ideas (gimmicks, etc.) are about the only way to interest people.
> People have to be entertained. Only way to get that done is give 'em something different.[48]

Paige did continue to deliver something different, to entertain on the field of play as well as in the sports pages. He made appearances in Lexington and Lincoln with Goose Tatum and the Harlem Stars against the Kansas City Monarchs. While with Tatum on Lincoln's Sherman Field, both men were eclipsed by rookie John Winston who wore a pair of bib overalls, backwards, and entertained fans from first base, at the plate, and in the stands.[49] In his article about the game, Jack Andersen noted that "[w]hat fans probably did not know was that Winston was one of the finest ball players [sic] on the field ... [and] was once the property of the Cleveland Indians."[50] In that contest, Paige pitched his traditional first three innings. In another contest, this time in a Monarch uniform against the Omaha Eagles at Rosenblatt Stadium, Paige arrived "unannounced in advance ... and worked out at third base before the game."[51] But the box score from that game does not suggest that Paige actually pitched.[52]

Back in Omaha in 1966, only this time wearing the uniform of the Indianapolis Clowns, Paige was described as "the ageless Negro pitching star,"[53] while again appearing in the River City with the Clowns in 1967, he was referred to as the pitcher who "has been going to the mound for half a century."[54] Both games were played at Rosenblatt Stadium, the first against the New York Stars and the second against the Baltimore Stars.[55]

In addition to the ball field, Paige came back to Omaha and Lincoln via the Harlem Globetrotters, returning to the Civic Auditorium in 1965 as part of the Globetrotter's entourage, which included the Czechoslovakian state folk dance troupe and Eva Bosakova, the winner of a 1960 gold medal in gymnastics.[56] The game was a reunion of Paige and Globetrotter owner Abe Saperstein, who had been instrumental in Paige's signing by the Cleveland Indians in 1948.[57] In the final minute of that game, Paige went up against Meadowlark Lemon, who had taken a batter's stance near the sidelines, and threw three strikes by him.[58]

On the local scene, the 1970s brought a quietness to the voices and characters of the '40s, '50s, and '60s. By that time, Pascale was retired from promotions of most kinds, and Wally Provost tipped his hat to him in a 1972 column recounting Pascale's part-time scouting efforts, including the push to put Bob Gibson on the radar of the Chicago Cubs. Cy Slapnicka, a full-time scout for the Cubs, came to Omaha and determined that the 17-year-old Gibson did not throw hard enough. Provost pointed out that Gibson earlier during the '72 season had become the winningest pitcher in the history of the St. Louis Cardinals. Wrote Provost, "Uncle Mat is part of our baseball tradition. A salute to the gentleman for his contributions," with contributions also including being the magnet drawing "Richie Ashburn, Johnny Hopp, Rex Barney[,] and Doyle Lade home on barnstorming tours, and [entertaining] thousands by booking Negro professional teams."[59]

In his mid–80s in 1977, Pascale was inducted into the Nebraska Semipro Baseball Hall of Fame for a journey that began when he "played his first money game of baseball in 1908 (for $2)."[60] During his relationship with sports that spanned over 70 years, Pascale wore many hats, but again Provost asserts that Pascale, "probably made more people happy through promotional efforts that brought the House of David, the baseball Globetrotters, Kansas City and Satchel Paige, Mickey Cochrane's Great Lakes team[,] and other attractions to this area."[61]

John Rosenblatt passed away in October of 1979. In common with Pascale, he began his long, varied career on the Omaha sandlots including League Park at 15th and Vinton. Long before he pushed for a new baseball park that would eventually bear his name and before he served as public properties commissioner, street commissioner, and mayor, he was a semiprofessional outfielder who played in a 1927 exhibition game with Babe Ruth and Lou Gehrig. Also, he stood in the box against Satchel Paige, running the count full, and then according to Rosenblatt, "He looked at me and announced that he was going to strike me out on the next pitch. He did. Never saw a pitch travel so fast in all my life."[62]

Reminiscing in the early days of retirement, *Omaha World-Herald* writer Robert Phipps remembered the Satchel Paige he interviewed in the 1930s. Paige had given his age at that time as 27, and in response to Phipps' comment that he was the fastest pitcher in baseball, Paige offered that this was not true. In the words of Phipps:

> He said he "used to be fast," but he named six pitchers in the Negro baseball league that were faster. He said his arm had seen its best days because he was forced to pitch every day without rest. He said white players who got days off for rest were pampered.[63]

At 27 with a tired arm, Paige was a fair distance from his major league debut in 1948.

On the national scene in the 1970s, Paige was in his 60s and still making noise and news. Poignant noise and news. In 1971, Paige was inducted into the National Baseball Hall of Fame (HOF), but not without establishment-induced controversy. Originally Paige was slated to be included in a section of the HOF reserved for Negro League stars, but he was approved for induction into the HOF proper after it was determined that he did not have to be held to the eligibility requirement of 10 years in the majors.[64] Jim Murray of the *Los Angeles Times* reminded readers of the significance of Satchel's induction:

> Let's hear it for two-a-day baseball, lunch in a paper sack, dressing in the back of the bus. Let's hear it for barnstorming baseball where nine or more of the greatest players in the game, not to say its history, had to show up at leaky-roof parks in hot minor-league factory towns and play jewelry store nines for pass-the-hat money, far from the microphones, headlines, endorsements, and 12-cylinder Phaetons of the big leagues.
>
> You're all invited to Cooperstown! Old Satchel Paige made [the] Hall of Fame, and not by the tradesman's entrance, and you all know he is [the] surrogate for you. When Satch makes it, the Homestead Grays make it, the Chattanooga Black Lookouts make it, [R]ed [A]nt [W]ickware, Jackson "Johnny"

Taylor, the best schoolboy pitcher I ever saw, and that includes Bob Feller, makes it. As long as Satch is there[,] their names will never die.[65]

Murray continues, pointing out that Cool Papa Bell, Josh Gibson, and Judy Johnson "had to play the game part-minstrel [sic] and part-athlete [sic]" and paved the way for Jackie Robinson, Henry Aaron, Willie Mays, and Vida Blue.[66]

Larry Tye takes us to the day of Paige's induction into the HOF, reminding us that the path to the Hall had not been easy for Paige who, "pitched his heart out during twenty years in the Negro Leagues, then reminded the [m]ajors of all that he could do at an age when most players were feeding beer bellies and watching from the bleachers."[67] Members of the press advocated that Paige should be in the Hall proper, and Tye quotes Bill Veeck as confiding, "Some dark night, I'm going to sneak into Cooperstown and find out where Satchmo's plaque is and put it in the front room where it belongs."[68]

Public outrage and pressure from the press ensured that Paige's plaque would hang in the HOF proper, and Tye provides snippets of Paige's acceptance speech, including "barnstorming across America in cars so tightly packed that his knees were 'sticking up in front of me. For five years I didn't know where I was going. I couldn't see.' He talked about the enigma of his age, of pitching 165 games in a row, and of never looking back."[69] Off stage that afternoon, Paige spoke out against the lack of black managers in the major leagues, as well as the lack of black ballplayers being brought up from the minor leagues.

An editorial in the December 31, 1982, *Omaha World-Herald* titled "Was 1982 a Good Year? The Question Is Personal" gave as three of its examples: "Henry Fonda's memory lived on at the Omaha Community Playhouse, Bear Bryant retired in Alabama, death overtook Satchel Paige."[70] For a larger-than-life persona such as Satchel Paige, death probably did in fact overtake him. Or caught him napping. Paige was a nine lives sort of figure, the individual you can never quite pin down for a definitive answer on anything, the person you sort of expect to still see walking down the street, whistling, even after reports of his demise. Paige is the sort of person you still hope to see because they have simply always been there.

A few months before Paige's death, Wally Provost made mention of a possible Paige speaking engagement in his column, calling

Satchel Paige in 1941. Little did he know then that 30 years later he would be the first person elected to the National Baseball Hall of Fame by its Committee on Negro Baseball Leagues (National Baseball Hall of Fame Library).

out Paige as the tentative speaker for the Nebraska Semipro Baseball Hall of Fame banquet to be held at Fayes Lounge and Restaurant in Fremont.[71]

But Paige did not speak at the event.

In the year before Paige died, a Jeff Jordan column carried a memory from Ross Horning, at the time the acting chairman of the history department at Creighton University. Horning remembered facing Paige in 1938. Paige was pitching for the Kansas City Monarchs in Watertown, South Dakota, against the semipro Watertown Elks. Horning, who was only 17 years old at the time, played second base for the Elks and had one at bat against Paige. As Jordan writes:

> "Batting against him," Horning said, was not exactly an accurate description of what happened: "I was at the plate against Satchel Paige as three pitches—like three shots out of a laser beam—went by."
> 
> Horning was also anxious to correct any erroneous latter-day impression that folks might have that Paige was loved by the crowds, even then, because he was a clown. He was not, Horning said. He was a craftsman on the mound, a dedicated athlete who, with every pitch, showed the irony that, because he was black, his skills would never be seen in the white major leagues of his heyday.[72]

Mat Pascale, Mr. Amateur Baseball, "a quiet little man with a ton of dignity and two tons of baseball yarns that could hypnotize listeners,"[73] passed in 1985, surviving Paige by three years and leaving Omaha and Nebraska with more than 70 years of baseball dedication and memories. My dad passed in 1997, the year that the Florida Marlins won their first World Series. In the years since, I have wondered at times what my dad might have thought about that, about the Marlins and the World Series win that was quickly followed by a mass trade-off of most of that Marlin team. It is not my place to put words in his mouth, but I offer that my dad was a bit of a purist. There are many conversations that my dad and I never had and all kinds of practical guidance that I refused by sheer stubbornness or that he never offered because he was a bit of an enigma himself. But my dad wanted me to know about Satchel Paige. Perhaps it was a case of one complex character showing respect for another complex character. Or admiration of Paige's moxie. Or maybe it was just the story itself and a father wanting his daughter to know the spine and whimsy of Satchel Paige.

NOTES

1. Paige's given first name can be found spelled "LeRoy" or "Leroy," depending on the source.
2. Satchel Paige Memorial Stadium, 5050 Swope Parkway, Kansas City, Missouri.
3. All the standard baseball reference works and websites agree on this date, but cf. Mark Ribowsky, *Don't Look Back: Satchel Paige in the Shadows of Baseball* (New York: Simon & Schuster, 1994), 21–25, and Larry Tye, *Satchel: The Life and Times of an American Legend* (New York: Random House Trade Paperbacks, 2009), viii–xi, 227.
4. Tye, vii.
5. *Ibid.*, viii.
6. Robert Phipps, "Hurling Born with Satchel," *Omaha World-Herald*, September 4, 1935.
7. Tye, ix.
8. *Ibid.*, vii.
9. "Short Short Sport Stories—Races Threatened," *Omaha World-Herald*, April 28, 1949.
10. Ribowsky, 11–12.
11. Tye, 266.
12. Donn Rogosin, *Invisible Men: Life In Baseball's Negro Leagues* (New York: Atheneum, 1983), 124.
13. LeRoy (Satchel) Paige as told to David Lipman, *Maybe I'll Pitch Forever: A Great Baseball Player Tells the Hilarious Story Behind the Legend* (Lincoln: University of Nebraska Press, 1993; originally published by New York: Doubleday & Company, 1962), 115. The citation is to the University of Nebraska Press edition.

14. Virgil Parker, "I May Be Wrong," *Lincoln (NE) Evening Journal*, June 7, 1973.
15. *Ibid.*
16. *Ibid.*
17. *Ibid.*
18. "Employment," *Omaha World-Herald*, November 4, 1923.
19. "Amateur Baseball," *Omaha World-Herald*, May 24, 1925.
20. "New Athletic Club," *Omaha World-Herald*, January 10, 1928.
21. "So Monarchs Join Satchell [sic]," *Omaha World-Herald*, September 19, 1935.
22. "Red Sox Play Packer Team," *Omaha World-Herald*, July 11, 1934.
23. "National League Stars Play Here," *Omaha World-Herald*, October 6, 1933.
24. "Paige to Pitch Here Tonight," *Omaha World-Herald*, September 27, 1935.
25. "Satchel Will Pack 'Em In," *Omaha World-Herald*, September 3, 1935.
26. *Ibid.*
27. Dennis E. Hoffman, "Scoop's Last Story: The Mississippi of the North," *Omaha Star*, May 17, 2007.
28. *Ibid.*
29. Walter E. Dobbins, "Negro All[-]Stars Use 14 Blows to Clip Powers, 10–5," *Lincoln (NE) Evening Journal*, August 13, 1937.
30. "Satchel Paige on Mound," *Lincoln (NE) Star*, August 19, 1939.
31. Walter E. Dobbins, "Worthington Plays Links in Twin Bill," *(Lincoln, NE) Sunday Journal and Star*, August 20, 1939.
32. Robert Phipps, "We Want Bergman!" *Omaha World-Herald*, July 25, 1946.
33. Maurice Shadle, "Mel Pleases Crowd with 4-Inning Chore," *Omaha World-Herald*, October 13, 1946.
34. Robert Phipps, "Slider Pitch is Not New," *Omaha World-Herald*, October 17, 1946.
35. "Monarchs Eye 2d Win Here," *Omaha World-Herald*, May 25, 1949.
36. "Satchel Paige," *Omaha World-Herald*, July 8, 1948.
37. Robert Phipps, "Alas, Good Old Days of Colorful Shows by Monarchs Are Gone!" *Omaha World-Herald*, May 27, 1942.
38. "Satch Says 'No' to Big Leagues," *Omaha World-Herald*, August 7, 1942.
39. Bob Considine, "Negro Sports Editor Says Paige's Career Behind Him," *Omaha World-Herald*, August 14, 1942.
40. *Ibid.*
41. "Old Satch on Strike for G.I. Joe: Plans Boycott on Star Negro Game if Owners Profit," *Omaha World-Herald*, August 2, 1944.
42. *Ibid.*
43. "Paige, Richards to Perform Here," *Omaha World-Herald*, October 4, 1952.
44. Grantland Rice, "Classic Lacks Past Luster," *Omaha World-Herald*, July 8, 1952.
45. "Semipro Group Salutes Satchel," *Omaha World-Herald*, December 26, 1953.
46. Robert Phipps, "Speaking of Sports," *Omaha World-Herald*, December 14, 1953.
47. Tye, 240.
48. Conde Sargent, "Ole Satch Pitches His Philosophy," *Lincoln (NE) Evening Journal*, August 2, 1960.
49. Jack Andersen, "Old Satchel, Goose Fine, But Rookie Big Attraction," *Lincoln (NE) Evening Journal*, July 17, 1962.
50. *Ibid.*
51. "Jays Outscore Offut—Eagles Keep Winning Touch Against Satch's K.C. Club," *Omaha World-Herald*, August 1, 1964.
52. *Ibid.*
53. "Satchel to Pitch for Clowns Here," *Omaha World-Herald*, August 17, 1966.
54. "Satch Here Tonight," *Omaha World-Herald*, June 21, 1967.
55. *Ibid.*, and "Satchel to Pitch for Clowns Here."
56. "Satchel, Abe Join Forces," *Omaha World-Herald*, December 13, 1964.
57. *Ibid.*
58. "Cage Clowns Treat 6,432," *Omaha World Herald*, January 6, 1965.
59. Wally Provost, "The Good Scout: A Valuable Man," *Omaha World Herald*, August 22, 1972.
60. Wally Provost, "Voice [f]rom the Grandstand," *Omaha World-Herald*, May 12, 1977.
61. *Ibid.*
62. Michael Kelly, "Rosenblatt One of Best Right Up to Last Bat," *Omaha World-Herald*, October 30, 1979.
63. Robert McMorris, "Phipps Has To Look Back—He's a Newspaperman," *Omaha World-Herald*, July 11, 1970. Since Paige was born in 1906, the "Negro baseball league" that Phipps mentions was probably the second Negro National League.
64. "Satchel to Move Directly Into Hall," *Omaha World-Herald*, July 8, 1971.
65. Jim Murray, "Satchel and Pals Now Riding High," *Omaha World-Herald*, August 13, 1971.
66. *Ibid.*
67. Tye, 268.

68. *Ibid.*
69. *Ibid.*, 269.
70. "Was 1982 a Good Year? The Question Is Personal," *Omaha World-Herald*, December 31, 1982.
71. Wally Provost, "Hall-of-Fame Candidate Not Best in This Family," *Omaha World-Herald*, April 25, 1982.
72. Jeff Jordan, "Pianist Had Special Thanks," *Omaha World-Herald*, June 14, 1981.
73. Wally Provost, "Time Machine Goes Too Fast," *Omaha World-Herald*, May 2, 1985.

# 7

# When Jackie Came to Town

### John A. Shorey

On the day that Adolf Hitler's head of the German Luftwaffe, Hermann Goering, took poison to cheat justice at the Nuremburg Trials of Nazi war criminals and Enos Slaughter made his mad dash home to help the St. Louis Cardinals win Game Seven of the World Series, history was being made in Omaha, Nebraska. October 15, 1946, was when Jackie Robinson came to town to play a composite team of local baseball players. Some historians have postulated that 20th-century America can be divided into two epochs: before and after Jackie Robinson. Whereas others may claim that assessment is a bit of hyperbole, there is little doubt that Jack Roosevelt Robinson left an indelible imprint on the United States at mid-century.

It was not quite a year earlier that Robinson made national news when the president and general manager of the Brooklyn Dodgers, Branch Rickey, Sr., scheduled a press conference for October 23, 1945, at which Hector Racine, the president of the Montreal Royals of the International League, Brooklyn's top farm club, announced that the Dodger organization had signed the 26-year-old African American.[1] Robinson caught the attention of Dodger scouts, not only because of his stellar season in the summer of 1945 in which he batted .345 for the Kansas City Monarchs of the Negro Leagues,[2] but also due to his multisport athletic prowess at UCLA, his military background, and his overall character.

The former Monarch shortstop's first year in Organized Baseball was spent as a second baseman with the Royals in 1946, when he captured the batting title with a .349 average and also lead the league in runs scored with 113.[3] In part because of Robinson, Montreal would win the International League pennant by 18½ games, and the team would set a new franchise attendance record. In fact, Robinson's presence not only increased the turnout at the Royals' home park, but it helped Montreal's opponents as well. As Jules Tygiel wrote:

> Almost three times as many fans in other cities saw Montreal play in 1946 as had appeared the preceding year.... [So,] [c]ounting the regular schedule and post-season [sic] play-offs [sic], over a million people saw the Royals perform in 1946, a remarkable figure in a minor league in which most arenas seated between ten and twenty thousand spectators.[4]

Thus, in the fall of 1946, Robinson was a nationally known figure who could draw a lot of spectators. Like a number of other professional baseball players of that time, notably Bob Feller, Dizzy Dean, and Satchel Paige, Robinson would try to capitalize on his newfound stardom by doing some baseball barnstorming in the fall after the conclusion of the regular season. Bob Feller, the Hall of Fame flame-throwing right-handed pitcher from Van Meter, Iowa, had been doing barnstorming tours for quite some time. He and Satchel Paige would travel with their respective teams made up of white players from major league baseball on Feller's roster and black players from the Negro Leagues playing on the team headlined by star pitcher Paige. Robinson, with his emerging celebrity status, was recruited by Feller, Paige, and Kansas City Monarch owner J.L. Wilkinson to join their barnstorming tour. However, as Tim Gay has noted, "Robinson ... was not happy with the financial terms presented [to him] by [the triumvirate], which prompted [him] to organize his own tour."[5] Feller spent months during the 1946 baseball season working on his postseason travel arrangements, including "[leasing] two state-of-the-art DC-3s from Flying Tigers Airlines and [then having] them [painted] 'Bob Feller All-Stars' on one fuselage [and] 'Satchel Paige All-Stars' on the other."[6] In addition to the planes, Feller also booked ballparks and motels for the tour. Even as late as August 30, the *Council Bluffs (IA) Nonpareil* reported that the scheduled October game of the Feller-Paige all-stars "probably [would] include Jackie Robinson."[7]

Along with being his generation's most celebrated major league pitcher, Bob Feller was a tough businessman. He held strong opinions, and he was not shy about sharing them. Feller, no doubt, realized the drawing card potential of adding Robinson to the roster of the Satchel Paige All-Stars. For him, the tour was all about making money. He actually scheduled a few day-night doubleheaders in two different cities hundreds of miles apart in order to get two gates in one day. But the likelihood of signing Jackie Robinson to the tour was probably slim. Although they did not know each other well, Feller and Robinson already had a troubled relationship. The bad blood between the two began about a year earlier when the news broke of Jackie's signing with the Brooklyn Dodgers in October 1945. Feller was on his 1945 postseason tour and had just beaten a black barnstorming team, which included Satchel Paige, by a score of 4–2. As Tim Gay describes:

**In his only season in the minors (1946), Jackie Robinson was a star for the Montreal Royals (National Baseball Hall of Fame Library).**

> After the game, Paul Zimmerman of the [*Los Angeles*] *Times* quizzed [Feller] about Dodger signee Robinson's big league potential. Jackie was a good athlete but too muscle-bound to be an effective major league hitter, Feller told the reporter. [He

maintained that] Robinson's football physique would make him susceptible to fastballs. "[Robinson] couldn't hit an inside pitch to save his neck," [Feller] ungraciously claimed.

[He went on to state], "If [Robinson] were a white man, I doubt if they would consider him big league material." Later that fall, Feller told [*Pittsburgh Courier* sports reporter] Wendell Smith, "I hope [Robinson] makes good. But I don't think he will."[8]

A year later, after Robinson's stellar season with the Montreal Royals, Feller doubled down on his views concerning Robinson and black baseball players in general. When during the course of his 1946 tour against the Satchel Paige All-Stars, he was asked by Steve George of *The Sporting News* if he had seen any African American ballplayers who could perform at the major league level. Rapid Robert replied:

> Haven't seen one—not one.... Maybe Paige when he was young. When you name him[,] you're done. Some are good hitters. Some can field pretty good. Most of them are fast. But I have seen none who combine the qualities of a big league ball player [*sic*].[9]

And when George retorted, "Not even Jackie Robinson? ... [Feller countered,] Not even Jackie Robinson."[10]

Bob Feller and Jackie Robinson did square off against each other a week after Feller made his initial disparaging remarks in the fall of 1945. As part of Feller's barnstorming tour that autumn, he had a few games scheduled against Chet Brewer's Kansas City Royals, a touring team of black baseball players which included Satchel Paige and the now famous Jackie Robinson. According to Tim Gay:

> [Prior to the game, a] disagreement surfaced ... over how much money the black players had been promised. Some accounts suggest that ... Brewer and Robinson were concerned that they ... [would be] receiving a percentage of the net rather than a percentage of the gross [profits], as had been promised. Robinson threatened to lead a boycott of the game unless more money was put up.
>
> When Feller got wind of the brewing mutiny, he stormed into the black team's clubhouse..., confronted Robinson, and demanded that the Royals take the field—or else. Harsh words were exchanged, ... [but the game was played as scheduled.][11]

Future National Baseball Hall of Famer Bob Feller in 1948. Two years earlier, he had said that he had not seen any black ballplayers who could compete in the majors, with the possible exception of Satchel Paige in his younger days (National Baseball Hall of Fame Library).

And this was not the only instance in which Feller ran into a problem with one of his barnstorming partners. On November 9, 1946, the *Chicago Defender* reported:

> Leroy ["]Satchel["] Paige filed suit in Los Angeles against Bob Feller ... who was on a tour with Paige's team. Paige ... is asking [for] $1,711.58[,] which he claims is still due for his services....
>
> The great Negro pitcher says that he is also [owed] ... sums of $598.37 due on Oct. 17 and $1,500 due on a contract entered on Oct. 20.[12]

In the words of Gay, "Paige and Feller eventually settled their differences out of court, but not before a spate of embarrassing publicity."[13]

However, even earlier in the '46 tour, Feller was sued for $42,500 by Davenport, Iowa, promoter Ray C. Doan, Feller's former barnstorming business partner. In his complaint, "Doan asked for an accounting and an adjustment in the amount of $7,500 for their joint operation of the Flying Tigers Air Circus and an accounting of profits and adjustment in the amount of $35,000 for engagements in a joint barnstorming venture."[14]

While Bob Feller and Satchel Paige put together their own segregated squads and played primarily against each other on their tour, Jackie Robinson's team was groundbreaking in that it, at least for part of the tour, was an integrated group made up of some of the best minor leaguers from various clubs and some Negro League players. Among the more notable of the latter group that toured on and off with Jackie in the fall of 1946 were future Hall of Famers Monte Irvin and Larry Doby.[15] Also joining Robinson's team were four fellow Negro League stars who had already been signed by the Brooklyn Dodger organization: Roy Campanella, Don Newcombe, Roy Partlow, and John Wright.[16] And among the white players touring with Robinson was his double play partner from the Montreal Royals, Al Campanis,[17] who, as a future Dodger general manager, lost his job years later when he "publicly question[ed] whether blacks had the 'necessities' to manage at the big league level."[18]

Unlike Feller's barnstorming tour, Robinson's minor league all-stars had to wait until their marquee player finished participating in the Little World Series, which pitted Montreal against Louisville. And thanks in part to the second sacker's stellar play, the Royals won the postseason series, four games to two.[19] Robinson's tour began in New York City in early October at two iconic major league venues: the Polo Grounds, home to the New York Giants, and Ebbets Field, residence of the Giants' hated rival, the Brooklyn Dodgers. In those two contests, the opposing team consisted of an assortment of current major league players from various clubs and were managed by Brooklyn Dodger coach Chuck Dressen. After their New York contests, Robinson's All-Stars made their way to Chicago, playing games in Harrisburg, Pittsburgh, Dayton, and Columbus. In Chicago, they played at legendary Comiskey Park, the domain of the Chicago White Sox, on Sunday, October 13.[20] The opponent was another assortment of major league players which formed the Hans Wagner Major League All-Stars. Robinson's minor league integrated team prevailed against their rivals by a score of 10 to 5, with Robinson contributing to the winning effort by helping to turn three double plays and being 2-for-4 at the plate, with a triple and a run scored.[21]

Fresh off of their victory against the Wagner All-Stars, Robinson's team came to Omaha, Nebraska, minus many of their well-publicized players, and also having to deal with direct competition from the Bob Feller–Satchel Paige tour. Even though the visiting teams stayed in Omaha, the games were not played in the Big O due to the fact that the city's premiere ballpark on Vinton Street burned down in the summer of 1936.[22] It would not be until 1948 that the River City built Omaha Stadium, commonly called Municipal Stadium and later renamed Johnny Rosenblatt Stadium, on a hill not too far away from the old Vinton Street park. In the meantime, the only ballpark in the metropolitan area that had the capacity to hold the expected large crowds for those barnstorming games was across the Missouri River in Council Bluffs, Iowa: American Legion Park located on 35th Street.

176   Section I—The Long and Winding Road

Bob Feller and Satchel Paige each pitched three scoreless innings in their duel on Saturday, October 12, before a chilled crowd of about 4,000 spectators. The Feller All-Stars ultimately prevailed, 3–2, but the game was not without its lighter moments. After walking Chicago White Sox catcher Frankie Hayes, Satchel Paige caught Hayes napping so soundly while he took his lead off first base that Paige was actually able to run over to the bag and tag him out rather than throwing the ball to first baseman Buck O'Neil.[23]

After their afternoon game, both teams boarded their chartered flights out of Omaha and flew down to Wichita, Kansas, where they played another game that night before 7,000 shivering fans. Feller's All-Stars prevailed in that contest, 5–3.[24] The tight schedule no doubt led to a possible disaster for the touring troupe as Feller left $10,431 in checks in a desk drawer of his suite at the Paxton Hotel in downtown Omaha. Fortunately for Feller and his entourage, an honest night maid found them and the housekeeper immediately airmailed the checks to the Phillips Hotel in Kansas City before Feller even knew they were missing.[25]

Robinson's team was slated to play three days later on Tuesday, October 15, also at American Legion Park in Council Bluffs. A mild warm-up followed the chilly game on Saturday, but unfortunately for the spectators, the forecast for Tuesday called for a return to the cold temperature that had been experienced the previous Saturday, as well as for rain and a threat of late-day snow showers.[26] Unlike the Feller-Paige All-Star tour, which featured two teams made up of renowned players who competed against each other at stops along the tour, the Robinson tour was different. Now that they had left the big metropolitan areas of New York and Chicago, Robinson's All-Stars had to scramble to line up local teams to play against them. The opponent for Robinson's men when they visited Omaha was touted as the Omaha Firemen, a local all-star team that was sponsored by the Omaha Fire Department, which was using the contest as a fundraiser for fireman Eddie Stanek. Stanek, who was the co-manager and shortstop of the Fire Department's regular team, had suffered a broken leg during the summer.[27] Another challenge for the Robinson game was that it was slated for an 8:00 p.m. starting time, whereas the Feller-Paige matchup started at 12:30 p.m. due to being scheduled on a Saturday. Ticket prices for the evening contest ranged from $2 for box seats to $1.80 for reserve seats to $1.00 for general admission.[28]

In the lead-up to the game, there was much speculation and reporting as to the makeup of the two teams that would square off against each other that evening. As reported in the *Council Bluffs (IA) Daily Nonpareil*, the Omaha Firemen would consist of members of that team, along with "a few better players from other Omaha clubs."[29] Most prominent among those speculated to play was a local pitcher named Roman Roh. Roh was considered to be the elite semipro pitcher in the area, so the Firemen team coveted his participation. As an article in the *Nonpareil* reported back in September, the Omaha region was not short on overall baseball talent, but "[p]itchers are a different story."[30] Earlier during the summer of 1946, Roh was recruited by the semipro team, the Council Bluffs Browns, to hurl against Ligon's California All-Stars, which was a traveling black club.[31] Roh was such a local legend that two days before the tilt, the *Nonpareil* offered the analysis that "[t]he Firemen may not be sacrificial offerings Tuesday because the famous Roman Roh will pitch if he doesn't work at Kearney, Neb., Sunday."[32] Creighton University's J.V. "Duce" Belford, the local handler of the game, and promoter Mat Pascale, the baseball director for the Council Bluffs American Legion and the local sponsor of the game, also offered the assessment: "Local fans, though, are underestimating the baseball ability of the Firemen—especially if Roman Roh pitches."[33]

The composition of the Jackie Robinson All-Star team was also open to widespread speculation. Much of the prognosis about who would be playing was, no doubt, based on the makeup of the Robinson All-Stars from their previous games in New York and Chicago against major league talent. In an article with the headline of, "Jackie Robinson to Bring Strong Ball Club Here," the October 14 issue of the *Nonpareil* listed a number of prominent players. Included among the four white players making up the roster were Marvin Rackley, the International League stolen base leader, and Al Campanis, Robinson's teammate from the Montreal Royals that summer. (Campanis was earlier misnamed "Kampouris" in several articles on the upcoming game.[34]) The speculation about the black players joining Robinson would today read like a who's who of future baseball Hall of Famers, including "Roy Campanella, home run king of the Negro National [L]eague in 1945 [sic]; Monty [sic] Irvin of the Newark Eagles, Negro National [L]eague batting leader; [and Larry] Doby."[35] Along with those Negro League and later major league baseball legends, the *Omaha Star* in its preview article also named future Brooklyn Dodger pitching standout Don Newcombe in the list of probable players on the Robinson team.[36]

Unfortunately for the fans, the men that ended up playing did not match the pregame hype. The lineup for the Jackie Robinson All-Stars included none of the advertised white or black players, other than Jackie Robinson. As the *Omaha World-Herald* reported

This ca. 1946 image of Robinson batting captures the essence of what fans witnessed at Legion Park when Jackie came to town (National Baseball Hall of Fame Library).

in its postgame summary, "The Robinson troupe was just another good touring Negro club. None of the other advertised Dodger farmhands was in the lineup."[37] Even Jackie Robinson was reported "under the weather" for the past few days, but he told a *Nonpareil* reporter "that he did not want to fail the fans" by not playing.[38] Robinson was in the lineup for six innings, but he went 0-for-3 batting and did not have any chances in the field. The Omaha Firemen team did feature some of the local baseball talent, but missing from their ranks was the much touted pitcher, Roman Roh.

However, what the game lacked in star power and favorable weather conditions, it made up for in excitement. In the seesaw contest, the Robinson All-Stars took an early lead with a single run in the top of the second inning. The Firemen tied the contest in the bottom half of the second and built a 4 to 1 lead, highlighted by Frank Mancuso stealing home in the sixth inning. But the All-Stars rallied with four runs in the top of the seventh inning, aided by a couple of errors by the Firemen, probably partially a product of the adverse weather conditions. The Firemen tied it up with their turn at bat in the seventh inning, only to have the All-Stars regain the lead with two more runs in the top of the eighth inning on a triple to deep center off the bat of Joe Atkins of the Pittsburgh Crawfords. The score remained 7 to 5 in favor of the All-Stars heading into the bottom of the ninth. The Firemen pushed across one run early in the frame to cut the lead to one. Then, with two outs and the bases loaded, Subby Manzitto grounded a single between first and second to rally the Firemen to an 8–7 triumph. Along with the exciting finale, the fans who braved the cold conditions were also treated to a bit of unintentional comedy. In the fifth inning, a player for the All-Stars with the last name Sutton swung and missed at an inside pitch for strike three. But the ball was so inside when he swung that it went inside his jersey and fell into the knee of his pants. So, Sutton was not only the batter but also the catcher for the strikeout pitch.[39]

Even though he had not yet made his major league debut, Jackie Robinson was already a national celebrity as the first black baseball player to be signed by a major league team in the 20th century, thus breaking the longstanding "gentlemen's agreement" of major league baseball owners and general managers not to sign African American talent. This dated back to the late 1800s when Chicago White Stockings star player Adrian "Cap" Anson refused to play against another team because it had an African American on its roster. Fearing loss of revenue, the other teams caved in to pressure and in an unwritten agreement unofficially barred blacks from playing major league baseball until Jackie Robinson trotted out to his position on April 15, 1947, for the Brooklyn Dodgers.[40] In the fall of 1946, no one knew for sure if Robinson would be the first black to reintegrate major league baseball, but after his stellar season with the Dodgers' top minor league team that year, there seemed to be a good chance that he would fulfill that destiny. So with such a person coming to town, it was much more than just a ball game to be played across the river at Legion Park in Council Bluffs. The Omaha black community especially wanted to take advantage of the opportunity to meet Robinson, with the YMCA and the City Recreation Department inviting him to appear at the Near North Side Branch YMCA on the afternoon of the game and the Frontier's Club scheduling a dinner at 5:30 p.m. to honor him.[41]

The *Omaha Star* newspaper, the weekly publication for the Omaha black community, covered Robinson's talk to the youth at the North Side YMCA in its Friday edition after his visit to town earlier that week. While he was there, he shared with the youngsters that:

[heavyweight boxing legend] Joe Louis was his idol, [sic] because he was such a clean cut [sic] sportsman. He told the boys to pay attention to the headman's advice[,] to watch their conduct[,] and above all[,] he emphasized [d]iscipline. [Also,] he brought out that the white man trys [sic] to own Joe [Louis] because he is great and honest, but as soon as Joe would do something wrong, the white man would point out that he was a Negro. He ... added that more Negroes should get into the baseball field, [sic] because it is a very promising one. He pointed out that more should go into this field, [sic] because those who did go into the field did not go in the background.[42]

Such blunt comments are not usually associated with Robinson at that time during his career, but he tended to be less guarded of his opinions when talking to a black audience.

Along with his stop at the North Side YMCA, Robinson visited the offices of the *Omaha Star* newspaper. While there he met *Omaha Star* sportswriter Robert Rogers and other employees. When asked about his experience thus far in Organized Baseball, Jackie replied "that he has received excellent cooperation from his team mates [sic] [and the] 'baseball fans.'" He went further to say "that it [was] his intention to give his best in order that he might pave the way for other qualified Negroes to enter [O]rganized [B]aseball."[43]

After Robinson's visit to the Omaha area, his team continued its trek westward, eventually making it to California. In California in late October, the weather was more conducive to playing baseball. It was there that the Robinson All-Stars faced the Feller All-Stars in a three-game series. The bad blood between Robinson and Feller would now spill out on the diamond over three days in San Francisco, San Diego, and Los Angeles. The Feller All-Stars prevailed in all three contests. After winning the first game 6–0 and the second 4–2, the most dramatic victory was the 4–3 finale at California's Wrigley Field. In the words of Tim Gay:

> Twelve thousand "screaming" fans saw Feller pitch a perfect game for the first five innings, striking out 10 of 15 batters. But it was Robinson's strenuous objections to the ball-and-strike calls of a [Pacific Coast League] umpire ... that grabbed the headlines in [*The*] *Sporting News*.
> Today, Robinson is justly praised for grace under pressure. But that night in his hometown, still seething over Feller's criticism and perhaps nervous about the presence of Dodger manager Leo Durocher, [he] took loud exception to several umpiring calls.... Robinson, who had kept his anger in check during the '46 International League season, may well have been frustrated that night by his inability to hit Feller. He struck out twice, going zero for three.[44]

Ironically, years later, only two players would be voted into the National Baseball Hall of Fame in 1962: Bob Feller and Jackie Robinson.[45]

Jackie Robinson's visit to Omaha in the fall of 1946 was a headline story for the *Omaha Star*. In addition to previewing the game, the *Star* reported on Robinson's talk at the Near North Side YMCA and included a photo in its October 18 issue of Robinson in the office of the newspaper with four of its employees.[46] A short follow-up article in the *Star* on October 25 mentioned that Robinson had started practicing with a professional basketball team associated with the National League that was operating out of Los Angeles.[47] The *Star*'s coverage over a three-week span of three issues included some quotations from Robinson, some of his comments to the boys he talked to at the YMCA, and additional background information about Jackie's athletic prowess while attending UCLA.

An interesting side story in the *Star* mentioned that the 1946 baseball tour was not Robinson's first trip to Omaha. He had first visited Omaha in 1942 as a member of the Fort Riley football team which played Creighton's football team. When asked about any future prospects of playing football, Robinson answered "that he isn't playing anymore

[sic] football, [sic] because baseball is easier."⁴⁸ The October 11 issue of the paper gave a brief preview of the game, along with Robinson's schedule of attending the Near North Side Branch of the YMCA and the dinner in his honor prior to the game at the Frontier's Club. Oddly enough, the October 18 issue of the paper a week later contained no coverage of the game itself. Perhaps that can be best explained by the fact that the newspaper did not come out until Friday and the game took place three days earlier on Tuesday. Another contributing factor may have been the fact that a local team of white semipro players triumphed over the Robinson All-Stars. The *Omaha Star* was not only a weekly paper but also not a very large paper which did not have a special sports section. However, the post-game edition did contain the stories about Robinson speaking to the boys at the YMCA and his appearance at the offices of the newspaper.

By contrast, coverage in the *Omaha World-Herald* mainly focused on the preview of the game and the game itself. The various issues of the *World-Herald* contained no quotations from or interviews of Jackie Robinson. The only mention of anything other than speculation about the composition of the teams and details about the game was a brief paragraph in the morning edition on the day of the game mentioning that "Jackie Robinson [would] appear at the Near North Side YMCA at [four that] afternoon to talk baseball with any boys who [wished] to listen."⁴⁹ While the *Omaha Star* had a photo of Robinson's visit to the newspaper offices, the only photo of Robinson in the *Omaha World-Herald* was an archive photo with the game preview article. In comparison, the day after Bob Feller and his All-Stars played in Omaha, which, as mentioned earlier, was just three days prior to Jackie Robinson's visit, the top of the *World Herald's* sports page featured a photo of Feller with Omaha native Mel Harder, Feller's Cleveland teammate, who actually started the game against the Paige All-Stars, and Johnny Rosenblatt, the man for whom the future Rosenblatt Stadium would be named.⁵⁰ In the evening edition of the *Omaha World-Herald* following that afternoon's game, sports editor Floyd Olds penned a lengthy column with glowing comments about Feller. The column's headline proclaimed, "An Amazing Youth Visits."⁵¹ No such accolades were showered upon Robinson's visit, but that may be attributed to the fact that Robinson's amazing story was just unfolding, whereas Feller was already an accomplished major league star.

The manner in which Jackie Robinson was described in the two Omaha newspapers also varied greatly. In its main story about Robinson's visit to Omaha, the *Omaha Star* concluded with the sentence, "Mr. Robinson is definitely an all-around athlete and is an encouragement to our young boys, as well as a credit to our race."⁵² In the preview article of the *Omaha World-Herald*, the caption under the image of Robinson read, "Jackie Robinson ... plans plenty of bunts for Omaha stars tonight at Legion Park."⁵³ The accompanying article in the morning edition of the *World-Herald* referred to Jackie as the "lithe Negro,"⁵⁴ while the evening edition described him as the "little Negro."⁵⁵ This appears to be a strange and condescending characterization of Robinson—especially after Feller had railed about his football physique and that Robinson was too muscle-bound to be a professional major league baseball player. The *Council Bluffs (IA) Daily Nonpareil* newspaper had extensive coverage of the lead-up to the game, along with the game itself. This was no doubt due to the fact that the contest was actually played in Council Bluffs, even though the players stayed in Omaha overnight. The *Nonpareil* tended to be more positive in its description of Robinson and the event compared to the reporting done by the *Omaha World-Herald*. An advance man for the Jackie Robinson troupe was quoted in the *Nonpareil* the morning of the 15th as saying, "We want to show you what a great Negro ball player [sic] this Robinson is."⁵⁶ The article went on to describe Jackie as "the sensational Brooklyn farm hand [sic] with Montreal."⁵⁷

Even as Jackie Robinson's visit to Omaha in October of 1946 garnered a considerable amount of attention, it is doubtful if anyone in the River City in the fall of that year truly appreciated the revolution that was unfolding before their eyes, spearheaded by the courageous former Kansas City Monarch player. Within 12 months of Robinson breaking the color barrier in America's pastime, President Harry Truman would issue an executive order integrating the U.S. military. Thus, two cornerstones of American society, baseball and the military, ended their policies of segregation in back-to-back years. The U.S. Supreme Court's landmark ruling in the *Brown vs. Board of Education* case in 1954 would strike down segregation in public schools and launch the full-scale Civil Rights movement. Jackie Robinson was perhaps an unwitting pioneer of that movement, but he accepted the leadership mantle with extraordinary discipline. And remember that discipline was the main point Robinson emphasized to the Omaha youth gathered to hear him speak prior to his game on that historic day when Jackie came to town.

In April of 1947, six months after visiting Omaha, Robinson would reopen the door for blacks to play in the majors (National Baseball Hall of Fame Library).

NOTES

1. Mary Kay Linge, *Jackie Robinson: A Biography* (Westport, Connecticut: Greenwood Press, 2007), 47.
2. James A. Riley, *The Biographical Encyclopedia of the Negro Baseball Leagues* (New York: Carroll & Graf Publishers, 1994), 672. But cf. Dick Clark and Larry Lester, eds., *The Negro Leagues Book* (Cleveland, Ohio: Society for American Baseball Research, 1994), 299; "Jackie Robinson," www.baseball-reference.com (accessed on February 12, 2017); and "Jackie Robinson," http://www.seamheads.com/NegroLgs/player.php?playerID=robin01jac (accessed on June 5, 2019). Perhaps Mary Kay Linge assessed the matter best when

## Section I—The Long and Winding Road

she wrote, "Robinson performed well as a Monarch, hitting an estimated .345 (statistics were never reliably kept in Negro League contests)." Linge, 43.

3. Lloyd Johnson and Miles Wolff, eds., *Encyclopedia of Minor League Baseball*, 3rd ed. (Durham, North Carolina: Baseball America, Inc., 2007), 401.

4. Jules Tygiel, *Baseball's Great Experiment: Jackie Robinson and His Legacy* (New York: Oxford University Press, 1983), 130.

5. Timothy M. Gay, *Satch, Dizzy & Rapid Robert: The Wild Saga of Interracial Baseball Before Jackie Robinson* (New York: Simon & Schuster, Inc., 2010), 224.

6. *Ibid.*

7. Jack Hand, "Bob Feller Has More Irons in Fire Than Mike Jacobs," *Council Bluffs (IA) Daily Nonpareil*, August 30, 1946.

8. Gay, 208.

9. Steve George, "250,000 See Feller-Paige Teams Play," *The Sporting News*, October 30, 1946, 9.

10. *Ibid.*

11. Gay, 210.

12. Fay Young, "Through the Years," *Chicago Defender*, November 9, 1946.

13. Gay, 210.

14. "Feller Game Slated Today," *Omaha World-Herald*, October 12, 1946.

15. "Jackie Robinson's Team Beats Major Leaguers, 10–5," *Chicago Defender*, October 19, 1946.

16. "Jackie Robinson's Team Will Play at Comiskey Park Sunday, Oct. 13," *Chicago Defender*, October 12, 1946.

17. "Jackie Robinson's Team Beats Major Leaguers, 10–5."

18. Gay, 220–221.

19. "Jackie Robinson's Team Will Play at Comiskey Park Sunday, Oct. 13."

20. *Ibid.*

21. "Jackie Robinson's Team Beats Major Leaguers, 10–5."

22. For details on the ballpark on Vinton Street, see "Nebraska Minor League Baseball: Rourke Park, 13th at Vinton, Omaha[,] Nebraska," http://www.nebaseballhistory.com/rourkepark.html (accessed on February 14, 2017), and Judy Horan, "Western League Park," http://omahamagazine.com/articles/western-league-park (accessed on February 14, 2017).

23. "Feller, Satchel in Scoreless Three Inning [sic] Mound Stints," *Council Bluffs (IA) Daily Nonpareil*, October 13, 1946.

24. Maurice Shadle, "Mel Pleases Crowd with 4-Inning Chore," *Omaha World-Herald*, October 13, 1946.

25. Jake Rachman, "$10,431 Forgotten by Feller Here," *Omaha World-Herald*, October 15, 1946.

26. "Showers, Cold Forecast Tuesday," *Omaha World-Herald*, October 14, 1946.

27. "Jackie Robinson Will Play Here," *Council Bluffs (IA) Daily Nonpareil*, October 9, 1946.

28. "See Jackie Robinson and His All[-]Star Team at Council Bluffs," *Omaha Star*, October 11, 1946.

29. "Roh May Hurl in Tuesday's Game," *Council Bluffs (IA) Daily Nonpareil*, October 10, 1946.

30. F.W.H., "Sports Digest," *Council Bluffs (IA) Daily Nonpareil*, September 23, 1946.

31. "Colored Crew Plays Browns Friday Night," *Council Bluffs (IA) Daily Nonpareil*, June 14, 1946.

32. "Robinson's All Stars [sic] to Play Firemen Here," *Council Bluffs (IA) Daily Nonpareil*, October 13, 1946.

33. "Stolen Base Leader Due," *Omaha World-Herald*, October 14, 1946.

34. For example, *ibid.* and "Jackie Robinson Will Play Here."

35. "Jackie Robinson to Bring Strong Ball Club Here," *Council Bluffs (IA) Daily Nonpareil*, October 14, 1946.

36. "Jackie Robinson's Baseball Team To Play in Bluffs," *Omaha Star*, October 11, 1946.

37. Maurice Shadle, "Omaha Stars Win in 9th, 8–7," *Omaha World-Herald*, October 16, 1946.

38. "Omahans Rally in Last Frame," *Council Bluffs (IA) Daily Nonpareil*, October 16, 1946.

39. *Ibid.*

40. "Jackie Robinson," www.baseball-reference.com (accessed on February 12, 2017).

41. "Jackie Robinson's Baseball Team To Play in Bluffs."

42. "Jackie Robinson, Famed Negro Visits Omaha," *Omaha Star*, October 18, 1946.

43. "Jackie Robinson Visits 'Star'[sic] Offices," *Omaha Star*, October 18, 1946.

44. Gay, 243.

45. "1962 Hall of Fame Voting," www.baseball-reference.com (accessed on February 8, 2017).

46. "Jackie Robinson, Famed Negro Visits Omaha," and "Jackie Robinson Visits 'Star'[sic] Offices."

47. "Robinson Will Play with L.A. Pro Five," *Omaha Star*, October 25, 1946.

48. "Jackie Robinson, Famed Negro Visits Omaha."

49. "Negro Aces Billed Tonight," *Omaha World-Herald*, October 15, 1946.

50. Maurice Shadle, "Mel Pleases Crowd With 4-Inning Chore," and "Pitchers Bob Feller (left) and Mel Harder (right) of [the] Cleveland Indians … tell Johnny Rosenblatt that [the] turnout was a pleasant surprise," *Omaha World-Herald*, October 13, 1946.

51. Floyd Olds, "An Amazing Youth Visits," *Omaha World-Herald*, October 12, 1946.
52. "Jackie Robinson, Famed Negro Visits Omaha."
53. *Omaha World-Herald*, October 15, 1946.
54. "Negro Aces Billed Tonight."
55. "Jackie & Co. Face Firemen," *Omaha World-Herald*, October 15, 1946.
56. "Jackie Robinson Will Play Here Tuesday Night," *Council Bluffs (IA) Daily Nonpareil*, October 15, 1946.
57. *Ibid.*

# 8

# African Americans in the College World Series

## Jerry E. Clark

The College World Series (CWS) that determines what is known today as the NCAA Division I champions of baseball began in 1947 in Kalamazoo, Michigan. In that first year, the University of California triumphed, defeating Yale University, whose first baseman was none other than George "Poppy" Bush, the future president of the United States. The 1948 CWS was again held in Kalamazoo, with Bush again playing for the runner-up Yale team, this time a loser to the University of Southern California (USC), whereas the following year it was held in Wichita, Kansas, with the University of Texas emerging as the winner. Then the Series moved to Omaha, Nebraska, in 1950, where it has been played ever since.[1]

Once in the River City, the College World Series was held at Omaha Stadium, a new ballpark that had been built for the professional Class A Omaha Cardinal baseball team and opened on October 17, 1948. In 1964, the park was renamed Rosenblatt Stadium in honor of the former mayor, Johnny Rosenblatt, who had championed baseball in the Big O and was instrumental in bringing the CWS to the city. The Series was played at that stadium for 61 years until 2011 when it was moved to TD Ameritrade Park in downtown Omaha.[2]

College baseball benefited from the popularity of the game during the 1950s and 1960s. Professional baseball was in its prime and this rubbed off on amateur ball from Little League to high school to town teams to college ball. Part of the reason for this celebrity was undoubtedly the presence of black players in Organized Baseball, which was reintegrated at the minor league level in 1946 and at the major league level the following year. Jackie Robinson, Larry Doby, Don Newcombe, Willie Mays, Ernie Banks, and Hank Aaron, among others, added an excitement to the game and increased its allure.

However, black players in the CWS lagged behind the professional game. Of course, identifying who was the first African American to be a member of a College World Series team is difficult, if not impossible. The NCAA has no idea who the person may have been and the author of this essay could not find another source that could provide any information on this matter. Earl Robinson of the 1957 University of California Golden Bears may have been the first black to play on a CWS championship team, though Wesley Mallette, associate athletics director of strategic communications at the University of California, told Angelo J. Louisa in 2015 that "Unfortunately, from what we can see, nothing we have ever put out, nor any obits (Cal produced or from other outlets/sources), or anything else about Robinson mentioned him as being the first black player to have played in, or be part of a team to have won the College World Series (in 1957)."[3]

The 1960s saw an increase in the number of African Americans on college baseball teams, and by the 1970s and early 1980s, many teams included six to nine black players. But in the last 25 years, the number of blacks on college squads has decreased. In 2004, only 4.5 percent of all NCAA ballplayers were African American. Even at historically all-black colleges, the number of African American ballplayers is diminishing. For example, Bethune-Cookman and Winston-Salem State boast baseball teams that are predominantly white.[4] The results of this drop-off were particularly evident in 2008 when there were only five black players among the eight programs competing in the CWS.

The decline in the number of African American ballplayers has not only been seen in the college ranks, but in major league baseball as well. In 1975, 27 percent of all major leaguers were black, but only 8.3 percent of the players on the opening day rosters in 2014 identified themselves as African American.[5] In 2007, the Atlanta Braves and the Houston Astros had no black players. This is partly due to the decline in the number of blacks in college ball. Thirty years ago, over 60 percent of professional baseball players were drafted out of high school, but now, 70 percent are drafted out of the college ranks.[6] And with fewer blacks in college ball, fewer blacks are entering the pros.

But why are there so few African American players in college ball today? Although a number of hypotheses have been offered as answers, opportunity seems to play a major role. Today, youngsters who want to make it on a college team must have a chance to play youth baseball. Increasingly, young ballplayers are being developed on select teams with long seasons, travel expenses, and high-level coaching. These teams focus on talent, and the parents of the players must have money, with it costing several thousand dollars to participate. Thus, this has become a suburban experience—not an inner city one—and poor and many minority youths have little opportunity to play on such teams.[7]

Another reason there are fewer blacks in college ball is the reduction in baseball scholarships. In the 1960s and 1970s, when a large number of African American athletes played college ball, coaches had a maximum of 25 scholarships to attract players. Today, college programs are limited to 11.7 scholarships that must be passed out among as many as 25 players. By comparison, football has 85 scholarships and basketball has 15.[8] Coaches are often blamed for avoiding black players, but while football and basketball coaches have the scholarships to take a chance on a Proposition 48 student,[9] baseball coaches cannot afford to tie up a scholarship on such an athlete.

Still, there have been a good number of African American ballplayers who have participated in the College World Series, though some who had great college or professional careers did not fare so well in Omaha. For example, Chris Chambliss came to Omaha with his UCLA team in 1969. He had hit .340 during the season, with 45 runs batted in (RBI) and 15 home runs, which was a school record before the use of aluminum bats.[10] The first draft pick by the Cleveland Indians in 1970, he went on to a remarkable career with the New York Yankees and the Atlanta Braves, as well as with Cleveland, where he received the Rookie of the Year Award in 1971.[11] But in the CWS, UCLA lost its first two games and Chambliss had only one hit in eight at bats.[12] Nevertheless, he should be considered a black star in spite of his disappointing Series performance.

On the other hand, there were African American players who had a fantastic College World Series experience, making the All-Tournament Team and leading their schools to championships. But for them, the CWS turned out to be the highlight of their baseball careers. They may have knocked around the minors for a while, but they never made it to the majors. One such player was Jerry Bond, an outfielder for Southern Illinois. The Salukis participated in the CWS in 1968 and 1969, finishing second in the former year, with Bond being named to the All-Tournament Team. Bond led his alma mater in hits, runs, and triples during the '68 season, and the following year, he was drafted by Cleveland in the seventh round and played five seasons in the minors but never made it past Double-A ball.[13]

Still other blacks who played in the CWS had careers in nonbaseball ventures that made them stars. Deion Sanders was a member of the 1986 and 1987 Florida State teams in the Series. Though he did not stand out in those games, he had an exceptional professional career in the National Football League (NFL), as well as playing nine seasons in the majors.

As mentioned earlier, possibly the first African American ballplayer on a CWS championship team was Earl Robinson, who was the shortstop for the 1957 University of California Bears. The sportswriters did not begin picking All-Tournament teams until 1958, but a case could be made for including the "Earl of Berkeley" on such a team based on his seven hits and .350 batting average for the Series. Earl was a two-sport star at California and an All-Pacific Coast Conference guard on the 1956, '57, and '58 basketball teams, the last of which he captained, while being named All-American in baseball in 1957. He went on to play in the majors with the Los Angeles Dodgers and Baltimore Orioles before becoming an assistant basketball coach at California in 1963 and the first black head coach in the California junior college system during the 1966–1967 academic year, when he accepted a job at Merritt College in Oakland. He also taught speech and communications at Laney College and English at Oakland's Castlemont High School. And he helped Ricky Henderson with his acceptance speech for his National Baseball Hall of Fame (HOF) induction.[14]

In 1958, Fred Scott of

In 1957, Earl Robinson helped lead the University of California Golden Bears to a 35–10 record and the College World Series championship (Cal Athletics).

the University of Southern California, made the CWS All-Tournament Team as a shortstop.[15] Scott played only three years in the minors, but his teammate Don Buford, who was not even a starter for the '58 Trojans, went on to a successful career with the Chicago White Sox and Baltimore Orioles before ending his playing days in Japan.[16] He then spent seven seasons as a major league coach and three as a minor league manager.[17]

In 1961, Julie Yearling was a left fielder for Northern Colorado. Though he did his part with four hits in two games, his team lost those games and was eliminated.[18]

The 1963 and 1964 University of Southern California's baseball teams made it to the CWS for their eighth and ninth times, winning the championship in 1963 and coming in third in 1964. An outfielder for the Trojans during those seasons, Willie Brown made the All-Tournament Team the latter year and also played I-back on USC's national championship football team in 1962 as well as captaining the 1963 football squad. Then he was hired by his alma mater in July of 1968 as an assistant football and assistant baseball coach, serving in the former position for eight years, 1968–1975, and in the latter position through the 1970 season. He would return again to his alma mater in the mid–1990s to become a staff member of the Student Athlete Academic Services, a job that he was holding at least as late as February 13, 2015, and in 2005, he was inducted into the USC Athletic Hall of Fame.[19]

Archie Clark was a member of the 1964 University of Minnesota CWS championship team. He had a rather lackluster Series until the semifinal game against Maine, in which he went three-for-four with two doubles and a triple. But it was his speed that made him such a threat. In the opening game against Texas A&M, he did not get a hit, but he did get to first on a fielder's choice. He promptly stole second and third, before scoring on a wild pitch. For the entire Series, he managed to steal four bases. Clark starred in both baseball and basketball at Minnesota, and in 1966, he was All-Big Ten in the latter sport and was chosen by the Los Angeles Lakers in the National Basketball Association (NBA) draft. He had a 10-year career in the NBA and was selected for the All-Star team twice.[20]

Besides Chris Chambliss and Jerry Bond, whose teams went two and out, African Americans in the 1969 CWS were represented by Lenny Randle, the second baseman for the champion Arizona State University (ASU) team, who also played on Arizona State's football team. In 1980, Randle was named to ASU's Hall of Fame. Although he had a good Series, he was not selected for the All-Tournament Team, an honor that went to a second baseman from Texas named Lou Bagwell. In 1970, Randle was a first-round draft pick of the Washington Senators (the Texas Rangers today) and went on to play 12 years in the majors on six different teams. He also played ball in Italy for a while. But he may be best remembered for a game he played against Kansas City, in which he got on his hands and knees and tried unsuccessfully to blow foul a slow roller that Amos Otis had hit down the third base line. Since retiring from baseball, Randle has operated a sports academy for inner city kids.[21]

The year 1971 might be remembered as the second of USC's five CWS championships in a row or as the debut of Fred Lynn as USC's freshman All-American. But the Cinderella team of the Series was Pan American University of Edinburg, Texas, which made its first and only College World Series appearance.[22] In the regional tournament, the Broncs knocked off the heavily favored University of Texas team, and though they finished the CWS with a 2–2 record and none of their players were chosen for the All-Tournament Team, they had a number of black members. One was James Tyrone, the center fielder, who was an All-American in both 1970 and '71. This speedster stole 51 bases during the 1971 season, followed by four in the CWS, including three in an opening game loss to Southern Illinois.[23] Tyrone played 11 seasons of professional ball in the United States with the Chicago Cubs and the Oakland A's and four more years in Japan.[24] His brother Wayne was a member of the Pan American team, too.

Another 1971 Bronc was pitcher Andre Rabouin. In the third game of the Series, he pitched a four-hit shutout against Harvard with 11 strikeouts. He had also pitched four shutouts during the 1971 season, including one against Texas. Drafted by the Cincinnati Reds, he played three years in the minors—two in Cincinnati's farm system and one in that of the Los Angeles Dodgers—14 seasons at various levels in Mexico, and part of a season for the Panama Bankers of the Triple-A Inter-American League. Then, for a number of years, he served as a pitching coach for several minor league clubs and for Howard University and Prince George's Community College. And as of January 1, 2017, he had been Gallaudet University's pitching coach for seven of the last eight seasons. In addition, Rabouin was an ambassador for Major League Baseball's (MLB's) Play Ball program in China, which teaches the Chinese how to play and coach baseball.[25]

In 1972 and 1973, Bump Wills, son of Maury Wills, played in the CWS for Arizona State. During the '72 Series, Wills batted .350 and was named to the CWS All-Tournament Team. He was drafted by the Texas Rangers, played two seasons in their minor league system, and then replaced Lenny Randle at second base on the parent club. After five years with the Rangers, he was traded to the Chicago Cubs, who in 1983 moved Ryne Sandberg to second base, making Wills expendable. He went on to play two seasons in Japan before becoming a minor league manager.[26]

Probably the best black CWS ballplayer, Dave Winfield, participated in the 1973 Series as a pitcher-outfielder for the University of Minnesota. Winfield, an excellent basketball as well as baseball player, was born on October 3, 1951, the day that Bobby Thomson hit the "shot heard round the world" for the New York Giants. In 1972, he helped Minnesota win its first Big Ten basketball championship in 35 years. Shifting sports, he pitched the Gophers to a 1–0 victory over Oklahoma, striking out 14 Sooners in the opening game of the '73 CWS. This was the first College World Series to use the designated hitter, but when Winfield pitched, Minnesota obviously did not use it. In the semifinals, the St. Paul, Minnesota, native pitched a one-hitter for eight innings against Southern California. But USC scored eight runs in the ninth inning—two with Winfield on the mound—to beat Minnesota, 8–7, and knock the Gophers out of the tournament. Nevertheless, the 6'6" star was picked as a pitcher for the All-Tournament Team and was voted the Most Outstanding Player (MOP) of the Series.

In 1973, Winfield was drafted by the San Diego Padres (MLB), Atlanta Hawks (NBA), and Utah Stars (American Basketball Association). He was even picked by the Minnesota Vikings (NFL), though he had not played football since high school. Winfield signed with the Padres and moved right into the starting lineup as an outfielder, never once playing in the minor leagues. After eight seasons with the Padres, he went to the New York Yankees, where he played for a little more than another eight seasons. He then spent the next five years with the California Angels, Toronto Blue Jays, Minnesota Twins, and Cleveland Indians. However, in spite of their inflated payroll, the Yankees never won a World Series during Winfield's tenure. Thus, the Minnesotan's only World Series ring came in 1992 with Toronto. In 2001, he was inducted into the National Baseball Hall of Fame and chose that his plaque would show him in a Padre, not a Yankee, cap.[27] According to Winfield:

When I look at everything, it's kind of like, who gave me the first opportunity, where do I come from, where did I emerge? All this started a long time ago. They saw me, drafted me first, gave me a chance to play in the big leagues right away. I was an All-Star there; I was their first captain.[28]

Marvin Cobb was the CWS All-Tournament shortstop in 1974 when he played for the champion USC team. He hit .280 in the Series, with seven runs scored and three stolen bases. Cobb had also played on the 1973 national championship team, in addition to the 1972 and, depending on the selector, 1974 national championship football teams. Upon graduating, he opted to sign with the Cincinnati Bengals in the NFL and was a defensive back for them for five years. He finished his football career with the Pittsburgh Steelers and Minnesota Vikings.[29]

Kenny Landreaux played outfield for Arizona State in the CWS in both 1975 and 1976. He performed well in the former Series, hitting .300, scoring four runs, and driving in two in five games, but he was even better the next year, upping his batting average to .318 and increasing his run production to four scored and six knocked in, again in five games, for which he made the All-Tournament Team. Landreaux came into the latter Series as an All-American, and for that season, he hit .406 with a .479 on-base percentage, a .686 slugging average, 96 runs scored, and 93 driven in. He was drafted in the first round by the California Angels in 1976, and the following season, he was named minor league player of the year by *The Sporting News* while playing for Salt Lake City in the Pacific Coast League. In 1979, he was traded to the Minnesota Twins, and a year later, he was selected for the American League All-Star team. He was then sent to the Los Angeles Dodgers, where he helped them win the World Series in 1981. Landreaux retired after the 1987 season, and in 2014, he fulfilled a promise to his mother by returning to Arizona State and earning his degree at the age of 60.[30]

The year 1977 was a notable one for black players in the CWS. Hubie Brooks, another ASU All-American, hit only .250 for the Series but did his part to help his team win the championship. However, he was even better

Dave Winfield in 1972 or 1973. A dual-sport athlete for the University of Minnesota, Winfield was chosen as the Most Outstanding Player of the 1973 College World Series (Minnesota Athletic Communications).

in 1978, when he batted .432, with a 36-game hitting streak, and was the third player taken in that year's draft, being chosen by the Mets. Brooks then performed for 15 years in the majors with five different clubs and was twice named to the National League All-Star team while playing with the Montreal Expos.[31]

Two other African American players on the 1977 ASU team were Rick Peters and Darrell Jackson. Peters was drafted by Detroit and played five years in the majors with the Tigers and Oakland.[32] Jackson pitched 15 and a third innings in the CWS without giving up an earned run and tossed a nine-inning shutout victory against Southern Illinois.[33] He later pitched for the Minnesota Twins for all or a part of five seasons.[34]

However, probably the most exciting player in the 1977 CWS was South Carolina outfielder Mookie Wilson, whose hitting—he batted .348 for the Series—and baserunning—he stole home in the opening game against Baylor—made him a unanimous pick for the All-Tournament Team. Drafted by the New York Mets, Wilson played for them from 1980 through 1989, then finished his career with the Toronto Blue Jays. But he is best known for his grounder that went through the legs of Boston Red Sox first baseman Bill Buckner in the sixth game of the 1986 World Series. Had Buckner fielded that ball, the Series would have been over and the Red Sox would have been the champs. Instead, a run was scored on that play, and the game was kept alive to be won by the Mets, who went on to capture the Series the next day. Since retiring from the playing field, Wilson has coached for the Mets and managed in the minor leagues.[35]

Andre Robertson, a University of Texas second baseman, hit .313 in the 1979 CWS. Though known primarily for his defensive abilities, Robertson had three hits in a win over Mississippi State. He was drafted in the fourth round by the Toronto Blue Jays, who promptly dealt him to the New York Yankees, where he played from 1981 through 1985. A promising infielder for the Pinstripers, he looked to become a fixture at shortstop, until a car accident in August of 1983 broke his neck and injured his right shoulder. Although he returned to the Yankees after rehabilitation, he was not able to regain his previous level of effectiveness, but in 1985, he had a successful spring before hurting his knee. Still, he batted .328 in 50 games that season. For his professional career, he played five years in the majors and 10 in the minors over an 11-year period.[36]

In 1981, Alvin Davis, Arizona State's black first baseman, made the All-Tournament Team. He hit .478 for the Series, leading ASU to another national championship. During his four years at his alma mater, Davis batted .362 and had 200 runs batted in, which led ASU to retire his #9 jersey in 2006. He was signed by Seattle out of college and played eight seasons for the Mariners, as well as part of one for the California Angels, making the All-Star team and being named the American League Rookie of the Year in 1984. Seattle sportswriters even dubbed him "Mr. Mariner," and he was inducted into the Mariners Hall of Fame in 1997. Davis went on to be an assistant baseball coach at Martin Luther King High School in Riverside, California, and in 2013, he was hired by the Mariners to be their minor league coordinator.[37]

The years 1983 and 1984 were banner years for African American ballplayers in the College World Series, when Barry Bonds, Barry Larkin, and Oddibe McDowell all played in it.

Barry Bonds is undoubtedly the most famous (or infamous) of the trio. The son of Bobby Bonds, Barry played outfield for Arizona State and was named to the All-Tournament Team in both his freshman and sophomore seasons. He hit .357 in the 1983 CWS and .500 in the one held in 1984. In a win over Oklahoma State in the latter Series, Bonds was five-for-five, tying a CWS record, with three stolen bases, while the ASU offensive attack garnered 23 hits and 23 runs in that game. And in that same Series, he tied another CWS record by having hits in eight consecutive at bats. Bonds was drafted by Pittsburgh after his sophomore season and played 22 years in the majors with the Pirates and the San Francisco Giants. His major league statistics, most notably home runs, would make him a shoo-in for the National Baseball Hall of Fame, but unfortunately for him, it seems likely that the physique that produced all that power was artificially created by performance-enhancing drugs. He has been cast in the same "Hall of Shame" as Pete Rose, Mark McGwire, and Sammy Sosa, among others.[38]

Shortstop Barry Larkin was an All-American at Michigan in both 1984 and '85 and played in the 1983 and '84 CWS, but his team won only two games in those Series. In 1984, he was a member of the United States Olympic team, and then, after college ball, he signed with Cincinnati in 1985 and was promoted to the majors the following year. He played 19 seasons for the Reds, helping to lead them to the 1990 World Series championship, and appeared on 12 All-Star teams. His honors include receiving the 1993 Roberto Clemente Award, the 1994 Lou Gehrig Memorial Award, and the 1995 Baseball Writers' Association of America's National League Most Valuable Player Award, as well as being inducted into the National College Baseball Hall of Fame in 2009 and the National Baseball Hall of Fame in 2012.[39]

One of Larkin's teammates on the U.S. Olympic team was Oddibe McDowell, an outfielder for ASU in the 1984 CWS. He hit .500 for the Series and was selected to the All-Tournament Team. A two-time All-American, McDowell batted .405, with 23 homers, 101 runs scored, 74 RBI, and 36 stolen bases out of 39 attempts his senior year. He was drafted by the Texas Rangers and played seven years in the majors with them, the Cleveland Indians, and the Atlanta Braves.[40]

When the topic of perennial CWS teams is discussed, usually LSU is mentioned, with its great fan base and regular participation in the Series. However, the Tigers did not make their first appearance in Omaha until 1986 and did not win the Series until 1991. One of the stars on the '86 team was Albert Belle. This young black man played three years at LSU and was an All-SEC player in 1986 (second team) and '87 (first team). During his college career, he batted .332 and slugged 49 home runs, drove in 172 runs, and whacked 30 doubles.[41] The Tigers won only one game in '86, but Belle had three hits, including two homers, in their elimination loss to Miami.[42]

LSU made it back to the CWS in 1987, though Belle did not accompany his teammates. He had been suspended for attacking a heckling fan in a regional game.[43] This form of behavior was to become a pattern throughout his professional career as well. The Cleveland Indians took Belle in the second round of the '87 draft and he played 12 years with them, the Chicago White Sox, and the Baltimore Orioles. He was a five-time All-Star and regularly among the leaders in home runs, RBI, extra-base hits, slugging average, and other offensive categories. But he was disliked by managers, players, and especially the press for his surliness and conduct both on and off the field.[44] Upon Belle's retirement, the *New York Daily News* columnist Bill Madden wrote:

> Sorry, there'll be no words of sympathy here for Albert Belle.... [H]e was a surly jerk before he got hurt and now he's a hurt surly jerk.... [H]e was no credit to the game. Belle's boorish behavior should be remembered by every member of the Baseball Writers['] Association when it comes time to consider him for the Hall of Fame.[45]

This seems prophetic in that in his second year of eligibility for the HOF, he did not garner enough votes to remain on subsequent ballots, while players of lesser abilities did get the votes.[46] Fortunately for the CWS, leaving Belle aside, LSU has probably brought the most gracious players and fans of any school.

Greg Vaughn also played in the 1986 College World Series but for the University of Miami. Even though he batted only .222, with no home runs, the Milwaukee Brewers picked him fourth in that year's draft, which led to him playing in the majors for 15 years with five different clubs, making the All-Star team four times. During those years, he slugged 355 homers, with his single-season high being 50 in 1998—third best in the National League, behind Sammy Sosa and Mark McGwire. At the same time, though, he had 1,513 strikeouts.[47]

In 1988, the NCAA introduced the two-division College World Series format to placate the television industry. Each division contained four teams, with the divisional winners playing for the Series championship. Although Fresno State competed in only two games before being eliminated, they had a black outfielder named Tom Goodwin who had three hits in 11 at bats, a stolen base, and a run scored in a losing cause. A member of the 1988 U.S. Olympic team, he finished his college career with 164 stolen bases and, in 1989, was named the Big West Conference Player of the Year. Also in 1989, he was drafted by the Los Angeles Dodgers and performed for 14 seasons in the majors with six different teams. After he retired from playing in 2004, Goodwin managed the Lewisville Lizards, coached for the Lowell Spinners, served as a roving outfield and baserunning coach in the Red Sox minor league system, and spent time as the first base coach for the New York Mets.[48]

Nineteen ninety-one was an exciting year for Omaha fans because the Creighton Bluejays made their first and only appearance to date (January 1, 2020) in the CWS. Creighton's two wins—over Clemson and Long Beach State—kept them in the Series, but two heartbreaking losses to Missouri Valley Conference foe Wichita State finally put them out of the tournament. Six of the Creighton players went on to the majors, including two African Americans: Dax Jones to the San Francisco Giants and Kimera Bartee to the Detroit Tigers.[49] In addition, one of the two Creighton players to be selected for the All-Tournament Team was Steve Hinton, though he did not make it to the big leagues. Hinton got a double and a triple with three runs batted in and a run scored during the win over Clemson and singled, homered, drove in three runs, and scored two against Long Beach State. For the season, he hit .338, with a .423 on-base percentage, a .604 slugging average, 10 triples (fourth in the NCAA Division I), and 90 RBI (third in the NCAA Division I), and was named to the Missouri Valley Conference All-Conference Team. Hinton was a ninth-round draft pick for the Kansas City Royals and played five years of minor league ball. Then, following his playing days, he went to Penn State to get a teaching degree, became a scout, and in 2008, was named the special assistant to the scouting director for the Chicago Cubs.[50]

In 1992, Charles Johnson was the starting catcher for the Miami Hurricanes in the CWS. He was not known for his hitting—though he did bat .278 for the Series and drove in the winning run in one game—but he was an outstanding defensive catcher. Twice a first-round draft pick, first in 1989, when he was chosen 10th overall by the Montreal Expos, and again in 1992, when he was the Florida Marlins' first-ever draftee, Johnson competed for the United States in the '92 Barcelona Olympics. He then went on to be a four-time Gold Glove winner who was the starting backstop for the 1997 World Series champion Marlins, hitting .357 for the Series, and had a 12-year major league career, during which he was selected twice to the National League All-Star team. In fact, he belongs to a small group of black catchers to play in the majors since the early '90s, and he is arguably the best African American backstop since Roy Campanella and Elston Howard in the 1950s and 1960s.[51]

Though his teammate Chip Glass was the CWS Most Valuable Player in 1994, Oklahoma's Darvin Traylor hit .467 for the Series and was 3-for-4 in the championship game against Georgia Tech, with a triple and three runs scored. A member of the All-Tournament Team, he batted .363 that year and was an All-Big Eight Conference selection in the outfield.[52]

Wes Rachels, a Southern California second baseman, was voted on the CWS All-Tournament Team during his freshman year of 1995 and again in his senior year of 1998 when he was also named the Most Outstanding Player of the Series.[53] In the championship game in '98 against Arizona State, Rachels had five hits, including a home run, and a CWS record seven runs driven in.[54] His coach, Mike Gillespie, said of him:

> Wes Rachels was the absolute best offensive player in all phases of the game I have ever seen in 36 years of coaching. He was a grand master at executing all the skills on offense such as the drag, push, sacrifice, squeeze, hit and run ... you name it.
>
> I'll never forget the 1998 College World Series where he was named [MOP]. Many people don't realize that from the first day of the College World Series to the last, Wes did everything offensively you can do. He got a squeeze down, drag bunt, hit and run, moved a runner over, hit two doubles and a home run.[55]

Rachels was drafted by the Philadelphia Phillies, but not until the 33rd round, and played only four years in the minor leagues before retiring.[56]

Another black All-Tournament selection in 1998 was Cedrick Harris, an outfielder for LSU, who was also on the LSU championship teams in 1997 and 2000. Harris

Kimera Bartee, shown here playing for Creighton University in 1991, spent 10 seasons in Organized Baseball (Creighton Athletics).

hit .357 in the '98 Series and had three home runs in the four games in which he participated. An All-American at Ashdown High School in Ashdown, Arkansas, and Mr. Baseball in the state of Arkansas, he played five years of minor league ball for teams in the Arizona and Milwaukee franchises and two independent leagues. In addition, he served as an assistant coach at the University of Arkansas at Pine Bluff, a coach for Alamo Elite, the head baseball coach at Antonian College Preparatory School, and an associate scout for the Texas Rangers.[57]

In the first decade of the 21st century, fewer and fewer African American ballplayers have shown up on CWS teams and only a handful could be considered stars.

Probably one of the best College World Series feel-good stories came in the 2001 season. Charlton Jimerson was born in San Leandro, California. His father had deserted him and his mother, who was a crack addict. At age 12, he moved in with his older sister Lanette, who raised him and his brother and made sure that they went to school and got involved in extracurricular activities. He excelled at his studies, and when he graduated from high school, he turned down being drafted by the Houston Astros and enrolled at the University of Miami on an academic scholarship. He then became a walk-on on the baseball team and saw limited action for three and a half years.

When Miami went to the CWS in his freshman and sophomore years, Jimerson sat on the bench. But toward the end of his senior year, he began playing regularly, hitting .299 (seventh best on the team), and when Miami got to the College World Series that year, Jimerson went on a tear. He played in all four of his team's games, led off the first two with home runs, finished with a .429 on-base percentage, seven stolen bases, and five runs scored, and was voted the Series MOP. Since that time, he has played 10 years in the pros, mostly in the minor leagues with the Houston Astro, Seattle Mariner, and Los Angeles Angel organizations.[58]

University of Texas second baseman Tim Moss made the CWS All-Tournament Team in 2002. An All-Big 12 selection whose batting average was .371 for the year, he hit .333 in the Series, including having two hits and scoring a run in the final game against South Carolina and having two more hits and scoring three runs in an 8–7 win over Stanford in Texas' second game. Also, he was on the Longhorn team that took part in the CWS in 2003, was drafted by the Philadelphia Phillies that same year, and played four seasons of minor league ball.[59]

Jonny Ash, Stanford's black third baseman, who is also part Native American—his mother is half Tohono O'odham—was selected to the CWS All-Tournament Team in 2003, after having a phenomenal Series.[60] Batting .396, he led all participants in hits with 14, RBI with 10, and total bases with 24, as well as slugging two homers—the first two of his college career.[61] A .314 batter during the regular season, he had an even better year in 2004, but Stanford did not return to Omaha that June.[62] Drafted by the Houston Astros the same month, he played in their minor league system until 2008 and was named MVP in the 2007 Texas League All-Star Game while a member of Corpus Christi.[63] He was let go by Houston in 2009 and signed on with the Chico Outlaws of the independent Golden Baseball League.[64]

In 2004, the University of Miami won only one game in the CWS, but Brian Barton, the Hurricanes' center fielder, was selected to the All-Tournament Team after batting .462. He had hit .371 for the season, but his forte was defense. Chosen by the Cleveland Indians in the draft, he played three years in their minor leagues before being traded in 2008 to the St. Louis Cardinals, for whom he saw action in 82 games, hitting .268. In

2009, he was sent to the Atlanta Braves in exchange for Blaine Boyer but was let go after just one game.[65]

Jared Mitchell of LSU was the 2009 College World Series Most Outstanding Player. He got lots of press because not only did he play on the national champion baseball team that year, but he was also a wide receiver on the Bowl Championship Series national champion football team in 2007. Just as impressively, while at Westgate High School in New Orleans, Mitchell was the Class 5A offensive MVP in football in 2005 and the Louisiana High School Gatorade Player of the Year in baseball in 2006. In the CWS, he hit two home runs, a triple, and two doubles, drove in seven runs, scored four more, and played well defensively. He was drafted in the first round by the Chicago White Sox in 2009 and became a career minor leaguer.[66]

The University of South Carolina had the honor of being the national champions in both the last Series in Rosenblatt Stadium in 2010 and the first Series in TD Ameritrade Park in downtown Omaha in 2011. The MOP of the 2010 Series was South Carolina's Jackie Bradley, Jr., who batted .345 with five runs scored, nine runs batted in, and two homers during the Series. Though he was only 1-for-6 in the Gamecocks' win over the Oklahoma Sooners, his hit with two strikes drove in the tying run in the 12th inning and he eventually scored the winning run later that inning.[67]

John Norwood after hitting the Series-winning home run for Vanderbilt in the championship game of the 2014 CWS (Vanderbilt Athletics).

In 2011, South Carolina won again, christening the new ballpark. Bradley, who had been out of action since hurting his wrist against Mississippi State on April 23, came back for his team's opener against Texas A&M. He made the most of the four hits and two walks that he got, scoring three runs, driving in two, and stealing a base, but the best black player of the "June classic" was Tony Kemp of Vanderbilt, who had two triples and four singles in 15 at bats—a .400 batting average—and scored the first CWS run in Ameritrade Park. For his accomplishments, Kemp was rewarded by being named to the All-Tournament Team.[68]

South Carolina made it to the championship round for a third time in 2012, but they were defeated by the University of Arizona in the final game. The black star for this Series was Devon Travis of Florida State. He scored runs in the first, third, and fourth innings in the Seminoles' opening win over Stony Brook, hitting a home run in the fourth and doubling in another run in the sixth. After the Series, Travis was named to the All-Tournament Team, and that year he was drafted by the Detroit Tigers but was later traded to the Toronto Blue Jays' organization.[69]

In 2014, Corey Ray, a freshman outfielder from Louisville, almost single-handedly led the Cardinals into the CWS. Having entered the starting lineup during only the last week of the regular season, he went three-for-four, including two doubles, and had an RBI in beating Kansas in the second round of the regional playoffs. He then doubled and scored in a win over Kentucky in the regional championship. And finally, in the super regional, he had two hits in three at bats with a stolen base and a run scored against Kennesaw State to send the Cardinals to the CWS. However, unfortunately for the Louisville team and its fans, he did not perform such heroics in the Series itself.[70]

Ironically, in a CWS dominated by pitching and good defense, it was a late-inning blast by Vanderbilt's John Norwood that won the 2014 title. His rare home run in the eighth inning led to a 3–2 victory over the University of Virginia and was the first round-tripper for the Commodores in 17 games. Norwood joined three other Vanderbilt players on the All-Tournament Team.[71]

What is the future of African Americans in the College World Series? In the first 15 years of this century, the teams coming to the CWS have had very few black players. Still, it is fitting to remember those African Americans who made their teams and their race proud while visiting Rosenblatt Stadium or TD Ameritrade Park. It would be great to see another Dave Winfield on the mound, a Barry Larkin pounding out hits, or a Mookie Wilson stealing bases. But that will have to begin in Little League and high school ball, where youngsters dream of being the next black star in college baseball's Mecca: Omaha, Nebraska.

## Notes

1. "CWS History," http://www.cwsomaha.com/index.php?option=com_content&task=view&id=58264&Itemid=247 (accessed on November 12, 2016).
2. "Rosenblatt Comes Down, Fans Mourn Stadium Loss," *Omaha World-Herald*, August 23, 2012.
3. Wesley Mallette, email message to Angelo J. Louisa, September 23, 2015.
4. Frank B. Butts, Laura M. Hatfield, and Lance C. Hatfield, "African Americans in College Baseball," *The Sports Journal*, March 14, 2008, http://www.thesportjournal.org/article/African-americans-in-college-baseball (accessed on November 12, 2016). Since the completion of this study, anecdotal evidence suggests that little has changed. See, e.g., Nancy Haggerty, "Youth to Majors, fewer African-Americans are playing baseball," USA Today High School Sports, http://usatodayhss.com/2015/youth-to-majors-fewer-african-americans-are-playing-baseball (accessed on November 12, 2016), and Michael Coker, "A Former HBCU Ballplayer's Take On the State of Black College Baseball," http://blackcollegenines.com/?p=1357 (accessed on November 12, 2016).
5. Jens Manuel Krogstad, "67 years after Jackie Robinson broke the color barrier, Major League Baseball looks very different," Pew Research Center, http://www.pewresearch.org/fact-tank/2014/04/16/67-years-after-jackie-robinson-broke-the-color-barrier-major-league-baseball-looks-very-different/ (accessed on November 12, 2016).
6. Jerry E. Clark's calculations.
7. Stephen F. Philipp, "Race and Gender Differences in Adolescent Peer Group Approval of Leisure

Activities," *Journal of Leisure Research* 30, no. 2 (Spring 1998), http://js.sagamorepub.com/jlr/article/view/766 (accessed on November 12, 2016).

8. Shaun Powell, "The New Face of Baseball," *Sports on Earth*, April 15, 2014, http://www.sportsonearth.com/article/72021954/white-players-making-up-majority-of-historically-black-college-baseball-teams (accessed on November 12, 2016).

9. "Proposition 48 was implemented in 1985. It stated that any student-athlete who did not have an S.A.T. score of at least 700 or 15 on the American College Test, and a grade-point average of 2.0 on a 4.0 scale, could be granted a scholarship, but would not be allowed to play or practice with the team in his freshman year and would lose that year of eligibility." Peter Alfano, "For Brian Shorter, Proposition 48 Is Working: A Proposition 48 Success Story at Pitt," *New York Times*, January 22, 1989.

10. "Results and Records," *2016 UCLA Baseball Information Guide*, 80, 81, http://www.uclabruins.com/sports/2016/2/9/210699570.aspx (accessed on December 6, 2016).

11. "Chris Chambliss," www.baseball-reference.com (accessed on December 6, 2016).

12. Robert Williams, "Texas Wins Opener; Tulsa Edge UCLA," *Omaha World-Herald*, June 14, 1969, and Robert Williams, "Mass. Slays Giants; Violets Don't Shrink," *Omaha World-Herald*, June 15, 1969.

13. The information used in this paragraph came from *2018 Saluki Baseball*, 120–121, 130, https://siusalukis.com/documents/2018/2/9/2018_BSB_Media_Guide_Web.pdf (accessed on February 7, 2020); "1968 NCAA University Division Baseball Tournament," https://en.wikipedia.org/wiki/1968_NCAA_University_Division_Baseball_Tournament (accessed on February 7, 2020); and "Jerry Bond," www.baseball-reference.com (accessed on January 25, 2016).

14. The information used in this paragraph came from Robert Phipps, "Cyclone Club Jolts Irish, 13–8," *Omaha World Herald*, June 9, 1957; Robert Phipps, "Cal, Penn State Clash Tonight; Sudden Death for Irish or T.U.," *Omaha World-Herald*, June 10, 1957; Robert Phipps, "Cal Earns Favorite Role on 8-to-0 Win," *Omaha World-Herald*, June 11, 1957; Robert Phipps, "Penn State Blocks Cal's Drive to Title," *Omaha World-Herald*, June 12, 1957; Robert Phipps, "California Annexes Title Without Loss," *Omaha World-Herald*, June 13, 1957; "1957 California Golden Bears Baseball Team," http://www.digplanet.com/wiki/1957_California_Golden_Bears_baseball_team (accessed on December 17, 2016); "Earl Robinson," www.baseball-reference.com (accessed on December 17, 2016); and Dennis Fitzpatrick, "Cal Great Earl Robinson Passes Away," http;//www.calbears.com/ViewArticle.dbl?ATCLID=209540921 (accessed on August 23, 2014).

15. "1958 College World Series," www.baseball-reference.com (accessed on November 12, 2016).

16. "Don Buford," www.baseball-reference.com (accessed on November 12, 2016).

17. *Ibid.*, and "Don Buford," www.retrosheet.org (accessed on November 12, 2016).

18. http://www.netitor.com/photos/schools/ncol/sport/m-basebl/auto_pdf/06-BASE-Guide27-52.pdf (accessed on November 12, 2016).

19. "1964 College World Series," www.baseball-reference .com (accessed on December 18, 2016); telephone conversation between Angelo J. Louisa and Rachel Caton, assistant sports information director, University of Southern California, March 2, 2017; Sarah Bergstrom, "Willie Brown: The Life Coach," http://www.uscbhm.com/willie-brown (accessed on March 3, 2016); and "2005 Inductees For USC Athletic Hall Of Fame Announced," http://www.usctrojans.com/genrel/102304aab.html (accessed on March 3, 2016).

20. The information used in this paragraph came from "1964 College World Series Box Scores," http://grfx.cstv.com/photos/schools/minn/sports/m-basebl/auto_pdf/1963--36/misc_non_event/boxscore-1964-cws.pdf (accessed on November 12, 2016); "Two-Sport Star, Archie Clark Leaves Legacy at Minnesota," http://www.gophersports.com/sports/m-baskbl/spec-rel/020205aad.html (accessed on January 19, 2016); and "Archie Clark," www.basketball-reference.com (accessed on November 12, 2016).

21. The information used in this paragraph came from "Lenny Randle," www.baseball-reference.com (accessed on December 17, 2016), and "Lenny Randle Sports Academy," http://lennyrandlesportstours.com/about-lenny (accessed on December 17, 2016).

22. Pan American merged with the University of Texas at Brownsville in 2015 to form the University of Texas at Rio Grande Valley.

23. "1971 College World Series Team," http://goutrgv.com/sports/2012/7/6/BB_0706125927.aspx (accessed on November 12, 2016).

24. "Jim Tyrone," www.baseball-reference.com (accessed on December 16, 2016).

25. The information used in this paragraph came from Maurice Shadle, "Pan Am's Rabouin Is 'On' in Tense CWS Situation," *Omaha World-Herald*, June 15, 1971; "1971 College World Series Team," UTPA Broncs, University of Texas Pan-American, http://goutrgv.com/sports/2012/7/6/BB_0706125927.aspx (accessed on November 12, 2016); "Gallaudet University Baseball Archive," http://www.gallaudetathletics.com/sports/bsb/archive/index (accessed on December 18, 2016); and "Andre Rabouin," Gallaudet Athletics, http://www.gallaudetathletics.com/sports/bsb/coaches/rabouin_andre?view=bio (accessed on December 18, 2016).

26. The information used in this paragraph came from "1972 College World Series," www.baseball-reference.com (accessed on November 12, 2016), and "Bump Wills," www.baseball-reference.com (accessed on November 12, 2016).

27. The information used in this paragraph came from Doug Skipper, "Dave Winfield," SABR Baseball

Biography Project, http://sabr.org/bioproject (accessed on November 12, 2016), and Murray Chass, "On Baseball—Winfield Chooses Padres Over Yanks," *New York Times*, April 14, 2001.

28. Chass.

29. The information used in this paragraph came from "1974 College World Series," www.baseball-reference.com (accessed on December 29, 2016); Steve Sinclair, "USC Magic Lives; Texans Blitzed, 9–2," *Omaha World-Herald*, June 9, 1974; Steve Sinclair, "N. Colorado Gambles in Saluki Showdown," *Omaha World-Herald*, June 11, 1974; Steve Sinclair, "Trojans' Nose Bloodied by the New CWS Bully," *Omaha World-Herald*, June 13, 1974; Steve Sinclair, "USC Vet, SIU Soph Pitted in Showdown," *Omaha World-Herald*, June 14, 1974; Steve Sinclair, "The King Is Still Alive; It's USC vs. No. 1 Miami," *Omaha World-Herald*, June 15, 1974; Steve Sinclair, "USC Streak Is Still Intact," *Omaha World-Herald*, June 16, 1974; "2015 USC Baseball," http://www.usctrojans.com/sports/m-basebl/archive/usc-m-basebl-archive.html (accessed on December 29, 2016); *USC Football 2015*, 115, 158, https://usctrojans.com/documents/2015/7/14/2015-media-guide.pdf (accessed on December 29, 2016); and "Marvin Cobb," www.pro-football-reference.com (accessed on December 27, 2016).

30. The information used in this paragraph came from Robert Williams, "Sun Devils, Texas Wins [*sic*] CWS Openers," *Omaha World-Herald*, June 7, 1975; Robert Williams, "Sooners Think Left for Mound Choice," *Omaha World-Herald*, June 9, 1975; Robert Williams, "Carolina Win Led by Bass," *Omaha World-Herald*, June 12, 1975; "Sun Devils Win 1–0; Texas Romps," *Omaha World-Herald*, June 13, 1975; Robert Williams, "South Carolina Foe for Texas in Finale," *Omaha World-Herald*, June 14, 1975; Steve Sinclair, "Arizona State Stays Bedeviling; Camp Hurls Cougars Past O.U.," *Omaha World-Herald*, June 13, 1976; Robert Williams, "Sun Devil Enhances Worth," *Omaha World-Herald*, June 14, 1976; Robert Williams, "Hurons Deal ASU 1st Loss," *Omaha World-Herald*, June 16, 1976; Tom Ash, "Devil 'Heats' Prior to Win," *Omaha World-Herald*, June 17, 1976; Robert Williams, "Finals Tonight Cut Short Celebration for Arizona," *Omaha World-Herald*, June 19, 1976; "1976 College World Series," www.baseball-reference.com (accessed on December 31, 2016); *Sun Devil Baseball 2015 Season*, http://www.thesundevils.com/sports/2013/4/17/208245301.aspx (accessed on December 31, 2016); "Ken Landreaux," http://thebaseballcube.com/players/profile.asp?P=Ken-Landreaux (accessed on December 31, 2016); "Ken Landreaux," www.baseball-reference.com (accessed on December 31, 2016); Patrick Reusse, "Holy Einstein! K.T. Landreaux is a College Grad," *Star Tribune Sports*, December 22, 2014.

31. The information used in this paragraph came from Robert Williams, "Relief in Ninth Inning Spoils Tigers' Party," *Omaha World-Herald*, June 11, 1977; Tom Ash, "Little-Used Saluki Delivers," *Omaha World-Herald*, June 14, 1977; Tom Ash, "LA Rewards Faith; ASU Bothers Gophers," *Omaha World-Herald*, June 15, 1977; Robert Williams, "Sun Devil Bat Star Calls Win Satisfying," Omaha World-Herald, June 17, 1977; Robert Williams, "Slider, Salukis Mashed by ASU," *Omaha World-Herald*, June 18, 1977; Robert Williams, "ASU's Black Sheep Are CWS Champs," *Omaha World-Herald*, June 19, 1977; *Sun Devil Baseball 2015 Season*; and "Hubie Brooks," www.baseball-reference.com (accessed on December 19, 2016).

32. "Rick Peters," www.baseball-reference.com (accessed on December 19, 2016).

33. Ash, "Little-Used Saluki Delivers," and Williams, "Slider, Salukis Mashed by ASU."

34. "Darrell Jackson," www.baseball-reference.com (accessed on December 19, 2016).

35. The information used in this paragraph came from Robert Williams, "Diablos Don't Need Magic to Produce Upset in CWS," *Omaha World-Herald*, June 12, 1977; "There, Scouts, Take That," *Omaha World-Herald*, June 14, 1977; Robert William, "King, '75 Gamecock Vet, Confident," *Omaha World-Herald*, June 16 1977; Williams, "Sun Devil Bat Star Calls Win Satisfying"; Williams, "ASU's Black Sheep Are CWS Champs"; "1986 World Series," www.baseball-almanac.com (accessed on December 20, 2016); and "Mookie Wilson," www.baseball-reference.com (accessed on December 19, 2016).

36. "6-Run Inning Boosts Texas Past Huskies," *Omaha World-Herald*, June 3, 1979; Robert Williams, "Survivors Tonight Get Rest, 'Have Chance,'" *Omaha World-Herald*, June 4, 1979; Steve Sinclair, "Razorbacks Spoil Longhorn 'Dance,'" *Omaha World-Herald*, June 6, 1979; Steve Sinclair, "Waves 'Rise to Occasion,' Splash Longhorns," *Omaha World-Herald*, June 7, 1979; "Andre Robertson," www.baseball-reference.com (accessed on January 4, 2017); Wayne Coffee, "Yankee Shortstop Andre Robertson and Ballet Dancer Reclaimed Their Lives After Horrific Car Crash," *New York Daily News*, December 20, 2008.

37. Robert Williams, "Gillespie Hometown Heroics Key Bulldogs; Sun Devils Roll," *Omaha World-Herald*, May 31, 1981; Robert Williams, "Arizona State Rallies Past Bulldogs," *Omaha World-Herald*, June 3, 1981; Robert Williams, "Cowboys Outslug Top-Rated ASU, *Omaha World-Herald*, June 6, 1981"; Steve Sinclair, "Sun Devils, Texas Battle Today for Spot in Finals," *Omaha World-Herald*, June 7, 1981; Robert Williams, "'Momentum Equal' in CWS Finals," *Omaha World-Herald*, June 8, 1981; Robert Williams, "Unusual Moves Help Sun Devils Claim Fifth Title," *Omaha World-Herald*, June 9, 1981; "1981 College World Series," www.baseball-reference.com; *Sun Devil Baseball 2015 Season*; "Alvin Davis," http://seattle.mariners.mlb.com/sea/history/hof_member.jsp?name=Davis; "Alvin Davis," www.baseball-reference.com; and Larry Stone, "Alvin Davis: Mr. Mariner Reconnects with His Old Team," *Seattle Times*, March 5, 2013.

38. The information used in this paragraph came from "1983 College World Series," www.baseball-reference.com (accessed on November 12, 2016); "1984 College World Series," www.baseball-reference.com (accessed on November 12, 2016); Steve Pivovar, "Tide Squeezes Past Arizona State," *Omaha World-Herald*, June 5, 1983; Robert Williams, "One-Hitter Silences Maine Bats," *Omaha World-Herald*, June 6, 1983; Robert

Williams, "Sun Devils Survive Rally by Cowboys," *Omaha World-Herald*, June 9, 1983; Robert Williams, "Tide Last Obstacle to Texas Title," *Omaha World-Herald*, June 11, 1983; "Baseball," *The Arizona Republic*, June 3, 1984; Steve Pivovar, "Four Hits From No. 9 Spot—Hot Sun Devil Bats 'Contagious,'" *Omaha World-Herald*, June 6, 1984; Robert Williams, "Texan Says Club Shows It Improves," *Omaha World-Herald*, June 8, 1984; "Cal State Fullerton Athletics," http://www.fullertontitans.com/sports/m-basebl/archives/pdfs/84CWSboxes.pdf (accessed on December 15, 2016); and "Barry Bonds," www.baseball-reference.com (accessed on December 15, 2016).

39. The information used in this paragraph came from Rick Kindhart and Sean Straziscar, *NCAA Baseball & Softball Records* (Indianapolis: National Collegiate Athletic Association, 2001), 141; "Barry Larkin," www.baseball-reference.com (accessed on November 12, 2016); "2009 College Baseball Hall of Fame Inductees," www.collegebaseballhall.org (accessed on November 12, 2016); and "Barry Larkin," www.baseballhall.org/hof/larkin-barry (accessed on November 12, 2016).

40. The information used in this paragraph came from Robert Williams, "Arizona State Is Eliminated—'Excited' Lefty Lifts Cal Fullerton," *Omaha World-Herald*, June 9, 1984; "1984 College World Series," www.baseball-reference.com (accessed on November 12, 2016); [Arizona State University] *2009 Baseball Media Guide*, 99, 164, http://www.thesundevils.com/sports/2013/4/17/208245301.aspx (accessed on December 8, 2016); and "Oddibe McDowell," www.baseball-reference.com (accessed on November 12, 2016).

41. For Belle's collegiate baseball career, see *LSU 2016 Baseball Official Yearbook*, 52, 53, 143, http://www.lsusports.net/ViewArticle.dbml?ATCLID=209882628 (accessed on January 25, 2017).

42. Fran LaBelle, "UM's Balancing Act Eliminates LSU 4–3," *(Fort Lauderdale) South Florida Sun Sentinel*, June 6, 1986.

43. Bob Carter, "Belle Battled Fans, Teammates, Self," http://www.espn.com/classic/biography/s/belle_albert.html (accessed on January 25, 2017).

44. For Belle's major league baseball career, see "Albert Belle," www.baseball-reference.com (accessed on January 25, 2017).

45. Bill Madden, "A Shef Salad of Offers Reds, Braves Still Cooking," *New York Daily News*, March 11, 2001.

46. For information on Belle's National Baseball Hall of Fame candidacy, see "Albert Belle," www.baseball-reference.com (accessed on January 25, 2017).

47. The information used in this paragraph came from Robert Williams, "4-Run Ninth Inning Boosts Miami Over OSU," *Omaha World-Herald*, June 1, 1986; Steve Sinclair, "FSU Hurler Changes Luck, Result," *Omaha World-Herald*, June 4, 1986; Steve Pivovar, "Hurricanes, OSU Keep CWS Hopes Alive," *Omaha World-Herald*, June 6, 1986; Steve Pivovar, "Newest Hero Keeps Miami Alive," *Omaha World-Herald*, June 8, 1986; Steve Sinclair, "Seminoles, Arizona Will Meet for Title," *Omaha World-Herald*, June 9, 1986; and "Greg Vaughn," www.baseball-reference.com (accessed on January 25, 2017).

48. The information used in this paragraph came from Robert Williams, "6th Seed Fullerton, 7th Seed Stanford Advance," *Omaha World-Herald*, June 5, 1988; Tom D'Angelo, "Hurricanes Stay Alive with 12-Inning 8–4 Win," *Palm Beach (FL) Post*, June 7, 1988; *2016 Fresno State Baseball Fact Book*, 55, 67, https://s3.amazonaws.com/sidearm.sites/gobulldogs.com/documents/2016/6/8/2016_fact_book.pdf (accessed on February 7, 2020); "Tom Goodwin," www.baseball-reference.com (accessed on December 21, 2016); and "Tom Goodwin," http://en.wikipedia.com/wiki/Tom_Goodwin (accessed on December 21, 2016).

49. The six were Bartee, Alan Benes, Mike Heathcott, Jones, Chad McConnell, and Scott Stahoviak. *Creighton Baseball 2016 Media Guide*, 83, https://gocreighton.com/documents/2016/2/25/2016_Baseball_MediaGuide_ALL_smaller.pdf (accessed on February 7, 2020).

50. The information on Hinton came from Tim Peeler, "Bluejays Outhit Tigers," *Greenville (SC) News*, June 2, 1991; "The Day in Sports," *Los Angeles Times*, June 5, 1991; and "Steve Hinton (U.S.)," www.baseball-reference.com (accessed on December 15, 2016).

51. Robert Williams, "Miami Pulls It Out in 13th," *Omaha World-Herald*, May 30, 1992; Lee Barfknecht, "Wild Night No Problem for Miami," *Omaha World-Herald*, June 1, 1992; Steve Pivovar, "Titans, Miami to Play It Again," *Omaha World-Herald*, June 4, 1992; Steve Pivovar, "Titans Splash Past Miami, Into the Final," *Omaha World-Herald*, June 6, 1992; "Charles Johnson," www.baseball-reference.com (accessed on December 22, 2016); and "Charles Johnson Stats," www.baseball-almanac.com (accessed on November 12, 2016).

52. The information used in this paragraph came from "1994 College World Series," www.baseball-reference.com (accessed on December 20, 2016); "Auburn (44–20)—vs—Oklahoma (47–17)," https://auburntigers.com/sports/baseball/stats/1994/oklahoma/boxscore/13244 (accessed on February 7, 2020); Tom Vint, "Sun Devils Fall in 11," *(Phoenix) Arizona Republic*, June 7, 1994; "The Day in Sports," *Los Angeles Times*, June 10, 1994; and "OU Baseball Tradition/1994 National Champions," Sooner Sport, http://www.soonersports.com/ViewArticle.dbml?ATCLID=208791693 (accessed on November 12, 2016); *2016 Oklahoma Baseball Guide*, http://www.soonersports.com/ViewArticle.dbml?ATCLID=208791712 (accessed on December 20, 2016); and "Three Husker Players Selected for All-Big 8 Baseball Team," *Omaha World-Herald*, May 24, 1994.

53. "1995 College World Series," www.baseball-reference.com (accessed on December 21, 2016), and "1998 College World Series," www.baseball-reference.com (accessed on December 21, 2016).

54. Jim Hodges, "Trojans Retire 12th Title with 21-Run Salute," *Los Angeles Times*, June 7, 1998.

55. Lou Pavlovich, Jr., "Top Coaches Explain Bunting Tactics," quoting Mike Gillespie, *Collegiate Baseball Newspaper*, October 11, 2002, found at http://www.baseballnews.com/old/features/stories/buntingtactics.htm (accessed on November 12, 2016).

56. "Wes Rachels," www.baseball-reference.com (accessed on December 17, 2016).

57. "1998 College World Series," www.baseball-reference.com (accessed on December 17, 2016); "1997 Roster" and "2000 Roster," http://www.lsusports.net/SportSelect.dbml?SPSID=27867&SPID=2173&Q_SEASON=1996 (accessed on December 17, 2016); Steve Pivovar, "Record 8 Home Runs Rally LSU," *Omaha World-Herald*, May 31, 1998; Steve Pivovar, "LSU Continues HR Barrage," *Omaha World-Herald*, June 2, 1998; Steve Pivovar, "USC Cuffs LSU to Stay Alive," *Omaha World-Herald*, June 5, 1998; Lee Barfknecht, "Perfect Play Puts USC in Final," *Omaha World-Herald*, June 6, 1998; "Cedrick Harris," http://www.zoominfo.com/p/-Cedrick-Harris/1196470704 (December 17, 2016); "Cedrick Harris," www.baseball-reference.com (December 17, 2016).

58. The information used in this paragraph came from Michael Corbo, "Older Sister Sacrifices for Baseball Dream," *St. Petersburg (FL) Times*, June 8, 2001, http://www.sptimes.com/News/060801/Sports/Older_sister_sacrific.shtml (accessed on January 27, 2017); Jim Callis, "Ask BA," May 7, 2002, https://www.baseballamerica.com/today/columnists/askba02may.html (accessed on January 27, 2017); "Tennessee vs. Miami (Fla.) (June 09, 2001)," http://dataomaha.com/cws/game/776 (accessed on January 27, 2017); "Southern California vs. Miami (Fla.) (June 11, 2001)," http://dataomaha.com/cws/game/780 (accessed on January 27, 2017); "Miami (Fla.) vs. Tennessee (June 14, 2001)," http://dataomaha.com/cws/game/783 (accessed on January 27, 2017); "Stanford vs. Miami (Fla.) (June 16, 2001), http://dataomaha.com/cws/game/784 (accessed on January 27, 2017); "2001 College World Series," www.baseball-reference.com (accessed on January 27, 2017); and "Charlton Jimerson," www.baseball-reference.com (accessed on January 26, 2017). When Jimerson's College World Series statistics are added to the rest of his statistics for 2001, his batting average rose to .302. "2001 Statistics" http://www.hurricanesports.com/ViewArticle.dbml?SPSID=658425&SPID=103774&DB_LANG=C&DB_OEM_ID=28700&ATCLID=205536330 (accessed on January 27, 2017).

59. "2002 College World Series," www.baseball-reference.com (accessed on December 23, 2016); *Texas Baseball: 2015 Fact Book*, 178, http://www.texassports.com/documents/2015/2/2/2015_Factbook_Full_Version_.pdf (accessed on January 30, 2017); "Texas Season Statistics: 2002 University of Texas Baseball," http://stats.texassports.com/sports/m-basebl/2001-2002/ba_02-final.html (accessed on December 27, 2016); "Texas vs. Rice (June 15, 2002)," http://www.dataomaha.com/cws/game/665 (accessed on December 23, 2016); "Texas vs. Stanford (June 17, 2002)," http://www.dataomaha.com/cws/game/669 (accessed on December 23, 2016); "Texas vs. Stanford (June 20, 2002)," http://www.dataomaha.com/cws/game/672 (accessed on December 23, 2016); "South Carolina vs. Texas (June 22, 2002)," http://www.dataomaha.com/cws/game/674 (accessed on December 23, 2016); "Texas vs. Miami (Jun 14, 2003), http://www.dataomaha.com/cws/game/649 (accessed on December 27, 2016); "Rice vs. Texas (June 16, 2003), http://www.dataomaha.com/cws/game/653 (accessed on December 27, 2016); "Miami vs. Texas (June 17, 2003), http://www.dataomaha.com/cws/game/654 (accessed on December 27, 2016); "Texas vs. Rice (June 18, 2003), http://www.dataomaha.com/cws/game/656 (accessed on December 27, 2016); and "Tim Moss," www.baseball-reference.com (accessed on December 17, 2016).

60. "2003 College World Series," www.baseball-reference.com (accessed on December 17, 2016).

61. http://www.gostanford.com/news/2013/4/17/208432459.aspx (accessed on November 12, 2016).

62. "Jonny Ash," www.thebaseballcube.com/players/profile.asp?P=Jonny-Ash (accessed on November 12, 2016).

63. *Ibid.*, and Lisa Winston, "Ash Ensures South Rules at Texas All-Star Game: MVP Second Baseman Singles in Winning Run in Bottom of 10th," http://www.milb.com/news/article.jsp?ymd=20070627&content_id=265870&vkey=news_milb&fext=.jsp (accessed on December 17, 2016).

64. "Jonny Ash," www.thebaseballcube.com/players/profile.asp?P=Jonny-Ash (accessed on November 12, 2016), and "Golden Baseball League," https://www.baseball-reference.com/bullpen/Golden_Baseball_League (accessed on June 13, 2019).

65. The information used in this paragraph came from "2004 College World Series," www.baseball-reference.com (accessed on December 29 2016); "LSU vs. Miami (Fla.) (June 19, 2004)," http://www.dataomaha.com/cws/game/632 (accessed on December 29, 2016); "Miami (Fla.) vs. Cal State Fullerton (June 21, 2004), http://www.dataomaha.com/cws/game/636 (accessed on December 29, 2016); "Miami (Fla.) vs. South Carolina (June 22, 2004)," http://www.dataomaha.com/cws/game/637 (accessed on December 29, 2016); "Brian Barton," www.thebaseballcube.com/players/profile.asp?P=Brian-Barton-3 (accessed on November 12, 2016); and "Brian Barton," www.baseball-reference.com (accessed on December 29, 2016).

66. The information used in this paragraph came from "2009 College World Series," www.baseball-reference.com (accessed on January 24, 2017); *2009 LSU Baseball Media Guide*, 77–78, http://www.lsusports.net/ViewArticle.dbml?ATCLID=204883742 (accessed on January 24, 2017); "Virginia vs. LSU (June 13, 2009)," http://dataomaha.com/cws/game/870 (accessed on January 24, 2017); "LSU vs. Arkansas (June 15, 2009)," http://dataomaha.com/cws/game/875 (accessed on January 24, 2017); "LSU vs. Arkansas (June 19, 2009)," http://dataomaha.com/cws/game/879 (accessed on January 24, 2017); "LSU vs. Texas (June 22, 2009)," http://dataomaha.com/cws/game/881 (accessed on January 24, 2017); "Texas vs. LSU (June 23, 2009)," http://

dataomaha.com/cws/game/882 (accessed on January 24, 2017); "LSU vs. Texas (June 24, 2009)," http://dataomaha.com/cws/game/883 (accessed on January 24, 2017); and "Jared Mitchell," www.baseball-reference.com (accessed on November 12, 2016).

67. The information used in this paragraph came from "2010 College World Series," www.baseball-reference.com (accessed on December 30, 2016); "South Carolina vs. Oklahoma (June 20, 2010), http://www.dataomaha.com/cws/game/855 (accessed on December 30, 2016); "Arizona St. vs. South Carolina (June 22, 2010)," http://www.dataomaha.com/cws/game/859 (accessed on December 30, 2016); "Oklahoma vs. South Carolina (June 24, 2010)," http://www.dataomaha.com/cws/game/862 (accessed on December 30, 2016); "South Carolina vs. Clemson (June 25, 2010)," http://www.dataomaha.com/cws/game/864 (accessed on December 30, 2016); "Clemson vs. South Carolina (June 26, 2010)," http://www.dataomaha.com/cws/game/866 (accessed on December 30, 2016); "South Carolina vs. UCLA (June 28, 2010)," http://www.dataomaha.com/cws/game/867 (accessed on December 30, 2016); and "UCLA vs. South Carolina (June 29, 2010)," http://www.dataomaha.com/cws/game/868 (accessed on December 30, 2016).

68. The information used in this paragraph came from "South Carolina 5, Texas A&M 4 (June 19, 2011)," http://www.dataomaha.com/cws/game/917 (accessed on December 30, 2016); "Vanderbilt 7, North Carolina 3 (June 18, 2011)," http://www.dataomaha.com/cws/game/914 (accessed on December 30, 2016); "Vanderbilt vs. North Carolina (June 18, 2011)," http://www.dataomaha.com/cws/game/914 (accessed on December 30, 2016); "Florida vs. North Carolina (June 20 [sic], 2011)," http://www.dataomaha.com/cws/game/919 (accessed on December 30, 2016); "North Carolina vs. Vanderbilt (June 22, 2011)," http://www.dataomaha.com/cws/game/919 (accessed on December 30, 2016); "Vanderbilt vs. Florida (June 24, 2011)," http://www.dataomaha.com/cws/game/924 (accessed on December 30, 2016); and "2011 College World Series," www.baseball-reference.com (accessed on December 30, 2016).

69. The information used in this paragraph came from "Florida State vs. Stony Brook (June 17, 2012)," www.dataomaha.com/cws/game/933 (accessed on December 22, 2016); "2012 College World Series," www.baseball-reference.com (accessed on December 22, 2016); and "Devon Travis," www.baseball-reference.com (accessed on November 12, 2016).

70. The information used in this paragraph came from "Corey Ray," http://www.gocards.com/roster.aspx?rp_id=3 (accessed on January 7, 2017).

71. The information used in this paragraph came from Steven Pivovar, "Norwood's Blast Lifts Vanderbilt to First National Crown," *Omaha World-Herald*, June 26, 2014, and "2014 College World Series," www.baseball-reference.com (accessed on December 22, 2016).

# 9

# The Pride of Omaha
## Bob Gibson

WILLIAM R. LAMBERTY *and* ROBERT P. NASH

Bob Gibson is without question one of the best athletes ever produced by the state of Nebraska. However, at the time of his birth during the Great Depression, no one could have possibly foreseen that he would grow up to become one of the most outstanding pitchers in baseball history. Born in Omaha in 1935, Gibson was the seventh and youngest child of a widowed mother who worked in a laundry and cleaned houses to feed her large family. His father, Pack Robert Gibson, had died three months before his birth. Gibson himself succinctly assessed his inauspicious start in life as: "I was fatherless. I was poor. I was black."[1] He was also a small, sickly child whose early illnesses included rickets and pneumonia.

Like a number of successful athletes, Gibson's career was built on the supportive efforts of many and sprung from neighborhood sandlots and high school gyms and fields. He competed against blacks and whites alike in the area of North Omaha where he grew up, facing other top-notch athletes but also segregationist racial mores of the mid–20th century. He received guidance—athletically and otherwise—from family members, drew inspiration from the highest level of competitive sports, and took full advantage of the opportunities presented him while working around obstacles—and all within a turbulent social context. Like most of America, Omaha during the 1930s, '40s, and '50s was highly racialized. Physical and social boundaries had to be constantly negotiated, and civil rights gains were continually met with resistance through both formal and informal means.

Before relocating to the Logan Fontenelle Housing Project on Omaha's North Side, Gibson's family lived for a time in what he later recalled as a "four-room wooden shack."[2] Built in 1935, under the auspices of the Works Progress Administration, Logan Fontenelle was constructed for working class families, most of whom were employed in the city's stockyards and railroad industry. While the project was home to both blacks and whites, the residents were nevertheless segregated along racial lines,[3] and as with many things in his life, the highly intelligent and analytical Gibson found complexity in the topic of his neighborhood:

> There were about twice as many whites in the project as there were Negroes, which may be surprising. We weren't the only ones who lived in the slums, we just got credit for it. The white person is in the ghetto too, but I can't feel sorry for him. He can get out ... some way. He can change his name to escape racial prejudice, but what can the Negro do? He cannot change anything. He can only sit there ... trapped.[4]

According to a childhood friend, Rodney Wead, Gibson's mother, Victoria, raised all her children to be self-reliant. "She was a tough, feisty woman who had her own way of doing things. Gibson's her—warmed over."[5] In addition to his stalwart mother, Gibson's greatest influence growing up was his oldest brother, Leroy "Josh" Gibson.[6] Josh Gibson, not to be confused with the famous Negro League National Baseball Hall of Famer of the same name, was 15 years older than his youngest brother. In part because of this, he would become a surrogate father for Bob but would also frequently serve as his brother's coach throughout his formative years. Josh was in the U.S. Army during the Second World War and subsequently earned a master's degree in history. He sought a postwar career as a teacher and coach, but despite his obvious talents and education, he was not able to secure a job in any of Omaha's schools. Blocked from teaching positions by the racial barriers of that era, Josh ended up working in the city's meatpacking industry. Undeterred, he channeled his love of sports into organizing and coaching youth teams. As Bob observed, "The neighborhood—basically the Logan Fontenelle Housing Project and rec center—became Josh's classroom."[7] That rec center ultimately evolved into the North Side YMCA, and over the years, Josh Gibson's guidance touched hundreds of children. In addition to his kid brother, they included such future sports luminaries as National Basketball Association (NBA) All-Star Bob Boozer; world-class sprinter Roger Sayers; Roger's younger sibling, Pro Football Hall of Famer Gale Sayers; All-Pro National Football League wide receiver Marlin Briscoe; American Basketball Association All-Star Ron Boone; and Heisman Trophy winner Johnny Rodgers.[8]

A rags-to-riches story, Bob Gibson overcame poverty, illness, and racial discrimination to become a National Baseball Hall of Fame pitcher (National Baseball Hall of Fame Library).

Josh was an exceptional athlete in his own right, having been a track star in high school and a center fielder on an adult fastpitch softball team. He was, his brother said, "bullishly strong" and "surprisingly agile."[9] As a coach, he sought to instill strength and toughness in his young charges. According to Bob, he "refused with all his heart, to be beaten, cheated, or demeaned, and expected the same of anyone who played for him—especially me."[10] Indeed, Bob attributed his well-known intensity as an athlete to his older brother's strong example:

> Over the years, quite a bit has been said and written about my competitiveness. I'm beholden to the teammates, opponents, and critics who have alluded to it and almost kept it relevant; but I'm even more beholden to the big brother who embedded it. The best thing I can say about my own competitiveness is that, giving myself the benefit of the doubt, it might have ranked second in our family to Josh's.[11]

Bob's youth was filled with sports, and as early as 1948, when he was still only 12 years old, his name was already appearing in the local sports pages for his exploits on the baseball field and the basketball court. Although he played for other coaches as he grew up, for much of his youth he played on teams coached by his uncompromising older brother. These included Josh's basketball club, the Omaha Travelers, and his baseball club, the North YMCA Monarchs—named in honor of the famed Negro Leagues club, the Kansas City Monarchs. In addition to facing local competition, both clubs traveled around Nebraska and the neighboring states of Iowa, Kansas, and Missouri. And Josh's teams were remarkably successful. For example, in 1950, a young Bob Gibson helped the Monarchs win Nebraska's State Midget American Legion baseball championship.[12] In doing so, they became the first black team to accomplish the feat.[13]

Despite his previous success, upon entering Omaha's Technical High School, Gibson found that racial discrimination would curtail his full participation in the institution's athletic programs. Although nearly half of the student body was African American, the football teams fielded only a handful of black players, and the baseball teams had none at all. Gibson believed that this was mostly due to Tech's football and baseball coach, Ken Kennedy, who "apparently hadn't heard of Jackie Robinson."[14] When he went out for football during his freshman year, Gibson was cut by Kennedy and told to "eat some potatoes and come back later."[15] While discrimination may well have been a factor, Gibson did acknowledge that as a freshman he stood less than five feet tall and weighed less than 100 pounds. Nevertheless, when Gibson had sprouted to 6 feet and 175 pounds by his senior year, he relished turning down a belated offer from Kennedy to join the football team.[16]

While Gibson starred on the school's track and basketball teams, it was not until his senior year, when Tom Murphy replaced Ken Kennedy as Tech's baseball coach, that he, along with shortstop Jerry Parks, finally broke the program's color barrier.[17] A standout at several positions—he had twice earned all-city honors in American Legion ball as a utility player—Gibson performed in the outfield and pitched. In doing so, he helped lead Tech to the 1953 Intercity League regular-season co-championship and the runners-up position in the Intercity League Tournament, tossing a one-hitter in the semifinal contest.[18] Indeed, although Gibson could throw hard, he believed if he had any future in baseball, it would most likely be as an outfielder, third baseman, or catcher.[19] Gibson's baseball skills were such that he had earlier received an offer from the Kansas City Monarchs of the Negro American League, as well as some interest from major league scouts. His family, however, preferred that he defer any potential professional athletic career in favor of obtaining a college education.

Despite his ability on the baseball diamond, never during his youth and high school athletic career did Gibson consider baseball his best sport. That distinction fell to basketball. His Tech basketball squad advanced to the 1952 state tournament in his junior season under the guidance of Neal Mosser, whose coaching style and competitiveness Gibson likened to that of his older brother. Furthermore, Coach Mosser "didn't care what color you were as long as you could play basketball."[20] In the tournament's semifinal game in Lincoln against Fremont, Mosser courageously started an all-black lineup. That represented a first for the state tournament, and Gibson said he would never forget the "eerie" atmosphere created by the "stone silence" of the crowd. Somewhat suspiciously, all the starters except Gibson fouled out in the first half, and he too fouled out very early in the second half. Fremont went on to bounce Omaha Tech from the tournament by a 40–39 score.[21]

After graduating from high school, Gibson had hoped to be offered a scholarship to play basketball at Indiana University (IU), the defending NCAA champions. However, he was surprised and disappointed when he was informed through his high school coach that Indiana's "quota of Negroes" had already been filled.[22] College basketball in the 1950s was still very much a racially segregated affair. In 1944, the University of Iowa was the first school in the Big Ten conference with an African American basketball player, Richard Culberson, but it was not until 1960 that the last school in the Big Ten finally integrated its basketball program. IU had become the second Big Ten institution to cross the unofficial color line in 1947, when it recruited Bill Garrett for its basketball team.[23] Then, the year before Bob Gibson graduated from high school, IU signed its second black basketball player, Wally Choice, an all-state performer from New Jersey. The following year, it added Hallie Bryant, the 1953 Mr. Basketball award recipient as the best high school player in the state of Indiana, who would later go on to have a lengthy and distinguished career with the Harlem Globetrotters. But Bryant's basketball talent notwithstanding, Gibson would later wryly observe that Indiana "got the wrong Negro."[24]

With Indiana University no longer an option, the only other colleges that had shown any interest in Gibson were some small schools in Nebraska and a few black institutions,[25] though he had no interest in any of them, and without an athletic scholarship, his hopes for a college education were looking bleak. With the new school year fast approaching, an opportunity suddenly arose from an unexpected source, and one very close to home. Creighton University, a private Catholic institution, was located only several blocks away from Tech High School. So, one day, J.V. "Duce" Belford, Creighton's athletic director, dropped by the North Side YMCA and surprised Gibson with a scholarship offer to play basketball for Creighton, an offer that appears to have been due in no small part to the influence of Gibson's brother Josh.[26]

Gibson was not, as is often reported, the first black basketball or baseball player to play for Creighton.[27] He was, however, the first to receive an athletic scholarship and to become a star player for the varsity. His initial year was spent on the freshman team, but on November 27, 1954, he made his debut for Creighton's varsity in a 66–51 victory over Buena Vista College of Storm Lake, Iowa. "Of all the rookies," proclaimed the *Omaha World-Herald*, "Bob Gibson made the most auspicious entrance. The sophomore jumping jack harvested 19 points, turned in a clever floor game, was pesky on defense[,] and teamed with [Dan] Simon for the two buckets which put the game on ice."[28]

Gibson went on to top Creighton's basketball team in points in both his junior and senior years, ending his varsity career as the Bluejays' third all-time leading scorer. Although standing only 6'1", he also led the team in rebounding in each of his final two seasons. He even held the school's single-game rebounding record (20) until a future NBA All-Star, Paul Silas, came along later to break Gibson's mark.[29]

Of course, Gibson starred on Creighton's baseball team as well, in this case, as both an outfielder and a pitcher. At that time, however, baseball was a minor sport at Creighton with a very short season against mostly in-state rivals. In his senior year, for example, Creighton played only 12 games, compiling a 10–2 record. Gibson was co-captain of the team that year and led the pitching staff with three wins against no losses, while batting .318.[30] And interestingly, the baseball team was led by Bill Fitch, a young coach not much older than Gibson himself. Fitch also served as Creighton's assistant basketball coach, and he would go on to have a distinguished coaching career, including 25 years in the NBA, where he won a championship with the Boston Celtics. "After baseball practice," Fitch recalled, "Gibson and I played one-on-one basketball back in the gym. We had some knock-down, drag-out battles—sometimes lasting well into the evening. I never thought I'd see the likes of him as a competitor."[31] Indeed, Fitch considered Gibson "as the toughest competitor" he had ever encountered, unrivaled until he crossed paths with another athlete who absolutely hated to lose, the Boston Celtics' future NBA Hall of Famer, Larry Bird.[32]

As Gibson's collegiate career wound down, he harbored dreams of playing either basketball or baseball at the professional level. He still considered basketball his best sport, and it also was the one which he preferred. He had completed a questionnaire sent to him by the Minneapolis Lakers, but did not hear anything more from them, and no other team had showed any interest. Despite the fact that integration had begun in the NBA in 1950, there still were not a lot of opportunities for African American players. In the season following Gibson's graduation from Creighton, only 13 black players appeared on NBA rosters,[33] though there were admittedly very few roster spots available for anyone. In 1957, the league had just eight teams, and those teams' collective rosters contained only around 100 players. Nevertheless, Gibson believed that he would have made it in the NBA if he had been given the chance.

Another outlet for talented black basketball players of that era was the famous Harlem Globetrotters. As it happened, in April of Gibson's senior year at Creighton, the Globetrotters arrived in Omaha on one of their cross-country tours. Their opponents were a travelling team of college all-stars. To increase

Gibson as a player on the 1957 Creighton University baseball team (Creighton Athletics).

interest and attendance, local players were frequently recruited for a game to play against the Globetrotters. So, Gibson was asked to suit up with the collegians for their appearance in Omaha. Although relegated to the bench for most of the game, midway through the third quarter he was finally sent in, much to the delight of the hometown fans. Making his first four shots and snagging five rebounds, the Creightonian sparked his team to a slim 79–77 win. The reporter for the *Omaha World-Herald* gushed that "there was no question about the place in the lineup being deserved once he got to display his wares."[34] The Globetrotters, who rarely lost whether or not they were clowning, were so impressed with Gibson's performance that they actually made him an offer to play for them. Gibson, however, was not ready to accept their terms at that time. Not only did he want to finish the school year and graduate, but he was also a newlywed, having just gotten married the day before his appearance against the Globetrotters.

As he completed his final season of baseball at Creighton, Gibson received some interest from several major league baseball teams, but nothing of any substance. A scout for the Yankees even went so far as to inform him that he "wasn't good enough to play Class D ball."[35] The exception to the rule was Runt Marr, the local scout for the St. Louis Cardinals who had had his eye on Gibson for some time and who had tried to sign him as far back as Gibson's high school days. Also, Josh Gibson knew Bill Bergesch, the general manager of the Cardinals' minor league affiliate in Omaha and evidently put in some good words with him on behalf of his younger brother.[36] Thus it was in June of 1957 that Gibson agreed to a minor league contract with his hometown Omaha Cardinals.[37] It was for far less than he had hoped, but he was able to augment his minor league salary by making arrangements to join the Globetrotters after the baseball season was finished.

As Gibson embarked on his professional baseball career, he did not have to travel very far. The Omaha Cardinals played their home games in Omaha Stadium—commonly referred to as Municipal Stadium—where Gibson had appeared previously during his collegiate baseball career. Gibson was not sure what position he would be assigned, and neither were the Cardinals. They believed he could end up as either a pitcher or an outfielder. Marr reported that Gibson had the "speed and defensive ability to play the outfield but there is a question about his hitting ability in Triple[-]A."[38] For his part, a determined Gibson stated that "I had no idea what I was going to do, how I was going to try to make it. I just knew I was going to make it. As an outfielder. As a catcher. As a first baseman. As a pitcher. I would play wherever they wanted me to, but I was going to make it."[39]

As it turned out, the Cardinals quickly decided where Gibson's future would lie. When he joined the team, manager Johnny Keane asked him to throw some batting practice. He told Gibson not to throw hard, but even so, the batters were not able to make good contact with his half-speed pitches. On the other hand, Gibson was so raw and inexperienced that when Keane asked him to toss some curveballs, he realized that he did not really know how to throw a proper curveball.[40] Nevertheless, Keane had seen enough of Gibson's powerful arm. From that day forward, Gibson would be a pitcher.

Growing up in Omaha, Gibson had never seen his hometown Cardinals play. The first professional baseball game that he ever saw was viewed from his team's own dugout in Municipal Stadium.[41] On June 16, 1957, only a week after signing with the Cardinals, Gibson made his professional debut in the second game of a doubleheader against the Indianapolis Indians. Coming in as a reliever with the score tied 2–2 in the ninth inning, he promptly loaded the bases by walking two batters and hitting a third. But he managed to work out of this self-inflicted predicament with no runs scored, and the Cardinals ultimately won the game, 3–2, in the 11th.[42]

On June 23, Gibson was given his first start against the Charleston Senators. Despite enduring "enough emergencies for a week's starts," he went 8⅔ innings and picked up his first win, 4–3.[43] In two months with Omaha, Gibson appeared in 10 games, starting four and compiling a record of two wins and one loss. At the end of July, however, he received the unwelcome news that he was being sent down to the Columbus, Georgia, Foxes in the Class A South Atlantic League, better known as the Sally League. The Cardinals needed to free up a roster spot due to personnel moves, and they also wanted to give Gibson more opportunities to pitch than he would have otherwise in Omaha. Gibson was less than thrilled to be relegated to Columbus, saying that it was "the last place in the world" he wanted to go.[44] Fortunately for him, it was just for the final month of the season, and Gibson was in fact able to get in more work on the mound, as he started eight games, winning four and losing three with a 3.77 earned run average (ERA).

At the end of the baseball season, Gibson returned home to Omaha, but only briefly, for by early October he was on the road again to join the Harlem Globetrotters. While he enjoyed his time with the team, the highly competitive Gibson ultimately found the Globetrotters' trademark clowning not to be to his liking. Also, the St. Louis Cardinals' management wanted him to concentrate his athletic efforts solely on becoming a better baseball pitcher. This was something that Gibson was happy to do, especially since the Cardinals increased his salary for the 1958 season as an inducement to put an end to his nascent basketball career. "Not only was I down to one sport," noted Gibson, "but one position in that sport."[45] However, no less an authority than the Globetrotters' famed "Clown Prince of Basketball," Meadowlark Lemon, was unequivocal in his assessment of Gibson's skills on the hardwood court. A young Lemon was Gibson's teammate on the Globetrotters, and also for a brief time, his roommate on the road. Many years later Lemon declared, "I thought Bob was a better basketball player than a baseball player.... I think Bob could have played with any NBA team. He was that good." Lemon was quick to add, though, that Gibson's choice to go with baseball "turned out better for him."[46]

Johnny Keane, who as early as 1958 recognized Gibson's potential to be an outstanding major league pitcher, was Gibson's St. Louis Cardinal manager from 1961 through 1964 (National Baseball Hall of Fame Library).

For the 1958 season, Gibson was invited to spring training with the St. Louis Cardinals. When the season began, however, he was back with the Omaha Cardinals. In mid–June, after appearing in 13 games for Omaha, he was shipped off to St. Louis' other Triple-A level franchise, the Rochester, New York, Red Wings of the International League. It was actually a promotion, since St. Louis considered the Red Wings to be its better farm team. Gibson spent the rest of the season at Rochester, appearing in 20 games and having his fastball voted as the International League's best. Commenting on that recognition of his improving pitching skills, Johnny Keane, Gibson's former manager in Omaha, asserted that "Bob can be a major league pitcher—a great one."[47]

Gibson began spring training with St. Louis again in 1959, and this time he qualified for the Cardinals' opening day roster. On April 15, he made his major league debut, pitching two innings in relief against the Los Angeles Dodgers in a 5–0 Cardinals' loss. But after just two more appearances on the mound for St. Louis, he was sent back down to Omaha. While in the River City, he played in 24 games, starting 18 of them and compiling a record of 9 wins and 9 losses with a 3.07 ERA. On July 12, in what would be his final performance at Omaha's Municipal Stadium, Gibson tossed all 12 innings against the Minneapolis Millers to pick up his eighth victory of the season, 3–2. Twelve days later in Dallas, Texas, he pitched his last game as an Omaha Cardinal, surrendering one unearned run and defeating the Rangers, 2–1. At the end of July, Gibson was rewarded for his solid performance in the Big O by being called up to St. Louis for the remainder of the 1959 season. His initial start as a major leaguer was on July 30 in Cincinnati, and not only did he pick up the win, but he did so in spectacular fashion, shutting out the Reds by a score of 1–0.

Gibson's final year in the River City turned out to be the Omaha Cardinals' last one there as well. At the close of the 1959 season, the St. Louis powers decided that they could no longer support two franchises at the Triple-A level. Attendance at Omaha games had declined for four straight years, so the powers opted to keep their farm club in Rochester at Omaha's expense. The departure of the Cardinals ended the city's 13-year association with the St. Louis parent club, and for the 1960 season, Omaha was left without a professional baseball team for the first time since 1947.

The beginning of the 1960 season saw Gibson again playing for St. Louis, but in May, after just five appearances, he was sent down to Rochester. This time, however, his stay in the minor leagues was only a brief one. By mid–June, he was back in the majors, where he would remain for good. His subsequent remarkable major league career is well documented and well known. In 17 years with the St. Louis Cardinals, Gibson proved himself to be one of the finest pitchers in the annals of Organized Baseball. He won 251 games, with 56 of them being shutouts. When he retired in 1975, his 3,117 strikeouts were second only to Walter Johnson on the all-time list. An All-Star for nine seasons, he earned two Cy Young Awards and nine consecutive Gold Gloves, the latter honors for being the best fielding pitcher in the National League. And on baseball's biggest stage, the World Series, Gibson was nothing less than outstanding. In his three World Series appearances, he compiled a record of seven wins and two losses with a 1.89 ERA and was named the Series' Most Valuable Player (MVP) for leading the Cardinals to championships in 1964 and 1967. Then, in overpowering fashion, he won the first two games he pitched in the 1968 World Series, and most certainly would have captured a third MVP Award, if he had not been outdueled in the deciding Game Seven by the Detroit Tigers' Mickey Lolich, the eventual MVP.

However, perhaps Gibson is best remembered for his otherworldly season-long performance in 1968. In what would be labeled the "Year of the Pitcher," Gibson was preeminent. He threw 28 complete games and won 22 of them, including 13 shutouts. His 1.12 ERA was the lowest since Dutch Leonard's 0.96 in 1914 during the aptly named Deadball Era. And not only did he earn his first Cy Young Award as the league's best pitcher, but he was also selected as the National League's MVP, one of only 11 pitchers to win both awards in the same year.[48] In fact, so dominant were Gibson and his fellow hurlers in 1968 that the rules of the game were changed in an effort to help out the overmatched batters. For the 1969 season, the pitching mound was lowered from 15 inches high to only 10 inches high and the strike zone was reduced. These modifications became known as the "Gibson Rules" in a tip of a hat to the man who best exemplified the reason for the changes. As to what Gibson himself thought of that distinction, he later revealed, "I can assure you I was not consulted. Nor was I flattered, much preferring not to be associated, in any fashion, with legislation that would diminish the power of the pitcher."[49]

Even during his playing career in St. Louis, Gibson had always maintained his off-season home in Nebraska. But in the mid 1960s, when he and his family purchased a house in Omaha in a previously all-white neighborhood, they discovered that although Gibson's status as a professional athlete may have mitigated some of the usual racial discrimination, it certainly did not remove it. Among the hurtful slights, new white homeowners moving into the neighborhood would be forewarned that a black family lived there, but that they should not be concerned because "it was only Bob Gibson, the ballplayer."[50] Nevertheless, Gibson ultimately retired to the Omaha suburb of Bellevue, just south of the city where he was born and raised. He lived there until his death on October 2, 2020, and when he was once asked why he resided in the Omaha area, he graciously replied that "[t]his is a nice place to live, and where people care for each other. This is the reason I still live here."[51]

Gibson's off-the-field and postbaseball pursuits have been many and varied. Like a number of former players, he hoped to continue his association with baseball in some fashion either through coaching or a front office position. However, as he had learned more than once in his life, racial barriers made that a challenge. Despite the fact that the color line on the playing field had already been broken, coaching opportunities were still limited. It was not until 1974, just before Gibson began his last year as a player, that a major league team, the Cleveland Indians, had hired its first black manager, Frank Robinson. Robinson went on to have a 17-year managerial career in the major leagues with four teams, but aside from short stints by Larry Doby with the Chicago White Sox in 1978 and Maury Wills with the Seattle Mariners in 1980–1981, another black manager would not be hired by a major league club until the Toronto Blue Jays signed Cito Gaston in 1989.

In 1981, Gibson joined the New York Mets' coaching staff of his friend and ex-teammate, Joe Torre. He then followed Torre to Atlanta in the next season, serving as the Braves' pitching coach until Torre was fired after the 1984 season. A decade later, in 1995, he linked up again briefly with Torre, this time with his old team, the St. Louis Cardinals. That position subsequently transitioned to work as a special instructor, or what Gibson called being a "celebrity coach" during the Cardinals' spring training.[52]

Like many former athletes, Gibson also found his way into sportscasting. Shortly after his playing career ended, he was hired in 1976 as a color commentator for ABC's Monday Night Baseball, the first of a series of jobs as a television and radio analyst. Other jobs included hosting a radio show covering Cardinal games for KMOX in St. Louis and briefly serving as a commentator for baseball games on ESPN. Although he generally enjoyed that line of work, neither of his jobs in the broadcast booth were long-lasting.

At home in Nebraska, Gibson was prominently involved in a number of local business ventures, including a bank and a radio station, KOWH, both of which he left for different reasons. As Gibson explained in his second autobiography:

> When I ultimately accepted a coaching job with Joe Torre and the Mets in 1981..., I had to resign from the board of the bank because the FDIC frowns upon directors who cannot attend meetings on a regular basis. I remained an investor in the bank but by that time had divested myself of any interest in the radio station. As the principal investor in KOWH, I had been operating at a personal liability that was eventually too much to handle.[53]

Gibson's belief was that the larger Omaha community did not adequately support businesses that had minority proprietors, saying that "[r]egardless of how good it is, any business that is known as black-owned, people just don't do business there."[54] In 1979, Gibson and two partners opened a restaurant and bar on north 30th Street in Omaha, one of his more successful business undertakings. Bob Gibson's Spirits and Sustenance was located near both Omaha's Technical High School and Creighton University, as well as Gibson's old neighborhood home. The restaurant served good food and offered live jazz, and Gibson took a very hands-on approach to the endeavor, saying that "running the restaurant was the thing that got me started on the second half of my life."[55] One of his partners attested to the fact, observing that "[h]e gave it 100 percent. He was there at 7 a.m., checking the beer trucks."[56] The restaurant lasted for 10 years, but Gibson said:

> By the time I joined Torre's staff with the Mets, however, I was unable to run the restaurant on a day-to-day basis and lost my handle on it.... [So,] I had to reluctantly close it down in part because city regulations would not permit us to expand our parking and in part because it was becoming increasingly difficult to maintain the kind of establishment I wanted without being there.[57]

One of Gibson's most notable off-the-field pursuits has been that of an author. Following his remarkable 1968 season, Gibson came out with his first autobiography, *From Ghetto to Glory: The Story of Bob Gibson*, written with Phil Pepe. That was followed 26 years later, in 1994, with a second autobiography, *Stranger to the Game*, this one authored with Lonnie Wheeler. In 2009, Gibson joined forces with his fellow National Baseball Hall of Famer, Reggie Jackson, and Wheeler to produce *Sixty Feet, Six Inches: A Hall of Fame Pitcher & a Hall of Fame Hitter Talk About How the Game Is Played*. Gibson's most recent foray into writing, his third collaboration with Lonnie Wheeler, was 2015's *Pitch by Pitch: My View of One Unforgettable Game*. In that book, Gibson discusses in fascinating detail the first game of the 1968 World Series against the Detroit Tigers, a game in which Gibson faced off against Detroit's 31-game winner, Denny McLain. Not only did Gibson win that game with a shutout performance, 4–0, but he also struck out 17 Tigers to set a still-standing record (as of November 1, 2019) for most strikeouts in a World Series contest.

Also, Gibson has been active in numerous philanthropic efforts. These include organizing and hosting a charity golf tournament in Omaha. Beginning in 1997 and continuing for several years afterward, the Bob Gibson All-Star Classic attracted notables for the world of professional sports to raise funds for charitable causes. Among them were the American Lung Association and the Baseball Assistance Team (B.A.T.), which provides support for former ballplayers who find themselves in difficult circumstances.

Gibson once said that he "would rather be known as Bob Gibson, great American, than Bob Gibson, great baseball player."[58] He will, however, probably always be best remembered for his accomplishments as an athlete. In 1981 he was elected to the National Baseball Hall of Fame in his first year of eligibility. He joined an even more select group in 1999 when he was named to Major League Baseball's All-Century Team, one of only nine pitchers and 30 players total that were so honored. Not surprisingly, his native state has been especially appreciative. When Gibson's alma mater, Creighton University, established an Athletic Hall of Fame in 1968, Bob Gibson became the first inductee. He would subsequently become an inaugural inductee of both the Nebraska High School Hall of Fame in 1994 and the Omaha Sports Hall of Fame in 2007.

In March 1999, the city of Omaha honored its famous native son by changing the name of a length of Deer Park Boulevard to Bob Gibson Boulevard. Appropriately, the newly redubbed street was located just north of Rosenblatt Stadium,[59] where Gibson had thrown his first pitch as a professional baseball player more than four decades before. "I think most anyone would enjoy that," said a moved Gibson. "You've got to be crazy if you don't appreciate something like that."[60] Among those in attendance for the ceremony was Gibson's old high school basketball coach, Neal Mosser.[61]

More than a decade later, in April 2013, a larger-than-life bronze statue of Gibson was unveiled outside of Werner Park, the home of the Storm Chasers, Omaha's current Triple-A baseball club. In honor of the occasion, Governor Dave Heineman issued a proclamation declaring it "Bob Gibson Day" in Nebraska.[62] Said an emotional Gibson, "There's really no explanation for the feeling I have inside. I'm elated."[63]

In 2005, the *Omaha World-Herald* embarked on a project to identify

Gibson during the first game of the 1968 World Series, a game in which he struck out 17 Detroit Tigers. Because of his continual prowess on the mound, the Omaha hurler was chosen in 1999— along with Roger Clemens, Lefty Grove, Walter Johnson, Sandy Koufax, Christy Mathewson, Nolan Ryan, Warren Spahn, and Cy Young—to be part of the pitching staff of Major League Baseball's All-Century Team (National Baseball Hall of Fame Library).

Nebraska's 100 greatest athletes. The list was revealed over a 10-day span, reminding readers of the state's many illustrious sports stars. Among them were Pro Football Hall of Famer Gale Sayers; National Baseball Hall of Famers Grover Cleveland Alexander, Richie Ashburn, Sam Crawford, and Arthur "Dazzy" Vance[64]; NBA All-Star Bob Boozer; and Heisman Trophy winners Eric Crouch and Johnny Rodgers. Sitting atop the list as Nebraska's greatest athlete was the Omaha-born and -raised Bob Gibson, who overcame poor health and economic circumstances, not to mention ever-present racial discrimination, to become one of the best baseball pitchers to toe the rubber. Amazingly, four of the top five athletes—Gibson, Sayers, Boozer, and Rodgers—along with several others on the list, had been mentored at some point in their youth by Josh Gibson. It is an impressive testament to Josh's powerful influence in Omaha's African American community. When the *World-Herald* revisited the list 10 years later in 2015, Bob Gibson's status as the state's number one athlete was reconfirmed. At the height of Gibson's professional career, a *World-Herald* columnist once crowed that he was "Omaha's gift to baseball."[65] It would be just as true to say that Bob Gibson was a gift to his hometown and native state.

## Notes

1. Bob Gibson with Phil Pepe, *From Ghetto to Glory: The Story of Bob Gibson* (New York: Popular Library, 1968), 5.
2. Ibid.
3. Ibid., 6.
4. Ibid., 7.
5. James Allen Flanery, "Wins and Losses: Hall-of-Famer [sic] Gibson Finds Post-Baseball Success Elusive," *Omaha World-Herald*, February 6, 1994.
6. In Gibson with Pepe, Josh Gibson's real first name is spelled "LeRoy," but in Bob Gibson and Lonnie Wheeler, *Stranger to the Game* (New York: Viking, 1994), it is spelled "Leroy." Cf. Gibson with Pepe, 11, and Gibson and Wheeler, *Stranger to the Game*, 10.
7. Bob Gibson and Lonnie Wheeler, *Pitch by Pitch: My View of One Unforgettable Game* (New York: Flatiron Books, 2015), 195.
8. Gibson and Wheeler, *Stranger to the Game*, 29.
9. Ibid., 19.
10. Gibson and Wheeler, *Pitch by Pitch: My View of One Unforgettable Game*, 195.
11. Ibid., 194.
12. "Omaha Monarchs Cop Midget Title," *Omaha World-Herald*, August 28, 1950.
13. Gibson and Wheeler, *Stranger to the Game*, 19.
14. Ibid., 20. See also Dennis E. Hoffman, "Impact Players: How Jackie Robinson, Mildred Brown, and Leroy Gibson Transformed the African American Experience with Baseball in Omaha, Nebraska, 1946–1950," *Black Ball: A Journal of the Negro Leagues* 4, no. 1 (Spring 2011): 47, 57n17.
15. Gibson and Wheeler, *Stranger to the Game*, 21.
16. Ibid.
17. Ibid.
18. Don Lee, "Benson High Finally Hits Baseball Jackpot; Clips Tech by 7–6 for Intercity Meet Crown," *Omaha World-Herald*, May 23, 1953, and "Creighton Prep's Tobin Is Intercity Golf King with 78," *Omaha World-Herald*, May 29, 1953. However, Gibson's memory of the results of the championship game differ from the information found in the *Omaha World-Herald*. Cf. Lee, "Benson High Finally Hits Baseball Jackpot; Clips Tech by 7–6 for Intercity Meet Crown," and Gibson and Wheeler, *Stranger to the Game*, 21.
19. Gibson and Wheeler, *Stranger to the Game*, 22.
20. Gibson with Pepe, 17–18.
21. Gibson and Wheeler, *Stranger to the Game*, 23.
22. Gibson with Pepe, 22.
23. See Charles H. Martin, "The Color Line in Midwestern College Sports, 1890–1960," *Indiana Magazine of History* 98 (June 2002): 85–112; and Tom Graham and Rachel Graham Cody, *Getting Open: The Unknown Story of Bill Garrett and the Integration of College Basketball* (New York: Atria Books, 2006).
24. Gibson and Wheeler, *Stranger to the Game*, 24.

## 214  Section I—The Long and Winding Road

25. Gibson with Pepe, 22.
26. *Ibid.*, 23.
27. In 1912, R.S. Taylor became the first African American baseball player at Creighton University, and for the 1925–1926 season, William Waldon Solomon was the first to suit up for the basketball team. See Dennis N. Mihelich, *The History of Creighton University, 1878–2003* (Omaha, Nebraska: Creighton University Press, 2006), 111, 216.
28. "Jays Subdue Buena Vista," *Omaha World-Herald*, November 28, 1954.
29. *Creighton Basketball 2016–2017 Media Guide*, 89 ff.
30. "Frank Zitka Named Jays' Most Valuable," *Omaha World-Herald*, May 28, 1957.
31. Bill Fitch quoted in Jack Ramsay, *Dr. Jack's Leadership Lessons Learned from a Lifetime in Basketball* (Hoboken, New Jersey: Wiley & Sons, 2004), 173.
32. *Ibid.*
33. See Ron Thomas, *They Cleared the Lane: The NBA's Black Pioneers* (Lincoln: University of Nebraska Press, 2002).
34. Howard Brantz, "Forte Paces Stars by Trotters, 79–77," *Omaha World-Herald*, April 16, 1957.
35. Gibson and Wheeler, *Stranger to the Game*, 42.
36. David Halberstam, *October 1964* (New York: Villard Books, 1994), 101.
37. "Bob Gibson of Creighton U. Signs for Omaha Card Play," *Omaha World-Herald*, June 10, 1957.
38. *Ibid.*
39. Gibson with Pepe, 32.
40. *Ibid.*, 34
41. *Ibid.*, 34.
42. Robert Phipps, "Cardinals Only 2½ Games Back of Leaders After Sweeping Bill," *Omaha World-Herald*, June 17, 1957.
43. Robert Phipps, "Barnes Faces Leading Saints Here Tonight in Loop Feature," *Omaha World-Herald*, June 24, 1957.
44. Gibson with Pepe, 37.
45. Gibson and Wheeler, *Stranger to the Game*, 48.
46. Lee Barfknecht, "Lemon says Gibson was NBA-ready," *Omaha World-Herald*, August 17, 2003.
47. Wally Provost, "Keeping the Tailor Busy," *Omaha World-Herald*, September 10, 1958.
48. As of November 1, 2019, the others to accomplish this rare feat are Don Newcombe (1956), Sandy Koufax (1963), Denny McLain (1968), Vida Blue (1971), Rollie Fingers (1981), Willie Hernandez (1984), Roger Clemens (1986), Dennis Eckersley (1992), Justin Verlander (2011), and Clayton Kershaw (2014).
49. Gibson and Wheeler, *Pitch by Pitch: My View of One Unforgettable Game*, 77.
50. Gibson and Wheeler, *Stranger to the Game*, 123.
51. Colleen Kenney, "For an Emotional Gibson, Street Name Overwhelming," *Omaha World-Herald*, June 9, 1999.
52. Rick Ruggles, "Gibson Honored by Omaha Street Designation," *Omaha World-Herald*, March 19, 1999.
53. Gibson and Wheeler, *Stranger to the Game*, 257.
54. Flanery.
55. Gibson and Wheeler, *Stranger to the Game*, 258.
56. Flanery.
57. Gibson and Wheeler, *Stranger to the Game*, 259.
58. Gibson with Pepe, 199.
59. Omaha Stadium was renamed Rosenblatt Stadium in 1964 in honor of former Omaha mayor Johnny Rosenblatt.
60. Ruggles.
61. Kenney.
62. Rob White, "Gibson is Aces with This," *Omaha World-Herald*, April 12, 2013.
63. Dirk Chatelain, "In the Pitching Arts, Gibson Breaks the Mold," *Omaha World-Herald*, April 12, 2013.
64. Although Vance was born in Orient, Iowa, he lived for a number of years in Nebraska.
65. Don Lee, "Black Sees Gibson as Broadcaster," *Omaha World-Herald*, December 3, 1968.

## Section II

# Voices from the Omaha Area

# Prologue

### Dennis E. Hoffman

This section presents readers with an impressive roster of players and coaches from the Omaha area telling stories about their experiences in "black ball"—that is, the involvement of African Americans in playing baseball—and in various other matters. Except for Heisman Trophy winner Johnny "The Jet" Rodgers, the lineup includes unsung heroes and forgotten faces. An obvious omission is Omaha's most famous black baseball player, Bob Gibson, but there is an essay on him in the first section of this book. Another significant omission is Omaha's most influential African American baseball coach, Bob Gibson's brother Josh. The Near North Side YMCA program director trained and nurtured a generation of young black ballplayers. In 1950, Josh Gibson's team, the Y Monarchs, led by Bob Gibson, became the first African American team to win the Nebraska American Legion Class A Junior State Tournament. I am sorry to say that Josh's voice has never been heard in published works because he is deceased, though if you listen closely to the voices of his former ballplayers and associates, you might hear the ghost of Josh Gibson exhorting you to be all that you can be.

However, to be understood, these voices must be given a sense of place. And that place is North Omaha, which is central to the identity of many of those interviewed for this book. Most of them have a deep connection to that locale that will never leave them. As a part of the River City, North Omaha is bordered by Cuming and Dodge Streets on the south, Interstate 680 on the north, North 72nd Street on the west, and the Missouri River and Carter Lake, Iowa, on the east. Just north of downtown Omaha, this region is the hub of a historically significant African American community. An important district within it is the Near North Side. This neighborhood was one of the first in Omaha, emerging in the 1860s as a home to the German and Irish immigrants and later, 1910–1970, as a home to blacks from the rural South.

North 24th Street, which runs through the heart of the Near North Side, has long been an avenue of commercial and social activity. From the 1920s through the 1950s, North 24th Street, or as it used to be called the "Street of Dreams," was a place where African American culture bloomed. It contained such establishments as the Dreamland Ballroom, which featured national black jazz talent as well as local legends, including saxophonist Preston Love.

North 24th Street has also been the scene of riots that destroyed many commercial buildings in the Near North Side and left vast stretches of vacant lots. July 4, 1966, marked the first of several riots in this area. A crowd of African Americans gathered at the intersection of North 24th and Lake Streets, the heart of the Near North Side. Police attempts to disperse the crowd triggered the demolition of police cars, the wrecking of businesses, and the firebombing of buildings along North 24th Street. A month later, police killed a 19-year-old black man during a burglary, setting off another riot in that area. On June 24, 1969, a white police officer took the life of an unarmed African American teenager named Vivian Strong at the Logan Fontenelle Housing Project, which had been built along North 24th Street. Young African Americans responded with looting and firebombing businesses there.

For 72 years the most prominent educational institution serving the African American community in North Omaha was Technical High School or "Omaha Tech." Located between Cuming and Burt Streets and between 30th and 33rd Streets, the Omaha Tech building stands four stories tall and sprawls over two blocks of land. During its years of operation, Tech High graduated 25,000 young people. Many alumni were outstanding athletes, especially in football and basketball. Some went on to stardom in college and professional sports. Among the football players were Phil Wise (Class of '67), a University of Nebraska Omaha (UNO) star who played for the New York Jets, and Johnny Rodgers ('69), who earned the Heisman Trophy and All-American football honors at the University of Nebraska–Lincoln. Basketball stars included Bob Boozer ('55), who became an All-American at Kansas State University and an Olympic gold medalist in 1960 before playing in the National Basketball Association (NBA), and Ron Boone ('64), who retired from pro basketball after setting a durability record of 1,041 consecutive American Basketball Association and NBA games. Last but not least, Bob Gibson ('53), a basketball and baseball star at Tech, became a National Baseball Hall of Fame pitcher and World Series hero with the St. Louis Cardinals.

Omaha Tech was a source of great pride for Omaha's African American community. Miss Black Tech beauty pageants held annually from 1971 to 1982 were so popular that black teenagers without tickets to the coronation once broke into the school. Their motive for "breaking and entering" was to witness the spectacle of talented and beautiful African American girls performing on stage in the auditorium of the Tech High School building. However, Tech faced tough times in the 1960s and 1970s when housing patterns and racial segregation reinforced its reputation as one of Omaha's "black schools." Citing shrinking enrollments, the Omaha Public School Board shut down Omaha Tech in 1984.

Other black schools in North Omaha have over the years also played a vital role in the education of Omaha's black ballplayers and other African American youth. Some of these include Kellom Elementary School, which was one of Bob Gibson's alma maters, Howard Kennedy Elementary School, Nathan Hale Junior High, Druid Hill Elementary School, Long School, Lothrop School, and Horace Mann School. Whereas black schools originated under legal segregation in the southern United States (U.S.) after the American Civil War and Reconstruction Era, the term "black schools" is commonly used today to refer to schools whose students consist mainly of African American youth. Public schools in Omaha and other U.S. cities were technically desegregated in 1954 by *Brown v. Board of Education*, but during the 1950s and 1960s, many schools remained (and still are) de facto segregated due to inequality in housing and patterns of racial separation in neighborhoods.

For young African Americans growing up in Omaha in the 1950s and 1960s, a vibrant sports-centered children's street culture provided opportunities for fun, friendship, and a sense of belonging. This street culture included kids playing ball outdoors, which took place on quiet backstreets and along routes that ventured into local parks, playgrounds, and sandlots. It often incorporated many found and scavenged materials such as sticks that substituted for bats and rocks that substituted for balls. Also, it imposed an imaginative status on certain sections of the urban realm in Omaha. For example, some youthful ballplayers pretended that the walls of buildings were outfield fences. Various contemporary cultural geographers, anthropologists, and sociologists mourn the loss of child-invented and child-sustained street culture or of children "playing outdoors." They attribute the loss to the advent of indoor distractions such as television and video games.

Today, North Omaha is one of the poorest communities found anywhere in the United States. Among America's 100 largest metro areas, the city of Omaha has one of the highest black poverty rates—largely due to a concentration of intergenerational poverty in North Omaha. Worse yet, the River City's percentage of black children in poverty ranks every year among the highest in the country. In some census tracts of the Near North Side, for instance, 80 percent of the black kids live below the poverty line.

One constant in this oral history is that those interviewed used sports—including ball-and-bat games—to rise above the racial and/or environmental hurdles that they encountered and to find ways to give back to their community.

\* \* \*

*Editor's Note*: The following interviews except for the one with James Redden, which occurred in 2014, were conducted in 2016. So, all personal details found in essays 10 and 12–21 are current as of 2016, and those found in the James Redden interview are current as of 2014.

# 10

# John Morse

There were and still are white people fighting for racial justice in baseball. Their stories can inspire and sustain all of us. One of these people is John Morse. At a time when some of Omaha's high schools and colleges discriminated against blacks who wanted to play baseball, this short, pudgy white coach dared to be different. As Omaha's Technical High School's baseball coach, John Morse scoffed at negative stereotypes about black athletes and rejected the racist notion that "a mostly black or all-black baseball team can't win."

John Morse began playing baseball with the Murphy's Midgets under Coach Duce Belford in 1950. While attending Benson High School, he made second team All-Intercity League Baseball as a catcher on Benson's baseball team. In college, he caught four years for Coach Virg Yelkin at the University of Omaha (now the University of Nebraska Omaha). A highlight of his baseball-playing career was catching future National Baseball Hall of Famer Bob Gibson for the Woodbine, Iowa, Whiz Kids in 1954.

While teaching history at Tech from 1958 to 1984, Morse coached a predominantly black starting nine in 1966 to the only state baseball championship ever won by Tech. The Tech team got off to a terrible start, winning two games and losing five. They entered the tournament with a 6–5 record and a dismal school history of always finishing last or near the bottom of the Metro Conference in baseball. When Tech disposed of Lincoln Southeast and Benson High School in the state tournament held at Rosenblatt Stadium on May 24 and 25, it sent shock waves through Omaha high schools. To have a highly segregated so-called black school win a championship in the "white sport" of baseball surprised veteran white coaches and white high school officials. This feat stunned many believers of popular racial stereotypes about the limits of African American baseball players.

"The rest of the story," as famous radio commentator Paul Harvey used to say, has to do with the little-known reason for Morse's success in coaching minorities: Morse was an extraordinary multicultural educator. Long before multiculturalism became fashionable in the Omaha Public School system (OPS), this American history teacher was busier than a one-legged shortstop advancing the cause of diversity and equity at Omaha Tech. During Morse's tenure at Tech, the educational institution was known as "Omaha's black high school" because the racial segregation of OPS dictated that most black students go there. Morse developed and taught the first African American Studies course in OPS as well as the first Chicano Studies course, the first American Indian Studies course, and the first Asian American Studies course. For 11 years, he was a sponsor of the Miss Black Tech pageant which enjoyed great popularity in Omaha's black community.

When I interviewed the spry 83 year old in his West Omaha apartment, we were surrounded by baseball and other sports memorabilia. He told me about the upcoming 50th reunion of his 1966 championship baseball team. Rattling off the names of all members of that group, Morse told me he couldn't wait to be with his ballplayers again.

\* \* \*

My most memorable moment in black ball was the last time I caught Bob Gibson in August of 1955. We were both 20 years old. I was a student at the University of Omaha. Bob was a student at Creighton. Bob and I were playing as ringers for a town team from Logan, Iowa. Except for Bob and me, everyone on Logan's team lived in Logan. Bob got paid a hundred bucks and I got paid 25 bucks.

Well, anyway, Logan was playing in a tournament in Treynor, Iowa. We played the championship game at night. The Treynor ballpark's lights were dim. With Bob's speed and the bad lighting, he was unhittable. Bob threw hard. On this night, I did what I always did when I caught Bob—I wore a sponge in my glove. Like all the other times I caught Bob, on this night I never knew what Bob was going to throw. Sometimes I'd call a pitch, but Bob would decide if he wanted to throw whatever I called. If I called for a changeup and he didn't want to throw it, I might get a big surprise in the form of a fastball. Bob never threw any curveballs as a kid. His older brother, Josh, wouldn't let him. As I recall, Bob struck out 18 of 21 batters in that seven-inning championship game. We won, 1-0. The game lasted an hour. Three years later, Bob was playing professional baseball.

Bob and I were also teammates on another town team, the Woodbine Whiz Kids. This was an independent team, unaffiliated with any league. We played games around the Iowa-Nebraska-Kansas area. Our coach, Red Brummer, used to coach the Cuban All-Stars and so we wore uniforms that had once been worn by the Cuban All-Stars. Two other black ballplayers from Omaha—Jerry Parks and Don Benning—played for the Whiz Kids. Bob usually traveled to Whiz Kid games with his brother Josh.

Not to be confused with the Josh Gibson who starred as a slugging catcher in the Negro Leagues during the 1930s and 1940s, Bob Gibson's big brother made a greater impact on black baseball in Omaha than Bob Gibson himself. Josh is most famous for making Bob Gibson one of the most tenacious competitors in major league history. Equally important, though, Josh molded economically disadvantaged, mostly fatherless, and mostly African American boys into talented teams and prepared these boys to excel in sports and in life.

Josh was Bob's mentor and he dominated Bob's life. When Bob was a very young guy, they tell me he was very active. Without Josh exerting a strong guiding fatherly hand, Bob might have gone astray and never made it to the majors.

Well, one time the Woodbine Whiz Kids went down to Kansas to play ball, and things got ugly. The local fans were hurling slurs at Bob. From my catcher's position, I could hear the fans sitting behind home plate yelling, "What's this 'N' doing down here playing ball?" And then they would boo Bob. As soon as the game was over, Josh hustled Bob to Josh's car and they got the hell out of there.

Speaking of Josh Gibson, he deserves much of the credit for Omaha Tech's state championship in baseball in 1966. Many of the players on my 1966 team had played previously on Josh's YMCA youth teams. Josh taught them the fundamentals. He was a friend of mine who used to come over to Adams Park where the Roberts Dairy Legion team that I coached during the summers played. I'd give him used baseballs and cracked wooden bats that we'd tape up for Josh's team.

If it hadn't been for white racism, Josh would've been coaching the 1966 Omaha Tech baseball team instead of me. You see, both Josh and I applied for the same job at Tech teaching American history and coaching the baseball team. But Josh never had a chance. OPS discriminated against him. In those days, OPS didn't hire blacks to teach high school. Due to white privilege, I was hired. Josh was bitter. And I don't blame him. It was wrong.

As a coach and teacher, I tried to be fair—regardless of what anyone else wanted me to do. Some local coaches objected to mostly black or all-black teams. They subscribed to the stereotype that "you can't win with an all-black team." What I heard from other white coaches was that I should mix in a few whites. They gave two reasons. First, they said black ballplayers were selfish and incapable of being team players. Second, some white coaches believed blacks weren't smart enough to assume leadership positions. You know what I'm talking about—the stereotype that blacks can't play quarterback on a football team or point guard on a basketball team.

Well, the 1964 freshman basketball team I coached at Tech proved that this was bullshit. With five black starters and five black reserves, my freshman basketball team rolled to a 14–0 season. There simply weren't any whites at Tech who could compete with any of the 10 black guys on that team. After we whipped Central, their freshman coach marveled at how disciplined my players were.

When I took over as head baseball coach at Tech, I inherited mostly white players. One of the best was Billy Wachtler. Ever heard of him? Great ballplayer. The Wachtlers had a family tradition of producing quality ballplayers. Billy led the Metro League in hitting. Charlie Skaggs may have been the first black to play on one of my Tech varsity baseball teams. That would've been around 1959. In case you're wondering how I got from one black player to having a majority of blacks as my starting nine on the 1966 team, I got my players from Josh Gibson's pipeline.

I always put my best players on the baseball field. Actually, there were some years at Tech when I had only nine players, and other years when Tech couldn't have a baseball team because not enough players tried out. You have to realize the glory sports for blacks back in the so-called heydays of blacks playing baseball in the mid–1960s were still track, football, and basketball—not baseball. Between 1960 and 1966, only a few blacks played on my baseball teams—so few I can name them: Ron Boone, Tilman Trotter, and Otis Bullion.

By contrast, six of the nine starters on my 1966 Tech team were black: Johnny Roper, Phil Wise, Kirkland Wise, Ferguson Hill, Rodger Ulmar, and Ron Bartee. These ballplayers had one thing in common. They had all played for Josh. By the time they tried out for the Tech varsity, they all had baseball in their blood and Josh had given them the transfusion. In addition to my second and third basemen who were white, my shortstop and sparkplug, Bobby Griego, was Hispanic.

Other than Central High School's Jerry Bartee, I don't recall any blacks starting on Omaha metro high school baseball teams in Tech's championship season of 1966. To my knowledge, no other state baseball champion in Nebraska history has featured as many black starters as my 1966 Tech team. Actually, I tried to recruit Jerry Bartee to play for me in 1966. If Jerry had transferred to Tech, I would have had an embarrassment of riches. I would have had the two best shortstops in Omaha playing for me. You know Jerry went on to play minor league ball for the St. Louis Cardinals. I tried to persuade Jerry to transfer by telling him that if he came to Tech, he'd play alongside his brother Ron. But Jerry stayed at Central. I think he wanted to graduate from Central because Central had a better reputation for academics than Tech.

In those days, Central was known as "the Jewish high school" because of all the Jewish students attending it. At the time, Central was maybe 20 percent black. By contrast Tech was regarded as a "Booker T. Washington School"—a place to get a technical education. With 50 percent of the city's black students going there, Tech was known as Omaha's "black high school." Omaha's African American community regarded Tech as representing it. Black youth attending Tech considered it to be "their school." Tech was the pride and joy of the African American community.

Racial bias of white umpires against blacks in Omaha high school baseball was real but difficult to detect. I don't recall any incidents when I was coaching the Tech varsity baseball team where the umps screwed us. Keep a couple of things in mind, though. First, most of my baseball teams, except for the 1966 and 1967 teams, were predominantly white. Second, the umps didn't have to beat us because most of the time we beat ourselves. The only years I had a bunch of Josh's players were 1966 and 1967. Other than those two years, we lost most of our games.

But let me tell you what happened to one of my freshman basketball teams—not the 1964 hotshot one. An all-black freshman Tech basketball team of mine was playing the Westside freshman, an all-white team, on Westside's home court. It must have been 1965 or 1966. My dad always used his station wagon to help me transport players to the games. At halftime of the game at Westside, Tech had 23 fouls and Westside had none. White refs. During halftime, my dad confronted the refs. He went wild. Westside authorities kicked my dad out of the gym. As far as racial bias of white umps in that baseball championship season of 1966 goes, you'll have to ask my players.

My favorite memory of that championship season is Bobby Griego stealing home against Benson High School in the final game at Rosenblatt. Bobby was our leader, our catalyst. His dad was Hispanic and his mom was white. Now, it might seem strange to have a Hispanic young man as the leader of a mostly black team. But if you think about it—it makes sense. Being biracial, Bobby could relate to everyone on the team. I guess you could say that, as a light-skinned, mixed-race American youth, Bobby "acted white." He was studious, super smart. In the top five percent of students I've ever had in my history and ethnic studies classes. Back in those days, Bobby probably found it easier to navigate life by acting white. After all, Mexican-Americans were not well accepted in 1966. White folks in Omaha called them "wetbacks." This ethnic slur was used to paint all Mexicans with a broad brush—to suggest that they all had immigrated illegally to the U.S. by swimming or wading across the Rio Grande River that separates the U.S. from Mexico.

All that year in 1966, I had never given Bobby the steal sign. He was on his own. Whenever Bobby was on base, he knew when a pitcher was going to go home. Bobby would watch the pitcher's shoulder and heel. Then, he'd take off. Most of the bases Bobby stole the catchers never had an opportunity to throw him out. He'd get incredible jumps. He'd be halfway down the baseline before the catcher got the ball.

Well, in that championship game, our big rally came in the third inning when we collected four runs. With two outs, Griego reached base on an error and then stole second. Phil Wise ripped a base hit into left field which should have easily scored Griego, but Bob tripped as he rounded third. So Bobby picked himself up. Went back to third base. He was fuming. Bobby was a heckuva a baserunner. He was kicking himself because he should have scored. He came over to the third base coaching box where I was standing.

"I can steal home," he whispered.

"Bobby," I said, "I've never given you a signal before and I'm not going to start now."

The next pitch was high. Bobby had been studying the Benson pitcher's delivery all game. When he saw the pitcher go into a full windup, he took off. He slid under the catcher's tag. I've got the picture of it from the *World-Herald*.

Kenneth Smith walked. Kirkland Wise and John Roper followed with base hits to score three more runs before the final out.

The Benson Bunnies scored one run in each of the next two innings, but excellent defensive play kept them from scoring again. Phil Wise, playing left field, smashed four hits in four times at the plate and made seven putouts at his position.

Before 1966, my Tech baseball teams were the laughingstock of metro baseball. We were like the New York Mets before the "Miracle Mets" upset the Baltimore Orioles in the 1969 World Series. Hapless and hopeless. Couldn't win a game to save our souls.

So, what was special about my 1966 team?

Athleticism. Solid team defense—we played errorless baseball in the championship game. Timely hitting. Outstanding defensive outfielders. With Kirkland Wise in center, Kirkland's brother Phil Wise in left, and Ferguson Hill in right, our speedy outfielders covered the outfield like a blanket. Whenever a fly ball was hit to the outfield, they tracked it down. Additionally, our 1966 team had excellent pitching. Our ace, Rodger Ulmar, won seven and lost one; Ron Bartee won two and lost two; and reliever Ernie

John Morse with his 1966 Technical High School baseball team (left to right): (front row) Pete Louvaris, Phil Wise, Ernie Boone, Kirkland Wise, Charles Plummer, Rick Mobley; (middle row) John Morse, Rodger Ulmar, Bobby Griego, Ken Smith, Ron Bartee, Steve Bauermeister, John Roper, Ferguson Hill, Robert Trumbauer; (back row) Robert Pederson, Walt Hannah, Tommy Hill, Robert Bednarz, Jeff Ahrens (personal collection of Steve Bauermeister).

Boone won two and lost two. Ulmar won one game in the district playoffs plus the championship game against Benson. Bartee was the winning pitcher in the first game of the district playoffs and in the first game of the state playoffs against Lincoln Southeast.

One more thing. Ever see the team picture taken after we won the championship in 1966? The *World-Herald* published it. The majority of the players and me have our arms draped around one another. This picture reveals camaraderie. We were tight.

After we won the Nebraska baseball championship, we defeated Council Bluffs Thomas Jefferson High School [which had won the Iowa high school baseball championship] in a game played at Rosenblatt. With Rodger Ulmar pitching, we topped off our championship season with one more victory. This made us champs in two states.

The following year a future Heisman Trophy winner, Johnny Rodgers, played on my Tech baseball team as a sophomore. Most people don't know it, but Johnny was a great baseball player. Fast. Quick. Good base stealer, but not as good as Griego. Johnny's first 10 steps were dynamite. Johnny was a switch hitter. First game he played for me he was 15 years old. We played Central High School at Central's home park which was Kellom Field. Johnny hit a double left-handed and an inside-the-park home run right-handed. There was no outfield fence at Kellom, so once the ball got by the outfielders there was no chance to stop Johnny from rounding the bases. Today—all these years later—I remain close friends with Johnny Rodgers and many of my other ballplayers.

In retrospect, I attribute my ballplayers' respect for me to the wonderful respect I received as a teacher from all the students at Omaha Tech. My black students and black ballplayers, in particular, knew I had their backs. After I retired from teaching, I had many black students from Tech tell me how much they appreciated the things I'd done. One black student said, "I still remember what I learned from you 50 years ago. It was so nice of you to do something no other teacher ever did for me—teach me my own history."

# 11

# James Redden

I first met James Redden on June 24, 2014, at the W. Dale Clark (Main) Library of the Omaha Public Library (OPL) system. I had just finished giving a presentation on several Omaha black baseball teams for a miniseries on African American baseball history that I had organized for Joanne Ferguson Cavanaugh, the director of the Washington Branch of the OPL system, and had opened the floor for questions. After several attendees had spoken, James raised his hand and asked me if I had ever seen any Negro League games. I told him that I hadn't. All my information came from talking with former Negro League players such as Buck O'Neil, Art Pennington, and Ernest "Schoolboy" Johnson; reading countless newspaper articles and the works of the great Negro League historians: Phil Dixon, John Holway, Robert Peterson, and James Riley, among others; and having conversations with the local black baseball aficionados: Dennis Hoffman, Robert Nash, and David Ogden.

"Well, sir," James replied, "I was a batboy for some of the Negro League teams when they visited Omaha." I responded, "You stick around after the show is over because I want to talk more with you." He did, and we scheduled a date—August 23—for me to interview him over lunch at the Upstream Brewing Company in downtown Omaha. That day, James arrived hungry and with some items that he wanted to show me. Here's his story.

\* \* \*

Twice in my young age—I must have been around 10 years old—I served as a batboy for Negro League teams that came to Omaha Stadium—the future Rosenblatt Stadium. This must have been 1954 or 1955. One time it was for the Kansas City Monarchs and I can't remember who the other team was or, for that matter, who those teams played. I was just awed to be there. What I do remember is that my grandfather took my grandmother, my mother, and me to watch the games. You see, when the Negro League teams came to town, all of North Omaha would dress up and go to the games.

Well, we were sitting in Row One at the ballpark and I got asked to be the batboy. That's all had to do—get the bats. Nobody had me getting them ham sandwiches or anything else—just bats. And after the game, the players took me into the dugout and gave me bats and balls.

Now I have some things for you to look at. Here's an authentic Jackie Robinson card that my mother got for me when I was four years old. And here's a 1924 Negro League World Series program. [We looked at photographs of the Kansas City Monarch club that won that World Series, including those of J.L. Wilkinson, Frank Duncan, José Méndez, and Bullet Joe Rogan, and I pointed out Newt Allen's image to James and told him that Allen had played for the Omaha Federals in 1922, tying his program back to the River

City.] Now here is a book with pictures of some of the Negro League greats: John Donaldson, Judy Johnson, John Henry Lloyd, Double Duty Radcliffe, and Buck O'Neil. And look at the size of O'Neil's glove—how small it was. We had small gloves when I played in the 1950s. They told us to put our gloves in a jar to soften them up. Or you could put water and a ball in the pocket of the glove and tie the glove up and that would soften it.

I also went to watch the Omaha Cardinals when they played at Omaha Stadium. Troy Richardson, a mighty fine semipro pitcher who played for the mostly black Omaha Eagles, lived down the street from me and would provide tickets. We used to walk to the park, or if we had the money, we would take the trolley, but we still had to walk to the trolley.

You see, I reside in the same house that I grew up in. It's about two blocks from the YMCA that Jackie Robinson visited in 1946. And I remember with fondness those days. That's when North Omaha was a self-sufficient community. From Cuming to Ames and from 16th to 33rd streets. We had three or four bakeries and seven drugstores. We also had our own YMCA—the Near North YMCA that Jackie Robinson had visited. Now, that was the time of segregation, so we were permitted to go swimming at the main YMCA on Farnam Street for only a few hours on Saturday mornings, but then we'd go back to our YMCA for other activities.

And we were a close-knit community. Everyone knew everyone else. So, if you got into trouble, someone would whup your ass, and then they would call your mother and you'd get your ass kicked again. There were white families living in our neighborhood, too—they lived on the corner. And that's when the Old Market was a real market. My grandmother and grandfather went there every Saturday morning.

We had fun when we were kids. There were about 30 of us—blacks and whites—who lived between Lake and Locust streets and we all played together. Sometimes, we played cowboys and Indians and slept out in each other's yards, using a rope and a blanket for a tent. Other times, we would gather in a vacant lot—girls, too—and play hide and go get it. And, of course, we played sports, which leads me to talking about two of the Gibson brothers: Josh and Bob.

I began playing baseball for real at the Y under John Butler in 1958. Josh was at the Y with Butler, and he ran the Y's baseball team. He was a no-nonsense person and a good teacher of fundamentals for both baseball and basketball. Now, basketball was the bomb at the Y, and Josh had the number one team, called the Travelers. They were very tough and they barnstormed.

I first encountered Bob when he was playing for Creighton. Bob would come down to the Y to stay in shape, so I got a chance to play against him. He was very competitive. Bob's wife would sit in the balcony at the Y and watch him play basketball.

And when it came to baseball, Bobby G. could play the whole game. I hate the designated hitter [DH] and I can't stand baseball games that go for three or more hours. But you didn't need a DH with Bobby G. He could do it all: pitch, field, and bat. And he didn't mess around when he pitched, so no game went three hours when he was on the mound.

Of course, today you have all the TV commercials and the instant replay that add a lot of time. Now, I refereed for 47 years—both football and basketball and every level of play below the NFL and the NBA—and I was told to call deadball timeouts, some that lasted for five minutes. The only reason for that was for the money. People are so damn greedy.

And I don't care for instant replay. Ain't nobody perfect except God. Now, it's OK to call over the other refs and ask them for help on a close play. What did you see? What did you see? That's just part of the game. You're always going to make someone happy and someone mad. As a referee, I focused on the game; if there were any comments, I didn't hear them. But the kids aren't the problem. The kids just want to play, and they won't play if the refs say so. The problem is the parents. The parents are bad—and the worst are the football parents.

Now, I was fortunate to have some great mentors when I was growing up. See, I didn't have any man around the house because my grandfather worked all the time. But I received my mentoring outside of the house by John Butler, Josh Gibson, Jon McWilliams, and my brother-in-law Charlie Bryant, who was the greatest man in my life, the man who had the greatest influence on me [an African American pioneer, Bryant was a successful teacher, administrator, coach, poet, and artist]. You see, in 1953,

A football and basketball referee for 47 years, James Redden twice served as a batboy for Negro League teams (personal collection of James Redden).

McWilliams and Bryant were the first blacks since 1913 to letter in football for the University of Nebraska–Lincoln [UNL prohibited blacks from athletic competition from 1917 until the late 1940s] and they both played in the 1955 Orange Bowl game. And McWilliams, who was an administrator for the Boys Club at that time, asked me to be a volunteer assistant football coach for the club. I accepted his invitation because I wanted to give back to the Omaha community what I had received. So, I got involved and ended up working for the Boys Club for approximately 10 years—and I even got to coach Johnny Rodgers! [Laughs by both of us]

After one year of being a volunteer assistant football coach, I became the assistant social director for the Boys Club, which led to me coaching Karl Webb, a city champion in track [Webb would go on to help lead Omaha North High School to a share of the 1970 Nebraska Class A boys track and field championship]. He became the fastest man in junior college in 1971 [the 1971 national junior college champion in the 220 when he was at North Platte Junior College, Webb was a member of the 1973 UNL winning mile relay team that contributed to the Cornhuskers' capturing of the Big Eight indoor track championship that year]. And I got to coach Charlie McWhorter, an outstanding running back who became a first team All-America for UNO [the University of Nebraska Omaha] in 1972 and set various football records for the school. We were bad. The Boys Club back in the '60s, we were tough. Man, that was the best job I ever had!

Kids need positive role models. But don't get me wrong—we didn't have gang problems then [the 1960s]. The gangs came later from California—they were imported—but the kids need direction.

Getting back to baseball, I didn't start off playing softball. When it comes to ball-and-bat games, all I ever played was baseball, which wasn't my best sport. Before I started playing for John Butler and Josh Gibson, there were about 25 of us boys and we had our own team. Of course, this was in the 1950s—after Jackie Robinson first visited North Omaha, and everybody wanted to be Jackie Robinson. And there were African American players from Omaha who probably could have made the majors, but they didn't get the opportunity. For example, there was Floyd Crandall. I called him "Cranman." He was a great shortstop, who I think played until he was about 50.

[I then asked James if he had heard of Jerry Bartee and his response caused me to laugh.]

Hell yeah. I knew the Bartee family before Jerry was born. We went to the same church. And I still see Jerry's cousin, Carmen. Yeah, Jerry not only played minor league ball, but he coached baseball for Creighton. I went to see him coach once when Creighton played Wichita State.

As for me, I didn't personally experience any prejudice in Omaha. However, after I graduated from Omaha Tech [Omaha's Technical High School], I went to Peru State. And that's when I first ran into prejudice. There's prejudice in southern Nebraska. When I was there, I wouldn't go any further than Auburn to see a doctor.

But looking back on it, I had a good life—the ups and the downs.

# 12

# Al Gilmore

Racism runs deep. To deal with it can seem like an insurmountable task. Al Gilmore's experiences inside and outside baseball have taught him a thing or two about how to overcome institutional racism and how to handle prejudiced individuals. Now in his second year of retirement, Gilmore sat down with me for a cup of coffee. Big, strong Al looks like he could still belt a ball out of Rosenblatt Stadium or shut down the Kansas City Monarchs for a few innings. Although his hair has grayed, this businessman's mind remains razor sharp.

Back in Gilmore's day, racial discrimination was par for the course in baseball in Omaha. But for racial discrimination, Gilmore might have played in the majors and some of his teammates on the Omaha Eagles, most notably Sherman Walker and Floyd Crandall, might have joined him. Gilmore would never make such a claim because he's too modest to ever brag about himself or his friends.

From watching and listening to Gilmore tell stories about his triumphs and trials in baseball and business, it's easy to get the false impression that his life has been smooth sailing. His manner is easygoing. His demeanor is calm and relaxed. His voice is velvety smooth, like a radio announcer's. Gilmore exudes the professionalism of a top-drawer businessman. Smiles come easily to his face. A classy guy, he carries himself with dignity. He's one of those people who seems to possess a tremendous amount of self-control, so much so that it's hard to imagine him in a situation where he's not in control.

But what Gilmore couldn't control and what he had to contend with in his prime as a ballplayer and a businessman were two kinds of white racism. One kind Gilmore confronted—institutional racism—consists of a set of deeply held stereotypes and practices woven into the fabric of American institutions. Institutional racism threw him a curve. Luckily, though, Gilmore has always feasted on curveballs. The other type Gilmore faced was everyday racism or individual prejudice. Although Gilmore couldn't control situations where his white teammates uttered racist remarks or behaved in racist ways, he found constructive ways to cope with racist people. In the end, Gilmore triumphed over ignorance and racism.

\* \* \*

My introduction to baseball came through playing softball at recess at Pleasant Hill Grade School. It was located at 27th and Chandler Road in an area today that is considered Bellevue. I went there through the eighth grade. Anyway, I was one of the best hitters in softball and really liked it. People showered me with attention because of my softball playing ability, leading me to want to play Little League baseball.

Gerry Kleinsmith, who I think used to play professional baseball, contacted my brother Gary, my cousin Chauncey, and me about playing for his Little League team. Gerry used to pick up the three of us in South Omaha and drive us to a Little League field near 24th and Poppleton for practices and games. The field was located in an area called Sunken Gardens. We were all good players. We learned a lot from Gerry. I was a right-handed pitcher and I also played the outfield. Back then, the *Omaha World-Herald* printed write-ups about Little League games. I remember one time I struck out a bunch of hitters in a game and it was reported in the paper.

From my father, I gained a solid work ethic that paid off in baseball and business. For 30 years, Dad worked in the packing houses in South Omaha. He worked in beef kill, slaughtering cows. My brothers, sisters, and I got a good work ethic from him. There were times in Sarpy County, when our car was broke down, that Dad would walk to work. He never missed a day of work.

From my mother, I got love, affection, and direction. My mom did day work in people's homes and hotels. You know, she did what you'd call at the time "odds and ends work for ladies." Spent a lot of time raising us. My mother was the one who insisted that my brothers, sisters, and I go to Central High School. Although it upset our friends who went to South High, it ended up best for us. At the time, Central was one of the top-rated high schools in academics in the country. My success in life is rooted in the good education I got at Central.

Jim Karabatsos, who later became an English professor at Creighton University, was my baseball coach. [Coincidentally, Karabatsos coached against John Morse when Morse was coaching Omaha's Technical High School. He played college baseball at Creighton University and then minor league baseball.] I could hit pretty good. In fact, I started in right field for the varsity about half the games in my freshman year at Central. Since I had a good arm, coaches put me in right. My brother Gary was a year behind me. I loved playing baseball with my brother. He was an outstanding player and a great teammate. There were times at Central when Gary would be in center and I'd be right.

An old Central classmate called me the other day to tell me about a website where you can look at Central's archives, and I dug up some of the old write-ups about my ball playing. They have the yearbooks. So I clicked on 1959, the year I graduated. And I found articles from the Central High Register in the spring of 1959. One game, I drove in the tying run in the seventh and then drove in the winning run in the ninth. From my sophomore year through my senior year, I started every baseball game for the Central High varsity.

I got a fair shot to play baseball at Central—which is more than I got later on at the University of Omaha [currently the University of Nebraska Omaha]. In terms of race relations, our teams at Central were mixed while teams from Omaha's other high schools were mainly white. Our teams performed at a high level, winning championships. Other black ballplayers who played on Central baseball teams with me include Charlie Dickerson, the quarterback of Central's football team; Jim Hall; and Art Reynolds, a pitcher who could throw both right- and left-handed. Later, Gary played for Central.

I'd like to say that my parents watched me play at Central, but they weren't at the games. My mom was too busy working to attend any of my games. My father, who happened to be an alcoholic, only went to one—a high school game at Brown Park. Because of all the attention I was receiving from the newspapers, I wanted Dad to see me. I was playing right field against South High. My father was trying to talk to me during the game. I was trying to ignore him. He got angry and loud, embarrassing me. I never asked him to come to another game.

During the regular high school baseball season, I didn't pitch for Central. Summers were a different story. In the summertime, I'd play for both Budweisers [the Central Legion team] and Josh Gibson's Y team. I pitched for Josh. Josh used to drive all the way to South Omaha to pick up my brother Gary and me to take us to games and practices. Josh was really heavy. I remember Josh used to have an old catcher's mitt in the equipment bag. It was too old to use, but it was the catcher's mitt they used when Bob Gibson played for Josh's team. It was paper-thin. Like a handkerchief. Looked like Bob's fastball had beaten the heck out of it.

I really liked Josh and I loved playing for him, but here again, transportation was an issue. My family was poor—very poor. Gary and I didn't have any way to get to ballgames. So Josh picked us up. Josh used to take us on road trips. We'd play these little towns in Iowa. We even played a game in Guthrie, Nebraska, which is out near the Panhandle. Mondamin, Treynor, West Point. All these little towns had teams and we played them. I pitched a lot for Josh. Fans would drive their cars right up along the baselines and park. Then, they'd sit in their cars to watch us play. This scene reminded me of a drive-in theater where you sit in your car and watch the movie.

Josh's teams were good. We won most games. How good? Well, one time I pitched for Josh against the Kansas City Monarchs at Rosenblatt. Roger Sayers was playing center field for us. We beat the Monarchs, 3–2. Mind you, this was not Satchel Paige's Kansas City Monarchs that once dominated the old Negro Leagues. Those were major league–caliber players. When I pitched against the Monarchs, it was 1957. By then, Jackie Robinson had broken the color line and major league teams had cherry-picked many of the best Negro Leaguers from the Monarchs and other Negro League teams. The team I beat was not "the real Kansas City Monarchs." On the other hand, I was a kid then and the Monarchs were men. Gary played left field that game. The Monarchs team we played that night was our speed. I mean they were comparable talent-wise to an average college baseball team of the 1950s. Back then, there was no such thing as middle relief, closers, and that sort of thing—the pitcher just pitched. Naturally, I went the distance against the Monarchs.

My dad got me an old Chevy my sophomore year so I could drive to Central. On my way home, I'd drive past the home of South High School varsity baseball coach Cornie Collin. After Central beat South a game or two, Cornie stopped me when I was driving by. He asked me how come I didn't go to South.

South Omaha was incredibly racist in the early 1950s. I used to walk from our house in Sarpy County to Omaha Stadium—whose name was later changed to Rosenblatt Stadium—so I could collect baseballs hit out of the park. That's how we got our balls to play sandlot ball. We'd stand outside the stadium for the first seven innings. We'd shag balls. Foul balls. Home runs. I can remember my brother and I had to fight our way through Brown Park in South Omaha just to get to the stadium. White kids would pick fights with us. After we'd whup 'em a few times, they'd leave us alone. I also recall Joe Tess' restaurant in South Omaha sold takeout fish to blacks but refused to allow blacks to dine in. Then, too, I'd be walking down the streets of South Omaha and people would call me all kinds of racial names. Racism was out in the open in South Omaha.

My promising baseball career hit a roadblock when I transitioned from high school to college baseball. The first indicator of stormy weather came when my Central High School baseball coach never encouraged me to go to college, never encouraged me to continue playing baseball. He made no effort to hook me up with a college baseball program. Everything was on me. My family, my dad—they didn't know anything about how to get a college baseball scholarship. It was a racial thing. Since I was black, the white coach didn't figure I could succeed in college. In all fairness, my grades in high school were average. In my high school classes, I did enough to get by. I was a C+ to a B student. So I personally made an appointment to meet with the University of Omaha's (OU's) head baseball coach, Virg Yelkin, and went to the campus to see if I could get a scholarship.

Yelkin listened and offered to pay for my books. Back then, paying for books wasn't that much money, but I accepted. Yelkin's "books only" offer was another bad sign. Since I'd outperformed some of the Omaha high school players Yelkin had given full-ride scholarships to, I felt Yelkin had treated me unfairly. Fact is, my senior year at Central I had hit .360. So before I even stepped onto the baseball field, I hit racial barriers at OU.

Up to this point, I'd been accustomed to baseball coaches recognizing and appreciating my skills and how hard I played. I was always one of the top two or three players, and coaches would call on me to hit or to demonstrate a skill. Whereas Josh and my other coaches had always made me feel special, I felt excluded at OU.

I became a first at OU—the first African American ballplayer to play there. Coach Yelkin was nice to me on the surface, but he made me a bench warmer. Assistant coach Don Clawson used to ask Yelkin to make me a regular. But I got to play only a few innings and had only five or six at bats my entire freshman season. Worse, my OU teammates, who were all white, ostracized me. The players made fun of me, directed racial slurs at me, and insulted me by talking in a real deep Southern accent to mimic the way blacks supposedly talk. My teammates did everything they could to make me feel uncomfortable. I never had a chance. Years later, George Casper, OU's white catcher from South High, apologized to me for the team's racist behavior.

While my memories of riding the bench at OU are unpleasant, I fondly recall getting inserted as a sub into a game for defensive purposes in an NAIA baseball tournament. I remember this particular game because OU was playing against Lou Brock and his Southern University team. Maybe the OU coaches thought sticking me in the outfield for defensive purposes would shut down the speedy Brock. I was good but not that good.

Even though OU Coach Yelkin thought I wasn't good enough to get playing time for OU, the Los Angeles Dodgers offered me a contract to play Class D professional baseball. The Dodgers had scouted me when I was a senior at Central High School, so they knew how good I was. At that time, Omaha's minor league team

Al Gilmore in 1993. A number of years earlier, Gilmore made history by becoming the first black person to play baseball for the University of Omaha (personal collection of Al Gilmore).

was the Omaha Dodgers. Actually, after I received this offer to turn pro, one of Omaha's Triple A players invited me to Rosenblatt to work out with the Omaha Dodgers. The workout was held prior to a game in which the Dodgers played Dallas–Ft. Worth.

I'll never forget what happened during that tryout while I was shagging fly balls. The Dallas–Ft. Worth guys were also in the outfield, and someone hit me from behind. It felt like I'd been blindsided in a football game. That player that hit me was Jim Fregosi. He was playing for Dallas–Ft. Worth. We talked a little bit. Fregosi went on to star in the majors with the American League. When I got a chance to hit, I jacked a curveball out in right-center field. It traveled 370 feet.

I could hit curveballs because my Little League coach Gerry Kleinsmith taught me how to do it. Gerry taught us to hit the ball where it was pitched. I always thought in terms of a right-handed hitter because that's what I was. If the pitch was outside, hit to right. If it's inside, pull it to left. If the pitch is down the middle of the plate, hit the pitch somewhere between left-center and right-center.

Following the workout, I asked the manager of the Omaha Dodgers what he thought my chances were of playing in the majors. He promised to check back with me after my next season at OU, but there never was a next season because I quit. What happened, though, was that the Dodgers remembered "Gilmore" and they tracked Gary. Gary followed me to OU. By the time he arrived there, the times were changing. Gary wound up starting on the OU baseball team. Omaha U also brought in another black player, Lew Garrison.

Ironically, the most satisfying game I ever pitched was against OU. I was playing summer ball in, I think, 1961 with the Omaha Eagles. We were pitted against a summer team consisting mainly of players from OU's baseball team. Warming up for the game at Brown Park, I wanted to get 'em. I could taste revenge. See I was a finesse pitcher, not a power pitcher. Fastball was just average. Good curveball. Changeup. Slow curve. Side-arm curve. Sinker.

I can remember OU had some good hitters. George Casper was one of 'em. My changeup had OU's hitters lunging. My sinker had them beating balls into the ground. After I started mowing down OU's hitters, their players yelled at me, "Stop throwing that junk up there!"

I beat 'em, 3–2. After the game, none of the OU players shook my hand.

Looking back, it would have made sense for me to join my brother Gary and play for the Omaha Blackhawks. I regret never playing softball for the Blackhawks. If I had it to do over again, I would. Back then, I saw playing softball as a step down. But they had some good ball clubs. Our catcher from the Eagles, Sherman Walker, played. He was a good hitter, excellent receiver, and showed good knowledge of the game.

I left baseball only to return for the sake of my sons when they were little bitty guys. I wanted to teach them to love baseball, so I became their coach in Country Club Little League. I made some good ballplayers. I had learned some tricks from Gerry Kleinsmith. I took an old bat that had been broken, cut a hole in the handle. Drilled a hole through it. Tied a rope to the bat. Drilled a hole through a baseball. Put the baseball on the rope. Spun the ball through the strike zone. Let the hitters hit the ball. That's how I made good hitters. Then, for pitching, I had two broomsticks. I tied a string across the top of the strike zone. Tied a string across the knees, and then put the two pieces of string 17 inches apart. Put a catcher behind the plate and then had my pitchers throw. The pitchers aimed inside the square. That's how I developed control pitchers.

I started out trying to make ballplayers out of my two sons and wound up making ballplayers out of two other kids. One of 'em was one of Jerry Bartee's sons, Kimera. Kimera could outrun everybody. He also hit towering fly balls. I told Kimera's parents if they worked with him, he could become a pro baseball player. Actually, two of my little league players, Kimera and Tim Decker, played on that Creighton University baseball team that went to the College World Series in 1991. Decker was a starter for CU during his junior and senior years.

One life lesson I learned from baseball is to be a team player. In baseball it's about "us," not about "you." When I got to the business world, I followed this principle. I started out at Blue Cross Blue Shield as a sales trainee in 1968. Ran into discrimination. The Blue Cross routine was to hire someone, train him or her for two weeks, and assign him or her a territory to work. But Blue Cross kept me as a trainee for six months. Apparently, I wasn't as good as the white trainees. They thought I needed "extra."

Well, the bosses didn't know what a big favor they were doing me. As a trainee, I made it a point to go out with as many different salesmen as possible. During that bonus six-month period, I learned how to get along and collaborate with a diverse bunch of people. When they finally gave me my own territory, I became the top producer. Earning a series of promotions led me to become Senior Vice President of Sales and Marketing for Blue Cross Blue Shield. After 31 years with Blue Cross, I retired early at 59. These days I like to spend time hunting and fishing with my brother Gary.

One of the most important things you learn as a black person in America is that racism exists, and if you are going to be successful in life, you must learn to accept this fact. Once you learn that reality, you must learn how to deal with it. You must accept the fact that you must do much better than your white competition in both the corporate world and in athletics. During my Little League days in South Omaha, there were restaurants where black people could purchase food on only a carryout basis. Seeing this discrimination as a black child, you learn quickly that things are much different for you than for whites.

On the streets, you fight. When my brother Gary and I were involved in fist fights while walking home from Rosenblatt, it was self-defense. In those days it was common for us to be called the "N-word" and to be physically confronted by white kids in certain South Omaha neighborhoods.

In the corporate world, you finesse. You study the rules of the game and leverage the rules to your advantage. By excelling in sales, I took control of my destiny. I learned to ignore many racial insults and get along with everyone on the job. I also learned that being a top sales producer made me lots of friends in the company. In the racialized environment of Blue Cross, I learned that making money for the company set me apart from others. In the role of a top producer, I became accepted by my white bosses and colleagues as one of those [black] people who was all right. As evidence of my acceptance, I became the first black Senior Vice President of Marketing in the Blue Cross Blue Shield system in the United States.

# 13

# Jerry Bartee

Ever since eight-year-old Jerry Bartee served as batboy for the mostly black Omaha Eagles baseball team almost 60 years ago, he has been at the center of Omaha's black baseball universe. One of Bartee's baseball mentors was Josh Gibson. After playing for Josh's Y team, the slick-fielding Bartee starred at shortstop for Omaha's Central High School from 1964 through 1966. Drafted by the St. Louis Cardinals in the latter year, the 6'2" 180-pound Bartee switched positions and became a center fielder. For seven years, Bartee bounced around the minors, languishing in the shadow of Curt Flood, one of the greatest defensive center fielders of all time. So, unlike Moonlight Graham in *Shoeless Joe,* Bartee never got a cup of coffee in the majors.

When Bartee returned to Omaha, he parlayed relationships formed while he played for an all-black slow pitch softball team called the Blackhawks into a successful career as an educator. His accomplishments include earning his bachelor's, master's, and doctorate in education; being the head baseball coach at Creighton University from 1978 through 1980; teaching at Nathan Hale Middle School; holding the positions of assistant principal and principal at South High School; and serving as assistant superintendent for business services for Omaha Public Schools (OPS). In his role as assistant superintendent, he oversaw a city-wide initiative aimed at reducing truancy and recovering lost youths. Recognized by his colleagues for his leadership and compassion, Bartee is known as a person who believes that every child should be valued and should have the right to a quality education.

I caught up with Bartee during his second year of retirement from OPS. Since retiring, Bartee has had four surgeries. As we ate breakfast together in a small café, he joked half-heartedly that his body is "breaking down." He shrugged off the physical challenges of aging, discounting his surgeries as something that "comes with age." Seeing such a once powerful and gifted athlete as Bartee struggling to stave off the ravages of old age reminded me of these verses from the poet Dylan Thomas: "Do not go gentle into that good night…. Rage, rage against the dying of the light."

\* \* \*

If my Uncle Dunk were alive, he wouldn't be surprised by my success. Howard S. Duncan was my mother's older brother. He once played for a semipro Negro team in Springfield, Missouri, called the Hyde Park Stars. Springfield is where I was born in 1948. Uncle Dunk's own coach on that team was Carl Thompson—the man who I would later in life discover was my biological father. Uncle Dunk and my mother moved our family to South Omaha near the packing houses in 1951. The Great Migration was in high gear. Black people were moving to Omaha from the South.

Along with six other kids and three adults, I lived in a semitrailer parked in Uncle Dunk's backyard. A few years after we all had been living in Omaha, Uncle Dunk became the "singing catcher" for the Omaha Eagles baseball team. From the time my brother Ron and I could walk, Uncle Dunk introduced us to Negro baseball. Uncle Dunk was our father figure. He was a strong male role model. He taught me to walk away from trouble and passed on a positive, can-do attitude.

During the 1950s and 1960s, Uncle Dunk was the guiding light for my brother and me. He taught us common sense, respect, and manners. He also stressed that beauty is on the inside, not the outside. He was at every one of my baseball games in Omaha. He was always in a good mood. I never heard him cuss. He was always helping someone. Not a hands-on parent, Uncle Dunk let me enjoy baseball.

As I said, Uncle Dunk attended every one of my baseball games, and his singing made me aware of his presence. When I was warming up to play a ballgame, I could hear him. Several blocks away from the ball field, he'd be singing "Hey, hey, hey." From my Uncle Dunk, I learned to always give it my all and to have fun playing baseball. He never pressured me. If you're playing baseball and you're not having fun, you're disrespecting the game. But from a technical standpoint, Uncle Dunk didn't know the game. It took Josh Gibson to refine me as a ballplayer.

My Uncle Dunk died at age 64—before he could even draw his first Social Security check. I'm 67 now. He worked 25 years in the hide cellar at Wilson's Packing House in Omaha. The hide cellar was the place where hides were graded, trimmed, salted, and cured. If you've never been in a hide cellar, you can't imagine what it's like. The workers in the hide cellar would take hides off cattle—hides that were wet, heavy, and smelly. They would spread those hides out in the cellar and shovel rocks and salt onto them. The atmosphere in a hide cellar was damp, moist, and moldy. Workers would breathe in the air, their lungs would get clogged up, and they would become susceptible to pneumonia. That's what happened to Uncle Dunk.

Uncle Dunk had a peculiar way of driving home the importance of getting a good education. On Saturdays, he took Ron and me to work in the hide cellar. After making Ron and me use knives to trim hides, he'd ask us, "Wanna to do this for the rest of your lives?" Just thinking of the hide cellar makes my hands hurt.

Believe it or not, softball played a key role in my baseball career and in my career as an educator. As a 10-year-old kid, I played third base for Rodney Wead's church youth softball team in an all-black church league. Seven or eight churches were in the league. We played at Kountze Park. It's a public park located near 19th and Pinkney in the Kountze Place neighborhood of North Omaha.

Rodney was a disciple of Josh Gibson. He'd played first base on one of Josh's Near North Side Y teams. You know Rodney is 6'6". He grew up with Bob Gibson in the Logan Fontenelle Housing Project. The project was a public housing site that used to be located from 20th to 24th Streets, and from Paul to Seward Streets in the Near North Side neighborhood. During the 1970s and 1980s, Logan Fontenelle was called "Little Vietnam" because of drug dealing and gang violence. The feds tore down the project in 1995 to replace it with new, low-density housing.

One thing I remember about being on Rodney's softball team was how passionately I felt about softball. After every loss, I would cry. I never could understand how I could play my hardest and yet we could still lose.

When I was in seventh grade in 1960, Josh Gibson became my first real coach. Josh worked at the Near North Side Branch of the YMCA, not to be confused with the North Branch Y which is now Miller Park. I knew of Josh through Rodney Wead who used to talk about Josh. Josh had a reputation in North Omaha for being a solid guy. If you played for Josh, you knew you were going to go places in life.

Josh was a heavyset, unassuming guy. Nothing charismatic or flashy about him. He spoke in a deep voice. With Josh, it was all about respect and caring. He truly cared about each of his players. Parents could see he cared about their sons and they loved him. Josh never cut players. Josh and his ballplayers were like family. Many of us didn't have fathers, so he served as a father figure. We were close. He taught us the importance of teamwork. Josh taught me team building and leadership skills that served me well later in life as an educator. The message Josh communicated was simple: If you're fundamentally sound and play with a big heart, then you're a winner.

Josh commanded respect. When Josh spoke, his players listened. He didn't tolerate nonsense. No talking. No jacking around. He demanded that you play hard all the time. He stressed fundamentals. A real perfectionist. He taught us the right way to play baseball. If you played for Josh, you played different positions. Josh didn't believe in pigeon-holing his players and sticking them in one position. Instead, he fielded a team of utility players.

From seventh grade on, all I wanted to do was play baseball. I got my start in the Near North Branch Y Baseball League. Josh ran the league. There were eight mostly black teams from various neighborhoods in North Omaha and we played at Burdette Field in North Omaha. One white kid played on Josh's team with me—Dave Garland. He became a principal at a Catholic school in Omaha. Teams wore Storz [beer] T-shirts and hats. By cherry-picking the best players from the neighborhood teams, Josh put together a seventh, eighth, and ninth grade all-star team. I played shortstop, second base, third base, and outfield for Josh's all-stars.

Josh's all-star team was a traveling team but not like today's select teams. At the time, we were the only "select" or traveling team in Omaha. This was before the Gladiators. We played other Little League teams from Omaha as well as teams from small towns in Iowa. Playing for Josh was fun and free. To cover the costs of equipment and travel, Josh got donations and lined up sponsors. For transportation, Josh and his brother, Freddie, drove cars.

I got to Central in the fall of 1963, graduated in the spring of 1966, and played baseball from 1964 through 1966. After my sophomore year at Central, I wanted to go back to play summer baseball for Josh so I could have fun. But the Central High baseball coach issued an ultimatum: Play for Central High's Budweiser Legion team in the summer or forget about playing baseball for Central High's varsity next spring. Josh understood. He knew it was time for me to move on.

As a star athlete at Central, I was privileged. I was more accepted by whites than other blacks who were not athletes. I was the only black player to start for Central's baseball team during the '64, '65, and '66 seasons. From time to time, I still see some of my white classmates. I might attend my 50th reunion this year. I've played golf with several of my white classmates, and they ask, "Why don't our black classmates from Central come to reunions?"

My response is always the same: "Because you don't make the reunions relevant to us. You hold them way out west in the suburbs at 190th and Dodge."

My social reality was different from the reality of my white classmates in the 1960s. I knew the "Rhythm Boys" of Omaha Central. Those hotshot basketball players were sophomores when I was a senior. During the historic 1968 basketball season when the Central High School basketball team made history with its first all-black starting lineup, I was playing baseball down South. Still, I heard about the Rhythm Boys because they were in my sister's class. I also heard about segregationist George Wallace making a campaign stop in Omaha in his third-party presidential bid and igniting a race riot in the city.

Both Cope Jones of the St. Louis Cardinals and Buck O'Neil of the Chicago Cubs scouted me at Central, attending my games and practices at Kellom Field. The field was located on the grounds of Kellom Elementary School. Baseball scouts in those days, you know, you could always pick them out. There were no radar guns then, but at my Central games, there weren't many spectators in the stands at Kellom—and I personally knew all the fans—so Cope Jones and Buck stood out sitting in the stands.

I was only 17 years old and I could turn pro or go to college. I was expecting Virg Yelkin, the University of Omaha's baseball coach, to talk to me about playing baseball at his school [the current University of Nebraska Omaha]. But he never showed up. Instead, he sent the school's wrestling coach, Don Benning, to recruit me. Since I had doubts about how welcoming Yelkin was to black ballplayers, I asked Benning: "Are you sure Omaha U is the place for me?" Benning assured me that there would be no problems. Unconvinced, I hoped to sign with the Cardinals.

After graduating from Central in June 1966, I didn't go out partying with my friends because I was expecting to hear from the Cardinals. The next morning my mom had to go out of town, and I got a call from Cope Jones.

"I want to talk to you and your mother," Cope said.

When I told him my mother was gone, he informed me that there had to be an adult present for him to make an offer. My cousin Rodney Wead was like a big brother to me, so Rodney came over to my house at two o'clock that afternoon. Rodney, Cope, and I talked. Then, Cope got on the phone and didn't say who he was talking to. That was part of the sales pitch. You know, like used car salesmen who get on the phone when you're trying to buy a car from them. Once Cope got off the phone, he offered me $5,000.

"Oh, no, no, no," Rodney moaned.

I'm thinking to myself, "Hell, man, that's more money than I've ever heard of in my life."

I signed for $10,000.

After I signed with the St. Louis Cardinals in 1966, I bought my brother Ron his first new glove. When Ron and I started playing ball together as little kids, our first gloves were raggy, hand-me-downs from two or three previous generations. But, hey, they were baseball gloves. That's all we cared about. So when I signed, Ron and I went to Russell Sporting Goods in downtown Omaha. I did it because I was financially able to do it, because both of us had always wanted new gloves, and because my mother couldn't afford to buy my brother a new glove. Actually, I bought things for every member of my family. I bought my mom an automatic washer and dryer, and I bought luggage for my sister.

My signing happened so fast it made my head spin. I got drafted on Tuesday, signed on Saturday, and on Sunday I was flying on a plane for the first time, heading for Sarasota, Florida. Away from home for the first time. Just a kid. Nobody took me under their wing. I found myself playing baseball with lots of Spanish-speaking ballplayers at the ballpark in Sarasota eight hours a day and unable to speak Spanish.

Luckily, Uncle Dunk had prepared me. He taught me to love the game of baseball and schooled me in how to cope with life. Toughest part of playing in that rookie league in Sarasota was homesickness. I missed my high school sweetheart who was back in Omaha. Still, it was an experience I'll never forget. There were ballplayers from six major league teams in that rookie league. We all lived in a big hotel. We practiced all day long and played night games. Practices were boot camps aimed at instilling "the Cardinal way."

As a style of play, the Cardinal way in the mid–1960s emphasized fundamentals. Some call it "old school." George Kissell, the greatest instructor of baseball who ever lived, drilled the Cardinal way into our heads. Kissell's exceptional ability to teach baseball earned him the nickname of "the Professor." From him, I learned how to play all nine positions on a baseball team and how to handle every situation that might come up in a game. Kissell taught me everything I needed to know to one day become a coach myself.

The Cardinals made me switch positions from shortstop to center field because they didn't think I could beat out the Cardinals' starting shortstop, Dal Maxvill. Of course, this threw an even bigger obstacle in my path to the big leagues—the Cardinals' All-Star center fielder, Curt Flood. Even though I never got called up, playing AA professional baseball taught me an important lesson: Never second-guess yourself.

I came back to Omaha jobless and homeless. At that time, Gary Gilmore was running the recreation program at Wesley House. In his leisure time, Gilmore was a player on an all-black slow pitch men's softball team called the Omaha Blackhawks. That team consisted mostly of black Omaha educators who had migrated to Omaha from the South. One day Gilmore and Sam Crawford (the principal of Omaha's Technical Junior High School) asked me if I wanted to play on their softball team.

"Softball?" I said. "I just got out of pro baseball. Get outta here!"

Crawford and I made a deal. In exchange for me playing for the Blackhawks, Sam would rent me a house for a decent price and get me a job as a security guard at Tech Junior High. This meant I'd be working in Omaha's Technical High School building. It also meant I'd be teaming up with Sherman Walker, Gary Gilmore, Floyd Crandall, and others—former members of the Omaha Eagles baseball team. Of course, I already knew these guys because I'd been the Eagles batboy. As a kid, I'd idolized Crandall. He was an infielder, and I was a shortstop coming up, so I patterned my game after his. A bonus of playing for the Blackhawks was those black educators on the team. Guys like Sam Crawford, Jim Freeman from Tuskegee, Tom Harper from Grambling, and Gene Haynes (who is now the principal at North High School). Later, knowing these guys would help me advance my career as an educator.

Anyway, after my first year of playing for the Blackhawks, the players asked me to coach the team. I said, "Well, if you want me to coach, I'm gonna do it the George Kissell way."

I explained that my way would include winter conditioning. The guys were all in. We had a great sponsor, George Thomas Real Estate. Every Sunday in the wintertime, my players and I hit the gym for conditioning and bonding.

During my first season of coaching, the team to beat in slow pitch softball was the Four Seasons Lounge. They had a team of former Creighton University jocks—basketball players. Their team included Tom Apke and Jocko Elkins. Big tall guys. Harold Weinstein was the owner. Our Blackhawk team came out of nowhere and started beating everybody—including the Four Seasons.

I'd get 'em going. We'd win, 2–1, 3–2. There were no fences on Omaha's slow pitch softball fields back then. Taking advantage of these fenceless fields, I preached speed and defense. We were the fastest team in the state. We played with four outfielders. Originally, I was the left-center fielder. Then, I moved to second base next to Crandall at shortstop. It was a kick "turning two" with my childhood hero. On third base, we had Harvey Gilbert. He was our only white ballplayer. At the time, Gilbert served as assistant basketball coach at Tech High under head coach Gene Haynes. Now Gilbert's an educator living in Kansas City.

After my second year of coaching the Blackhawks, Creighton University was starting an NCAA summer camp called the National Youth Sports Program (NYSP). The purpose was to bring minority students onto a college campus and expose them to the possibility that they could get a college education. The plan was to bring 400 minority students from North Omaha to Creighton University for five hours every weekday, but Creighton didn't have any culturally competent staff members to work with these kids. So the school recruited the entire Blackhawk softball team to run NYSP on Creighton's campus. The program featured cultural enrichment, antidrug education, and off-campus field trips. Eventually, I took over as director.

When I was ready to return to my job as security guard at Tech Junior High, Eddie Sutton buttonholed me. Creighton's head basketball coach and athletic director asked me to stay on to direct Creighton University's intramural program. I rejected his offer. Eddie persisted.

"You don't understand," Coach Sutton said. "I'm gonna pay you $500 a month and give you tuition so you can earn your bachelor's degree."

Jerry Bartee in 1979, his second of three seasons as the head baseball coach at Creighton University (Creighton Athletics).

I ain't crazy. I know a good deal when I see one. By going to summer school, I was able to earn a bachelor's in three years. My job with intramurals proved to be a stepping stone to becoming Creighton University's baseball coach.

Coaching college baseball wasn't enough for me, though. I wanted to make a bigger impact. So I applied for and landed a teaching job with OPS. By subbing at different schools every day, I learned the entire school district. Spent six years at Nathan Hale in the classroom. Moved on to become assistant principal and then principal at South High School. Later, became assistant superintendent of OPS. Ironically, I finished my career as assistant superintendent in the Tech High building—the same building where I'd started as a security guard.

Looking back, there are a lot of "what ifs." What if there was no Josh Gibson? Without Josh Gibson, there would be no Jerry Bartee. What if OPS had hired Josh Gibson? The fact that Tech's 1966 championship team was mostly black is, of course, a significant occurrence in black baseball in Omaha. But John Morse coached at an all-black high school [Actually, Technical High School was not an all-black high school. See John Morse's, Ron Bartee's, and Phil Wise's interviews.], so he didn't have a choice—if he wanted to win, he had to start black ballplayers. If Tech High School had hired Josh Gibson instead of John Morse as its head baseball coach, I would have gone to Tech and played for Josh. I never would have attended Central in the first place. If the civil rights movement hadn't happened, OPS might not have hired me as assistant superintendent.

# 14

# Steve Bauermeister

What does it feel like to be in the minority? Steve Bauermeister enjoys the distinction of being one of the few white youths to ever play for one of Josh Gibson's illustrious Near North Side Y teams. Bauermeister's other claim to baseball fame is that he played on Tech's 1966 championship team—a ball club whose starting nine was predominantly black.

When I sat down to interview Steve in a Barnes & Noble cafe, he noted that his parents gave him the middle name of Gordon in honor of Detroit Red Wing and Omaha Knight hockey great Gordy Howe. Despite being pregnant with Steve, his mother never missed a Knights' game at the old Ak-Sar-Ben Coliseum. That was back in 1948–1949 when Howe was playing hockey in Omaha.

Sporting a St. Louis Cardinal jersey, the tall, balding Bauermeister raved about how talented the Omaha Cardinals were and gushed about how much he loved watching Bob Gibson pitch for them at Rosenblatt. When he lectured me on the importance of fundamentals in baseball, I had no doubt that Bauermeister had played for Josh Gibson.

Pointing to his chrome dome, Bauermeister announced that he has no hair because he was a workaholic during his 45-year career in marketing. Now in his sixth year of retirement, he's finally starting to get the hang of relaxing.

"Life is too short," he opined. "I've had two heart attacks due to stress, and I'm getting back into shape by walking. My future goal is to bike with my grandson this summer."

\* \* \*

My mother, father, brother, and I moved to Omaha from Millard around 1957 when I was eight years old. Before that, my father was a foreman for a feedlot operation in Millard. During the early 1950s, I was going to an old one-room schoolhouse. I attended the old Pratt School, a private school that used to be located at 31st and Dodge for two years. Then, I entered Omaha Public Schools. When my family moved into Omaha, we never missed an Omaha Cardinal game at Rosenblatt. We'd sit in the right field bleachers where I would chase down foul balls.

Growing up on Decatur Street near the Logan Fontenelle Housing Project on Parker [near where the Salem Baptist Church stands today], we played ball with the kids in the neighborhood on the old Franklin Elementary playground. We'd play nine-inning wiffle ball games with a plastic bat. We'd reenact our own version of that old TV show *Home Run Derby*.

My favorite player was Bob Gibson. Gibson was number one in the Omaha pitching rotation. Frank Barnes was number two. My second brother was named Don after the Omaha second baseman Don Blasingame. The Cardinals played real baseball. The Pacific

Coast League [which the Omaha Storm Chasers play in today] can't compare to the old American Association.

In the sixth grade, I got my baptism in sports. Our female gym coach at Franklin grade school took five of us kids to Kellom School to compete in a basketball tournament. Kellom was a hub for sports in those days. Our first and only game was played inside in a

From 1961 through 1963, Steve Bauermeister (on the left) was a minority on Josh Gibson's Near North Side YMCA baseball squads: a white player on predominantly black teams (personal collection of Steve Bauermeister).

gymnasium. Kellom's all-black team defeated us, 56–2. They whupped us. You're looking at the guy who scored all of Franklin's points. As a country boy from Millard, I was in awe of the talented big city basketball players at Kellom.

My first baseball coach was Josh Gibson. I played for him during my junior high years, 1961–1963. Josh was like another father to me. My real father worked long hours as a construction worker and, in the winter, drove semis, so I walked from our home at 3127 Decatur to places I needed to go. One of those places was the Near North Side Y located at 22nd and Lake. Josh held tryouts for his baseball team there. Like Kellom School, the Y was a center for excellence in sports. Another white ballplayer, Dave Garland, played on Josh's team with me. Dave Garland, who went on to pitch for Omaha U [the University of Nebraska Omaha today], and I were the only two white kids on Josh's team.

Josh never played favorites, never favored black players over whites. I played the outfield for Josh's team because I had speed. I thought I was fast until one day I was playing on the Tech Junior Varsity football team and I had an opportunity to tackle Johnny Rodgers. I got ready to take him down but he zoomed around me like a jack rabbit. I never even laid a hand on him.

Let me tell you how I felt about Josh. Ohhhh, I just loved that man. He was a father figure to me. Josh Gibson stood about 6'4". He wasn't fat. He knew baseball. One day after watching me hit, he pointed out that I had a hitch in my swing—I was dropping my shoulder. I never heard Josh yell or scream at a player. He would quietly tell you what you were doing wrong and suggest how you could improve. I played for him during my junior high years.

Josh taught me the fundamentals. The basics. Inside knowledge of the game. The proper way to throw, catch, and hit the baseball. Teamwork. Nine players working in unison. Each player thinking one step ahead. Backing up your teammates on defense.

One year I was with Josh's team, we played 20, maybe 30 games. We may have had a losing record, but our games were close. We played our games all over the city. One game was at Carter Lake. I got there late. My dad dropped me off. While I was playing center field, a fly ball was hit to shallow center. The second baseman, shortstop, and I converged. The ball dropped between us. After the game, Coach Josh pulled me off to the side. He put his arm on my shoulder.

"The center fielder is the captain of the outfield," he said softly. "Next time, you call off everyone and catch the ball."

While playing for Josh, I had no fear about being a white kid walking through black neighborhoods in North Omaha. As I walked from my home down to the Near North Side Y, I felt proud. Wearing the baseball uniform of Josh's team made me part of the community. As I walked by, some folks on the street would give me high-fives and others would ask, "Did you win or lose?" The uniform was a typical Legion baseball uniform for AAA midget baseball. The jersey was white with the Legion patch on one of the shoulders and NNY [Near North Y] printed across the front. The hat had NNY on it. One day I was walking away from the Near North Side Y with two other players on Josh's team. They were black. Before each of the other guys broke away to go their respective homes, we gave each other the "brother handshake." That made me feel like we were family.

From 1961–1963, I ran track at Tech Junior High [Technical High School] and discovered how seriously some athletes took sports. I mean "bragging rights serious." While competing in the 440 and the 880, I was running against mostly black kids. Elbows were thrown. Runners jockeyed and pushed for position. That kind of rough and tumble was good for me. I took it in stride.

Playing for Tech High School's varsity baseball team in 1966 was a once-in-a-lifetime opportunity, but you have to put things in context. Keep our age in mind. We were 15- and 16-year-old kids playing a game. What do kids that age do? Well, we weren't civil rights activists. In 1965, while I was riding on the bus with the Omaha Tech junior varsity to play a game in Lincoln, players in the back of the bus were playing poker. On a more serious note, the players knew some of the leaders of the civil rights fight.

Take Mildred Brown [the publisher of Omaha's black-owned newspaper, the *Omaha Star*]. God, I loved that woman. She was like a mother to me. I used to work in a grocery store on North Locust where she used to shop. She'd come in. We'd talk. Some days we'd wind up having lunch together at Charlie Hall's café. Charlie was another icon in North Omaha.

As I kid, it was easy to get caught up in sports and get distracted from academics. I played sports by Dad's Rules. One of his rules was that "It's a privilege to play high school athletics." Dad would get with my high school teachers and check my grades. There was one year my dad put me on academic probation and barred me from playing any sports because I hadn't met his minimum grade point average. Having to sit out a year made that championship season all the more special.

Winning that championship was sweet. Our team was loaded with juniors. I was a junior that year. The keys to our winning were pitching and defense. While other metro teams had one good pitcher, we had two: Rodger Ulmar and Ron Bartee.

Our team captain, Bob Griego, was low-key like Coach Morse. Bob would never argue or scream. He was well respected, well liked. I believe the players voted Griego captain. The Bauermeister and Griego families were like two peas in a pod. You've got to remember our team was a multi-racial, multi-ethnic family. Of the 15 players, 10 were black and five were white.

We got off to a slow start during the regular season, were a dark horse in the districts, and peaked at the right time. During districts, Coach Morse assigned me to coach first base. He picked me because, he said, I was mature for a high school kid. I had it upstairs. But if it hadn't been for Josh Gibson and his assistant coach, Mr. Hill, I never would've made the Tech varsity baseball team in 1966, never would have known enough about baseball for Coach Morse to turn me loose coaching first.

For the state title game with Benson, I coached first and Coach Morse coached third. One time when Phil Wise singled, Coach Morse flashed the steal sign. I relayed it to Phil. Concerned that Phil had missed the sign, I tried to call time out. The ump told me I couldn't do it, so I tried to get the sign to Phil without Benson knowing it. Well, Phil never attempted to steal second. At the end of the inning, I told Phil he'd missed the sign.

Later in that same inning, Benson scored a run. I got on top of the dugout. Even though I was just a substitute player, I wanted to fire up the guys. From my perch, I stared at all of my teammates.

"It ain't over yet," I screamed. "Let's get some runs!"

Toward the end of the sixth inning, Coach Morse asked me to pinch hit. I protested. I told him that I wanted to win just as badly as he did and that I could help the team more as a coach than as a hitter. Afterwards, Ron Bartee and Phil Wise told me that if I hadn't been coaching first, we wouldn't have won. Fifty years later, their kind words still mean a lot to me.

# 15

# Gary Gilmore

The Gary Gilmore story features more than a passing resemblance to *The Natural*, a sports drama starring Robert Redford. In case you are too young to have watched this 1984 film classic, *The Natural* recounts the experiences of a baseball player named Roy Hobbs. The film begins by showing Hobbs as a boy who has baseball skills and who often plays catch with his father. In 1923, a 19-year-old Hobbs is a promising pitcher. He can't miss becoming a major league player. But on the way to a tryout with the Chicago Cubs, Hobbs is seriously injured, putting an apparent end to his promising career.

Like Roy Hobbs, Gary Gilmore was a natural. Whereas Hobbs played catch with his father in the open fields on a Midwestern farm, Gary played catch with his brother Al on the streets of South Omaha. Just as Hobbs could do it all on a baseball diamond, Gary was a five-tool player. This rare breed of baseball player, usually a nonpitcher, has five of the tools pro scouts look for: (1) hitting for power; (2) hitting for average; (3) fielding ability; (4) throwing ability; and (5) speed.

Majoring in general education at the University of Omaha (OU; the future UNO), Gary told everyone he wanted to be either a teacher or a social worker. The truth was Gary wanted to be a professional baseball player. Gary was damn good and he knew it. To hone Gary's gifts, Josh Gibson worked with him. Maybe Josh didn't push Gary as hard as Josh had pushed Bob Gibson—but Josh worked Gary hard. Gary was damn good and Josh knew it. Even OU's head baseball coach Virg Yelkin, who had sat by in silence and done nothing while Gary's teammates ostracized OU's first African American baseball player—Gary's brother Al—had no choice but to start Gary—who became OU's second African American baseball player. Gary was damn good and Yelkin knew it.

Although both Hobbs and Gilmore were injured in freak accidents that could have been avoided if they had exercised better judgment, this is where their paths diverge. Whereas a 35-year-old Hobbs re-emerged as a hard-hitting right fielder, Gilmore never had a second shot at playing big-time baseball. Following the receipt of his bachelor's degree in general, Gary landed a job as a social worker in 1966. But after a couple of years of being employed at that occupation, he was recruited by State Farm to become an insurance agent, a position in which he served the Omaha community for 40 years.

When Gary and I met at the historic Joe Tess Place fish restaurant in South Omaha (whose house specialty has long been fried carp), the wiry strong Gilmore was wearing a blue Kansas City Royals' cap and t-shirt. Over lunch Gary told his story. Besides baseball, he fondly reminisced about coaching his daughters' sports teams. He had no regrets about not getting a second chance to play pro baseball. An easy smile came over his face when he talked about how much he likes retirement. In addition to going on trips with his wife, he enjoys hunting and fishing with his brother Al.

\* \* \*

My baseball career started on a dirt street in front of our home at 26th and Harrison in South Omaha. At the age of 10, my brother and I were playing street ball—hitting rocks or bottle caps with sticks from trees or broomsticks. The next step was playing softball in the street with five or six neighborhood kids. From there, we took our ball playing to McKinley Park at 26th and Harrison. The park is still there. I still have a big gash in my arm where I reached over a fence at the park to catch a fly ball. Although I caught the ball, I ripped up my arm pretty bad. [He laughs.]

At Pleasant Hill Grade School, we played softball at recess. Mr. Peterson, my grade school principal, developed softball teams, basketball teams. We started playing other schools and that's when I ran into Roger Sayers who was attending Howard Kennedy. Both Roger and his brother, football great Gale Sayers, attended this school which is located on North 30th Street in North Omaha. Roger and I competed against each other. Later, I crossed paths with Gerry Kleinsmith. He was a former professional pitcher coaching Little League teams. Al and I got on his team. Gerry stressed fundamentals, coming to practice on time, playing for the team instead of for yourself, and knowing how to bunt to move runners around the bases.

About the same time, I started playing for Josh Gibson. Josh had a reputation for emphasizing fundamentals. Even though Josh was nearing the end of his trail, he was instrumental for my development in baseball. Josh had a pretty good team. Roger Sayers was on the team. I tried out and made the team. Played for him when I was in seventh and eighth grades in the late 1950s.

Josh would always work with me individually before or after practice at the field at Kellom School. He would send me to the outfield, hit my fly balls, and make me run to catch them. He'd hit those balls over my head, in front of me, to my right, to my left. After making the catch, I'd fire the ball on a line to him. He'd really work me. That's how I learned to really "go get 'em." Of course, Josh would have a big jug of water there for me to drink. I'd come in and rest for a while and then go out and catch fly balls for another 10 minutes. He taught me how to position myself to catch fly balls, how to catch balls over my head.

Kellom Field had partial dirt on the infield and the infield wasn't kept up. In the grassy outfield there was a huge fence. But when I was playing outfield, I was in the open because the fence was 600 feet from home plate. When Josh would be hitting me fly balls, I'd be out in the grass. Josh would have a catcher. Josh would toss the ball up and hit it. Josh would tell me to get into a good starting or athletic position, catch everything I could with two hands, and make accurate and low throws so if an infielder needed to cut off a throw, he could do it. Josh would tell me to catch balls below the waist with the fingers of my glove pointing down and to catch balls above my waist with the fingers of my glove pointing up. For balls over my head, he would constantly remind me to take the proper angle and keep an eye on the ball as much as possible. Sometimes he'd hit 10 balls in a row over my head.

One of my major league heroes was Paul Blair. He was a great defensive outfielder for the Baltimore Orioles. I modeled my defensive game after Blair's.

As a coach, Josh was relentless. He never would give up. He expected all players to work as hard as he did. Sweat would be rolling off Josh during a practice and he wouldn't even stop to wipe it off. He drove me. Similarly, he drove Bob Gibson hard.

Josh was a huge, huge man. Weighed close to 300 pounds. Deep voice. Very intimidating guy. He demanded that players be on time for practice. Loved to work with kids. He had a great big heart. He'd raise his voice. But he never used his size to bully an umpire. I never saw him get out of line with an umpire.

Josh believed speed and defense win games. His teams loved to bunt, steal bases, take extra bases. We had a fast team. Roger Sayers would hit a routine ground ball to shortstop and beat it out most of the time. Small ball. We played small ball because we didn't have big sluggers. Josh was a stickler for fundamentals. Moving runners over. Sacrifice flies. Proper positioning of his defensive players. He'd always shade hitters. Additionally, he stressed teamwork. Whenever we won, he emphasized that we had done it together. As he said, "We win together, we lose together."

Considering how I was an all-city outfielder for Central High School three years in a row, I'd say Josh did a good job of preparing me for the next level. At Central High School, I played for Coach Jim Karabotsos, another guy who stressed fundamentals. I played freshman ball at Central, and then, as a sophomore, I made varsity. Wound up making the all-city team in baseball as the center fielder three years in a row. I was a defensive outfielder. Anything hit to center, I'd catch it. Good arm at that time.

When Al was a senior, I was a sophomore, so we played together on Central's varsity. Al was a right fielder who did some pitching. It was great to be in center with my brother in right. I'd played with Al previously on one of Kleinsmith's Little League teams. Al didn't play for Josh. [But see Al Gilmore's interview.] Under Karabotsos, Al and I played together on Central's summer Legion team. Later on, we played semipro baseball together on the Eagles.

After graduating from Central, I had a reputation for being a good baseball player, so I went out to OU to talk with OU's baseball coach, Virg Yelkin. My Central High coach didn't set anything up. I went on my own. Now you have all these clinics where high school players can showcase their talents to college coaches. Back then, we had only Legion ball and college coaches didn't have time to watch Legion games. Yelkin said he'd heard about me playing ball and offered me a full ride. A lot of the seniors had full rides. His style was to give an incoming freshman a partial. If you made it, he would give you a bigger scholarship in subsequent years.

I made OU's baseball team as a freshman and played baseball for OU from 1961 through 1965. I got along pretty well with most of my teammates. There were a few guys—seniors who played for OU when Al was on the team and who had shown prejudice against Al—that I sensed were not happy that I was on the team. I was a five-tool player. My skill set is probably the reason I didn't have any problems at OU. Plus my brother, Al, kicked in the door there. You know, he was the first black to ever play for a OU baseball team. I didn't have to deal with any of the crap Al had to deal with. By the time I came along, Coach Yelkin had grown accustomed to having a black player on his team. Al suffered all the hardships and racial stuff, paving the way for me.

While playing for OU, I thought I had a shot to play pro baseball until I hurt my arm in my senior year. On the opening travel trip of the season to Pittsburg, Kansas, our team bus stopped in St. Joe, Missouri, to get ice cream. I was sitting in a park with Jim Collin [OU's big, strong first baseman and a son of South High School baseball coach Cornie Collin] and we started arm wrestling. That led to a tussle. I heard something pop

Gary Gilmore (at the left end of the front row) as a member of the 1964 University of Omaha baseball team. Gilmore was a five-tool player until he hurt his shoulder in 1965 (personal collection of Gary Gilmore).

in my shoulder. While my OU teammates were playing 10 games in Pittsburg, I rode the bench due to my arm injury. I could barely lift my arm. My shoulder took a month to heal. Although I played the rest of the year, I could never zip the ball the way I used to. So I became, in effect, a player who could hit, field, and run—but not throw.

Despite my bum arm, I made the NAIA all-tournament team in 1965. OU finished second to Carson-Newman out of Tennessee in an eight-team field. Carson-Newman had a lefty by the name of Clyde Wright. He was drafted later and played for the Angels. He beat us, 2–1, in the championship game. We had opportunities. We should have won. I had some chances to throw out a runner or two and I didn't do it. Major league scouts were there. They could see that I had speed, that I could hit the ball. Unfortunately, they could also see that I couldn't throw. None of the scouts contacted me. Consequently, I didn't get drafted. If I hadn't got hurt, I could've played in the minors and worked my way up.

Following my OU career, Al was playing with the Eagles and he hooked me up with them. Playing for the Eagles from 1966 through 1969, my coach was the mild-mannered, laid-back Johnny Dixon. He was a "friendship guy." He let his friends play whatever positions they wanted to. After the games, he'd go to the bars and drink with some of his buddies on the team. He loved baseball. He moved to Little Rock, Arkansas, and developed a semipro team there. We would travel to little towns like Missouri Valley and Underwood [both Iowa towns]. Whenever the home team did something, the fans watching from their automobiles would honk their horns. We'd get a nice check after each game. Typically, we'd get $40 or $50. A lot of those town teams would recruit ringers—ex-professional pitchers. Gene Hines, who grew up in Omaha and was signed by the Dodgers, would be hired by some of those teams to pitch against the Eagles.

Let me set the Eagles' lineup for you. Sherman Walker was behind the plate. Walker was a strong guy who handled pitchers well, could hit home runs. He was our cleanup hitter. More importantly, he was the glue of the Eagles. George Wright played third. Troy Richardson pitched and played first base. This lefty had a good curve and was a solid reliever. Henry Hamilton was our best starter. He's still alive, moved to Oklahoma. Hamilton was a righty who threw high heat that nobody could hit. Floyd Crandall anchored the infield at short. A real gamer, Floyd was 5'11" and weighed 175 pounds. A big strong guy, a solidly good number two hitter, a good bunter, a hitter who could hit behind the runner, an excellent base runner, a sound defensive player with a great arm—Floyd could go into the hole and gun guys out at first. Without a doubt, Floyd could have played in the majors. Don't know why he didn't.

The Eagles' toughest opponents were the Kansas City Monarchs. We played two games against the Monarchs at Rosenblatt and I took part in the second one, which we won. Al pitched the second game, so I'll let him tell you about that one.

After the Eagles, I was part of the Omaha Blackhawks, a softball team. In fact, I was the first coach of the Blackhawks. I got that thing started. Later on, I passed it on to other coaches. As the Blackhawks' first coach, I patterned my coaching style after my OU baseball coach. Coach Yelkin taught his players to be fundamentally sound. Detailed oriented, he paid attention to the little things. He drilled into my head that "baseball is a game of inches." Just a few inches on a pitched or hit ball can determine whether you win or lose. Don't overlook the importance of little things like bunting, taking an extra base, and switching signs when you think the other team is stealing your catcher's signs. Like Yelkin, I was a strategist. I'd spend time dreaming up ways to beat another team. I also followed Yelkin's example when it came to recruiting—I tried to recruit talented, intelligent players for the Blackhawks. Sometimes the Blackhawks were victorious because we outsmarted our opponents.

In 1971 the Blackhawks won the city championship, beating Four Seasons down at Boyd Field in North Omaha. Four Seasons had a good pipeline for acquiring inner-city softball players. They recruited the best players in Omaha—guys who'd made all-city in baseball. When we beat Four Seasons, we felt like the Brooklyn Dodgers did in 1955 when they defeated the New York Yankees in the World Series.

The Blackhawks were built on speed and defense. We picked up a guy by the name of Jerry Bartee, don't know if you've ever heard of him. He came out of the Cardinal organization. Eventually, we made him our coach. Jerry was the coach when we beat Four Seasons. Jerry was a tough competitor. As a coach, he always put the Blackhawks in the best position to win. If Jerry had to, he'd get into an umpire's face. Never pushed or shoved an ump. Very cordial. Never used any bad language.

As a player for the Blackhawks, Jerry had a rifle for an arm. From his position in left-center field (we played with four outfielders), threw ropes from the outfield all the way on the fly to the catcher. He was a five-tool player. With Bartee in left-center, I'd play left field and hit third or fifth in the batting order. Jerry could do it all. And he was a class act—just like the rest of the Blackhawks.

Gene Haynes was the catcher and cleanup hitter for the Blackhawks. Currently, he's the principal of Omaha North High School. Before migrating to Omaha, he grew up in Mississippi. He's worked for OPS since 1967. He began as a teacher and basketball coach at Omaha's Technical High School and was the first African American basketball coach for OPS. We always hit Gene fourth because he had an uppercut swing that produced towering drives.

When Sherman Walker wasn't pitching for the Blackhawks, he played first base. Whenever we wanted to stack our lineup with more hitters, Sherman would pitch. Harvey Gilbert played second base, excellent hands and quick release—remember Bill Mazeroski of the Pittsburgh Pirates? Harvey turned double plays like "no touch" Mazeroski—before the ball was in Harvey's hands, it was gone. Our Blackhawk infield was so good that we routinely pulled off double plays—in slowpitch softball! We used a lot of guys on third base. Sam "Doc" Crawford was another pitcher for us. The great Floyd Crandall played shortstop.

The Blackhawks traveled to tournaments in Kansas City, St. Louis, and other places, and we won a few. More important than winning was the bond that developed amongst the players. Many of the Blackhawks worked in local school systems. Besides Gene Haynes, Sherman Walker worked at North High School, Tom Harvey and Jerry Bartee became assistant superintendents, and Jim Freeman has held various administrative positions at UNO. The team is still close. So close that Jerry Bartee invites the Blackhawks to a Super Bowl party at his house every year.

During the early years of both the Eagles and the Blackhawks, I'd sometimes look into the stands and I'd see Charlie Washington at ballgames. He'd be there covering the game for the *Omaha Star*. He was a good sports fan. He attended more Eagle games than Blackhawk games. Charlie was a short, stocky guy. Weighed between 250 and 275 pounds. Sometimes I'd see Charlie hanging out with Josh Gibson.

I first met Charlie Washington at an Eagle game played at the Nebraska State Penitentiary. The Eagles would go to Lincoln once a summer to play against inmates at the penitentiary. At one of these games—it must have been between 1966 and 1969—I spotted Charlie in the stands sitting with the inmates and cheering for both teams. Don't know why Charlie was incarcerated. I do recall that every time a batter hit a ball over the prison wall in left field for a homer, the inmates went wild.

Umps were almost always white, but I remember a game when a black ump cheated the Blackhawks. Petey Allen, a famous black fastpitch softball player who was inducted into the Omaha Softball Hall of Fame, was umpiring. Petey had starred in a fastpitch softball league in Omaha in the 1950s, 1960s, and maybe into the early 1970s. At one time, Petey also had played on a slow pitch team called Stage Two (after the lounge in North Omaha by the same name). Stage Two was a rival of the Blackhawks. We would play each other around holidays. We'd usually beat them 'cause we had all the good players. Well, anyway, Petey had stopped playing for Stage Two and had become an umpire. So the Blackhawks were playing Stage Two on the Fourth of July at Boyd Field under the lights with Petey umpiring. The score was tied. It was late in the game. I muscled up and whacked the ball over the right fielder's head. As I tore around the bases, Stage Two's right fielder hit a relay man and the relay man fired the ball to their catcher. I slid into home plate ahead of the throw, but Petey Allen called me out. We ended up losing the game because of Petey's bad call at home. That was the worst call by an umpire I've ever seen. And he was a black umpire!

I'll close on a positive note. One of my favorite baseball memories. As I said earlier, defense was my specialty. When I played outfield for Central High School, I had a McGregor glove. My McGregor is what I made a lot of nice catches with. My McGregor was bigger than most gloves of the time. Now the major league players use huge gloves because they want to catch everything with one hand. I always protected my McGregor and sometimes I wanted to take it to bed with me. I oiled it and took good care of it. A good ol' glove will bail you out of a lot of tight ballgames.

Well, I was playing center field for Central High against South High School at Brown Park in South Omaha. This ball diamond has been around for more than 100 years and it's seen a lot of baseball. You know, Babe Ruth and Lou Gehrig once played there. Brown Park is the home field for the South High School baseball team and the South Omaha American Legion team.

It was late in the game with the score tied. South had runners on base. South was the home team. A South batter hit a low, sinking liner to center field. To save the game, I had to catch it. I sprinted after the ball as hard as I could and dove headfirst. I caught it, but broke my wrist in the process. Central went on to win the game and it took eight weeks for my wrist to heal.

# 16

# Rodger Ulmar

The plan was for me to interview Rodger Ulmar in a grocery store café in Omaha, but there was a catch: we'd never met before and we needed a way to pick each other out. I promised to wear my blue 1947 Brooklyn Dodgers' baseball cap. Of course, I forgot to wear it. Luckily, I'd seen the photo taken of the 1966 Tech High School state baseball champs after they'd won the championship. In that photo, a smiling Ulmar has his arm around a grinning Coach John Morse. In that same photo, the tall, lanky Ulmar is wearing glasses. I'd also talked to Coach Morse prior to the interview and Morse had given me a tip.

"Look for someone with big hands," Coach Morse suggested. "Rodger's huge hands helped him develop pinpoint control and made it easier for him to throw a hellish curveball."

Walking up to a tall, thin fellow wearing glasses in the café, I extended my hand and said, "Sir, you look like you could still pitch a few innings."

When the man shook my hand, I knew I had found the right person.

Before Rodger Ulmar and I settled into a conversation about his baseball playing days, I told him I wanted to throw him a "curveball." Instead of starting with a baseball question, I asked him to think back to the night of July 4, 1966. To refresh his memory, I informed him that this was the night that the first riot between the black community and the Omaha police broke out at the Safeway grocery store which used to be located in the heart of North Omaha near 24th and Lake. I wondered if Rodger remembered that riot.

\* \* \*

My best pitch was a curveball, so you asked an easy question. [He laughs.] I had three pitches: a fastball, a curveball, and a knuckleball. Gary Hunter, one of my catchers at Tech High, taught me how to throw the knuckleball. Gary and I used to play catch, and he'd throw knuckleballs back to me. The ball would dance and dart. Naturally, I asked him how he made the ball move. By throwing each other knuckleballs, I learned how to throw it. As for my curveball, it broke sharply from right to left. I'd start the ball at the batter and hit the outside corner. My strong suit was control. I could hit spots.

So now that I've told you about my curveball and my control, you're wondering if I forgot your question. [Laughter] I was an eyewitness to the riot on July 4, 1966. I was playing for Roberts Dairy [which was the Tech High School affiliate] that summer, but there was no Legion game that night. I was at home and we lived near where the riot broke out. The riot began at Safeway. Kids used to congregate there. While I was on our front porch, I saw smoke and followed the smoke to Safeway. Saw everything burning. My clothes were at the cleaners that the rioters burned down. Things were in chaos.

People were breaking into stores and running out. I saw the National Guard come in. Police had their clubs out and they were using them. I didn't see any weapons drawn but I saw the authorities arresting people. As things got more serious, I returned to the safety of my home.

Baseball was on my mind in those days, not rioting. Born in 1948, I started playing ball in the street with my brothers. During my early years, my family and I lived at 27th and Burdette in North Omaha. As a little kid, I started playing baseball with my dad and brothers. My dad used to take my brothers and me out to a field at Carter Lake when I was seven years old. Back in those days, there was a baseball park at every school. Kids did everything outside. We were always outside playing some kind of ball. Today, kids play inside.

We played softball during recess at school and in the neighborhood parks when school was out. Three or four times a week. The first thing we did at recess was put some bases out so we could start playing softball. I played mainly softball up until I was in the sixth or seventh grade. Then I switched to baseball.

My dad, Frank Ulmar, worked at a packing house. He looked like me. About 6'1". I'm 6'3". A bit taller than him. He played for a short time in the Negro minor leagues. I can't recall the name of the teams he played with. He taught my brothers and me how to play ball, but he never talked about his own playing days.

I had three brothers. Two are deceased. The brother who was three years older than me—James—my father would take the two us to a field at Carter Lake and hit us fly balls. He helped us develop our fundamentals. My brother's softball team won a national tournament. He was in the seventh grade. My brother James was the best player. He played shortstop on one of Coach Morse's Tech varsity teams. After he graduated from Tech, the Phillies offered him a contract. The Phillies wanted him as an outfielder. But instead of signing with the Phillies, he went into the military and never came out of the military until he retired. James was three years older than me. He passed away. Strong arm. Really fast. He could play the outfield also.

Jerry Parks, the head of Parks and Recreation, ran these green houses in the summer. From these places you could check out softball bats, gloves, and other sports equipment. The availability of equipment made it easier for us kids to be outdoors playing all the time. Jerry was about 5'9", slight build, very personable, everyone liked him. He made sure the parks were in excellent condition. He dragged the baseball and softball fields every day. The fields looked almost as good as Rosenblatt [Stadium in Omaha]. The lines were chalked. The pitching mounds were smoothed out.

I played for Coach James Shaw. Strictly speaking, Shaw wasn't my first coach. I'd been around coaches. You see, my brother James had played for Josh Gibson out of the YMCA, so I was around Josh. Josh was like an extended family member to all the kids. He would go out of his way to make sure the kids were treated fairly and to teach kids right from wrong. He made sure kids had equipment they needed to play. He was a fatherly, chunky guy. He wasn't six feet tall, but he was stocky, dark-complected—kinda the same color as Bob Gibson … nice man. When I started playing baseball, Josh was getting out of coaching youth baseball.

Shaw was a Josh Gibson clone, but he was more vocal, louder, with a harder edge. Shaw had played baseball at Tech before Morse became Tech's baseball coach. He was older than my brother James by a couple of years. By the time I got to the seventh grade, Shaw was in his early 20s and working for the Y. Shaw is hard to describe. [He chuckles.]

Since Shaw was a former Tech High School football player, he was known to be a roughhouser. Six feet tall. Muscular.

What stands out in my mind is that we had a really good all-black team called Cole's Sundries. I played right field and first base. We wore yellow baseball caps and yellow jerseys. We played our games at Burdette, Druid Hill, Kountze Park, and Kellom. All located between Cuming and Ames streets in North Omaha. Each of these places had its own league.

Burdette was a nice field. It was fun to play there. That's where the Boys Club was located. The ball field used to be located in the back of the building now occupied by the Hope Center. [The Hope Center is a faith-based youth development facility located in the Near North Side.] Lots of fans attended ballgames there. Even the Eagles [a mostly black Omaha baseball team] played there. The field faced from southwest to northeast. It was a good-sized field with a fence.

At some point, ball fields started disappearing in North Omaha. An example is what happened at Long School where I attended grade school. [Once located in the Near North Side of North Omaha, Long School was identified in 1952 as being the only school in Omaha with a 100 percent African American student body population. The first two African American teachers in public education in Omaha were assigned to Long School in 1940.] Because Long School was only a block and half from where I lived, we used to walk there on the weekends to play softball. That ended when the Omaha Public School system built portable classrooms on our ball fields, wiping out our open space to play ball. Our search for another ball field led us eight blocks away to Kellom. Each year more of our ball-playing space was taken away. Pretty soon kids stopped playing softball and hardball.

With no baseball fields available in North Omaha, my son, who was born in 1976, and all of his friends played soccer. When I was a kid, we were always outdoors playing catch. My son didn't want to play catch. It hurt my feelings. [He laughs.]

My short career as a ballplayer took off once I started pitching for Tech. I met Robert Weir. We were playing catch one day, and he threw a curveball back to me. I asked him to show me how he made the ball break and he showed me how to grip a curve. I started practicing throwing curveballs to him. By the time I was a freshman at Tech, I could throw a good curve. Funny enough, in my first start as a freshman playing for Roberts Dairy in the summer league, I pitched a no-hitter. The other team's hitters couldn't touch my curve. I was surprised. This was the first time I'd ever pitched a game at any level of baseball. I went on to pitch for the Tech varsity baseball team in my sophomore, junior, and senior years. Coach Morse says I had a 7–1 record my senior year. I had winning records every year but I didn't keep track of that stuff.

I do recall that before the championship game in 1966, I was calm. I would never get nervous before or during a game I was pitching. Baseball never made me nervous. I recall some games when I'd be playing right field and, with the other team having the bases loaded and we were one run behind, Coach Morse would call me in and have me relieve whoever was pitching. I wasn't nervous. My main thing was control. I could throw strikes. I never walked any hitters. Our catcher would move his target around to the corners of the plate and I'd hit his mitt.

Going into the championship game against Benson at Rosenblatt, I felt relaxed. I'd played at Rosenblatt before, so I was comfortable. With its elevated pitcher's mound, I loved playing there. Winding up and throwing from that mound made me feel powerful. My mom and dad sat behind home plate. My mom was a yeller. She was emotional. My brother, James, was in the military at the time, but he also attended that game. Ron Bartee, who was a good catcher, caught me. Whereas Bartee was tall, my previous catcher, Gary Hunter, was stocky and short. Hunter's targets were a little easier to hit. Because of his long legs, Bartee had difficulty setting up low. Phil Wise caught sometimes. Wise was shorter, and his target was easy to hit.

My strategy for that championship game was the same one I used every game. As a pitcher, I tried to get batters to hit fly balls and ground balls. I never tried to strike anyone out. I was pretty successful until the final out. No long balls were hit off me. Besides throwing different pitches, I kept hitters off balance by changing speeds.

I remember the final out. A Benson hitter belted one of my pitches pretty good to left field. I wasn't sure it was going to stay in the ballpark. Phil Wise drifted back. I could see his eyes following the flight of the ball. From the way Phil set up his feet, I knew he was going to catch it, and he did near the warning track.

I pitched the interstate championship game against Thomas Jefferson High School, but I don't remember it. We're talking 50 years ago.

Even though I pitched well throughout the 1966 season, Tech's success was due to team effort and athleticism. Some of my previous teammates from other Tech teams—Lewis Garrison and Ron Boone—they're haters [He laughs.] and they insist our 1966 team wasn't any good. They claim we got lucky. Well, they're wrong. [Laughs heartily.] In reality, our team was loaded with highly talented athletes. Kirkland Wise—Phil Wise's brother—played center. Kirkland was a good basketball player, excellent fielder, and very fast. He died two or three years ago. Our shortstop Bob Griego could hit, steal bases, field well, and throw. Another good athlete was Ron Bartee who caught, played right field, and got clutch hits. I remember a game—it might have been in Auburn, Nebraska—there was this big scoreboard. Ron Bartee hit a ball harder than I've ever seen a ball hit in high school, knocking it over that scoreboard. And what about Phil Wise? He was one of Tech's greatest athletes of all time.

After graduating from Tech, UNO's baseball coach Virg Yelkin offered me a scholarship, but I turned him down. I didn't think I threw hard enough to pitch college baseball. You see, when I graduated from high school, I weighed 160 pounds. Yelkin talked to me personally. He

Rodger Ulmar in 2014. Ulmar was the ace of the 1966 Technical High School baseball team's pitching staff (personal collection of Rodger Ulmar).

seemed like a decent guy. Following a year at UNO as a student, I joined the military and became an administrative specialist in the Air Force. I typed top secret documents. Upon leaving the military, I worked for Union Pacific for two years and then I went back to UNO to earn my bachelor's degree. After that, I worked for the state as an employment interviewer. Did that for five years and then worked for Frontier Airlines for nine years. Finally, I returned to the state and wound up working there until I retired. Now that I'm retired, I don't have a routine. No itinerary. My wife and I travel. We take cruises. Go for drives. We're enjoying retirement.

Now, when I look back 50 years, I am struck by how much I loved playing ball outdoors. We were "outside kids" in those days. But the day of the young black ballplayer is gone. Kids today are wrapped up in playing video games indoors. I can't see black ball making a comeback. The neighborhood baseball and softball fields are gone in North Omaha. Where are the kids gonna play? It used to be a Saturday outing for a family to get out and find a game in North Omaha. Kellom Field was kept up. Carter Lake. Burdette. Within walking distance of 24th and Lake in North Omaha, a baseball game was always going on. Today, I live in northwest Omaha. Northwest High School's baseball field is nearby. Every now and then at night, I see the lights on and kids playing a ball game—but the stands are practically empty. Nobody's watching. I feel like stopping to watch a game, but never do. Maybe I should.

# 17

# Ron Bartee

Making smart decisions is a key to success in baseball as well as in life. Bad decisions can lose a baseball game and ruin a business career. As a rule, few people can consistently exercise sound judgment in decision-making. A former pitcher and catcher on Technical High School's state baseball championship team by the name of Ron Bartee is an exception to the rule. If Ron ever writes an autobiography, he ought to title it "Smart Decisions." Throughout his baseball and professional careers, he has demonstrated a knack for making gutsy, intelligent decisions.

During a phone interview with Ron (who now lives in Salt Lake City, Utah), he regaled me with stories about tough decisions he made as a parole officer and as chairperson of the Nebraska Parole Board. Bartee served on the Nebraska Parole Board from March 1983 until February 1992 under three different governors. He left the Parole Board in 1992 to take a job with the U.S. Parole Administration in Kansas City. Moreover, he earned a bachelor's degree in criminal justice from the University of Nebraska Omaha. Nebraska Governor Ben Nelson was one of the three governors who Bartee served under as chairperson of the Parole Board. In 1994, Governor Nelson publicly acknowledged Bartee's penchant for making smart decisions. To quote Governor Nelson, "Throughout his years as a parole officer and Parole Board member, Ron has demonstrated excellent judgment."

In our phone conversation, Ron also told stories about evaluating the risks and benefits of investment opportunities that have come his way. He must not have done too badly with those decisions either. When he sold his interest in a drug testing and safety latex glove company, Ron walked away with a lot of money.

\* \* \*

I started playing organized ball when I was seven or eight at Kellom Field. The baseball field was filled with rocks, sticks, and dirt clods. Nobody dragged the field. So prior to practices, Josh Gibson would have us walk the field and pick up rocks. Josh Gibson was my first coach. Uncle Dunk [Ron's uncle Howard Duncan] was my mother's brother and was like a father to my brother Jerry and me. We would watch him when he was a trash-talking catcher for the Omaha Eagles. He also played in a Negro baseball league in Springfield for a team called the Hyde Park Stars. His brother Bobby played with him. Dunk taught us to love baseball. From an early age, Jerry and I knew baseball was going to be an important part of our lives.

Jerry and I played catch all the time. Often, we played "burn out." Jerry could throw harder but I had better control. Our throwing ability came from throwing rocks in rock fights in our neighborhood. I was born in Missouri, and my family would return there in the summers to visit our cousins. We'd be there for a month or so. In Missouri, my brother and I discovered slate rocks—they're flat. Let me tell you what, the first time we threw slate rocks, we knew we had a powerful weapon. Slate, if thrown the right way, catches the wind and turns corners. When we got into rock fights back in Omaha, our opponents would say, "Man, those Bartee boys can not only throw hard and straight but they have rocks that can turn corners." [Laughter]

Actually, I played softball in a church league for about two years before I played organized baseball. Jerry, our two cousins—Reggie and Howard Duncan—and the other neighborhood kids won every softball game. We hit the ball so far that the other team's coach would protest playing against us, claiming we were too old. Once Jerry and I figured out that a softball came at you as a hitter on an arc, not straight at you like a baseball, we understood to adjust our swings and follow that arc with our bats. We would hit the ball so damn high that the average outfielder couldn't judge it in order to catch it. Jerry and I got to the point in our hitting in softball, that if a pitch wasn't thrown on an arc—if it came in on a line—we'd undress the pitcher—that is, we'd hit line drives right at the pitcher.

Switching coaches from Rodney [Wead] to Josh was a natural progression. Rodney talked about Josh, so we looked forward to playing for Josh. Actually, Jerry and I played for Josh and his brother Freddie, who assisted Josh. Those two used to load all the players up in their vehicle and travel as far as Kearney to play other teams. I owe being a catcher to Josh and Uncle Dunk.

One day while taking infield practice at Kellom Field, the ball took a bad hop and hit me in the throat. I threw my glove down and ran home. After practice Josh came to my house and tried to encourage me to come back.

"Hell no," I said.

Josh laughed.

I was still rubbing my neck. Josh asked me to think about it and then he left. Later, Dunk asked me if my throat was still hurting. I nodded.

"There is one position on the field," Uncle Dunk said, "where you don't have to worry about getting hit or hurt, it's catching. Just remember three things in this order":

    1. Wear a cup.
    2. Keep your throwing hand out of the way to make sure it doesn't get hit by the bat or a foul ball.
    3. Watch out for the freight train coming from third base—the base runner.

Josh always told us to never leave the decision of the game to the umpire, hit hard, don't commit any errors, and score runs. Playing on Josh's team gave you an education in the fundamentals and in sportsmanship. If you applied these keys, you would come out ahead.

Playing ball with my brother Jerry when we were little kids was one the best times of my life. As kids, Jerry and I played together all the way up to the 10th grade. We both could place hit the ball. We both could jack the ball out of the park. When you got that type of weaponry on a team, you go into every game figuring that you're gonna win. We weren't cocky—we were quietly confident. I knew that if a game came down to either Jerry or me coming through with our bats, we could do it. I had that same feeling of supreme confidence every time I was Jerry's teammate and walked onto a ball field with him.

Jerry was the greatest baseball player I've ever seen. Jerry always did what a baseball player is supposed to do. He conditioned himself. Even as a little kid, Jerry practiced, practiced, practiced. When I got a little older—I really didn't get crazy about baseball until my junior or senior year in high school—I saw that all of Jerry's hard work had paid off and made him into a highly talented ballplayer. I loved to watch Jerry play baseball. Playing shortstop he was so smooth. He glided to the ball. He fielded like a vacuum cleaner, sucking up balls. Had a helluva an arm. He'd catch a grounder and play with a runner before throwing the ball. I admired that. Catch the ball, take a few steps, skip—and the runner would think he was going to beat it out because Jerry was taking too much time—then Jerry would unleash a rocket across the diamond to the first baseman. Jerry took the basic fundamentals of baseball that Uncle Dunk and Josh Gibson taught him, owned those fundamentals, and turned himself into a ball-playing work of art. While playing on the same teams with him, I'd get distracted from watching how graceful he was.

As a hitter, Jerry could knock the hell out of the ball. Jerry threw right and batted left. When Jerry was a tyke, one day he took his stance at the plate as a right-handed hitter but he mistakenly gripped the bat cross-handed. A coach by the name of Charles Page corrected Jerry. Instead of just moving Jerry's right hand over the top of his left hand (which is the correct hand position on the bat for a right-handed hitter), Coach Page told Jerry to keep his hands the same way on the bat (with the left hand on top of the right hand) and to switch sides of the plate. That's how Jerry became a left-handed hitter.

Some folks wonder how Jerry could be so damned good and not make it in "the bigs." Things happen for a reason. When Jerry was drafted, he assumed he'd be with the St. Louis Cardinals for the rest of his career. In reality, trading a player was like changing underwear. If the Cardinals had traded Jerry, he would've excelled and made it to the bigs. He could play any position. Jerry got to be 22, 23, or 24, he wasn't in the bigs yet, and he did something that shocked me. Jerry all of a sudden wasn't playing minor league baseball. I asked him what the hell happened.

"Man," he said, "it's a different ballgame."

I was stunned.

"Up above me in the St. Louis organization," Jerry said, "the Cardinals are two players deep in the position I'm in, so I quit."

"Man," I said, "you never quit anything."

"I'm not going anywhere," Jerry replied. "I'm not on a track to play in the majors. I gotta think of my future. I must get my education. I went into the pros straight out of high school. I don't want to be a common laborer."

So Jerry started his bachelor's degree at Creighton and the rest is history. Even though Jerry never made it to the bigs, he's still my favorite baseball player.

A highlight of my baseball career was winning the state high school baseball championship in 1966. This made me part of the history of baseball at Tech High. We didn't win many metro games my three years at Tech, but we won when it counted, winning district and state in '66 and coming back in '67 and winning district.

One of the reasons we won that championship is Coach Morse. Morse was a young coach in 1966 and 1967, but he knew baseball. Over and over he drilled us on fundamentals at every practice and game.

"Can of corn," Coach Morse would say.

As a baseball term, "can of corn" refers to a high, easy-to-catch fly ball hit to the outfield. Coach Morse used the phrase in a more general way. He would say, "If you follow the fundamentals, the game of baseball is a 'can of corn.'" In practice, Morse would hit a grounder to ya, and he'd say, "Can of corn." He would always say it—even if it was a hot grounder or a hard-to-catch fly ball. In a tense, difficult situation on the baseball field, Morse would holler out to us, "Can of corn." By repeating that phrase, he conditioned us to think that we could do anything on a baseball diamond.

The first time I met Coach Morse he asked if I was kin to Jerry. I told him Jerry was my brother. Coach Morse was probably thinking if I had half the ability of Jerry, then I was a keeper. That same day, my departing words to Coach Morse were: "Before I leave Tech, we will win a championship in baseball." Coach was probably thinking, "Poor soul, doesn't he know that Tech has never won a championship in baseball or had a winning season?"

Coach Morse got along with everyone on the team and the players had the utmost respect for him. We did not see color. We saw baseball players working toward the common goals of having fun and winning. I had many friends on the '66 team. I would say Rodger Ulmar (pitcher), Bobby Griego (shortstop), Phil Wise (outfield-catcher), Ernie Boone (pitcher), and Steve Bauermeister (first baseman-coach) were the closest.

Coach Morse frequently complimented me for making smart decisions. Whatever intelligence I had came from being both a pitcher and a catcher. Being a pitcher and a catcher gives you the best inside straight against a batter. From the catcher's point of view, you could ask for a pitch based on where the batter was lining up in the box. That's why catchers call for certain pitches. As a pitcher, you know what pitches to throw to avoid the fat or meat of the bat. It's like a game of chess.

In 2016, pitcher-catcher Ron Bartee was reunited with some of the other members of the 1966 Technical High School baseball team (left to right): Ron Bartee, John Morse, Ernie Boone, Steve Bauermeister, Rodger Ulmar, and Charles Plummer (personal collection of Steve Bauermeister).

I also want to praise my mother. My mother was a single mom. She loved me and kept me out of trouble. For example, she kept me out of harm's way the night of July 4, 1966. My mother told my sister and me (Jerry was gone because Jerry had already left Omaha to go to play in the pro instructional league), "You're going to stay in this house and you're not going down to 24th and Lake."

We were living at 25th and Ames in North Omaha, so I wanted to go down and see the riot. My mom said, "No, your ass is stayin' in the house."

My mother raised all three of us. As a single parent, she knew the riot was nuttin' but trouble.

"Any viewing of the riot you do will be by watching TV," she said.

We never would defy our mother.

My family started living close to Kellom near 24th and Indiana in North Omaha when I was a kid. From there, we moved to the projects. From the projects, we moved just off Lake Street and we attended Howard Kennedy School. From there, we moved onto Spalding Street and attended Horace Mann Junior High. Next, in my sophomore year at Tech, we moved to 25th and Ames. My mom still lives there.

We lived in South Omaha for a short period right after our family moved here from Missouri. My mother and her sister and brother (Uncle Dunk or Howard Duncan) moved to Omaha, and we stayed with my great-uncle Herman who lived in South Omaha. Herman got Howard a job at a packing plant. Many African Americans worked at packing plants in South Omaha. When my mom moved our family from South to North Omaha, Uncle Dunk came with us. It's common in African American families to find adult siblings living together in a large home. Uncle Dunk, my mother, and my mother's sister lived together near 24th and Indiana Street in a large home. By the way, all the schools I mentioned had predominantly African American student populations. Where we lived on Ames Street, we lived in the district of North High School—it was right up the street. But I wanted to attend Tech. That's where my buddies were. Kids gravitate toward their friends. It's all about comfort.

I was comfortable crouching behind home plate catching Rodger Ulmar for the championship game. Coach Morse's high school coach Scotty Orcutt and my brother Jerry were in the stands watching that game. The only comment my brother made and kept repeating over and over was, "I'll be damned, they did it."

Yes, we did!

One of my favorite memories from that 1966 season happened in a regular-season metro game that I pitched against Jerry's Central High School team. The first time Jerry batted against me in that ballgame, he hit me pretty hard, so I walked him the second time he came to bat. With Jerry taking a lead off first, I threw over one time. The next thing I knew Jerry stole second base. Our shortstop, Bobby Griego, came to the mound. Bobby said, "If Jerry starts to lean toward third, turn your head toward me, turn back and look toward home plate, count to three, turn and fire to second."

Low and behold, Bobby snuck in behind Jerry. Jerry was like a deer caught in the headlights. I pivoted on the mound and fired toward second base. Bobby caught my throw and slapped the tag on Jerry. We picked him off! I taunted Jerry the whole way back to the bench. Tech lost the game, but we got Jerry. It felt good!

When Jerry signed with the St. Louis Cardinals in '66, I was happy and excited for him. My brother and my best friend was leaving. Before Jerry left, he said, "Let's go for a ride."

We stopped at Russell's Sporting Goods Store in downtown Omaha. We walked in and Jerry told me to pick out a glove. Neither Jerry nor I had ever had a brand new baseball glove. We always used a found or a second-hand glove. Jerry bought me my first new glove, a Wilson A2000. I still have that glove today.

Another special memory of mine about that championship season is the "secret advantage" Tech had whenever we hosted an opponent at Adams Field in North Omaha. Home field advantage at that park meant more than any of our opponents would ever know. We always tried to hit the ball to right field. Why? Because we knew right field was uphill and full of gopher holes. Not knowing right field like we knew it, outfielders on opposing teams would stumble and fall while chasing fly balls there. To add to our advantage, before each home game a few of us Tech players would pour honey on the opposing team's bench. Of course, our unsuspecting opponents would sit in the honey. What followed was hilarious. Bees drawn to the honey would try to sting our opponents. If any of our opponents discovered our mischief today, we'd have to forfeit the few metro home games we won in 1966 on account of "trauma inflicted" upon our opponents. [Laughter]

The following baseball season at Tech was my worst nightmare—I emphasize "mare" because our catcher's name was "Mayer" pronounced "mare." Let me tell you, Tech won district. I pitched and won both games. The headline in the newspaper read, "Hope for Rain, So Bartee Can Start Again." It rained. So I got to pitch the first game in state. We were leading by one run in the bottom of the seventh inning in a seven-inning game. There were two outs with a runner on first. The runner stole second. I called the catcher out to the mound.

"I own this batter," I said. "I've faced him many times this year, and I know I can strike him out. If the runner tries to steal third, don't throw the ball."

As I threw the next pitch, the runner broke for third.

"No, no, no!" I yelled at my catcher.

I'll be damned if the catcher didn't throw the ball to third. The throw went right through our third baseman's legs and into the outfield. The runner scored, tying the game. We lost, ending Tech's bid to repeat as state champs.

I had it. I had that game in the palm of my hand. If we had won that game, I know I could have pitched well enough for us to win state again. Ever since 1967, that last inning has been a recurring nightmare for me.

After graduating from Tech in 1967, I joined the military and served in Vietnam. When I got out, University of Nebraska Omaha (UNO) Coach Virgil Yelkin gave me a partial baseball scholarship. I played baseball one year—1972. I was the only African American on UNO's team. I played left field. I made the starting lineup for a three-game road trip to Texas. The dugouts were cement in Texas. The left lens of my glasses popped out, hit the cement floor, and shattered. I needed glasses to see. Without my glasses, I failed to produce with the bat. By the time UNO returned to Omaha, I was riding the pine. I tried to tell Virg, "Coach, it was the glasses." But he never gave me a chance to win my position back. It was unfair. Hell, I could run, throw, hit, and catch. Playing the outfield is a piece of cake compared to the pitching and catching I'd done in high school.

After playing ball at UNO for a season, the academic advisor for UNO's criminal justice program called me in and told me that the state of Nebraska was looking for a minority parole officer. I was in my sophomore year. I applied and got the job. I was allowed to continue to attend classes; they even gave me a car. There was only one catch: I would have to give up my baseball scholarship. I wrestled with that decision. But I realized I was 26 years old and I had no prospects of playing pro baseball. So I took the job.

I thought quitting baseball at UNO was the end of the line, but my ball playing was not quite over. By joining the Thomas Reality's Omaha Blackhawks, I became reunited on the ball field with my favorite ballplayer. It gave me that same great feeling of confidence that I used to get as a kid when Jerry and I were teammates. A lot of educators played for our team. They might not have been the greatest baseball talents, but they could run. They could run so damn fast that when they would get to the ball, they'd sometimes over-run it. Jerry had to teach some of them how to catch. We played in the top competitive slow pitch league in the state. As our coach, Jerry was adept at using everyone on the team in a ballgame. This helped get all of the players involved and made us work together as a team. Eventually, the Blackhawks broke up and the players joined other softball teams.

Looking back on my journey in baseball in Omaha, it's important to put my Tech baseball experience in context. It starts with the fact that Tech was a multicultural school. Attending Tech you had white, black, Hispanic, and Asian kids as classmates.

It also requires that you realize Tech High was exactly what the name says it is—technical. No other school in Omaha was like Tech. It was almost like a reformatory. All education was skills based. We had electrical. Auto body. Everything you needed to have a career.

Additionally, it's crucial to recognize Tech High had the great spirit of the Trojans. Trojans don't fight each other; they fight others. Trojans work toward a common goal—WINNING. Track, basketball, wrestling, and football had all won championships. It was past the time for Tech to win a championship in baseball.

In closing, let me tell you, talking about black ball has evoked many memories. I feel so strongly about this subject that I'll be happy to continue the conversation any time, any place in the future. To quote the great Satchel Paige, "I don't have to warm up. I ain't cooled down from the last game."

# 18

# Phil Wise

"One of the reasons people don't say much about me in Omaha," Phil Wise remarked to me in a telephone interview, "is because I'm outspoken." Phil personifies Frank Sinatra's signature song, "My Way." Anyone who knows Phil Wise will vouch for his "tell it like it is" manner of speaking. When discussing any topic under the sun, Phil often shoots from the hip and gives you his unvarnished takes and opinions.

Born in 1949 in Omaha, one of the most magical moments in this former National Football League (NFL) player's sports career came in 1966 when his disrespected, disregarded, and downgraded predominantly black Technical High School baseball team shocked Omaha's mostly white high school baseball teams by winning the Nebraska state championship. Asked about that 1966 team, Phil couldn't curb his enthusiasm. Fifty years after Omaha Tech—as the school was better known—had won the championship in baseball, Phil Wise was raving to me about how amazing this feat was. To hear Phil tell it, Tech winning the 1966 baseball title was comparable to the New York Mets winning the 1969 World Series.

Phil talked baseball nonstop for an hour. Every once in a while, he'd pause to catch his breath. Then, he'd reflect.

"You know, it's interesting," he'd say.

Then, he'd reflect.

So much baseball talk coming from the 6-foot 190 pound strong man who played in the NFL for six years with the New York Jets and three years with the Minnesota Vikings. So much pride in his high school's baseball team that you'd expect him to still be wearing his old letter jacket or letter sweater bearing the letter he won in baseball in 1966. So much passion for baseball that he barely mentioned how outstanding he was as a football player for the University of Nebraska at Omaha (which later became the University of Nebraska Omaha, but continued to be referred to as UNO).

Since Phil didn't brag about his record as a running back in college, I will. It drives home what a great athlete Phil Wise was. During his 1968–1970 college football career for UNO, he rushed for a total of 1,146 yards, highlighted by a 231-yard performance in one game. As a junior, he ranked ninth in the nation in the NAIA in scoring with 15 touchdowns. He still holds the UNO record for longest run from scrimmage, a 95-yard dash against Fort Hays State in 1969. He was an all-conference selection twice, once at defensive back and once at running back.

After nine years of playing in the NFL, Phil walked away. He loved the game of pro football but hated the business of pro football. In his view, the NFL was a business. A lot of times teams punished black athletes for their mistakes because, according to Phil, they could get away with it. Typically, the pro teams would draft white players and players from the Big Ten and pay them big salaries. To complete their rosters, pro teams would sign good black players from small colleges, like Marlin Briscoe, who played for UNO when its name was the University of Omaha, and Phil, and underpay them.

Out of pro football and armed with a bachelor's degree in criminal justice from his alma mater, Phil sold pots and pans. It took a year for him to get a job in insurance with The Equitable. He was living in Minneapolis then, the same place he lives today. His next job was in security at Honeywell where he earned a pension. Made real good money. Better money than police officers—and he didn't even have to carry a gun. Then, he began working in security at Mystic Lake, the Native American casino in Minneapolis. Eventually, Phil landed his current job as a host of the radio station KQRS Morning Show in Minneapolis.

Phil enjoys coming home. He returns to Omaha to see his sister, to reminisce with old college and high school friends, and to lay plans for creating a positive youth development program. He talked to me about starting a program in Omaha that addresses the root causes of Omaha gun violence and gang problems. In explaining his motives, Phil said simply, "Somebody's gotta care about the kids of North Omaha."

\* \* \*

My late brother, Kirkland, was my hero. He played center field for the 1966 Omaha Tech High baseball team and for the Tech-affiliated Roberts Dairy summer Legion team. I was next to him in left field. My brother was a year ahead of me. He and I came up playing ball with Josh Gibson. Kirkland was a great all-around athlete. My brother was a version of Joe Orduna, the running back at Nebraska. Orduna went to Central High where he was also a track star. My brother could do the things Orduna could do, including run the 440 in track. Weighing only 165 pounds, Kirkland captained a very good Tech football team and earned all-state honors at offensive guard. Kirkland even received a football scholarship offer to attend Nebraska. At that time, the dominant teams in Omaha football were Creighton Prep and Boys Town. You're talking about my brother playing against teams that had 200-pound linemen.

You know, it's interesting.

When folks talk about great Omaha athletes, nobody mentions my brother. He was quiet. A different kinda guy. Instead of playing football for the Big Red, Kirkland wound up going into the military. Ended up serving in Germany. My father was dead and my mother didn't know anything about sports. We had a cousin of ours who was a police officer, Jimmy Smith, who helped us. Black athletes didn't have much help in those days when it comes to going to college. Anyway, my brother was lucky to be stationed in Germany. He was one of the few who didn't go to Vietnam.

When I was in high school, I didn't know anything about baseball. I didn't know anything about bat speed. I used a bat that was way too big—I should have used a lighter bat. I was real strong. The Baltimore Orioles were interested in me, but I planned to play pro football. The Orioles weren't going to waste a draft pick on someone who didn't want to play baseball. I was going to go to whichever college offered me a football scholarship. If I wouldn't have received a scholarship from South Dakota to play football, I probably would've played baseball in college. I like baseball.

Actually, a friend of mine was drafted to play pro baseball: Jerry Bartee. Jerry was known for one sport—baseball. Unlike my brother who was an all-around athlete, I was mainly known for football and baseball. You know it's funny, people always told me I could play any sport and play it well. I could play baseball well. I could play football well. I even had a wrestling scholarship to Nebraska in the Big Eight. But Kirkland was a better athlete than me.

This may shock Nebraska fans, but I turned Nebraska down and went to South Dakota. My reason was that I knew Nebraska wouldn't let me play quarterback. Then, Nebraska tried to give me a wrestling scholarship. I didn't want to wrestle any more. If I'd wanted to wrestle, I'd gone to UNO. Under Coach Benning, UNO had a great wrestling squad. Coach Benning coaxed me out for wrestling for a few days. I wrestled Mel Washington, a great wrestler.

I went to South Dakota cause I wanted to be a quarterback. It took me one semester there to know that I wouldn't be a quarterback. I probably would've had a chance to be a quarterback had I went to UNO like I was supposed to. Marlin Briscoe was there. I would have been his backup for one year. It was interesting. I came back to UNO. While on UNO's football team as a running back, I got to play against South Dakota several times. I never made All-American but I did make Honorable Mention. From UNO, I got drafted by the New York Jets and I signed with the Jets. Majoring in criminal justice at UNO, I graduated in my second year of pro football. I played six years with the Jets, and I forced them to trade me.

We talk about it today—the decisions we had to make by ourselves as black athletes. If you were a black athlete in Omaha in the 1950s and 1960s, most high school coaches didn't help. Very few. Johnny Rodgers is the exception. Johnny had help. But see, Johnny was behind me. Some other guys paved the way for Johnny. See, I had a really good college football career. That helped Johnny. I had no problems with eligibility. I could have

The outspoken Phil Wise (on the right), an outfielder-catcher on the 1966 Technical High School baseball team, played nine seasons in the National Football League, four of those—1971–1974—with Steve Tannen (on the left) (personal collection of Phil Wise).

played at any college. I could pass any SAT. A lot of athletes couldn't. Johnny paved the way for other black athletes who came after him. You have to remember those were the late 1960s. It wasn't easy for black athletes.

You know, it's interesting.

Most black high school athletes went to either junior colleges or the Vietnam War. People tell me all the time that I was dodging the draft because as long as I was in college, I had a deferment and the military couldn't draft me. While I was going to college, all my friends were being drafted. Nam and all that. A lot of my friends went to Vietnam. They came back not right in the head or they came back in a body bag.

You know, it's interesting.

When I went to South Dakota tryin' to be a quarterback, South Dakota had ROTC. I'm dodging the draft like all the other male college students in America, and South Dakota's got me takin' military classes. How ironic!

It seems like a long time since Vietnam. I'm 67 years old. I can still remember a few things. [Laughter] You know I just took that National Football League (NFL) concussion test. Former NFL players have to take these tests. The test consists of a series of tests or games. Neurological tests. Oh man, when you start taking those you're wondering to yourself, "Is my mental state a function of hits to the head or is it just old age?"

One of the things we all worry about in our 60s is getting Alzheimer's. They say when you get that you lose a lot of things and put things in strange places. You put things where you normally wouldn't put them. That's scary. These days I spend too much time lookin' for stuff. I put my keys and wallet in the same place or I lose them.

You should take the NFL test. They ask you at the beginning ... show you different pictures of stuff, ya know. When the test is over 30 minutes later, they show you pictures and ask what you recall seein'. Taking that test can be terrifying. You take the test over three days. It becomes confusing. I scored in the average range, but I always want to be above average in everything I do. It's interesting. They don't have a baseline—they don't know the condition of a typical former NFL player's brain. By collecting baseline information, scientists hope to observe neurological deterioration. If you're one of the players who shows deterioration, you qualify for an award you don't want to get. [Laughter]

I was raised in a neighborhood in North Omaha near the Logan Fontenelle Housing Project. I went to Kellom grade school. It's interesting. Kellom is still there. When I'm in Omaha, I drive past it. The projects were located right across the street from Kellom. Man, they were somethin'. Not far from 24th Street. I drive down 24th Street all the time, and it doesn't remind me of anything about the 24th Street I grew up on. They're redeveloping North Omaha. A friend of mine from Tech High, Mike Maroney, is spearheading economic development initiatives aimed at revitalizing North Omaha. Many Tech grads are doing well. Yet, they closed Tech [The Tech building today is the headquarters of Omaha Public Schools.].

Why would the city shut down a place where many minorities were acquiring the tools they needed for success? The city closed a great high school that had great teachers. The people in power in Omaha pretty much tore up the entire African American community living in North Omaha.

My sister lives in a building down there near where the Tech building stands. It's a place Mike Maroney developed. So I go over there to see her. She's sick. She's an old Trojan. When I go to visit her, I notice that there's not a single store in her neighborhood. No place to buy groceries. No place to shop. Isn't that interesting?

The African American community in North Omaha has been displaced and destroyed. It's happening in cities all over the country. After a sense of community is lost in a place, the authorities wonder where the gangs came from. I'll answer that: you reap what you sow. Segregation is part of the problem. You segregate by economics. Occupation and income dictate where you can live.

The solution for reviving North Omaha is to bring back business. I compare North Minneapolis to North Omaha—places where gangs roam and where minorities live. A business wasteland. Lots of cities have this stuff. What's lacking is jobs. Jobs give residents of a community a vested interest or a stake in that community. A great community has small businesses. Eighty percent of the American economy is small business.

You know, it's interesting.

My first recollection of baseball is playing baseball in the projects. There was a building—a trucking building—down by Kellom School where I lived. Next to this trucking business building there were other big buildings. Those buildings served as our outfield fence. To hit a home run, our rule was that you had to hit the ball high off the wall. Those buildings were a long way from the home plate on our sandlot diamond.

Josh Gibson was my first coach in a Near North Side YMCA league. Back in those days, black kids in North Omaha played baseball against other black kids. If you were black, you "stayed in your lane." Don't think you're going to high school at Creighton Prep. You were limited to where you played and limited to who you could play for. Black athletes had limited choices. Jerry Bartee, who was a great baseball player, went to Central High School. I went to Tech.

You know, it's interesting.

As I look back, baseball in my time was so segregated.

Everyday life was so segregated—and still is.

In America, we segregate by economics. America's not free. You're free to live wherever you want—if you've got the money to live in the area where you want to live.

When I was playing baseball, baseball was so segregated that blacks thought of baseball as "the white man's sport" or "the thinking man's sport." You had to THINK to play baseball. White athletes in my day didn't want to compete against black athletes in football, track, and basketball. You know, because of the stereotypes about black athletes—black athletes are fast and all of that. But it was okay to play against black athletes in baseball 'cause blacks were "too dumb" and because baseball was "too cerebral" for us. You have to remember this—it's context. I recall that when I started playing baseball, most of my black friends used to focus on offense—they were always trying to swing as hard as they could in order to hit home runs.

You know, it's interesting.

Josh Gibson changed how black kids played baseball in Omaha. Gibson's challenge of teaching us to play baseball was heightened by the fact that many of us came from undisciplined backgrounds. It took a father figure like Josh to gain the respect of kids and instill discipline in them. You didn't mess with Josh. It's interesting. There's a direct line between Josh and Tech winning the 1966 state high school baseball championship. Before 1966, Tech baseball was the laughingstock of high school baseball in Omaha. All the other high schools in town wanted to play us. They figured they'd 10-run us. Baseball was a chance for the predominantly white high schools to pay Tech back for whupping them in football, basketball, and track.

Both Josh Gibson and Coach John Morse worked hard. Certainly, when we were kids, we were clueless about baseball. The coaches who taught us the game had to be in love with baseball. They had to have patience.

For Tech to win the high school baseball championship in 1966 and for us to win the district in baseball the next year—that was a miracle. Those were the only two years Tech was a force to be reckoned with in baseball.

Nevertheless, people still don't give those 1966 and 1967 Tech baseball teams the respect we deserve. I was talking to Jerry Bartee the other day. We were talking about 1966.

"You lucky suckers," Jerry said.

"How dare you call us lucky," I said.

"You all got hot," Jerry replied.

We got hot? We were the only metro team with two really good pitchers. We had outstanding catchers. We had some excellent athletes. What about our shortstop—Griego. He was arguably the best baseball player in Omaha in 1966. And my brother, Kirkland. A great athlete. But he wasn't disciplined as a hitter. Since he was always trying to hit a home run, he struck out a lot. When he occasionally made contact, he'd hit towering home runs.

Keep in mind, Tech wasn't all black. It was the school that most of the blacks in Omaha attended. Tech had the highest percentage of black students. In its history, Tech had black sports stars and white sports stars. But the public's image of Tech was that it was a "black school."

Keep in mind also that Josh Gibson's brother was one of the greatest athletes to come out of Omaha. Tech's Bob Gibson was more than just a great baseball player. He was a great athlete. Great basketball player.

I had major scholarships offered to me in three sports. With respect to baseball, Josh taught us that raw athleticism wasn't enough in baseball because baseball was cerebral. To win at baseball, you've got to be smart. You have to know the game.

White high school baseball teams used to like to play Tech. They expected our infielders to throw the ball around and eventually throw it away. They expected our outfielders to throw behind the runners and allow runners to take an extra base.

This disrespect toward black baseball players in Omaha carried over into the 1966 high school baseball season. Our opponents assumed we were dumb and undisciplined. They assumed we didn't know how to hit a curveball. They expected our hitters to swing on a count of three balls and no strikes. They figured their base runners could take big leads on our pitchers. They assumed their base runners could steal whenever they wanted to without any risk that our catchers would throw them out. The mentality of the fans and players from these white schools prior to a baseball game against Tech was "We'll get these guys today just like we always do—we'll run their black asses off the field."

By the middle of the 1966 high school baseball season, all those white high schools—their players and their fans—were mad at Tech. They had grown accustomed to beating up on our baseball teams. Making us look foolish. Our team got off to a slow start but went on an eight-game winning streak. Any team that played us during that streak got the message from us real quick: "Game on now, brother! You ain't gonna get revenge for what we did to you in football and basketball today. You're gonna get your ass kicked."

In midseason, our Tech team jelled. It was game over in five innings. I was a starter on the Tech varsity baseball team since my freshman year. Great athletes raised me in baseball. White athletes! Gary Hunter. He was like my big brother. A white catcher. He used to teach me all kinds of stuff about baseball.

I'll tell you somethin'. By the fifth inning, our games were over. Once we took the lead in a baseball game, these white teams would tighten up. They knew they weren't invincible any more. Whenever a team got behind us, they knew we were different from Tech baseball teams from the past. Unlike previous Tech teams, we were built on speed, defense, and pitching, so we weren't going to give away games. You had to take it from us.

After Tech beat Creighton Prep in the districts in 1966, a brawl broke out in the parking lot at Rosenblatt Stadium where we had played the game. Creighton Prep was one of the elite schools in athletics in Omaha, you know that. If you go back to the sixties, you'd see Prep was a force in high school sports. Shoot. Our Tech team was one of the few predominantly black sports teams to defeat Creighton Prep in anything. Tech never beat Benson—except we beat Benson in the championship game.

Tech winning the state championship embarrassed Omaha's white establishment. I was so proud about winning the championship that I ran around school with my letter jacket with my baseball letter on it. To anyone from another high school who would express shock that I would choose to wear my letter for baseball instead of my letters from other sports because Tech had a reputation as being worthless in baseball—I'd say, "Suck on that one."

After we won that championship, all those great athletes from rival Omaha high schools who had been laughing their asses off and making fun of Tech's baseball team had to shut up. [Laughter]

You know, it's interesting.

I took Ron Boone, who graduated from Omaha Tech—a guy who played all those years for the Utah Stars in the American Basketball Association—to dinner. One of the greatest basketball players ever to come out of Omaha. They called him the "Iron Man" because of all the pro basketball games he played. Ron and I love each other. We respect each other. He had a great career in pro basketball. I had a great career in pro football. I played pro football 9 years. Ron played pro hoops for 10 years or so.

What do you think our dinner conversation centered around? Coach John Morse and baseball! We both had played for Coach Morse—like Ron's brother Ernie Boone who was a pitcher on Morse's '66 and '67 Tech baseball teams. Ron Boone played Tech baseball before me. He's tight with Coach Morse. Ron was an infielder.

I never had Coach Morse as a teacher, but as a player on Tech's 1966 varsity baseball team, I understood that if Tech won the championship in baseball, then Coach Morse was going to allow Ron Bartee (who at the time was enrolled in one of Morse's classes) to teach his class for one day. The next thing you know—it happened—we won the championship and there was Ron Bartee teaching Coach Morse's class. Me and all of the other players were walking by Coach Morse's classroom and laughing.

Let me tell you. Coach Morse put up with a lot. Compared to Coach Morse, the other coaches in the metro had it easy. Morse was a basketball coach, too. Did you know that? I was on his best basketball team—it was a freshman team. I didn't have to score. We had George Hicks. We won the Boys Town tournament. We were up and comin'. Coach Morse did things none of the high school coaches who got all the publicity in the *Omaha World-Herald* did. In basketball, he took a team of black freshman, played the toughest competition in Omaha, and went unbeaten. Coach Morse developed basketball players for Coach Mosser who ran the varsity program. It's interesting. Morse developed talent for the basketball teams and Josh Gibson did the same thing for the two successful Tech baseball teams.

Morse guided a predominantly black team playing a white sport to a championship. That's embarrassing to white teams. The white high school baseball teams could not "hold serve" against us. The white teams almost gave up a second baseball championship the next year to our 1967 team. If Tech hadn't lost in the semifinal game in 1967, we'd have been playing for a second state championship. To go from being the team everyone made fun of to almost winning back-to-back championships is amazing.

Do you know how wonderful it feels to go from the big underdog to become the only state champ? Just look how happy we were in that team picture. All of us realized we'd done something that wasn't supposed to be done. Take a closer look at that team picture. There's two great coaches in that picture. Besides Coach Morse, Coach Trumbauer is in that picture. Coach Trumbauer was the assistant baseball coach and the head football coach. He developed me as a quarterback. He's the one who told me to keep working hard to improve as a quarterback because eventually I'd get my shot to play that position.

Let me tell you something. All of the players on that team had gone through hell together. We were not only the laughingstock of other high school baseball players in Omaha but also the laughingstock of our Tech classmates. Say a bunch of Tech baseball players would be walking through the halls of Tech wearing their baseball uniforms. Say they bump into a bunch of their classmates. The razzing starts.

"They gonna get ten-runned. They gonna get killed."

Our classmates would be laughin' in our faces.

Before 1966, Tech had a tradition of terrible baseball teams with horrible records.

You know, it's interesting.

To appreciate what we did, you gotta realize baseball was a white man's sport. It ain't about how gifted you are. But when you look at that 1966 team, you see black and white ballplayers. I'm looking at the team picture now. I'm looking at the late John Roper. A big black athlete. He was mainly a baseball player. He looks like Cecil Fielder who used to play for the Detroit Tigers. Both Roper and Fielder were big and gifted. They moved like small men.

You gotta remember, the black athletes on the 1966 Tech team were boys growing into men. When you grow up black and you're discriminated against all the time, your self-esteem isn't the greatest. We all blossomed at the same time. It wasn't just one of us having a great year in 1966. We all did.

Look at that team picture. Why are my teammates and I looking jubilant? Because we knew that we had just given a black eye to white baseball in Omaha—that's why.

# 19

# Johnny Rodgers

On June 1, 1969, Johnny Rodgers' high school baseball career ended as something only Bill Veeck could stage. The center fielder from Omaha's Technical High School took a couple of pitches while batting right-handed in his final trip to the plate. Then, he backed out of the batter's box and stepped to the other side of home plate. Batting left-handed he got a base hit. Those who had followed the baseball career of this Tech senior didn't bat an eyelash. They had become accustomed to super feats. While lettering in four sports for three years at Tech, Rodgers had dazzled fans. Nicknamed "The Jet" for his quick starts and speed, Rodgers was voted Nebraska High School Athlete of the Year when he was a senior.

Standing 5'10" and weighing only 170 pounds, Rodgers was better physically suited for baseball than for football. As a testament to Rodgers' potential as a baseball player in his senior year at Tech, the *Omaha World-Herald* called Rodgers "pro material in baseball." But after playing baseball his freshman year at the University of Nebraska–Lincoln (UNL), Rodgers quit the sport to focus on football.

In 1972, the year after leading the Huskers to a national championship in football, Rodgers won the Heisman Trophy for most outstanding player in college football in the United States. He served as a punt return specialist, pass receiver, and running back. He broke every offensive team record and was twice named to the college football All-America team. Rodgers played professionally in the Canadian Football League (CFL) with the Montreal Alouettes and in the National Football League (NFL) with the San Diego Chargers.

I interviewed Rodgers while drinking cold beverages with him in the friendly confines of his former coach and friend John Morse's apartment in West Omaha. Rodgers recalled his involvement with black baseball in Omaha, offered a social history of his athletic career, and mentioned he's getting knee surgery. Most importantly, he exploded my preconceived image of him as a self-centered, dumb jock. Dressed in a red dress shirt and slacks, the Omaha businessman was sharp, on point, and generous to a fault.

\* \* \*

Josh Gibson was my first baseball coach. Josh was a black Bob Devaney, but Josh never got the credit Devaney did. Both Devaney and Gibson were master coaches. All of Bob Gibson's fame can be attributed to Josh. Without Josh, there would never be Hall of Famer Bob Gibson. Josh was hard on Bob. Heck, Josh was hard on everybody.

I remember how I got started playing for Josh. My mom and I met with Tommy Davis, a recreation worker, at the Boys Club. Tommy looked my mom in the eye.

"Johnny has a unique talent for baseball," Tommy said, "but he's in desperate need of a coach—somebody to teach him the finer points and strategies of the game. If I can get Johnny onto Josh Gibson's team, playing for Josh will take Johnny's athletic career to a whole new level. But you've got to get him to the games and the practices. Can you do this?"

My mom said she couldn't and laughed Tommy down. Tommy turned to me.

"Johnny, what do you want to do?" he asked.

"I want to make $100,000," I said.

My mother slapped me.

"Stop saying that shit," she said. "Black people don't make $100,000."

Tommy volunteered to drive me to Josh's practices and games. Four years later, I graduated from Tech and I had earned All-State honors in several sports.

Josh took losing seriously. Josh's players would get rides to the games but catching a ride back was predicated on winning. If Josh's baseball team, which I played on, lost a ballgame in South Omaha, Josh would make us walk back to North Omaha. It was a straight shot on Twenty-Fourth Street. [Twenty-Fourth Street connects the heart of North Omaha to the heart of South Omaha.] Following a loss to a South Omaha team, Josh used to escort us to 24th Street, point north, and tell us to keep walking until we got home. We turned it into a fun walk. All of the players were laughing and talking. Today, it seems bizarre to be doing that to kids, but if you knew Josh, you would say he was acting in character. He treated us kids like adults. He expected us to conduct ourselves in a professional manner. We had to bunt well. Catch with two hands. Play hard. We rarely lost.

Few people know this, but baseball was my first sport. I loved baseball more than football. I was better at it. And that was because of Josh. The first time I played organized baseball was at the Near North Side Y. Of course, when I was four or five years old, I was throwing and hitting balls in the street in my neighborhood in North Omaha. I played both baseball and football in the streets of North Omaha. Basketball we played in people's driveways. I played with Paul White, Jimmy White, Jimmy Long, Julius Harris. We also played a lot of baseball in Kountze Park. It's located right across the street from the King Science Center which used to be called Horace Mann School. I would go to Kountze Park, stand around, and wait for an opportunity to play ball with the bigger guys. Kountze Park was where Gayle Sayers, Marlin Briscoe [Marlin "The Magician" Briscoe played football at Omaha South High in Omaha, earned All-American honors as a quarterback at the University of Omaha—now the University of Nebraska Omaha—in the mid–1960s, and played nine seasons in the NFL], and almost every other athlete from North Omaha who you can think of played baseball, football, and basketball.

To play for Josh, you had to try out and make his team. We'd practice on a field down behind Horace Mann. Josh would select a team, the team would travel, and we'd play our games in a white baseball league. I remember Larry Zachary, Lloyd Smith, Aaron Hall.... I can't remember all of them. We had an all-black team. I was eight or 10 years old. We played all around Omaha but didn't travel out of town for any games. You have to understand, Josh raised Omaha's black baseball players. Most of them went to Omaha Tech. If they didn't go to Tech, chances are they wouldn't be allowed to play high school baseball.

If Josh was alive, he wouldn't be sitting here having a beer with us. Josh was a big man. Heavyset, dark-skinned guy. Josh's personality was standoffish. He was unapproachable. He was "the coach." A very intimidating guy. On the ball field, Josh was yelling most of the time.

Josh built me to be a baseball player. He taught me to switch hit. Originally, I batted right-handed. Josh explained that it was easier to get bunt singles by hitting from the left side than the right side. A left-handed batter is much closer to first than a right-handed batter. Josh taught me to bat left-handed and drag bunt. I would stand in the batter's box on the left side of the plate, bunt the ball right along the first base line, and beat it out. It worked almost every time.

I could run the bases so well that once I got on, I would score. I used to steal home all the time. Josh must have taught me how to steal home. With Josh, you didn't figure shit out yourself. You did what he said. Josh was a strict disciplinarian. You played Josh's way or you didn't play. If you played for Josh, you didn't make errors or mental mistakes. You didn't screw around.

Of course, I was lucky to have a coach like Josh. He taught me life lessons. Most importantly, he taught me discipline. By the time I was playing high school and college ball, Josh had turned me into a "coachable" athlete. Other players on my high school and college teams weren't prepared to play for somebody like Devaney. Some of them may have been pampered by their coaches. Josh did not pamper. Josh taught me to respect my coaches, to carry myself like a professional. Josh made us "little professionals." There's a difference between having raw athletic talent and being an athlete with a professional mindset. The professional-minded athlete knows you never make mistakes, never argue with umpires or referees. I learned this from Josh.

During my days of playing ball in Omaha, I never saw a black umpire. It was taboo for us players to question the calls of white umpires, but Josh would stick up for us. He would never be intimidated by umpires or anyone else. Nobody ever treated Josh's players unfairly and got away with it. Josh himself was an intimidating guy. He would have "talks" with white umpires from time to time. Josh was a great role model and coach. If an umpire or another team attempted to take advantage of us in a baseball game, Josh had trained us to retaliate through our aggressive style of play. One time a guy asked me "how aggressive were Josh's baseball teams?" I gave him an "are you serious?" look. And then I said with a straight face, "I used to steal home." If I was a base runner on third base and the pitcher went into a full windup, it was over. Before the pitch reached the batter, I'd be sliding across home plate.

I played for Josh from the time I was at the Y until I went up to the Boys Club when I was 12 or 13 years old. I hit a lot of inside-the-park home runs. Some right-handed, some left-handed. I played shortstop and centerfield for Josh. I had a strong arm, a quick start, and good speed. I could run down balls in center field. I seemed destined to become a baseball player.

Growing up in North Omaha was special in the sense that I had opportunities to play with great athletes. We had quite a few young guys like myself who were busy playing sports. I never thought about joining a gang. My gangs were all the baseball, football, and basketball teams I played for. All year long I played sports so I never had idle time to get into trouble. I was into sports. If you had been a kid living in my neighborhood, you'd be going to Kountze Park. You'd see the Bartees, Marlin Briscoe, and a bunch of other good athletes there. Everybody who excelled as an athlete came through Kountze Park. The baseball field there was the same field we played football on. It wasn't really a baseball field. It was a softball field.

I played baseball for Coach Morse at Tech from 1966 through 1969. When I was a sophomore, we won district in 1967. I was playing shortstop. This was a period of racial unrest in North Omaha. When the riot following the police murder of Vivian Strong was going on in 1969, I was playing at Boyd Field near Carter Lake for Tech's Roberts Dairy summer Legion team. We heard all the noise. I wasn't on 24th Street involved in the riot because I was with Coach Morse on the baseball field. Busy playing ball.

My first game on the varsity baseball team at Tech, I hit a home run and a double at Kellom Field. My mom who had me when she was 14 years old came to all my games. She'd yell and clap. She'd supported me earlier when I'd played for Josh at the YMCA and then at the Boys Club. From my birth to 10 or 12 years old, I was involved in a lot of sports activities. My mom was there for me.

I don't recall ever seeing Josh at any of my Tech baseball games. Sometime in the late 1960s, Josh quit coaching. He confided in me that he couldn't get a job in the Omaha Public Schools as a high school teacher and baseball coach because of his race. He was sad and pissed. He had a master's degree from Creighton University. OPS didn't have any black teachers or coaches in high school, period. That's straight out racism. Without Josh Gibson, Johnny Rodgers would have never played high school or college baseball.

As a kid I also played football and tried wrestling, but wrestling was so goddamned tough and it was so hot in the wrestling room that I decided to be a basketball player. I became all-city in basketball. But football and baseball were my sports. At 5'10" the odds of me going very far in basketball were not good. Football as a career seemed iffy. At that size, I could play shortstop, second base, or center field—and be just fine. I had choices.

**Football great Johnny Rodgers (fourth from the left in the back row) was also an outstanding baseball player. Here he is as a member of the 1967 Roberts Dairy American Legion team, and notice the glasses that he is wearing (personal collection of Steve Bauermeister).**

Ten major league teams scouted me when I played high school baseball. A bunch of 'em showed up at my games. Several colleges also sent scouts to my baseball games. One was UNL baseball coach Tony Sharpe. I wound up playing baseball for Sharpe. After the Los Angeles Dodgers drafted me out of high school, I flew to California. My dad picked me up and took me around. The Dodgers offered me $25,000 a year for three years. There was a problem. I had always dreamed of making $100,000. Now, I really didn't know how much $100,000 was, but it was the biggest number I'd ever heard of. When the Dodgers offered me 25 grand, I wasn't enthused.

My dad drove me around to the Los Angeles Coliseum. He rattled off the names of African Americans who had won the Heisman Trophy: Ernie Davis, a running back from Syracuse, in 1961; Mike Garrett, a running back from the University of Southern California (USC), in 1965; and O.J. Simpson, a running back from USC, in 1968. I knew that Davis had died, and that Garrett and Simpson were each making over $100,000, so I figured, hell, if I could play for USC, then I could make $100,000. So the plan was for me to play football for USC.

Back in Omaha, I contacted my mentor, Charlie Washington. Charlie was a big guy, not quite as dark as Josh. Charlie was the "Governor of the North Side" of Omaha. If you wanted something in North Omaha, you had to go through Charlie. He was the spokesperson for black folks on the North Side. Whenever money was needed for business development or a family needing a helping hand, Charlie would go to white people to get it. Charlie didn't have any money, but he could go get money. He had influence and respect. Everybody listened to Charlie. Charlie hung out with Malcolm X and other national leaders of the black community who would come to town. He wrote for the *Omaha Star*. That's where I met Charlie. I used to sell papers for the *Star*. I'd get a nickel for every paper I sold. Charlie showed me how to sell newspapers. That's how I got close to him. As I got older, I depended on Charlie to help me make decisions. If Charlie were here now, he would be having drinks with us. You know, he was very social. He would have parties at his house at 25th and Lake in North Omaha.

As an advocate for the North Side, Charlie arranged a meeting between Bob Devaney, the head coach of Nebraska's football team, and me. Devaney wanted to talk me into coming to Nebraska. The thing that bothered me about Nebraska is that back in those days the Cornhuskers hadn't won a championship since Jesus was a kid. So I wasn't interested. But because of Charlie, I agreed to meet Devaney. When Bob Devaney came into my house and he was telling me how great he was, he cracked me up. The guy looked like Mr. Potato Head. [Laughter] I figured this guy couldn't be for real. I mean, I was used to these tough-assed coaches like Josh Gibson and Don Benning. Devaney didn't look like he could coach anybody.

Devaney told me he wanted national champions, not Big Eight champions. He wanted All-Americans, not all-Big Eight players. He predicted that if I came to Nebraska, then Nebraska would become the national champion. According to Devaney, I needed to do this for the state.

"Coach, I'm sorry," I said. "But I've got my own plan. I gotta get on outta here."

I was thinking about that $100,000.

Being a master salesman, Devaney offered scholarships in both baseball and football—and he assured me that after four years of playing both sports, I could make $100,000 by going pro in two sports. Even though I wanted to go to USC and follow in the footsteps of Garrett and Simpson, USC wasn't trying that hard to recruit me—so everything worked out for the best. Despite my initial doubts, Devaney turned out to be a master recruiter, trainer, and coach.

My freshman year at Nebraska I played for Coach Tony Sharpe on the baseball team, and then Coach Devaney told me he wanted me to quit baseball because he had figured out all of these ways he was going to get me the football.

"Coach, that's crazy," I replied. "You promised me—you gave me your word."

Of course, at the time, you know what's running through my mind? I'm thinking I need $100,000.

"I'll make a deal with you," Devaney said. "If you give up baseball, I'll endorse you for the Heisman."

Realize something about the timing of this offer. Coach Devaney approached me about quitting baseball at a time in my life when I was vulnerable. I had gotten into trouble on the last day of school my freshman year at UNL in 1970. I was only 18 years old and did something stupid—I was screwing around drinking with two other guys. We were just playing a prank. Without any weapons, three of us robbed a gas station in Lincoln. We got $90 or $30 apiece. Most expensive $30 I ever had in my pocket. Making my life at the time even more complicated, I had three kids.

Quitting baseball allowed me to focus. My goals were to earn $100,000, win a national championship, and win the Heisman Trophy. Bob Devaney promised to help me. Together we devised a system for me to follow. We called it the "Heisman Factor System." "H" was for holding myself to a higher standard. "E" was I had to expect to win. "I" was for I had to invest in yourself and others. "S" was for setting goals and sticking to them. "M" was for being mentally tough and for making things happen. "S" was for staying strong. And "N" was for never giving up—no fair catches on punts.

This system kept me on track to win a national championship and the Heisman Trophy. I became the fourth African American to win the Heisman. The San Diego Chargers were the first to make an offer: $50,000 a year for three years.

"Goddamn," I said. "I still can't get my $100,000—even after I spent all this damn time playing football."

So I flew to Montreal.

"What will it take for you to bring that Heisman Trophy to Canada and to play for the Alouettes?" the owner of the Montreal Alouettes asked.

You know what I said, right?

# 20

# Kimera Bartee

Since Kimera Bartee made his debut on April 3, 1996, at the Hubert H. Humphrey Metrodome as a defensive replacement in the outfield with the Detroit Tigers against the Minnesota Twins, no other African American ballplayer from Omaha has entered the majors. Kimera spent 10 years as a player in professional baseball, including 243 major league games with Detroit, Cincinnati, and Colorado. Beginning with his rookie season in 1996, in which he stole 20 bases, Bartee embarked on a career in "The Show" where he played all three outfield positions, though he was primarily a center fielder. During his time in Organized Baseball, Kimera was also named by *Baseball America* as the fastest base runner and best defensive outfielder in the International League while playing for Toledo in 1997.

Before his pro playing days, Bartee was part of Creighton University's (CU's) NCAA College World Series team in 1991. The 1991 Bluejays finished with a 51–22 record, including a 9–4 mark in the postseason. The 51-win total remains a Creighton program high for victories in a season. The following season, Bartee was named to the 1992 Missouri Valley Conference All-Tourney team. His brother Khareth was also an outfielder, playing in the Kansas City minor league system in 2000. Prior to his time with CU, Kimera starred in baseball at Central High School in Omaha.

After 10 seasons of playing professional ball, Bartee retired and later became a baseball coach, beginning his career in 2005 with the Delmarva Shorebirds, the Baltimore Orioles Low Class A affiliate in the South Atlantic League. And as of the 2016 major league season, he is the Pittsburgh Pirates' minor league outfield and baserunning coordinator.

Given his native Omaha coaching pedigree, it seems only right that Bartee himself would become a major league coach. After all, he received tutelage from great baseball teachers in the River City. These included his father, Jerry (who had played for Josh Gibson's Y team and who had been the Creighton Bluejays baseball coach); Kimera's great-uncle Dunk (a former player on all-black clubs in Missouri and a former catcher for the Omaha Eagles); his great-cousin Dr. Rodney Wead (who also had played for Josh Gibson's Y team and someone who had been a local church softball coach); Al Gilmore (who had been a member of Josh Gibson's Y team and who had been a Country Club Little League coach); and the entire Omaha Blackhawks' slow pitch softball club.

When I interviewed Kimera over the phone, he was on the road in Charleston, West Virginia. The next day he planned on working with outfielders on the Pirate-affiliated West Virginia Power. Being a family man, however, Kimera was especially looking forward to returning home to Phoenix, Arizona. He yearned to sit in the stands on the third base side at a small baseball field so he could watch his youngest protégé roam the outfield. In his mind's eye, Kimera envisioned a batter hitting a foul tip, his protégé gazing into the stands, Kimera raising his arm up to signal the young outfielder where to position himself for the next pitch, and the outfielder seeing the sign and repositioning himself. This young ballplayer, who happens to be Kimera's son, is living proof that the circle of Bartees playing baseball will not be broken.

* * *

Growing up, my dad will tell ya, he used to say, "If baseball's not in ya, ya need to get out of the house." Baseball's a lifestyle. The Bartees still hold baseball dear to our hearts. The tradition of baseball in our family traces back to my father, his uncle—Howard Duncan, who ignited a passion for baseball in our family—and my uncle Ron. When I started playing baseball myself, I realized I was carrying a torch. I'm continuing a tradition that goes way deeper than myself. To this day, our family treasures the pictures we have of Uncle Howard Duncan from his baseball-playing days.

Some of my baseball roots are in the backyard of my family's home on Raven Oaks Drive where I used to play wiffle ball. We had one of the best-kept yards in the neighborhood. We had hedges put in which I helped Dad trim. In addition, we had a wire fence surrounding our backyard that we could knock the wiffle ball over. The combination of the manicured lawn, the hedges, and the fence turned our backyard into a field of dreams. With a little imagination, I saw our well-groomed backyard as a miniature major league ballpark—the perfect place to play wiffle ball. Even though there were five acres of open land across the street, I felt like the only place to play ball was in my backyard. Often, the wiffle ball games involved neighborhood kids and me. Other times my dad, my brother, and my dad's best friend—Mose Turner [an Omaha Softball Association Hall of Famer]—would play home run derby in our backyard. It'd be two on two. Serious wiffle ball battles went on there.

Even into my college years, my brother, my dad, Mose Turner, and I were playing home run derby in the backyard. I can still see big Mose standing at the plate. Mose epitomized a home run hitter. He had the look, he had the walk, he had the build. To this day, whenever I think of an intimidating home run hitter, I think of Mose Turner.

More of my baseball roots are in Country Club Little League. [Country Club Little League serves residents of a mostly white, affluent, middle class neighborhood whose boundaries extend from 52nd to 56th streets and from Blondo to Corby Street.] My first experience in organized baseball involved a coach in Country Club Little League by the name of Al Gilmore. I had him my third year of Little League and he coached me for two or three seasons. One of my teammates on coach Gilmore's team, Tim Decker, played with me on that Creighton team that went to the College World Series in 1991.

In Country Club Little League, Coach Gilmore taught me a lot about the fundamentals of baseball. At that time, I was a catcher. He would always say to me, "Get up on your haunches."

I didn't know what that meant. It means that whenever there's a guy on base and you're catching, you need to get up on the balls of your feet so you're in a position to throw in case the runner tries to steal. What I remember most about Coach Gilmore is what he taught me about the relationship between a player and a coach. A real coach cares. Coach Gilmore cared about me, and I knew it. To this day, the coaches who have made the greatest impression on me as a player were the ones who believed in me. As far as the specific fundamentals Coach Gilmore taught me, I don't remember them as much as I remember him teaching me how to be a man. By being a good role model, he was a man I could emulate.

Coach Gilmore emphasized that as baseball players we needed to "exercise our brains." He taught me to exercise my brain in school so I learned how to make fast, smart decisions—a talent that's important in life as well as on the baseball field. He stressed quickness in thinking and in reacting to situations. Coach Gilmore taught me to anticipate on the baseball field. Always think a play ahead.

In the fourth grade, I played on the Cardinal Country Club Little League team for Coach Gilmore. A friend of mine, Andre Gilmore, was my teammate. Andre is the first friend I can remember. We were friends before kindergarten. He's still a close friend. Recently, he attended the banquet in honor of Creighton University inducting the entire 1991 CU baseball squad into its Hall of Fame. Everything I did as a kid, I did it with Andre. We've always had each other's backs. The three longest years in my life were when I went to Nathan Hale Junior High and he went to Lewis and Clark Junior High. I was lost for three years. He is as close to me as any blood relative could be.

When Andre and I played in Country Club Little League, about 75 percent of the players were white and the other 25 percent were black. Some folks might think I was at a disadvantage coming up in Little League instead of playing for a select or travel team, but I disagree. There are too many problems with select teams. First, playing year round causes burnout. Second, too often coaches on travel teams are concerned with winning instead of player development. And third, select coaches have a tendency to pigeonhole kids to win—limiting kids to playing one position is not smart because you never know how a little kid is going to develop physically.

Actually, as a kid, I played in three leagues. I went to Lil Vikes for football [Lil Vikes is a youth football program supporting the North Omaha area], Kellom Elementary School for basketball, and Country Club for baseball. Looking back, I can see how my dad and Mr. Gilmore did a good job of making sure black kids who played football and basketball in the fall and winter tried out for baseball in the summer. Equally important, I was encouraged to play football and basketball on fields and courts in North Omaha.

The first time I noticed race was when I made the All-Star team in Country Club Little League. I was the only African American on the team. It seemed like there was an agenda. We wore yellow pinstriped uniforms. [And] even though I was one of the best players in the league, the coaches stuck me in the outfield. From my vantage point today, the outfield was where I was supposed to be. [He laughs.] But, at the time, I saw being in the outfield as a demotion. The mindset of a Little Leaguer is that the best players play infield and the weakest play outfield.

Please keep in mind, though, that I was only seeing this All-Star experience through my eyes, my lens. No doubt it looked different from the perspective of the coaches of that Little League All-Star team. As I've gotten older, I've learned to look at things through other people's lens. Nevertheless, I can still recall standing in the outfield in the practices and games for that All-Star team, looking around at the infielders and thinking to myself, "Hey, what am I doing in the outfield—I'm better than them."

At the time, my main positions during the regular season in Little League were catcher and second base. I've always tried to be versatile and I've always sought to make things look easy when I do them. I'd rather be good at a lot of things than great at one thing. If you're good every day, that makes you great. As opposed to, bad one day and great another day—then, bad—then, good. Seek consistency and balance. Life is a marathon, not a sprint.

As a little kid, I didn't know my dad was preparing me to play outfield. By launching tennis balls into the air with a tennis racket, my dad taught me how to catch fly balls. I still use a tennis racket and tennis balls to this day when I work with outfielders in the Pirate organization. They love it. I even invented a drill. It's a Spanish name. Mano de chibo. It means "hands of a goat."

For the drill, I don't allow the players to use gloves. I launch balls into the air and they catch the balls barehanded. The drill instills in players the habit of watching the ball into their hands, teaches them how to set their feet properly for an athletic catch, and also makes their hands softer. Whenever a player drops a tennis ball, we say he has "hands of a goat." Get it. The hands of a goat are the goat's hooves.

Faith, family, and baseball are the top three things in my life. God first and foremost, family next, and baseball is third. I feel so blessed.

Along the way, I've faced a few challenges. When I tried out for the Gladiators [a select or travel baseball team in Omaha], I went to tryouts when I was one year younger than the other players. Age didn't matter to me. Although my best position was catcher, I ran my butt out to shortstop. I didn't want anything to do with catching. I wanted to make it as a middle infielder. I wanted to play shortstop, the position I grew up watching my dad play.

At the end of tryouts, the coaches posted the roster listing all the kids picked for the team. I read the list but didn't see my name. Then, the coaches addressed the players.

"All you kids who didn't make the team," one of the coaches announced, "should use this failure as motivation. Hopefully, three or four years from now, you'll run into us, and you can say, 'Remember me? I'm the one you cut.'"

I never forgot that moment. I used it as motivation.

My senior year in high school, I was playing in the Metro spring senior all-star game, and I slugged a triple at Seymour Smith Field. I slid into third, popped up, and looked into the stands behind third base. Lo and behold there were the same Gladiator coaches who'd cut me. I looked them in the eye.

"Remember me?" I shouted. "I'm the one you cut." [He laughs.]

Thinking back about that tryout, I have a few regrets. Would I have made the team as a catcher? I don't know. The lesson I learned was "Always position yourself to thrive, not merely survive." By failing to try out at my strongest position, I situated myself to survive. From that point on, I've always played to my strengths.

At Central High School, I made the junior varsity as a freshman. I was playing high school baseball as a ninth grader and I was still in junior high! [At that time, junior high in Omaha ran through the ninth grade.] It was heady stuff for a kid. While playing baseball for Central, I was walking around Nathan Hale Junior High wearing a Central baseball jacket. Eventually, toward the end of the high school baseball season, I got called up to the varsity for the playoffs. It was fun. Some of the seniors who didn't see me as a threat taught me a lot. But the sophomores and juniors were not so happy that I was playing varsity. They looked at me as someone who would take one of the starting positions away from their buddies the next year. And they were right. That summer, I played with the varsity and learned even more.

I never talked at Central. I would sit back and analyze. Take things apart. I observed and studied those Central High varsity players from the bench and learned things that

I knew would eventually benefit me. In particular, I witnessed how mental toughness could be a powerful factor. I thank my Central High teammates to this day. At the time, the seniors didn't even know they were teaching me.

One of the seniors was Marcus Harvey. He took me under his wing. Marcus was a black ballplayer whose dad used to play for the Omaha Blackhawks. His father, who recently passed away, was an administrator in the Omaha Public Schools. Marcus had known me since I was five years old. Our relationship went deeper than Central High, so it was easier for Marcus to take me in. Wendell Young, another black ballplayer on the Central High team, also mentored me. Today, Wendell runs the Omaha Royals' youth travel baseball team. Both Marcus and Wendell got on my case when I needed it. They cared.

During my junior year, Elvis Dominguez [a four-year starter at shortstop for the Creighton Bluejays from 1983 through 1986 and who now is the head baseball coach of the Bradley University Braves] took the helm as Central's baseball coach. Knowing that if I was going to make it as a pro that it would probably be as a middle infielder, Elvis would work out with me for half an hour after practice. For these after-practice workouts, he designed a wooden glove for me to use catching ground balls. He figured the glove would help me to develop softer hands and to learn how to funnel ground balls. Elvis also taught me situation assignments, such as where to go if the ball was hit into a gap in the outfield. He taught me everything I needed to know to play second base, including double cuts, my responsibilities on bunts and on relays. None of this was for the benefit of Central High School. All of it was for my personal development. I've been blessed to have people like Elvis in my life—people who saw something special in me and worked to make me better.

At Central, I was All-Metro in my junior year, and in my senior year, I was All-Metro, All-District, All-State—all that stuff. You have to keep in mind, however, track, football, and basketball were the big sports at Central in those days. My friends would ask, "Why aren't you playing other sports?" The football coach asked me to come out and promised he would start me at safety. Whenever I'd get tempted to go out for football, I'd look at my friend at Central, Calvin Jones. [After starring as a running back in football at Central, Calvin Jones played collegiately for the Nebraska Cornhuskers and professionally for the Los Angeles/Oakland Raiders and the Green Bay Packers.] Calvin was bigger and faster than me. I was afraid Calvin would run me over.

My freshman year at Creighton University, I was back at square one—not talking. I got off to a bad start. The first meeting of the CU baseball team—I think it was an orientation to the CU Athletic Department—I arrived late because my mom was sick. Jim Hendry, the CU head coach, chewed me out. I thought to myself, "Is this what college is really about? I'm here five minutes, and I get yelled at."

Again, I was lucky to have a whole new group of guys who were willing to take me in. Dax Jones, Steve Hinton, and Scott Stahoviak reached out to me. Those were my guys. Jones, Hinton, and Stahoviak were all juniors. The year of 1991 was their year to shine. They took me in as their little brother. They forced me to talk. Took me to parties. Showed me everything. That day I got yelled at, they were the first ones in my corner. They pulled me aside and said, "No excuses, no explanations."

After my freshman year, Coach Hendry took a job with the Florida Marlins and Todd Wenberg, who previously was the pitching coach under Hendry, took over as CU head coach. My sophomore year is a blur. Whereas in my freshman year I was one of the first guys off the bench, in my sophomore year I was adjusting to oftentimes being a starter. My sophomore year, we went to the NCAA tournament and lost to Virginia Commonwealth. My junior year, CU was ranked in the top 25 all year, but we slumped at the end, and didn't get an NCAA bid. That was back when there were only 48 teams in the tournament instead of the 64 they have now.

Out of CU, the Baltimore Orioles drafted me. Former Northwest High School coach Bill Olson put the word in for me, had the national cross-checkers come out…. He … yeah … he's the one who put me on the pro track. I'll be forever grateful to Coach Olson. Still friends with him to this day.

After getting traded to Detroit and at the end of the 1996 baseball season, I returned to Omaha and went to the school where my mom was principal—Lothrop School. Lothrop is a public elementary school located on North 22nd Street in the Kountze Place neighborhood of North Omaha. My mom asked me to come and talk to the kids. It was a chance to give back. I didn't hesitate. I knew what North Omaha was about—I realized how important a black professional ballplayer was to the kids at Mom's school.

While I was talking to the kids in a cafeteria, I made eye contact with Mom. The look she had in her eyes I'll never forget. She was proud that I was serving as a positive influence for her students. With kids sitting all around me, I asked what was most important in their lives. After listening to their answers, I repeated what Coach Gilmore had taught me about the importance of exercising your brain in school.

As I continued my conversation with the kids, my mind flashed back to my own childhood—times when I was a little kid and Nebraska Cornhusker football players would come to visit my elementary school in Omaha. As a kid, I'd never heard a baseball player speak at any of my schools in Omaha. It had always been Nebraska Cornhusker football players. Seeing my superheroes at my schools always made me feel special.

My conversation with the kids took an unexpected turn when they asked two questions: "Who taught you how to play baseball?" and "Who is your idol?"

Former major leaguer Kimera Bartee was part of the 1991 Creighton University baseball team, which finished 51–22, including a 2–2 record in the College World Series (Creighton Athletics).

Without a moment's hesitation, I blurted out one answer to both questions.

"My mom," I replied.

I explained to the kids how when I was seven years old, my mom used to throw batting practice to me with real baseballs in our backyard! To hit off Mom, I positioned myself to hit away from the house and up a hill. No net to catch the batted balls. No nothin'. If there were no kids to play with, my mom would come out in the backyard and play catch with me. She had no idea what she was doing with the glove or the ball. She just wanted to help. I needed her to be there. And she was. She's always been there.

As I drove away from Lothrop School, my mind drifted back to days when I was a kid playing basketball at Kellom School and my mind started racing. Did Dad have a hidden agenda when he signed me up to play basketball at Kellom in North Omaha? Was Dad's intention to set me up for failure—to put me on Kellom's basketball court where I wouldn't be "The Man" that I was on the baseball diamond. Was he teaching me how to deal with adversity?

The reality hit me that at Kellom I was playing basketball against the guys who my dad and Mr. Gilmore had persuaded to play baseball even though their best sports were football and basketball. Baseball was my arena. Dad had to be aware that it would take some work on my end to compete in their arena at Kellom. Playing basketball against players who were better than me in North Omaha tested me, forced me to grow, and helped me to develop friendships that I have to this day.

They say, "It takes a village to raise a child," and I'd be remiss if I didn't mention the Omaha Blackhawks. I never knew why Dad wore 15. I do now. He wore 15 because one of his teammates with the Omaha Blackhawks—a guy my dad grew up idolizing and copying, the late Floyd Crandall—wore 15. Floyd Crandall and the Blackhawks also helped raise me. Crandall's son and I are still friends. Today, in my job as a roving instructor for the Pittsburgh Pirates, guess what number I wear? 15. Guess what number my son wears?

I've been with the Pirates nine seasons now as their coordinator. When I started, we were not very good. Now we're solid. Our starting three outfielders are products of our developmental process. They're all from our system. All guys that I had since they were babies. We take a lot of pride in developing our own. We love the fact that we're on top. We're solid. The icing on the cake is that we are winning with our own players. The Pirates are winning with the same model that the 2015 World Series champion Kansas City Royals used.

As a Pirate, there is the matter of Pirate pride. While talking to my outfielders, I often invoke the name of the greatest Pirate of all time. We instill tradition in our players. We stress character, integrity, and identity. We firmly believe that it takes men to win in the big leagues. There is no better model for being a man and being a great baseball player than Roberto Clemente. In the Pirate organization, we talk about Clemente all the time. His memory and glory will never fade.

One thing bothers me about my own legacy in black ball in Omaha—I'm the last African American to play in the majors. My first year in the majors was 1996. It's been 20 years. That's too long. I need to get back home. I need to stay involved in the Omaha community. Shame on me for being the last African American from Omaha to play in the majors. I need to come back to Omaha and change that.

I'd like to see little black kids playing baseball again in Omaha and across the country. I would love to be in the forefront on this. I've been talking to the president of the Major League Baseball Players Association about this issue. Plans are being drawn up to get black baseball players back in the game. We're a dying breed.

# 21

# Peaches James

By the numbers, there has arguably never been a more dominant home-grown prep and collegiate pitcher in the history of baseball and softball in either the city of Omaha or the state of Nebraska than Peaches James. Not National Baseball Hall of Famer Bob Gibson. Not National Baseball Hall of Famer Grover Cleveland Alexander. Not Baltimore Orioles 1989 Rookie of the Year Award winner Gregg Olson. As Casey Stengel used to say, "You could look it up."

Stats don't lie: Peaches James left hitters in the dust. After being named to the All-State Second Team as a freshman playing for the powerhouse Papillion-LaVista varsity in 1996, this phenomenal high school star earned first-team all-state honors three straight years. The *Lincoln Journal Star* and *Omaha World-Herald* selected her as honorary captain of the all-state teams in 1998 and 1999. In those same two years, she was chosen the Metro Conference Player of the Year. According to the University of Nebraska–Lincoln's (UNL's) athletic website, she set 10 Nebraska state softball records. These include consecutive pitching wins (31), consecutive shutouts (19), consecutive shutout innings (162⅓), consecutive innings with no earned runs allowed (257⅔), lowest season ERA in 1999 (0.04), lowest career ERA (0.13), most no-hitters in a season (11), most perfect games in a season (five), most career perfect games (six), and most consecutive perfect games (three).

When discussing who was the greatest home-grown high school and collegiate pitcher, it is important to recognize that James' amazing individual accomplishments translated into team championships. With Peaches leading the way, Papillion-LaVista won four straight state championships from 1996 through 1999. She also helped the Echoes Spirit (a summer team) to a second-place finish at the 2000 American Softball Association nationals. Pitching for UNL from 2000 through 2004, James led her team to three Big 12 championships (two regular season crowns and one tournament title) and eight victories in the NCAA tournament.

James capped four seasons of heroic collegiate performances by winning second-team National Fastpitch Coaches Association All-America honors in her senior season in 2004. In the Big 12 Tournament, James threw the second perfect game in UNL's school history against Oklahoma. She finished her senior season with a 37–9 record and a 0.70 ERA. During her junior season, she was named first-team All Midwest Region, first-team All-Big 12, and second-team academic All-Big 12. For her sophomore season, she earned first-team All-Big 12 honors with a 22–9 record and a 1.33 ERA. Highlights of her freshman season include compiling a 16–7 record, posting a 1.37 ERA, and pitching four shutouts against Big 12 teams. Following her NU career, Peaches pitched in the National Pro Fastpitch league and was an All-Star in 2005.

I interviewed the woman whose name has become synonymous with softball in Nebraska on the campus of the University of Nebraska Omaha where Peaches now works as a senior financial support counselor. Although she still gives girls pitching lessons, James has moved on from softball. Armed with a Master of Business Administration, she is carving out a new career for herself in higher education leadership. During our conversation, Peaches was humble and high-spirited, with a sparkle in her eyes.

\* \* \*

Shortly before I enrolled at Papillion-LaVista High School, my dad pulled me aside and said, "Just think, Peaches, Jackie Robinson played in the Negro Leagues for the Kansas City Monarchs and now you're going to be playing softball for the Papillion-LaVista Monarchs." That remark prompted me to select the number 42 at Papillion-LaVista. After that, I refused to wear any other number for the rest of my career. I wore 42 to give African Americans a sense of pride. Every time I stepped onto a softball field wearing 42 on my back it made me feel proud to be a strong, young black woman. Because Jackie was so impactful, I wanted to be like Jackie. Even though Jackie and I played during different times in history—he played during Jim Crow and I played later on—I saw myself breaking barriers just like Jackie. When I was playing high school and college ball, there were few black softball players. Black female softball pitchers were a rarity. I wanted little black girls to see me pitch and say, "Hell yes, I can be a pitcher just like Peaches!"

When I started playing softball as a little girl, I wasn't the best. Once I got into high school, a light went on. It dawned on me that I could get a college scholarship for softball. For a time, there was a professional women's softball league. Its existence inspired me to believe that I could become a professional softball player. Then, the pro league folded. Reality set in. My chances of making a living playing the game I loved would be slim. Sometimes I would think to myself, "What if I was a guy?" If I was a guy playing baseball, I could have been playing in the majors as a full-time job instead of playing softball as a summer job. Even today, playing pro softball doesn't pay enough to support a woman—you need a job for the rest of the year. I would've loved to have had the opportunity to play in a professional women's softball league equivalent to major league baseball.

The first time I picked up a softball I was 10 years old. I showed up at a preseason tryout for Keystone Little League in West Omaha. Until then, I'd never even played catch with my brother who was a baseball player. Keystone was a big challenge. I wasn't good. Didn't know the game. Playing just for the fun of it, I never saw myself as becoming good.

At the age of 11, my mom encouraged me to try pitching. There was only one big problem: I couldn't throw strikes. It was me and my mom. My dad loves watching sports but he wasn't the type to get out into the yard and play catch. My mom played slow pitch softball growing up in Omaha. She used to wear a yellow and black jersey, but I can't recall the name of the team she was on. Mom was my catcher. She was the most influential person in my development as a softball player. She was encouraging. Whenever I needed to practice, Mom would be out there on the field with me.

Mom instilled passion and competitive drive in me. She's always been a very driven woman. She works hard. For a living, she managed an insurance business. I took it seriously when my mom and, later on, my coaches would say, "Pitching takes hard work." I still coach pitching. I don't think my girls understand how much hard work it takes. When I got faster as a pitcher, I broke mom's thumb. Mom was like, "Okay, I need to retire and let your teammates catch you."

To be great, you need passion. On some days, passion is all you have in the gas tank. When you're tired and you don't feel like pitching, if it's cold outside or if you're losing or if you have things going on in your personal life that are getting to you emotionally—sometimes the only thing that gets you through is your love of the game.

As I matured as a pitcher, I developed mental toughness. When dealing with pressure, a pitcher must be mentally tough. As a youngster, I lacked that strong mental aspect. I would get out of tight situations because athletically I was more physically talented than other girls. It took time for me to build a different mindset, to train my brain to deal with different pressure situations and to not let the pressure get to me. I credit the University of Nebraska coaches with training my mind as a freshman to handle pressure.

I also made adjustments relating to my body and my personality. In softball pitching, the taller you are, the longer your stride. To compensate for being short, I was big on using my legs. If you see photos of me in my windup, you'll see my front leg jumping out there. I'd be flying toward the hitter. Personality-wise, I was too nice. From time to time, I addressed this weakness. I was tentative in my early years. Afraid to throw inside because I didn't want to hit a batter. I needed to grow out of that.

To conquer my fear of hitting batters, I intentionally hit a batter in a game against DePaul University. This batter was crowding the plate. To move her off the plate, I hit her. I didn't say I was sorry. As she trotted to first base, I turned my back on her. It was the only time in my career that I ever hit a batter intentionally. If I would've have known how good this works, I would have intentionally hit more batters. [Laughter] After hitting this batter, I never again hesitated to come inside. My new attitude was, "If I hit a batter, oh well."

Quiet off the field but overpowering on it, Peaches James displays her famous pitching style during a game in 2004 (personal collection of Peaches James).

My senior year at Nebraska I was one of the leaders, but it took a long time for me to assume a leadership role. "Natural me" wasn't vocal. Off the field, I was introverted, quiet, shy. I lacked confidence, doubted my abilities. During my freshman and sophomore years in high school and again in college, my coaches would challenge me to "Be a leader." When I resisted, they would say,

"Okay, she's still young. Let her grow into being a leader." My leadership style evolved to where I led by example. My actions as a player spoke louder than my words.

In my senior year at the University of Nebraska, I started wearing sunglasses whenever I pitched. Up until then, I'd never worn sunglasses while pitching. There was something magical about those dark green sunglasses. It was an unspoken thing. Before a game, my Husker teammates and I would be in the dugout. My teammates would be putting on their gloves, getting ready to run onto the field and take their positions. I'd put on my dark green shades. Suddenly, I transformed from a meek woman into a bold dominator.

My attitude was "Give me your best hitter, I'm ready for her. We're going to win this game; we're going to win a championship."

Funny how putting on those sunglasses triggered positive messages flashing through my mind. I was only 5'6", but when I put on those shades, I felt 6'5". As far as my teammates were concerned, it was like I'd turned the key in the ignition of a car. Putting on the glasses caused them to start yelling and shouting, "Now we're ready!" My teammates knew those glasses changed me. In their eyes, sunglasses on meant "game on."

Looking back, the one moment from my entire softball career that I'd like to put into a time capsule would be the game I pitched during my senior year against Oklahoma in the Big 12 tournament. Honestly, I didn't know I was pitching a perfect game until the game was almost over. It's an unspoken rule in baseball and softball that nobody mentions the perfect game while it's happening—and never ever mention it to the pitcher who is throwing the perfect game. Mentioning jinxes the pitcher.

After I struck out the last batter to end the game, the crowd and my teammates went wild. I was so pumped to have beaten Oklahoma in the Big 12 tournament that I assumed everyone's excitement was simply about the fact that we had just won the ballgame. I didn't realize I'd thrown a perfect game against one of the top teams in the country.

The first person I hugged was my catcher. Every game I felt like it was her and me against the batter. When you have that connection with the catcher, it feels like you're unstoppable. She worked just as hard as I did to get the batters out. She told me I'd thrown a perfect game. I corrected her. "No," I said, "'we' threw a perfect game."

My mother was nowhere to be found. She was in the stadium parking lot because she couldn't bear to watch. She was always nervous when I was pitching—so nervous that she couldn't sit still. Once someone informed her that I was pitching a perfect game, it made her even more nervous and she had to leave the stands.

You'll notice that I haven't mentioned race once—even though I was often the only black person on the diamond in Little League, select, high school, and college. As a little girl playing softball, I never noticed race. Things changed in my late teens; I began feeling like I was "the only one." I never saw another African American pitcher. Never had a role model. Starting out in Keystone Little League, when I was 10 to 12 years old, there were no other minority players on my team. [Keystone is a predominantly white, middle class suburban community located in Northwest Omaha.] Even though my parents were living in West Omaha, I was new in Keystone Little League. Few kids on my first Keystone team knew me because I had attended Druid Hill Elementary School in North Omaha.

From 12 to 18 years old, I was the only African American playing on an American Softball Association select or travel team called the Echoes. No other minorities. I didn't play with an African American teammate until I played with Tiffany Jones at Papillion-LaVista High School. She was a couple years older than me. When I started as a freshman, she was a junior. Until an African American joined the UNL softball team in my senior year, I had had only one minority teammate there. After Nebraska, I played for a Texas team in the pro league. There were two other African Americans on that team. Then, I played for a diverse New York team. My last two years I played with one African American for the Chicago Bandits.

When I was playing ball, I never really understood my own "privilege" that came from being a star athlete. My experience as an African American female star athlete was probably different from what it would have been if I had been just your average African American non-athletic female student. High school can be tough. Kids get bullied; kids pick on each other, make fun of each other. But if you're a good athlete, you're immune to this stuff. While pitching in high school and college, for example, I never experienced racial slurs. Being out of athletics today, however, I see and feel things that I never experienced as an athlete.

During my softball career, my Caucasian friends and teammates learned more about my culture than I learned about theirs. By the time I started playing ball, I already had a basic understanding of white culture. I'd picked it up from growing up with white friends. There were so many things my white teammates didn't understand about African American women. For example, they didn't know that rain does different things to a black woman's hair compared to a white woman's hair. When it rained during a game, my white teammates looked at me and said, "Why are you freaking out about covering your hair." I explained how rain can wreak havoc with a black woman's hair.

Today, I'm more sensitive to racial issues. I played for Chicago in 2006 and 2007, plus lived in Chicago for six years before moving to Omaha. I hadn't been living in Omaha since I'd played here in high school. Now I see racial issues in Omaha that other African Americans shared with me but that I didn't see before. Because I was an athlete, my experience was different. Other African Americans tell me that they experienced racism at local schools. They asked, "How did you handle it?" My response is always the same: "I didn't experience it."

Right now, I'm in a different place. I see life through a different lens. I mean, I notice it when people talk to me but don't look me straight in the eye. Other times I feel invisible. I'm standing with a friend. Someone comes by. Engages my friend in conversation, but ignores me and acts as if I'm not even there.

Now that I'm back in Omaha, what has heightened my awareness of racial issues is being in the normal workforce rather than the sports world. It's very interesting to me how differently someone will act towards me when they don't know who I am. I don't get the same level of respect as I do when someone knows me as the Peaches James who played Nebraska softball. Growing up I was very naïve, and probably still am a bit to this day. I always wanted to believe that racism didn't exist anymore and that everyone is treated fairly and equally. Unfortunately, that's not reality.

I live life just like I learned to pitch—control the controllables. My pitching coach at the University of Nebraska, Lori Sippel, taught me this. Things like the umpire making a bad call, a teammate making an error, or a pitch not working on a given day. These things I couldn't control. But I could control how I responded. Many times we create unnecessary pressure on ourselves. If we just concentrate on what we can do in throwing the next pitch, it keeps us in the moment and helps us to focus.

Of course, controlling the controllables applies to racial issues. I can't control what people think about me or the racist thoughts in their minds, but I can control myself and how I respond to prejudice or discrimination. I can control how I'm going to raise my six-year-old African American son. I'm going to teach him that diversity is a beautiful thing and to never discriminate against someone based on their race.

Although racism is all around us, not everyone lives with that mindset. I've met some fantastic individuals from various races throughout my life. God has blessed me. He deserves all the credit for every success I've had throughout my years of playing softball and in my personal life. He continues to bless my life each and every day.

# About the Contributors

Jeremy S. **Bloch** has contributed an essay on the College World Series to *Rosenblatt Stadium: Essays and Memories of Omaha's Historic Ballpark, 1948–2012* and served as the assistant to the program director for the events accompanying the traveling exhibition *Pride and Passion: The African American Baseball Experience* when it was in Omaha. He is best remembered for his portrayal of Pee Wee Reese during a number of performances for the River City's *Pride and Passion* activities.

Jerry E. **Clark** is an associate professor emeritus of anthropology at Creighton University in Omaha, Nebraska. A former high school and college infielder, he is the author of *Nebraska Diamonds: A Brief History of Baseball Major Leaguers from the Cornhusker State* and *Anson to Zuber: Iowa Boys in the Major Leagues* and co-author of *Alexander the Great: The Story of Grover Cleveland Alexander*.

Dennis E. **Hoffman** is a professor in the School of Criminology and Criminal Justice at the University of Nebraska Omaha. In addition to publishing books and articles on criminal justice topics, he has given presentations at the Jerry Malloy Negro League Conference and for the Omaha *Pride and Passion* program and is the author of "Scoop's Last Story: The Mississippi of the North" and "Impact Players: How Jackie Robinson, Mildred Brown, and Leroy Gibson Transformed the African American Experience with Baseball in Omaha, Nebraska, 1946–1950."

William R. **Lamberty** is the assistant athletic director of athletic communications at Montana State University. A member of the Society for American Baseball Research (SABR) since 1981, he was the vice chairperson of the organization's Deadball Era Committee and is the author of biographical articles on Sam Crawford, Amos Otis, Harry Pulliam, George Sisler, Mike Sweeney, and Roy Thomas.

Angelo J. **Louisa** is a researcher, writer, and community educator who lives in Omaha, Nebraska. The author of *The Pirates Unraveled: Pittsburgh's 1926 Season*, he has contributed articles to books, periodicals, and websites and is co-editor of two works on baseball history. Co-creator of McFarland Historic Ballparks, he served as a general editor of the series for 11 years and was the program director for the events accompanying the traveling exhibition *Pride and Passion: The African American Baseball Experience* when it was in Omaha.

William H. **Lyons** is the Richard H. Larson Professor of Tax Law Emeritus at the University of Nebraska–Lincoln College of Law. A member of the Society of American Baseball Research (SABR) since 1995 and a Boston Red Sox fan whose research interests include the former Boston National League club, 19th-century baseball, and the origins of baseball, he is the author of books, chapters, and articles on tax law topics. His chapter on William H. Conant in *The Glorious Beaneaters of the 1890s* was his first baseball history publication.

Robert P. **Nash** is a retired special collections librarian and professor emeritus at the University of Nebraska Omaha. A member of the Society for American Baseball Research (SABR) since 1993, his baseball-related publications include, among others, contributions to *Rosenblatt Stadium: Essays and Memories of Omaha's Historic Ballpark, 1948–2012*; *Kansas City Royals: A Royal Tradition*; and *Sports in American Culture: From Ali to X-Games*.

## About the Contributors

Devon M. **Niebling** continues to enjoy the simple elements of the game … the grass and dirt of the field, wooden bats, 108 stitches on a baseball, and the stories—especially the complexity of the stories as evidenced by the life and times of Satchel Paige. Co-author of *Baseball in Omaha* and author of an essay on Rosenblatt Stadium icons for *Rosenblatt Stadium: Essays and Memories of Omaha's Historic Ballpark, 1948–2012*, she resides, writes, and teaches in Omaha, Nebraska.

David C. **Ogden** is a professor emeritus of communications at the University of Nebraska Omaha. His research focuses on baseball and culture, with specific emphasis on the relationship between African American communities and baseball. Besides contributing articles to various journals and giving presentations at a number of national and regional conferences, he is co-editor of three works on sports history and co-author of *The Call to the Hall: When Baseball's Highest Honor Came to 31 Legends of the Sport*.

John A. **Shorey** is a professor of history and political science at Iowa Western Community College, where he teaches a course on baseball and American culture. He has conducted research on various baseball topics and has presented at a number of conferences, including the annual symposium at the National Baseball Hall of Fame.

# Index

Numbers in ***bold italics*** indicate pages with illustrations

Aaron, Henry "Hank" 168, 184
ACIPCO *see* American Cast Iron Pipe Company
Acme Giants 91
Adams Park 220
Adrian, Michigan, Demons 20, 36
Adrian, Michigan, Page Fence Giants 1, ***18***, 20, 21, 36, 37, ***52***, 74, 75
Ahrens, Jeff ***223***
AkSarBen Coliseum 242
Alamo Elite 194
Alexander, Grover Cleveland 213, 286
Alexander, John H. 78
All-American Girls Professional Baseball League 54$n$12, 165
All-Inter City League Baseball 219
All Nations 4, 91, ***91***, 94, 104, 106, 149$n$7
Allen (Omaha Rockets) 132, 144
Allen, James "Jim" 146
Allen, Newton Henry "Colt" or "Newt" 3, 91, 92, 93, ***93***, 94, 100, 104, 107, 149$n$10, 225
Allen, Petey 251
Amarillo Colts 101
American Association (major league) 55$n$19, 58$n$93
American Association (minor league) 243
American Basketball Association 188, 203, 217, 271
American Cast Iron Pipe Company 98, 99, 123, 151$n$9
American Legion Park 124, 127, 131, 133, 162, 164, 175, 176, 177, 178, 180
American Softball Association 286, 289
Anson, Adrian "Cap" 69, 178
Antonian College Prep School 194
Apke, Tom 239
Arizona Diamondbacks 194
Arizona State University 187, 188, 189, 190, 191, 193
Arizona State University Hall of Fame 187
Arries, Alex 58$n$90
Arvin, Mary 101, 102, 103
Ash, Jonny 194
Ashburn, Richie 164, 167, 213

Ashby (Twenty-fifth Infantry) 84
Ashdown High School 194
Aspen Aspens (Silver Kings) 19, 21, 37
Association Ballpark 11
Atkins, Joe 178
Atlanta Braves 185, 191, 195, 210
Atlanta Hawks 188
Atlantic City Bacharach Giants 96, 105, 122
Austin (Omaha Rockets) 133, 146
Austin, C.F. 61$n$170

Bagtime (Omaha Rockets) 148
Bagwell, Lou 187
Baker, Norman Leslie 32, 33, 38, 45, 57$n$72, 57$n$75, 58$n$92, 58$n$93, 60$n$149, 62$n$192, 62–63$n$204
Ballingall Hotel 72
Baltimore Orioles (American Association) 54$n$10, 58$n$93
Baltimore Orioles (American League) 186, 187, 191, 223, 247, 266, 284, 286
Banks, Ernie 184
Banks, Harry 21
Barnes (Lead City, South Dakota, baseball team) 63$n$234
Barnes, Frank 242
Barney, Rex 164, 167
Barrett (Barnett), A.G. 133, 146
Bartee, Jerry 2, 221, 228, 235–241, ***240***, 250, 251, 266, 269, 270
Bartee, Khareth 279
Bartee, Kimera 192, ***193***, 234, 279–285, ***284***
Bartee, Ron 221, ***223***, 223, 241, 245, 256, 258–264, ***261***, 271
Barton, Brian 194
Baseball Assistance Team (B.A.T.) 211
Baseball Writers' Association of America's National League Most Valuable Player Award 191, 210
Battle of the Little Bighorn 79
Bauermeister, Steve ***223***, 242–245, 261, ***261***
Baylor University 190
Beardsley (Kearney, Nebraska, baseball team) 64$n$238
Beatrice (baseball club) *see* Nebraska State League

Bednarz, Robert ***223***
Belford, J.V. "Duce" 176, 205, 219
Bell, Cool Papa 102, 152$n$84, 158, 161, 168
Belle, Albert 191, 192
Benes, Alan 199$n$49
Benjamin, Jerry 161
Bennett (Omaha Rockets) 134, 146
Benning, Don 220, 238, 277
Benson (Omaha Tigers) 113, 114, 121
Benson High School 219, 222, 223, 224, 245, 255, 256, 271
Benteen, Frederick W. 79
Benteen Base Ball Club 79
Bergesch, Bill 207
Bethune-Cookman University 185
Beymer (Missouri Valley, Iowa, baseball team) 17
Big Eight Conference 193, 227, 277
Big West Conference 192
Binga, Bill ***18***, ***52***
Bird, Larry 206
Birmingham Black Barons 99, ***99***, 110, 121, 123, 146, 151$n$60
Birmingham Industrial League 98
Bishop (Biship; Omaha Rockets) 142, 143, 148
Bishop (Bishoff), Donald "Don" 132, 133, 136, 139, 146, 147
Blair, Paul 247
Blasingame, Don 242
Blue, Vida 168, 214$n$48
Bob Feller All-Stars 159, 162, 173
Bob Gibson All-Star Classic 211
Bond, Jerry 186, 187
Bonds, Barry 190, 191
Bonds, Bobby 190
Boone, Ernie ***223***, 223–224, 261, ***261***, 271
Boone, Ron 203, 217, 221, 256, 271
Boozer, Bob 203, 213, 217
Borders (Omaha Rockets) 146
Bosakova, Eva 166
Boston Red Sox 1, 99, 158, 166, 190, 192
Bowman (Twenty-fifth Infantry) 84
Bowman, Charles 33, 61$n$70
Boyd Field 250, 251, 276

295

Boyer, Blaine 195
Boys Club 227, 228, 255, 273, 275, 276
Boys Town 162, 266, 271
Bradford (Beatrice, Nebraska, baseball team) 32
Bradford (Plattsmouth, Nebraska, baseball team) 34
Bradley, Jackie, Jr. 195
Bradley University 283
Bretzer, Johnny 113, 161
Brewer, Chet 93, 174
Brewer, Harry 41, 42, 71
Bridges, Tommy 160
Briscoe, Marlin 203, 266, 267, 274, 275
Broadus (Lincoln Giants) 21
Brock, Lou 232
Brooklyn Dodgers 1, 87, 162, 172, 173, 175, 177, 178, 181, 250
Brooks, Hubie 189, 190
Brooks, Smiling 122
Brown (Omaha Federals) 104, 108
Brown, Jesse 12, 19, 23n48
Brown, Mildred 245
Brown, Ray 161
Brown, Willard 102
Brown, Willie 187
Brown Park 230, 231, 233, 252
*Brown v. Board of Education* 80, 181, 217
Brummer, Red 220
Bryant, Charlie 227
Bryant, Clarence 144
Bryant, Hallie 205
Bryant, Paul "Bear" 168
Bubbles (Bubber, Bubbe, Bubler, Burber; Omaha Tigers) 111, 112, 113, 114, 121
Buchpest, A.W. 58n95
Buck, John **83**
Buckner, Bill 190
Bud Fowler Way *see* Fowler, Bud
Budweiser American Legion team 237
Buena Vista College 205
Buffalo Soldier regiments: Ninth Cavalry 78, 79, 80, 81, 82, 87, 88n6; Tenth Cavalry 78, 79, 82, 83, **83**, 85, **86**, 87; Twenty-fourth Infantry 78, 79; Twenty-fifth Infantry 78, 79, 82, 84, 85, 86, **86**, 87; Thirty-eighth Infantry 78; Thirty-ninth Infantry 78; Fortieth Infantry 78; Forty-first Infantry 78
Buford, Don 187
Bullion, Otis 221
Bullock, James 19, 21
Burch, J. Feagin "Barney" 90
Burch Rods 90
Burdette Field 237, 255, 257
Burgin (Omaha Rockets) 129, 144
Burgin (Burdin, Bergin, Berrigan, Barrigan), Clifford "Cliff" 132, 133, 146
Burns, Pete **18**, **52**
Burt, Andrew S. 80, 84

Burt, Reynolds 81
Bush, George "Poppy" 184
Butler, B. 61n170
Butler, Horace 33
Butler, John 226, 227, 228

Calhoun, Will 100, 101, 104, 162
California Angels 188, 189, 190, 249
Campanella, Roy 175, 177, 193
Campanis, Al 175, 177
Canadian Clowns 163
Canadian Football League 273
Cannon (Omaha Rockets) 135, 146
Cannon (Connon), Ernest "Cannonball" 139, 142, 143, 147, 148
Carald (Omaha Federals) 104
Carr, Ed 16, 19, 21, 23n48, 55n28
Carson-Newman University 249
Casper, George 232
Castlemont High School 186
Castone, George William "Will" 10, 11, 14, 15, 16, 17, 18, 19, 21, 23n48, 28, 29, 34, 35, 37, 38, 40, 41, 44, 48, 53, 55n28, 57n67, 59n126, 61n154, 61n156, 64n238, 67, 68
C.E. Mayne Base Ball Club 9
Central High School (Omaha) 221, 222, 224, 230, 231, 232, 235, 237, 238, 241, 248, 251, 252, 262, 266, 269, 279, 282, 283
Chambliss, Chris 185, 187
Charleston Senators 208
Chattanooga Black Lookouts 167
Chavous, James **18**
Chicago American Giants 92, 104, 121, 146, 147
Chicago Bandits 290
Chicago Cardinals 104, 144
Chicago Cubs 54n5, 54n16, 165, 167, 188, 192, 238, 246
Chicago Union Giants 1, 20, 21, 105
Chicago Unions 24n91
Chicago White Sox 175, 176, 187, 191, 195, 210
Chicago White Stockings 178
Chicago Whitings 15
Chico Outlaws 194
Chiles, Pierce 63n231, 50, 51
Choice, Wally 205
Cincinnati Bengals 189
Cincinnati Reds 188, 191, 209, 279
Ciudad Trujillo All-Stars 161
Civic Auditorium 166
Clark (Kearney, Nebraska, baseball team) 41, 61n153
Clark (Plattsmouth, Nebraska, baseball team) 34, 58n105
Clark, Archie 187
Clark, Ed "Eddie" 146
Clark, James or Eddie 132, 144, 162
Clawson, Don 232
Claybrook Tigers 161
Clemens, Roger 214n48, **212**

Clement, Thomas 82
Clemente, Roberto 191, 285
Clements, Charley 161
Clemson University 192
Cleveland (Western League club) 25
Cleveland Indians 162, 163, 164, 166, 180, 185, 186, 188, 191, 194, 210
Clink Clair's All-Stars 160
Cobb, Marvin 189
Cobb, Ty 1
Cole (Kearney, Nebraska, baseball team) 70
Cole, A.T. 57n81
Cole's Sundries 255
College World Series 3, 8, 184–186, 196; *see also* individual players and teams
Collin, Cornie 231, 248
Collin, Jim 248
Collins (Omaha Rockets) 143, 148
Collins, Eugene Marvin "Gene" 124, 144
Colorado Rockies 279
Colorado State League 10, 19, 21, 37, 67
Colored Western Giants 73
Colored Western League *see* Western League of Colored Baseball Clubs
Columbus, Georgia, Foxes 208
Columbus, Ohio (Western League club) 55n20
Columbus, Ohio, Blue Birds 92, 104
Coman, S.C. 29, 30, 31, 33, 34, 41, 43, 57n68, 58n90, 68
Comiskey, Charles 54n5
Comiskey Park 164, 175
Conley (Connely), Buford "Tex" 138, 139, 147
Cooley (Omaha Rockets) 139, 147
Cooper, Cecil 158
Cooperstown Seminary 65
Corcoran (editor of the *York Democrat*) 55n23
Corcoran, David **66**
Cotton (Omaha Rockets) 142, 143, 148
Cotton, Hurler 137, 147
Council Bluffs Browns 131, 176
Council Bluffs Maroons 21, 37
Council Bluffs Nonnpareils 11, 14, 17
Country Club Little League 233, 279, 280, 281
Cox, Georgia 97
Cram (Kearney, Nebraska, baseball team) 64n238
Crandall, Floyd 228, 229, 239, 240, 250, 251, 285
Crawford, Sam 213
Crawford, Sam "Doc" 239, 251
Creighton Preparatory School 266, 269, 271
Creighton University 3, 169, 176, 179, 192, **193**, 205, **206**, 206, 207,

## Index

211, 212, 214n27, 220, 226, 228, 230, 234, 235, 239, **240**, 240, 260, 276, 279, 280, 281, 283, **284**
Creighton University Athletic Hall of Fame 212
Crouch, Eric 213
Cuban All-Stars 220
Cuban Giants 1, 17, 18, 19, 20, 21, 24n91, 28, 35, 36, 75
Cuban Giants (Lincoln, Nebraska, baseball club) 3
Cuban House of David 150n43
Cuban Stars 150n43
Cuban X Giants 20, 36
Cudahy Packing Company 95, 108
Cudahy Rex 3, 95
Culberson, Richard 205
Currie (Curry), Reuben "Rube" 92
Curry, Callie 95
Curry, Christopher Columbus "C.C." 95, 98
Curry (Currie), Homer "Blue Demon" or "Goose" 95, 96, **96**, 111, 112, 113, 121
Cutright, J.W. 29
CWS *see* College World Series
Cy Young Award 209, 210

Dallas Rangers 209
Dandridge, Ray 93
Daniels (Omaha Federals) 104, 108
Daniels, Robert Lee "Lefty" 124, 144
Davenport (Northwestern League club) 25, 54n5
Davis (Omaha Federals) 104, 106, 107
Davis (Omaha Rockets) 144
Davis, Alvin 190
Davis, Benjamin O., Jr. 78
Davis, Benjamin O., Sr. 78
Davis, Ernie 277
Davis, John West 97
Davis, Lorenzo "Piper" 3, 97, 98, 99, **99**, 100, 115, 116, 117, 118, 119, 120, 121, 123, 151n58, 151n59, 151n60, 151n61
Davis, Tommy 273
Davis, Virgil 150n34
Day, Jewel (Jewell) "Mighty" 124, 126, 144
Deadball Era 210
Deadwood Metropolitans 20, 36
Dean (Lincoln Giants) 19, 21
Dean, Jay Hanna "Dizzy" 159, 160, **160**, 172
Decker (Keokuk, Iowa, Hawkeyes) **66**
Decker, Tim 234, 280
Delmarva Shorebirds 279
DeMoss, Elwood "Bingo" 93
Denver (Western Association club) 32, 55n17, 55n18, 55n19, 55n28
Denver (Western League club) 15, 26, 30, 54n9, 54n13

Denver Black Champions 19, 21, 37
Denver Claytons 21, 37
Denver Grizzlies 21, 37
Denver Gulfs 21, 37
Denver Mountain Lions 26
Denver Post Tournament 118, 160, 161
Denver tournament *see* Denver Post Tournament
Department of the Missouri 84, 85, **86**
Depaul University 288
Dern, John 58n90
Detroit Lions 104, 144
Detroit Stars 105
Detroit Tigers 160, 190, 192, 196, 209, 211, **212**, 272, 279, 284
Detroit Wolves 92, 104
Devaney, Bob 273, 275, 277, 278
Dickerson, Charlie 230
Dihigo, Martin 93
Dixon, Johnny 249
Dizzy Dean All-Stars 159
Doan, Ray C. 175
Dobbs (Dodds), Robert 21
Doby, Larry 175, 177, 184, 210
Dominguez, Elvis 283
Donaldson, John 4, 226
Doubleday, Abner 66, 79
Doubleday Field 75
Douglas, Del 144
Drake, E.G. 29, 57n81, 57n68, 60n149
Dreamland Ballroom 216
Dressen, Chuck 175
Druid Hill Elementary School 217, 255, 289
Dubose (Dubos, Dubsow, Dufos, Dufose, Dufore; Omaha Tigers/Monarchs) 97, 117, 120, 123
Dubuque (Northwestern League club) 25, 54n5
Duffy, Dubb 103
Duffy, W.C. "Billy" 124, 126, 144
Dugdale, Dan **66**
Duluth Dukes 103, 145
Dunbar (Omaha Rockets) 124, 144
Duncan, Frank, Jr. 92, 225
Duncan, Howard S. 235, 236, 238, 258, 259, 260, 262, 279, 280
Duncan, Reggie 259
Dunning, H.D. 58n90
Durocher, Leo 179
Dwyer, John 57n81

East-West All-Star Classic *see* East-West All-Star Game
East-West All-Star Game 92, 99, 157, 164
Eatmon (Eatman, Eastman, Eaton), Lefty 115, 118, 119, 120, 123
Ebbets Field 87, 175
Eckersley, Dennis 214n48
Edinger, J. 32, 46, 58n82, 63n232
Eighth Infantry 80
Elkins, Jocko 239

Elliot, J.A. 58n90
English, Bud 10, 19
Espinosa (Ecpinosa, Epinosa, Espinola), Teddie (Teddy, Ted) 125, 126, 128, 144
Ethiopian Clowns 121, 163
Ewing, H.L. 29, 57n81
Executive Order 9981 87

Fayes Lounge and Restaurant 169
Feller, Bob 158, 162, 163, 168, 172, 173, 174, **174**, 175, 176, 179, 180
Feller-Paige All-Stars 159, 162, 173, 174, 175, 176, 179, 180
Finch, L.J. 33
Findlay Sluggers **35**, 73
Fingers, Rollie 214n48
Finley, Charles O. 166
Finn, Michael J. "Mike" 90
First Nine 98, 123
Fiske, I.L. 57n81
Fitch, Bill 206
Flipper, Henry O. 78
Flood, Curt 235, 239
Florida Marlins 169, 192, 283
Florida State University 186, 196
Foley, James 58n95
Fonda, Henry 168
Fontenelle Athletic Club 161
Forby (Tenth Cavalry) **83**
Ford V-8s 97, 112, 113, 160
Fort Hays State 265
Fort Hood 87
Fort Leavenworth 85
Fort McKavett 79
Fort Missoula 84
Fort Reno 84, 85
Fort Riley 84, 85, 86, 87, 179
Fortieth Infantry *see* Buffalo Soldier regiments
Forty-first Infantry *see* Buffalo Soldier regiments
Foster (Omaha Federals) 105
Four Seasons Lounge 239, 250
Fowler, Bud 2, 3, 8; post-Nebraska 36, 53, 73–75; pre-Nebraska career 25, 26, 35, **35**, **36**, 65–67, **66**, 76n21; time in Nebraska 34, 36, 38, 40, 41, 42, 48, 57n67, 59n126, 60n148, 61n154, 64n239, 67–73
Fowler, Frank 58n90
Freeman, Jim (educator) 239, 251
Freeman, Jim (Omaha Rockets) 148
Fregosi, Jim 233
Fremont (baseball club) *see* Nebraska State League
Fresno State University 192
Fried (mayor of Fremont, Nebraska) 33, 58n90
Frontier Airlines 257
Frontier's Club 178, 180
Fuller, Kid 34
Fulmer, John M. 56n55, 60n142, 62n192

## Index

Gallaudet University 188
Garland, Dave 237, 244
Garrett, Bill 205
Garrett, Mike 277
Garrison, Lewis "Lew" 233, 256
Garvis, G.B. 58$n$90
Gaston, Cito 210
Gatewood, Harry 29, 32, 39, 46, 58$n$82, 58–59$n$105
Gauger (Lincoln, Nebraska, baseball team) 41
Gehrig, Lou 158, 167, 252
Gehringer, Charlie 160, 161
Genoa Indians 15
George Thomas Real Estate *see* Omaha Blackhawks
Georgia Tech University 193
Ghost Dance movement 88$n$6
Gibson (Plattsmouth, Nebraska, baseball team) 34, 58–59$n$105
Gibson, Bob 1, 3, 8, 75, 167, 208, 216, 217, 219, 220, 226, 231, 236, 242, 246, 248, 254, 270, 273, 286; career in the majors 209–210, *212*; career in the minors 207–209; at Creighton University 205–207, *206*; post-1975 210–213; youth and adolescence 202–205, *203*, 213$n$18
Gibson, Freddie 237, 259
Gibson, Josh 1, 158, 161, 168
Gibson, Leroy "Josh" 2, 203, 204, 205, 207, 213, 213$n$6, 216, 220, 221, 222, 226, 227, 228, 231, 232, 235, 236, 237, 241, 242, 244, 245, 246, 247, 248, 251, 254, 258, 259, 260, 266, 269, 270, 271, 273, 274, 275, 276, 277
Gibson, Pack Robert 202
Gibson, Victoria 203
Gibson (Gipon), Welda H. 128, 130, 131, 132, 144
Gilbert, Harvey 240, 251
Gilkerson's Union Giants 91, 160, 163
Gillespie, Mike 193
Gilliam, Jim 93
Gilmore, Al 229–234, *232*, 247, 248, 279, 280, 281, 284, 285
Gilmore, Andre 281
Gilmore, Gary 230, 231, 233, 234, 239, 246–252, *249*
Gitchell, O. 61$n$170
Glass, Chip 193
Glass, Edward 82
Glen (Glenn), Edgar 127, 128, 144
Goering, Hermann 172
Gold Glove Award 192, 209
Golden Baseball League 194
Goodwin, Tom 192
Graham (Omaha Tigers) 121
Graham, Moonlight 235
Graham, Vasco 52
Grand Island (baseball club) *see* Nebraska State League
Grant, Charlie *18*, 52
Grant, Frank 1, 71, 72

Graver, J.L. "Lou" 33, 61$n$170, 63$n$234
Gray (Omaha Federals) 105, 106
Great Depression 202
Green, A.V. "Ves" 44, 45, 46, 62$n$192
Green, Dalbert P. 84, 85, 86, 88$n$46
Green, Harry 60$n$143
Green, John E. 78
Green, Robert 147
Green Bay Packers 283
Greenlee, Gus 159
Greusel, Phil 29, 39, 56$n$55
Griego, Bobby 221, 222, *223*, 224, 245, 256, 261, 262, 270
Griffin, Pug 161
Grimm (Omaha Tigers) 113, 121
Grove, Lefty 163, *212*
Guelph Maple Leafs 66
Gunn (Omaha Tigers) 121

Hack (Hock; 1949 Omaha Rockets) 139, 147
Hack (1950 Omaha Rockets) 143, 148
Hall, Aaron 274
Hall, Jim 230
Hambright (Tenth Cavalry) *83*
Hamilton (Omaha Federals) 105, 106, 107, 108
Hamilton, Henry 250
Hannah, Walt *223*
Hans Wagner Major League All-Stars 175
Harder, Mel 162, 180
Harding (Lincoln Giants) 21
Hardins, John J. 9
Harlem Globetrotters 151$n$61, 165, 166, 205, 206, 208
Harlem Stars 166
Harolds Club 101
Harper (Omaha Federals) 105, 107, 108
Harper, Tom 239
Harrington, William *66*
Harris (Tenth Cavalry) *83*
Harris, Cedrick 193
Harris, Julius 274
Harris, M. "Steel Arm" 116, 118, 123
Harrison, W.H. 55$n$23
Hart, Frank E. 40, 56$n$55, 60$n$134
Harter, George *66*
Harvey, Marcus 283
Harvey, Paul 219
Harvey, Tom 251
Harvey's Wallbangers 158
Hastings (baseball club) *see* Nebraska State League
Hastings (Western League club) 26, 30, 54$n$13
Haverlys 16, 23$n$77
Hay, Richard *83*
Hayes, Frankie 162, 176
Haynes, Gene 239, 240, 250, 251
Hays, Hobart "Hobe" 102
Healy, J.A. 41

Heathcott, Mike 199$n$49
Heineman, Dave 212
Heisman Trophy 203, 213, 216, 217, 224, 273, 277, 278
Henderson, Ricky 186
Hendry, Jim 283
Henson (Omaha Tigers) 121
Herman, Booker 123
Herman Independents 165
Hernandez, Willie 214$n$48
Hickey, T.J. 29, 31, 41, 56$n$46
Hickok, George O. (George A.) 42, 58$n$90
Hickox, I.B. 58$n$90
Hightower, George 19
Hightower, James 10, 14, 15, 19, 21, 23$n$48, 64$n$238
Hill, Ferguson 221, 223, *223*
Hill, Tommy *223*
Hillis (Lincoln, Nebraska, baseball team) 40, 41, 57$n$67
Hines, Gene 250
Hinton, Steve 192, 283
Hobbs, Roy 246
Hockenberger, E.C. 58$n$95
Hofer (Grand Island, Nebraska, baseball team) 38
Hoffmaster (Hoffmeister; Grand Island, Nebraska, baseball team) 33, 58$n$97
Holland, Billy *18*, 52
Holmes, Fred 32, 47, 63$n$229, 63$n$230, 64$n$236
Holohan (Beatrice, Nebraska, baseball team) 32
Holtscher, George 159
Homestead Grays 1, 2, 92, 96, 104, 122, 161, 167
Hondo Ligons 164
Hoover, Charlie 14, 15, 23$n$56
Hopp, Albert 40, 48, 70
Hopp, Johnny 164, 167
Horace Mann School 217, 262, 274
Horning, Ross 169
House of David 124, 132, 157, 159, 160, 161, 165, 167
Houseworth, Will 28, 29, 30, 31, 32, 34, 40, 41, 55$n$36, 55$n$37, 61$n$153, 67, 68, 76$n$26
Houston Astros 185, 194
Howard, Elston 193
Howard Kennedy Elementary School 217, 247, 262
Howard University 188
Howe, Gordy 242
Howe, Shorty 46, 50, 58$n$82, 63$n$230
Hubert (Omaha Tigers) 121
Hubert H. Humphrey Metrodome 279
Hudson, Nat *66*
Hughbanks, George 11, 12, 19, 21, 23$n$48
Hughbanks, Hugh 11, 12, 14, 19, 23$n$48
Hughes (Omaha Tigers/Monarchs) 123
Hughes, Sammy T. 93, 161

# Index

Hunter, Gary 253, 256, 270
Hyde Park Stars, 235, 258

Indiana University 205
Indianapolis (Western League club) 54n6, 55n20
Indianapolis Clowns 92, 104, 144, 163, 166
Indianapolis Indians 207
Intercity League 204
Intercity League Tournament 204
International Association 36, 66
International League 71
Iowa-Nebraska Powers of Lincoln 97, 113, 120
Irvin, Monte 175, 177
"I've Been Everywhere" *156*

Jackie Robinson All-Stars 177, 178, 179, 180
Jackson (Omaha Rockets) 124, 144
Jackson, Darrell 190
Jackson, Guy 90, 91, 94, 105, 107
Jackson, J.J. 81
Jackson, John W. *see* Bud Fowler
Jackson, Reggie 211
Jackson, William 10, 19
Jahn (John; Omaha Rockets) 135, 146
Jamerson (Jameson), Londell "Tincy" 139, 147
James (Omaha Tigers) 113, 121
Jesse (Jessie; Omaha Tigers) 112, 113, 122
Jimerson, Charlton 194, 200n58
John J. Hardins 9
Johnican (Johnsicano, Johnson?; Omaha Tigers) 114, 122
Johnny Roseblatt Stadium *see* Rosenblatt Stadium
Johnson (Omaha Rockets) 134, 146
Johnson (Omaha Tigers/Monarchs) 97, 115, 120, 123
Johnson, Charles 192
Johnson, Ernest "Schoolboy" 100, 225
Johnson, Grant "Home Run" *18*, *52*, 73
Johnson, Judy 168, 226
Johnson, Lou 64n235
Johnson, Oscar "Heavy" 87
Johnson, Richard 84, 85
Johnson, Walter 209, *212*
Johnson, William "Big C" 87
Jones (Beatrice, Nebraska, baseball team) 32, 58n82
Jones (Tenth Cavalry) *83*
Jones, Calvin 283
Jones, Cope 238
Jones, Dax 192, 199n49
Jones, Tiffany 289
Jordan (Omaha Tigers) 122

Kansas City (Western Association) 26, 30, 54n15, 55n18, 55n19
Kansas City (Western League) 54n6, 54n13, 55n20

Kansas City Athletics 166
Kansas City Maroons 16, 19, 20, 21, 36
Kansas City Monarchs 4, 90, 91, *91*, 92, *93*, 100, 101, 104, 105, 106, 118, 122, 144, 145, 146, 147, 160, 162, 163, 166, 167, 169, 172, 204, 225, 229, 231, 250, 287
Kansas City Royals (American League) 187, 192, 246, 285
Kansas City Royals (black touring team) 174
Kansas City Stars 20, 101, 164
Kansas City Tigers 92, 104
Kansas State University 217
Karabatsos, Jim 230
Keane, Johnny 207, *208*, 209
Kearney (baseball club) *see* Nebraska State League
Kearney Independents 97, 112, 114, 119, 120
Kearney Kearneys 11, 12, 13, 64n238
Kearney Stewarts 73
"Kearney's Wail of Woe" 12
Keefe (Grand Island, Nebraska, baseball team) 38, 63n232
Kelley, Tom 164
Kellom Elementary School 217, 238, 243, 244, 262, 268, 269, 281, 285
Kellom Field 224, 238, 247, 255, 257, 258, 259, 276
Kemp, Tony 195
Kennedy (Plattsmouth, Nebraska, baseball team) 34, 49, 58n82, 58-59n105, 62-63n204, 63n226
Kennedy, A.S. 63n231
Kennedy, Ken 204
Kennedy, Ted *66*
Kennedy, William 44
Kennesaw State 196
Keokuk, Iowa (Western League club) 25, *66*, 67, 69
Kershaw, Clayton 214n48
Keystone Little League 287, 289
Kimerer (Lincoln, Nebraska, baseball team) 41
Kimmel, B. 61n170
King (Lincoln Giants) 20
Kipp (Grand Island, Nebraska, baseball team) 42
Kissell, George 239
KITTY League 101, 102, *103*, 152
Kleinknecht, Merl 92
Kleinsmith, Gerry 229, 233, 247, 248
Klum (Omaha Tigers) 114, 122
Koufax, Sandy *212*, 214n48
Kountze Park 236, 255, 274, 175
Kroner Silver Grays, 3, 21

Labor Temple team 161
Lade, Doyle 167
LaMarque, Lefty 162
Landis Field 120, 160, 161
Landreaux, Kenny 189

Lane (Lainne, Layne), Richard "Night Train" 104, 127, 144
Laney College 186
Langford (Omaha Tigers/Monarchs) 115, 116, 117, 118, 119, 120, 123
Lansing Colored Capital All-American team 75
Larkin, Barry 190, 191, 196
Larue (Omaha Federals) 105
League Park *see* Western League Park
Lee (Omaha Federals) 105, 108
Lee (Omaha Tigers) 112, 113, 122
Lee (Omaha Tigers/Monarchs) 123
Legion Park (Council Bluffs, Iowa) *see* American Legion Park
Leland Giants 1, 21
Lemon, Meadowlark 158, 166, 208
Leonard, Buck 161
Leonard, Dutch 210
Leroy (Omaha Federals) 105
Lewis (Tenth Cavalry) *83*
Lewis, William "Blackest" 10, 11, 14, 18, 20, 55n24
Lewisville Lizards 192
Ligon's California All-Stars 176
Lincoln (Western League club) 26, 55n18
Lincoln, James/William "Dorcas" or "Will" *13*, 14, 19, 20, *45*
Lincoln Air Force Base All-Stars 166
Lincoln All-Stars 160
Lincoln Giants establishment 9-10; 1890 season 10-17, 19-21, 22-23; 1891 and beyond 17-19, 21-22, 24
Lincoln/Kearney (baseball club) *see* Nebraska State League
Lincoln Kroner Silver Grays (Lincoln Greys or Silver Greys) *see* Kroner Silver Grays
Lincoln Links 161
Lincoln Southeast High School 219, 224
Little World Series *see* World Series (minor league)
Lloyd, John Henry 226
Lockwood, N.A. 29
Logan Fontenelle Housing Project 202, 203, 217, 236, 242, 268
Lolich, Mickey 209
Lomax (Omaha Tigers) 114, 122
Lonezo (Omaha Tigers) 122
Long, F. M "Froggy" 63n232
Long, Jimmy 274
Long Beach State 192
Long School 217, 255
Longley (Longlgey; Omaha Tigers) 112, 113, 122
Los Angeles Angels 194
Los Angeles Coliseum 277
Los Angeles Dodgers 186, 188, 189, 192, 209, 232, 277
Los Angeles Lakers 187
Los Angeles/Oakland Raiders 283

Los Angeles Rams 104, 144
Lothrop School 217, 284, 285
Lou Gehrig Memorial Award 191
Louis, Joe 155, 179
Louis and Clark Junior High School 281
Louisville (American Association major league club) 58n93
Louisville (American Association minor league club) 175
Louisville Colonels 54n10
Louvaris, Pete **223**
Love, John 90
Love, Preston 216
Lowe, Albert S. 83
Lowell Spinners 192
LSU 191, 192, 193, 195
Lynch, John R. 87n3
Lynn, Fred 187

Mack, Geoff **156**
Magic City team 81
Maglie, Sal 165
Major League Baseball's All-Century Team 212, **212**
Major League Baseball's Play Ball program 188
Malarcher, Dave 94
Malcolm X 277
Mancuso, Frank 178
Manzitto, Subby 178
Mariners Hall of Fame 190
Maris, Roger 158
Marnell, Ed 17
Maroney, Mike 268
Marr, Runt 207
Marsh, Mel 61n170
Martin Luther King High School 190
Mason (Macon, Magon), Charles "Charlie," "Corporal," or "Suitcase" 95, 96, 98, 99, 109, 111, 112, 113, 114, 115, 116, 117, 118, 119, 120, 122, 123, 150n43
Mason, Jim 150n43
Mason, Scoop 161
Massey (Massie; Omaha Rockets) 127, 145
Massie (Massey, Massy), James "Jim" 134, 136, 146, 147
Massingale (Massingole), Mack 138, 140, 141, 147
Mathewson, Christy **212**
Maupin, Frank 10, **13**, 16, 19, 20, 22, 23n48, 34, 36, 37, 38, 39, 40, 42, 44, 45, **45**, 46, 53, 55n28, 59n125, 60n143, 60n144, 62n178, 62n191, 64n238, 64n240
Maxvill, Dal 239
Mayfield Blackhawks 101, 102, 103, 145
Mayfield Clothiers 101, 102, 103, **103**, 145
Mays, Willie 99, 168, 184
Mayweather (Mayweathers, Maeweathers, Maweathers, Maryweathers), Submarine 115, 116, 120, 123

Mazeroski, Bill 251
McCarley (Omaha Rockets) 135, 146
McConnell, Chad 199n49
McCook Cats 102, 145
McCrary, William L. "Bill" or "Youngblood" 146
McCreary (McCrary, McCray, Macrae), William 140, 141, 146, 147, 162
McCullough, Joseph 13
McDowell, Oddibe 190, 191
McGwire, Mark 191, 192
McKay (McCarey, McCrey; Omaha Rockets) 132, 145
McKibbon, Byron 34, 49, 58–59n105, 59n107
McKinley, William 87n3
McKinley Park 247
McLain, Denny 211, 214n48
McNeil (Omaha Tigers) 114, 122
McParea (Omaha Rockets) 130, 145
McWhorter, Charlie 227
McWilliams, Jon 227
Meadows (Omaha Tigers) 112, 122
Memphis Red Sox 115, 121, 122, 123, 148, 160, 150n43
Méndez, José 4, 225
Merritt College 186
Metro Conference 219, 286
Metropolitan League 159, 160
Michaels, Thomas F. 157
Michie (Omaha Rockets) 127, 145
Michigan State League 10, 20, 36, 70, 75
Mickey Cochrane's Great Lakes team 167
Millard Hotel 9, 10, 55n24
Miller (Plattsmouth, Nebraska, baseball team) 62n198
Miller, H.C. 55n23, 55n26
Miller, Joseph "Joe" or "Kid" 10, 11, 14, **18**, 19, 20, 22, 23n48, 23n51, **52**
Miller Park 161, 237
Milwaukee (American Association club) 55n19
Milwaukee (Western Association club) 54n15, 55n17, 55n18, 55n19
Milwaukee (Western League club) 54n6, 55n20
Milwaukee Brewers 192, 194
Minneapolis (Western Association club) 54n15, 55n17, 55n18, 55n19
Minneapolis (Western League club) 54n10, 55n20, 75
Minneapolis Clowns 141, 142, 165
Minneapolis Lakers 206
Minneapolis Millers 209
Minnesota Twins 188, 189, 190, 279
Minnesota Vikings 188, 189, 265
Mississippi State University 190, 195
Missouri Valley Conference 192, 279
Mitchell, Jared 195

Mizeur, Bill 161
Mobley, Rick **223**
Mohr, Rhinie 90
Montreal Alouettes 273, 278
Montreal Expos 190, 192
Montreal Royals 172, 173, 174, 175, 177, 181
Moody (Omaha Tigers/Monarchs) 118, 119, 121, 123
Moore, Walter "Dobie" 87
MOP *see* Most Outstanding Player
Morgan (Omaha Tigers) 111, 122
Morledge (justice in Hastings, Nebraska) 63–64n234
Morris, Kenny 133, 145, 146, 162
Morse, E.N. 33, 58n90
Morse, John 2, 219–224, **223**, 230, 241, 245, 253, 254, 255, 260, 261, **261**, 262, 269, 271, 272, 273, 275, 276
Moss, Tim 194
Mosser, Neal 204, 212, 271
Most Outstanding Player Award 188, 193, 194, 195
Most Valuable Player Award *see* Baseball Writers' Association of America's National League Most Valuable Player Award
Most Valuable Player Award (Texas League All-Star Game) 194
Mulehearn (Plattsmouth, Nebraska, baseball team) 62n198
Municipal Stadium *see* Rosenblatt Stadium
Murphy (Omaha Rockets) 146
Murphy, Sylvester "Syl" 127, 130, 131, 145
Murphy, Tom 204
Murphy's Midgets 219
Musial, Stan 158
MVP *see* Writers' Association of America's National League Most Valuable Player Award
Myers, W.M. 44

NAL *see* Negro American League
Napoleon (Napolian, Napoline), Charles "Lefty" 124, 126, 127, 129, 131, 145
Napure (Nepure; Omaha Federals) 105, 107, 108
Nash, Jim 147
Nathan Hale Junior High 217, 235, 240, 281, 282
National Baseball Hall of Fame's Committee on Negro Baseball Leagues **168**
National Basketball Association 187, 188, 203, 205, 206, 208, 213, 217, 226
National College Baseball Hall of Fame 191
National Fastpitch Coaches Association 286
National Football League 104, 186,

## Index

188, 189, 203, 226, 265, **267**, 268, 273, 274
National Football League's All-Time All-Pro Team 104
National Football League's 75th Anniversary All-Time Team 104
National League Most Valuable Player *see* Baseball Writers' Association of America's National League Most Valuable Player Award
Nature (Omaha Federals) 105, 108
NBA *see* National Basketball Association
Near North Side YMCA 178, 179, 180, 216, 236, 237, 242, **243**, 244, 269, 274
Nebraska American Legion Class A Junior State Tournament 216
Nebraska High School Hall of Fame 212
Nebraska Independent League 102, 104
Nebraska Parole Board 258
Nebraska Semipro Baseball Hall of Fame 167, 169
Nebraska Semipro Baseball Tournament 2, 97, 112, 113
Nebraska State League establishment 27–37, 55–59; season 37–48, 59–63; what went wrong 48–52, 63–64
Nebraska State Penitentiary 251
Nebraska's State Midget American Legion baseball championship 204
Negro American League 99, 101, 204
Negro Leagues 1, 87, 91, 156, 157, 159, 163, 164, 168, 172, 173, 204, 220, 231, 287
Negro Leagues Baseball Museum 67
Negro Leagues Committee 19
Nelson, Ben 258
New Orleans Pickwicks 66
New Orleans Pinchbacks 20, 46
New York (American Association) 58n93
New York (softball team) 290
New York Bacharach Giants 122
New York Black Yankees 121, 122
New York Colored Giants 20
New York Cuban Giants *see* Cuban Giants
New York Giants 175, 188
New York Gorhams 24n91
New York Jets 217, 265, 267
New York Mets 190, 192, 210, 223, 265
New York Stars 166
New York Yankees 1, 185, 188, 190, 250
Newark Eagles 147, 177
Newcombe, Don 175, 177, 184, 214n48

Newman, William 14, 120, 23n48, 23n51
NFL *see* National Football League
Nicodemus, C.B. 58n90
NIL *see* Nebraska Independent League
1966 Technical High School baseball champions *see* Technical High School
1924 Negro League World Series 225
Ninth Cavalry *see* Buffalo Soldier regiments
North High School (Omaha) 227, 239, 250, 251, 262
North Loop Sluggers 3
North Omaha Athletic Club 159
North YMCA Monarchs 204, 216
Northern League 103, 146
Northwest High School (Omaha) 257
Norwood, John **195**, 196
NSBT *see* Nebraska Semipro Baseball Tournament
Nuremburg Trials 172

Oakland A's 188, 190
O'Brien, Darby **66**
Oklahoma State University 190
Oliver, Herschel 124, 127, 145
Olson, Bill 284
Omaha (Northwestern League club) 25, 54n5
Omaha (Western Association club) 14, 15, 26, 55n17, 55n18, 55n28, 58n93
Omaha (Western League club) 25, 26, 27, 30, 54n13, 55n20, 67, 90, 111, 160
Omaha Black Panthers 99
Omaha Blackhawks 233, 239, 250, 264, 279, 283, 285
Omaha Cardinals 162, 207, 208, 209, 226, 228, 242
Omaha City Steams *see* Omaha Reserves
Omaha Colored Nine 19, 20, 36
Omaha Concrete Stars 159
Omaha Eagles 166, 226, 229, 233, 235, 236, 239, 248, 249, 250, 251, 255, 258, 279
Omaha Evans Laundrys 3
Omaha Federals 3, 90, 91, **91**, 92, **93**, **94**, 95, 100, 104–108, 149n33
Omaha Firemen 176, 177, 178
Omaha Gladiators 237, 282
Omaha Lafayettes 3, 9, 10, 11, 19, 20, 21, 36
Omaha Pickwicks 3, 9, 19
Omaha Reserves 10, 11, 13, 14, 15, 23n43, 33
Omaha Roberts Dairy (American Legion team) 220, 253, 255, 266, 276, **276**
Omaha Rockets 3, 90, 100, 101, 104–148, 162, 164, 165
Omaha Sports Hall of Fame 212

Omaha Stadium *see* Rosenblatt Stadium
Omaha Storm Chasers 212, 243
Omaha Storzes 131, 164
Omaha Tech *see* Technical High School
Omaha Tigers/Monarchs 2, 3, 90, 95, 96, 97, 98, 100, 104, 109–123
Omaha Travelers 204, 226
Omaha Umpires' Association 162
Omaha University *see* University of Nebraska Omaha
Omaha Western Stars 3
Omaha Wilcox & Drapers 3, 19, 20, 21, 37
O'Neil, Buck 93, 155, 158, 176, 225, 236, 238
Orcutt, Scotty 262
Otis, Amos 187
OU *see* University of Nebraska Omaha

Pacific Coast League 87, 179
Page, Charles 260
Page Fence Company 74
Page Fence Giants *see* Adrian, Michigan, Page Fence Giants
Paige, Lula 164
Paige, Satchel 1, 2, 3–4, 69, 102, 155–169, **156**, **160**, **164**, **168**, 169n1, 172–173, 174–176, 180, 264
Palmer, B. 61n170
Pan American University 187, 188, 197n22
Panama Bankers 188
Papillion–La Vista High School 286, 287, 289
Pappio (Omaha Federals) 105, 107
Parker, Virgil 159
Parks, Jerry 204, 220, 254
Parsons, Gus **18**, **52**
Partlow, Roy 175
Parvin (Plattsmouth, Nebraska, baseball team) 46, 62n198
Pascale, Mat 159, 161, 162, 164, 165, 166, 167, 169, 176
Patterson, John F. 55n23
Patterson, John W. "Pat" **18**, 19, 20, 22, 23n48, 34, 36, 38, 39, 42, 44, 45, 46, 53, 55n28, 59n107, 60n143, 64n238, 64n240
Patterson, Sam 34, 58n105, 60n143
Patterson, Tom 29, 32
Pederson, Robert **223**
Pedie (Omaha Rockets) 131, 145
Penn State University 192
Pennington, Art 225
Perrine, Al 34, 44, 58–59n105
Peru State College 228
Peters, Rick 190
Philadelphia Giants 1, 20
Philadelphia Phillies 193, 194
Philadelphia Stars **96**, 121, 146, 147, 162
Philippine-American War 79, 82
Philippine Insurrection *see* Philippine-American War
Pine Ridge Reservation 79

# Index

Piper First Nine  98, 123
Pittsburgh Alleghenys  58*n*93
Pittsburgh Crawfords  4, 160, 161
Pittsburgh Keystones  105
Pittsburgh Pirates  191, 279, 285
Pittsburgh Steelers  189
Plattsmouth (baseball club) *see* Nebraska State League
Pleasant Hill Elementary School  229, 247
*Plessy v. Ferguson*  80
Plummer, Charles  **223**, 2**61**
Pollock's Cuban Stars  150*n*43
Polo Grounds  175
Pond, Lee  45
Pope, William M.  1, 9, 10, 14, 15, 16, 18, 23*n*75, 27, 55*n*23, 55*n*24
Porter, C.W.  34
Porter, William K.  **83**
Powell, Joe "Step Infetchit"  118, 123
Pratt School  242
Press All-Stars  166
Prince George's Community College  188
Providence (National League baseball team)  54*n*5
Purcell (Percell), Dick  33, 61*n*170

Rabouin, Andre  188
Rachels, Wes  193
Racine, Hector  172
Rackley, Marvin  177
Radbourne, Charles "Hoss"  54*n*5
Radcliffe, Ted "Double Duty"  161, 226
Ragan, Pat  90
Ragion (Omaha Federals)  105, 106
Randall (Beatrice, Nebraska, baseball team)  32
Randle, Lenny  187, 188
Ray (Omaha Federals)  105, 106
Ray, Corey  196
Red Ant Wickware  167
Redd (Omaha Federals)  105, 106
Redden, James  4, 218, 225–228, **227**
Redford, Robert  246
Reed (Omaha Tigers/Monarchs)  117, 123
Reese (Omaha Tigers/Monarchs)  123
Reeves, John "Jack"  11, 12, 13, 15, 19, 21, 22, 23*n*48, 34, 36, 38, 39, **39**, 42, 44, 45, **45**, 46, 53, 55*n*28
Reitz, Gus  58*n*90
Reynolds (Omaha Tigers)  111, 122
Reynolds, Art  230
Rhodes, Dusty  126, 127, 145
Richards, L.D.  58*n*90
Richardson, Troy  226, 250
Richie (Omaha Federals)  105
Richmond Black Swans  66
Rickey, Branch, Jr.  102
Rickey, Branch, Sr.  172
Rickey, Don  80
Rickey, Frank  102
Right (Wright; Omaha Federals)  107

Rinitz (Omaha Rockets)  135, 146
Roan, Howard C.  **83**
Roberto Clemente Award  191
Roberts, Frank  58*n*90
Roberts Dairy [American] Legion team *see* Omaha Roberts Dairy
Robertson (Lincoln Giants)  21
Robertson (Omaha Rockets)  145
Robertson, Andre  190
Robinson, Brooks  158
Robinson, Earl  184, 186, **186**
Robinson, Frank  210
Robinson, Frazier  94
Robinson, Jackie  181; Omaha visit  175–181, **177**; post–Omaha  179, **181**; pre–Omaha  172–175, **173**, 182*n*2
Rockford (Northwestern League club)  25, 54*n*5
Rodgers, Johnny "The Jet"  203, 213, 216, 217, 224, 227, 244, 267, 273–278, **276**
Roe (Omaha Rockets)  145
Roe, Preacher  165
Rogan, Wilbur "Bullet"  87, 225
Roh, Roman  176, 177, 178
Rohrer, Kay  54*n*12
Rohrer, Ulysses S.  28, 30, 32, 33, 34, 38, 42, 43, 53, 54*n*12, 56*n*61, 56–57*n*62, 58*n*105, 60*n*149, 61*n*167, 61*n*168, 63*n*234, 71
Rohrer, William  54*n*12
Rollins (Rolon; Omaha Federals)  106
Rookie of the Year Award  185, 190, 286
Roper, John "Johnny"  221, 223, **223**, 272
Rose, Pete  191
Rosebud Reservation  79–80
Roseburg Chiefs  101
Rosenblatt, Johnny  165, 167, 180, 184
Rosenblatt Stadium  166, 175, 180, 184, 195, 196, 212, 214*n*59, 219, 222, 224, 225, 229, 231, 233, 234, 242, 250, 254, 255, 271
Ross (Omaha Rockets)  135, 146
Rourke, James  58*n*95
Rourke, W.A. "Pa"  29, 30, 32, 33, 38, 42, 48, 60*n*149, 70, 71, 72, **72**, 148*n*3
Rourke Park *see* Western League Park
Rowe, Dave  15, 23*n*5
Rowe, Schoolboy  160
Russell (Omaha Rockets)  138, 147
Ruth, Babe  1, 156, 157, 167, 252
Ryan, Nolan  **212**

St. Louis (Western Association club)  54*n*15
St. Louis Black Sox  66
St. Louis Browns (American Association)  58*n*93
St. Louis Browns (American League)  159, 165

St. Louis Browns (National League)  54*n*93
St. Louis Cardinals  3, 167, 172, 194, 207, 208, 209, 210, 217, 235, 238, 260, 262
St. Louis Maroons  54*n*10
St. Louis Stars  92, 104, 105
St. Louis West Ends  21, 36
Sally League  208
Salt Lake City (Pacific Coast League club)  189
Sam Ellas team  159
San Diego Chargers  273, 278
San Diego Padres  188
San Francisco Giants  191, 192
Sandberg, Ryne  188
Sanders (Omaha Rockets)  124, 131, 145
Sanders, Deion  186
Sanderson (Omaha Rockets)  145
Santa Fe (Omaha Rockets)  136, 146
Saperstein, Abe  159, 161, 165, 166
Satchel Paige All-Stars  159, 162, 173, 174
Satchel Paige Appreciation Night  166
Saunders (1950 Omaha Rockets)  148
Saunders (Sunders; 1948 Omaha Rockets)  134, 135, 136, 146
Saunders (Sanders), Horatius "Dedee" or "Dee Dee"  126, 127, 128, 129, 130, 131, 132, 145, 148
Sax, Steve  158
Sayers, Gale  203, 213, 247, 274
Sayers, Roger  203, 231, 247, 248
Schomberg, Otto  **66**
Scott, Fred  186–187
Seattle Mariners  190, 194
Selee, Frank  54*n*16
Senter (Senters), John  133, 136, 146
Seventh Cavalry  79
Seymour Smith Field  282
Sharpe, Tony  277, 278
Shaw, James  254, 255
Shepherd, A.J.  55*n*23
Sherman Field  128, 132, 166
Shiled (Omaha Federals)  106, 108
Shorter (Tenth Cavalry)  **83**
Silas, Paul  205
Simon, Dan  205
Simpson, O.J.  277
Sioux City (Western Association club)  26, 54*n*15, 55*n*18, 55*n*19
Sippel, Lori  290
Skagges (Schaggs), Edward  143, 148
Skaggs, Charlie  221
Slagle, John A.  32, 39, 47
Slapnicka, Cy  167
Slaughter, Enos  172
Smith (Lincoln Giants)  21, 22
Smith (Lincoln/Kearney, Nebraska, baseball team)  40, 41, 57*n*67, 60*n*148

# Index

Smith (Omaha Federals) 106, 107, 108
Smith, Bruce E. 33, 42, 58n90
Smith, Kenneth "Ken" 223, *223*
Smith, L. 122
Smith, Lloyd 274
Smith, R. 112, 113, 114, 122
Smith, Rufus 123
Smith, Wendell 174
Snow, Felton 161
Solomon, William Waldon 214n27
Sosa, Sammy 191, 192
South Atlantic League 208, 279
South High School (Omaha) 252
South Omaha American Legion team 252
Southern Illinois University 186, 188, 190
Spahn, Warren *212*
Spanish-American War 79, 82
Springfield Blues 21
Springfield Reds 21, 36
Stafford, Clifford "Lefty" 145
Stage Two 251
Stahoviak, Scott 199n49, 283
Stanek, Eddie 176
Stanford University 194
Staple (Staples; Omaha Federals) 106
Stephens, James 139, 147
Stephenson (Omaha Rockets) 147
Stevens (Omaha Rockets) 143, 148
Stevens, James "Jim" 146
Steward, Theophilus 84
Stewart (Staurt; Omaha Federals) 106, 107, 108
Stockham Pipe and Fittings Company 98, 123, 151n58
Stockham Valves and Fittings *see* Stockham Pipe and Fittings Company
Stoney, Harry 33
Stony Brook 196
Strong, Vivian 217, 275
Stubblefield, Harrison 100–101
Stubblefield, Mary Wilker 100
Stubblefield, Ollie Bee 100
Stubblefield, Wilker Harrison Thelbert (or Thelbert W.) "Little Satch," "Mickey," or "The Mayfield Mounder" 3, 100, 101, 102, 103, *103*, 104, 125, 128, 132, 145, 162
Sunny (Omaha Federals) 106
Sutton (Jackie Robinson All-Stars) 178
Sutton, Eddie 240

Tatum, Goose 163, 166
Taylor (Omaha Tigers) 109, 111, 122
Taylor, Candy Jim 159
Taylor, George H. "Colored Prodigy," "Colored Wonder," or "Nellie" 12, 16, *18*, 19, 21, 22, 23n48, 32, 37, 39, 40, 46, 47, *52*, 53, 55n28, 58n82, 62–63n204, 64n238

Taylor, Jackson "Johnny" 167–168
Taylor, R.S. 214n27
T.D. Ameritrade Park 184, 195, 196
Tech High *see* Technical High School (Omaha)
Technical High School (Omaha) 2, 3, 204, 205, 211, 217, 218, 219, 220, 221, 222, 223, *223*, 224, 228, 230, 239, 240, 241, 242, 244, 245, 251, 253, 254, 255, 256, 258, 260, 261, *261*, 262, 263, 264, 265, 266, *267*, 268, 269, 270, 271, 272, 273, 274, 275, 276
Tennessee Coal and Iron 98, 123, 151n58
Tenth Cavalry *see* Buffalo Soldier regiments
Texas A&M University 187, 195
Texas Rangers 187, 188, 191, 194
Thirty-eighth Infantry *see* Buffalo Soldier regiments
Thirty-ninth Infantry *see* Buffalo Soldier regiments
Thomas (Thompson; Omaha Rockets) 125, 145
Thomas, Dylan 235
Thomas Jefferson High School 224, 256
Thomas Realty's *see* Omaha Blackhawks
Thompson (Beatrice, Nebraska, baseball team) 32, 46, 58n82, 61n172, 63n232
Thompson, Carl 235
Thomson, Bobby 188
Thornton, Beverly F. *83*
Timms, C. 61n170
Timpson, George 22
Toledo Maumees 54n10
Topeka (Western League club) 26, 30, 54n9, 54n13
Topeka (Western League of Colored Baseball Clubs) 94
Toronto Blue Jays 188, 190, 196, 210
Torre, Joe 210, 211
Travis, Devon 196
Traylor, Darvin 193
Trotter, Tilman 221
Trout, Mike 1
Truman, Harry S. 87, 181
Trumbauer, Robert "Bob" *223*, 272
Turner, Mose 280
Twelfth Infantry 81, 82
Twenty-fifth Infantry *see* Buffalo Soldier regiments
Twenty-fourth Infantry *see* Buffalo Soldier regiments
Tyrone, James 187, 188
Tyrone, Wayne 188

UCLA 172, 179, 185
Ulmar, Frank 254
Ulmar, James 254, 256
Ulmar, Rodger 221, 223, *223*, 224, 253–257, *256*, 261, *261*, 262

Union Pacific Gold Coast Limiteds 3, 95
Union Pacific Railroad 257
U.S. Olympic team 191, 192
U.S. Parole Administration 258
University of Arizona 196
University of Arkansas at Pine Bluff 194
University of California 184, 186, *186*
University of Iowa 205
University of Kansas 196
University of Kentucky 196
University of Louisville 196
University of Miami, FL 192, 194
University of Minnesota 187, 188, *189*
University of Nebraska Omaha 217, 219, 220, 228, 230, 232, *232*, 233, 238, 244, 246, 248, 249, *249*, 250, 251, 256, 257, 258, 263, 264, 265, 266, 267, 274, 287
University of Nebraska at Omaha *see* University of Nebraska Omaha
University of Nebraska–Lincoln 9, 11, 14, 217, 227, 273, 277, 278, 286, 288, 289, 290,
University of Oklahoma 188, 193, 195, 286, 289
University of Omaha *see* University of Nebraska Omaha
University of South Carolina 190, 194, 195, 196
University of South Dakota 266, 267, 268
University of Southern California 184, 187, 188, 189, 193, 277
University of Texas 184, 187, 188, 190, 194
University of Texas at Brownsville 197n22
University of Texas at Rio Grande Valley 197n22
University of Virginia 196
UNL *see* University of Nebraska-Lincoln
UNO *see* University of Nebraska Omaha
USC Athletic Hall of Fame 187
Utah Stars 188, 271
Utley, Charles 148

Van Arnam, William 32, 49, 58n82, 58n84, 58n85, 60n148
Vance, Arthur "Dazzy" 213
Vanderbilt University 195, *195*, 196
Van Dyke, Bill *66*
Van Dyke, Fred *52*
Varona (Verono, Verone, Verno, Vanora), Gilberto (Jilberto) 139, 148
Vaughan (Tenth Cavalry) *83*
Vaughn (Omaha Federals) 106
Vaughn, Greg 192
Veeck, Bill 162, 166, 168, 173
Verlander, Justin 214n48

Vertam (Omaha Rockets) 145
Vinson, Billie 138, 139, 140, 148
Vinton Street Park *see* Western League Park
Virginia Commonwealth University 284

Wachtler, Billy 221
Walker (Adrian, Michigan, Page Fence Giants) *18*, *52*
Walker (Omaha Tigers) 111, 113, 122
Walker, Moses "Fleet" 25
Walker, Sherman 229, 233, 239, 250, 251
Wallace, George 238
Walter (1947 Omaha Rockets) 131, 145
Walters (1947 Omaha Rockets) 131, 145
Walters (Walter; 1950 Omaha Rockets) 142, 143, 148
Walters, Chophouse 135, 136, 147
Warfield, Frank 93
Warzer (police chief of Hastings) 63–64n234
Washington (Omaha Federals) 106, 107
Washington, Charles "Charlie" 251, 277
Washington, Mel 267
Washington Browns 98, 123, 151n59
Washington Elite Giants 121, 161
Washington Nationals 54n10
Washington Pilots 150n43
Washington Senators 187
Watertown Elks 169
Watson, Al 61n170
Watts (Wall, Walts; Omaha Tigers/Monarchs) 97, 123
Watts, Al 147
Wead, Rodney 203, 236, 237, 238, 259, 279
Webb, Jim 132, 147

Webb, Joe 138, 139, 140, 141, 148
Webb, Karl 227
Webb, Zip 147
Weinstein, Harold 239
Weir, Robert 255
Welch, Winfield 99
Wells (Omaha Rockets) 143, 148
Wenberg, Todd 283
Werden, Percival Wheritt "Perry" 54n10
West, Tom 145
Western Colored League *see* Western League of Colored Baseball Clubs
Western League of Colored Baseball Clubs 3, 5n5, 92, 94, 95, 107
Western League of Negro Baseball Clubs *see* Western League of Colored Baseball Clubs
Western League Park 4, 90, 106, 107, 108, 111, 115, 148n3, 160, 161, 167, 175,
Westgate High School 195
Westside High School 222
Wetzel, Dutch 160
White, Jimmy 274
White, Paul 274
White, Sol *18*
Wichita State University 192, 228
Wilkinson, J.L. 91, *91*, 93, 149n7, 159, 173, 225
Wilkinson, Richard 93
Williams (Omaha Federals) 106, 107, 108
Williams, Chet 161
Williams, Cotton 147
Williams, Jesse 93
Williams, L. 106
Williams, Ralph 124, 145
Wills, Bump 188
Wills, Maury 188, 210
Wilson, George *18*, *52*
Wilson, Mookie 190, 196
Winfield, Dave 188, *189*, 196

Winston, John 166
Winston-Salem State University 185
Winters, William 58n95
Wise, Kirkland 221, 223, *223*, 256, 266, 267, 270
Wise, Phil 217, 221, 222, 223, *223*, 241, 245, 256, 261, 265–272, *267*
Wood (Grand Island, Nebraska, baseball team) 93
Woodbine Whiz Kids 219, 220
Woodson, Speedball or Lefty 115, 116, 117, 123
Works Progress Administration 202
World Series 169, 172, 188, 189, 190, 191, 192, 193, 209, 211, *212*, 217, 223, 250, 265
World Series (minor league) 175
World Series Most Valuable Player 209
Wright (Omaha Rockets) 124, 145
Wright, Bill (Baltimore Elite Giants) 161
Wright, Bill (Omaha Rockets) 145
Wright, Charles 145
Wright, Clyde 249
Wright, George 250
Wright, John 175
Wrigley, Phil 165
Wykoff, Dick 161

Yale University 184
Yapp, George 34, 38, 45, 58n105
Yearling, Julie 187
Yelkin, Virgil "Virg" 219, 232, 238, 246, 248, 250, 256, 263
York Colored Monarchs 24n91
Young (Omaha Federals) 106, 108
Young, Charles 78
Young, Cy 165, *212*
Young, Wendell 283
Yount, Robin 158

Zachary, Larry 274